Cities of the Prairie

Cities of the Prairie is a volume in the series, "Studies in Federalism," sponsored by the Center for the Study of Federalism, Temple University.

CITIES OF THE PRAIRIE

The Metropolitan Frontier and American Politics

DANIEL J. ELAZAR

Basic Books, Inc., *Publishers*

NEW YORK LONDON

Library of Congress Catalog Card Number: 76–94297
SBN 465–01137–3
Manufactured in the United States of America
DESIGNED BY VINCENT TORRE

TO MY WIFE

Harriet

who was born and raised
in the greatest city
of the Illinois prairies
and who has come to know
the lesser ones.

Preface

AT THE BEGINNING of this decade, when community studies were all the rage among political scientists, I began a study of the eight "lesser" metropolitan areas in Illinois under the auspices of the University of Illinois Institute of Government and Public Affairs. My first intention in designing that study was to prepare "community maps" of each of the areas. Each map was to provide an outline of a particular metropolitan political system (or systems), emphasizing the distribution of power within it and indicating where further studies of decision-making could profitably be undertaken. It soon became apparent that this "photographic" approach to community politics was not likely to produce an accurate or even an adequate picture of the political systems being studied. Not only was the search for an abstraction—in this case, "the distribution of power"—doomed to failure without some points of references to concrete political issues, but the attempt to isolate any local political system at a particular moment and without a detailed understanding of its larger environment could only lead to an incomplete view of the system in question.

In this way, the effort to properly study certain specific metropolitan areas—the cities of the prairie—led me to seek an understanding of the processes that have shaped politics in metropolitan America more generally, even as I attempted to explore current political patterns within them. Almost at once, the connections between those processes that shaped the setting of the cities of the prairie and those I had encountered in my other studies of the American system became apparent. Local political systems in the United States are tied into a federal system that has fostered extensive intergovernmental collaboration, and are much influenced erstwhile by that system. Similarly, the cities of the prairie are not simply frontier settlements in a particular part of the country grown large but continue to be shaped by the forces of the frontier as they are felt in the Upper Mississippi Valley, the heartland of the United States. Finally, the sum of the differences that came to view in the several metropolitan areas studied could be understood only as reflections of the differences in the cultural backgrounds of the respective settlers. Consequently, proper understanding of the communities in question seemed more and more to demand an investigation of their place in the federal system, the impact of frontier and section upon them, and a study of the cultures that inform them as civil communities.

In the end, I was left with the profound impression that before much could be said about the political systems of the cities of the prairie or any other civil communities, it was necessary to discuss the problems of their setting. The chapters that follow are directed toward doing just that and are based on the studies of the cities in question and, to no small degree, on my research into the American system over the past fifteen years. The discussion of the particular setting of these metropolitan areas is necessarily a discussion of the setting of American urbanization and metropolitanization in microcosm; a delineation of the framework of contemporary urban politics within the context of the American political system. As such, it is necessarily as much an agenda of what must be done in the field of community studies as a summary of what has been done in certain specific communities.

From the outset, it should be clear that a study as modest as this one—a preliminary effort, as it were—must rely heavily on the work of others, making its specific contributions through the limited investigation of the specific communities studied and the synthesis of the data gathered with other works.

The ten metropolitan areas covered here are only a few of the medium-size metropolitan areas that qualify as "cities of the prairie." Sponsorship of this study by the Institute of Government and Public Affairs of the University of Illinois meant that the first criterion for choosing the metropolitan areas to be explored would be their location all or partly within Illinois. It was also agreed that, for comparative purposes, at least two metropolitan areas of similar size located in states with different political traditions but within the same general segment of the country should be studied as well; hence the inclusion of Pueblo and Duluth-Superior. Both of these metropolitan areas were chosen because my previous background in studying politics in their respective states satisfied me that despite other similarities they would be likely to reflect significant political differences compared to those in Illinois.

The larger study from which this volume is derived was conducted over a three-year period from September 1959 through July 1962 on the campus of the University of Illinois, in the communities studied, and in the capitals of their respective states. The timing was fortuitous, making it possible to focus that aspect of the study concerned with the current politics and government of the communities selected on the events and decisions of the half-generation after the end of World War II. That period, roughly from 1946 to 1961, saw the opening of the metropolitan frontier in all the cities of the prairie and the reconstitution of their respective political orders as a result of the impact of the new frontier. By 1961, the first stage of these postwar developments had run its course. The New Frontier-Great Society round of national innovations had yet to begin, so the locus of postwar progressivism and reform was still overwhelmingly on the local plane. Local adjustments to the new wave of federal programs were still in the future. The civil rights revolution was just beginning to be felt outside the South and had yet to make a significant impact on the cities of the prairie. While the early 1960's were not the end of an era, they did mark the midpoint of the postwar generation when the forces generated in its first half were beginning to coalesce, to emerge as the dominant ones in its second half.

The methods used in this study combined historical probes of the metropolitan areas, their cities and hinterlands, using both documentary and quantitative evidence; site visits designed to utilize unobstructive measures; extensive open-ended interviews in depth with politicians, public officials, and other key informants; and review and analysis of available (and limited) documentary and quantitative data for the period immediately under consideration (see Appendix A).

The decision to go beyond immediate issues to examine the larger setting led to further examination of crucial selections from the mass of materials on American society and politics. While this approach admittedly lacks the rigidity and "hardness" associated with structured interviews, survey research, and quantitative analysis, it may well be even more revealing because of its utility in uncovering the meaning of more visible data. Furthermore, the medium-size communities of concern in this study represent a "dark continent" in American political and social research. Hence the "ethnological" approach is as important for their initial exploration as it was for the initial explorations of primitive tribes that laid the foundation for today's more sophisticated research in the developing nations.

In the larger sense, the ideas presented in this book are not new. Alexis de Tocqueville expressed or outlined most of them in *Democracy in America.* Frederick Jackson Turner offered variations of those same ideas in creating his great synthesis of the American frontier experience. I modestly hope that the following discussion will help open the way for a similar synthesis for our times, for the age of the metropolitan frontier. The great Frenchman, in the introduction to his classic work, set down an apologia that deserves to be repeated by all those sufficiently audacious or foolish to attempt syntheses of this nature:

> Those who look closely into the whole work will, I think, find one pregnant thought which binds all its parts together. But the diversity of subjects treated

is very great, and whoever chooses can easily cite an isolated fact to contradict the facts I have assembled, or an isolated opinion against my opinions. I would therefore ask for my book to be read in the spirit in which it was written and would wish it to be judged by the general impression it leaves, just as I have formed my own judgments not for any one particular reason but in conformity with a mass of evidence.

Any study of the length and magnitude of this one, conducted in such a variety of locations, is made possible only through the assistance of many people. My gratitude is due the more than five hundred people who consented to be interviewed and who cooperated as fully as possible in my efforts, the many people who responded to my requests for documentary materials, the librarians in the ten metropolitan areas who helped me search out relevant historical materials, and the newspapers and their staffs who provided political insights and, frequently, documentation of those insights in their columns and files. Particular thanks are due Kenneth E. Gray, whose cooperation in developing the pattern for the field research was invaluable; James G. Coke, Everett Smith, Herbert Gamberg, and Nason Hall of the Office of Community Development, University of Illinois, who, while studying some of the same metropolitan areas for different purposes, were generous with their findings and their advice, both of which proved of inestimable value; Seymore Z. Mann and Eleanor Schwab of the Bureau of Public Administration and Metropolitan Affairs, Southern Illinois University, Edwardsville Campus, who made it possible for me to gain some knowledge about the highly complex metropolitan area they serve; Dennis Sullivan, who made his data on Champaign-Urbana freely available; and Charles S. Liebman, whose data on Decatur and general counsel was of considerable importance. Rondal Downing shared his experiences studying judicial politics in Illinois that so frequently reaffirmed from another vantage point my assessments of local politics in the areas of this study.

My greatest debts are to my colleagues of the Institute of Government and Public Affairs. Gilbert Y. Steiner, director of the Institute, was most generous in providing financial support during a seemingly long four years of research. He was equally generous with his frank and forthright criticisms of the product of that research. Samuel K. Gove and Glenn Fisher were always available to give me the benefit of their specialized knowledge. Tom Page and James B. Holderman, Jr., contributed suggestions and ideas at critical points in the research. During our two years of association at the Institute, and since, Thomas J. Anton has served as a constant source of social comment and healthy criticism, always available as a sounding board, ready to respond with ideas of his own. My particular thanks are due him for his critical reading of the manuscript in its penultimate draft.

The institute's secretarial staff, particularly Doris Falk, Mrs. Jean

Baker, and Mrs. Loretta Ward, were unfailingly patient with me and my demands. The quality and constancy of their services never wavered.

During the course of my work, I was greatly aided by three excellent research assistants. Miss Nancy Anderson helped me begin the study in 1960. Mr. (now Professor) Lyman Kellstedt, Jr., was of considerable assistance to me during the middle stages of the fieldwork. During the period in which the first draft of this book was written, Miss Nancy Bilow served devotedly and conscientiously in many capacities.

The final revision of this volume was carried out under the auspices of the Center for the Study of Federalism, Temple University. It benefited greatly from the assistance of Vincent Pinto, James Quesenbury, and Benjamin Schuster, graduate research assistants at the Center. The task of preparing the manuscript was ably handled by Linda Scherr and the Center's very capable secretary, Mrs. Mary Ann John. My deepest thanks are due to Mrs. Bernadette A. Stevens, my assistant, who undertook to complete the myriad editorial tasks needed to turn a manuscript into a book.

My wife, Harriet, to whom this book is dedicated, calmly and sympathetically endured the trials of fieldwork and writing that are periodically inflicted on academic wives and went beyond that by enabling me to endure them. My appreciation for her is unbounded and increases with each new "endurance."

Needless to say, despite all debts, the final product is my own, for which I must accept full responsibility.

As fate would have it, this book, whose perspective emerged out of research begun in the Workshop on American Federalism of the University of Chicago, inaugurates a new series of publications sponsored by the Center for the Study of Federalism of Temple University, the Workshop's heir. This new series of "Studies in Federalism" will include products of original research and synthesizing works that range widely across the concerns of federal democracy in the United States and elsewhere. The subject matter of this particular volume, which attempts to combine both aspects, should reflect something of the series' scope.

D.J.E.

Jerusalem
March 1970

Contents

PART III

CITIES, STATES, AND NATION

Cities of the Prairie

Introduction / Themes and Issues

Metropolitanism and American Civilization

AMERICAN CIVILIZATION has been shaped by four decisive forces: *the frontier, migration, sectionalism,* and *federalism.* The American frontier has offered access to abundance to all who would (or could) take advantage of its opportunities, has stimulated technological innovation, and has been the source of pressures for continuous change in social structure and economic organization. The phenomenon of continuing large-scale migration to the country, across and within it, has not only provided the people with which to conquer America's successive frontiers but has been responsible for the transplantation of cultures from the Old World and their diffusion, with appropriate modifications, in the New. Through the crystallization of the several sections and their periodic adjustment to the various frontiers without losing their distinctiveness, the United States has developed its fundamental pattern of social organization and has harnessed the thrust of both the frontier and immigration to create distinctively American forms of settlement, including the cities now containing an increasing majority of our people. Finally, American federalism has set the tone for the nation's political and social organization by providing the fundamental operating principles for American constitutionalism and popular government and the framework for social response to the relatively impersonal phenomena of the frontier and the city.

These four forces, operating in concert, have produced a number of corollaries including such generally acknowledged phenomena as agrarianism, reform, industrialization, urbanization, metropolitanization, and democracy. They are not simply interrelated in their operations or in their effects but are equally joined in the thrust of their influence and the scope of their impact. They are, in short, parts of one bundle, tied together within the fabric of the American experience, interacting sometimes harmoniously and sometimes in tension with one another, to produce the civilization characteristic of the United States.

Permeating these four forces is a common mystique: the American sense of vocation as expressed in a sense of obligation to create "a city on a hill" to be a model for the world. This sense of vocation, like the forces it influences, has special nuances of meaning for Americans in varying circumstances. These nuances change from era to era as well. Yet the mystique as a whole persists to color the four forces in every generation, reinforced by the peculiarly American character of the forces themselves. Tocqueville rightly saw as the basis of this mystique a synthesis of "the *spirit of religion* and the *spirit of freedom*" (his emphasis).

This particular study of contemporary metropolitan politics is focused on several very specific communities. However, in a larger sense, it represents an effort to begin exploration of the combined influence of the four forces on contemporary American politics and metropolitan society. The uniquely American metropolitan society of today is the product of the interaction of these four forces and the American mystique. Those who must live in that society, those who want to understand it, and even those who wish to change it must come to grips with the factors that have created it.

The Civil Community

This study does not focus on cities, pure and simple, though the city stands at the core of its concern. Nor does it focus on metropolitan areas as such, though the metropolitan area is the immediate environment of that concern. Its focal point is the *civil community*; a species of locality (in this case urban) containing many governmental institutions not necessarily coterminous with city boundaries or metropolitan limits, but served by a single comprehensive local political system.

Every locality with its own comprehensive political system is a civil community. Such a system is composed of a variety of political institutions, ranging from formal governments (state and federal agencies as well as local) through the public nongovernmental institutions and the local party system which serve local ends, to include the organized interest groups which take a continuing role in shaping those ends. It provides a wide variety of governmental services for those who live under it, ranging from the maintenance of law and order to the provision of recreation and welfare services, the extent and character of which depend, in great measure, on local demands. It also functions to manipulate activities not of local concern alone, such as the selective service and public education systems, so as to make them conform with local values.

In brief, a local political system can be identified as *the organized sum of the political institutions which function in a given locality to provide it with the bundle of governmental services and activities that can be manipulated locally to serve local needs in light of local values.* Hence a locality becomes a community insofar as its existence is defined by its organization for political—or civil—purposes. Such a community can be properly called a *civil community*, imputing to it neither more nor less of a communal character than that which stems from its existence for political, or public, purposes.

The political definition of communities in this manner embraces much that is characteristically American. It takes into consideration the very real paradox of American life (and perhaps of modern life generally); high social and geographic mobility prevents the formation of traditional communities based on stable populations, while functioning, self-perpetuating local communities clearly do exist and may be even more powerful politically than in premodern times.

American civil communities have existed in a variety of forms, urban and rural, ranging from the traditional New England town or rural southern county of yesteryear to the metropolitan center of today. The New England town and the southern county were easily visible as civil communities because, in a simpler age, the community and its political boundaries were identical. Today, the complexities of government are reflected in the complexities of governmental structure, at least at the local level. While city, town, or county lines may indeed delimit the civil community adequately in many cases, the limits of specific civil communities may be less easily discovered within formal political boundaries. In metropolitan America, city boundaries do not necessarily encompass the entire population of the civil community, and city governments but partially encompass the institutions of the local political system. At the same time, counties are usually too large or politically complex to serve as political structures for the civil community, either because urban-rural divisions within them are sharp or because they contain too many different forms of urban life.

With the universalization of what were previously considered to be local concerns and the absence of clear-cut political boundaries to delineate local political systems, the student of politics soon discovers the difficulty in even determining the manner in which elements of population in a particular locality are bound together politically. At the same time, the high mobility characteristic of Americans makes the *political* definition of a local community even more important because it may be the only possible definition under the circumstances.

While the problem of "community" in its largest sense cannot be solved by a study of politics alone, for purposes of political analysis a local community may be properly considered as the entity served by an identifiably distinct local political system. The civil community is necessarily the basic unit of local political decision-making and control and, as such, is the basic unit of study for students of local politics.

In practice, it is necessary to determine the character and limits of each specific civil community, based on certain common politically significant components shared by them all. These include: (1) the formally established local governments which, taken together, are designed to supply the bundle of formal governmental services provided locally (the municipality, the school district, the township, special districts); (2) the local agencies of the state and federal governments which have been referred to as "governments locally" because they are, for all intents and purposes, also providers of services specifically tailored for the locality (the post office, the various local committees of the U.S. Department of Agriculture, the local state employment office); (3) nongovernmental public bodies which serve local governmental or quasi-governmental purposes (the community welfare council, the chamber of commerce, the human relations council); (4) the political parties or their equivalents, which function locally to mobilize political activities and structure political activity across the fragmented lines of formal jurisdictions; (5) the system of interest groups which functions in the local political arena to represent the various local interests in their development of public concerns, advancement of proposals to meet those concerns, and the shaping of local political ends; (6) the shared public concerns as reflected in the bundle of public services and activities provided locally in a manner congruent with the political institutions and population of the locality; and (7) the locality's body of written constitutional material and unwritten political tradition which serves as a framework within which sanctioned political action must take place and as a check against unsanctioned political behavior.

The urban civil community almost invariably has a city at its core, no matter how much its population and political system may transcend the formal municipal limits (both geographic and political). Similarly, county lines almost invariably mark its potential outer limits. Consequently, it is very easy to think of the civil community as a city or a county, even though this may not be accurate in many cases. This tendency often becomes a matter of necessity since the statistical data available are usually based on either city or county boundaries. Thus it is often necessary to follow the path of least resistance in using quantitative measures in the study of local political systems, at least until it is possible to qualitatively delineate the actual boundaries of specific civil communities.

The Question of "Location"

It is already clear that a civil community, no matter how self-contained it may seem to be as a political system, is located in some larger political system. It is also located at some point in space and in a particular segment of time. At the risk of seeming pedantic or restating the obvious, it is necessary to emphasize the importance of location in *both* space and time in the study of the civil community or any other social phenomena. The importance of geo-historical location becomes particularly evident when the "external" or "objective" influences on urban political systems are considered as limiting and directing factors shaping the range of possibilities for what is known as "local decision-making."

A central premise of this study is that it is neither possible nor desirable to study local political systems apart from their larger setting in time and space because of the very intimate nature of their relationship to the larger universe of which they are part. Consequently, while the limitations of research and the dictates of research strategy make it necessary to study segments of a humanly unattainable spatial and temporal whole, the choice of the segments must be dictated by some perception of the whole.

In this study, space and time will be considered as two dimensions of the same phenomenon of location. When Champaign-Urbana, for example, is "located" by the reader, it is not enough for him to perceive its spatial location as a mapmaker might—in the state of Illinois on the Illinois Central Railroad main line 130 miles southwest of Chicago, 165 miles northeast of St. Louis, 90 miles east of Springfield, and 40 miles west of the Indiana border, in the heart of the corn belt. The reader's perception of that metropolitan area's location must include an implicit understanding of such geo-historical factors as:

1. The relationship of both cities to the settlement of central Illinois in the third through sixth decades of the nineteenth century and the nature of frontier settlement in that place and period;

2. The differences between the two cities that stem from their founding at different points in that period, for quite different reasons, at the spatial and temporal meeting point of the old "pre-industrial" frontier of subsistence farmers and crossroads villages and the new frontier of railroads, urban centers, commercial farming, and a clearly national (even international) economy;

3. The course of metropolitanization as it has developed in central Illinois, moving in from the east since the end of World War II.

The reader concerned with politics must further consider Urbana's political development in light of the developing tension between the city's traditional position as the seat of an agricultural county with secondary commercial characteristics "ruled" by a local "oligarchy," and its recently developed concern with industrial and commercial development that has brought with it certain demands for fundamental political change. Similarly, Champaign's political development has to be considered in relation to its origins as the direct product of the new industrial frontier, which also coincided with the rise and continued dominance of the Republican party as the area's voice and as the political spokesman for its particular commercial interests.

What this suggests is that the cumulative effects of each local community's evolving location in time and space on its political system must be considered as fundamental elements in determining community patterns. Particularly in the modern age, the simple passage of time alters every community's relative spatial location to the point where its overall geohistorical setting is affected. There is a commonsense perception of this on the part of most Americans, often sharpened upon return to the "hometown" after many years' absence. Thomas Wolfe's phrase, "You can't go home again," has become part of the language, in implicit recognition of one aspect of this kind of change. Change in this sense does not necessarily mean progress. Communities that "stand still" also change, because their relationship to the larger setting changes. Communities that have avoided such changes—which are manifested physically as well as in other ways—are invariably small villages tucked away in eddies of the national current. They are often referred to in the popular literature as "towns that time forgot," an expression that perfectly illustrates the idea of changing temporal location.

As the temporal aspects of community location are altered, the patterns of its previous history accumulate "geologically" to influence subsequent patterns and events in myriad ways, some easily visible but many imperceptible to the casual observer. All contribute to the limitation, direction, and shaping of local decisions in any period regardless of who ostensibly holds the power of decision-making. Two consequences of this must be emphasized here. First is this "geological" limitation on the independence of action of any particular generation of community powerholders. The layers of culture and experience subjected to the folding, fracturing, and erosion of time and events combine to create a structure for every community that is far less malleable under normal conditions than its surface manifestations alone might indicate. Proper understanding of those surface manifestations—what is usually called the "community power structure"—necessarily means an understanding of how those manifestations reflect the community's social geology. The second consequence is the expansion of possibilities for community development and change through the local impact of nationwide changes in temporal location. The social geology of every community is most easily loosened by changes that occur in the nation as a whole, whose repercussions often reverberate in earthquake-like fashion to upset "fixed" local patterns, sometimes to local advantage and sometimes not.

It should be stressed that while the cumulative effects of geo-historical location are limiting in many ways, the very passage of time in a civilization oriented to change, such as our own, also represents the opening of new opportunities. In one sense, at least, this is a new phenomenon. The opening of the modern age in the seventeenth century, which coincided with the settlement of English-speaking North America and the foundation of American civilization, not only initiated an epoch of change but initiated a chain reaction that has accelerated the process of change continuously since. The result has been the virtual institutionalization of change in all modern societies and most particularly in the United States. As change became institutionalized, time lost its premodern character as a factor whose impact was well-nigh imperceptible from generation to generation, to become an almost visible force, opening new frontiers for human development in every generation.

Brought down to the community level, the dynamics of geo-historical location change every community's location virtually every generation. Changes in location make it necessary for American communities to perpetually reconstitute themselves politically much as they must reconstruct themselves economically and physically. Indeed, such changes can transform previously prosperous communities into depressed ones through no apparent fault of their own. It can also make it possible for benighted local communities to transcend the limits of past location by capitalizing on the potentialities of future location. Implicit in all this is the understanding that each generation adds its mite to the record and, in doing so, contributes to the determination of the contributions of future generations.

The "historical geology" of social phenomena is such that there is some "beginning" in every social order at the point where space and time are first linked in the life of a particular social system. The bedrock upon which the subsequent strata of human activity are deposited is located at the point where particular men first begin to function in systematic relationship to one another on a particular territory. The continued effects of that first linkage and their modification by the deposits of later human activity, the upheavals of subsequent events, and the simple erosion of time provide the framework within which social systems develop and, as such, constitute basic matter for social investigation.

Every political system has its own particular location in space and time. Consequently, every system rests upon its own "geological" base. The geology of each system plays a fundamental role in dictating the context in which the system must operate, the broad limits of its discretion, the structuring of its political concerns, and the continuing character of the political interaction within it.

Fortunately, the United States provides one of the very best settings available for the study of social and political systems from the foregoing point of view because of its "New World" qualities. It is one of the few countries in which the interaction between space-time, political systems, and political processes can be traced "from the beginning" with reasonable accuracy and within a manageable time span. We possess detailed information about the development of this country from the days of the first settlers, and the entire process has taken place within a span of less than four centuries (or less than twelve generations). Scholars and scientists who study social phenomena in the United States are thus given an unparalleled opportunity to develop a multi-dimensional analysis of a society from its first foundation with a thoroughness that can be duplicated in few other parts of our planet. This opportunity is increased when much younger political systems west of the Appalachians are studied.

This study, though broadly historical throughout, is particularly concerned with the most recent time segment of each local political system's respective geo-historical universe and the larger geo-historical universe of which all are part—the half-generation following the close of World War II, roughly 1946 to 1961. This period has witnessed a series of "revolutions" at the local level which have redrawn political boundaries, revamped established patterns of political control, and activated groups that had previously been politically quiescent. These local developments have not occurred in a vacuum of local interest but have been vital elements in a pattern of profound national change that is itself an outgrowth of the cumulative effects of the experience of the immediately preceding generation.

The Medium-Size Urban Community

Approximately 40 per cent of all the inhabitants of metropolitan America, or some 25 per cent of the nation's total population, live in urban civil communities of 50,000 to 250,000 population. As cities, these medium-size civil communities comprise the largest single class in the United States and have done so for better than half a century. More than that, urbanization on one hand and metropolitan decentralization on the other are rapidly making them the principal custodians of the nation's growth.

Yet the medium-size urban community, be it an independently designated metropolitan area or located within a larger metropolitan complex but possessing an internal cohesiveness of its own, has rarely been the subject of social research. Urban studies in the United States have largely been concerned with either the very largest or the smallest urban areas: the great metropolis because of its highly visible position at the forefront of American development; the "little community" because of its "manageability" and the face-to-face social relationships which may be studied within its bounds.

This seeming neglect is due partly to the relatively recent emergence of the medium-size civil community as a well-developed type on the American scene. Even a generation ago, the population range defined here as "medium size" was one that most urban communities simply passed through on their way to "large city" status. Of the sixty-three cities that had a population of between 50,000 and 250,000 by 1900, only thirty-six can still be classified as of medium size today. All the rest have grown up out of that category in the intervening two generations. Now, however, with the essential preemption of the "metropolis" category by existing cities and the decentralization of the population in the great metropolitan centers, cities of medium size have emerged that are unlikely to grow significantly larger. Indeed, in some cases, cities limited to this size category are being planned from the ground up. In 1964, for example, Irvine, California, was but an open plain and some plans on a drawingboard, but it was designed to become a city of 100,000 people even before ground was broken. Columbia, Maryland, is an eastern version of a "new town" planned to be in the same size category.

Irvine will represent one example of the new type, an urban community with its own identity and political system located within a larger metropolitan region. Columbia will represent another, located outside a Census Bureau-defined standard area but in the heart of the East Coast megalopolis. Both represent increasingly prevalent urban settlement forms, particularly in the eastern megalopolis and the larger metropolitan regions west of the Great Lakes. The Los Angeles metropolitan region alone has at least twenty-five such communities, most of them hemmed in by other cities and limited in their future growth so that they will almost certainly remain medium size.

Medium-size cities are also centers of free-standing metropolitan areas of their own that, because of their geographic position, are unlikely to grow significantly larger. East of the Great Lakes and north of the Ohio River, counties defined as medium-size metropolitan areas are frequently linked to one another in a continuous band, each remaining a separate standard metropolitan statistical area (SMSA) and, in fact, containing separate civil communities. To the west and south, such SMSA's are more frequently "free-standing" and often contain two or more medium-size cities coexisting as joint centers either in a single civil community or as distinct ones.

As a newly developed "type" standing between both extremes, the medium-size urban civil community occupies an increasingly important place in the framework of American metropolitan society. Though it has still to acquire an image of its own, it is in the process of developing a "politics" that is somewhat unique. While it has too many people for communitywide face-to-face relationships, it is still small enough to afford all who are so inclined the opportunity to develop such relationships with the circle (or circles) of actors who shape the community affairs. In practice, this means that no member of the community is more than one person removed from the local decision-makers. At the same time, the medium-size civil community is of sufficient size to develop governmental institutions of some complexity and to employ specialists to manage them. The specialists, in turn, must function in direct contact with the larger public and cannot rely upon a large bureaucracy or a complex structure to shield them from the community. At the same time, the continuous necessity for the civil community to rely on voluntary services to supplement the work of the specialists has led to the development of unique lay-professional relationships in the governmental sphere.

The medium-size community has enough people to develop an industrial base of its own, making it either internally self-sufficient as a source of work for its residents or an active contributor to the commercial and industrial system of its metropolitan region, yet each of its local enterprises is important to the community in its own right. Just as significant, it also has the wherewithal to develop a cultural life of its own, to maintain institutions—such as an art museum, a symphony orchestra, a theater, bookstores, a daily newspaper, radio and television stations—that directly enrich community life on one hand and also symbolize urbanity to the world at large. Through these institutions it may serve as the center for its own hinterland or contribute significantly to the cultural life of the region of which it is a part.

These common elements in the life of the medium-size urban community, induced by the size factor, often mask wide differences in the functions that the various communities in this class perform within the general framework of American society. Depending less on size than on geographic location and the pattern of development, communities in this category run the gamut from smaller versions of "empire cities" dominating extensive hinterlands of their own to large "dormitory" satellites of even larger cities, located in complex metropolitan regions. They serve a wide variety of economic purposes, from mill towns to agricultural centers. They are governed by political institutions covering the full range of possibilities developed in the United States, from traditional mayor-aldermanic government to city manager systems where professional managers are virtually custodians "minding the store" without citizen "interference." Their political systems and styles range from tightly knit oligarchies to nearly chaotic fragmented pluralisms. All these options for the citizen offer advantages for the student as well. In short, the recent growth of the medium-size urban civil community (be it city or metropolitan area) has opened up new choices for urban settlement in the United States and new possibilities for the comparative study of community politics.

The Cities of the Prairie

The medium-size metropolitan civil communities upon which this study is based are all located in the greater West—more specifically, in the area between the Great Lakes and the Continental Divide. Those located in Illinois are all within the "Land of Lincoln"; every one was touched by the Great Emancipator during his days as a prairie lawyer and most were within the ambit of his regular haunts. Thirteen civil communities, located in ten standard metropolitan statistical areas in five states, were studied intensively. Each is not only worthy of study in its own right but also exemplifies civil communities found elsewhere in America. They are:

1. *Pueblo, Colorado:* A civil community representative of the cities of the mountain and plains West, located in its own free-standing metropolitan area that consists of the city of Pueblo and the urbanized fringes included in its governmentally defined planning area in Pueblo County.
2. *Belleville, Illinois:* One of several medium-size urban civil communities located in the Illinois section of the St. Louis SMSA (which is better described as a bi-state metropolitan region), consisting of the city of Belleville, its satellite villages, and the urbanized fringes around them in St. Clair County; exemplary of the satellite city absorbed into a metropolitan region that strives to maintain its own life style in the face of new pressures.
3. *Champaign* and *Urbana, Illinois:* "Twin" civil communities, located in their own free-standing metropolitan area, consisting of the two central cities, their urbanized fringes, and the University of Illinois complex, in Champaign County; in part representative of the American "college town."
4. *Decatur, Illinois:* A civil community located in its own free-standing metropolitan area consisting of the city of Decatur and its urbanized fringes in Macon County, it has been recognized as a typical farmers' metropolis and is based on the processing of the products of its agricultural hinterland.
5. *Joliet, Illinois:* A civil community, located in the six-county Chicago SMSA (which is better described as a metropolitan region) but substantially

autonomous within it, consisting of the city of Joliet and its census-delineated urbanized area in Will County; exemplary of a small manufacturing center in the northeastern industrial belt.

6. *Peoria, Illinois:* A miniature metropolis, located in the center of its own extended free-standing three-county metropolitan area, consisting of the city of Peoria and its suburban townships in Peoria County; viewed in American folklore as a typical midwestern city, symbolic of grassroots America.

7. *Rockford, Illinois:* A manufacturing civil community exemplary of the Upper Midwest socioeconomic pattern and civic culture, located in its own free-standing metropolitan area, consisting of the city of Rockford, suburban Loves Park, Rockford Township, and the urbanized fringe around it in Winnebago County.

8. *Springfield, Illinois:* The capital of the state of Illinois, located in its own free-standing metropolitan area typical of the half a hundred civil communities devoted to politics and government, consisting of the city of Springfield and its surrounding suburban townships in Sangamon County.

9. *Rock Island* and *Moline, Illinois,* and *Davenport, Iowa:* Three civil communities sharing the same bi-state, free-standing metropolitan area, each consisting of a central city and its suburban fringes; Rock Island and Moline in Rock Island County and Davenport (with suburban Bettendorf) in Scott County. Straddling the edge of the Trans-Mississippi West, these three civil communities are miniature versions of such multi-centered metropolitan areas as the San Francisco-Oakland SMSA while at the same time exemplifying many western patterns in their development.

10. *Duluth, Minnesota:* A civil community located in a Census Bureau-defined bi-state metropolitan area consisting of the city of Duluth with only the barest urban fringe outside the city limits in St. Louis County; representative of American cities dependent upon the extraction of natural resources for their existence.

Six civil communities located in the same SMSA's were also studied less intensively in order to complete the metropolitan-wide scope of the project and to better delineate the civil community characteristics of the basic thirteen. They are:

1. *Alton* and *East St. Louis, Illinois:* Two medium-size civil communities located, with Belleville, in the Madison-St. Clair Counties section of the St. Louis SMSA (two counties which, together, should be considered a separate metropolitan area in the St. Louis metropolitan region), each of which serves as a center in its county.

2. *East Peoria* and *Pekin, Illinois:* Two smaller civil communities located in Tazewell County, part of the Peoria SMSA.

3. *East Moline, Illinois:* A smaller civil community located in Rock Island County, part of the so-called Quad Cities SMSA.

4. *Superior, Wisconsin:* Located in Douglas County, officially part of the Duluth-Superior SMSA but actually an independent civil community in its own right, particularly representative of the declining boom town whose economic

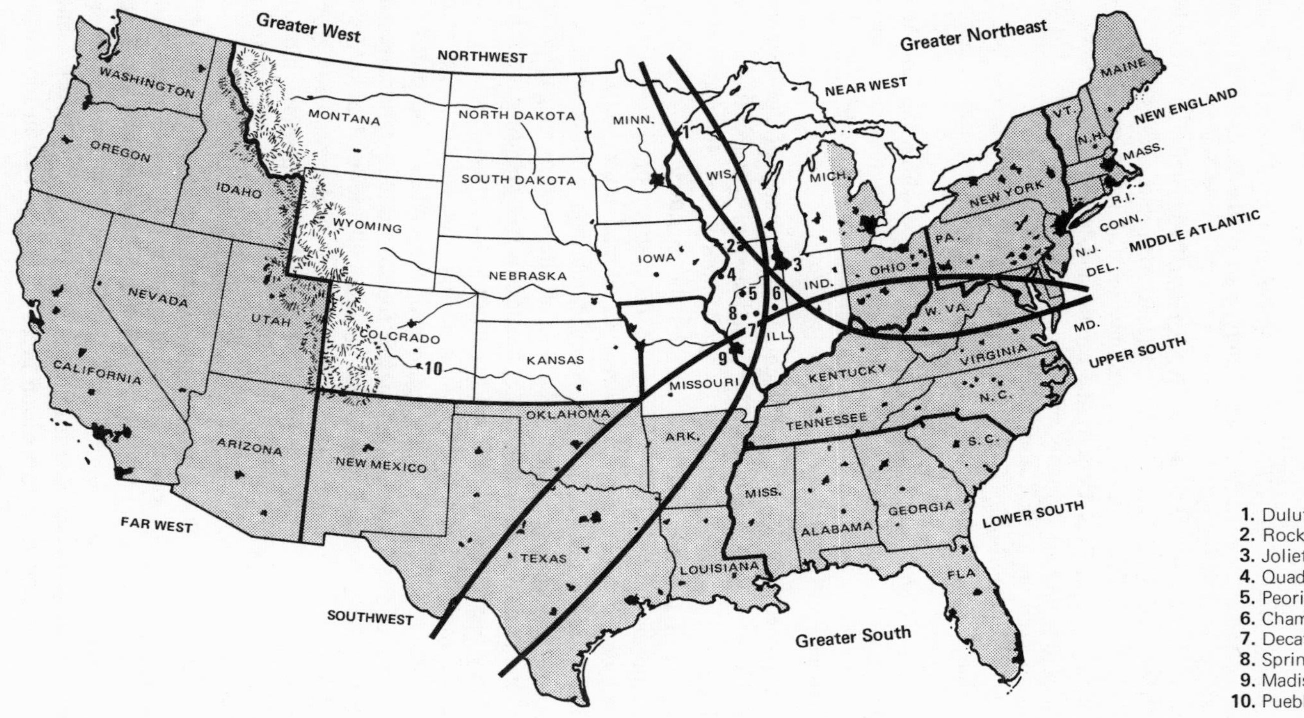

1. Duluth-Superior
2. Rockford
3. Joliet
4. Quad Cities
5. Peoria
6. Champaign-Urbana
7. Decatur
8. Springfield
9. Madison-St. Clair Counties
10. Pueblo

Map 1 The Cities of the Prairie in Their Countrywide Setting

base has disappeared as a result of natural resource depletion and technological change.

Comparative data were also gathered through site visits to six more small or medium-size civil communities:

1. *Bloomington-Normal, Illinois:* A twin-centered civil community at the threshold of SMSA status in McLean County, part of the central Illinois multi-metropolitan region.
2. *Colorado Springs, Colorado:* A civil community located in a free-standing metropolitan area in El Paso County, adjacent to Pueblo.
3. *Des Moines, Iowa:* A civil community located in its own free-standing metropolitan area in Polk County, the capital and largest city of Iowa.
4. *Oak Park, Illinois:* A highly suburbanized civil community located within the Chicago SMSA in Cook County adjacent to that city.
5. *Palo Alto, California:* A civil community located within the San Francisco-Oakland SMSA (actually the Bay Area metropolitan region), a part of highly urbanized Santa Clara County.
6. *Pasadena, California:* A civil community located within the Los Angeles-Long Beach SMSA (actually the Los Angeles metropolitan region), the commercial and cultural center of the western San Gabriel Valley and a focal point in Los Angeles County.

The cities of the prairie are all located in five states of the broadly defined prairie-plains region of the Upper Mississippi River Valley, a region often described as the "heartland" of the United States. By and large, this area, a part of the greater West, includes the territory last settled by the pioneers of the land frontier. Excepting only some of the southernmost cities included in this study, they were developed after 1830, even after 1850, and near those at its farthest reaches, the land frontier persisted into the twentieth century. Unlike the cities of the eastern megalopolis, the cities of the prairie are, by and large, located in free-standing metropolitan areas. They are "oasis cities," rising out of often undistinguished prairie lands and providing centers of human shelter and culture amid territory that supports relatively few people. Indeed, the cities of the prairie often tend to enhance the aesthetic qualities of the surrounding landscape simply because they have been cultivated as human settlements. Unlike the cities of the South, almost all of which appear to be rural crossroads grown to uniform size as metropolitan centers serving their immediate hinterlands only, the cities of the prairie come in varying sizes and serve quite varied and often specialized functions of regional and national importance.

No claim is made that these civil communities and their metropolitan areas are "typical." Nevertheless, they appear to cover the range of metropolitan types found in the Midwest and West and, because of the centrality of the Mississippi Valley in American civilization, the location of five of them at the edges of the South and the East adds to their representative character in respect to metropolitan areas of similar size in those spheres.

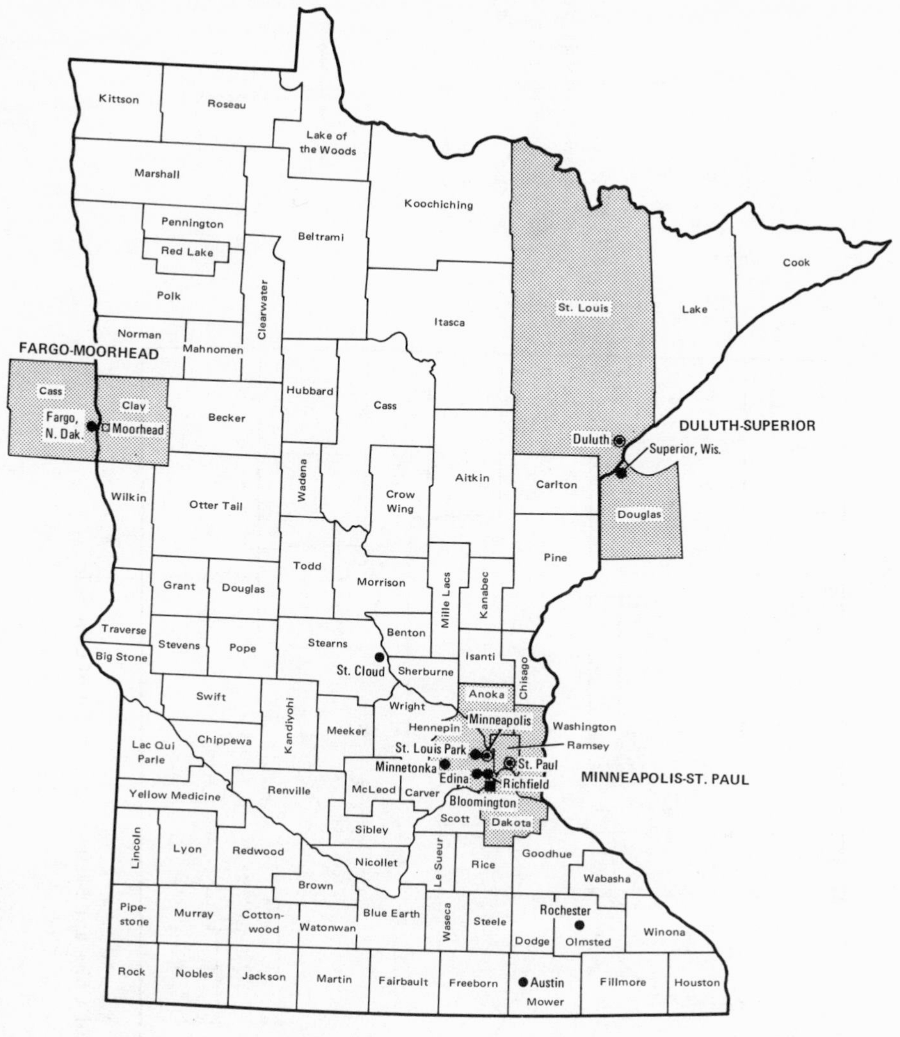

LEGEND

- ◉ Places of 100,000 or More
- ■ Places of 50,000 to 100,000
- ● Places of 25,000 to 50,000
- ◻ Central City Under 25,000
- ▒ Standard Metropolitan Statistical Areas

10 0 10 20 30 40
MILES

Map 2 Major Cities and Metropolitan Areas of Minnesota

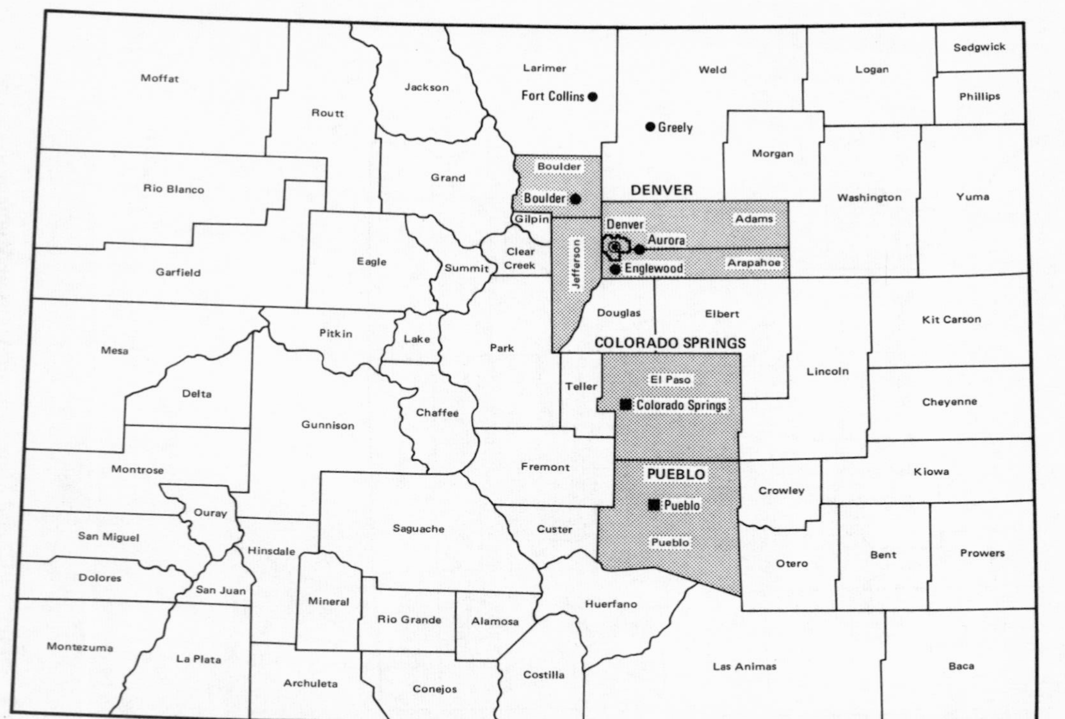

Map 3 Major Cities and Metropolitan Areas of Colorado

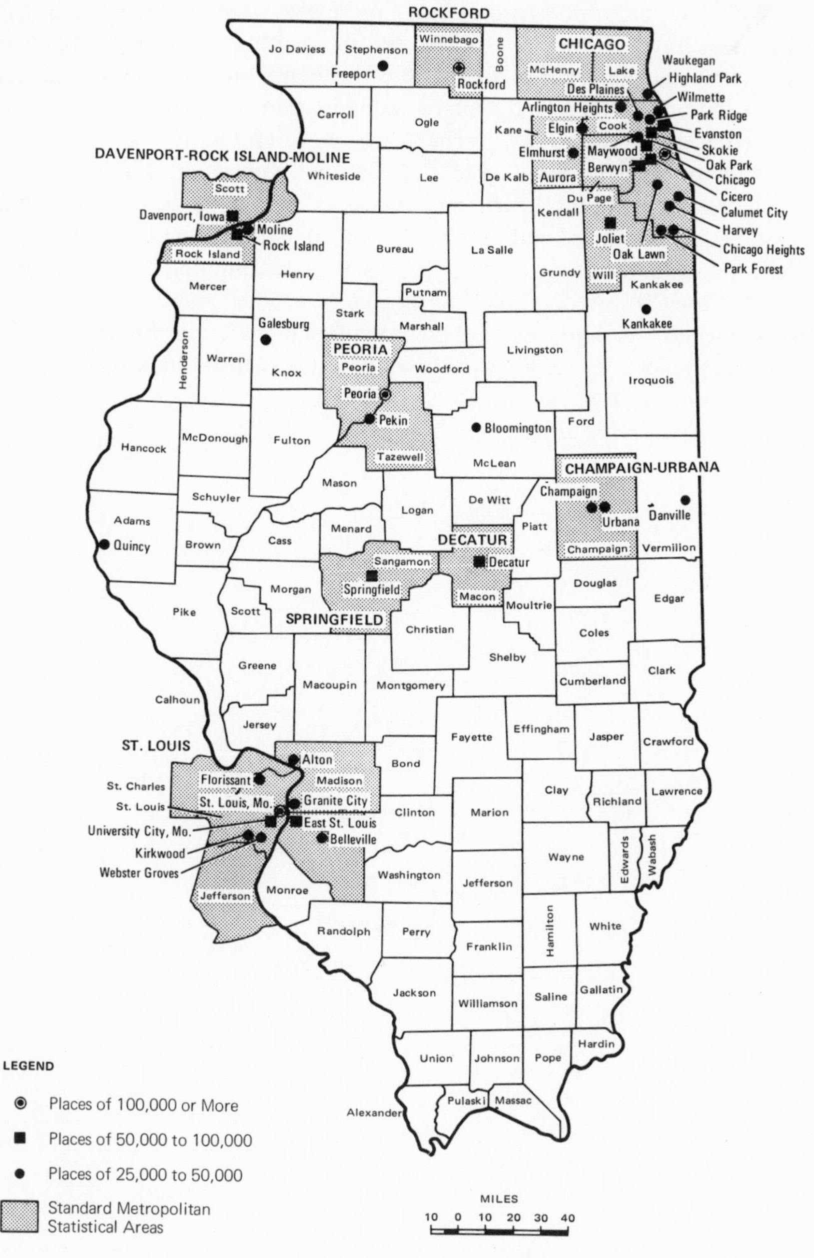

Map 4 Major Cities and Metropolitan Areas of Illinois

As cities they range in population size from 30,000 to 135,000 and are located in ten metropolitan areas ranging in size from 118,000 to 487,000. The states in which they are located run the gamut from Illinois, the highly heterogeneous centerpin of the nation, through Colorado, Iowa, and Wisconsin with their clearly distinctive combinations of population and economic base, to Minnesota, perhaps the most culturally self-sufficient of all states outside the South. Most of the civil communities are in Illinois, which, as the nation's heartland, embraces within its limits the coming together of the varied cultural and political currents that shape the nation's life, a factor of no mean importance in determining their own political development. Accordingly, if the limits of size and regional location are taken into account, the civil communities included in this study can be studied as reflecting many basic elements of the metropolitan pattern in the United States as a whole.

PART I

CITIES, FRONTIERS, AND SECTIONS

Chapter I / The Metropolitan Frontier

The Metropolitan Frontier and Its Antecedents

IN THE THREE YEARS following the end of World War II, the cities of the prairie, in company with many of their sister civil communities in the vast territory between the Appalachians and the Pacific, passed into the metropolitan stage of America's continuing frontier. Since the opening of the metropolitan-technological frontier, population growth, social change, economic development, and political reform all have been centered in the metropolitan areas of this nation. The rise to prominence of this new metropolitan frontier as the focal point of American development and the major source of individual and communal opportunity marked the second reopening of a process which has been characteristic of American civilization since its beginning. The metropolitan or, more properly, the metropolitan-technological frontier represents the third great manifestation of the frontier process in the United States, a manifestation whose major contribution has been to modify the essentially urban form of contemporary American settlement by applying new technologies to reorder urbanization so that it meets the "anti-citification" demands of the American people while retaining the advantages of urban society.

After 1945 America's major cities either became centers of new metropolitan areas or had to cope with rapid suburbanization in older ones. Consequently, the opening of the metropolitan frontier marked a new stage in their history, political and otherwise. In the half-generation since their emergence as metropolitan communities in the contemporary sense of the term they have become focal points and embodiments of social and economic development in their respective regions and have come to virtually monopolize whatever dynamic elements that exist or have been added in their sections of the country.

Accompanying this concentration of social and economic dynamism within metropolitan areas that encompass less than 7 per cent of the total land area of the United States has been the emergence of an extensive body of frontier-generated problems, most of which have invariably had to be translated into political terms. These problems have grown from matters of private interest to become public concerns and then political issues, requiring the mobilization of all available political resources, located in a variety of political institutions, governmental and nongovernmental, to meet them. In more than a few cases, they have required the development of new political resources and institutions to do so.

The very concentration of the intense dynamism of American life—the ingredient that orders "ordinary" socioeconomic change and compounds it into a frontier manifestation—has so increased the magnitude and complexity of the public concerns and political issues in the metropolitan civil communities that nothing short of considered reconstitution of major aspects of the local political order could enable the communities to begin to cope with them. Since the close of World War II, just such reconstitutions—perhaps even revolutions—have begun in every one of the cities of the prairie, leading to substantial sociopolitical change in most of them and a measure of political reform in all.

The political revolutions in the cities of the prairie and in the nation's other metropolitan centers may someday be viewed as the most substantial and far-reaching American manifestations of the postwar "age of revolutions" that has characterized world history since 1945. If this is ever the case, it will be in recognition of those aspects of the revolutions which, to date, have received the least attention because they are least visible. Political reconstitution in the cities of the prairie has infrequently taken the forms advocated by the more vocal reformers. The reforms proposed by the latter, which are often considered to be synonymous with "local reform," invariably have been structural in nature: designed to alter political boundaries, jurisdictions, and forms of government. Reforms such as the adoption of council-manager government, the annexation of suburban fringe areas, the election of "reform" tickets to local office, or even the closing of major "red light" districts, when and where they have been adopted, have been but manifestations of more important changes and have not been coextensive with the revolutions in most of the cities of the prairie.

The real revolution in those civil communities has involved political change considerably more basic and far-reaching in nature. It has meant the elimination of the previously existing political separation between older and newer immigrant groups into "two cities," an "upper" city of established "Americans" governed in a reasonably republican manner and a "lower" one of "immigrant" or "minority" groups ruled autocratically through political machines or bosses. It has meant the introduction of broader conceptions of the "proper" role of local government and government generally in serving public purposes. It has meant the development and recognition of politically articulate leadership from virtually every segment of the civil community. And it has meant the introduction of professionalized civic administration at the local level to cope with the new demands placed on local government.

This revolution, whatever its visible manifestations, is an outgrowth of the continuing frontier experience of the American people. The manner of initiation of the revolution and its consequences fall into a classic pattern that, in its general form, accounts for much of the continuing uniqueness of politics in this country. This is because the bundle of interacting factors which comprise the frontier experience has been and continues to be a major influence in the shaping of American society. As such, an understanding of the politics of American cities is contingent upon an understanding of the American frontier process and the cities' relationship to it.

The "Classic" Land Frontier and the Frontier Hypothesis

The original and classic American frontier was, of course, the land frontier opened by the very first English settlers on these shores in the early seventeenth century.[1] The land frontier or, more properly, the rural-land frontier was the first frontier in every state and section of the United States as it moved progressively westward. The rural-land frontier persisted as a major force (though not the only frontier) on the American scene until its passing at the close of World War I, when the extended settlement of virgin land anywhere in the country virtually ceased.[2] The first permanent white settlers in every one of the cities of the prairie came as parts of the westward tide of the rural-land frontier, and the great majority of the cities themselves were initially founded in response to the demands of that first frontier. As the classic American frontier, it has become the model of the frontier process, against which all subsequent frontier phenomena and phenomena seeking the "frontier" designation must be compared.

The dominant characteristics of the rural-land frontier period were the preoccupation of a predominantly rural American society with the settlement and development of the land itself through the establishment of a socioeconomic system based on agricultural pursuits. The cities that emerged in that period were, from the first, highly important institutions in American society but were developed as products of this rural-land frontier. Their primary functions were to engage in "agribusiness," serving as commercial, social, intellectual, and political centers for agricultural regions and secondarily as workshops to supply the increasing number of manufactured "necessities" required by the farmer. Needless to say, it was during the three-hundred-year epoch of the rural-land frontier that the basic social and political institutions, as well as the basic political culture of the United States and of its subdivisions, were formed.

Frederick Jackson Turner, the classic analyst of the classic frontier, whose views must serve as a starting point for any discussion of the frontier concept, described the land frontier epoch as the period when the conquest of the land was the most important factor in shaping American life and democracy, associating both the forms of American civilization and its social and political functions with the peculiar set of challenges and commitments which were generated by the existence of the frontier. Accordingly, he viewed American institutions as adaptations to the changes of an expanding people whose expansion took place in an apparently open-ended arena (in Tocqueville's terms, the southward sloping half of North America). Contrasting the blessings of open-ended expansion with the problems other peoples have had in trying to expand in clearly limited space, Turner concluded that it is only in the former, where the same "pie" need not be divided and redivided through internecine struggle but continues to grow so that it can potentially provide enough for all comers, that democratic institutions are born and are able to take root.

American social development on the land frontier was viewed by Turner as a "beginning over again" at the edges of civilization. Though the people who come to the frontier bring with them the cultural "baggage" of centuries, even millennia, that cannot ever be dismissed, their interaction with the wilderness at the edge of the frontier leads to a virtual "rebirth" of society, a reshaping of the frontiersmen's cultural heritage to meet the demands of the frontier. Continuous contact with the "primitive," in the sense of that which is not refined but raw, provides a means for men to come to grips with their essential natures, while the meeting of the primitive and the civilized in the amorphous area between the wilderness and "civilization" leads to the emergence of a new type of man in a new type of society.

Turner saw the frontier as a series of successive waves, each of which had to go through the same process of making contact with the primitive and becoming re-formed in the process. In each of these waves, similar problems emerged: the Indian question, or what to do with the denizens of the wilderness who were in the way of "civilization"; the problem of disposing of the public domain, or how to ensure the best possible use of the resources of the wilderness in line with society's public (and democratic) purposes; the problem of maintaining relationships with the older settlements in the hinterland, or the question of "commerce," broadly construed;

the problem of extending political organization to the newly settled areas; the problem of adapting the religious aspects of life to the demands of each new frontier and its newly settled areas; the problem of providing an education suitable for frontier conditions and needs, yet also connected with the larger universe of knowledge; and the problem of providing for the common defense, be it against Europeans, Indians, or others who would threaten American institutions. In dealing with these problems by successively more elaborate means, Turner saw a process of social evolution, from the simplest forms of society to the level of complexity which we call "modern civilization." He also saw a process of social "feedback" in which the experiences accumulated in the erection of societies on the frontier became useful in advancing or reforming the more established societies of the hinterland.

One aspect of this system of development by waves was the order of arrival of those who participated in the conquest of the frontier. First came the explorers, who discovered the new lands and mapped them out for settlement. Then came the transients, who made the first social uses of the land, the hunters and trappers or the pioneer squatters. Following them were the first "permanent" settlers, who came with the intention of staying. They included both producers (farmers, cattlemen, and the like) and entrepreneurs (the bringers of commercial activity) and they created the first organized society in the land.

Turner saw the frontier as encompassing only a relatively small portion of American society at any one time but as exercising a profound influence on all segments of that society. It was the frontier that made possible the formation of a common American experience, or civilization, by synthesizing the diverse groups who conquered it. It was the frontier that provided the social and economic wherewithal, the resources and the experience needed to increase American social, economic, and intellectual independence. It was the frontier that stimulated the development of new industries and occupations in the United States, providing new economic and social opportunities even in nonfrontier areas. It was the necessity for increased government action, particularly on the part of the national government and the concomitant development of a deeper spirit of American nationalism. It was the rough and ready equalitarianism produced by frontier conditions that led to the promotion of democracy in America and even in Europe by setting precedents and "proving" that democracy could "work." Among other things, the frontier strengthened the autonomy of the nuclear family and of its individual members, if only by physically removing people from the places of residence (and spheres of influence) of their extended families and forcing them to function on their own. It was on the frontier that the franchise was extended, first to include all adult males and then, on a farther frontier, to embrace females as well. Finally it was the frontier that provided the opportunity for power—economic, social, or political—to be made accessible to many rather than concentrated in the hands of a few.

Turner also saw that the frontier contributed certain negative influences to society. It was the frontier and the opportunities it offered for accumulating vast wealth which contributed substantially to the development of unsound fiscal and business policies, lax business morality, and even criminal activities. It was on the frontier that the cruder forms of religious revivalism originated to the detriment of the more stable and beneficent churches. Frontier conditions did much to weaken standards of political morality by making it possible for people to engage in politics for the sake of pecuniary profit without being censured for doing so. Finally, frontier life could produce an easing of restraints upon individuals that bordered on anarchy to the detriment of overall moral values and even of family life.

In Turner's eyes, both the good and the bad effects of the frontier process reflected the fact that the frontier stood for freedom, freedom for the individual to pursue his own chosen goals and freedom for society as a whole. This freedom had its positive and negative aspects precisely because it was both freedom to do new things in new "unspoiled" places and freedom from bondage to past tradition, to entrenched custom, and to the formal influences of ancestry. Turner highly valued this freedom, but he saw that its consequences were mixed, leading to great individual and social good and also to actions that could seriously debilitate society and the individual.

Though Turner saw each of the successive waves of the land frontier as emerging naturally from its precursor as a matter of course, he believed that the passing of the land frontier inevitably meant the end of the frontier phase of American history. He considered this country fortunate in that its frontier phase came first, to mold the basic institutions and attitudes of American civilization, to give us our basic culture and our fundamental mystique, but he foresaw radical changes in the future as Americans would have to learn how to maintain their civilization and its pace in an environment with no open end—no more unconquered frontiers.

Many of Turner's hypotheses about the influence of the frontier on American life have since had to be revised to take into account the evidence provided through more detailed research, including his own and that of his students. Still, the main thrust of his conceptualization remains a valid and useful tool for understanding American life. What Turner apparently did not foresee was that the frontier which he discovered and explored initiated a chain reaction that, even in his time, had led to the opening of a new frontier as the old one was fading, a frontier which has since generated another. Turner's frontier was but one manifestation of a greater frontier which transcends the three-hundred-year conquest of the lands of North America.

What is suggested here is that the bundle of phenomena described above which made the land frontier a distinctive kind of human experience has recurred in essentially similar, if progressively more complex, forms in other "media" as the result of the opening of new frontiers. The great frontier has been established as the primary force promoting and directing American social development and economic change. The validity of this thesis is demonstrated by the striking and patterned reappearance of certain elements originally associated with the classic land frontier at every stage of American development, including the present one. A proper understanding of these elements, the "constants" present on every frontier, can lead to an understanding of the successive frontiers which have challenged the American people and their impact on American civilization, including its cities.

This enlarged frontier thesis is not simply a dramatic way to describe change in a dynamic society. The frontier situation involves something much more fundamental than that; a social commitment and a series of social tasks directed together against specific "natural" obstacles that, taken together, provide the essential stimuli for the periodical remaking of American society. The process of conquering the various frontiers regularly induces radical change in certain aspects of American society but in a way that, to date, has served to preserve the basic social and psychological characteristics of the American people, their institutions and their society's fundamental mystiques. In this respect the word "frontier" is particularly apt because, as its usage has evolved in American English, it has come to serve as a dynamically descriptive term for a multi-dimensional wilderness (or primitive) "area," both transient and temporal, which invites human entry for purposes of "conquering" or "taming" it for "civilization." One major characteristic of the frontier in its American usage is that it represents an advance directed primarily against "nature" rather than against other men.[3]

By examining the historical record using a modified version of Turner's "model," it is possible to abstract ten basic conditions present in every frontier situation:

1. Frontier activities are those devoted to the exploration of that which was previously unknown and the development of that which was previously "wild" or undeveloped.

2. The frontier involves extensive new organization of the uses of the land, uses so new that they are essentially unprecedented but so much a part of the process in question that they will be applied across the length and breadth of the continent.

3. The frontier involves an expanding or growth economy based on the application of existing technologies in new communities or new technologies in settled communities.

4. The frontier movement, though manifesting itself as a single "whole," actually coalesces a number of different "frontiers" both geographic and func-

tional that exist simultaneously and successively, each with its own goals, interests, character, and frontiersmen, yet all tied together by their common link to the central goals, interests, and character of the larger frontier of which they are parts.

5. The frontier generates opportunities to grow, change, risk, develop, and explore within its framework amid elements of risk and action and demands responses involving courage, freedom, and equality.

6. There must be reasonably free access to the frontier sector of society for all who want it.

7. A frontier situation generates a psychological orientation toward the frontier on the part of the people engaged in conquering it, endowing them with the "frontier spirit."

8. The "feedback" from the frontier leads to the continuous creation of new opportunities on many levels of society, including new occupations to be filled by people who have the skills to do so, regardless of such factors as family background, social class, or personal influence, thus contributing to the maintenance or extension of equality in the social order.

9. The frontier feedback must influence the total social structure to the point where the society as a whole is significantly remade.

10. The direct manifestations of the frontier can be found in every section of the country at some time (usually sequentially) and are visible in a substantial number of localities that either have, or are themselves, frontier zones.

These ten criteria can be found recurring in every stage of the American frontier. Because each stage is more complex than its predecessor, the manifestations of the criteria are also more complex. Moreover, they obviously have differential impacts at different times and, as the critics of Turner have strenuously pointed out, are never as fully realized as the model. It is not likely that everyone or even the majority in a frontier society will be involved in realizing them or even be committed to their realization. In any society, the frontier sector is a relatively small one and the frontiersmen occupying it are relatively few in number, but a frontier society is not only a perennially "emergent society," growing and changing, but is marked by the fact that the frontier sector and its frontiersmen set its tone.

All ten criteria were substantially fulfilled on the classic rural-land frontier. In the first place, there was obviously the land, a wilderness to be settled, conquered, and tamed for a wide variety of new uses. Exploration of unknown territories and their subsequent settlement for essentially rural purposes was the essence of the frontier process. The people who came to explore or tame the land were conscious of their involvement in a great task, no matter how they defined it. They had the "frontier spirit" that led them to attempt things thought insane or inane by people from established, nonfrontier environments. During the entire life of the rural-land frontier, excepting only temporary periods of depression and recession, the American economy was an expanding one growing at what would generally be considered a phenomenal rate. The overall land frontier combined several very specific frontiers: the agricultural frontier, the mining frontier, the cattlemen's frontier, the transportation frontier, as well as various regional frontiers from the Atlantic seaboard to the Pacific slope.

It is hardly necessary to delineate the role that risk played in the conquest of the land frontier, whether the risk of the eastern capitalist building a railroad or the risk of a sodbuster trying to create a farm on the prairie. Action was, of course, the basic requirement and the major emphasis of the frontier "way of life." Courage was required, usually in the sheer physical sense of the term. And freedom and equality were concomitants of the first three, since the courage to take risks by acting invariably led to freedom and, on the whole, promoted social equality as well. There was a freedom to do all this out at the end of settlement, or at the limits of previous human activity, where greater equality of condition was the general rule. Indeed, society's greatest rewards went to those who made use of that freedom (though obviously only to a few of them) in any number of ways.

Generally speaking, access to the frontier was unlimited, except insofar as government imposed limits equally on everyone. Though this was not entirely true in practice, one of the major tasks of politics in the days of the land frontier was to keep making the adjustments necessary to insure a reasonable degree of equal access. Every section of the country and every locality went through the land frontier stage at some time as the frontier moved generally westward. The land frontier profoundly affected the development of American society, both in the frontier zone and in the hinterland, in myriad ways, keeping American society in flux, ending certain categories of privilege by rendering them obsolete, and providing the means whereby the society could continue to grow and change. The land frontier stimulated the creation of new opportunities for people in every segment of American society and offered many opportunities for people to begin "on their own" and to succeed on their own merit. Perhaps its greatest success in this regard is the manner in which it gave rise to the urban-industrial frontier out of its own accomplishments, setting off the chain reaction that has enabled one frontier to breed another.

The Urban-Industrial Frontier and Its Impact

The second American frontier was the urban or urban-industrial frontier which opened along the Atlantic coast after the War of 1812 and predominated in the greater Northeast after 1830 as the rural-land frontier moved westward. The urban-industrial frontier was to spread across the continent by the end of the century, directly manifesting itself in every section and in most cities. By 1860 the outlines of the still dominant greater Northeastern industrial heartland, stretching from southern New Hampshire past Lake Michigan, were already clear. It was within this latter area touching upon the eastern fringes of the "cities of the prairie" region, that the essential characteristics of the urban-industrial frontier were to be most intensely expressed. From the early to mid-twentieth century, these same characteristics were to find expression in the greater South and greater West, with appropriate sectional modifications.[4]

The primary characteristic of the urban-industrial frontier period was the development of the city as the major form of organized land use. New cities were established and established ones expanded, not merely as service centers or workshops for the rural areas, but as independent centers of opportunity, producers of wealth, and social innovators. In those cities there developed basic manufacturing industries that were not devoted simply to manufacturing for agricultural purposes. This new industrial frontier stimulated the development of intensive urban concentrations in the latter two-thirds of the nineteenth century and the first third of the twentieth, as it transformed the United States into an industrialized nation. It was in this period that the cities of the prairie emerged as urban communities, at least partly detaching themselves from dependence upon the land frontier for growth.

As in the case of the land frontier, the opening and progress of the urban frontier led to great changes in American life in a manner which substantially met the ten conditions of the frontier hypothesis. The assault upon nature was transformed from the relatively simple matter of turning wildlands into productive land (usually agricultural), into a continuous effort to inventively exploit natural phenomena (steam, electricity) or to extract and re-form raw materials (coal, iron) in unprecedented ways. It involved extensive new organization of the uses of the land through the development of cities with concentrated urban populations as the dominant form of social and economic organization in American life.[5] In place of the explorer of new lands, the scientific inventor became the source of new discoveries and the trailblazer into the unknown, while the industrial entrepreneur and the factory worker replaced the commercial entrepreneur and the agriculturalist as the pioneers in the development of the discoveries of the inventor-explorer.

Despite periodic depressions, the nation's economy continued to expand at an even more rapid rate, past the "takeoff" period described by Rostow and through the period of rapid industrialization with its corresponding increase in national wealth.[6] A new technology, fostered in great part by the demands of the land frontier, emerged to become a major force in the promotion of urbanization, industrialization, and economic growth, creating new secondary frontiers of its own. Cities grew up to produce not only ever more sophisticated agricultural implements but also the machine tools needed to make the former. The railroad, itself a revolutionary instrument in the realm of transportation technology, created other revolutions in the patterns of settlement on both frontiers. These, in turn, led to the emergence of new specialized function frontiers (textiles, steel, food processing) or reorientations of old ones (transportation, mining, merchandising), as well as new geographic frontiers.

As Horatio Alger, Frank Norris, and Arthur M. Schlesinger have told us, for people who were willing to respond to its lure, the urban frontier provided new opportunities for making fortunes, for getting away from home, for taking financial and personal risks, and for achievements based on the willingness to act. There also existed the same kind of freedom to engage in the enterprises previously associated with the land frontier, both for the entrepreneur interested in the development of a new product and a new market and for the "man in the street" interested in new forms of earning a livelihood. The same "boom or bust" spirit, sense of boosterism, and feeling of pioneering found among the pioneers of the land frontier could be found among the developers of the industrial cities on the urban frontier, for good reason. The popular literature of the day reflects this quite clearly.[7]

As on the classic frontier, talent remained more important than either family background or inherited money, so access to the challenges and benefits of the urban frontier remained reasonably free. This access was extended broadly as new occupations developed at a rapid rate, with openings for people from all levels in the society. The new occupations, coupled with the professionalization of old ones, served to break down developing inequalities in the agricultural sector. Also, as in the case of the land frontier, where the promise of the frontier did not appear to be materializing as a matter of course, seekers of the promise took political action to rectify matters. Despite the tendencies of the new industrialism to promote large fortunes (almost invariably made by entrepreneurs from humble backgrounds), the forces of the urban frontier still operated to promote a rough equality of condition for the majority by destroying the established inequalities of the past.

The coming of urbanization transformed the social structure of American life, moving first the most energetic and ultimately the majority of the nation's population into the cities where they had to modify aspects of their agrarian outlook in an effort to meet the problems of high-density living in a complex, highly organized society. It also changed the nation's demographic base by adding a polyglot population of Catholics and Jews from all over Europe to a previously overwhelmingly Protestant Anglo-Saxon base. Industrialization, with its introduction of recurring technological obsolescence, introduced a level of continuing change unheard of in any earlier society.

The urban frontier began the urbanization of American society before it became recognizable as a major frontier manifestation in its own right. There has been a growing migration to urban areas at least since the eighteenth century. Since 1790, the year of the first Census, the nation's urban and rural populations have grown at the same rate in only one decade, between 1810 and 1820, before the emergence of the urban frontier as a force to be reckoned with. Since 1820, the rate of urban growth has been accelerating while the rate of rural growth has been declining. The city rapidly became the center of American life even when city dwellers still represented a small minority of the total population. Virtually every city was taken in hand by its boosters, who had a continual desire to enlarge its size and position as a metropolitan center, to make each city a bigger and supposedly grander metropolis than any other city, and, in the process, to glamorize urban living.

By 1850, urban life as a reflection of the urban frontier had become the dominant way of life in the East, and the city had become the vanguard of the land frontier in the West. In general, the period between 1816 and 1876 was the "heroic age" for the foundation, incorporation, and growth of what are now the nation's largest cities, just as it was the heroic age for the conquest of the last land frontier.[8] Indeed, the two phenomena went hand in hand; a significant overlapping of frontiers at a time when the shape of the United States was being crystallized. It is significant that the bulk of the nation's population growth in the past two generations has taken place in the metropolitan areas surrounding the cities created in that era. This was also the period during which the leading cities included in this study were founded (Table 1–7) as part of the spread of settlement into the Mississippi Valley, where they became urban service centers for their rural hinterlands and outposts on the land frontier.

During this period when the distinctive American urban pattern took root, the largest cities in the United States were, with one or two exceptions, no bigger in population than the medium-size cities of today. It was only after 1890, when the land frontier had become secondary to the urban frontier that had become the primary source of individual opportunity and social development in this country, that most of these cities grew really large. In the years between the Civil War and the turn of the century, the combined influence of the two frontiers stimulated a process of "natural selection" that transformed some of those cities into national and world centers while limiting others equally as old to lesser positions. In the case of the greater West, while cities like Chicago (founded 1829, incorporated 1837), St. Louis (1764 and 1822), Minneapolis (1856 and 1867), St. Paul (1842 and 1853), and Denver (1859 and 1861) were becoming "empire cities," the cities of the prairie founded in the same period were growing from villages to become small or medium-size cities within the hinterlands of the aforementioned centers. By the turn of the century, the bright hopes of each budding metropolis had been altered by the realities of history and geography that assigned it a "proper" position vis-à-vis the others, within the larger pattern of urbanization in the central and western Mississippi Valley.

The Opening of the Metropolitan Frontier

The history of the urban frontier in the United States appears to envelop two contradictory trends. On one hand, the urban frontier has brought about the urbanization of American society. On the other hand, even as the rate of urbanization began to accelerate, a counter, almost anti-urban trend began to develop as well, a trend that would not become dominant until the physical setting of American society had become thoroughly urbanized four generations later. After 1820, the nation's largest cities, such as New York, Boston, Philadelphia, Baltimore, and New Orleans, began to experience an outmigration to newly created suburban areas. Though most of these early suburbs were later annexed by their central cities in the fashion of the urban frontier, the suburbanization process continued throughout the nineteenth century, gaining new impetus as new means of transportation were developed that made movement from the city possible. First the railroad, then the electric trolley, and finally the automobile stimulated suburbanization past the "horse and buggy" stage.

Though the progress of urbanization in the United States has proceeded steadily, Americans have moved to the cities with seeming reluctance. Only in 1890, when the urban frontier was entering its highest stage of development, did the number of urban places in the United States exceed one thousand and the urban population exceed one-third of the total population (Table 1–1). It was not until after 1900 that cities of over 50,000 came to include as much as one-quarter of the nation's total population. In light of this slow development of large urban centers, it is understand-

TABLE 1-1

Distribution of U.S. Population by Size of Place: 1790-1960

Year	% Urban	No. Urban Places	Urban Places 1 million +		500,000-1 million		250,000-500,000		100,000-250,000		50,000-100,000		10,000-50,000[b]		Less than 10,000		% Rural
			No.	% of Pop.	No.	% of Pop.	No.	% of Pop.	No.	% of Pop.	No.	% of Pop.	No.	% of Pop.	No.	% of Pop.	
1790	5.1	24	–	–	–	–	–	–	–	–	–	–	5	5.1[b]	19	–	94.9
1800	6.1	33	–	–	–	–	–	–	–	–	1	1.1	5	5	27	–	93.9
1810	7.3	46	–	–	–	–	–	–	–	–	2	–	9	–	35	–	92.7
1820	7.2	61	–	–	–	–	–	–	1	1.3	2	1.3	10	4.6	48	–	92.8
1830	8.8	90	–	–	–	–	–	–	1	–	3	–	19	–	67	–	91.2
1840	10.8	131	–	–	–	–	1	1.8	2	1.2	2	1.1	32	6.7	94	–	89.2
1850	15.3	236	–	–	1	–	1	–	4	–	3	–	52	–	174	–	84.7
1860	19.8	392	–	–	2	4.4	1	0.8	6	3.2	7	1.4	77	10	299	–	80.2
1870	25.7	663	–	–	2	–	5	–	7	–	11	–	143	–	495	–	74.3
1880	28.2	939	1	2.4	3	3.8	4	2.6	12	3.6	15	1.9	188	13.9	716	–	71.8
1890	35.1	1348	3	5.8	1	–	7	–	17	–	30	–	296	–	994	–	64.9
1900	39.7	1737	3	8.5	3	2.2	9	3.8	23	4.3	40	3.6	362	7.3	1297	–	60.3
1910	45.7	2262	3	9.2	5	3.3	11	4.3	31	5.3	59	4.5	588	10.4	1665	8.7	54.3
1920	51.2	2722	3	9.6	9	5.9	13	4.3	43	6.2	76	5.0	608	11.5	1970	8.8	48.8
1930	56.2	3165	5	12.3	8	4.7	24	6.5	56	6.1	98	5.3	791	12.6	2183	8.6	43.8
1940	56.5	3464	5	12.1	9	4.9	23	5.9	55	5.9	107	5.6	878	13.2	2387	8.7	43.5
1950	64.0[a]	4743[a]	5	11.5	13	6.1	23	5.5	65[a]	6.3[a]	126[a]	5.9[a]	1030[a]	13.7[a]	3479[a]	10.1[a]	36.0
1960	69.9[a]	6041[a]	5	9.8	16	6.2	30	6.0	81[a]	6.5[a]	201[a]	7.7[a]	1566[a]	18.1[a]	4142[a]	10.1[a]	30.1

[a]Current Urban Definition. Not included in this table is the population of unincorporated parts of urbanized areas, which equal 4.9 per cent of the total in 1950 and 5.5 per cent in 1960.

[b]Percentage of population includes all cities of less than 50,000 through 1900.

Source: U.S. Census Bureau, *Historical Statistics of the United States* and *Statistical Abstract of the United States.*

able that cities like Duluth and Peoria ranked among the nation's largest in 1900 and why Davenport, Springfield, Rockford, Pueblo, and Superior were considered miniature metropolitan centers as well.

The urban population did not exceed the rural population until 1920, when the urban frontier was already passing the peak of its influence. That same year, the total population in cities of 100,000 and over came to exceed the total population in all smaller urban places. The age of the big city had seemingly arrived. However, no sooner did the big city become the apparent embodiment of the American style of life than it began to be replaced by a less citified style in turn. As Table 1–1 indicates, the upward trend in the growth of big cities came to an end during the Depression, giving way to the development of medium-size and smaller cities within large and medium-size metropolitan areas as a new embodiment of American urban life and a major aspect of the third American frontier.

The positive yet reluctant response of most Americans to urbanization reflects a basic desire on their part to have their cake and eat it too; to have the economic and social advantages of urbanization, which they value for essentially hedonistic reasons, while preserving the erstwhile "rural" amenities of life—both physical and social—which they value for essentially moral reasons. As long as city life was able to offer most of the amenities of "rural" living, as well as the economic, social, and cultural advantages of the city, to those who were in a position to determine the city's growth, the expansion of cities as cities continued. Throughout the nineteenth century, newly settled suburbs and smaller cities brought into the big city orbit were annexed to already large cities because their residents, or those holding power locally, felt reasonably confident that loss of their suburb's independent political status would not mean an end to their suburban style of life. Not only did large cities continue to grow larger, but small cities still aspired to become great metropolitan centers. The full impact of big city life in its less attractive aspects—crowding, apartment living, tenement slums, lack of such natural amenities as clean air, grass, and trees—had not become sufficiently apparent to the majority of the residents in the cities and so had evoked no negative response to the idea of indefinite city growth.

The truth of the matter was that, before 1890, big cities in the United States had not yet become big enough to evoke these negative reactions, except in a few isolated cases along the eastern seaboard. This is not to say that cities like New York, Philadelphia, Boston, Baltimore, and Chicago, or even smaller industrial towns, did not have extensive tenement sections before 1890, but even in those "great" cities, the majority of the socially and politically articulate population could still live in private or semiprivate homes along tree-lined streets. Tenement living remained the preserve of newly arrived immigrants who as yet had little or no voice in civic affairs and no wherewithal with which to escape the tenements to which they were, in effect, confined.

There came a point in the development of most of the larger cities, however, when even the politically articulate citydwellers found it difficult to maintain their semi-urban style of life within them. Even enlargement of the city limits came to mean the enlargement of the city's problems without any reasonable recompense. At the same time, several other factors coalesced to encourage metropolitanization in place of simple urbanization.

As maintenance of even the simpler rural-style amenities began to cost more money within the large cities, the wealthier citydwellers began to seek new residences outside the city limits. The cities themselves began to encounter increased difficulties in their attempts to annex new areas, coming up against already existing cities which, while being suburbanized socially and economically, desired to retain their political independence in order to better maintain their distinctive character. It had become apparent that annexation to the great cities was tantamount to absorption into a citified environment with little or no possibility of controlling the extent of citification. Hence neither old residents nor new settlers fleeing the big city were willing to be brought into its embrace. Annexation, which had been relatively easy under the law in most states, was made more difficult as the small cities on the fringes of the giants went to the legislatures with their demands for self-preservation. In fact, as these fringe area cities began to attract settlers from the central city, they frequently began to annex vacant land themselves, often in competition with the central city, growing from villages to small and even medium-size cities within the larger metropolitan region that was in the process of formation.

Simultaneously, improved transportation technology made it possible for more people to move out of the great cities into surrounding areas while retaining jobs within the cities they left. This movement, begun in the days of the railroads, was intensified by the development of the automobile and the construction of roads suitable for heavy motor traffic. At the same time, the previously deprived groups living in the substandard areas of the great cities prospered sufficiently to seek alternatives to their relatively poor city living conditions, and the offspring of recent immigrants among them acquired the American taste for a semi-urban environment. Following the "old tenement trail" to the suburbs, they began to move out to a new metropolitan frontier where it became possible to live in the same style that earlier prestigious groups had endowed with considerable status.[9] Moreover, as the movement to the metropolis accelerated in the country as a whole, many rural residents moved directly into the suburban fringes of the major cities, preferring them over city living from the first.[10]

"Permanent" metropolitanization (as distinct from the "temporary" suburbanization of earlier years) began in the East in the last third of the nineteenth century in response to the urban frontier and spread to the larger cities in the middle and far West by the turn of the century (just as the urban frontier had begun in the heyday of the land frontier as a response to the needs of the land frontier and spread in the same manner). Students of society were already becoming interested in it in the 1920's, but it was not until the close of World War II that the metropolitan frontier came into its own. At that time, the pressures to leave the great cities, which had been building up through the Depression and war years, burst their bounds. By 1950, the trend toward big city living had been reversed and the number of people living in cities of over 100,000 had declined to less than the number of people living in smaller urban places. By 1960, only 28.5 per cent of the total population in the United States lived in urban places of more than 100,000 population, the lowest figure since 1920. The percentage of population living in cities of over one million, which had peaked in 1930, had declined sharply since then and was back at the 1920 level. All this occurred despite the increasing metropolitanization of the country's population. By 1960, 63 per cent of the nation's people lived in the two-hundred-and-twelve Census Bureau-defined standard metropolitan statistical areas, which grew 26.4 per cent between 1950 and 1960, in contrast to the overall national growth of 18.5 per cent.

The great migration to the suburbs was simply one aspect of the new metropolitan frontier. The urban-industrial frontier lost its primacy in the Great Depression. With the completion of the nation's basic urbanization and industrialization, the complex of opportunities needed for frontier-style development temporarily disappeared. Urbanizing and industrializing trends did persist in regions till then on the peripheries of the urban-industrial frontier, just as pioneering on the land frontier has continued in isolated areas. However, the opportunity of fostering the continuous reconstruction of the social order associated with the frontier was no longer available through simple urbanization and industrialization.

So, after a brief hiatus due to the Depression and World War II, the third great manifestation of the American frontier began to unfold. Its reappearance as the metropolitan-technological frontier of science, suburbia, and space led to the emergence of new versions of old frontier situations. Even more so than in the case of the land and urban frontiers, the metropolitan frontier is most immediately a local phenomenon that has spread within and across the continent in a generally east-west direction to become manifest nationwide. While the metropolitanizing trend moved across the continent, almost every one of the nation's urban centers responded to the new frontier locally by developing a metropolitan frontier of its own. Thus frontier areas of new growth have emerged around the fringes of the great majority of the nation's urban centers while, within those same urban centers, areas of decline have developed that have been unable to respond positively to the new frontier's demands. These "inner city" areas have come to resemble the "backwash" regions left in the wake of the earlier frontiers with all the problems of areas returning to "wilderness" (in today's parlance, "jungle"). While this particular kind of localization of the frontier process can be partly traced back to the urban frontier, it did not become a significant aspect of the great frontier until the rise of metropolitanism. With its advent, the great frontier entered into a truly new stage reflecting its generally increased complexity.

On the metropolitan frontier, land is once again a crucial factor. The "metropolitan fringe"—the area of expanding urbanization and the non-urban area into which it expands—is the arena of frontier expansion. Within the metropolitan area, it is even possible to delineate a frontier line (where settlement falls below a density of 500 per square mile) that marks the limit of metropolitanization and can be seen to move as settlement expands. The metropolitan frontier has organized the use of land in a new way, combining densities that would be considered rural in much of the Old World with urban social and economic organization to create quasi- (or sub-) urban metropolitan complexes encompassing cities of all sizes, towns, and villages, and rural dwellings. By the standards of the urban frontier era (which are all too often still applied in discussions of contemporary metropolitanization), the land uses of the metropolitan frontier are considered "urban sprawl," but, in view of the goals of deconcentration implicit in the development of these variegated metropolitan land use patterns, this so-called sprawl is what makes urban living tolerable to many (if not most) Americans. Even with the spreading of metropolitan forms of land use, as of 1960 less than 7 per cent of the land area of the United States was within standard metropolitan statistical areas, and only about 4 per cent was actually urbanized, leaving near-limitless area for future expansion of metropolitan settlement in this country, a key manifestation of its frontier character. Though land is no longer "free" or unoccupied, and there is no longer the once-prevalent feeling that it is limitless, the facts of availability of new land for metropolitanization do not differ substantially from similar *facts* regarding the land frontier.

Though the physical world of the metropolitan frontier appears highly tamed to the naked eye, it is likely that man has never before in his history confronted the "wilds" of nature to the extent that he does today. Of course, these wilds (or the wilderness they add up to), whether they be on the earth, below, or beyond it, must be approached through the intellectual techniques of science rather than through the simple exertion of brute physical force (not that science did not supplement brute force on the land frontier or that physical power is no longer needed). This shift to the primacy of intellectual effort, with all its consequences for society as a whole, is itself one of the most profound impacts of the contemporary frontier.

The metropolitan land boom and the growth of brain industries are but two manifestations of the twenty-year economic boom that began with the opening of the new frontier and, though occasionally slowed down by recessions, has continued as the feedbacks of the frontier (ranging from the demands of space exploration to the needs of newborn babies) have exerted increasing influence on the economy. The results of scientific exploration on the new frontier have stimulated the pioneering of many new technologies, so important that technological change has surpassed land and industrialization in significance to become the motive force of the metropolitan frontier.

As in the past, changes in transportation and communications technology have been crucial in opening the metropolitan-technological frontier. On this new frontier, the key to the expansion of settlement is the automobile, whose development is illustrative of the frontier impact of science and technology. From certain theoretical principles of physics, "discovered" by the first scientific explorers a century or more ago, the inventor-pioneers of the urban-industrial frontier were able to create the internal combustion engine and, ultimately, the automobile. The new vehicle and the technology it represented rapidly revolutionized society, creating a myriad of new industries—the oil industry, for example—which had never existed before and which provided a wide range of opportunities for those willing and able to take advantage of them. By 1963, over seven million jobs were directly dependent on the automobile, none of which had existed two generations earlier.

American society became automobile-oriented, which, in turn, led to a revolution in its physical organization, its social structure, and its moral sense. The automobile, like the railroad before it, made possible the opening of a new geographic frontier. Whereas pre-automobile communities could develop only along rail lines, new ones could develop wherever roads could be built. This fact was of particular importance around the nation's cities. Suburbs offering better housing, lands and open space, and greater feeling of community, previously few in number and the preserves of the rich because they were dependent upon railroad service, now became accessible to the vast majority of the people. This, in turn, radically changed the uses of land in potentially suburban areas, the social structure of urban populations, and the political organization of metropolitan regions.[11] The automobile also extended freedom of travel to people who were unable to travel before, transforming isolated villagers into participants in wider regional communities.[12]

The impact of the automotive frontier had some important (and often unforeseen) byproducts as well. The new automotive society enriched numerous automobile manufacturers and dealers, as well as manufacturers and dealers of subsidiary products, creating a whole new class of millionaires with interests and values reflecting the culture that made them. It transformed the socioeconomic structures of whole states, creating, among other things, modern Michigan, contemporary Texas, and twentieth-century California (the very acme of the new frontier). The automotive frontier also contributed the five-dollar day, making it possible for Negroes to earn a living wage for the first time in their history on these shores and promoting their migration northward. In this and other ways, it broadened both the opportunities and horizons of a people previously restricted in every way with ease and contributed mightily to stimulating the present drive for Negro equality. Thomas H. McDonald, for thirty-four years head of the Federal Bureau of Public Roads, put the matter succinctly:

> . . . the roads themselves helped us create a new wealth, in business and industry and land values. . . . So it was not our wealth that made our highways possible. Rather, it was our highways that made our wealth possible.[13]

Not the least of the automobile's effects was the change it induced in family life, giving children greater freedom from parental control than at any time in history. These changes, in turn, forced a variety of adjustments in traditional American political institutions, particularly in the structure and scope of government—local, state, and national—raising new problems of police, changing the span of political control and pressure, and making new demands on government in the social realm as well.

The metropolitan frontier, like its predecessors, is also a composite of many specialized geographic and functional frontiers. The automotive and suburban frontiers have already been mentioned. The recreation and space frontiers are yet others, not to mention the particular frontiers of the eastern megalopolis or southern California. Each of these specialized frontiers has offered many opportunities for exploration, growth, and development. All have required the taking of risks and active pursuit of frontier-style goals while offering great material and moral rewards. The builders of subdivisions, the creators of franchised "chains," the researchers in the laboratories, and perhaps even the promoters of psychedelic art all potentially share this aspect of the frontier experience insofar as their courageous application of effort brings them the exhilarating rewards that came from exploring or pioneering.

The very complexity of the metropolitan frontier and the variety of specialized frontiers within it heighten the freedom of access to the frontier zone in one form or another. In particular, the existence of a standard body of scientific and technical knowledge formally (if not actually) available to all on the basis of ability alone, whose mastery offers access to the frontier, is simply a more complex variation of the kind of equality of access that prevailed in the days of the land frontier.[14] Then the "standard body of techniques" grew out of physical prowess rather than intellectual ability but served the same general purpose. Moreover, the use of intelligence as a prime means of access to the frontier is not confined to the realms of science and technology.

If the publications and pronouncements of the press and mass media and the orientation of recent political campaigns are at all indicative of public attitudes, popular awareness of the frontier-like opportunities present in American society is very high, and public responses to the challenges of the contemporary frontier are no less impressive than in earlier periods in American history. All in all, the repeated references to "new frontiers" are not simply a matter of rhetoric. This frontier psychology exists despite the strong tendency in American society to view the problems of each era as unique, an outlook that itself reflects the thinking of people engaged on the frontier.

Rapid technological change has stimulated the creation of new industries, creating new occupations on all levels of society that demand talents not transmittable by heredity and that consequently must be open to those who qualify regardless of their social backgrounds. It has been reliably estimated that some 80 per cent of the jobs that exist in the United States today were not in existence two generations ago when the urban-industrial frontier was at its peak. Moreover, there has been a shift in the character of American occupation structure from production to service, comparable to the shift from agriculture to industry that was produced by the advance of the urban frontier. At the same time, the social "feedback" from the advancing frontier continues to have strong pro-democratic effects on American social structure and civil society, promoting both freedom and equality through its continued fostering of social mobility and an expanding conception of the rights of all to participate equally in social life and the political process. In a decade that has seen a civil rights revolution, a war on poverty, and the proclamation of new forms of individual freedom from many quarters, all avowedly in response to developments in American society since 1945, this assessment need hardly be formally documented.

The greatest social contribution of the metropolitan frontier has been the impetus it has given to the breakdown of major social and economic differences among population groups. As a result, the older institutions of the Republic and its subdivisions, which had more or less excluded those not white, Protestant, and Northern European, have had to readjust to include the rest of the country's population in the system of politics and power, public and private, through which decisions are made. We are presently in the throes of this readjustment, and the bulk of America's political energies are being directed toward that end in order to achieve it in a manner consonant with the American mystique and the basic institutions and traditions through which that mystique is expressed. As the very designation of the new frontier indicates, most of these adaptations have had to be made on the metropolitan level. Indeed, the best expression of the sociopolitical consequences of the new frontier has been found in the transformation of urban America into metropolitan America. The key to the adaptation lies in that very transformation.

The Agrarian Ideal and the Metropolitan Frontier[15]

The present concentration of population in great conurbations is a world-wide phenomenon, but in the United States the continuing frontier has given it a unique character. Behind America's great metropolitan migration lies a complex of special attitudes about cities and urban living. Nobody conversant with American history need be reminded of the agrarian roots of American civilization. Beginning with the settlement of the Puritans in New England and the emergence of a Southern agrarian squirearchy, both of which invoked Biblical, and hence divine, support for their views, articulate Americans viewed the rural life (on separated farms or in agricultural towns, depending on one's cultural heritage) as the good life or, indeed, the best life, where the vices inherent in man by virtue of Adam's fall would be least likely to flourish while proper community could be developed. Until the middle of the nineteenth century, this doctrinal position was reinforced by an agrarian economic system and a pattern of political organization that rested on individual agricultural freeholders. Furthermore, social equality, always a basic element in the American mystique, found its closest approximation in the overwhelmingly middle-class agricultural society of early America, a fact which was not lost upon those who seriously concerned themselves with the problems of creating the good society.

In the eighteenth century, the agrarian ideal was restated in sweeping philosophic terms to become part of the world view of the Enlightenment. Thomas Jefferson, the foremost American spokesman for philosophic agrarianism, saw the agrarian life as that best suited to bringing out man's natural virtues and most likely to prevent the social evils always possible in organized society. He saw the city as the source of collective, even more than individual, corruption; to be avoided as a source of inequality, class distinction, and social disorganization that could lead to tyranny in one form or another.

Both views of agrarian virtue versus urban corruption became part of the mainstream of American thought, articulated by intellectuals from

Thoreau to Frank Lloyd Wright and made the basis of political movements from Jeffersonian Democracy through Populism and the New Deal to the "new conservatism" (and segments of the new radicalism as well) of the 1960's. The city was and continues to be viewed by many as a breeder of crime, corruption, social disorganization, and anomie, not fit to be lived in by "honest middle-class folk" and valuable only for its economic utility.[16]

With the exception of certain of its Southern manifestations, the American agrarian ideal differs significantly from its Old World counterparts. Essentially a complex of middle-class, progressive (in a liberal sense), equalitarian, democratic values, American agrarianism was never committed to the promotion of rural villages populated by aristocrats and peasants rooted generation after generation in the same soil where they lived out their respective roles in "organic" symbiosis. Rather, it combined a middle-class orientation linking agriculture with commerce to create a new synthesis designed to assure individual liberty, essential equality, and mutual advancement through self-created communities with a broad attachment to the land, communities which could be planted anywhere as the frontier demanded through the initiative of those who were on the spot. This new synthesis was best manifested in the real world in the New England town and its lineal descendant, the Upper Mississippi Valley township, where individual freeholders engaging in agriculture or agribusiness were morally and practically linked in communities whether they lived close together or were divided by the large acreage of most American farms.[17] To a lesser extent, it was also manifested in the counties of the Middle States and the South, where more individualistic farmers and businessmen pursued their less communally oriented vision of rural independence.

Because it was not bound by traditional rural limitations, the American version of the agrarian ideal survived and grew even as the actual process of urbanization accelerated and the cities became the pace-setters in American life, leading to a perhaps curious but important ambivalence in most Americans' approach to the city. While desiring to gain economically and socially in certain ways by exploiting the benefits of urban concentration, Americans have, time and again, rejected the classically urban styles of living basic to the Old World and the Old World style "ghettos" in our major cities populated by the more recent immigrants from Europe (and now by those from the American South).

Accepting the necessity and even the value of urbanization, Americans have, by and large, distinguished between living in cities and what may be termed "citification"—the adoption of the sophisticated values and interests classically associated with city living—rejecting the latter at every turn. They have tried to bring their version of the old agrarian ideals into the urban setting and to reinterpret them through the establishment of patterns of living within urbanized areas resembling the rural patterns they had known previously. The result has been the conversion of urban settlements into metropolitan areas whose very expansiveness provides the physical means for combining a variety of rural and urban life styles into a new pattern which better suits the American taste. This pattern is intended to combine the advantages of an urban environment with the preservation of the essence of those virtues that have traditionally informed the "American way of life."

Nowhere is this tendency more pronounced than in the region of the cities of the prairie. There the synthesis of agriculture and commerce into an American agrarianism reached its apex. And, while almost every kind of concrete expression of that agrarian vision can be found within that region, the township pattern and its later variations are clearly the most pronounced. No doubt that is why their region is invariably considered to be the most typically American in this nation's folklore.

As part of the effort to transplant American agrarianism into an urban setting, a whole set of symbols and mechanisms has developed that evokes rural and small-town America and its traditional values. In almost every case, they have been induced or supported by developments on the metropolitan frontier. And, in almost every case, they have either taken political form or have found expression through politics. Suburbia has become the equivalent of small-town America as the symbol of the country's grass roots and the fountainhead of "the American way of life." This is so regardless of whether suburbia is praised or condemned in that role. The popular literature defending suburbia and that attacking it are both strongly reminiscent of the popular literature devoted to small-town America two to four generations ago. If some see virtue in the small community—whether it is typified by a dominant small-town society or a dominant suburban society—others (Sinclair Lewis and Edgar Lee Masters, from the very area of this study, come immediately to mind) see ignorance, provincialism, and even corruption in the same situation.[18]

In essence, the development of suburban—and exurban—communities ranging in size and scope from cities of 100,000 people or more to collections of scattered homes on multi-acre tracts served by common "crossroads" institutions has now made available to urban Americans numerous options for sub-city living, creating new kinds of "grass roots" settlements. The accepted value of these new kinds of communities in preserving or reforging a way of life that allows for the development of local interests in a complex national society can be seen in the continued resistance of the residents of suburban communities to any efforts, real or imagined, to absorb them into the political sphere of the central city or otherwise limit their existence as autonomous political entities.

The sphere of community political organization is only one manifestation of this "neo-agrarianism." The continued emphasis on home ownership and the complex of activities and symbols which surround it represents the private corollary to the effort to re-create the town in the public sphere, one which is found in both cities and suburbs. Owner-occupied, free-standing homes, each with its lawn and garden, represent a major expenditure of energy and resources in contemporary American society. The emphasis on widely extended home ownership is not an accidental consequence of the convergence of separately initiated policies. On the contrary, it is the product of conscious design. The foundations for today's widespread home ownership were laid during the 1930's by the New Deal, which, in general, prepared the way for the opening of the metropolitan frontier, reflecting the agrarian outlook of that great movement. As Henry Bamford Parkes has persuasively argued, the New Deal represented a major resurgence of traditional American agrarianism, and its major contribution was an effort to translate those values into terms and programs appropriate to the new urban setting.[19]

Consequently, while urbanization and metropolitanization in other countries have led to the development of official policies to encourage high-density living, federal, state, and even local policies (other than the property tax) in the United States are heavily weighted in favor of the home owner and low-density development. Mortgage guarantees, home-financing funds, homestead exemptions, zoning regulations, and many other specific devices have been enacted into law to encourage widespread home ownership. Even the recent apartment boom has had to come to terms with the American penchant for home ownership. The rapid spread of condominiums indicates the vitality of this tradition even in unlikely quarters. Still, except for New York and Chicago, apartments remain the home of unmarried young adults, newly married couples, and the retired. The recent spurt in apartment construction is apparently designed to meet the needs of these groups rather than to replace the single-family home. Furthermore, much of the apartment "boom" is taking place in the suburbs, reinforcing their developing self-sufficiency as communities.

In light of all this, it is not surprising that the percentage of owner-occupied homes has been increasing rapidly since 1940, when only 43.6 per cent of the nation's housing units were owner-occupied. By 1950, the figure had risen to 55 per cent and by 1960 to 61.9 per cent. This compares well with the 64.16 per cent owner-occupied farm housing units in 1900 (when only 36.5 per cent of the urban housing units were owner-occupied), a figure which reflects the land frontier ideal of farmers owning rather than renting their farms.

The cities of the prairie fully exemplify this trend. Despite their progressive population growth, urbanization, and metropolitanization, every one of them is built around the owner-occupied single-family home, which represents the cornerstone of the good life for the overwhelming majority of their citizenry and which functions as the fundamental physical and social (and, indeed, political) building block in each civil community. Owner-occupancy is on the increase in the cities of the prairie in much the same manner as in the rest of the country and has led to even higher percentages of home ownership than in larger cities.

As Table 1–2 indicates, in 1940 home ownership was still basically a rural phenomenon, even in the heart of the Middle West. While home owners predominated in the rural areas and villages near the cities of the prairie, renters predominated in the cities proper, even in the smaller ones. Of the seventeen central cities, only Belleville, always a predominantly middle-class residential community, and Pueblo, located much farther West and subjected to a different order of external pressures, had more owner-occupied than renter-occupied housing units within their boundaries. By 1950, only Davenport had more renter-occupied units, and by 1960 the gap in favor of owner-occupied units in all the cities except one had widened considerably.[20]

Perhaps the most revealing aspect of all this is that the increase in owner-occupied units has been generally constant in all seventeen cities, regardless of other factors such as population growth, extent of metropolitanization, and the like. Superior, with an absolute decline in population, and Duluth, with the barest growth, have changed as radically as Rockford, Pueblo, and Champaign, which have grown so greatly since 1940. This uniformity is indicative of the universal character of the shift to home ownership. It undoubtedly is, in part, a reflection of government housing policies, which make home ownership the easiest way for families to improve their living conditions.

If the shift had taken place primarily in centers of considerable population growth, this explanation of the phenomenon might suffice. However, the universal character of the change indicates that there is something more involved. It is very likely that the agrarian-rooted ideal of home ownership was frustrated by the limited financial resources of most families and the equally limited lack of mortgage funds in the early days of American urbanization but again became feasible, even in the urban setting, in the prosperity that followed World War II. It is apparent that one of the great motivating forces behind the opening of the metropolitan frontier was this popular, near-universal drive for home ownership and "space."

The trend to owner-occupied housing has revived such symbolically rural occupations as gardening and "do-it-yourself" home maintenance. The public response to these activities indicates that they are, in effect, an urban recrudescence of a vernacular artistic tradition long associated with rural and small-town life. The importance of this vernacular tradition in American life is often overlooked, as those who are generally deemed to be the custodians of the arts in this country tend to be products of the more cultivated traditions of Western civilization as a whole. Similarly, the impact that private maintenance of lawns and gardens has on the maintenance of the esthetic qualities of American urban areas has generally been ignored by students of urbanization, but it is readily apparent when slum areas where no such private contributions are made are contrasted with even the most commonplace suburban tract developments where lawns and gardens are a social "must." The private expenditure for lawn and garden maintenance far exceeds the public expenditure for parks and other forms of public beautification and represents a virtually irreplaceable contribution to the "public good."[21]

The effort to limit the exercise of governmental powers in each locality and to fragment those that are exercised has been another aspect of the transplantation of agrarian values into urban settings. The reasons for this are complex and the effort itself is by no means consistent. Particularly in the region of the cities of the prairie, but throughout the nation as well, there is a hesitancy about strengthening local government in the provision of amenities for fear that the addition of more local services will increase the urban character of the environment. In the fringe areas of most cities in the South and West and many in the East as well, large numbers of people resist sidewalks because sidewalks represent citification. Certainly, the notion of controlling power by involving as many citizens as possible in its exercise is part of the emphasis on fragmentation, though there are other reasons as well.

Here the impact of widespread home ownership converges with the public aspects of neo-agrarianism. To take one example, in a political system which relies heavily on the property tax for local revenue, widespread home ownership tends to reinforce the already great reluctance of the citizenry to increase local government responsibility for public facilities and services. This, in turn, helps limit the expansion of local governmental activity and expand federal and state involvement in local affairs, since the latter generally possess better (less painful) means of raising revenue.

All told, this neo-agrarianism is part of the general impact of the metropolitan-technological frontier in American life much as the original agrarianism was a product of America's first frontier. The combination of ideology, economic development, and technological advance that has made this metropolitan migration possible has led to the substantial decitification of American society within decades after it became recognizably urban in the first place. The metropolitan movement, then, appears to be an effort to reconcile two apparently contradictory forces: the agrarian bias built into the American conception of the good life and the real need for urban concentration to satisfy the frontier aspirations of the American people.

TABLE 1-2

Home Ownership in the Cities of the Prairie: 1940-1960

SMSA	1940		1950		1960	
	Owner-Occupied	Renter-Occupied	Owner-Occupied	Renter-Occupied	Owner-Occupied	Renter-Occupied
Champaign-Urbana	8,859	10,584	14,374	12,521	20,358	15,876
Champaign	3,015	3,972	5,421	4,462	8,116	5,582
Urbana	2,063	2,305	3,109	2,951	4,081	4,112
Remainder of county	3,781	4,307	5,844	55,108	8,161	6,182
Decatur	8,861	10,146	20,335	10,301	26,649	10,461
Decatur City	7,838	9,460	13,673	7,447	17,685	7,916
Remainder of county	1,023	686	6,662	2,854	8,964	2,545
Duluth-Superior	22,006	21,042	49,614	25,906	99,801	25,108
Duluth	13,422	14,397	19,340	11,972	22,257	12,234
Remainder of St. Louis County	2,186	591	21,480	9,058	68,033	8,698
Superior	4,352	5,292	6,105	4,403	6,684	3,770
Remainder of Douglas County	346	110	1,689	473	2,827	406
Joliet	13,448	12,159	24,155	13,065	38,534	14,974
Joliet	5,139	6,399	8,832	6,365	12,622	7,318
Remainder of SMSA	8,309	5,760	15,323	6,700	25,912	7,656
Peoria	24,044	21,801	47,377	26,742	61,742	26,101
Peoria	13,851	16,608	18,298	15,410	19,056	14,586
Pekin	3,363	2,211	4,746	2,128	6,796	2,210
East Peoria	1,037	913	1,521	1,075	2,442	1,386
Remainder of SMSA	5,793	2,069	22,812	8,129	33,448	18,182

TABLE 1-2 (continued)

SMSA	1940		1950		1960	
	Owner-Occupied	Renter-Occupied	Owner-Occupied	Renter-Occupied	Owner-Occupied	Renter-Occupied
Pueblo	8,833	7,538	15,509	8,848	23,083	9,229
Pueblo	7,143	6,798	12,365	6,786	18,333	7,422
Remainder of SMSA	1,690	740	3,144	2,062	4,750	1,807
Madison-St. Clair	43,147	43,406	72,514	40,623	103,929	40,654
Alton	3,770	4,893	5,590	4,311	9,073	4,310
Belleville	4,662	3,901	6,577	3,845	8,738	3,340
East St. Louis	7,626	13,522	12,505	11,378	13,634	11,324
Granite City	2,535	3,801	5,624	3,246	8,694	3,385
Remainder of SMSA	24,554	17,289	42,218	17,843	63,790	18,295
Quad Cities	23,894	25,636	41,803	26,999	55,173	26,594
Davenport	8,426	10,715	8,426	10,715	17,406	9,933
East Moline	1,340	1,359	2,014	1,320	3,160	1,257
Moline	5,113	5,133	7,170	4,536	9,362	4,578
Rock Island	5,805	6,552	8,572	6,278	10,230	6,346
Remainder of SMSA	3,210	1,877	15,621	4,150	15,015	4,480
Rockford	13,204	17,216	27,714	17,931	42,584	20,135
Rockford	9,880	14,942	15,673	13,054	24,665	15,223
Remainder of county	4,324	2,274	12,041	4,877	17,919	4,912
Springfield	12,255	13,084	25,123	15,536	31,354	16,160
Springfield	9,833	11,752	14,656	11,284	16,797	11,955
Remainder of county	2,422	1,332	10,467	4,252	14,557	4,205

Source: U.S. Census, *Characteristics of the Population, 1940, 1950, and 1960.*

The Medium-Size City and the Metropolitan Frontier

At the local level, the major beneficiaries of the metropolitan frontier have been cities in the 10,000 to 100,000 population range; the medium-size ones and their immediately smaller counterparts, many of which are on their way to medium size.

It is within these medium-size and small metropolitan centers that the greatest population growth has taken place in recent years. Some of this growth has been a product of the exodus from the central cities into suburban satellites, and some has come into both "suburban" and "free-standing" cities from the rural areas as part of the continuing process of urbanization. According to the data presented in Table 1–1, the cities in the 10,000–100,000 class are the fastest growing in the United States, in absolute population, in per cent of total U.S. population, and in number of cities. In Table 1–3, the facts of American urbanization become

TABLE 1-3

The Growth of Cities, by Class, 1920-1960

	Great Cities			Large Cities			Medium-Size Cities			Small Cities			Towns		
Year	No.	Total Pop. (1,000's)	% of Nat. Pop.	No.	Total Pop. (1,000's)	% of Nat. Pop.	No.	Total Pop. (1,000's)	% of Nat. Pop.	No.	Total Pop. (1,000's)	% of Nat. Pop.	No.	Total Pop. (1,000's)	% N P
1920	3	10,146	9.6	22	10,765	10.2	119	11,784	11.2	608	12,110	11.5	1970	9,354	8
1930	5	15,065	12.3	32	13,720	11.2	154	14,032	11.4	791	15,523	12.6	2183	10,615	8
1940	5	15,911	12.1	32	14,285	10.8	162	15,137	11.5	878	17,384	13.2	2387	11,708	8
1950	5	17,404	11.5	36	17,429	11.6	191[a]	18,410[a]	12.2[a]	1030[a]	20,675[a]	13.7[a]	3479[a]	16,207[a]	10
1960	5	17,484	9.8	46	21,877	12.2	282[a]	25,488[a]	14.2[a]	1566[a]	32,519[a]	18.1[a]	4142[a]	18,050[a]	10

[a]Current urban definition.

Source: U.S. Census Bureau, *Statistical Abstract of the United States, 1962.*

Key: Great Cities 1,000,000+
Large Cities 250,000-999,999
Medium-Size Cities 50,000-249,999
Small Cities 10,000-49,999
Towns less than 10,000

even more apparent. Examine the five categories of cities in the United States: "great cities" (one million and over); "large cities" (250,000–999,999); "medium-size cities" (50,000–249,999); "small cities" (10,000–49,999); and "towns" (less than 10,000).[22] Within the framework of massive urbanization, the overwhelming majority of the American people still reside in relatively small political units, either in rural areas (36.6 per cent) or in cities of medium size or smaller (42.4 per cent). While the percentage of population in rural areas and in the great cities is declining, that in the towns is only holding its own and that in the large cities is increasing slightly; the population in the medium-size cities is increasing substantially, and that in the small cities is booming.

Many of the small cities and some of the medium-size ones are located in larger metropolitan regions where they have been benefiting from the out-migration of the residents of the central cities. Of the eighteen cities with populations in excess of 500,000 in 1950, fourteen lost population to their own suburban areas between 1950 and 1960. It is this phenomenon of the accelerating population decline of the very large cities, coupled with the rapid growth of the suburban areas surrounding them, reflecting the frontier of "the old tenement trail," which has captured the attention of most students of urban affairs and the public at large. It has meant that, as metropolitan area populations grow ever larger, so do the number of independent political jurisdictions in which those populations live. Some of the suburban political jurisdictions, generally the smallest ones, serve as little more than neighborhood governments designed to protect their citizens from central city encroachment and to provide minimal municipal services. The ones of concern here, however, whether they are either newly created satellite communities or formerly "free-standing" cities brought into the metropolitan orbit, have become or are becoming nuclei of civil communities in their own right.

TABLE 1-4

Number and Total Population of SMSA's by Class, 1900-1960
(Population in Millions)

	1960		1950		1940		1900	
Size Group	Pop.	No.[a]	Pop.	No.	Pop.	No.[b]	Pop.	No.[b]
Over 500,000	80.8	53	63.8	37	42.5	24	14.8	10
Under 500,000	32.2	159	25.5	125	27.4	106	16.5	43
TOTAL	113.0	212	89.3	162	69.9	130	31.3	53
Percentage of total under 500,000	28	75	28.5	76	39.2	80	53	81

[a]Standard metropolitan statistical areas as defined for 1960 Census, not directly comparable with other columns.
[b]Standard metropolitan areas computed for earlier decades according to criteria used in 1950 Census.
Sources: *Municipal Year Book*, 1961; and Donald J. Bogue, *Population Growth in Standard Metropolitan Areas, 1900-1950.*

Most of the medium-size cities and some of the smaller ones are free-standing metropolitan centers in their own right. They too have benefited substantially from the metropolitan frontier. Though far outmatched by the larger metropolitan regions in total population, today there are far more free-standing medium-size metropolitan areas than any other kind, even according to the often misleading definition used by the United States Census Bureau (Table 1–4). Their development provides other important clues to understanding the American attitude toward urbanization and the manner in which Americans are choosing the forms of urbanization that, on the face of it, are best calculated to preserve those aspects of the agrarian tradition they value within the framework of contemporary society. These medium-size or small metropolitan civil communities are very definitely attractive to certain types of individuals, commercial concerns, and industrial corporations. They are large enough to offer urban advantages yet small enough to maintain suburban-style amenities even in their older areas, have sufficiently complex populations to encourage a variety of occupational and recreational possibilities, and are governmentally strong enough to provide a wide range of public services. As urban alternatives to citification they avoid many of the pitfalls of the smaller suburbs, which, by ignoring the realities of urbanization, are blinded to the need for coping with its problems.

These medium-size and small metropolitan centers continue to attract people from rural areas or smaller cities who emigrate to them purposely because of these attractions. Most of these people, even those who otherwise qualify as local "boosters," have ceased to hope that their cities will grow to "great city" size, nor do they regret it. This is in large part a recognition of reality, but it also reflects an apparent contentment with a more modest level of growth that will bring "progress" but will not disrupt the pleasant features of their particular style of urban living.

These free-standing cities have developed metropolitan areas of their own, quite different from those of their larger sisters, since even their level of urban living is too high to satisfy the quasi-agrarian desires of many Americans. Many people, involved though they may be in the urban economy, seek homesites outside all municipal jurisdictions, regardless of size. In many cases the suburbanites of this group choose to live outside the city not so much because of a desire to escape the city's style of life—which still offers most of the semi-urban amenities to its residents—as to escape the obligations of city living, which usually take the form of higher taxes and assessments. They do not move out to create new suburbs, except where they wish to control local zoning or where they find it necessary to do so to provide the most minimal urban services. On the contrary, they seek the autonomy of ruralism within the metropolitan setting. To the extent that this has become the dominant motive for the suburban migration in these communities, suburbanization in the medium-size metropolitan areas is of a different order than suburbanization in the large metropolitan regions. Where emigrants from the large cities most frequently seek smaller cities, those from the smaller cities often seek no city at all.[23]

All told, the *number* of medium-size cities, free-standing or within larger metropolitan regions, increased by 50 per cent between 1950 and 1960 (from 1,030 to 1,566) while the number of smaller cities increased by almost as great a percentage. The metropolitan frontier has fostered the emergence of the medium-size city as an urban type in its own right.

The growth and spread of these cities while both larger and smaller ones are declining may well be indicative of the emergence of a new version of the classic American town—larger, to be sure, as it must be to meet the more complex demands placed upon the civil community today, but not large enough to impair true efficiency (which, in human affairs, after all, is something more than purchasing in bulk) and still small enough to offer elements of community unavoidably absent in the big cities. The returns are not yet in, and it is too soon to draw conclusions as to the reasons for the growth and spread of such cities, much less evaluate their achievements. But it is certainly possible to conclude that they represent a special product of the metropolitan frontier and bear watching.

Metropolitanization and the Civil Community Concept

One paradox remains. The census figures indicate a relative decline in the medium-size metropolitan areas' share of the total metropolitan population, in direct contradiction to the increase of the medium-size cities' share of the total urban population. This is partly a problem of classification, but it is even more important for what it reveals about the weakness of the metropolitan area as an accurate indicator of the boundaries of

TABLE 1-5

SMSA's and Size of Largest Central City, 1960

SMSA's by Population Category (1,000's)	Central City Size (1,000's) 1,000 +	500-999	250-499	100-249	50-99
2,000 +	5	5			
1,500-1,990		2	1		
1,000-1,490		7	3	1	
500-999		2	18	8	1
250-499			5	28	13
100-249				25	66
50-99					22

real or potential political communities. Ten of the fifty-three metropolitan areas with populations exceeding 500,000 have no central city that exceeds 250,000 (Table 1–5). In these ten metropolitan areas, the fragmentation of the population among different political jurisdictions is so great that the "model" metropolitan relationship of one central city with a dependent urbanized fringe cannot be said to exist. Though this condition is usually confined to the medium-size metropolitan areas at present, it is a portent of future developments in the largest SMSA's as well.

Furthermore, the Census Bureau definition upon which the delineation of independent metropolitan areas is based often does not permit proper subdivision of the great metropolitan complexes. Many of these, still formally defined as single metropolitan areas, include an increasing number of substantial cities with suburban fringes of their own that deserve designation as metropolitan areas in their own right. Almost all of these would be considered medium-size metropolitan areas by virtue of their size. The Census Bureau has begun to recognize this fact by dividing some of the larger standard metropolitan areas of 1950 into smaller standard metropolitan statistical areas (adopting the new term, SMSA, to imply that the idea is useful statistically but not necessarily valid sociologically) and by delineating some separate urbanized areas within others. Joliet has been designated the center of one such urbanized area within the Chicago SMSA. While this procedure is more accurate than simply including the Joliet area within the larger SMSA, even it does not accurately reflect the degree of political separation of Joliet and its Wills County hinterland from the Chicago–Cook County areas.

Even this is not sufficient, however. "Hidden" within the large SMSA's are over one hundred medium-size cities, many with fringe areas as well, which should be separated, at least as political systems, from the overall metropolitan areas of which they are formally a part. In 1960 there were eighty-five cities of 50,000 to 100,000 population and fifteen cities of over 100,000 population so hidden that they are not even classified as separate urbanized areas. In the nation's five largest metropolitan areas alone, there were forty-six cities of between 50,000 and 250,000 in 1960 containing from 5 to 24 per cent of each SMSA's total population. When cities the next size smaller are included, the total rises to 290 and the percentage ranges from 16 to 46 (Table 1–6).

Half a decade later, this number has certainly increased, even without taking into consideration those cities with just below 50,000 population which serve as centers for larger civil communities with the SMSA. The Madison–St. Clair County situation is a case in point. Both counties, though located in Illinois, are formally included in the St. Louis SMSA. They are not even delineated as a separate urbanized area, despite the fact that East St. Louis is a city of 82,000 people and Alton, Belleville, and Granite City, each with city populations near or over 40,000, are centers of civil communities with populations of well over 50,000 each.

Similar difficulties arise even within officially designated medium-size metropolitan areas which include more than one central city. Even in those cases, the boundaries of the metropolitan area do not necessarily correspond with the boundaries of the various local political systems that function more or less autonomously within it. This study includes

TABLE 1-6
Small and Medium-Size Cities in the Five Largest SMSA's
(Population in 1,000's)

Small and Medium-Size Cities in SMSA	SMSA and Its Population				
	New York 10,695	Los Angeles 6,743	Chicago 6,221	Philadelphia 4,343	Detroit 3,762
Number					
Population size					
10 to 50	68	60	49	40	27
50 to 250	6	19	8	5	8
Total	74	79	57	45	35
Total Population					
Population size					
10 to 50	1,159	1,511	946	674	710
50 to 250	510	1,609	509	487	612
Total	1,669	3,120	1,455	1,161	1,322
Total population as a percentage of SMSA population					
Population size					
10 to 50	11	22	15	13	19
50 to 250	5	24	8	11	16
Total	16	46	23	24	35

several cases where metropolitan designations embrace two or more central cities, each of which is the center of a separate civil community that goes unrecognized in the available statistics. Duluth and Superior and Davenport, Rock Island, and Moline are prime examples of this, while the Peoria and Champaign-Urbana metropolitan areas represent variations of the same situation. Even in single-centered metropolitan areas, the metropolitan boundaries as defined are not of great use in dealing with community political systems. Rarely does a medium-size community political system embrace an entire county or even the greater part of one. Pueblo, Rockford, Springfield, and Decatur are centers of single-county metropolitan areas, and none are centers of county-wide community political systems.

When the civil community is recognized as a factor in the development of options for avoiding citification, the initial political thrust of the metropolitan frontier becomes apparent. By creating new and viable civil communities or maintaining established ones within large metropolitan areas, or outside them, those who seek a less citified (or a differently citified) way of life have a political instrument that can do much to safeguard their interests in the face of pressures from the central city, neighboring civil communities, or the larger world, sometimes by gaining the autonomy to make crucial political decisions locally but more frequently by assuring their community a role in areawide and even nationwide political decisions affecting their destiny.

The data available in 1960 indicated that 44 million people resided in medium-size civil communities of all kinds, nearly one quarter of the population of the United States and approximately 40 per cent of the nation's total metropolitan population. Both the population and number of these medium-size civil communities is rising. They and their sisters approaching medium size include major segments of the total population in the fifty states. Moreover, if present trends continue, the bulk of the population of the great megalopolitan aggregations of the future—and a large share of the political power—will be located in medium-size and small civil communities.

The political importance of the nation's medium-size civil communities is enhanced by their geographic distribution. In eighteen of the fifty states the largest civil communities are in the medium-size category. In four others, the census of 1960 recognized no medium-size cities or metropolitan areas, but in all four the largest civil communities were on the verge of moving into that category. Of the twenty-eight remaining states, the total population in medium-size civil communities is greater than the total population in large civil communities in six. Large cities, then, predominate in only twenty-two states, and only nine of these states have more than one large city within their boundaries. Even when formally defined metropolitan areas are considered, the largest SMSA's in eighteen states are medium size, four states have no SMSA's, fourteen have only one larger SMSA, and the remaining fourteen, eight of which are in the northeastern third of the country, have two or more. In Illinois, slightly under 20 per cent of the state's total population lives in civil communities included in these two categories. In Minnesota the figure is slightly over 10 per cent, and in Colorado it is slightly under 17 per cent. In Iowa, approximately one-third of the state's population lives in such civil communities and in Wisconsin approximately one-fourth. These percentages generally compare favorably with the percentage of population residing in the largest metropolitan centers in each state, and in Iowa and Wisconsin the smaller categories are dominant.

Not only are the economic, cultural, and political centers of nineteen states located in medium-size civil communities, but the state capitals of twenty-four are similarly located. Only eleven state capitals are located in larger civil communities, and the remainder are in even smaller ones. Of the states of the cities of the prairie, Iowa has no civil community larger than medium size. Illinois, Colorado, and Wisconsin each have one larger city, and only Minnesota has two. The state capitals of Illinois, Iowa, and Wisconsin are located in medium-size cities as well.

The evidence is clear. The medium-size civil communities have become a significant alternative to "citification" in the minds of many Americans and a growing alternative at that. Their significance in this respect may

TABLE 1-7

1960 Population in Medium-Size and Small Metropolitan Civil Communities in Five States (in 1,000's)

	Ill.	Minn.	Colo.	Iowa	Wisc.
Medium-size metropolitan civil communities	1,218	132	204	706	457
Small metropolitan civil communities	764	212	86	190	540
Total medium-size and small metropolitan civil communities	1,982	344	290	896	997
Total large metropolitan cities	3,550	796	494	–	741
Total state population	10,081	3,414	1,754	2,758	3,952

not be articulated by many of their inhabitants, but it will be seen to have an important effect on the formulation of public policy within them and in the approach taken by their citizenry to the problems they face. This, in itself, provokes great conflict as the problems of urbanization come to confront the anti-urban biases of those who must meet them. The differing ways in which the issues confronting American cities are handled in each civil community often reflect differing interpretations of the conflict between the desire for the advantages of urbanization and the bias in favor of an agrarian way of life. Each civil community must resolve this apparent paradox in its own way. It is the manner of its resolution which frequently provides a major share of the central dynamism of community politics.

The civil communities included in this study are representative of both urban alternatives to citification. All of them have been affected by the opening of the metropolitan frontier, which has created new problems for each of them and has also given them the impetus needed for attempting to meet those problems in the political arena. It is their confrontation with the frontier problems of the age which has become the most important aspect of their political life, in our day as in the days of the earlier frontiers. Their respective response to those frontier problems and the reasons behind each response are of central concern in this study.

NOTES

1. The land frontier has been intensively studied at least since the days of Frederick Jackson Turner. Many of those studies are of considerable interest to students of the contemporary metropolitan frontier. The central works in the study of the

frontier are, of course, those of Turner himself, particularly *The Frontier in American History* (New York: Henry Holt, 1920), which includes his famous essay setting forth the frontier hypothesis as well as other essays of general theoretical interest. Extensions and modifications of Turner's thesis can be found in Walter Prescott Webb, *The Great Frontier* (Boston: Houghton Mifflin, 1952), which adds an international dimension; David Potter, *People of Plenty, Economic Abundance and the American Character* (Chicago: University of Chicago Press, 1954), which adds the dimensions of abundance of resources and effects of technology; Turner's own *The Significance of Sections in American History* (New York: Henry Holt, 1932), which adds the dimension of sectionalism; John Kouwenhoven, *Made in America, The Arts in Modern Civilization* (New York: Doubleday, 1948), which discusses the social impact of frontier technology; Vernon L. Parrington, *Main Currents in American Thought* (New York: Harcourt, Brace, 1927 and 1930), which adds an intellectual perspective; Robert E. Spiller, *The Cycle of American Literature* (New York: Mentor Books, 1956), which discusses the impact of the several frontiers on literature; and Merle Curti, et al., *The Making of an American Community* (Stanford, Calif.: Stanford University Press, 1960), which traces the validity of the thesis in accounting for the development of a particular community. Ray Allen Billington provides a thorough history of the frontier movement in *Westward Expansion, A History of the American Frontier* (New York: Macmillan, 1949) and an important reassessment of the Turner thesis in *America's Frontier* (New York: Holt, Rinehart and Winston, 1967). Worthy modifications of the Turner thesis from sources unfriendly to it include Henry Nash Smith, *Virgin Land, The American West as Symbol and Myth* (Cambridge, Mass.: Harvard University Press, 1950), which does much to clarify the real impact of the land frontier as a "safety valve"; Louis M. Hacker, *The Triumph of American Capitalism* (New York: Simon and Schuster, 1940), which adds the dimension of Eastern capitalistic influences; and Oscar Handlin, *The Uprooted* (Boston: Little, Brown, 1951), which discusses the contribution of mass immigration to the successive frontiers.

Among the contributions to the study of the frontier in America of most value in the study of urban politics are Carl Bridenbaugh, *Cities in the Wilderness: The First Century of Urban Life in America, 1625–1742* (New York: Ronald Press, 1938) and *Cities in Revolt: Urban Life in America, 1743–1776* (New York: Alfred A. Knopf, 1955); Richard C. Wade, *The Urban Frontier: The Rise of Cities in the West, 1790–1830* (Cambridge, Mass.: Harvard University Press, 1959); and Anselm Strauss, *The Images of the American City* (Glencoe, Ill.: The Free Press, 1962), George R. Taylor, ed., *The Turner Thesis Concerning the Role of the Frontier in American History* (Boston: D. C. Heath, 1956) contains an excellent summary of the "pros and cons" of the debate over the validity of the Turner hypothesis while *The Frontier in Perspective* (Madison: University of Wisconsin Press, 1957), edited by Walker D. Wyman and Clifton B. Kroeber, offers a survey of recent thought about the meaning of the frontier.

2. The prevalent notion in American history is that the land frontier was closed by 1890. This notion, popularized by Frederick Jackson Turner as a means of introducing his frontier thesis (in 1893) and based on the United States Census report of 1890, is actually misleading. The last great burst of land settlement did not come until after 1900 when the marginal plains area that reached from northern Minnesota to eastern New Mexico was homesteaded. That period, which saw the transfer of more lands under the Homestead Act of 1862 than any other, came to an end at the close of World War I. With its passing, the rural-land frontier was, for all intents and purposes, closed. Though a minimal amount of homesteading still continues in the United States today, it is not a significant factor in American life.

See Ray Marvin Robbins, *Our Landed Heritage; The Public Domain, 1776–1936* (Lincoln: University of Nebraska Press, 1962).

3. The emphasis here and in this chapter generally is on the positive aspects of the frontier experience and its impact. Since the overall impact of the frontier experience has been more positive than negative, judged by the standards of the system, the author deems such an oversimplification warranted. However, it should not obscure the negative side of the frontier phenomenon: the degree of social disorganization, the disorientation of certain kinds of individuals, the weakening of traditional forms of community, the renewal problems of access to the rewards of American society produced by the cumulating inequalities of each frontier, to name only a few. Nor are these simply problems of the current frontier. It is a mistake to think that past frontiers did not generate or inherit problems of equal or greater magnitude. In fact, the study of American politics must be, to a great extent, the study of the uses of politics to overcome frontier-generated problems as well as to open new frontiers. Turner himself recognized this clearly. While this entire volume is concerned with those two faces of American politics, they will be discussed more explicitly in the concluding chapter.

4. Unfortunately, there is no body of literature on the urban-industrial frontier comparable to that available for the rural-land frontier. Not only have the frontier aspects of nineteenth-century American urbanization gone largely unnoticed but, until very recently, there have been few studies of American urban history from any perspective. The students of American immigration who have come closest to recognizing the frontier character of urban development in the United States have generally argued against the frontier hypothesis in opposition to Turner's supposed agrarian biases, disregarding the links between the two frontiers. See, for example, Handlin, *op. cit.* Among the other relevant immigration studies are Marcus L. Hansen, *Atlantic Migration: 1607–1860* (Cambridge, Mass.: Harvard University Press, 1940); Oscar Handlin, *Boston's Immigrants, 1790–1865: A Study in Acculturation* (Cambridge, Mass.: Harvard University Press, 1941), *Immigration as a Factor in American History* (Englewood, N.J.: Prentice-Hall, 1959), and *Race and Nationality in American Life* (Boston: Little, Brown, 1957). See also Arthur M. Schlesinger and Dixon R. Fox, eds., *A History of American Life*, 13 vols. (New York, Macmillan, 1927 and 1948); Edith Abbott, *Historical Aspects of the Immigration Problem* (Chicago: University of Chicago Press, 1926); and A. M. Schlesinger, "The Significance of Immigration in American History," *American Journal of Sociology*, Vol. XXVII (July 1921). The best sources for the study of the opening of the urban frontier include Schlesinger's classic, *The Rise of the City, 1878–1898* (New York: Macmillan, 1933); Constance McLaughlin Green, *American Cities in the Growth of a Nation* (New York: J. DeGraff, 1957), and *The Rise of Urban America* (New York: Harper and Row, 1965); and Charles N. Glaab, ed., *The American City: A Documentary History* (Homewood, Ill.: Dorsey Press, 1963). Perhaps the best synthesis of the two approaches is Moses Rischin, *The Promised City: New York's Jews, 1870–1914* (Cambridge, Mass.: Harvard University Press, 1962). See also Harvey Perloff, et al., *Regions, Resources and Economic Growth* (Lincoln: University of Nebraska Press, © 1960), and Jean Gottman, *Megalopolis: The Urbanized Northeastern Seaboard of the U.S.* (New York: Twentieth Century Fund, 1961).

5. In this respect, it is interesting to note the common use of population density as a means of determining the "frontier line" on both the land and urban frontiers. The U.S. Census Bureau early determined that the frontier line on the land frontier would be marked by the limits of settlement to the density of 2 per square mile, that the frontier zone would be the area with a density of 2 to 6 per square mile, and that "civilization" could be said to exist in any area with a density exceeding

18 per square mile. Using this system of measurement, it was possible to draw the limits of the frontier with considerable accuracy. With the rise of the urban frontier, similar measures were devised. It was generally agreed that a density of 1,000 people per square mile meant the elimination of the agricultural uses of land as a general means of livelihood and the achievement of urbanization. This measurement scheme was ably advanced and justified by Walter F. Willcox, "A Redefinition of 'City' in Terms of Density of Population," *American Journal of Sociology*, XXXII (July 1926), 97–102. Utilizing this measurement system, it is possible to clearly delimit the urban frontier line with equal precision. Projecting the same kind of divisions used in reference to the land frontier, less than 1,000 per square mile would be considered "beyond the frontier"; 1,000 to 2,000 people the frontier zone; and 2,000 to 6,000 people (the latter density represents something of a consensus as the desirable level for garden cities) the zone of "civilization." On the other hand, it may well be that at the highest reaches of urban density, perhaps over 30,000 per square mile, the city is transformed into a jungle, another form of wilderness that must be reconquered. The foregoing projections are supported by the available data on urban population densities in the United States as supplied by the U.S. Bureau of the Census. This theme is discussed further in Daniel J. Elazar, "Land Space and Civil Society in America," in Ivan Hanson, ed., *Land Settlement Policy* (Raleigh: Agricultural Policy Institute, North Carolina State University, 1969).

6. Walt W. Rostow's *The Stages of Economic Growth, A Non-Communist Manifesto* (Cambridge, Eng.: Cambridge University Press, 1960), provides a theory of economic growth that harmonizes well with the frontier theory presented in outline here. Harvey Perloff and Lowden Wingo, Jr., "Natural Resource Endowment and Regional Economic Growth," in Joseph J. Spingler, ed., *National Resources and Economic Growth* (Washington, D.C.: Resources for the Future, 1961), pp. 191–212, provide data for applying the scheme to America's frontier development.

7. A summary of the literature reflecting this spirit can be found in Strauss, *op. cit.*, Part I, "The Symbolization of Cities."

8. Before 1816 (which can be considered the end of the first generation of independence), only seven of what are today the fifty largest American cities had been incorporated. Between 1816 and 1876, thirty-nine were incorporated, leaving only four incorporated since 1876. Most of today's medium-size cities were founded and incorporated in the same period. See Daniel J. Elazar, "Urban Problems and the Federal Government: A Historical Inquiry," *Political Science Quarterly*, LXXXII, No. 4 (December 1967), 505–525.

9. Samuel Lubell was the first to describe this migration as a frontier phenomenon and to discuss its political meaning in Chap. 4 of his very important book, *The Future of American Politics* (New York: Harper, 1952). The phrase quoted in the above paragraph is his.

10. This oft-neglected fact can be documented by simple comparison of suburban growth and central city out-migration adjusted for natural increase, for any or all metropolitan areas.

11. Recognition of the role of highways in promoting and changing development patterns and social structures has spread in recent years, and has led to a growing number of highway impact studies by social scientists and others. The Bureau of Public Roads, U.S. Department of Commerce, has published a summary of the more than one hundred economic impact studies it financed through 1961 under the title *Highways and Economic and Social Changes* (Washington, D.C.: Government Printing Office, 1964). It provides a good overview of the role played by highways on the metropolitan frontier as well as a bibliography of the specific studies and other relevant materials.

12. The full impact of this revolution on the cities of the prairie is made apparent

when Sinclair Lewis' description of the isolation of the towns of the middle border in *Main Street* is contrasted with the contemporary situation. In central Illinois, for example, a region no more than one hundred and fifty miles across, once isolated cities and villages have now become parts of a unique kind of metropolitan region with a population of over 2 million. In that region, where it is possible to drive one hundred miles to a meeting, concert, or dinner and back in an evening, Champaign, Urbana, Decatur, Peoria, and Springfield have emerged as specialized centers, each offering certain kinds of services unique to it and together providing most, if not all, of the services commonly offered in more compact metropolitan areas with similar populations. The people of central Illinois not only travel from urban oasis to oasis but are now creating regionwide associations to encompass their regionally based activities. For a discussion of this new phenomenon, see *Highways and Economic and Social Changes*, p. 1.

13. An excellent recent compendium of analyses of this kind of feedback can be found in Garth L. Mangum, ed., *The Manpower Revolution* (Garden City, N.Y.: Doubleday, 1965).

14. The sanguine tone and somewhat oversimplified style of this paragraph, while reflecting what is essentially true, is not meant to obscure the sometimes harsh realities of American society that can operate to limit equality of access to the frontier or, for that matter, opportunity to benefit from working on the frontier. This was as true of past frontiers as it is of the present one, as critics of the Turner thesis have not hesitated to point out; see Henry Nash Smith, *op. cit.* What is important, however, is that the frontier-produced desirability of having equality of access has always reinforced the society's commitment to same, to foster a higher degree of actual equality than in other societies or nonfrontier situations.

15. This section represents a very brief treatment of what I believe to be a highly significant aspect of contemporary American society and its politics. Classic sociological theory, developed mainly in Europe where urbanization did indeed represent a radical cultural innovation, has traditionally assumed that urban living by its very nature produces a distinctive way of life which breaks down the old traditions of agrarianism and gives rise to a new set of norms, outlooks, and behavior patterns. See, in particular, Ferdinand Tönnies, *Community and Association,* trans. Charles P. Loomis (London: Routledge, 1940); also Louis Wirth, "Urbanism as a Way of Life," *American Journal of Sociology,* LXIV (July 1938, May 1939); and Georg Simmel, "The Metropolis and Mental Life," *The Sociology of Georg Simmel,* Kurt H. Wolff, trans. and ed. (Glencoe, Ill.: The Free Press, 1950). This theory was long held to be valid for describing urbanization in the United States. In recent years, however, it has been challenged as empirical research has revealed that urban areas can be constructed by their inhabitants (not necessarily consciously) so as to enable them to retain primary-type relationships and values brought in from the rural areas even within great urban complexes. See Morris Axelrod, "Urban Structure and Urban Participation," *American Sociological Review*, XXI, No. 1 (1956), 13–18; Floyd Dotson, "Patterns of Voluntary Association Among Urban Working Class Families," *ibid*., p. 16; and Gerhard Lenski, *The Religious Factor* (Garden City, N.Y.: Doubleday, 1961). My study of the first attempt to establish a metropolitan government in Nashville-Davidson County, Tennessee, *A Case Study in Metropolitan Integration: Nashville and Davidson County, Tennessee* (Chicago: National Opinion Research Center, 1961), discusses some of the political implications of this. This new perspective makes it both possible and necessary to reassess the meaning of urbanization and metropolitanization along the lines suggested in this section.

16. The literature reflecting this agrarian outlook is large and varied, as are the studies of its meaning. Two of the most recent discussions of the place of the

agrarian ideal in relation to American cities are Anselm Strauss, *Images of the American City* (Glencoe, Ill.: The Free Press, 1961), and Morton and Lucia White, *The Intellectual Versus the City* (Cambridge, Mass.: Harvard University Press-M.I.T. Press, 1962). Some classic or near classic works on the subject include: Vernon L. Parrington, *Main Currents in American Thought* (New York: Harcourt, Brace, 1927); Ralph H. Gabriel, *The Course of American Democratic Thought* (New York: Ronald Press, 1940); and Henry Bamford Parkes, *The American Experience* (New York: Alfred A. Knopf, 1947). There also exist some excellent studies of specific manifestations of the agrarian anti-city bias, among them: Daniel J. Boorstin, *The Lost World of Thomas Jefferson* (Boston: Henry Holt, 1947); Marvin Meyers, *The Jacksonian Persuasion* (Stanford, Calif.: Stanford University Press, 1957); and Richard Hofstadter, *The American Political Tradition* (New York: Alfred A. Knopf, 1948). It should be noted that the "agrarian" bias is not unlike that found in the Bible, which no doubt has profoundly influenced the attitudes toward urbanization of millions in this country, consciously or unconsciously. While it is apparently dominant in American life, there also exists a minority which values the city as the center of civilization in the classic (Greco-European) manner. This view, most frequently found among certain intellectuals, particularly those who concern themselves with the "failures" of the American city, is also shared by some of the older members of the last wave of European immigration. It has recently found expression in Jane Jacobs, *The Death and Life of Great American Cities* (New York: Random House, 1961).

17. Page Smith, *As A City Upon A Hill: The Town in American History* (New York: Alfred A. Knopf, 1966) offers an excellent description of the town as a classic American institution.

18. See Strauss, *op. cit.*, for an elaboration of these conflicting images. The transformation of the image of the small community from small town to suburb is nearly complete. The *Chicago Tribune*, traditional champion of the agrarian virtues as it perceives them, now features suburban settings for its "rural virtue" cartoons.

19. Parkes, *op. cit.*, Chap. 13.

20. Urbana, the one exception, had in all likelihood reverted statistically to a predominance of renter-occupied housing because of its unique character as a dormitory city for the University of Illinois. If only the permanent residents were considered, it too would reflect the general pattern.

21. John A. Kouwenhoven, *Made in America* (Garden City, N.Y.: Doubleday, 1948), offers a thorough and enlightening discussion of the vernacular tradition and its larger meaning.

22. The effects of differences in population size of cities and metropolitan areas is sufficiently important to demand an explicit size classification scheme. While there are arbitrary elements in this scheme, as in all systems of classification, by and large it separates cities at the most reasonable points of division, following Census Bureau categories in every case for comparability. A medium-size metropolitan area is defined as one with a central city (or cities) of at least 50,000 population and containing no central city or combination of central cities in excess of 250,000 population. This generally includes all standard metropolitan statistical areas with populations of under 500,000, though it also includes some whose populations exceed 500,000 but that do not have central cities with populations of 250,000 or more. This definition also includes some medium-size cities and their immediate fringes that are included in larger SMSA's by the Census Bureau but that are substantially independent in point of fact. By the same token, small metropolitan areas are those with central cities of less than 50,000 population which display the other characteristics of metropolitanization. Large metropolitan areas are those that include

central cities of over 250,000 but that do not exceed 1 million in total metropolitan population. Where more than 1 million people live in a single metropolitan aggregation, there exists a metropolitan region which can include several metropolitan areas of various size categories. Here again there is a degree of arbitrariness involved in the classification but, on the whole, it appears justified by what we know of urban social and political life.

23. A distinction must be made between those who settled the suburban fringes of the medium-size cities with the intention of being annexed to their parent city and those who moved out to escape the city entirely. The former are apparently in the majority in many of the cities of the prairie as the recent history of annexation indicates. They emigrated from the central city in search of better residential facilities, not in an effort to escape the city whence they came. In most cases, they subsequently encouraged the city to extend its boundaries to include their new residential areas.

Chapter 2 / The Cities of the Prairie and the Three Frontiers

The Stages of Frontier Growth

IT WAS IN RELATION to the land frontier that each of the cities of the prairie was founded and began to grow. However, it was not until they were engulfed by the westward movement of the urban frontier that the embryonic civil communities took on the characteristics of cities. Since then, each city has reached and passed through the different stages of urbanization and metropolitanization in its own time and at its own pace in response to different combinations of external and internal factors. Quite naturally, the political system of each city grew and was progressively adapted to the needs and nuances of that growth pattern.

Table 2–1 offers some useful indicators of the impact of each manifestation of the frontier on each of the civil communities.[1] Population growth is one of them. In general, each successive frontier has brought with it a population boom so pronounced that its very measurement can serve as an indicator of the different frontier eras. In addition, five significant dates mark important stages in the development of each city, reflecting its relationship to the great frontier beyond its borders. Each city's "birth" can be dated from the surveying and registry of its first plat. The plat represented the first public effort to organize its pattern of development; and since, in most cases, the first plat became the heart of the future city, the location of its central business district, and the source of its basic street pattern, it has continued to exercise a profound influence on the civil community's development. By giving the cities structural identities of their own, platting also began to cut their ties with the agricultural pursuits of the rural-land frontier and ultimately to lead them onto the urban-industrial frontier.

Each city's first incorporation (usually as a town or village) was a second milestone, marking its first acquisition of legal identity and the formal power, however limited, to manage its own affairs. Again, this marked another step in the ultimate separation of the cities of the prairie from the land frontier and their advancement onto the urban frontier. Communities not platted could not be incorporated, and communities not incorporated could not become urban centers, capable of self-sustenance. In contrast, the fortunes of those communities that remained unincorporated were so tied to the rural-land frontier as to virtually insure their decline with the passing of rural hegemony in America.

The date of the arrival of the first railroad is particularly significant in the history of the cities of the prairie. In the greater West (see Chapter Three) the coming of the railroad opened the vast and locked prairies for settlement and then served (with the telegraph that paralleled the tracks) as the link between the embryonic cities, the land frontier, and the settled parts of the country, bringing the first two into the web of national social and economic life created by the latter. Comparison of the population figures in the census years before and after the arrival of the railroad gives some indication of how important the railroads were in the early development of the cities. Every one of the ten metropolitan areas grew and prospered because of its connections with railroad operations, either as a major rail center or, at the very least, as a division point.

The ascendance of the urban frontier and the invention of the automobile at the end of the nineteenth century created a demand for good roads to end the dependence of America's cities and towns on a single transportation form and to increase intercity communications opportunities manyfold. The first paved road connection between a city and its neighbors was another landmark in its development. Paved roads were products of the urban frontier that also helped open the metropolitan frontier, following the classic pattern of frontier advance.

Finally, access to the metropolitan frontier requires air as well as automobile transportation with inter-metropolitan connections added to the intercity connections of the latter. The inauguration of regularly scheduled airline service in the early 1930's was an extremely important step in all but two of the metropolitan areas (which utilize the air services of the great cities adjacent to them) and the improvement of such service remains a political goal of some importance in most of them.

TABLE 2-1

Settlement, Incorporation, and Growth of the Cities of the Prairie

City	Date of First Plat[a]	Date of Incorporation[b]	Date of Arrival of R.R.	Paved Road Connection	Population 1840[c]	1850	1860	1870	1880	1890
Champaign	1854	1861	1854	1923	—	—	1,727	4,625	5,103	5,839
Urbana	1822	1833	—	1923	—	210	1,370	2,277	2,942	3,511
Decatur	1829	1839	1854	1923	—	600 (est.)	3,839	7,161	9,547	16,841
Joliet	1834	1845	1852	1921	2,558	2,659	7,104	7,263	11,657	23,264
Alton	1816	1821	1852	1921	2,340	3,585	6,332	8,665	8,975	10,294
Belleville	1814	1819	1871	1921	—	2,941	7,520	8,146	10,683	15,361
E. St. Louis	1818	1865[d]	1855	1921	—	—	—	5,644	9,185	15,169
Peoria	1825	1839	1852	1921	1,467	5,095	14,045	22,849	29,259	41,024
Davenport	1833	1855	1854	1923	—	—	2,028	4,166	7,800	12,000
Moline	1836	1839	1855	1923	—	1,848	11,267	20,038	21,831	26,872
Rock Island	1828	1841	1854	1923	—	1,711	5,130	7,890	11,659	13,634
Rockford	1835	1852	1852	1923	—	—	6,979	11,049	13,129	23,584
Springfield	1821	1840	1845	1921	2,579	4,533	9,320	17,364	19,743	24,963
Duluth	1856	1870	1870	1926	—	—	80	3,131	2,645	33,115
Superior	1852	1858	1870	e	—	—	—	—	—	11,983
Pueblo	1860	1870	1872	1931	—	—	—	—	3,217	24,558

[a] Not necessarily platted under the present name of the city.
[b] Illinois Secretary of State's records for each city under its present name.
[c] No census data are available for the cities prior to the 1840 Census.
[d] Incorporated as Illinois town in 1859.
[e] No data.

TABLE 2-1 (continued)

	Population						
	1900	1910	1920	1930	1940	1950	1960
Champaign	9,098	12,421	15,873	20,348	23,302	39,563	49,583
Urbana	5,728	8,245	10,244	13,060	14,064	22,834	27,294
Decatur	20,754	31,140	43,818	57,510	59,305	66,269	78,004
Joliet	29,353	34,670	38,442	42,993	42,365	51,601	66,780
Alton	14,210	17,528	24,682	30,151	31,255	32,550	43,047
Belleville	17,484	21,122	24,823	28,425	28,405	32,721	37,264
E. St. Louis	29,655	58,547	66,767	74,347	75,609	82,295	81,712
Peoria	56,100	66,950	76,121	104,969	105,087	111,856	103,162
Davenport	17,248	24,199	30,734	32,236	34,608	37,397	42,705
Moline	35,254	43,028	56,727	60,751	66,039	74,549	88,981
Rock Island	19,493	24,335	35,177	37,953	42,775	48,710	51,863
Rockford	31,051	45,401	65,651	85,864	84,637	92,927	126,706
Springfield	34,159	51,678	59,183	71,864	75,503	81,628	83,271
Duluth	52,969	78,466	98,917	101,463	101,065	104,511	106,884
Superior	31,091	40,384	39,671	36,113	35,136	35,325	33,563
Pueblo	28,157	44,395	43,050	50,096	52,162	63,685	91,181

The cities of the prairie became metropolitan centers in due course. Table 2–2 shows their population by metropolitan area since 1900, the first census to attempt to measure metropolitanism in the United States, indicating the census year in which each was first considered metropolitan. It should be noted that, by 1900, Duluth and Peoria were already centers of population equivalent to today's metropolitan areas at a time when only fifty-two such areas could be said to exist in the entire United States. However, while Peoria already displayed metropolitan characteristics, Duluth's growth remained urban (well within its city limits and without a satellite suburban hinterland) as it has through 1960. Though the Madison-St. Clair Counties area is not yet officially designated by the Census Bureau as a separate SMSA or even an urbanized area, by 1910 it had met the major population and demographic criteria of metropolitanism. By 1920, the Quad Cities and Springfield areas had qualified. Decatur and Rockford were added in 1930, while Joliet and Pueblo qualified by 1950. Champaign-Urbana was the last area to reach metropolitan status, being so designated in 1957. By the mid-1950's, then, all the cities of the prairie had come fully within the orbit of the metropolitan-technological frontier.

In responding to the three frontiers, each of the cities of the prairie has developed one or more special frontier-oriented functions which, while generally determined by regional factors, have transcended the limits of their immediate region to have national and even international significance and which have been crucial factors in securing the civil community's place on the frontier. In most cases, the relatively early development of those special functions made the difference between the growth of the medium-size civil communities and their smaller sisters' "retardation," just as the multiplication of the number and extent of special functions enabled the big cities to outpace them in turn. Thus Springfield as state capital (a choice influenced by the city's position on the land frontier of Illinois in 1837), Decatur as an internationally important food processing center (a development made possible by its location as a railroad junction in the heart of the richest agricultural region in the state), and Champaign-Urbana as the seat of the University of Illinois (an institution created to serve the rural-land frontier through education and research) became centers of medium-size metropolitan areas through the development of region-wide and transregional services connected with the land frontier, while equally urbanized and industrialized cities in the same central Illinois area—Bloomington, Danville, Kankakee, and Quincy—which did not develop special functions of larger-than-regional significance in appropriate relationship to the frontier, did not.

Table 2–3 summarizes the major economic functions of the cities of the prairie today, indicating (with italics) those special functions particularly directed to clients beyond their immediate trading areas. It also indicates which frontier manifestations stimulated the initial development of each function. This emphasis on the impact of economic functions is not to be taken as an expression of simple economic determinism. The questions of community development and politics are too complex to be explained so easily. Recognizing this, however, it is necessary to give economic factors their due. One of the virtues of the frontier hypothesis is that it can do so without reducing social science to simplistic economics.

Each special function stimulated a migratory wave of its own to the civil community as well as different forms of economic and social organization and a different set of economic and social concerns. Consequently the combination of special functions in each locality has made a significant contribution to the differentiation of the political systems in the several civil communities. The same economic impacts have contributed substantially to the periodic political upheavals that have occurred in each civil community.

The Southwestern Illinois Complex

The civil communities of Madison-St. Clair Counties are located at the original point of intersection of the Northeast, the South, and the West and have been influenced by all three spheres. The majority of their settlers came from the South to work for Eastern industrial and commercial interests involved in exploiting the wealth of the West or trading with its people. The balance of sectional influences has been set by the ebb and flow of the three frontier stages. Today the two Illinois counties across the river from St. Louis contain within their boundaries nearly half a million people in a complex pattern of cities, towns, and open country settlement that combines a crazy-quilt mosaic of municipalities reminiscent of the Los Angeles area with Southern-style rural nonfarm living. Their major civil communities are the oldest of the cities of the prairie, having been founded in the decade before Illinois achieved statehood as westerly outposts of the Southern Appalachian frontier made famous by Daniel Boone.

The leading population center of southern Illinois, the state's least metropolitan region, the two counties are related only peripherally to that region's concerns. With the largest concentration of population in the state outside Chicago, the two counties have no recognized center and no city with as many as 100,000 inhabitants. Statistically a part of the St. Louis SMSA, the area is really centered around six Illinois cities, two in the bottomlands, three on the bluffs, and one (Alton) where the bluffs

TABLE 2-2
The Growth of the Ten Metropolitan Areas

SMSA	1900	1910	1920	1930	1940	1950	1960
Champaign-Urbana	47,622	51,829	56,959	64,273	70,578	106,100	132,436[a]
Champaign City	9,098	12,421	15,873	20,348	23,302	39,563	49,583
Urbana City	5,728	8,245	10,244	13,060	14,064	22,834	27,294
Urbanized area[b]	c	c	c	c	c	c	78,014
Decatur	44,003	54,186	65,175	81,731[a]	84,693	98,853	118,257
Decatur City	20,754	31,140	43,818	57,510	59,305	66,269	78,004
Urbanized area[b]	23,249	23,046	21,357	24,221	25,388	32,584	89,516
Urban	—	—	—	—	—	—	—
Rural	23,249	23,046	21,357	24,221	25,388	32,584	—
Duluth-Superior	119,267[a]	210,696	256,162	251,179	254,036	252,777	276,596
Duluth	52,969	78,466	98,917	101,463	101,065	104,511	106,884
Superior	31,091	40,384	39,671	36,113	35,136	35,325	33,563
Urbanized area[b]	35,207	91,846	117,574	113,603	117,835	112,941	144,763
Urban	9,431	37,597	56,576	54,820	51,497	49,662	—
Rural	25,776	54,249	60,998	58,783	66,338	63,279	—
Joliet	74,764	84,371	92,911	110,732	114,210	134,336[a]	116,585
Joliet City	29,353	34,670	38,442	42,993	42,365	51,601	66,780
Urbanized area[b]	—	d	d	d	d	d	127,781
Urban	d	d	d	d	d	d	d
Rural	d	d	d	d	d	d	d
Madison-St. Clair	151,379	209,717[a]	243,415	301,605	316,248	388,302	487,198
Alton	14,210	17,528	24,682	30,151	31,255	32,550	43,047
Belleville	17,484	21,122	24,823	28,425	28,405	32,721	37,264
East St. Louis	29,655	58,547	66,767	74,347	75,609	82,295	81,712
Granite City	3,122	9,903	14,757	25,130	22,974	29,465	40,073
Urbanized area[b]	d	d	d	d	d	d	276,295
Urban	d	d	d	d	d	d	d
Rural	d	d	d	d	d	d	d

TABLE 2-2 (continued)

SMSA	1900	1910	1920	1930	1940	1950	1960
Peoria	121,829[a]	134,282	150,250	187,426	211,736	250,512	288,833
Peoria	56,100	66,950	76,121	104,969	105,087	111,856	103,162
Pekin	8,420	9,897	12,086	16,129	19,407	21,858	28,146
Urbanized area[b]	65,729	67,332	74,129	82,457	106,649	138,656	151,060
Urban	8,420	12,565	15,901	24,435	34,124	52,225	–
Rural	57,309	54,767	58,228	58,022	72,525	86,431	–
Pueblo, Colorado	34,448	52,223	57,638	66,038	68,870	90,188[a]	118,707
Pueblo	28,157	41,747	43,050	50,096	52,162	63,685	91,181
Urbanized area[b]	6,291	10,476	14,588	15,942	16,708	26,503	103,336
Urban	–	–	–	–	–	–	–
Rural	6,291	10,476	14,588	15,942	16,708	26,503	–
Quad Cities							270,058
Davenport	35,254	43,028	56,727[a]	60,751	66,039	74,549	88,981
Moline	17,248	24,199	30,734	32,236	34,608	37,397	42,705
Rock Island	19,493	24,335	35,177	37,953	42,775	48,710	51,863
Urbanized area[b]	34,812	38,842	43,611	44,583	54,649	73,600	227,176
Urban	–	2,665	11,216	15,525	18,492	22,100	–
Rural	34,812	36,177	32,395	29,058	36,157	51,500	–
Rockford	47,845	63,153	90,929	117,373[a]	121,178	152,385	209,765
Rockford City	31,051	45,401	65,651	85,864	84,637	92,927	126,706
Urbanized area[b]	16,794	17,752	25,278	31,509	36,541	59,458	171,681
Urban	–	–	–	–	2,825	8,587	–
Rural	16,794	17,752	25,278	31,509	33,716	50,871	–
Springfield	71,593	91,024	100,262[a]	111,733	117,912	131,484	146,539
Springfield	34,159	51,678	59,183	71,864	75,503	81,628	83,271
Urbanized area[b]	37,434	39,346	41,079	39,869	42,409	49,856	111,403
Urban	–	–	2,660	–	–	–	–
Rural	37,434	39,346	38,419	39,869	42,409	49,856	–

[a]First census year in which area met the major criteria of the current Census Bureau definition of a metropolitan area.
[b]Through 1950 ring area as given in *Population Growth in Standard Metropolitan Areas 1900-1950.* 1960 figures from U.S. Census.
[c]Not existent.
[d]Not separated from figures of larger metropolitan areas.
Source: *Population Growth in Standard Metropolitan Areas, 1900-1950* (Washington, D.C.: Housing and Home Finance Agency, December 1953).

TABLE 2-3

Major Economic Functions of the Cities of the Prairie

Civil Community	Primary Function	Primary Area Served	Secondary Area Served	Secondary Function	Primary Area Served	Secondary Area Served	Other Functions
Champaign	Educational (L)	Ill.	U.S., world	Commercial (L)	Immediate	Central Ill.	Transp. (L)
Urbana	Educational (L)	Ill.	U.S., world	Commercial (L)	Local	Immediate hinterland	Small indus. (U,M) Local govt.[a] (L)
Decatur	Commercial (L)	S.E. Ill.	Central Ill.	Farm products indus. (L)	U.S.	World	Other indus. (L,U,M) Local govt.[a] (L)
Joliet	Metal indus. (U) Heavy equip. indus. (M)	U.S.	World	Commercial (L)	Immediate hinterland	None	Transp. (L) Local govt.[a] (L)
Alton	Commercial (L)	Immediate hinterland	S. Ill.	Oil and chem. indus. (U)	U.S.	World	Other indus. (U)
Belleville	Commercial (L)	Immediate hinterland	S. Ill.	Dormitory (M)	American Bottoms	St. Louis	Local govt.[a] (L)
E. St. Louis	Agricul. indus. (L) Transp. (U)	S.W. U.S.	U.S.	Commercial (U)	Local	Immediate hinterland	Education (M)
Peoria	Commercial (L) Transp. (L)	Central Ill.	Central U.S.	Farm products indus. (L) Heavy equip. indus. (U)	U.S.	World	Other indus. (U) Local govt.[a] (L)

TABLE 2-3 (continued)

Civil Community	Primary Function	Primary Area Served	Secondary Area Served	Secondary Function	Primary Area Served	Secondary Area Served	Other Functions
Davenport-Bettendorf	Commercial (L) Transp. (L)	Immediate hinterland	Central Miss. Valley	Metals indus. (M)	U.S.	World	Local govt.[a] (L)
E. Moline-Silvis	Agricul. indus. (L)	U.S.	World	Commercial (L)	Local	None	
Moline	Agricul. indus. (L)	U.S.	World	Commercial (L)	Immediate hinterland	None	
Rock Island	Commercial (L) Transp. (L)	Immediate hinterland	Central Miss. Valley	Agricul. indus. (L)	U.S.	World	Other indus. (U) Local govt.[a] (L)
Rockford	Machine tool indus. (U)	U.S.	World	Comm. transp. (L)	Immediate hinterland	N. Ill. & S. Wisc.	Agricul. indus. (L) Local govt.[a] (L)
Springfield	Government (L)	Ill.	U.S.	Commercial (L)	Immediate hinterland	S.W. Ill.	Agricul. indus. (L) Local govt.[a] (L)
Duluth	Commercial (L) Transp. (L)	Lake Superior region	N.W. U.S., Can. prairie	Mining (U)	U.S.	World	Metal indus. (U), *Tourism* (U), Local govt.[a] (L) Education (M)
Superior	Commercial (L) Transp. (L)	Lake Superior region	N. Wisc.	Mining indus. (U)	U.S.	World	Local govt.[a] (L)
Pueblo	Commercial (L) Transp. (L)	S. Colo.	S.W. U.S.	Metal indus. (U)	W. U.S.	U.S.	*Defense indus.* (M), Local govt.[a] (L) *State govt.* (L), *Tourism* (U)

[a]County seat.

KEY: (L) - Rural-land frontier (U) - Urban-industrial frontier (M) - Metropolitan-technological frontier and the river meet. While the bottomlands cities developed as economic satellites of St. Louis from the very beginning, the area as a whole is only part of that city's larger metropolitan region for certain limited purposes. In sum, the two-county area is a miniature megalopolis masquerading as part of a metropolitan area.

What is now East St. Louis originated as a ferry landing on the Illinois shore in the late eighteenth century and developed as a formed civil community only with the rise of the urban frontier when it became the western terminus and transfer point for lines coming into the larger city from the east and south. The railroad yards made it an attractive location for heavy industries that gravitated to the Illinois shore to be near St. Louis. The leading local industry is the National Stockyards, part of the East St. Louis civil community though it is located just outside the city limits. It has been the community's second specialty since it was founded in 1873, primarily to process animals shipped into the St. Louis area from the southwest. First the railroads, then the stockyards, and then the industrial development of the late nineteenth century combined to produce a more or less continuous population boom from the Civil War to World War I. A creature of the urban frontier, East St. Louis has suffered the fate of all cities that have been unable to attach themselves to the metropolitan frontier and has been losing population since 1950.

East St. Louis attracted the kind of population needed to man its heavy industries but never proved attractive to the industrial or commercial managers who would have given the city a basis for solid growth. Never having played a significant independent role in the conquest of the land frontier in its area, it had no tradition of independent existence and developed no independent local economic or civic leadership to guide its urbanization. Hence it was at the mercy of St. Louis industrial interests from the beginning.

Alton grew originally as the first steamboat center in Illinois, one of the nation's earliest gateways to the upper Mississippi Valley. Unlike East St. Louis, it had two population booms influenced by the land frontier which, combined with its location upriver from St. Louis, enabled it to emerge early as a civil community in its own right. The first reflected the city's development as a river port before 1840 and the second, the coming of the railroad between 1850 and 1860. The urban frontier began to influence Alton's growth after 1890, initiating a boom along the Mississippi River below the city which continued until 1930. The new industries, which were not particularly attractive, were located in company towns along the river while Alton became the managerial and commercial center serving them. As a result, population growth within the city limits was only mildly affected, but the city became more firmly established as a subregional center. The impact of the metropolitan frontier did not begin

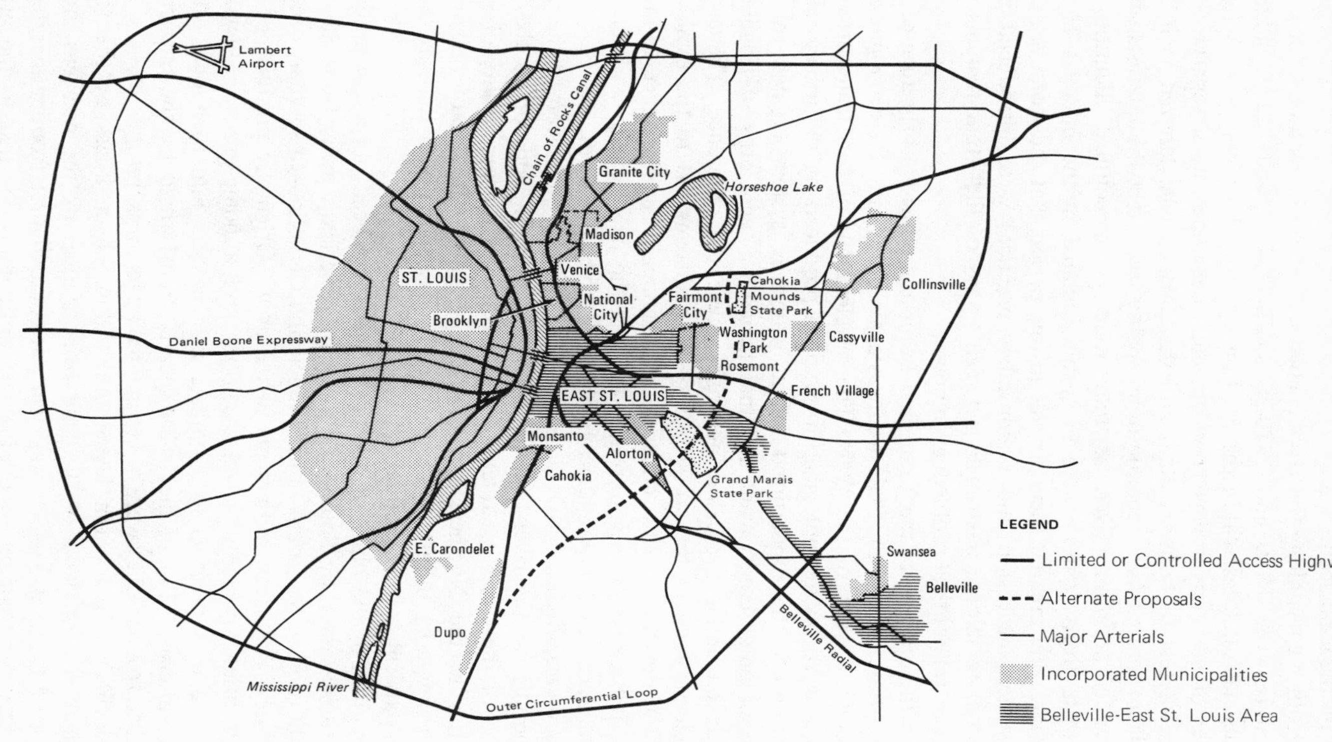

Map 5 Cities of the Belleville-East St. Louis Area

to reach Alton until after 1950 when industrial modernization became a factor on the local scene.

The other cities along the river (between East St. Louis and Alton) developed between 1870 and 1920 as specialized—usually single-industry—industrial satellites within the St. Louis metropolitan complex. A large number of company towns grew up, each developed by a separate corporate interest to house a plant and the workers who labored in it and each incorporated as a separate municipality to protect the interests of its founder corporation. Even as they were given political identities of their own, these "cities" were being manipulated in the interests of the companies that created them. It was in this period that the worst features of absentee ownership and unfair labor practices were introduced into that area, to initiate a struggle between "ways of life" that remains the area's central political problem even now.

With the opening of the Texas and Louisiana oilfields at the turn of the century, the Madison-St. Clair area was again drawn into the economic and technological orbit of the West. The development of two transportation systems based on technological innovations produced by the urban-industrial frontier—the modernized inland waterway system created by the system of dams constructed and maintained by the Corps of Engineers and the oil and gas pipeline network—made the difference. The area's strategic position at the crossroads of both systems led to the establishment and development of refineries and chemical plants designed to make use of petroleum products brought in from the new oilfields and the development of new communities and industries to handle them.

The metropolitan frontier has added yet another dimension to the sectional pulls on the river-front civil communities. In addition to the expansion of these new petroleum-based industries, the availability of railroad ties to the Northeastern megalopolis led to the establishment of branch plants by industries more generally associated with that area. Alton, in particular, has benefited in this regard.

The cities of the bluff, on the other hand, had been purposely founded in territorial days by Southern Protestant Americans away from the immediate orbit of St. Louis—then French and Catholic—to serve as centers of the new American settlements in the area.[2] Originally products of the land frontier, with established traditions and a home-grown leadership, they were in a position to assimilate urbanization into their own established patterns. Though they were clearly transformed by the impact of the urban frontier, they were not inundated by its pressures.

Belleville's initial boom lasted until 1860, affected less by the technological developments of the land frontier than by the overseas immigration of Germans, which was also part of that first frontier manifestation. The development of mining and craft industries tied to the urban frontier, after 1880, led to a small boom during that decade and steady growth thereafter in a civil community never noted as a center of frontier activity. The city's biggest boom in two generations came after 1950, reflecting the opening of the metropolitan frontier in the St. Louis region and the migration of people and industries out onto the Illinois bluffs, particularly from the Illinois bottom communities. A full-fledged, variegated civil community in its own right for four generations, Belleville is united by a strong common interest in maintaining its way of life in the face of metropolitan pressures. Its past experience has given it the economic, political, and civic leadership necessary to do so.

As the larger cities in the Madison-St. Clair Counties complex developed, they began to seek their own hinterlands and to compete with St. Louis for local commerce, creating a tension between the centrifugal force of St. Louis and their own centripetal counterpressures. Of them, East St. Louis, the largest city but the one closest to St. Louis, has succeeded least in its efforts to become more than a collection of residences serving an industrial complex while Alton, the farthest removed from the Missouri city by virtue of the physical barriers interposed between the two, has indeed become a center of commerce in its own right. Belleville, equally isolated from St. Louis by choice as well as by distance, became a local trading center serving eastern St. Clair County.

Since the end of World War II, the relationship of the various civil communities within the St. Louis metropolitan region has been further complicated by the opening of the metropolitan frontier, certainly the most revolutionary development in the region since the post-Civil War period. The still-increasing migration of suburban settlers from St. Louis and from the Illinois bottomland cities out into the bluff communities is altering established patterns of settlement and is beginning to affect established patterns of politics as well. It is too early to determine the lasting effects of these migrations on the established political patterns, but they have already led to serious efforts to change the status quo in the civil communities that have received the highest percentages of in-migrants.

The Civil Communities of Central Illinois

Central Illinois, one of the three great regional bands crossing that state, is generally typical of the farming region that dominates the low prairies east of the Mississippi River or the eastern half of the corn belt. Today the area combines urban and rural pursuits in such a way that its agricultural base remains the most significant factor in its local economy but in the most modern sense. Agriculture has become a highly professionalized and specialized pursuit, which needs the support of a whole range of "agri-business," "agri-industrial," and today even "agri-educational" functions, all of which are supplied by the area's cities. Nowhere in the country has this combination of urban and rural skills for the production of food and fiber reached a higher level of development than in central Illinois. The four metropolitan areas located in that region are all products of this relationship. They are linked with one another through important regional ties with each providing certain specialized functions for the larger whole.

With one exception, the major civil communities of central Illinois began to develop in the first decade of Illinois statehood as part of the thrust into the region of settlers from Ohio and Indiana as well as southern Illinois. They were among the last settlers to avoid the locational problems of the open prairies, locating their towns in the woodland strips that penetrated the grasslands, along watercourses, where they could benefit from the best of both worlds. At the same time, each of the civil communities in the four metropolitan areas typifies a particular manifestation of and response to the successive American frontiers.

Though Urbana and Champaign are twin cities, they were founded separately for entirely different reasons—the first in the 1830's as a local trading center for farmers pushing westward into east central Illinois from the Ohio River Valley woodlands, and the second twenty years later as a railroad division point on the Illinois Central, which was thrusting southward from Chicago to open the prairies of the great West. It was only after 1867, when the state legislature located the University of Illinois, the state's land grant college, between them that they began to develop as parts of a single metropolitan area. The cities had their first great population boom in the two decades that saw the coming of the railroad and the university, between 1850 and 1870, when the land frontier in Illinois was in its last stages. The two cities were absorbed by the westward movement of the urban frontier after 1890. In the decade immediately following the emergence of a local agricultural processing industry, the establishment of a number of foundries, and the reorganization of the University as research center—the major local impacts of the urban frontier—the populations of the cities increased by better than 60 per cent. The continued impact of that frontier led to continued population growth at a rate of better than 25 per cent per decade until 1930. The opening of the metropolitan frontier after 1945 initiated a new population boom connected almost entirely with the University, which has produced growth rates equal to those of the earliest ones.

The University, founded in response to demands of pioneers on the land frontier, has been elevated to major importance on the metropolitan frontier by virtue of its new position as a center for exploration on that frontier. The impact of the frontier on the University and of the University on the community in this regard follows the very model of the frontier process. The old frontier was given its impetus by its concern with conquering the land, a very specific segment of nature. The social consequences—in this case the development of an institution to conduct basic research and teaching to improve "agriculture and the mechanic arts"—of the old frontier were also related to the land. The new frontier takes all of nature as its "wilderness" in place of an undeveloped land mass and has devised means to explore it and to open its undeveloped areas to development through the application of appropriate technologies. The social consequences—in this case the metropolitanization of Champaign-Urbana—and the scientific concerns—in this case the adaptation of the University to undertake the basic research (exploration) and applied research (surveying and initiating development) that opens and tames the new frontier and to provide education (equal means of access to those interested in becoming the explorers and pioneers on that frontier)—are equally related to the great frontier of nature spread as it is throughout the universe as a whole.

The great acceleration of the University's growth since 1945 to serve the metropolitan-technological frontier has been reflected in the great growth of both cities and their elevation to metropolitan status in the past decade. It is now being reflected in an increase in their urbanity as well. Furthermore, such active partisan political conflict as exists in Champaign-Urbana is being fostered by the differences between the immigrants of the new frontier, particularly the new University people, who have party attachments and political demands different from those of the traditionally Republican townspeople and older University faculty in both civil communities.

Despite the leveling influence of the University, the differential impact of frontier and section has had its effect on the two civil communities. As a minor agricultural-products processing center and home of local foundries, Champaign has served the immediately local needs characteristic of its sphere for many years. With the development of the automobile, one of its local foundries expanded as a producer of auto parts. Urbana, on the other hand, had virtually no industrial base until the opening of the metropolitan frontier. Then, perhaps as an outpost of the greater East as well as a university town, it attracted a branch electronics plant, an industry uncommon on the Illinois prairies in the early 1960's.

The metropolitan frontier, with its new transportation systems, appears to be affecting Champaign-Urbana in yet another way. There is some reason to believe that the cities' regional importance has begun to expand as a consequence of changes being wrought by the interstate highway system. The cities are located at the crossroads of important east-west and north-south links in the system, which give them full cross-continental ties that, coupled with the development of a central Illinois freeway to link the two cities with the Mississippi River, gives Champaign-Urbana a chance to become the alternate motor gateway to the trans-Mississippi West between Chicago and St. Louis, and to play a role similar to that played by Peoria for railroads seeking to avoid the congestion of the two larger centers. The very recent expansion of industry, particularly in Champaign, offers some evidence to this effect. Major companies have begun to erect distribution facilities adjacent to Interstate 74, the east-west highway, near the point where it will ultimately intersect with Interstate 57, the north-south highway, and the Central Illinois Freeway. In 1963, a large industrial park, the first of its kind in that part of the country, was established to take advantage of the same junction. The evolving combination of university and freeway, itself a major phenomenon of the metropolitan frontier, could make Champaign-Urbana the leading metropolitan area of central Illinois.

A rural village until the railroad arrived in 1854, Decatur's land frontier boom was also initiated by the railroad and lasted for approximately two decades. The civil community quietly developed into a railroad service center, acquiring the maintenance shops of the Wabash Railroad. It was engulfed by the urban frontier after 1880 in a boom which lasted until 1930, during which time it became a minor manufacturing center of some importance with an agricultural processing industry now centered around soybeans and the Staley Company and a regionally oriented metalworking industry whose major function was to supply parts for the railroads and plumbing equipment for housing built in the area. Since 1945, and particularly after 1950, the coming of the metropolitan frontier has brought more industrial and population growth. The three established industries have continued to expand, but it is the last of the three which has brought Decatur's economic base into the province of the newest technology.

Very early, Decatur's specialty became the processing and export of agricultural products in a variety of ways, and the civil community quickly became the exemplar of the American city devoted to agribusiness. Growing first as a railroad and a small agricultural processing center serving the needs of its immediate hinterland, its development was impressively stimulated by the arrival of the urban frontier and the civil community's successful combination of both agriculture and manufacturing into an economic package. Between 1900 and 1930 the city's population almost tripled as it became an important center for refining the raw products of the land for export. Decatur's success with this one specialized function gave the city a reputation as an ideal industrial location and has since enabled it to add the offerings of the metropolitan frontier to its package. In the postwar period, a large number of subsidiary plants of nationally known companies were established there, to exploit the civil community's locational advantages and its reputedly good labor market.

Decatur has been able to keep abreast of changing frontier demands through the continual introduction of new industries in the same general field or the transformation of old ones in light of the latest technological developments. Thus the manufacture of auto parts effectively replaced the declining railroad parts industry while the manufacture of gas and water main equipment for private homes developed nationwide markets. A Caterpillar Tractor plant was established after World War II to build heavy construction equipment in conjunction with those at Peoria and Joliet. A molded plastics industry has been introduced by General Electric and the automobile parts industry has been expanded.

Decatur's economic development, emphasizing specialization as a manufacturing and processing center through industrial diversification, has encouraged similar development in the civil community's social and political spheres as well. The city's population is highly diverse, containing northern and southern elements in nearly equal proportions. It is particularly unique in the spread of its religious affiliations. The Decatur metropolitan area is one of only six metropolitan areas in the United States in which no single religious denomination accounted for at least 25 per cent of the reported religious membership in 1950.[3] Politically the civil community is equally diverse, being one of the few of its size and in its area of Illinois to have a competitive two-party system.

Of all the cities in central Illinois, Peoria was the first to attain national prominence as an urban center that figured significantly in the industrial and commercial life of the nation as a whole and the only one to acquire a national image (albeit a far from flattering one) as a city. It remains a miniature "large city" in its economic, social, and political characteristics and the butt of slighting remarks when anyone wants to refer to a city that is not citified. The civil community's special functions are derived from its early importance as a "river town" and a transportation gateway to the greater West in the days of the land frontier.

Peoria's first boom began with the opening of the Illinois and Michigan Canal connecting the Great Lakes and the Mississippi River via the Illinois River after 1840 and, clearly reflecting the influence of the land frontier, continued through the early years of railroad development until the 1870's. It first grew as a regional meat packing center serving hog and beef raisers from the surrounding prairies, who took advantage of its steamboat connections to eastern and southern markets. Its real growth began with the arrival of the railroad in 1855. In a smaller way but similar to Chicago and St. Louis, Peoria became a transfer point for eastern and western railroads in the latter half of the nineteenth century, connecting the cities of the East Coast, Ohio Valley, and Upper South with points west.[4] Utilizing this transportation advantage, the Peoria civil community moved onto the urban-industrial frontier and developed two specialized industries with national—now worldwide—markets: the production of alcoholic beverages (both beer and whiskey) and the manufacture of heavy construction and earth-moving equipment, both of which play equally or increasingly important roles on the metropolitan frontier as well.

After 1880 the city's growth was again stimulated by the urban frontier in a boom which lasted until the Depression. As center of the Cattle Feeders' and Distillers' Trust, the nationally famous "Whiskey Trust," which was "busted" by Theodore Roosevelt at the turn of the century and destroyed by Prohibition, Peoria converted its position as a gateway to the greater West into national business success, based on the exploitation of the natural produce of its region. Despite this specialization, which brought it a national reputation, Peoria also came to serve as a center for the manufacture of the standard products of Western technology from the beginning of its industrialization: farm implements, barbed wire, nails, barrels, and the like to serve the land frontier of the greater West. With the opening of later frontiers, Peoria continued to keep pace with this tradition, becoming the international center for the construction of earth-moving equipment as headquarters of the Caterpillar Company and a major manufacturer of related products as well.

Because of the early emergence of several special functions which flowered in the period of the urban frontier, Peoria's growth was rapid; its population exceeded 50,000 by the turn of the century to make it one of the fifty largest cities in the country and the second largest in Illinois. It was the largest of the cities of the prairie between 1850 and 1910 and again between 1930 and 1960 and, since 1890, has had a major impact on the national economy. Its Commercial National Bank remains Illinois' only major bank outside of Chicago.

Peoria's early blooming did not flower into really great population growth, perhaps because of its relative proximity to Chicago and St. Louis. Still, unlike most of its sisters of similar size, the Peoria civil community has passed through the stages of urban and metropolitan frontiers in a manner more characteristic of far larger metropolitan centers and has come to face the same problems: urban decay in its older sections, the assimilation of ethnic and racial minorities, suburbanization at the expense of the central city, and the like. Peoria proper began to lose population with the opening of the metropolitan frontier, though it remained the center of life and the economy in its metropolitan area. For many years it was unable to add the territory necessary for it to continue to grow as a city. Though it finally did annex the more fashionable suburban township north of the old city limits, the metropolitan frontier line generally lies far beyond its borders in suburban cities and townships that reach out onto the prairies on both sides of the Illinois River.

The political manifestations of Peoria's problems are also much like those in the larger metropolitan centers, appropriately miniaturized. Its partisan politics are more complex than in its sister's, as are its reform movements. Moreover, the problems of inter-metropolitan coordination are exacerbated by the size of its metropolitan area, which extends over three physically, socially, and demographically diverse counties.

If Peoria has a certain cosmopolitan tone unusual in cities of its size because of its far-flung industrial and commercial operations, Springfield has attained a similar level of sophistication as a consequence of its role as the governmental center of a great state. Orginally created as a rural county seat at the farthest limits of the land frontier, Springfield blossomed by virtue of its early citizens' successful efforts to make it the state capital. In 1837, the year Chicago became a city, Springfield became the capital of Illinois.[5] Its subsequent development all flows from this early benefit derived from the movement of the land frontier northward in Illinois. The growth that began with the relocation of the capital continued until the last echoes of the land frontier passed from Illinois after the Civil War. While this boost in Springfield's status was not sufficient to create a population center of great magnitude, considering the proximity of Chicago and St. Louis, over the years it has served to lift Springfield to the status of a cosmopolitan center whose immediate interests reach beyond the limited trading hinterland of its sister medium-size civil communities to the outer limits of its state and beyond. Thus, though not a particularly important center of industry, Springfield's political position made it respond to the urban frontier after 1880 with a population boom that lasted until 1930. During that time it too became the seat of an agricultural implements industry developed originally to serve the needs of prairieland cultivation and since expanded as part of a larger corporation to serve national and international markets. It has also become the seat of an insurance industry of considerable magnitude, which developed to serve the region to the west of it.

The opening of the metropolitan frontier with its attendant expansion of government has changed Springfield from a quiet capital city that came to life every two years when the legislature was in session into a constantly busy community, second only to Chicago as a locus of important day-to-day decision-making in the state. The new frontier has had less of an effect on the population of the city proper. As in the case of Peoria, the frontier of suburban settlement has extended out into the surrounding townships beyond the city limits of Springfield.

As the center of the state government, politics has been the all-embracing interest in Springfield, an interest which has affected virtually every phase of life in the civil community during every frontier period. Community life and the local economy have been inextricably bound up with the state government and the concerns of the politicians and administrators who serve it. One consequence of this has been the evolution of a politically conscious society in which every articulate element in the local community, from the downtown businessmen to the local pursuers of "culture," is visibly attuned to the political life, a situation unique among the cities of the prairie and apparently unique in American society generally. Springfield's political sensitivity has led it to respond to the changes in the American frontier process with unusual rapidity, even though it has never been at the forefront in inducing those changes. Because of its political role, it is always involved, willy-nilly, in the latest manifestations of the frontier.

The Quad Cities

The cities at the top of Illinois' western bulge developed in the second decade of statehood at a crossroads point in American history and geography. Founded just before the last of the Indian wars east of the Mississippi, they opened the third and last tier of settlement in the Prairie State and at the same time helped open the way for settlement of the northern trans-Mississippi region, which began at the same time. Today, located in America's agricultural and communications heartland, still at the crossroads between east and west, the Quad Cities interstate metropolitan area (formerly known as the tri-cities of Davenport, Rock Island, and Moline) differs substantially from its cornbelt neighbors to the south and east and, indeed, is rather unique when compared to other metropolitan areas in both Illinois and Iowa. A metropolitan complex in every way as variegated as the central Illinois group but compacted into two counties, its overall character is far more western than its geographic location would indicate, primarily because of its long-lasting relationship to the railroading and lumbering frontiers. The three central cities and their satellites have prospered from their strategic location on the banks of the Mississippi in the heart of the river's upper valley, equidistant from Chicago and Des Moines on the axis of American movement from east to west and St. Louis and Minneapolis-St. Paul from north to south. Their position is further enhanced by their situation at the gateway to the west, the far edge of the northeastern industrial heartland.

The Quad Cities first grew as centers of commerce on the land frontier, where they served both their immediate trans-Mississippi hinterland and the larger Northwest. As early as 1850, their primary specialized function as a regional transportation center was combined with a second one—at first regional, then national and international as well—that of producing farm implements, establishing the industrial potential of the area and providing the basis for relatively early and rapid advance onto the urban frontier. As in the case of Peoria, the combination of special economic functions spurred the growth of the three cities, raising them as a unit to national significance before the turn of the century.

The fragmentation of their metropolitan area among two states, three core cities, and four satellites has prevented Quad Cities from achieving a national image equivalent to that of Peoria (there is no famous ragtime song for any of the Quad Cities similar to "I Wish I Was in Peoria," nor did any of them achieve the somewhat perverse fame of their sister city as the instantaneously recognizable butt of early urban humor). At the same time, it has also kept the area free from the large-scale problems of urbanization and suburbanization which have plagued that other city, despite a metropolitan population virtually the same. Much of the strength of the Quad Cities metropolitan area resides in the uniqueness and compactness of its cities. Both stem from the circumstances of the area's development, which gave each city specialized functions and populations within the whole.

Part of the diversity of the Quad Cities area which led to the development of four civil communities instead of one is a direct product of the sequence of local responses to the technological revolution stimulated by the opening of the greater West. Rock Island, the first of the cities to be settled, profited immensely from the great technological innovation in waterway transportation, the steamboat, which though invented in the East, was one of the first of the creations of the new technology to find its proper milieu (after appropriate modifications by westerners) in the West. The 1840's and 1850's were the great years of steamboating when Rock Island became the jumping-off point for settlement of the upper Mississippi River. After the railroad came in 1854, the city became a center for the second stage of the revolution in transportation technology, particularly since the first railroad bridge to span the Mississippi connected Rock Island and Davenport after 1855.

The railroad brought the city's first population boom, which continued until the 1870's. From 1890 until the 1920's, it experienced a second boom based on a different combination of influences from the urban and land frontiers.

After the Civil War several lumber companies, including the Weyerhaeuser Company, later to become of national importance, were established in Rock Island to exploit the timber resources of Wisconsin and Minnesota and, later, of the Pacific Northwest. Rock Island and, to a lesser extent the other cities, served as a major center of the lumber industry in

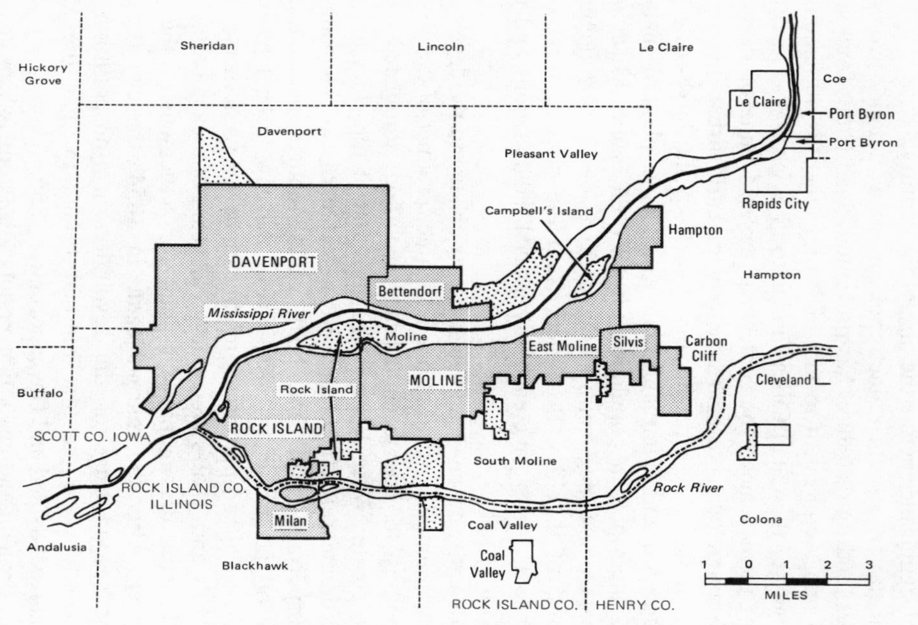

Map 6 Cities and Townships in the Quad Cities Urbanized Area

the late nineteenth century. Timber floated down the Mississippi from the Upper Midwest in the spring and summer of each year was milled in Rock Island. Until the turn of the century, when the last log rafts arrived, the lumbermen who accompanied them added a distinctive flavor to the city and, coupled with the railroad men and steamboatmen, contributed to the development of another major industry tied to the old frontier—elaborate, legalized prostitution (closely connected with local government), which Rock Island provided for that clientele as a matter of course. All in all, Rock Island retained its "Wild West" character longer than any of its neighboring cities, partly because of its commercial connections with the late nineteenth-century frontier and partly because it was connected to this one industry based on the land frontier later than any other city in its area.

The Rock Island Arsenal, a federal installation located on Rock Island (a large island in the center of the metropolitan area) was established in 1862 to supply weapons for the Union Army. After the war it remained in existence to supply weapons for the troops engaged in subduing the Indians on the great plains. Always a major industry in the community, the effective nationalization and internationalization of its markets since World War I have enabled its expansion to keep pace with that of the other local industries. The Arsenal has been particularly important as a unifying force in the industrial life of the Quad Cities, since it draws its workers from the entire area.

The development of the agricultural implement industry locally gave Rock Island a direct stake in the manufacturing frontier, even as it maintained its role as a transportation entrepot. Taken as a whole, the area became the world's largest center of farm implement production, but here, too, different farm implement manufacturers chose different cities in the area for the location of their plants. Thus the smaller farm implement companies established in Rock Island in the mid-nineteenth century, in the entrepreneurial tradition of that era, to serve the region's needs, grew in number and importance until they were consolidated and merged with what became the International Harvester Company shortly after the turn of the century and expanded into national and international markets. The new concern became the dominant manufacturer in that city, though still not the only producer of farm implements.

The city's expansion was limited, however, by the river to the north and west and Moline to the east. This problem did not become a serious factor in the city's growth until the opening of the metropolitan frontier, most of whose impact has been outside the city limits though within the Rock Island civil community.

Davenport, now the largest of the Quad Cities, originated slightly later than Rock Island (settlement on the west bank of the river was prohibited until 1833, when the federal government concluded a treaty with the Indians opening the land to white settlers) but has pursued a somewhat similar course of development. Its first role as a river town was as a port of debarkation for settlers seeking a livelihood in Iowa. Location on the west bank of the river held up its development until the railroad bridge was completed, giving it connections with the East and sparking a population boom that lasted through the 1860's. It was then that Davenport became "The Gateway to the West," as it has since advertised itself, combining steamboat and rail traffic in a package that enabled it to grow as the merchandising center for the prairie settlements beyond it.

A second boom, in part associated with the opening of the urban frontier along the upper Mississippi River and in part a continuation of the impact of the land frontier by then located further north and west, began after 1880 and lasted until the middle 1920's. It was during this period that Davenport's commercial role emerged as one of more than regional significance. At the point where river and rail transportation intersected, Davenport offered the best distribution point west of Chicago. Though this, in turn, led to the location of some industries on the Iowa shore to take advantage of these distribution facilities, Davenport was not really caught up in the region's first industrial boom. Retaining its preeminence as a wholesaling and retailing center, its trade territory was actually extended eastward into Illinois, along the railroad routes that fed into it. Though it developed an agricultural products processing industry of some importance, it remained clearly secondary to the Illinois cities in manufacturing. Only since the opening of the metropolitan frontier, whose technologically more sophisticated industries were better able to take advantage of Davenport's location, has the Iowa shore added significantly to the Quad Cities' industrial base. The largest plant in the Davenport civil community, the Alcoa Aluminum plant, located near suburban Bettendorf in an even smaller incorporated suburb of its own creation, is a typical representative of the new industry of that new frontier. It and the increased distribution facilities developed for the trucking industry gave Davenport a mild population boom after World War II, most of which has been contained in its considerably expanded city limits.

Unlike its two larger sisters, Moline's source of growth has always been tied to the urban-industrial frontier. It was founded along the Mississippi River rapids, a source of water power, and its first boom came when John Deere moved his agricultural implement plant to the new community to take advantage of its site as well as the good rail and water transportation of the area. This synthesis of the land and industrial frontiers gave Moline a population growth of 50 per cent or more per decade through 1900 and in excess of 30 per cent for two more decades. Unlike the absentee-owned International Harvester Company in Rock Island, which has been interested in the city of its location only insofar as is necessary to protect its interests, John Deere is based in Moline. Hence the latter company has always taken an interest in local affairs and at one time dominated the civil community politically as well as economically.

Never a commercial rival of either Davenport or Rock Island, though it competes with the latter for local retail trade, Moline has continued to exist as a provider of the implements necessary to make the prairies, plains, and plateaus of the greater West agriculturally productive. Virtually a one-industry town, Moline's response to the frontier is still conditioned by the John Deere Company. With the opening of the metropolitan frontier, the company moved its headquarters into a suburban area south of the city and, in doing so, transferred the center of the civil community's frontier activity and growth outside the city limits.

East Moline, in turn, was developed in the later stages of the urban-industrial frontier in response to the wave of industrialization generated by the demands of the greater West. The city was created at the turn of the century to handle new farm implement plants which the two leading companies in the area (and others) wished to build outside of existing taxing jurisdictions; to envelop the expanded railroad yards which were built on the available "free land" there, at the entrance of the Quad Cities area; and to accommodate the new immigrants who came to work in them, whom many of the older settlers wished to keep out of their established communities. As a product of the major areawide industry, East Moline has been a creature of the Quad Cities rather than a molder of civic patterns, since its creation.

The position of the entire Quad Cities area as a commercial center was later enhanced by the third stage in the transportation technology revolution, this one connected with the metropolitan frontier, when it became a trucking center for the area between Chicago, Minneapolis-St. Paul, Omaha, and St. Louis. The favored position of the Quad Cities as a medium-size urban oasis served by United Airlines as well as by several feeder airlines and its position as a port on the modern inland waterway system has further enhanced its regional importance. Rock Island, as the site of the area's major river port; Davenport, as the area's major trucking station; Moline, as the site of the area's major airport; and East Moline-Silvis, as the center of the area's major railroad yards, have all shared in this locational advantage by contributing distinctive elements to it.

Each of the Quad Cities is as unique ethnically and socially as it is economically, and so politics in the area is as fragmented as the area itself. On the more industrialized Illinois shore, it is a politics of industrial areas, with two-party competition and a tendency to Democratic predominance. Rock Island is the stronghold of the Democratic party, patronage-oriented politics, and interparty competition while Moline is far more conservative and Republican and has much less two-party competition or interest in the material rewards of politics, but with strongly

Republican leanings, Davenport combines both tendencies within a predominantly Republican base. In no case have the problems considered to be typically urban occupied an important place in the public mind.

Despite the great increase in commuting within the Quad Cities area and the corresponding increase in the interchange of the labor force among the several civil communities, each of the Quad Cities maintains something of a distinctive industrial pattern as well as a firmly established political identity. Their respective patterns can, in every case, be traced back to the original and continued responses of the residents of each city to the demands of successive frontiers in the greater West. At the same time their continued growth can be traced to the successful adaptation of their basic industries to national and international markets that transcend the regional economy they were originally designed to serve.[6]

Satellite and Metropolis in Northern Illinois

The civil communities of northern Illinois were settled at the very end of the state's second decade of statehood, to complete the occupation of its lands and capitalize on the opening of its prairies to intensive human use. They were the first of the state's cities to rely primarily on technological innovations—in transportation and manufacturing—for their development and, led by Chicago, soon outpaced their sisters as a result of their readiness to cope with the new age. Today they inevitably live in the shadow of Chicago and derive their distinctiveness from the way in which they adapt to that fact of life. Joliet and Rockford represent two very different kinds of adaptation: the former by playing the economic role of quasi-independent satellite and the latter by using a combination of politics and economics to maintain its independent character. As a result, Joliet comes close to typifying a city of its class in Illinois, and Rockford is the most atypical city of that class in the state.

Like many of the other cities of Illinois, Joliet's early development was tied to the incipient regional transportation network that began to radiate from Chicago in the 1830's to open the prairies and plains of the greater West. Its first boom rested on the construction of the Illinois and Michigan Canal, but its real growth did not begin until the Rock Island Railroad arrived in 1852. From the first, Joliet specialized in manufacturing necessities for its regional market, the greater West. From limestone to rails, from barbed wire to nails, it produced exactly those items needed for the taming of the prairies, attracting or creating new industries to meet each new frontier. Though other cities manufactured similar products, the location, concentration, and timing of their manufacture in the Joliet civil community became a specialty in and of itself.

During the 1850's, Joliet grew as a supplier of a major need on the treeless prairie—building materials. From the quarries near town came limestone blocks for central and western Illinois, as well as for places to the east of the city. After the Civil War, further technological advance eliminated the West's dependence on stone as a building material as the locally devised balloon-frame construction and prefabrication techniques were combined with lumber obtained from the northern fringes of the sphere to create the distinctive architecture of the greater West.

Joliet responded by shifting its industrial base without entirely eliminating the need for the acquired skills of its quarrying industry. The civil community began to exploit the nearby coal resources and became a center for the manufacture of steel products of regional importance. At first its mills produced steel items for the railroads and products for western homesteads, such as barbed wire and nails. From this developed later adaptations of local industry to the demands of new frontiers, specialized steelmaking and railroad equipment repair in the steel industry and the introduction of the manufacture of wallpaper, which served much the same purpose as the furniture industry in Rockford. More recently, with the advent of the great highway construction programs and the opening of the metropolitan frontier, a heavy-construction-equipment industry has been added to the Joliet industrial base.

As the city closest to the northeastern industrial belt, Joliet was one of the first in Illinois to be engulfed by the urban frontier, some time after 1870, in a boom that spent itself by 1900. It was not until the opening of the metropolitan frontier, after 1945, when the Chicago metropolitan region began to expand in depth, that Joliet again began to experience great population growth. Thus it was relatively slow in achieving medium size.

Sociologically, the Joliet civil community is very similar to the overall Chicago metropolitan region in which it is located. As part of that region, yet also a county seat on the fringes of downstate Illinois, politics in Joliet is generally in a state of flux. The combination of metropolitan style industrialization and traditional downstate political attitudes has led to a continuing political dichotomy in the civil community, usually expressed through the separate city hall and courthouse circles.

Rockford's special function, the machine-tool industry which began locally in the mid-nineteenth century, turned out to be a harbinger of the contemporary metropolitan-technological frontier. In an age of increasing automation that industry is making Rockford an internationally known center of technological change.

Rockford was established at a ford below the falls of the Rock River, as its name indicates. Originally intended to be a way station for travelers from Chicago to the Galena lead mines and a service center for farmers beginning to settle in the area, its founders immediately recognized the possibilities for industrial development using the available water power. They capitalized on the river from the very beginning to make Rockford a local milling center. After the advent of the railroad from Chicago in 1852, the civil community enjoyed its first boom, which lasted through the 1860's. Rockford became a leading center for the manufacture of farm implements, one of the major technological innovations designed to make human settlement of the prairie-plains feasible. As the city's industrial "ante," which put it in a key position on the land frontier even after the frontier line had moved well west of northern Illinois, the industry remains important locally. As the land frontier moved westward, Rockford and the smaller cities associated with it in northern Illinois continued to pioneer in the development of technological tools, such as barbed wire, for its conquest.

Rockford was the first of the cities of the prairie to build an economic base within the framework of the urban-industrial frontier. Already in the 1850's the farm implement industry in other cities located closer to the prairie markets began to outclass Rockford's, so the city's rising industrial leadership turned to the development of machine tools as a step to better production of a wide variety of products, and to the manufacture of furniture to meet the growing demand for upgrading the quality of home living in a section which was just emerging from the life of the raw frontier. Both industries were manifestations of the urban frontier which burst full force on Rockford in the early 1880's, starting a wave of population growth that continued until the Great Depression.

The machine-tool industry, an early precursor of what is presently called "automation," soon became the civil community's most important industry. Its expansion and development from a regional to a nationally oriented industry has become the main factor in Rockford's successful participation in the development of subsequent frontiers, since its economic importance has increased along with the need for more advanced technology. Rockford's history is a prime example of the chain reaction effect of the new technology whereby certain industries established to serve one frontier generate others to serve subsequent frontiers.

In all, however, the growth of Rockford in the nineteenth century was stimulated by less specialized manufacturing and commercial functions. It was not until the city's particular specialty came into demand in the years that marked the turning point between the industrial and technological frontiers that Rockford's growth was spurred accordingly. As a consequence, from fourth place among the cities of the prairie in 1920, it had risen to first place by 1960. The metropolitan frontier has had an impact on Rockford unexcelled in any of the other cities of the prairie.

Rockford is relatively unique among cities of its size in contemporary

America in that so much of its industry is locally owned. This relative economic self-sufficiency, combined with other factors, has assisted in the maintenance of a strongly developed sense of social and political self-sufficiency—even isolationism—in the Rockford civil community, which has been sustained for better than a century. Reinforced by a high degree of internal social homogeneity and a common fear of nearby (90 miles) Chicago, politics in Rockford reflects the pride of community fostered by a home-owned industrial base, the conservatism bred of isolation from the larger currents in state and nation, and something of the spirit of innovation that has given Rockford its home-grown industries.

The Cities of Lakehead and Mountain Gate

Far removed from the prairie cities of Illinois are Duluth and Superior, located at the head of Lake Superior, and Pueblo, at the western edge of the Great Plains. Yet, in common with their sisters to the south and east, they too are situated at an important crossroads between east and west; the junction between the Great Lakes-St. Lawrence waterway to the Atlantic and the overland crossing to the Pacific and the gateway to the mountains that link the Mississippi Valley with the far West. Their crossroads locations, combined with the rugged, mineral-rich, and still basically unsettled environment surrounding them have given them an economic base that uniquely synthesizes commerce and the extraction of natural resources. Dependent upon the vagaries of the latter for prosperity, they have proved to be able to avoid total economic disaster because of their commercial functions.

In most respects, Duluth and Superior exemplify those cities east or west that boomed because of mining or lumbering efforts nearby and which have found little else to sustain them. Pueblo, on the other hand, is a paradigm of the western city that would have hit the same economic snags except for the fact that it was in the mainstream of the nation's westward movement. Developed, for the most part, several decades after their Illinois counterparts, their beginnings as cities reflect the more mature land frontier of the 1870's, which was already heavily influenced by the urban frontier back East. In fact, it was the application of the new technology, much of it pioneered in the Illinois cities, that made possible the establishment of the cities farther north and west.

Duluth came into existence in the early 1850's when a scattering of settlers made their way over from Superior and up from St. Paul as a vanguard of the advancing frontier. The settlement virtually ceased to exist during the 1860's after the panic of 1857 had wiped out any possible economic advantage for settlement there. It came back to life with the beginning of construction of the Northern Pacific Railroad in 1869 and became a city in 1870, six months before the first passenger train arrived in town and in expectation of that event. The panic of 1873 destroyed the railroad enterprise and the city. Duluth, reduced to village status, was not to revive until the railroad did.

Since Duluth profited from the impact of both the land and urban frontiers simultaneously, its great boom—when it came—was all the more intense, but since its relationship to both frontiers was marginal, its periodic "busts" were equally great. That boom began in the late 1870's with the completion of the transcontinental line and the beginning of large-scale lumbering operations at the Lakehead. The opening of the Mesabi iron range after 1880 led Duluth into a period of spectacular growth.

Like Peoria, Duluth was considered a major American city at the turn of the century, with a population that exceeded 50,000 by 1900. Duluth's growth was due to its successful combination of two, perhaps three, special economic functions, all related to the land and urban frontiers. It was the gateway to and headquarters for the great iron ranges of Minnesota, then the nation's major source of iron ore, which fed the urban-industrial centers of the greater Northeast. It was the center of substantial lumbering operations which exploited the virgin wilderness and pushed back the land frontier. And it was the eastern rail terminus of the overland route for transshipping imports from the Orient, from the Pacific to the Atlantic coast.

Duluth reached its economic peak on the eve of World War I. Then the Panama Canal was opened and trade from the Orient was deflected southward, the timber played out, and the mining industry ceased to expand. (It is now in decline.) The combined stagnation of all three functions reflected the end of the land frontier and the stabilization of the urban frontier in the country as a whole. Duluth maintained its population but virtually ceased to grow, a large city becoming relatively smaller with each passing decade as no new special function able to relate the city to new frontiers was acquired.

Duluth's major problem has been the failure of its economy to move from the stage of its dependence on the land frontier into a positive relationship with the subsequent frontiers. Geared primarily to the then new technology of the frontiers opened up in the nineteenth century—based either on the exploitation of limited natural resources or the provision of rail transportation to places now served by other means of transportation—Duluth stagnated as those frontiers began to close.

The nearly static social structure that has resulted from the stagnation of Duluth's economic base has sharpened an already high level of political cleavage between workers and managers in the civil community by forcing the local interests to fight over the division of a pie whose size remains the same rather than enabling them to concern themselves with cooperating to obtain larger shares of a growing pie. Moreover, the high level of absentee ownership has robbed the community of an indigenous leadership capable of doing something to remedy the situation.

In the early 1960's, as the recoverable iron ore played out, the city was sinking into a deep depression, modified only because its location led the state of Minnesota to step in and create some basic institutions related to the metropolitan frontier to sustain it. The University of Minnesota at Duluth was established to serve the youth of northern Minnesota. A substantially state-financed port was built to put Minnesota in a competitive position for trade coming up the St. Lawrence Seaway. And, finally, the state's efforts to stimulate the development of the taconite industry offered Duluth its first chance to recover from the blows of a half-century ago.

Thus in recent years there have been some signs that Duluth may be able to leap directly out onto the metropolitan-technological frontier. The development of the taconite industry has been a case in point. The opening of the St. Lawrence Seaway may provide the means for Duluth to recapture much of the trade of its natural hinterland. Most recently, a major electronics plant, a branch of a California company, has been established in the city. The electronics industry, which has been intimately associated with the trans-Mississippi West from Minnesota to California, is particularly suitable to a city like Duluth, with its highly skilled labor force and relatively poor situation in regard to markets for bulk products. Yet despite these scattered signs of change, the city's overall economic position is still in doubt.

Superior has passed through a cycle similar to Duluth's but more extreme because of the city's even closer ties to the land frontier. Though actually established before the arrival of the railroad, the city became significant as an urban center only after the Northern Pacific was built to connect it with national and regional markets. The city remained significant while the railroad, the mines, and the trees held out and has never recovered from the nearly simultaneous decline of all three. The combination of frontier impacts after 1880 led to a great boom that lasted through 1910. Then the passing of the land frontier and the lumbering industry and Superior's failure to readjust to the urban frontier—the mining ranges it served were much smaller—turned the boom into a since continuous decline that is reflected in the accelerating decline of the city's population. Unable to make the transition from old to new frontiers, it has been more or less abandoned by the corporate interests that gave it life in the first place. It has retained the trappings of a larger city without the population to support them, surviving on the vestiges of its earlier economic functions and reflecting the old political issues that originated when those economic functions were strong.

Pueblo, like Duluth and Superior, did not begin to develop until the land frontier had begun to merge with the urban frontier, and its first boom reflects the influence of both. Starting after the coming of the railroad in 1870, it accelerated with the opening of the smelters and the steel industry after 1880 and ended with the passing of the land frontier after 1910. However, Pueblo was in an excellent position to capitalize on the opening of the metropolitan frontier, particularly since it is located on the fringes of the Southwest, the section which has benefited most from the recent migrations connected with that frontier. Hence it is now in the midst of a great new boom that equals its original one.

More than any other city in its part of the greater West, Pueblo developed as a consequence of advances in both transportation and manufacturing technology. The city was initially settled by "Anglos" just prior to the Civil War, and urbanization did not begin in earnest until the Denver and Rio Grande Railroad arrived from the north in 1872. Shortly thereafter, the great silver strikes in the Leadville area led to the creation of the first important Pueblo industry, the smelters developed by the Guggenheim interests to utilize new smelting processes designed to process the ores of the American West with greater efficiency. The smelters lasted as long as the silver could be profitably mined and then disappeared. They were replaced by the Rockefeller interests' Colorado Fuel and Iron Company, the first substantial iron and steel works west of the Mississippi River. The C.F.&I., still the major industry in Pueblo, was developed, like its counterparts in the other cities of the prairie, to produce items for the railroads, the mines, and the homesteaders of the West. Until World War II, Pueblo was the only steel-fabricating center of any significance between the Mississippi River and California. This special function, a product of the urban-industrial frontier, raised otherwise undistinguished Pueblo to major city status by World War I.

Today the C.F.&I. and the railroads play less of a role in Pueblo's economy. The U.S. Army's Pueblo Ordnance Depot, a number of auto parts manufacturers, and a service center for the great commercial jet airplanes, all industries attuned to the newer frontiers of technology and space, are growing to rival them, marking Pueblo's transition from the old frontier to the new. Within its regional framework, however, Pueblo's *relative* importance has declined, though its population growth has been great by national standards. A major and articulated concern of the community leaders in contemporary Pueblo is the development of a special economic function suited to the new frontier to replace its older counterpart.

The existence of an old-style industrial base has given Pueblo a social structure and political system markedly distinct from that of the rest of

Colorado. Demographically, it is more like the industrial centers of the other cities of the prairie; hence it has had to make adjustments unfamiliar to the state's other major cities. Its system has apparently been successful in combining the style of politics common in other urban industrial communities to the east with the style of politics indigenous in the rest of Colorado into its own particular package.

NOTES

NOTE: The major data sources for this chapter are listed in Appendix D.

1. The population figures in Table 2–1 are for the cities only and, accordingly, exclude sections of the civil community as a whole which in each case lie outside the city limits. In some cases, these represent substantial exclusions. Figures for the civil community as defined are not available as such in the Census records and even where they could possibly be abstracted, could be calculated only with great difficulty and questionable accuracy for the earlier years. At the same time, use of the statistics on a county basis would be even less accurate. Since the cities of the prairie have continued to respond to population growth by annexing at least part of their newly settled fringe areas to the central city, the basic city population figures are useful for conveying the general pattern of civil community growth, particularly as qualified in the text.

2. Aside from Belleville, founded in 1814, both Collinsville and Edwardsville were established before 1820.

3. According to the map prepared by John Tremblay for *Historical Atlas of Religion in America* (New York: Harper and Row, 1962). This measure of religious diversity is highly significant and will be discussed at greater length in subsequent chapters. The oligopolistic character of local religious patterns in the United States is quite marked. According to Tremblay, approximately 45 per cent of all counties in the United States are dominated by one religious group, having better than 50 per cent of the reported religious membership. Approximately 50 per cent of all counties are dominated by one religious group with 25 to 50 per cent of the reported religious membership. Only 96 counties in the entire country have no religious group with at least 25 per cent of the total reported religious membership and most of them are located in the sparsely populated areas of the West.

4. Peoria is even the headquarters for its own railroad, the Toledo, Peoria, and Western. Without implying a cause-and-effect relationship, it is evident that cities that have continued to be headquarters of Class I railroads (Duluth is another) invariably conceive of themselves to be "Class I" cities, in competition with the nation's major cities. This is certainly true of Peoria and Duluth, and sets them somewhat apart from the other cities of the prairie which have yet to evolve the institutions required to change the local "small-town" self-image, in their interests and their problems.

5. By virtue of the efforts of Abraham Lincoln and the famous "long nine" in the State Legislature. The apparent coincidence of dates was, in reality, not a coincidence but the consequence of a conjunction of statewide interests desirous of opening the northern two-thirds of Illinois to intensive settlement, which also created the

state's two great centers. The local consequences of what were, in effect, state-level decisions were of utmost importance, even at that early date.

6. For a further examination of the respective economic bases of the three major civil communities and some of their political ramifications, see Benjamin R. Schuster, "Industrial Ownership and Political Involvement in Three Midwestern Cities" (Philadelphia: Center for the Study of Federalism, 1966).

Chapter 3 / The Cities of the Prairie and the Greater West

The Frontier and Sectionalism

THE VARIETY of frontier experiences in the cities of the prairie is limited and conditioned by their common location in the eastern half of the greater West. The previous chapter indicates some of the ways in which that common location is the key to many of the civil communities' similarities despite the demographic, economic, and cultural factors making each unique. Location is the key to most of the characteristics which set them apart from their sisters in other parts of the country. The expression of social, cultural, economic, and political differences through territorial location is known classically in the United States as sectionalism.

Sectionalism, as both the concept and the reality have developed in America, embodies the interaction between geography and history that has forged the set of social patterns which make up the specific universe of each sectional entity. Each of the three spheres and eight sections into which the United States is divided is a grouping of contiguous states tied together by long-term common interests shaped by common historic patterns. Unlike the country's regions which encompass essentially homogeneous areas, each of these spheres and sections is a complex entity combining highly diverse states, communities, and subregions that remain linked within an enduring framework because of their complementary attributes, which enable them to satisfy common needs.[1]

The frontier emphasizes the workings of men in time—as embodied in the advances of succeeding generations—to change space; sectionalism reflects the crystallization of the actions of specific times in specific spaces. Appropriately enough, Frederick Jackson Turner formulated the classic theory of sectionalism as a corollary to the frontier hypothesis. He saw the twin forces of sectionalism and the frontier as the most important sources of political, economic, and social development, as well as political conflict, in the American scheme of things. In his most forceful formulation of the sectional idea, he said:

> The United States is, in size and natural resources, an empire, a collection of potential nations, rather than a single nation. . . . Within this vast empire there are geographic provinces, separate in physical conditions, into which American colonization has flowed, and in each of which a special society has developed, with an economic, political, and social life of its own. . . . Between these sections commercial relations have sprung up, and economic combinations and contests may be traced. . . . American industrial life is the outcome of the combinations and contests of groups of States in sections. And the intellectual, the spiritual life of the nation is the result of the interplay of the sectional ideals, fundamental assumptions and emotions.[2]

Turner's search for a sociological basis for geographically measurable political differences in the United States remains the starting point for all considerations of the place of sectionalism and regionalism in American life, particularly in line with the new awareness of the influence of geographic differences on American society which has developed in recent years. As the first impact of such nationalizing devices as the automobile, the airplane, and the mass media gives way to the process of learning to live with these new pressures toward a uniform culture, and as the class cleavage that became apparent in politics during the Depression and immediate post-Depression years is modified by the more recent period of prosperity, sectional differences that follow along the lines outlined by Turner have again become apparent.[3]

Sectionalism and the Three Spheres

American sectionalism does indeed emerge as a product of the interaction between the frontier process and "raw" geography. Its most notable characteristic is the way in which it unites regions by tying together a hierarchy of "easts" and "wests" in metropolis-hinterland relationships which reflect the country's basic cultural, social, and economic realities. Unlike the metropolis-hinterland relationships common in the Old World, which are generally dual in character, with a center and its peripheries, the internal pattern of American sectionalism is generally triadic or quadrilateral. On the map, the pattern is usually linear, with a major metropolis on the east, a hinterland region west of it, and a secondary metropolis at the section's far western edge. Where there is a fourth side, it is generally a region economically tied to the major metropolis but culturally and socially too distinct to be able to share equally in the general development of a larger whole.

This pattern is reflected in the United States as a whole. The northeastern megalopolis centering on New York and Washington is the national metropolis, the classic "East." Its "west" fans out over the Appalachians to embrace the Mississippi Valley and its border areas as the classic national hinterland. Along the Pacific coast, Los Angeles and San Francisco form a secondary metropolis, neither "east" nor "west" in classic terms but combining something of the culture and social patterns of one with something of the economic and social opportunities of the other. The South, economically tied to the northeastern megalopolis as fully as any part of the country, has been outside the nation's mainstream for nearly two centuries for significant cultural and social reasons. The pattern is repeated on a smaller scale within the country's three great historical, cultural, and economic spheres which form the underlying basis for American sectionalism: the greater Northeast, the greater South, and the greater West (Map 7).[4] Thus the already familiar megalopolis also serves as the metropolis of the greater Northeast. Its Appalachian hinterland to the west gives way to a secondary center that forms the Great Lakes industrial belt. Northern New England is its backwater region. The pattern is repeated on an even smaller scale in the major states of the Northeast. Thus New York has metropolitan New York City, an upstate hinterland leading to the Rochester-Buffalo secondary center, and Pennsylvania has metropolitan Philadelphia, an outstate hinterland, and greater Pittsburgh. Finally, the pattern is even repeated within the Northeast's great metropolitan regions. Similar hierarchies can be found in the greater South, which will not be explored here, and in the greater West, which will.

What distinguishes the nation's spheres from one another, however, is not simply the relatively clear pattern of "easts" and "wests" to be found within each but also the unique meaning of that particular pattern in the social, economic, and political life of the nation as a whole.

The greater Northeast includes all or the major parts of three sections: New England, the Middle East, and the Near West (or Old Northwest). It embraces the nation's urban industrial heartland and contains over 40 per cent of the country's population in hardly more than 10 per cent of the country's land area. It is the area where most of the patterns of American civilization originated and where most of the nation's power is concentrated.[5] The sphere developed from a series of "seed" settle-

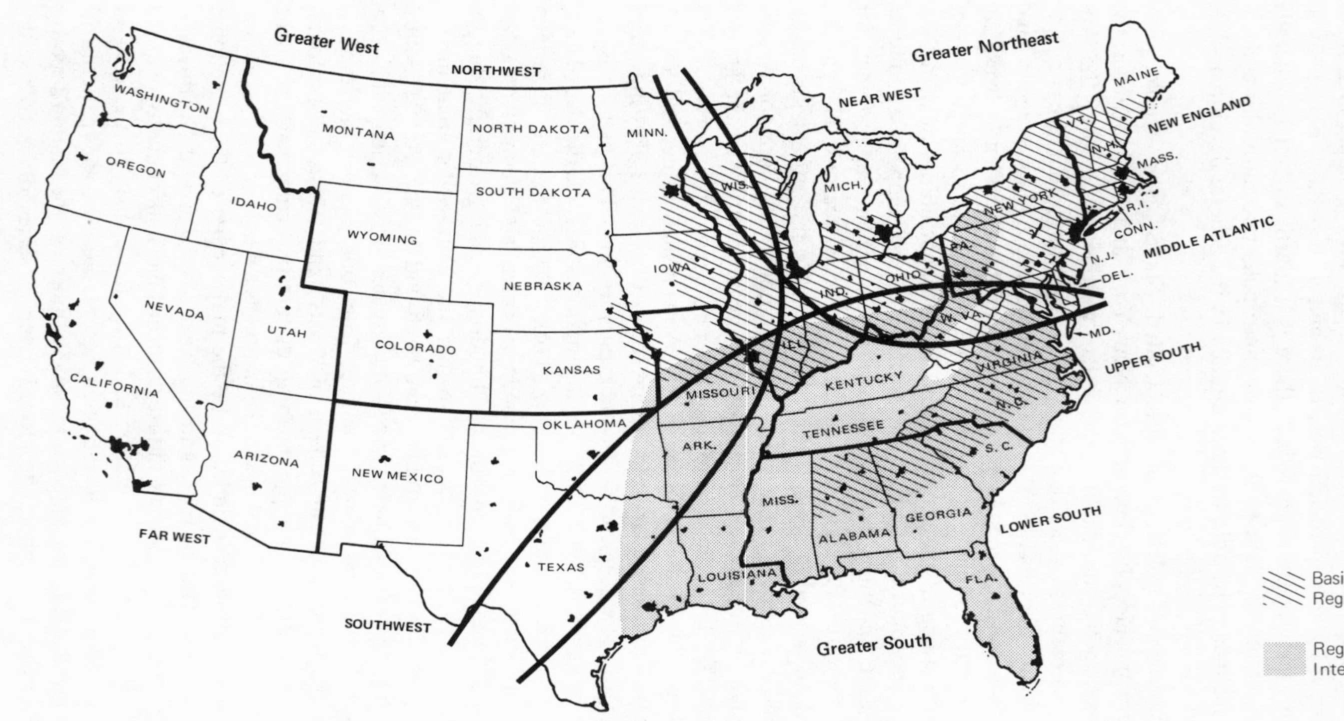

Map 7 The Three Spheres: Selected Characteristics

ments along the east coast above the Potomac River and includes the area due west of those settlements to a point just beyond Lake Michigan. Its core is the highly urbanized megalopolis that extends from Maine to Virginia, almost the entire length of the Atlantic coast within the sphere. The sphere's second concentration of urban areas begins in the western foothills of the Appalachians on a line from Buffalo to Pittsburgh and extends westward via the cities of Ohio, Indiana, and southern Michigan to the Chicago area, which is already a borderland. Most of the greater Northeast is located within the eastern time zone. Its western limits coincide with those of the natural eastern woodland, past which begin the great prairies. The greater Northeast as a whole is the area of greatest population density in the United States. Half of the nation's twenty-eight metropolitan areas of one million or more inhabitants are located within it, as are four of the six cities of over one million and half of those over 500,000. Dominated by these great cities and their suburbs with their densities of thousands of people per square mile, the sphere also has a very high open country density, because urban style settlement in rural areas is relatively easy. While the concentration of population stimulated by the metropolitan frontier has created substantial areas of open space reminiscent of land frontier days in the Appalachians and northern New England, overall the sphere is marked by a contiguous belt of settlement to its western limits with an open country (excluding urban places of 20,000 or more) density that exceeded 45 per square mile in 1960 (Map 8).

The sphere also contains the dominant manufacturing regions in the United States. While the manufacturing belt continues beyond the limits of the greater Northeast, the great contiguous bloc of manufacturing counties ends along approximately the same line. This concentration of industry has enriched the greater Northeast to the point where its three sections account for over half of the nation's personal income, a figure which has remained remarkably stable since at least 1929.

The greater Northeast was preeminently shaped by the urban-industrial frontier which superseded its commercial and agricultural economy as a major developmental force early in the nineteenth century. Contemporary metropolitanization in the sphere is rooted in the social and economic patterns established during the urban frontier stage, ranging from the transplantation of inner city ethnic communities to the suburbs to the necessary adaptations of an industrial plant designed for the coal and iron age.

The greater South, in many ways the most easily distinguishable of the spheres, also began from a number of "seed" settlements along the eastern seaboard but south of the Potomac River and ultimately advanced westward to include all or major parts of the former slave states plus certain peripheral areas to their north originally settled by Southerners. It embraces three sections: the Upper South, the Lower South, and the

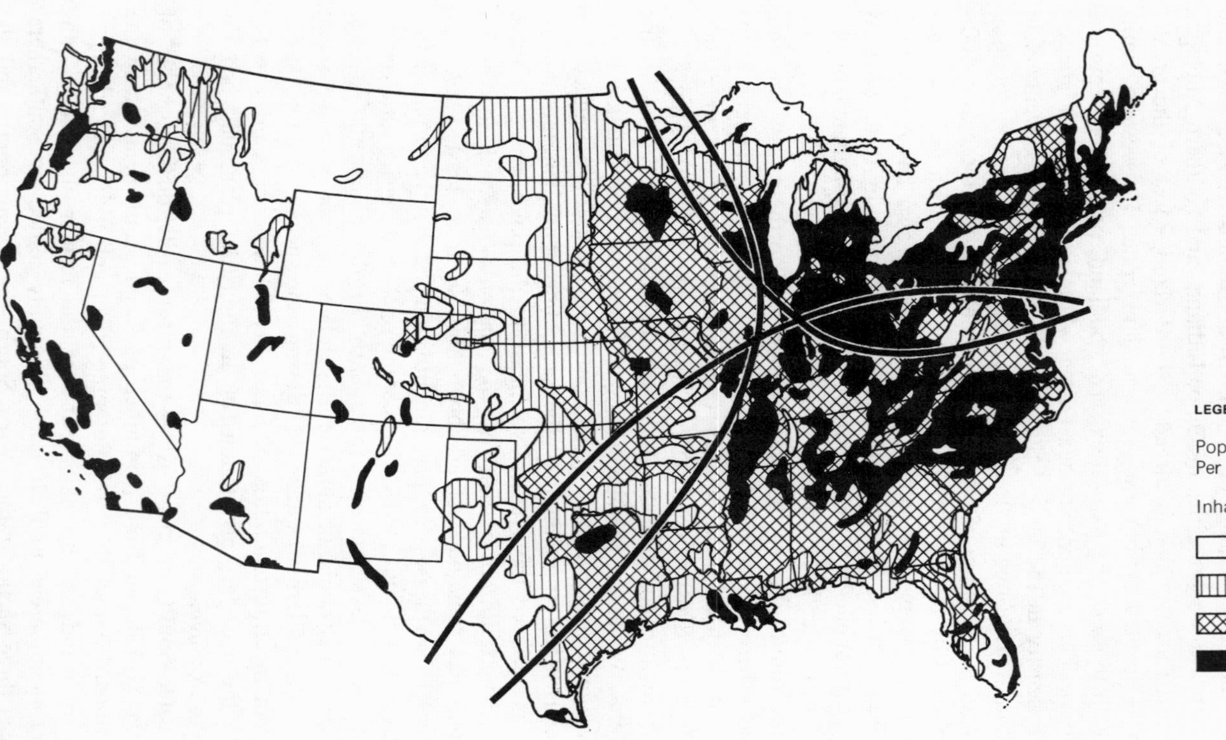

Map 8 The Spheres and the Density of Population, 1960

Western South (see Map 7). Until recently, it was clearly distinguishable by the mandatory segregation of Negroes within its territory. It is still held together by a perceived common concern (positive or negative) with "the Southern way of life" as expressed through the mythology of the "lost cause."[6]

The greater South is clearly identifiable in every one of the common statistical measures.[7] Agriculturally, the sphere is marked by the prevalence of cotton or tobacco farming supplemented by widespread timber farming and cattle feeding and sustained by an annual rainfall of more than 45 inches in all the states that are wholly or partly within the sphere. It is religiously distinctive in a way that no other major part of the United States is, with a marked predominance of Southern Baptists from the Atlantic to West Texas.[8] Much larger and considerably more varied in the spread of urbanization and economic activity than the Northeast, its metropolitan-hinterland patterns have been more sectional than sphere-wide. Moreover, the South's historic economic dependence on the Northeast has kept it from developing independent metropolitan centers of its own until the recent rise of Miami, Houston, and Dallas. At the same time, the relatively even spread of population in its rural areas—which support isolated homesteads and settlements even more easily than the Northeast—gives the sphere a distinctive population and settlement pattern that has reduced the pressure for the development of large cities. While the contemporary South has many metropolitan areas, few of them rank among the nation's twenty-five largest. In 1960 the entire sphere had only ten cities with populations in excess of 250,000 and only twenty-two others that exceeded 100,000, far fewer than either of the other two spheres.

The contemporary South is still substantially shaped by the land frontier as it was originally manifested in that sphere. The plantation agrarianism of antebellum days gave way to an industrial version of the plantation system when the urban frontier moved southward, substantial remnants of which still survive.[9] Today the urban frontier pattern of medium-size and small city industrialization has given way to industrial development in the medium-size and small metropolitan areas that have grown up around the older cities—often with twice the population—without being absorbed by them. While the desire to avoid citification is found nationwide, it is most intense in the greater South, where most urbanites have come directly from the farm in this generation. Many of these people retain possession of their farms, earning enough by growing trees for lumber companies to pay their taxes and in this manner maintaining tangible agrarian attachments. Many more work in the metropolitan areas but continue to live on their farms, often commuting long distances daily to avoid living in the city, even when the city is as rural as these Southern communities are. Both groups help maintain the homogeneous life style that unites urban and rural Southerners.

In its broadest sweep, the greater West has been delineated by many geographers and historians to include the entire area west and south of the Appalachian Mountains settled during or after the Revolutionary period primarily or initially by pioneers who were already products of American culture rather than unassimilated immigrants from the Old World.[10] There is much in this definition to recommend it; however, the character of the settlements established in the eastern and southern reaches of that vast territory was so firmly fixed by their first settlers into patterns operative in the other spheres that it makes better sense to exclude those parts from the sphere as here defined.

In the South's west, any fundamental Western qualities and influences had to take second place to the influences generated by a slave-based civilization. The continued overwhelming impact of the race question, still the central "problem" of the South, and the other characteristic economic and social features of Southern life have so diluted the impact of Western ways that, for political purposes at least, the latter must be considered to be secondary.

Similarly, the territory immediately west of the Alleghenies, while partly the product of typically Western influences, was so influenced by the first generation of Easterners who came over the mountains to settle and, a century later, by the great European migrations that responded to the urban frontier on both sides of the mountains that its Western characteristics had to take second place to those of the East. The urban planning of cities of this "Near West," which reaches from the Alleghenies to the Wabash River, illustrates this fact clearly. Though surveyed in the Western manner under the rectangular land survey system established by Congress in 1785, the cities of Ohio and Indiana were laid out in the then dominant Eastern (or Southern) patterns. In most, their local streets were developed in the interstices of the system of roads which converged on the center of town rather than in a grid tied to the survey lines. Others were consciously modeled after the Philadelphia city plan.[11] Like their coastal sisters, most of those cities grew primarily as a result of local influences—as products of colonization companies, as local trading centers, or as local milling centers—not as a result of larger regional and even national concerns like those that stimulated the cities of the true greater West. Moreover, the cities of that section were transformed by the urban frontier in much the same way as their East Coast sisters, becoming centers of heavy industry based on the availability of coal, with only sectional differences based on their proximity to iron ore. Thus the cities at the western end of the greater Northeast grew as parts of the northeastern industrial belt from the very beginning.

The authentic greater West, then, can be said to include all free-soil territories which had not emerged from the land frontier stage of their development by 1850: the free states west of the Mississippi River plus major parts of Illinois, Wisconsin, and Michigan. This is the area in which the national democratic ideals of the nineteenth century were given concrete expression. In the process, the greater West endowed itself with a unique character of its own. Primarily products of Jacksonian democracy and its influences, in the radically new physical environment of the greater West these national democratic ideals were combined with an entirely new technology. The combination stimulated an economic system in which laissez-faire ideas predominated but which was strongly influenced by corporate organization and governmental intervention from the beginning. The same combination gave rise to a populist approach to politics characteristic of the Jacksonian and post-Jacksonian eras which was intrinsically different from traditional or elitist approaches to politics characteristic of the other spheres. The greater West also gave birth to as unstructured a social system as the modern world has ever seen, which allowed and even expected great and rapid mobility both vertically and laterally within it. The sphere as a whole was populated through an implicit if unwitting system of recruitment that placed a premium on those with a psychology of individual initiative in economic pursuits and social conformity in most others.

The greater West includes all of two sections, the Far West and Northwest, and part of the Near West. The cities of the prairie are located within the latter two, on the sphere's fringe but in the nation's heartland. Along the borders of the three spheres (generally speaking, between and along the points of intersection of the semicircles on Map 7) lie three transition zones—the Ohio Valley, the western South, and the western Great Lakes—that share the characteristics of two or more spheres and have particularly diverse and complex patterns of culture and politics. With the exception of Pueblo, the cities of the prairie lie within the most complex of these three zones, the western Great Lakes, at the cultural and historical center of the United States. Though roughly falling within the limits of the greater West, their location in the transition zone at its eastern fringe does much to account for their diversity and representative character. As a result of location alone, every section of the country has its echoes in one of the cities of the prairie or another while, at the same time, the combination of characteristics of the greater West has endowed the cities with a common basis from which they have developed.

Landforms, Space, and Settlement Patterns

The pattern of urbanization in the greater West is rooted in three general factors: (1) an initial aspiration on the part of virtually every city in the area to become a great metropolitan center while remaining an uncitified "home town"; (2) the actual development of a very tightly and even "hierarchically" structured region-wide network of interrelated urban oases, sharply graded in size, each with a hinterland tributary to it roughly proportionate to its size (as "adjusted" for regional location); and (3) the location of all the larger urban oases and most of the medium-size ones either on the fringes of the sphere or along breaks in its normal landform patterns.

The landforms of the greater West are central to the development of its human settlements. Basically an interior region (to true Westerners, coastal-oriented California is the Orient), the greater West is characterized by a relatively high altitude (most of its land is more than one thousand feet above sea level, falling below that figure to as low as six hundred feet only on its peripheries) and massive landforms. Sweeping prairies and high plains, great forests and wide rivers, rugged mountains and desert plateaus dominate different parts of the sphere. All have one thing in common: the challenges they present to human settlement considerably exceed those of the other two spheres. The landforms and the climatic conditions associated with them have been the crucial "built-in" influences on the forms of human settlement in the greater West. Indeed, recent work done by physiologists and geographers indicates that the very character of society and the health and personalities of its individual members are strongly affected by these environmental influences everywhere.[12] The influence of landform and climate is readily apparent in the settlement patterns of the cities of the prairie. As Walter Prescott Webb has demonstrated, the great expanse of prairie-plains environment that reaches from western Indiana to central California is the heartland and characteristic environment of the West. Two major and universal characteristics mark this central great plains landform: treelessness and an oasis culture.

The plains area is naturally treeless overall, leaving animals and man with virtually no natural protection against a harsh climate. Intensive settlement on the plains is possible only in scattered "oases." Urban civil communities in the greater West have always been located in such oases, many of them manmade. While the benefits of modern technology have increased the number of potential oases and expanded the size and settlement capacity of others, this fundamental fact remains. During the late nineteenth and early twentieth centuries, attempts were made to intensively settle the plains with farmers on a uniform density basis. These efforts not only came to grief in the 1920's and 1930's, but accelerated a trend away from rural living in the entire prairie-plains area that is continuing to empty the land outside the cities. This trend has not only restored the oasis pattern of settlement on the plains by producing oasis-like metropolitan centers but has extended the metropolitan oasis system into the lowland prairies, which had previously supported more uniformly dense rural settlement patterns. Throughout the greater West, these metropolitan oases are growing even more rapidly in relation to their surrounding nonmetropolitan hinterlands than are similar metropolitan centers in either the greater Northeast or the greater South, where the land is hospitable to exurban settlement. Improved technology has expanded the size of these oases so that now several relatively large civil communities may exist in a single oasis where only one or two small ones could exist in the past. In point of fact, the differences between the spheres in this regard are increasing, as the territory between metropolitan centers or oases in the greater West becomes more sparsely populated while that of the greater South remains much the same in density (except for the Western South, a section with its own characteristics) and the density of the greater Northeast increases.[13]

The contrast between the oasis character of the greater West and the character of the other spheres is graphically illustrated in the spread of urban areas shown in Map 8. Not surprisingly, the relative isolation of the oasis civil communities changes the character of the problems —interareal, intergovernmental, and even interpersonal—that they must face as metropolitan areas.

One contemporary manifestation of the oasis culture in the metropolitanization of the greater West is the minimizing of severe "urban sprawl" caused by the disorderly development of subdivisions and housing developments or the construction of individual homes at varying distances from the area of concentrated urbanization. The difficulties of the region's landforms make it unattractive to build far away from the major concentrations of population where urban services cannot be found, since the cost of providing such services becomes prohibitive unless shared as widely as possible. Thus in the arid regions of the greater West, the cost of supplying water keeps settlement compactly within the "oasis" and keeps the expansion of the oasis reasonably uniform. In the humid regions, the need for concentration is not as great, though the necessity for artificial drainage has much the same effect. Topographic barriers such as rivers and mountains are more effective as limiting factors in the greater West than in the other spheres, because they are more rugged or more dangerous. Finally, the absence of natural forest cover tends to direct developers toward use of land near the oasis or its manmade extensions in order to enhance the quality of their developments.

This sectional difference is quantitatively demonstrable.[14] Despite the general inclination to larger lot sizes for individual buildings in the greater West, and the smaller population size of most of its metropolitan centers, its urbanized areas as a whole tend to be more densely settled than those in any other section of the country, excepting only the largest urban concentrations in the heart of the megalopolis.

Finally, the harshness of the heartland of the greater West has not only forced urbanization into an oasis pattern, but has tended to confine the major oases to either the fringes of the sphere or to obvious breaks in its general topography. From Chicago on the east, located where Lake Michigan and the prairies meet, to Los Angeles on the west, located where the treeless belt meets the Pacific Ocean, this imposition of nature has been important despite the possibilities for manmade settlement patterns which have been carried farther in the greater West than in any other sphere. Recent interurban growth patterns in the sphere reflect the continuing influence of this natural determinism. Where urban areas are growing together, they are growing together in corridor-like arrangements, following the natural breaks in the topography, albeit without formal planning to that end. In effect, despite the great victories of the new technology of the metropolitan frontier in emancipating settlement patterns from an overweening dependence upon the dictates of nature, the natural environment continues to subtly direct the course of settlement in the greater West.

The ten urbanized areas among the cities of the prairie conform nicely with the overall pattern of their sphere. All except Joliet (which is now part of the incipient Great Lakes megalopolis) are themselves oases or parts of larger oasis areas. Even Duluth and Superior are carved out of uninhabitable forests surrounding them. As such, they are reasonably compact centers of population surrounded by territory in varying states of emptiness, and often increasing emptiness at that. The Quad Cities, Joliet, Peoria, Pueblo, Rockford, Springfield, Alton, and East St. Louis are located in river valleys which cut more or less deeply into the prairie. Duluth and Superior are located on the shores of a great inland sea. Even Decatur, Champaign, and Urbana, apparently located on the open prairie, are actually located on glacially created moraines—often barely perceptible today. These are high points that break the flow of the prairie along the edge of the original break between the woodlands of the greater Northeast and the grasslands of their sphere.

Urban sprawl is a major problem only in the Madison-St. Clair Counties area, partly because of the influence of St. Louis but primarily because the landforms of that area are virtually Southern and encourage scattered individual settlement and subdivision development throughout the two counties. Noncontiguous development can also be found in varying degrees in the other civil communities on the edge of the woods—on the southern side of Springfield, on the northern side of Rockford, and east of Joliet—but it is the exception rather than the rule. In Duluth and Superior, the settled areas do not even extend to the city limits, having become more compact over the years because of the difficulties in providing urban services on the Laurentian shield where they are situated.

The impact of the prairie is nowhere better illustrated than in the case of Champaign and Urbana. While both civil communities are highly compact, Urbana, located on somewhat better-drained lands at the western edge of the eastern woodlands, has a scattering of subdivisions to the east of its boundaries while virtually all of urbanized Champaign (located on a once swampy prairie) is contiguous. While it may be argued that this is as much a consequence of differing policies toward the extension of municipal services outside the city limits, the possibilities for policy differences in this regard are not simply dependent on the distribution of local influence but are also contingent on the dictates of topography. Where drainage costs are prohibitively high, it is most unlikely that any exceptions to a policy limiting city services to annexed areas will be made, no matter how much pressure is exerted.

The declining open country density in the greater West is reinforcing another prime characteristic of that sphere, its sheer spaciousness. In the greater West, metropolitan concentration has meant the increase of aggregate open space. Examination of maps showing population density changes over the past three decades reveals that the decline of population in nonmetropolitan counties west of the Great Lakes and north of the forty-fifth parallel has been so great that, excluding the urban oases, most of the area has less than ten people per square mile, much of it has less than six (the Census Bureau-defined limit for the frontier zone), and more than a third (including areas in Champaign County, for example) has less than two. Even when the urban population is included, vast areas from western Illinois to the Pacific have less than eighteen people per square mile, the standard measurement for maintenance of the range of social institutions requisite for "civilized" settlement in the nineteenth century. Contiguous population density is increasing only on the sphere's eastern and western fringes, along the Pacific Coast and the Great Lakes.

Open space is a characteristic made all the more striking by the large scale of the landforms of the greater West, which not only provide physical space of a magnitude unavailable in other parts of the country but contribute to a psychology of spaciousness which is further reinforced by the architecture and city planning of the urban oases. The cities of the greater West are characterized by wide, tree-lined streets, large residential lots, and by a dominant tradition of low-rise, single-story construction surrounding the central towers that command the oasis. Approaching them by land, their oasis-like character is sharply delineated by the concentration of trees that covers all but the central core. As "oases," they stand out against the open treeless landscape that surrounds them. Though they are situated on the prairie, the visage these cities present frequently comes closer to concretizing the image of the "city upon a hill" than that presented by cities hidden in more rolling terrain; a visage often enhanced by their location on glacial moraines or low bluffs whose slight rise above the surrounding countryside not only offers them better drainage and soil better suited for planting trees but makes them stand out more sharply against the flatlands.

In the large cities of the greater West, the skyline is generally dominated by skyscrapers that appear to rise up out of the prairie itself, since around them the buildings drop off in size to one, two, or occasionally three stories almost immediately. This effect is even more pronounced in the newer cities. The medium-size metropolitan areas rarely have buildings more than twelve stories high. Hence the trees conceal most of the urban development within their limits. Occasionally a few of the taller structures will stand out above them, as does the Illinois State Capitol in Springfield or the Staley Elevators in Decatur. The smaller cities and towns, like the larger cities to which they are tributary, are characterized by both the skyscraper and the oasis. Grain elevators, located along the railroad tracks in the business district, rise high above the trees and all other structures in the town.[15]

Another urban manifestation of the spaciousness of the greater West is the declining density of population within the sphere's cities. This aspect of the metropolitan frontier, characteristic of suburbanization throughout the country, is also related to the anti-city tendencies in American life. In recent years urban renewal and slum clearance have lowered populations in the cities' most densely populated areas while suburban migration has led to a general loss of population by the central cities. In the cities of the prairie, their respective annexation programs have also contributed to this trend, reducing the relative density of population within their limits even though their absolute populations have increased (Table 3–1). Of the fifteen cities for which data are available, ten had lower population densities than in 1950. Only Rock Island, which lost out in its attempt to annex a large territory south of the Rock River, and Duluth, which has had a great deal more vacant land within its city limits than it has needed for expansion for sixty years or more, increased in population density in the past decade. Regardless of cause, the overall effect has been remarkably similar—to increase the amount of spaciousness within the cities and, in several cases, to increase the amount of municipally controlled vacant land on which future growth can be planned.

TABLE 3-1

Cities of the Prairie, Land Area and Population Density, 1940-1960

	1940		1950		1960	
City	Area (sq. m.)	Density (per sq. m.)	Area (sq. m.)	Density (per sq. m.)	Area (sq. m.)	Density (per sq. m.)
Alton	6.4	4,884	6.4	5,086	9.8	4,393
Belleville	5.5	5,165	6.4	5,113	8.5	4,384
Champaign	N.A.[a]	N.A.	4.7	8,418	6.4	7,747
Davenport	18.1	3,649	18.1	4,119	46.7	1,905
Decatur	9.5	6,243	9.3	7,126	19.7	3,960
Duluth	62.3	1,622	62.3	1,678	62.6	1,707
E. St. Louis	13.4	5,642	13.4	6,141	13.8	5,921
Joliet	5.8	7,304	7.7	6,701	14.2	4,703
Moline	6.9	5,016	7.1	5,267	9.2	4,642
Peoria	12.4	8,475	12.9	8,671	15.2	6,787
Pueblo	10.0	5,216	10.6	6,008	17.1	5,332
Rockford	12.0	7,053	14.0	6,638	26.0	4,873
Rock Island	9.1	4,701	10.5	4,639	10.9	4,758
Springfield	9.5	7,948	10.4	7,849	21.4	3,891
Superior	36.6	960	36.6	965	36.6	917
Urbana	N.A.[a]	N.A.	N.A.	N.A.	5.0	5,459

[a]N.A. means not available from Census because city had less than 25,000 population.

The magnitude of the landscape in the greater West is matched by the difficulties of the climate. Water is a perennial issue, not only in the semi-arid and arid lands west of the one hundredth meridian where it has been an agricultural problem since the first white farmer arrived, but in the cities located in the better watered regions where urban demands create the kinds of shortages previously associated with rainless areas. The cities of the greater West must be prepared to regularly meet everything from blizzards and floods to droughts and earthquakes. Tornadoes are a common hazard for most of the cities of the prairie. Their snow removal bill is a matter of annual concern. So is the cost of proper storm sewers. These and other very mundane matters, such as street maintenance, are more difficult—and more expensive—propositions as a result. The regular diet of climatic extremes is not only a major factor in the private lives of the residents of the greater West but adds considerably to the cost of providing normal municipal services.

The Impact of the Rectangular Survey

The greater West is visibly marked off by its geometric pattern of land use, a legacy of the federal land survey system which permanently imposed its rectangular pattern on all human settlement in the sphere when it was first opened up for colonization. The rectangular land survey represents the greatest national planning effort in American history. Its orderliness, regularity, and relative ease of management were significant factors in taming the vastness of the greater West and its inhospitable landforms in no more than three generations. In the greater West proper, the rectangular survey system is as influential today as when the land was first marked off into mile-square sections and six-mile-square townships by degrees of latitude and meridians of longitude, affecting virtually all land-use patterns in the sphere and the setting of boundaries for its major political subdivisions.

The rectangular system took hold in this sphere because, as a general rule, federal surveyors were able to complete their work before all but a few squatters had occupied the land. Furthermore, the reasonably level nature of most of the lands that were settled permanently made them eminently suited to a rectangular system of land division. Neither of these facts was true in the other spheres. In most of the greater South and all but a fraction of the greater Northeast, the rectangular survey system was never applied.[16] Where the land was continuously hilly, the nature of the topography, combined with the strong influence of the Atlantic and Gulf coast cultures on the patterns of settlement, generally nullified much of its effect. This was particularly true in the urban areas, which were most subject to outside cultural influences and least dependent on the local survey system.

Quite the contrary was true in the urban settlements of the greater West. There, even if squatters had infiltrated into an area prior to its being surveyed, urban settlements could not be permanently established until the land was officially opened for settlement. In most cases, the original sites of the new towns were granted to the local settlers by the federal government, under the various townsite land grant programs in operation from 1812 to the 1870's, by the state from previously granted federal lands, or by internal improvement corporations, particularly railroad companies disposing of federal or state grants. All of these devices served to reinforce the connection between the townsite and the national survey system since the grants themselves were almost invariably based on the rectangular survey. Consequently even the pattern of city streets in most of the cities of the greater West is based in whole or in part on the national survey system. Equally important, all parcels of land—including all city lots—in those cities continue to be registered, identified, and transferred on the basis of their location in the national survey system.

Of the cities of the prairie, only those located in the Madison-St. Clair Counties area and settled by the French or by Southerners before the federal survey were not platted according to the grid system, though it was partially imposed on them later as they annexed fringe areas that had been surveyed according to the rectangular method. Even where the origi-

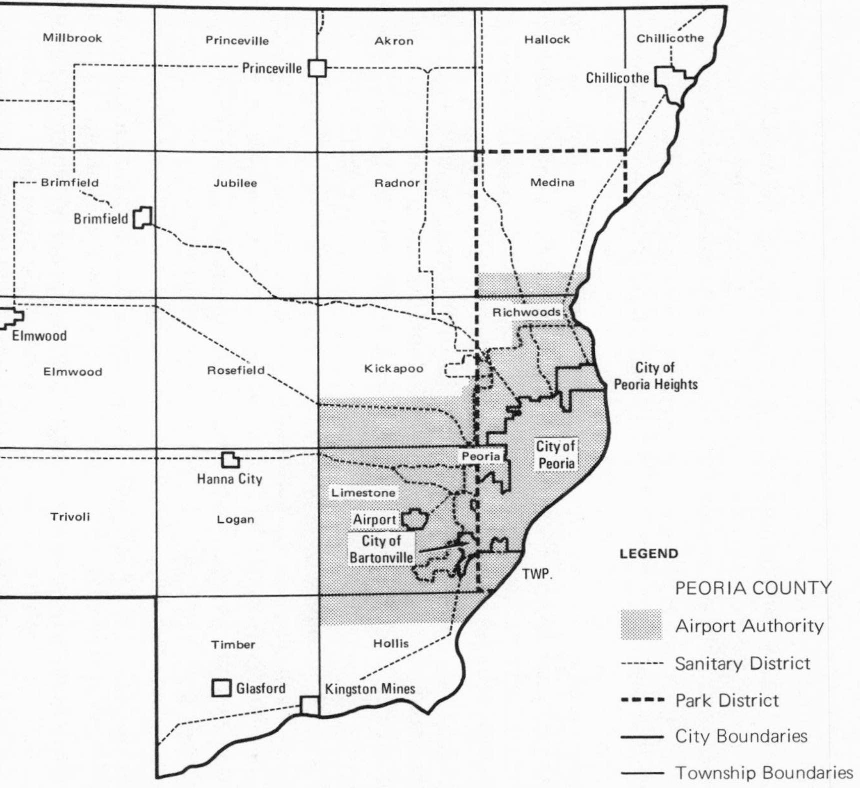

Map 9 The Governments of the Peoria Civil Community

nal plats were located in conjunction with a river (Peoria, Rockford), lake (Duluth), or railroad (Champaign) and diverged slightly from the standard east-west, north-south pattern of the overall survey, the subsequent plats reoriented the city in the standard direction. In some cases (Joliet, Rock Island, Davenport, East Moline, and Superior) a true-direction grid was set down in the first plat despite the existence of an important waterway nearby.

Thus, the rectangular survey has been etched into the very fabric of the civil communities through the street and real property system that governs all land use within their limits. If only because of purchase convenience, their subdivisions are almost invariably developed on parcels of land whose boundaries were established by the survey (quarter sections, half sections, and the like). Annexations and incorporations generally follow survey line boundaries, particularly since they must be adjusted to already existing rural roads and property lines which follow those boundaries.

The reasons for this are not hard to come by. The federal government rarely departed from its policy of disposing of the public domain in no less than quarter-section (160-acre) tracts. Homestead sales and grants were based on the 160-acre standard while land grants for public purposes involved no less than sections and, in some cases, townships. The 160-acre standard was formalized for the humid lands at the eastern end of the greater West as the ideal farm size for the region. In the nineteenth century, it was indeed that. Consequently, even after the initial transfer of land to private hands, parcels were frequently sold in quarter-section lots or, if broken up, in rectangular acre plots. At the same time, public improvements (first roads, then utility lines, and perhaps drainage or irrigation systems as well) were put in along property lines or at regular intervals coincident with the survey lines. Thus township roads would be built at one-mile intervals along section lines where they would provide adequate coverage while not interfering unduly with farming. As more public improvements were introduced, they all reinforced the original survey system in different ways, creating patterns which became increasingly difficult to alter. Later, as the cities grew out into the rural areas, they found it easier to adjust to the established patterns than to try to change them.[17]

In sum, contemporary urban land-use plans are prepared within the limitations imposed by that original planning effort. Even where communities have followed contemporary planning doctrine calling for residential streets to be laid out along the contours of the land rather than by the grid pattern fully or in part (and not all of them have), their major arteries are still laid out along the lines of a standard grid and usually in relation to the original federal survey lines.

In the greater West, the major political subdivisions are also products of the survey system—a matter of very real significance since political parties are organized by county in most of the fifty states. The boundaries of every county in the ten metropolitan areas of the cities of the prairie follow the rectangular survey lines wherever they do not follow natural features. Four counties (Champaign, Macon, Will, Winnebago) are bounded by survey lines in their entirety. Pueblo County is bounded by survey lines on three sides and by the adjusted boundaries of an old Spanish land grant on the fourth. All the rest are bounded by the survey lines on two (Rock Island) or three (Douglas, Madison, Peoria, St. Clair, St. Louis, Sangamon, Scott, Tazewell) sides and by some natural boundary (river or lake) on the others. In every case, those boundaries are of immense political importance. At the very least, they set the outer limits of direct political power in the locality. Such is the case in Pueblo. More often than not, the county political organizations formed in accordance with these lines are the nerve centers of local politics, the channels through which communications are cleared and influence is distributed. In some cases—Madison and St. Clair Counties are prime examples—the county organizations simply dominate local political decision-making. Where metropolitan areas embrace two or more counties, as in the Peoria area, the county-based political structure effectively divides what is at best an economic unit and often forms the basis for the flowering of separate civil communities that, statistically speaking, appear to be parts of a single urban area.

In Illinois, the township remains an active, if limited, governmental entity of considerable political importance. Almost all Illinois townships are Congressional townships, so called because their boundaries were fully determined by the federal survey and used as the basis for the Congressionally authorized common school land grant of two sections within each. Though many of the township boundaries within the ten metropolitan areas have been adjusted to the changes in city boundaries in one way or another, in Rockford, in Rock Island County, and in suburban Peoria and Springfield, politically significant townships which follow the survey lines still have considerable influence within their civil communities.

Not infrequently, the limits of the civil community itself are best delineated by the survey lines. The Rockford civil community is contained within the boundaries of Rockford Township, which provides the political jurisdiction needed for organizing the civil community's independent stance within the context of Illinois politics. So important is the township to the Rockford leadership as a unit of political control that one of the goals of the local revolution in the early 1960's was to obtain state enabling legislation to make it possible for Rockford Township to take in the one or two adjacent townships settled primarily by Rockfordians in the suburban migration but excluded from the political decision-making of the civil community by the lines of the federal survey. To Rockford's political "establishment," amalgamation was clearly more important than the city's annexation of the territory in question since it was political control they sought (which control of townships politics could provide), not administrative uniformity adjusted to reflect the changing urban growth patterns.

In Rock Island County, townships are politically important as centers of the city party organizations. Formally nonpartisan city elections in Rock Island and East Moline have forced the two major political parties—who participate in the city elections quietly with the tacit consent of the voting public—to strengthen the township party organizations, which have become, in reality, surrogates for city organizations. Though Moline retains partisan city elections, the overwhelmingly Republican character of the city has encouraged the Democrats to make use of the township structures to maintain a local political foothold. The division of each of the cities between two townships has encouraged a degree of intraparty competition, particularly within the majority party in each city, by making it possible for rival party factions to each capture one of the townships and compete from their own political bases.

In the Peoria area, six of the old Congressional townships in three counties outside the city gained new importance as political entities in the past decade as a consequence of suburbanization. Suburban settlers in several of these townships have carried their rejection of citification to the point of rejecting any attempts either to annex their new subdivisions to Peoria or to incorporate as separate cities. Those townships, with their guaranteed representation on the county board and their independent school districts, apparently serve to meet the perceived local government needs of their residents and have accordingly gained their (generally passive) support.[18]

The metropolitan frontier has given rise to much the same situation in those civil communities which had earlier taken steps to avoid it by creating city townships. The city township is an Illinois device designed to coordinate township and municipal government in cities choosing to do so by making the township and city boundaries coterminous. The adoption of the device is a matter of local option, and only those cities with the politically strongest municipal governments have done so, an oblique tribute to the political strength of the regular townships. Capital Township (the city of Springfield), like the other city townships in Illinois, is the end result of a process which, through annexations, has all but obliterated the original rectangular boundaries. Nevertheless, Capital Township still occupies only minor fractions of adjacent Springfield and Woodside Townships, whose boundaries, except for those minor fractions, follow the old survey lines. As those two townships become increasingly suburbanized, they are developing new political identities as providers of (minimal) suburban-type services and as formal vehicles for the presentation of the suburban viewpoint in county politics and metropolitan issues. This is particularly true of Woodside Township, which is receiving the heaviest and most organized emigration (through subdivision development rather than individual home construction) from Springfield. Woodside Township has gained no little recognition as an entity in public counsels in the Springfield civil community in the past decade.

In both Duluth and Superior, the township and section lines of the rectangular survey have been used to delimit the municipal boundaries, which, because of their initial vast extension and the slow growth (or even decline) of the cities, have not been changed in better than two generations. The boundaries of both Duluth and Superior encompass literally thousands of acres of forest, making them more like urbanized townships than cities. This is apparent in the very low density of population within the city limits of each. The one quasi-suburban area near Duluth, Herman Township, is also a direct product of the survey system, even to the point of maintaining township organization as its major local government.

The pervasiveness and apparent inviolability of the federal survey boundaries are so great that few political jurisdictions in the greater West can be said to really ignore them. Echoes of township and section lines can be seen in municipal and school district boundaries, which, even after they depart from those larger survey divisions, follow quarter-section and lot lines that are merely subdivisions of the original survey. Only recently have some special district boundaries been drawn without apparent regard for the survey lines, a difficult and rare matter since, as taxing jurisdictions, they are generally drawn to wholly include existing taxing jurisdictions for the sake of easier administration.

By and large, the geometric boundaries established by the federal rectangular survey in the last century, on lands whose topography has been most conducive to their perpetuation, have continued to influence the development of new cities in the greater West. In fact, they have frequently been infused with new political meaning as a consequence of recent metropolitan growth. Thus the trend toward formally municipalizing the six-mile-square townships has become quite significant around the larger cities of the Near West and Northwest. Thirty-one incorporations of former Congressional townships were recorded in Michigan, Minnesota, Ohio, and Wisconsin by 1960, with fourteen in Minnesota alone. Four of the thirty-one had populations that made them medium-size cities by that year, and, since all encompass more than twenty square miles and are located in the path of the metropolitan migrations, it is likely that their destiny is also to grow to medium size. This linkage of Congressional township boundaries and medium-size cities in the greater West offers a potential solution to the twin problems of suburban municipal incorporation and viable city size that represents an unforeseen benefit of the rectangular survey.[19]

Perhaps the ultimate impact of the various land survey systems has been cultural and psychological, shaping the spatial perceptions of those who live tangled—wittingly or not—within their barely visible webs. The people of the greater West, living within the ambit of the rectangular survey, are oriented toward straight lines and true directions in their spatial thinking. This is particularly—but not exclusively—true on the open prairies and plains (and in the cities on those prairies and plains) where north, south, east, and west have more meaning than any particular physical landmarks. To take but one example, alluded to previously, it is no accident that the new city planning with its curved streets and irregular lots has made greater inroads along the East Coast, where land is surveyed under the old metes and bounds system and town plats have been irregular since they were first laid out. Even on the West Coast, where the topography is not conducive to the grid system, the tendency has been to keep at least the major lines of urban development within a true directional framework, particularly where the first settlers or subdividers came from other parts of the greater West. There are surely more subtle impacts latent in these various spatial orientations, which may affect politics in hidden ways.

The New Technology and the Interlocking Transportation Network

As much as the immediate local patterns of human settlement in the greater West are products of the rectangular survey system, the larger sectional patterns are the end products of a radical reorientation of the thrust of American settlement, the frontier's response to the sphere's new and unprecedented landforms and climate. This reorientation was made possible by the rise of a new technology designed to fit the demands of the terrain and the needs of its settlers, a technology that was created, in large part, because of the need to "civilize" the most difficult wilderness to be confronted by the advancing land frontier. In turn, the newly devised uses of this technology were to spread beyond the greater West to become the basis for twentieth-century technological society in America and much of the world. In the process, the new technology provided the basis for transforming the cities of the prairie, as they became the centers for its development.[20]

This new technology of the greater West embraced many diverse elements but was, in every case, keyed to developments in the fields of transportation and communications that enabled men to conquer the prairies spatially and mechanical innovations that enabled men to stay on the land permanently. There it once again demonstrated the power of the instruments of commerce to stimulate agriculture, industry, and settlement by providing that most important of commodities—opportunity.

Foremost among all the innovations was the development of the railroad, the first major advance in land transportation in three thousand years. The railroad was first developed in the East, but its greatest success was not in its service as a better link between existing settlements in that part of the country but as the forerunner and initiator of settlement over much of the greater West.

The railroad was perfected in the West, which, as an interior basin with few navigable rivers penetrating its vast territories, demanded a new and necessarily man-created means of transportation for taming the land. Except for certain "natural" townsites along the sphere's few waterways, the land itself made the location of communities arbitrary as well as difficult. Accordingly, communities did not develop first and then seek connections with the outside world, as in the other two spheres, but were created in response to larger regional and national needs at locations dictated by railroads radiating out of the few urban centers whose settlement was more or less dictated by nature.[21]

With the trains came the telegraph. Invented separately, it made large-scale railroad operations possible by providing a means of coordinating mass movements at relatively high speeds; hence no tracks were laid that were not paralleled by telegraph lines. Independently, the telegraph revolutionized life by establishing the first method of instantaneous communication over long distances in the history of man. Through it the settlers of the greater West conquered the frontier without losing direct and immediate contact with the rest of the world and its influences.

The web of urban oases created by the railroad and telegraph network between 1850 and 1900 remains the basic settlement pattern of the greater West today. The railroad network has also done much to determine the relative size of each oasis. Without formal regional planning of the kind advocated today, a regional "plan" did emerge out of the combination of sectionally imposed limitations, national and regional economic needs, and local initiative, which in two generations led to the creation of a network of cities of varying sizes, almost hierarchically graded in size. As Chicago became the hub of the railroad network, it was guaranteed a place as one of the three great empire cities of the nation, outdistancing rivals such as St. Louis and ultimately transcending its regional limitations. Other lesser empire cities, whose positions were more closely entwined with their regional functions, developed in the Northwest, in a clearly defined pattern linked to Chicago. Minneapolis and St. Paul, Omaha and Council Bluffs, and the two Kansas Cities represent three regional centers (each containing twin cities) that feed into the Chicago-based railroad network, each approximately five hundred miles from the

Windy City. Denver represents a midpoint in the communications system of the greater West, some five hundred miles beyond. West of Denver, the major urban oases, such as Salt Lake City, are oriented to those of the West Coast as parts of a Far Western network which is, in turn, a somewhat self-contained westward extension of the Chicago-based pattern.

These cities-and-their-hinterlands were all interrelated economically from the start, parts of the same overall marketplace, which is why their growth could be so largely determined by their relationships with one another. Between the Great Lakes and Great Basin the various cities drew on tributary territories which stretched more or less westward and were in turn drawn more or less eastward into the orbits of even larger cities. On the Pacific slope, which was settled from west to east, the progression was exactly reversed.

The medium-size metropolitan oases developed as links within this overall pattern. Among the cities of the prairie, Rockford, Joliet, the Quad Cities, and Champaign-Urbana developed as interstitial settlements on the network running from Chicago to points west and south. Peoria and Decatur were developed partly within the Chicago network and partly as separate links between the greater West and the other spheres. The civil communities of Madison and St. Clair Counties developed as part of the St. Louis-centered network connecting the three spheres at the one point where all three nearly converge. Duluth and Superior developed both within the Minneapolis-St. Paul network and as northern anchors for two major transcontinental routes. Pueblo developed as part of the Denver network, serving as a junction point for it and the network that came out of Chicago via Kansas City, as well as a major gateway to the mountains. The impact of the railroad on each has already been made apparent in Chapter Two. Almost without exception, the opening of railroad service was a major factor in the elevation of each civil community from village to city status.[22] Today the cities of the prairie reflect both facets of this pattern quite well. They are directly or indirectly within Chicago's hinterland, with that city acting as a powerful magnet, providing markets, distribution facilities, newspapers, sources of education and entertainment, jobs, and many other things for the residents of the urban oases within its orbit. At the same time, they have hinterlands of their own, which tend to stretch beyond them, away from the empire cities to which they are tributary. More often than not, Chicago's great hinterland and their lesser ones thrust in a westerly direction.

The particular receptivity of the greater West to technological innovations is not a thing of the past. Nor is the influence of such innovations on urban settlements in the sphere a relic of the last century. Transportation systems remain among the first and foremost products of new technologies. Each new transportation system is brought into being as a product of national influences that can be only minimally shaped by local communities and each enhances or alters the competitive positions of the different civil communities within the overall regional and national framework. As in the case of the railroads, the decisions as to how each civil community is to fit into the new system are made in a manner that excludes formal local participation almost entirely though they influence the character of the community for generations, setting the pattern of its land use, determining the rate of its growth, and greatly influencing the sources from which its new settlers are drawn.

Take aviation. Large-scale commercial aviation first proved to be of greater value than the railroads for the conquest of distances in the greater West where distance remains an ever present factor. Even now, after a generation of consolidation and rearrangement and despite the tendency toward the concentration of corporate headquarters in New York, seven of the eleven trunk airlines operating within the United States have their home offices in that sphere, and ten of the sixteen local service airlines are headquartered in and service it. Moreover, the manufacturing of airplanes and aviation equipment is predominantly a Western industry. Indeed, the airline industry is one of the few which has remained decentralized in the United States, even after its initial period of growth, with headquarters of major trunk lines located in cities like Minneapolis, Denver, and Kansas City, as well as Chicago, and major manufacturing complexes located in St. Louis, Wichita, and Seattle, as well as Los Angeles.

While the airlines came on the scene too late to alter the nation's fundamental urban settlement patterns, they have played an important role in reinforcing or modifying existing patterns of communications and commerce. These, in turn, have significantly affected the growth rates of the nation's metropolitan centers. By and large, the positions of the greater and lesser empire cities have been solidified by the airline network, thus reinforcing the existence of the three spheres as meaningful sectional entities in our own time. In the greater West, the hierarchy of empire cities has also remained intact, with the possible exception of the growth of Los Angeles at the expense of San Francisco. Furthermore, the division of functions between trunk and local service (or "feeder") airlines, established within the last half generation, has reaffirmed the distinction between the major and medium-size cities in the sphere. And while the trunk lines' regional character is less visible than that of the railroads, the feeders rarely cross the lines separating the spheres except in the transition zones.[23]

By 1961, all the cities of the prairie except those located within the Chicago and St. Louis metropolitan regions had been assigned places within feeder networks by the airlines and the Federal Aviation Administration. This was the result of a decade and a half of political struggle to organize what is still a relatively new transportation system into an economically viable package. The Quad Cities and Peoria, which are served by trunk lines, are faced with and continually engaged in a struggle with the major airline companies, which seek to eliminate those stops as vestigial and costly.

The struggle for air service has been an important public concern in the free-standing metropolitan areas of this study, one which has involved the leading members of the local business community in every one of them and which shows no signs of letting up. Pueblo has been particularly active and successful in obtaining connections to various other parts of its region, particularly to the Southwest and Texas, via Central and Frontier Airlines, though it still remains tied to Denver and, via that city, to Chicago by the trunk lines as it has been by rail. Duluth has also been active in this regard, seeking to replace its declining rail ties with its western hinterland and Winnipeg with air service via North Central. It, like Pueblo, has remained in the orbit of the empire city which captured its market during the railroad era—in its case, Minneapolis-St. Paul. The Illinois cities of the prairie are all served by Ozark Airlines and remain tied directly to Chicago. Springfield lost in its fight to retain the service of American Airlines, which had inaugurated a local stop years ago before it had become a major trunk line. Champaign-Urbana successfully acquired a position in the Ozark system only after considerable negotiation substantially expedited by the University of Illinois. The other cities, which were brought into the Ozark system at the time of its creation, have by dint of continued effort been able to maintain the service.

The history of the last half-generation of air route adjustments is much like that of the rail route adjustments which took place in the Northwest roughly between 1860 and 1875. In both cases, the issue was forced upon each civil community by technological changes beyond its control, and the final decisions were made outside the community. In both cases, local effort was required to secure the most advantage from the impact of those technological changes, and in both cases the sectional integrity of the greater West was reaffirmed in the final resolution of the issue, binding the cities of the prairie to their sphere in new ways.

The other great contemporary transportation system, the road network, has also influenced and been influenced by the greater West. The development of the automobile found the country already settled but poorly provided with roads. As new roads were built, they were designed to connect already existing communities rather than to chart new paths. The combination of commercial necessities and local political pressures operated to ratify that pattern of settlement in its major outlines. The subsequent impact of the highway system is too well known to require much comment here. By making it possible for rural dwellers to travel farther to cities for marketing and other purposes, the highway system killed the rural village, intensified the process of urbanization, and increased the mobility of the nation immeasurably.

Here, too, sectional differences are noticeable. In the greater Northeast, where large and very large cities had developed earlier in response to the urban-industrial frontier, the coming of the automobile was a decentralizing factor. It intensified suburbanization by making it possible for people who worked in the city to move out to pleasant living sites in the surrounding areas and commute to work in their cars. The automobile not only accounts for much of the so-called urban sprawl in that sphere, but also for the increased density of population in its erstwhile "rural" areas, which have converted into exurbia in one form or another. Meanwhile, the older cities of the sphere, designed and built up as they were in horse and buggy days, were confronted with an internal transportation problem of unprecedented dimensions, which functioned to promote decentralization of business and industry to accompany residential decentralization. The first intercity highways in the greater Northeast were rapidly converted into urbanized strips connecting the sphere's many cities and towns, effectively reducing the open country to patches divided by urban development. Traffic on these highways soon became as heavy as in the cities, further intensifying the urban character of the entire sphere.

In the greater South, the automobile age came while urbanization was still in its early stages. It functioned less to promote city growth (which came about for other reasons) than to provide Southerners with a means to maintain their basically rural attachments by living in the country and working in the city. In fact, the automobile probably prevented the development of very large cities. Instead, the established crossroads market towns grew bigger and more diversified, confining urbanization in all but a few cases to the development of medium-size metropolitan areas, which, taking advantage of the new mobility, were suburbanized from the first. As in the greater Northeast, the land itself was favorable to scattered semi-urban settlement. So the automobile, which in the Northeast caused urban decentralization, has virtually prevented citification in the South. At the same time, political pressures in the states of the greater South demanded that every city be equally favored with highway connections even though this meant that very limited resources had to be divided up in many ways. The result was a system of second-rate roads that made long distance travel in the sphere quite difficult, again reinforcing the pattern of many scattered settlements rather than a few large ones.

Though the cities of the greater West obviously antedate the automobile, their streets were laid out for wagons and trains rather than for horses and buggies. Hence they were better prepared to cope with the new traffic and have suffered less from it. Intercity highways in the greater West were designed from the first to connect oases. Since the latter had developed in a more or less orderly network as a result of the railroads, the highway network emerged as an equally orderly one, often paralleling the railroad tracks exactly to speed travelers between the sphere's cities.

Since the various landscapes of the greater West are not conducive to open-country settlement, the primary effect of the automobile age has been to heighten the sphere's oasis pattern of settlement. The automobile has functioned to empty the smaller farming villages and market towns and concentrate commerce and population in the cities, thereby increasing the open space between settlements. Suburbanization in the sphere's largest metropolitan areas involves both decentralization from city to suburb and reconcentration from rural to urban locations, expanding their size as urban oases. The present regional economic relationships of the cities of the prairie reflect the automotive modifications of the basic patterns established by the railroads. Their hinterlands continue to follow along the lines established by the laying of the tracks, but their area has expanded as a result of the reduction in travel time and expense brought about by the building of highways. Table 3–2 summarizes the city-and-hinterland relationships for each of the ten metropolitan areas.

The interstate highway system authorized by Congress in 1944 and actually started in the 1950's represents the first attempt to create a national highway network corresponding to that of the railroads and airlines, which would link the nation's major cities with limited-access free highways and bypass the others. After intense political pulling and hauling, the network that has emerged has basically reinforced previously established regional patterns with one major innovation. By providing new north-south routes, which, particularly within the greater West, were never provided by the railroads, the interstate highway system will actually heighten the internal cohesion of each of the three spheres.

As in the case of railroad development one hundred years ago and the concurrent development of the airlines, the future development of the urban oases of the greater West was recognized by local influentials as intimately bound up with their respective positions in this highway network. The decisions as to highway location, like those of railroad and air route location, are formally made outside the civil community, at the federal and state levels. Each civil community has been accordingly concerned with presenting its case as forcefully as possible before the decision-making powers.

All the cities of the prairie except Decatur and Belleville were included in the interstate system as finally accepted by Congress and the states. The two exceptions struggled valiantly for inclusion and, in losing, were given "consolation prizes" in the form of equivalent limited access freeways to connect them with the interstate system at some appropriate junction point. Each of the cities of the prairie, then, was ultimately assured of its continued position within the pattern of its sphere. Even so, the alteration of the transportation pattern brought about by the new highway system is bound to have consequences in determining their relative future growth. The Quad Cities and Champaign-Urbana stand to gain, and are already gaining, from their enhanced positions as junction points on the interstate system, which enhances them as regional gateway cities. Champaign, Decatur, and Springfield in Illinois and Pueblo in Colorado are presently engaged in political activity designed to add other links to the freeway system that will give them a junction position or, in the case of Champaign, further enhance its junction status as an alternate highway gateway to the West (see Chapter Two).

The development of the interstate system has possibilities of immediately local value as well. Several of the civil communities have utilized their positions on the interstate system to provide intracity freeway connections and to develop slum clearance programs that might otherwise have been hard to initiate. By 1963, Peoria, Rockford, Champaign-Urbana, and Pueblo were already making use of the interstate freeways for intracity travel, and the Quad Cities and Springfield were making plans to do the same. Belleville, East St. Louis, and Joliet have gained better access to the centers of their respective metropolitan regions. Duluth and Superior have gained a long-sought intercity connection. By designing its leg of the project to pass through the city's most deteriorated neighborhood, Rock Island has gained in the realm of slum clearance, as have several other communities with less planned effort.

Just as the land survey systems have shaped the spatial perceptions of Americans, so too have the various transportation technologies shaped their perceptions of time. When men began the settlement of the North American continent, the impact of space was far greater than that of time. The state of transportation technology was such that the former was formidable and the latter, expendable. As the key technologies have been improved, time has progressively reduced the impact of space until, with the coming of the airplane and the auto in the twentieth century, men began to measure space primarily in terms of time, merging the two dimensions by giving primacy to time. In a very real sense, the shift began with the development of the new steam-and-rail technology in the mid-nineteenth century. Unlike the Northeast and the South, whose civilizations antedate those developments, the greater West was born with the change and was, indeed, created by it. Within its precincts, the relationship between space and time has never been the same as in the other spheres.

TABLE 3-2

The Cities of the Prairie and their Regional Economic Relationships

Metropolitan Area	Basic Trading Area (Counties)[a]	ABC Retail Trading and Newspaper Circulation Zone (Counties)[b]	Major Trading Center[c]
Champaign-Urbana	Champaign, Douglas, Ford, Piatt	Champaign, Coles, DeWitt, Douglas, Ford, Iroquois, McLean, Moultrie, Vermilion	Chicago
Decatur	Macon, Clay, Coles, Cumberland, Effingham, Fayette, Jasper, Moultrie, Richland, Shelby	Macon, Champaign, Christian, Coles, DeWitt, Douglas, Effingham, Fayette, Logan, Montgomery, Moultrie, Piatt, Sangamon, Shelby	Chicago
Joliet	Will, Grundy	Will, Grundy	Chicago
Madison-St. Clair	Madison, St. Clair, Bond, Calhoun, Clinton, Jersey, Monroe, Randolph[d]	Madison, Jersey, Macoupin, St. Clair, Clinton, Monroe, Randolph	St. Louis
Peoria	Peoria, Fulton, Marshall, Mason, McDonough, Schuyler, Stark, Tazewell, Woodford	Peoria, Fulton, Marshall, Mason, Putnam, Schuyler, Stark, Tazewell, Woodford	Chicago
Quad Cities	Rock Island, Henry, Mercer (Ill.); Scott, Muscatine (Ia.)	Scott, Cedar, Clinton, Jackson, Johnson, Jones, Louisa, Muscatine, Washington (Ia.); Rock Island, Bureau, Henry, Mercer, Warren, Whiteside (Ill.)	Chicago
Rockford	Winnebago, Bonne, Lee, Ogle	Winnebago, Boone, Carroll, DeKalb, JoDaviess, Lee, McHenry, Ogle, Stephenson, Whiteside (Ill.); Green Rock, Walworth (Wisc.)	Chicago

TABLE 3-2 (continued)

Metropolitan Area	Basic Trading Area (Counties)[a]	ABC Retail Trading and Newspaper Circulation Zone (Counties)[b]	Major Trading Center[c]
Springfield	Sangamon, Cass, Christian, Logan, Macoupin, Menard, Montgomery	Sangamon, Cass, Christian, DeWitt, Green, Jersey, Logan, Macon, Macoupin, Mason, Menard, Montgomery, Morgan, Pike, Scott, Tazewill	Chicago
Duluth-Superior	St. Louis, Carlton, Cook, Itasca, Koochiching, Lake (Minn.); Douglas Ashland, Bayfield, Price, Sawyer, Washburn (Wisc.)	Aitkin, Beltrami, Carlton, Cass, Crow Wing, Hubbard, Itasca, Kanabee, Pine, St. Louis (Minn.); Ashland, Barron, Bayfield, Burnett, Douglas, Polk, Sawyer, Washburn (Wisc.)	Minneapolis-St. Paul
Pueblo	Pueblo, Alamosa, Baca, Bent, Colfax (N.M.); Conejos, Costilla, Crawley, Custer, Fremont, Huerfano, Kiowa, Los Animas, Mineral, Otero, Prowers, Rio Grande	Pueblo, Crowley, Custer, Fremont, Huerfano, Otero	Denver

[a]Based on Rand McNally calculations, 1960.
[b]Overlapping of counties indicates the counties are divided among two or more central cities.
[c]Based on Rand McNally calculations, 1960.
[d]The Illinois portion of the St. Louis basic trading area.

The New Technology and the Development of an Economic Base

Paralleling the development of the railroad networks as a means of taming the greater West was a burst of mechanical innovation the likes of which had never previously been seen. From those innovations came the means to capitalize on the commercial opportunities created by the new transportation and communications systems.[24] These means included the development of sophisticated agricultural implements and elaborate farm machinery (developed in northern Illinois) to make possible the breaking and cultivation of the heavy sod of the prairielands. They included the development of such items as barbed wire (invented in northern Illinois) for fencing the prairies and plains and cheap nails for use in constructing shelters for humans and animals in a timberless region. The shelters themselves were "vernacular" adaptations to the unfamiliar landforms. The balloon frame house (developed in Chicago) represented the first great architectural adaptation to the conditions of exposed living in a harsh climate where traditional building materials were scarce.

Chapter Two has sketched out the way in which the cities of the prairie were prominently involved in the development and diffusion of these inventions, to their benefit. Indeed their growth as industrial centers has been predicated on their ability to attract industries creating those products of the new technology of particular use in the greater West. Illinois, the keystone of the prairie states, was not only the scene of pioneering efforts to create the needed technology but also created the industrial plant that made the inventions operational. Its cities owe their existence and development to those pioneering efforts as much as to the railroads that enabled them to distribute the fruits of their creativity.

Two factors, in particular, have influenced the way in which the new technology has provided the cities of the prairie with an economic base appropriate to each age. One is their sectional location. The greater West's needs and natural products have provided both the *raison d'être* and the wherewithal for local economic development. The other is the changing American frontier, which constantly places new demands on the American economy as a whole and on the local economies of sections, states, and communities, periodically rendering established economic structures and industries obsolete while at the same time opening new possibilities for economic development and industrial pioneering. Since the greater West itself is, in great measure, a product of certain economic necessities, it is not surprising that the economic bases of its cities have been shaped substantially by sectional factors. Nor was this true only of the past century, of the period of the land frontier. The economic base of each of the cities of the prairie remains related to its sphere or to the sections within that sphere. Related, too, are the possibilities for the cities' future economic development. Even the cursory review of the economic bases of the cities of the prairie offered in Chapter Two reveals the impact of the new technology and the influence of both factors in each. The cities' manufacturing activities were, virtually without exception, sired by a union of the necessities of the greater West and the inventiveness of its settlers. Even where their primary markets today stretch far beyond the sphere's confines, their products remain of primary use within the sphere as well. This is true even in those cases where the local "industry" seems to be far removed from sectional considerations. The University of Illinois, the greatest economic force in Champaign County, ostensibly offers a non-regionalized "product." In fact, not only does it primarily service the state of Illinois in its undergraduate teaching and extension work but it draws the great bulk of its graduate and professional students from Illinois and the states to the west and southwest as far as the Rockies, to become dependent upon a sectional market, willy-nilly.

The once new technology that was developed to make the settlement of the greater West possible and worthwhile is no longer new and is certainly no longer confined to that sphere. However, the cities it helped to create have, by and large, been able to retain their preeminent positions in the manufacture and servicing of its products by adapting themselves to new times and to expanding forms of the once new technology itself. While the farm implement industry no longer serves the same pioneering tasks in the greater West, the cities of the prairie continue to be the largest producers of farm implements for the sphere and for world markets. Railroads have declined and with them the industries developed to support them, but the distances of the greater West have been tamed again, by airways and highways. The cities of the prairie have become the great centers for the production of earth-moving and other heavy equipment for the construction of airports and highways (and similar large-scale public works), centers of the trucking industry which links them to each other and their sphere, and, in some cases, centers for servicing the airplanes which serve the sphere and the country. The original processes of extraction of the natural resources of the greater West, which brought many of the original settlers into the area and created great refining industries to transform them into workable materials have now declined in importance, but new processes for the extraction of many of the same resources have been developed through technological advances and have stimulated new local processing industries to replace their dying predecessors.

Of course, industries that stand out as exceptions to the overall sectional pattern can be found in each of the cities of the prairie. They are the exceptions, however. Close scrutiny of the cities' overall economic base makes clear the extent to which sectional needs have influenced the development of what are normally considered national industries and continue to do so, even in a day when, in many quarters, sectionalism is thought to have been transcended. Decatur is a strong case in point. For a decade or more after World War II, it seemed as if Decatur would transcend the implicit limits imposed on medium-size cities in its region to become an industrial center producing items with no particular connection to the greater West or with no special use within it. This trend, heightened by conscious efforts on the part of Eastern manufacturing interests to decentralize industries that were strong in that period, has apparently been reversed since 1960, by the latest manifestation of the new technology. Automation and the changes in production methods it has brought about have made decentralization less attractive and has even encouraged reconcentration of industry to take advantage of the computers. Some of the industries with no particular sectional ties have begun to leave Decatur. By 1962 it was apparent that Decatur's industrial boom, insofar as it had no relationship to the patterns or demands of the greater West, had passed, due to the negative impacts of the newest technology.

Still other civil communities are now in the process of discovering (or rediscovering) the necessity to develop and maintain a proper relationship with sphere and section for their economic health. Springfield, whose economic position has always been rooted in its role as state capital, probably has the most perceptive civic leaders of any of the cities of the prairie when it comes to sensing social and political trends. Thus it is significant that, as its leadership becomes increasingly concerned with broadening its economic base, there has been a local turning westward. Recent studies of possibilities for local economic development refer specifically to Springfield's advantageous position at the western end of the nation's manufacturing belt and at the transportation gateway to the western areas beyond it. They recommend the exploitation of its regional position in any program of industrial development.[25]

Duluth is a prime example of the consequences of sectional self-alienation. Though totally dependent upon the resources of its successive hinterlands for survival, Duluth's economic leaders—for the most part managers of absentee-owned enterprises—were, from the first, much more interested in directing their attentions to corporate headquarters "back East." As a result, they let other cities in the region siphon off trade from the areas further north and west or acquire the relatively few new industries which were located in the Upper Midwest for reasons of regional advantage or necessity. Consequently, when Duluth's economic mainstays collapsed, the city settled into a forty-year-long depression. Only with the reawakening of interest in meeting the problem of Duluth's location through the utilization of new technological developments of regional import in the late 1950's and early 1960's have there been signs of revival.[26]

A similar revival of sectional concern has been taking place in the St. Louis area, of particular interest because of the size of the metropolis involved. Sometime after the middle of the nineteenth century, around the time when Chicago took over its place as the great entrepot of the West, St. Louis turned southward and eastward to become dependent upon New Orleans, on one hand, and a satellite of the seaboard cities, on the other, virtually abandoning its position in the greater West to Kansas City. Soon its economy began to suffer accordingly, but, since it continued to grow in absolute terms and suffered only relative losses, much time had to elapse before its leadership became conscious of the problem. In the mid-1950's, St. Louis initiated a reversal of direction in an effort to develop stronger ties with the commerce and technologies of the greater West. This reversal has been dramatically stated in the city's public revival of its old title, "Gateway to the West," and the abandonment of its previous public relations stance that it was a cultural outpost of the East (always in contradistinction to Chicago). The shift was further symbolized by the city's successful efforts to have the federal government establish a national park on its waterfront to commemorate the nation's westward expansion. The new park is crowned with the great Saarinen arch, rising over five hundred feet above the river to serve as a material manifestation of St. Louis' gateway position and as the new symbol of the reoriented city.[27]

In the crucial realm of economics, the old links between frontier and section continue strong in the greater West and in the country as a whole. While political implications of these links will be explored in the following chapters, one major point must be made here: the crucial factors that do much to determine the economic health of the civil community not only exist and function external to it, but are subject to the operation of forces which are not even directly amenable to the decisions of national economic leaders. One need not be a Marxist to realize the importance of the economic base in civil society nor to conclude that the men of any given generation have relatively limited power over many economic factors. The history of the cities of the prairie is clearly a case in point. Much of their development is predicated on patterns established a century or more ago, which can be altered only slightly even by the great national economic powers—public and private—that command today's headlines.

Political Attitudes and the Frontier Tradition

One of the most lasting and influential characteristics of the greater West is its persisting frontier tradition. This tradition grows out of the sphere's closeness in time to the classic land frontier. The days of the land frontier are just around the corner in the greater West. Belleville, one of the very oldest American-founded cities in the entire sphere, was settled only 150 years ago, and its hinterland did not emerge from the frontier stage until the eve of the Civil War. Belleville's relative age is exceptional, even in Illinois, the first state of the greater West to be extensively settled by Americans. As we have seen in Chapter Two, most of the cities included in this study did not pass out of the land frontier stage until the Civil War decade had come to a close. There are still living men in most of these cities who, in their younger days, personally knew veterans of the conquest of the land frontier.

In Iowa, Wisconsin, Minnesota, and Colorado the land frontier is that much closer. The cities studied in the latter three states were frontier outposts for some time after the Civil War. For them, the land frontier was an immediate reality until after the turn of the century. Some of the county officials serving Duluth in the early 1960's were actually officeholders in their present departments in the very last days of the land frontier in St. Louis County, not forty years before. These men are not heirs of the frontier tradition; they are parts of it. The civil communities they serve were barely inhabited a century ago and, as cities, are not yet one hundred years old.

Whether at one end of the greater West or the other, the classic frontier tradition persists in the social patterns and outlook of the region's residents. So many students of the area have commented on this that the point need not be belabored here.[28] However, its political meaning still needs some clarification.

At the root of the political manifestations of this classic frontier tradition is a combination of agrarian and commercial values and attitudes which, while ultimately national in scope, are synthesized most thoroughly in the greater West. The land frontier in the United States had a commercial orientation from the first. Its pioneers were not peasants seeking binding ties to the land for security's sake; they were men who sought markets and profit even as they believed in the virtues of working the soil. Only in the South did something like a feudal commitment to an agrarian ideology develop—in the midst of a plantation economy that required outside markets. Unlike the ideological agrarianism of the greater South, the Westerners' attachment to the land was openly commercial from the first. Love the land though they might, the farmers as well as the businessmen of the greater West have been concerned with raising a cash crop for the market and have shown a willingness to abandon farming as a way of life if it could not be commercially profitable. At the same time, unlike the commercialism of the greater East, the Westerners have not considered those who work the land as an inferior breed but rather as the custodians of the nation's best qualities. In essence, they have combined both interests in a single socioeconomic package and endowed it with high moral value.

Socially, agrarianism in the greater West is less a matter of rural living than the maintenance of a certain style of life—in urban as well as rural surroundings—that places great value on religiosity, individual self-reliance, and family solidarity within the framework of a relatively classless, co-operating community built upon the widespread ownership of real property to give its members a "stake in society." Economically, the sphere's agrarianism continues to be manifested in the extensive dependence of its urban areas on agriculture. "Agri-business" is the Western term coined to describe these urban activities based on agriculture. It describes the occupations of the still very high percentage of Westerners whose livelihood is provided through a connection with agriculture and who wish to be so identified despite their urban location and habits.

The cities, as products of an agrarian-commercial society have shared in the sectional outlook as fully as have the rural areas, and perhaps even more so. Indeed the public expression of the agrarian-commercial ideal has come from the cities of the greater West more than it has from the rural areas, at first in order to justify the very existence of cities in a society that had mixed feelings about urban living and then in order to justify the city's victory over the farm and the transformation of the greater West into an urban society. The people of Illinois, a state whose population was 80.7 per cent urban in 1960 and had been more urban than rural for half a century, appear hardly more citified in attitude, outlook, and political behavior than the people of Iowa, only 53.1 per cent of whom lived in urban areas in 1960, in a state whose urban majority dates back no farther than the close of World War II.

In Illinois, this bias against citification is apparent in the perennial Chicago-"downstate" political feud, which finds the downstate cities of all sizes and Chicago's own suburban areas, all of which share so many of the same problems as Chicago does, pitted against the big city in matters political because of their deep and abiding distrust of the "big city." A review of the political strategies used in suburban and downstate areas in statewide political campaigns in Illinois reveals consistent and perennially successful efforts to appeal to popular suspicion of the "evil" big city and its "evil" political "machine," whose evil is considered intrinsic, an inevitable element in large cities. It is even used by downstate Democrats to oppose their Chicago brethren.

The irony of all this is that the Chicagoans are far from being the city slickers they are made out to be in downstate mythology. Except for a thin veneer of committed city dwellers at the top, the young unmarrieds who need the city's active social life, and a declining number of European immigrants who are used to living amidst a dense population and who can find that style of living only in the city, most Chicagoans, like their brethren in smaller communities, do not seek the advantages of the city, nor do they show any particular affection for the urban way of life as such. In fact, with the migration of Southern Negroes and whites into the city in great numbers, a majority of Chicago's population is no more than a generation removed from the farm, if that.

The political expression of this agrarian-commercial outlook was written into the fabric of American history in the last third of the nineteenth century and the first third of the twentieth as the Populist-Progressive revolt, a product of the cities and farms of the greater West from Michigan to California. The belt of political protest, whose roots lay in a popular reaction to the social and economic colonialism of the greater Northeast, stretched in a great western arc, which extended "fingers" southward and eastward from time to time. While this great movement periodically gained adherents in the other spheres, in particular from among the subsistence farmers of the greater South and the urban intellectuals of the greater Northeast, its roots, long-term existence, and lasting qualities were most pronounced in the greater West, where its aspirations were also most clearly defined. The Populist-Progressive revolt with its agrarian overtones was endowed with a particular quality in the greater West and, in turn, left an endowment of its own to that sphere.[29]

The heritage of Populism remains strong in the cities of the prairie. The contemporary heirs of that tradition were to no little extent responsible for triggering the reconstitution movements in the cities of the prairie during the past half-generation. In this way, they have carried on the tradition of urban reform that, though neglected in the popular history of the period, was part and parcel of the Populist-Progressive movement in the greater West. These neo-populists are interested in local political reform as the necessary means for improving (or restoring) traditional patterns of American democracy, not simply as a means to achieve desired "businesslike" efficiency and economy. As populists, believing in the efficacy of democratic politics, they see local problems as political issues capable of political solution. Consequently, their major function is to serve as catalysts who stimulate "unpolitical" economic notables and citizens to political action to meet the problems. As catalysts, they often drop from sight once more powerful—and more conservative—elements in the community pick up their reformist ideas and work to implement them, wholly or in part; hence the significance of their role is often overlooked. This strain of populist progressivism behind the civic improvement movements in the greater West is the greatest single political legacy of the Populists in the sphere.

Another persistent legacy is a latent distrust of the East, which grew out of the very real problems of Eastern economic colonialism vis-à-vis the greater West that contributed heavily to the Populist revolt in the first place and persisted well into the twentieth century. This distrust was further nurtured by the isolationist-internationalist conflict of the 1930's, which again pitted East against West for all intents and purposes.[30] The earlier economic roots of this distrust have been largely eliminated as the greater West has become urbanized, industrialized, and prosperous in its own right, but in its place there have developed new forms of sectional economic subordination to the concentration of corporate headquarters in the Northeast. If the greater West has acquired industry, it remains a branch plant area. This means that in community after community, in area after area, and even in whole states and regions, management decisions drastically affecting the "little" economies of the country—decisions which had previously been made within the areas affected, by people familiar with local conditions and with at least some concern for local needs—are now being made in Eastern offices by people who do not even know the communities, states, and regions involved. In many cases a local industry has been purchased by a major national concern with the full, even excited approval of the community involved, only to have its plant, transformed into a specialized branch of an industrial complex, closed down a few years later for reasons of corporate efficiency that have little or nothing to do with local needs and its most enterprising personnel transferred to other communities. Since this is done by "nameless" corporate managers, in a highly impersonal way, there is no one to blame, in the way the victims of the old colonialism could place blame on highly visible "robber barons."

Though the locally controlled industries of earlier days had been at the mercy of a national market, their owner-managers had to sink or swim with their communities. Hence they provided a continuing pool of community leadership that remained at home in good times and bad. The new centralization of economic control, on the other hand, drains communities of their best manpower and divorces the men with local economic power from serious community concerns. Insidiously, if unintentionally, the interests of men who in an earlier day would have sought influential roles in their local communities on the assumption that they would remain, are redirected to a concern with pleasing the national office in order to secure promotions that will ultimately lead them into the great Atlantic coast megalopolis where the economic power of the country is substantially concentrated.

The postwar growth of industrial and governmental power in the Northeastern megalopolis reinforced an already great concentration of cultural and intellectual power in the same area. Ever since the beginning of the Republic, this nation's "high culture" had been concentrated in such cities as Boston, New York, and Philadelphia. While this concentration was actually greater a generation ago, and continues to be proportionately reduced in a number of ways, its effects became more profound after the war, as the role of artists, scholars, and scientists as contributors to the nation's growth became more important to the American public, transforming them into significant molders of the nation's opinions.

As the Eastern intellectuals' influence grew, their somewhat parochial (from the Westerners' point of view) assessment of contemporary problems began to rankle. Whether in regard to urban affairs, where their megalopolis-oriented analyses had little relevance to the problems of the oasis West, or foreign affairs, where their commitment to a mythical "Atlantic community" obviously exceeded their interest in America west of the Appalachians, their newfound influence seemed to be in opposition to basic Western interests and values. Perhaps more crucial was the Eastern intellectuals' assault on the traditional manners and morals of the American heartland, an assault made especially potent by the development of television and especially galling because of the opinion-molders' apparent assumption that their "sophisticated" way of life was the necessary pattern for the entire country. Moreover, the Eastern megalopolis, as the national economic, cultural, artistic, and governmental center, continues to attract many first-rate talents from the greater West, draining that sphere of much talent. Their departure is felt most keenly in the cities.[31]

Thus the feeling of cultural colonialism, once associated with the sphere's rural areas and small towns, has moved to the cities along with the people. Today it is most impressively expressed in Chicago. Hardly a year goes by when that city does not become embroiled in controversy over its "subservience" to the Eastern megalopolitan center. The newspapers discuss this avidly. Chicago's "second city" complex subtly extends to the cities of its hinterland, carried there by the Chicago press and feeding on the old underlying distrust of Eastern "exploitation."

All those factors reinforce the profound feeling that the East still dominates and exploits the greater West. While no longer the overriding consideration it once was, this anti-Eastern bias is particularly visible among economic and religious conservatives, on one hand, and quasi-radical heirs of the Populists, on the other.[32] Politically, it is particularly noticeable among Republicans who have championed the conservative cause in the Far West. Barry Goldwater found much of his original support in the area from the Great Lakes to the Pacific among those in sympathy with his own anti-Eastern stance (much of which he later lost by giving the appearance of radicalism, which alienated the sphere's true conservatives). This attitude is more consistently emphasized by the Chicago *Tribune*, which reaches into almost every corner of the sphere east of the divide. Since the voters and the leaders of cities of the prairie are, with three exceptions, predominantly Republican in allegiance and, in the early 1960's "Goldwater Republican" at that, this attitude is particularly pronounced within their civil communities. While it is by no means a constant preoccupation in local politics, resentment and suspicion of the "East" remain beneath the surface to reappear from time to time and to color local attitudes toward national politics.

Nonpartisanship or, more accurately, popular anti-party bias is another legacy of the western frontier. No longer as strong on the state level as formerly, this anti-party bias survives at the local level and even flourishes there. The cry of many local government reformers continues to be "nonpartisanship," and it is one of their stands that is most appealing to the public at large. Illinois, for example, is one of the most politically nonpartisan states in the union in matters of state and national politics. Despite some penchant for maintenance of partisan politics on the local level, only six of the fourteen Illinois cities included in this study have formally partisan municipal elections which involve the major political parties. Though this formal nonpartisanship is frequently ignored in practice, its continuation is almost an article of faith among civic reformers and the citizenry at large. The underlying reasons for this anti-party bias will be examined in Chapter Ten.

Finally, the particular frontier tradition of the greater West has insured that the agitators for reform would be drawn primarily from the middle class, particularly from those in the middle class who are extensively involved in their communities. This was true of the farmers from whom the Populists drew their strength and the urban business and professional men who comprised the Progressive movement. It is equally true of today's reformers. This is, no doubt, in large measure because the majority of the population of the greater West has always identified itself with the middle class. The tradition goes beyond this, however. Almost without exception, both the leadership and the rank and file of the protest movements maintained their identity as members of the middle class regardless of the extent to which they embraced radical solutions to the problems of their time. Despite the "cover" of rural manners many of them adopted, the Populist leadership was, by and large, exceptionally well educated and cosmopolitan (in the sense of defining their community of concern very broadly). Neither they nor their followers allowed themselves to be reduced to the level of agricultural "proletarians" or peasants, no matter how difficult conditions were. This was even true, to no little degree, among radicals in the sphere's mines and mills.[33]

Needless to say, the populist element in the middle class is always a small one, but middle-class populists represent the major body of reformers in the greater West. Contrast this with the situation in the greater South and the greater Northeast, where reformers have almost invariably come from either the upper or lower classes. In the former, the first social reformers were of the plantation "aristocracy." Since the mid-nineteenth century, they have been drawn from the excluded groups: "rednecks," Scotch-Irish mountaineers, or, more recently, Negroes. In the latter, reform traditionally has been advanced by a coalition of "old family" liberals and the labor movement.

In the cities of the prairie, the labor movement, by and large, has played little role in civic reform, no matter how powerful the unions might be locally in securing economic benefits for their members. The two or three exceptions are in communities where the union members have been overwhelmingly middle class themselves and are responsive to middle-class concerns. By the same token, the few "upper-class" types to be found in cities in that size range, while not necessarily opposed to local reform, rarely if ever take the lead in reform movements. Even where their services are decisive in achieving political change, they have almost invariably been stimulated to take action by the handful of middle-class populists who can be found in almost every one of the cities.

The process of conquering the land frontier in the greater West also led to the development of strong nationalist and unionist sentiments among its population. All of the sphere's states, possibly excepting California and New Mexico, came into existence as civil societies as a result of national efforts significantly aided and abetted by the federal government. This was rarely true in either of the other spheres. All but two of the states of the greater Northeast were given political shape prior to national independence. All but three of the states of the greater South were either among the original thirteen or were organized as entities by other powers prior to their acquisition by the United States.

Having felt the hand of the federal government prior to the creation of their states, the early settlers who came to the greater West from other parts of the Union developed an immediate sense of national identification that went hand-in-hand with the frontier experience.

This tradition of nationalism proved to be of decisive importance during the Civil War, when the loyalty of what was then called the "Northwest" (an area which included most of the then settled parts of the greater West of today) made it possible to preserve the Union intact. It has been of great importance in the development of a national culture and in the broadening of the powers of the national government in general. Today it remains what it has been from the first, a combination of national and state attachments perceived to be complementary and inseparable. The people of the greater West, used to migrating across state boundaries but not accustomed to commuting across them, are nationalists at heart. But, excepting the minority in the largest cities of the region's eastern fringes, they are equally aware of the meaning of state lines and their common bonds as citizens of their respective commonwealths. Here, too, the greater West differs from its sister spheres. In the South, the Union is traditionally viewed as the creature of the states to be judged only from the "states-rights" point of view while in the Northeast both common and sophisticated opinion has it that the states have become outmoded as policy-making governments and that the nation—whose interests are assumed to be best articulated in their sphere—has an exclusive right to the citizenry's political loyalties.

The combination of nationalism and state loyalties is quite apparent in the cities of the prairie. The business, political, and civic leadership in every one shows awareness of their state ties, partly because of the important role played by state government in determining the destiny of their cities and partly because of the multitude of shared concerns which exist among them and their counterparts throughout their respective states. Yet in only one civil community, Rockford, does any significant segment of the leadership reflect what would be considered a states-rights ideology. In the others, the role of the national government, if not always acceptable, is invariably accepted. The community leadership of Springfield—the archetypal political community of the group—reflects this dual commitment most clearly, accepting the national role in their community's development and their role as a national shrine (the home of Abraham Lincoln) while remaining deeply immersed in the interests and operations of the State of Illinois.

In general the greater West has accepted the idea of partnership among the three planes of government in the United States as part of the American system (see Chapter Nine). Indeed, it was in the greater West, where the demands of the region's landforms and the technological revolution needed to conquer them were of such magnitude that local enterprise alone could not manage to meet them, that this partnership was given the shape it presently has.[34] Since the beginning of American settlement in the greater West, the states and localities of that sphere have looked to Washington for assistance and have been dependent on federal aid in a wide variety of ways. In much of the sphere, federally sponsored explorations revealed the possibilities for settlement. Federal negotiations with and protection from the Indians enabled settlers to enter the land. The federal land survey made it possible for them to occupy it. Federally assisted roads and railroads, some built in cooperation with the states and some constructed before the creation of states, opened the country up to settlers, starting with the National Road into southern Illinois and the Detroit-Chicago road that provided the first northern route into Illinois and culminating with the great transcontinental railroads connecting the Mississippi Valley to the Pacific Coast. Federal aid was made available to the states and localities for schools, public institutions, agricultural development, and many other activities vital for the establishment of civilization on the far frontiers of the greater West. The services of trained federal personnel were in great demand throughout the sphere. In this respect, as in others, the era of the land frontier was the father of the present.

It is true that federal assistance was available and important in the other spheres as well, but in a much less visible way. The universality of the demand, the similarity of intrasectional needs, the concurrence of local and national interests, and the availability of land as a uniform medium of financing improvements led to the early development of the system of universally applicable federal aid programs in the greater West. This system, which laid the foundations for contemporary American federalism today and shaped its essential features, stands as a pioneering political achievement of that sphere.[35]

NOTES

1. For an elaboration of this definition, see Daniel J. Elazar, *American Federalism, A View from the States* (New York: T. Y. Crowell, 1966), pp. 111–116.

2. Turner's theoretical writings on sectionalism can be found in *The Frontier in American History* (New York: Henry Holt, 1920) and *The Significance of Sections in American History* (New York: Henry Holt, 1932). The above quotation is from the first source, pp. 158–159. Turner's effort to develop a sociological basis for national political conflict rests on an implicit sense of the interrelationship of space and time within the American framework.

3. Critics of Turner's theory have argued that Turner placed too much emphasis on the sections' distinctiveness. They, in turn, posit the replacement of the sectional concept with the idea of regionalism, which is advanced as a more accurate reflection of the country's subnational divisions. Many of the regionalists have argued that, in an age of intensive nationalization of culture and an apparently growing class cleavage in politics that transcends geography, regionalism is useful for the description of latent and declining influences only.

Though Turner developed the larger part of his theory of sectionalism before the character of twentieth-century American culture had become apparent, the national character of even pre-twentieth-century American society was such that his ideas, in the main, take the patterns of nationwide cultural penetration into account. A more valid criticism of the Turner thesis lies in his occasional tendency to downgrade the position of the states. In his later reformulations, Turner himself did much to remedy this defect so that his theory of sectionalism, as it finally emerged, made a distinction between the sections, which were based on the states (if not always drawn along state lines), and regions, which could be drawn entirely without regard to state lines.

For a relatively recent reassessment of sectionalism and regionalism in the United States see Merrill Jensen, ed., *Regionalism in America* (Madison: University of Wisconsin Press, 1951). This volume is particularly valuable as a source of information concerning Turner's later thought on the subject and for its comprehensive bibliography. Harvey Perloff et al., have made a valuable contribution to the study of regional influences in *Regions, Resources, and Economic Growth* (Baltimore: Johns Hopkins Press, 1960). John Friedmann and William Alonso, eds., *Regional Development and Planning: A Reader* (Cambridge, Mass.: M.I.T. Press, 1964) offers a comprehensive view of contemporary regional theory often applied to the American scene. See, particularly, Part III for articles of special relevance to this study. John Gunther's *Inside USA* (New York: Harper, 1947) is a journalistic excursion into the same field and for all its weaknesses remains the most comprehensive recent study of sectionalism in the nation as a whole. Theodore H. White applies a rough regional classification as part of his analysis of the 1960 presidential election in *The Making of the President* (New York: Atheneum, 1960). His efforts, though often imprecise, attempt to describe the interrelationship of region, culture, and politics in a major national election. Several recent books have appeared analyzing state politics in regional perspective. Among them are: V. O. Key, Jr., *Southern Politics* (New York: Alfred A. Knopf, 1949); and John H. Fenton, *Politics in the Border States* (New Orleans: Hauser Press, 1957). An older study with the same regional orientation is that of Thomas C. Donnelly, *Rocky Mountain Politics* (Albuquerque: University of New Mexico Press, 1940).

4. While there is no literature specifically devoted to the three spheres as such, other than the works of this writer cited above, the idea of the three-fold division has appeared in various forms in the literature of American history and social science for nearly a century. Turner, *op. cit.*, discusses the United States as consisting of the Northeast, the South, and the West, using somewhat different boundaries than those suggested here. Anselm Strauss devotes Chapter 8 of *Images of the American City* (Glencoe, Ill.: Free Press, 1961) to a full discussion of the impact of the kind of influence here attributed to the spheres, on differing attitudes toward urbanism and city styles in what he calls the East, South, and Midwest. In his discussion of the latter, however, he finds urbanism in the far West to be so similar to urbanism in the Midwest that he does not formally distinguish between them. W. Lloyd Warner's series of studies of American cities in New England, the Southeast, and the Middle West, whether intended to do so or not, also projects the existence of these three major spheres of American culture. Perloff et al., *op. cit.*, use the same three-fold distinction in their regional economic analysis. One of the best indicators of the limits and extent of each of the three spheres is the spread of American religious denominations. Edwin Scott Gaustad traces the historical geography of American religions in the *Historical Atlas of Religion in America* (New York: Harper, 1962). John Tremblay's map, "Religion in America: 1950," prepared to accompany that atlas, confirms the sectional division in outline and even in detail. Also very useful in this connection are the U.S. Census Bureau publications organizing census data according to state economic areas and subregions for the 1950 and 1960 censuses. I am greatly indebted to the aforementioned works and those cited in the following notes for crystallizing my own observations as to the best delineation of the three spheres. My observations are based on some 250,000 miles of travel for research purposes in all forty-eight states of the continental United States in the past fifteen years, as well as intensive examination of library and documentary source materials in the field of regionalism.

5. The megalopolis of the East Coast is the heart of the greater Northeast. For a thorough study of that region, see Jean Gottman, *Megalopolis* (New York: The Twentieth Century Fund, 1961). While Perloff et al., *op. cit.*, include all of Illinois, Wisconsin, and Michigan in their Northeast, because they properly follow state lines, their mapped data are particularly useful because in many cases they trace the patterns that delineate the three spheres on a county-by-county basis, thus revealing the

westward projection of the greater Northeast as defined here, as well as the eastward projection of the greater West. Another important source of data which confirms this delineation can be found in the Rand McNally *Commercial Atlas*, issued annually. See also Edward L. Ullman, "Regional Development and the Geography of Concentration," reprinted as Chapter 8 in Friedmann and Alonso, *op. cit.* Robert A. Dahl's *Who Governs?* (New Haven, Conn.: Yale University Press, 1961) is an excellent study of a city political system which may well be characteristic of urban political systems in the greater Northeast. The Warner "Yankee City" series is an older study of urban society in the same area. W. Lloyd Warner et al., "Yankee City" series, Vols. 1–5 (New Haven, Conn.: Yale University Press, 1959).

6. The literature describing the greater South is quite extensive. The best works are W. J. Cash, *The Mind of the South* (New York: Alfred A. Knopf, 1941) and V. O. Key, Jr., *Southern Politics* (New York: Alfred A. Knopf, 1949). William H. Nicholls has some insightful comments about the South in "Southern Tradition and Regional Economic Progress," reprinted in Friedmann and Alonso, *op. cit.*, Chapter 23. Perloff et al. and Gaustad are particularly relevant for data on this sphere. Howard W. Odum and H. E. Moore, in *American Regionalism* (New York: Henry Holt, 1938), the first major work to challenge Turner's sectional theories, are at their best when describing the South. Floyd W. Hunter's *Community Power Structure* (Chapel Hill: University of North Carolina Press, 1953), does for Atlanta what Dahl's study does for New Haven. I would suggest that many of the differences in the empirical conclusions reached in those two studies (abstracting those conclusions which were products of the different research methods used) can be explained by the differences in the sectional settings of the two cities.

7. See, for example, Thomas Dye, *Politics, Economics and the Public; Policy Outcomes in the American States* (Chicago: Rand McNally, 1966).

8. Gaustad, *op. cit.* This phenomenon is so important that Gaustad's data can be used to trace Southern migration in the other spheres as well.

9. Cash, *op. cit.*, discusses this phenomenon in considerable detail. See also John K. Moreland, *The Millways of Kent* (Chapel Hill: University of North Carolina Press, 1958).

10. This greater West of the historians is thoroughly described in Ray Allen Billington, *The Westward Movement in the U.S.* (Princeton, N.J.: D. Van Nostrand, 1959) and D. E. Clark, *The West in American History* (New York: Thomas Y. Crowell, 1948). Turner talks of the West in these broad terms, at least for certain purposes. In a more recent comprehensive history of the westward movement, Richard M. Ketchum, ed., *The American Heritage Book of the Pioneer Spirit* (New York: American Heritage, 1959), the greater West as defined here emerges implicitly from the overall organization of the book.

11. Richard C. Wade, *The Urban Frontier: The Rise of Western Cities, 1790–1830* (Cambridge, Mass.: Harvard University Press, 1959).

12. Ellsworth Huntington's massive study, *The Mainspring of Civilization* (New York: John Wiley, 1945) is perhaps the most comprehensive and thorough presentation of the influences of location and climate on human social organization and the manner in which they interact with human physiology and culture to produce different regional civilizations. Frederick Sargent, a University of Illinois physiologist, has been studying the effects of geography and weather on human health for UNESCO and has come to conclusions that fit in well with the Huntington thesis. The greater West has been examined as an environment-based social order in Walter Prescott Webb's classic, *The Great Plains* (Boston: Ginn, 1931). While Webb's focus is on the high plains that lie at the base of the Rocky Mountains, which he sees as the central core of the West, his discussion extends to the peripheral zones around the

high plains, which include the bulk of the greater West as defined here. Webb's West, defined as the great, level, treeless area of the country and its wooded "islands" and fringes, is very close to what I here call the greater West.

13. Gottman, *op. cit.*, describes this phenomenon in the East in great detail.

14. Data on the population densities of SMSA's and urbanized areas are available in the U.S. Bureau of the Census, *City and County Data Book, 1962* (Washington, D.C.: Government Printing Office, 1962). When these data are correlated with the average lot size of dwellings in each civil community, a more or less accurate ranking of average densities can be obtained.

15. Christopher Tunnard and Henry Hope Reed, *American Skyline: The Growth and Form of Our Cities and Towns* (Boston: Houghton Mifflin, 1955) not only offers a full discussion of the impact of regional and historical factors on American cities but elucidates most of the aspects of urban cityscapes in the greater West mentioned here.

16. All of the twenty-two continental states entirely or partly located in the greater West were fully surveyed according to the rectangular system. Only five of the states wholly located in the greater South were surveyed under the federal survey act and three of them were surveyed in a unique system of small parcels unrelated to the national system of base lines and principal meridians. Of the fourteen states of the greater Northeast, only one (Indiana, which is a borderline case) was fully surveyed under the rectangular system and one other (Ohio) partly surveyed. See Benjamin Horace Hibbard, *A History of Public Land Policies* (New York: Macmillan, 1924) and U.S. Bureau of Land Management.

17. For a brief chronology and description of public land policy in the United States, see Richard B. Morris, ed., *Encyclopedia of American History* (New York: Harper, 1953), pp. 436–441.

18. Since the completion of this study, the most populous of these six townships, Richwood Township, located immediately adjacent to Peoria and the destination of upper and upper-middle class Peorians seeking more attractive homesites since the late 1940's, has been annexed by the city. The annexation was engineered by the township residents who had previously resisted the step for many years. Their change of attitude reflected their concern for the future of Peoria once it became apparent to them that they were losing control over the city's destiny by living outside it. Their response was typical of "cosmopolitans" faced with this problem in other urban areas. The other townships have been settled predominantly by "locals" or people who have moved into the Peoria area from elsewhere without ever having lived in the city; hence Peoria and its problems have little attraction for them. For a discussion of the impact of the "cosmopolitan"–"local" division in such issues, with special reference to the cities of the prairie, see Daniel J. Elazar and Douglas St. Angelo, " 'Cosmopolitans' and 'Locals' in Contemporary Community Politics," *Proceedings of the Minnesota Academy of Science,* XXXI, No. 2 (1964).

19. For a discussion of this development and its implications in the metropolitan area, see Thomas F. Hady and Clarence J. Hein, "Congressional Townships as Incorporated Municipalities," *Midwest Journal of Political Science* (November 1964).

20. Turner was among the first to note the importance and impact of this new Western technology and counts it among the great contributions of the frontier to the shaping of American society. See Turner, *op. cit.* It remained for Webb to pin down and give expression to its rise and consequences in *The Great Plains.* The importance of the greater West in the initiation and application of this technological revolution has been somewhat obscured by its general adoption by the nation as a whole. This major impact of the Western frontier on American life has not yet run its course. John Kouwenhouven discusses some of its larger impacts on American

society in *Made in America* (Garden City, N.Y.: Doubleday, 1948). Warner et al. discuss its cultural impact on the Illinois prairie settlements in *Democracy in Jonesville.*

21. Marshall McLuhan presents a fascinating and occasionally insightful discussion of the larger impact of the railroad on nineteenth-century social organization and communications patterns in his *Understanding Media* (New York: McGraw-Hill, 1964). While I believe that he confuses a number of issues in his analysis, he is one of the first to give the railroad its due as an agent of social change.

22. No mention has been made of the other two major transportation systems of the greater West, also products of changes in transportation technology generated in that sphere. The oldest of these is the waterway system which serves East St. Louis, Alton, Peoria, Joliet, and Quad Cities via the Mississippi and Illinois waterways and Duluth and Superior via the Great Lakes-St. Lawrence Seaway system. The first efforts at government waterway development date back to the 1820's, but ongoing federal programs for waterway improvement and the technology to make them feasible really took hold in the greater West after 1850. While the development of waterway facilities has been of continuing importance to those civil communities situated on navigable waters, the overall significance of water transportation in the greater West has clearly been secondary, in part because navigable waterways have been so unevenly distributed throughout the sphere. Thus their impact has been considerably more localized in character. More recently, the system of oil and gas pipelines stretching from the Great Plains to the Great Lakes has added another dimension to the overall regional transportation network—one, however, that has barely affected the politics of the communities served by those pipelines. While the location of both systems and their improvement have been matters of political concern to the cities of the prairie, this concern has clearly been secondary for better than a century.

23. This is not to imply that aviation has not had a special impact on the development of the nation's cities. The air age has certainly benefited Miami at the expense of New Orleans by making it the South's new gateway to Latin America. Phoenix and Tucson are, in many respects, products of the air age in the West as is Dallas in the Southwest. But, for the key cities in the nation's transportation network, such as New York, Chicago, and Atlanta, and their lesser subsidiaries, the airplane has simply reinforced and intensified patterns established by the railroads.

It should also be noted that the radio is to aviation what the telegraph was to railroading; the communications device that made the transportation vehicle operational while at the same time transforming the space-time relationship in society at large in its own right.

24. "Commerce" in the sense used here includes the commerce of ideas and intangibles as well as the more tangible commerce of traditional goods and services. The former are important particularly as they are "merchandized" by the press and the later mass media or by institutions of learning (schools, universities, museums, and the like). The local newspapermen, in particular, have been boosters of this type of metropolitanism.

25. See Robert O. Harvey, *An Economic Base and Potential Study of Springfield and Sangamon County, Illinois* (1958) and *Economic Potentials* (Regional Plan Report #1, 1959), both issued by the Sangamon County Regional Plan Commission.

26. For further discussion of this theme, see Daniel J. Elazar, "Constitutional Change in a Long-Depressed Civil Community: A Case Study of Duluth, Minnesota," in *Proceedings of the Minnesota Academy of Science,* XXXIII, No. 1 (1965).

27. Strauss, *op. cit.*, has done a most thorough job of examining the popular literature that reveals this apparently conflicting set of desires.

28. Among the best of these works is Graham Hutton's *Midwest at Noon* (Chi-

cago: University of Chicago Press, 1946). While confined to the Midwest as popularly defined, his book includes an excellent discussion of the continuing influence of the frontier in the region, as well as an excellent elaboration of much of the background material presented in this chapter. John T. Flanagan's anthology, *America is West* (Minneapolis: University of Minnesota Press, 1945), though also confined to the traditional "Middle West," is a broad-gauged collection of representative writings on this theme. Lewis Atherton's careful study of small-town life in the greater West east of the Rockies, *Main Street on the Middle Border* (Bloomington, Ind.: Indiana University Press, 1954) provides extensive documentation of the progression of social practices and attitudes discussed here, as well as in the earlier sections of this chapter. While all three of these studies start with a definition of "Middle West" that ranges from Ohio to the Dakotas, they are ultimately reduced to distinguishing between the western edges of the greater Northeast and the greater West as defined here, at least implicitly, in their descriptions and analyses, and, in Atherton's case at least, to extend their descriptions of the same phenomena westward into Colorado and beyond as well. In this regard, the previously cited sources of Turner, Webb, and Anselm Strauss add much to the discussion. The monographic literature available is even more extensive.

29. There are a number of good studies of the Populist-Progressive movement from the Western (as distinct from the national) point of view. Perhaps the best of these is Russel B. Nye's *Midwestern Progressive Politics* (East Lansing: Michigan State College Press, 1951). Nye, like many of the others whose works are cited here, tried to separate a Middle West from the greater West in his theoretical framework. The data within his chapters, however, of necessity take him beyond his limited "Middle West" into the area of the greater West as defined here. *The Wild Jackasses* (New York: Hartings House, 1956) by Dale Kramer treats the farm revolt as a phenomenon of the greater West, as do Webb and Turner, *op. cit.*

30. See Selig Adler, *The Isolationist Impulse* (New York: Abelard-Schuman, 1957) for a probing yet sympathetic discussion of the meaning of isolationism in the greater West.

31. For a more detailed discussion of this new sectionalism, see Daniel J. Elazar, "Megalopolis and the New Sectionalism," *The Public Interest,* No. 11 (Spring 1968), pp. 67–85.

32. The West Coast, centered around Los Angeles and San Francisco, is so convinced of its regional superiority within the country as a whole that it has had little time to worry about "colonialism." That section's confidence is further enhanced by its magnetic attraction for so many of the nation's immigrants. Moreover, it is in the process of developing its own independent economic base so that it will no longer be dependent on outside capital for development. To some extent this is leading to a turning of the axis of the greater West westward, toward California rather than Illinois. At the same time, the anti-Eastern feeling typical of the West may well be even stronger along the Pacific coast.

Though the greater South suffers from much the same cultural imperialism and accompanying talent drain, it appears to be less affected by it. The sphere's strong internal cohesion and commitment to the maintenance of a "Southern way of life," coupled with the strong undercurrent of feeling among its citizenry that the "Yankee North" does not understand their problems in any case, has created an isolationist impulse that makes participation in the national cultural arena much less desirable. Hence the loss of local talent is less felt.

33. This middle-class aspect of Populism has been described in Nye, *op. cit.* See also George Mowry, *The California Progressives* (Chicago: Quadrangle, 1963) and Walter T. Nugent, *The Tolerant Populists* (Chicago: University of Chicago Press, 1963). For a discussion of the cosmopolitanism of Populist leadership, see G. B.

Tindall, *The Populists* (New York: Harper, 1966). The cosmopolitan-local phenomenon as an aspect of political behavior has been described in Robert K. Merton, *Social Theory and Social Structure* (Glencoe, Ill.: Free Press, 1949). See also Alvin Gouldner, "Cosmopolitans and Locals: Toward an Analysis of Latent Social Roles," *Administrative Science Quarterly*, I, No. 2 (1957), 281–306; II, No. 2 (1958) 444–480.

34. My study of cooperative federalism in the nineteenth century, *The American Partnership*, develops this thesis more fully, particularly in Parts II and III.

35. The myth of frontier self-sufficiency and pioneer individualism need not be explored again in these pages. However, it does bear consideration for its contribution to the development of sectional differences. The myth itself is primarily a product of the southern and western frontiers of the greater South and the northern and western frontiers of the greater Northeast. Those frontiers, settled at an earlier date, in wooded, well-watered country which offered the bounties of nature without demanding the concerted cooperative effort that led to the development of the new technology necessary to subdue the lands of the greater West, did produce a type of self-reliant frontiersman, in the person of the subsistence farmer and his family. The subsistence farmer could take up land in the woods and, with a minimum of assistance, clear and cultivate it himself, with the aid of his family and perhaps a few neighbors. Since such families frequently preferred this independence, they often moved on once the area in which they had settled began to be filled up. All this came to a virtual end once the prairies were reached, leaving behind a myth of self-sufficient individualism that has colored the popular view of the meaning of the frontier experience to this day. More characteristic of the Western pioneer in any age is the pattern of cooperation between governments, corporate enterprise, and private individuals that is perhaps best represented by the colonization of the prairies. The cowboy, that vaunted individualist, is perhaps the best case in point. An employee, often serving corporately organized ranches, his individualism was limited to a willingness to quit his job at the drop of a hat. But even the homesteader, though nominally his own boss, was dependent on a complex economic system for survival, as the Populist revolt itself indicates.

PART II

STREAMS OF MIGRATION AND POLITICAL CULTURE

Chapter 4 / The Cities of the Prairie and the American Migrations

The Geology of Settlement

ULTIMATELY, the environmental unity which shapes the greater West reflects the multifarious influences of the peoples who have settled the sphere's different states and localities. The various ethnic and socioreligious groups who came to the cities and countryside of the greater West brought with them their own diverse patterns of culture to be integrated, modified —and unified—by a new environment. In order to understand the way in which the elements of environment and culture have combined to influence politics in the cities of the prairie, it is necessary to explore the "geology" of settlement in their sphere and the differing manifestations of that geology in each civil community.

This geology is given shape by the human "deposits" of fifteen migrational streams that have flowed across the United States at various times and with varying intensities since the initial settlement of North America. Each of these fifteen streams, taken in the aggregate, represents a population which, while composed of myriad individuals and many different groups, possesses certain unique cultural characteristics shared in some measure by the people within it, all of whom must somehow respond to the way of life it embodies. Through its deposits—determined in significant measure by sectional factors and the dictates of each successive frontier—each stream has contributed its special ingredients to the evolving social and political structures of the states and localities through which it has passed. Moreover, since the pattern of deposits (and the effects they have on each other) differs from locality to locality, the very movement of the streams has created unique social combinations from place to place.[1]

The "streams" are, of course, abstractions and, as abstractions, settle no places. Settlement is made by the individual households—families and individuals—that, combined, make up the several streams. Thus, in the last analysis, when we speak of migrational streams, we are speaking of the aggregation of small impacts of household after household. Families, in turn, tend to be bearers of traditional values and behavior patterns brought over in their essence from previous generations. This is found to be true even in rapidly changing American society. Nor is this to be wondered at. The first years of human socialization are the most crucial in the development of personality, the establishment of behavior patterns, and the inculcation of values. These early years are normally spent within the family group.

This tendency for families to act as bearers and transmittors of established values and patterns of social behavior is reinforced by the normal pattern of religious attachment in our society. Nuclear families not only share membership in the same religious community more often than not, but their members tend to marry endogamously within their religious community, thus perpetuating basic family religious ties over the generations. This is particularly important in American society where religious pluralism plays a vital social role. The streams themselves tend to take visible shape primarily through the religious affiliations of their constituent households, reinforced by the tendency of friendly cliques (the other major type of primary group in our society) to be religiously homogeneous. Such cliques, moreover, usually involve households occupying reasonably adjacent space.[2]

The composition of the streams and the manner in which they flow have tended to strengthen this collective pattern of cultural transmission. By and large, people who intended to settle permanently in the West moved westward in family groups. These family groups, whether originating in other parts of the United States or overseas, generally moved with other families from the same place of origin and with similar interests and attachments. Whether this movement took the form of formal colonization in which a group of families would actually form a colonization company to promote the settlement of a particular site, or whether it was simply a matter of friends attracting other friends in a less systematic manner, settlements usually developed along homogeneous lines in their early stages. From then on it was often a matter of like following like.[3]

As settlements grew into cities and gained larger populations, their demographic composition became more diverse. Other groups, representing other streams, would come in. They, too, would generally come to settle in groups of families, sometimes displacing established groups in the older neighborhoods and sometimes creating new neighborhoods of their own, adding new "deposits" to the evolving community. Even where the later arrivals have submerged the original streams, making them well-nigh invisible to the naked eye, the latter often continue to exist within the community, perpetuated through the complex of family ties, religious communalism, and friendship patterns while their original influence on the patterns of community life and politics to some degree continues to shape the ways of the later arrivals.

In most cases the various streams that have located in each city continue to be reinforced by new immigrants. Though the heyday of land settlement passed with the passing of the land frontier and the closing of unlimited immigration, migration in the United States continues undiminished, and the flow of the streams also continues, though perhaps at a somewhat diminished rate. Southerners continue to flow into areas settled by Southerners and even expand into contiguous ones, Yankees follow old migration lines established by their forbears, and new immigrants from overseas go where their families and friends who preceded them have already gone. In not a few cases reciprocal relationships have developed between the original sources of each stream and their cultural hinterlands (for example, sending the young "back East" to college) which tend to reaffirm the social influences of the streams as well.[4]

The Three Native Streams

The first settlers who founded colonies and communities at various points along the Atlantic coast from Maine to Georgia between 1607 and 1732 brought with them a cultural heritage from the countries or areas of their origin in the Old World which was reflected in the institutions—social, political, and religious—which they established on these shores. These colonists of the seaboard and their descendants spent anywhere from two to five generations rooting themselves in the American environment east of the Appalachians and then plunged into the wilderness to start the great westward movement that took them across the continent. As they became Americanized during their period of confinement to the coast, there developed not only the beginnings of a national culture but also three sectional subcultures which flourished within the framework of the emerging American civilization: (1) the Southern subculture of Virginia, the Carolinas, and Georgia, based on slavery, the plantation system, a radically individualist conception of social obligation, and a gentry-dominated political order; (2) the subculture of the Middle States (New York, New Jersey, Pennsylvania, Maryland, and Delaware) based on commercial enterprise, ethnic and religious pluralism, freehold agriculture, and a political order which, virtually from the first, was maintained by professional politicians; and (3) the Yankee subculture of New England based on Puritanism, with its emphasis on individual enterprise within the context of an organized and powerful community, dedicated to social improvement and individual redemption, and fostering a political order which encompassed a tension between an oligarchy deemed to be the guardians of religious orthodoxy and the fundamentally democratic town meeting.[5]

When the westward movement began, each section launched its own particular subcultural stream across the mountains. Each was carried westward by the people who were its products and the transmittors of its characteristics, flowing across the continent in the course of the late eighteenth, nineteenth, and early twentieth centuries, separately or together embracing wide bands of territory all the way west and depositing settlers who carried their cultural traits with them. Though these traits were modified in the course of their adaptation to fit into the new geohistorical environments into which they were transplanted, they were also transmitted from generation to generation with much of their essence intact and even sharpened as people who could not live comfortably within the mores of the subculture of their birth were able to move out and find more suitable environments.

For all intents and purposes, the first stream to affect any of the cities of the prairie was the Southern stream.[6] Examination of a map of the United States reveals why this was so. The southern third of Illinois lies well below any westward projection of the Mason-Dixon line, in the same latitude as much of Virginia and Kentucky. It is separated from the South only by virtue of the southwestwardly course of the Ohio River. Indeed, if state lines were disregarded, most of southern Illinois would be considered part of the greater South.

The Southern stream had crossed the Appalachians from Virginia and North Carolina by the eve of the Revolution, and its front was located in what are now the states of Kentucky and Tennessee. During the Revolutionary War, a Virginia expedition conquered the Illinois country for the new United States and gave it a political identity of its own as a county of the Old Dominion. It was not until the end of the war, however, that Americans began to settle in the area when Southerners came down the Ohio and up the Mississippi into what are now Madison and St. Clair Counties. The civil communities of those two counties, located as they are on the upper edge of the greater South, have remained quite Southern in culture and orientation. This is particularly true of those situated in the

"American Bottoms" (as the area along the river is called). Even on the bluff, only Belleville, with its strong combination of Southern and German elements, deviated from this pattern. Though different types of Southerners—from different states or districts—founded or settled in different civil communities to give each certain distinctive characteristics, the area's overall pattern continues to reflect Southern attitudes, values, and styles.

The Southern stream continued to flow northward up the numerous rivers that drain the Illinois prairie where its vanguard settled Springfield and Decatur and helped settle Urbana, Peoria, and Rock Island. In all of these civil communities, substantial colonies of Southerners can still be found, and Southern mores have penetrated in varying degrees into the overall fabric of their civic affairs. Remaining generally in the wooded river valleys and rarely venturing out onto the open prairie, the Southerners came primarily as individual families or in extended family groups which included brothers, sisters, and cousins with nuclear families of their own. At first, they were mainly hunters and trappers who developed subsistence farms or occasionally small businessmen who established mills and stores to serve the subsistence farmers. From the beginning there also came a minority of larger entrepreneurs, either men of wealthy backgrounds back in "the States" or men who aspired to the wealth and aristocratic pretensions of the Southern gentry. Many of these men came to Illinois as territorial officers, political appointees of the administration in power in Washington. They generally remained in the settlements near St. Louis, where they speculated in land and held or sought political preferment.

Few of the Southerners showed any inclination to found urban or even semi-urban settlements. Except in a few cases where individual entrepreneurs promoted townsites, the towns first settled by people from the South either "just growed" where farmers came to drink, play, or market their goods or were virtually forced into existence by the territorial and, later, state legislatures which had to create seats of government for newly formed counties. Belleville, Springfield, Decatur, Urbana, Peoria, and Rock Island were founded in this manner.

Southern settlers and the institutions they established formed the underlying matrix of settlement in the aforementioned civil communities. They brought with them an extremely individualistic attitude toward society as a whole whereby they minimized any sense of social responsibility beyond the family circle. Their churches, primarily Baptist and secondarily Methodist and Presbyterian, functioned as the major public agents for the transmission of these and other traditional values in the new communities. Their families, often related before locating in each settlement, grew more closely interrelated as intermarriage among them increased, reinforcing the role of kinship ties in their public life. Their politics began with efforts to imitate the traditional gentry-dominated politics of the states from whence they came with its system of interlocking family alliances struggling for political control primarily as a means to wealth and social position. It became the accepted brand, the base upon which the edifice of civil society was raised and the norm against which political behavior was measured.

The demands of the frontier, however, soon forced significant changes in those traditional institutions. In a new country without an inherited aristocracy and without the slave system needed to create one, gentry politics failed to take hold. Its proponents were either driven from public life by democratic politics or abandoned their claims to special social status and joined the democracy. What remained as the bases for political life were the family alliances and the search for wealth and status. They, too, were democratized. Kinship ties became as important in controlling the meanest county offices as they were in determining the government of the state, while the sharing of rewards became a pronounced and legitimate goal of the politically active of all social backgrounds. The politics of traditionalism gave way to a politics of individualism whereby no man had a greater intrinsic claim on public office and its perquisites than any other man, and the preservation of traditional patterns was reduced from the maintenance of an overarching social order to the support of an established infrastructure of kinship ties which continued to put certain brakes on individual drives for political preferment.

Traditionalism gave way to individualism in the churches as well. The high mobility of the frontier population not only prevented the development of strong intergenerational ties in specific churches but seriously weakened denominational attachments as well. Men went to church when they could and where, often as they were motivated to do so by good preachers who stirred their concern with the ultimate questions of life and death in the most direct manner, regardless of such formalities as membership or doctrinal demands. The personalities of the ministers became important factors in drawing people. The revivalism that resulted from this development institutionalized the most individualistic elements in Christianity, promoting individualism equally in the ministers and in the ministered to, even as it promoted a new tradition of literalistic fundamentalism that was exceptionally well suited to an increasingly individualistic society.

Southern-style individualism, then, was nurtured in a tradition that made organized community life, and the responsibilities it engenders, suspect. So long as this individualism was contained within a traditional society, preservation of the tradition served as a primary political goal. As the impact of the traditional patterns of Southern culture diminished in a new place, a new spirit of "rugged individualism," overlying the traditional infrastructure and reinforced by both the political and religious institutions, grew up. It continues to flourish even in the urban areas, wherever the Southern stream has predominated.

After reaching Rock Island and Peoria, the Southern stream turned westward again, continuing its course across Missouri and on to the Pacific coast, occupying most of the territory below the thirty-eighth parallel and sending "fingers" northward into Wyoming, Montana, and Idaho along the eastern slope of the Rockies and the western slope of the Sierras and Cascades. Pueblo, situated less than half a degree north of the thirty-eighth parallel, received its share of the Southern migration beginning when a party of Southerners established the first American settlement on its site during the Gold Rush of 1859, some twenty-five years after the current had reached its northern limits in Illinois. Except for isolated familes and individuals who continued northward in search of a new El Dorado, Duluth and Superior were unaffected by the Southern stream and never had to assimilate it or adjust to its style.

Close on the heels of the Southern migration into the greater West came representatives of the Middle stream, which originated in the Middle Atlantic states. The first people from those states to reach Illinois actually came via the Southern migration routes. Descendants of the Scotch-Irish who had moved down the Great Valley from central Pennsylvania in the second half of the eighteenth century found Virginia and the Carolinas unsatisfactory for one reason or another and so turned westward. Hill-dwellers by cultural background, they eschewed even the wooded lowlands to settle in the southern Illinois hill country. Some of them, however, did move up into western Illinois, where they joined the other settlers in the Madison-St. Clair Counties and Springfield areas and, to a lesser extent, in the other areas where they added the social, religious, and political institutions associated with Presbyterianism and its denominational offshoots.

Still, the bulk of the Middle stream flowed almost due west from New Jersey, Maryland, Delaware, and Pennsylvania via Ohio and Indiana into central, south central, and western Illinois, particularly after the close of the War of 1812. By that time the main elements of the Middle current had found an intermediate resting place on their way west, in Ohio, and had produced another generation. Many of the "emigrants" to the Illinois country whose fathers had started out in Pennsylvania were themselves natives of Ohio. One such group of Ohioans founded Urbana in 1822 and named it after their native city in the Buckeye State, just as Champaign County was later named after its Ohio forebears.

Like the Southerners, the Middle Staters also remained within or near the wooded areas in the regions they settled and did not at first venture far out onto the prairies. They, too, were primarily subsistence-type farmers at first, whose agricultural practices were not geared to distant markets but to self-maintenance. However, unlike so many of the Southerners, who tended to be marginal people, interested in making a subsistence living with a minimum of effort and invariably ready to move on to ostensibly greener pastures, the Middle stream farmers generally came to settle permanently and were interested in improving their farms and even in founding communities. Many of them later made the transition to commercially oriented agriculture once the prairies were opened up. Their children were among the first to migrate to the emerging cities that grew up in their midst. In the end, most of the cities in central and western Illinois grew from the crossroads settlements founded by earlier Middle stream migrants who had come west to engage in commerce, albeit on a local scale.

As the Middle stream crossed Illinois and entered Iowa, it laid down substantial cultural deposits in Urbana (and later Champaign), Decatur, Springfield, Peoria, Joliet, Rock Island, and Davenport. Its distinctive institutions were the Methodist Church and moderate Whig (later conservative Republican) political ties.[7] Both of these institutions contributed to the development of an ethos of moderate conservatism, essentially but not extremely individualistic in their general culture. Their primary orientation toward commerce as a means for achieving success as individuals carried over into the social and political life of their communities. Since political order is a precondition for commerce, the people of the Middle stream as a matter of course fostered a modicum of community organization based on what appeared to be necessary for maximizing commercial opportunities. At the same time, within their social order, men chose to go into politics for the same reasons that they chose any other career: for personal advancement defined in material ways. Politics, then, was primarily a matter of services rendered for appropriate rewards with the nature of both the services and the rewards defined primarily in commercial terms.

This culture of commercialism (not used here in any pejorative sense) remains dominant in the communities influenced by the Middle stream to this day, whether they are metropolitan or rural. A comparison of the predominant religious groups by county in Illinois and the state's county-by-county voting patterns in national elections during the mid-nineteenth century with those of the mid-twentieth indicates the extent to which the culture of their populations has remained constant.

Though products of the Middle stream did filter northward into Wisconsin and Minnesota, its main flow was westward across south central Iowa and into the southern half of Nebraska, Kansas, and eastern Colorado. It diminished in influence immediately west of the continental divide, though it reappears in some strength in the Pacific Northwest, particularly in parts of northern California and southern Oregon.

The current most influential in shaping the basic social and political patterns of the greater West—and most of the cities of the prairie—was the Yankee stream of New England. Originating in the seventeenth century in a small area from Cape Cod north into New Hampshire and south into Connecticut, it expanded to cover all of New England proper. In the late eighteenth century, the main current of this stream turned westward and propelled itself across the entire continent to create a greater New England that covers much of the present day greater West. By stages it took in much of upper New York State and northern Pennsylvania. It then jumped into Ohio, capturing the northern third of that state and moved hesitantly on across a narrow strip of northern Indiana (never a good land for Yankees) until it was blocked by the great Kankakee swamp. With characteristic vigor, the New Englanders of this Yankee migration captured approximately half of the greater Northeast for their own. However, in doing so, they had to share those states with other streams whose strength effectively diluted the impact of Yankee ways from the first.[8]

After the opening of the Erie Canal in 1825 and particularly after the publicity that accompanied the Black Hawk War, the Yankee stream took to the Great Lakes, sailed past the western lands of the greater Northeast and entered Michigan, Wisconsin, and Illinois in force. By the end of the decade, the Yankee emigrants had become the dominant group in the first two commonwealths and, in the northern two-thirds of Illinois, were rapidly superseding the other two native streams in political influence by virtue of their superior organization and intense exertions. From 1840 on, the three states and most of those to the west of them became New England outposts. In the end, the basic social patterns of much of the greater West were built on Yankee foundations and have continued to reflect Yankee values in some form even though the proportion of Yankees in the overall population has since declined in the face of subsequent migrations.

Among the very first Yankees to reach Illinois were those who came to the Madison-St. Clair Counties area early in the nineteenth century as casual settlers and as scouts for the home missionary societies of Massachusetts, Connecticut, and New York. Their reports, which dealt with both the fertility of the land and the spiritual poverty of its settlers, were instrumental in stimulating their brethren to come west, in person, as settlers and missionaries. Indeed, much of the subsequent settlement of the area was brought about through the organized effort of missionary societies, some supported in part by their parent states, to implant a new Puritan commonwealth on the prairies. This consciousness of purpose was one of the most notable features of the Yankee emigrants. Of course, not all Yankees were consciously concerned with society-building, no more than all Southerners were radical individualists, but the pacesetters, the public leadership, and the men of prominence among them at least shared this concern along with their interest in economic self-improvement.

When the Yankee stream hit Illinois in force two and three decades later, it entered the state through Chicago and spread out onto the prairie, rapidly engulfing the two northern tiers of counties, then thrusting south and southwestward. The Yankees who pioneered in the northern two-fifths of Illinois were responsible, in the main, for the development of the technology that was needed for the conquest of the prairies. In applying that technology, they created some of the Illinois cities of the prairie and raised the others from village to city status. Joliet was created by Yankees at the eastern end of this area, Rockford in the center, and Moline at its western end. Rockford and Moline became centers of the proposed Yankee Eden on the prairies. Even after their original Yankee settlers were engulfed by Scandinavians, their basic flavor was preserved. Joliet, on the other hand, was settled simultaneously by elements that differed considerably in values, outlook, and behavior from the Yankees, to the point where the Yankee influence was ultimately submerged. Two branches of the migration spread southward, one into western Illinois, where the remaining vacant prairielands were colonized predominantly by Yankees, much as northern Illinois was. Peoria, as that region's central city, was heavily invaded by the Yankees who followed the Illinois waterway southwestward. The other branch flowed into central Illinois, following the Illinois Central Railroad to fill in the unoccupied prairielands in that area, creating the city of Champaign and influencing the development of Decatur, Urbana, and even Springfield.

Reexamination of the historical tables in the first three chapters reveals how this initial urbanization progressed. The first half-generation of mass Yankee settlement (approximately 1835-1850), was devoted to developing a foothold on the land and establishing local trading centers as nuclei around which to build a settled society. In this respect, the Yankee mores coincided very handily with the objective demands of prairie living. The New England tradition of settlement dictated that the frontier be conquered by community groups and that every settled area be centered around a town which, in turn, was to be built around a church, a school, and a democratic local government. This social doctrine was a product of a religious doctrine which held that individuals were liable to gross error if left entirely to their own devices without the beneficent effects of community influence and communal responsibility. It, in turn, fostered the political institution of the town—or the township, its Western manifestation—famous in American tradition as the seat of American grassroots democracy. Indeed, the first major political contribution made by the Yankees who settled in Illinois was the establishment of the township system as a legitimate local government option. Southern-dominated Illinois had made no provision for township government, and the New Englanders hurried to remedy this in the Constitution of 1848 (a document which generally ratifies the migration-induced sectional realignment of the state).

The Yankees not only established the township system but founded towns as well, to serve as the nuclei for the farmers in the townships who were forced to settle on separate and independent tracts by the nature of the federal land system (which New Englanders had earlier opposed as national policy for just that reason) or who chose to do so in the manner of western settlers generally. These towns were urban communities—in the American style—from the start. They were platted and incorporated at local initiative within the first few years of their initial settlement, and, as Yankee technology connected them by railroad, they became centers of industry as well as commerce. Fulfilling the Yankee desire for community, the best of them were also well designed for the oasis culture of the prairie. A century later, when the attempt at scattered rural settlement had passed its peak and the once open prairies began to become open again, the originally obscured oasis character of those cities came into focus. Already available as urban hubs, they began to draw in large numbers of people who had previously resided out on the prairie, to become the urban or metropolitan centers many presently are.

At first, most of the cities serving the prairie farms were founded on the fringes of that great sea of grass. The founding of cities out on the prairie was primarily the result of Yankee activity channeled through the Boston-financed railroad companies which translated federal-state land grant programs into railroads that changed the face of Illinois. Of these, the Illinois Central was the most important. Built primarily through as yet unsettled territory, it was the first of many in the greater West that were faced with the task of colonizing the prairies and plains in order to make their existence profitable. This task neatly combined both the technological skills and the colonizing bent of the Yankees with considerable success. Through judicious combination of propaganda, land grants for townsites, and concessions to farmers, the railroad managed to attract settlers to the open prairie where none had lived before.

Since those early days the Yankee subculture has been transmitted through the Calvinist-originated churches brought into Illinois by the original New Englanders. The structures of local government they introduced, and the well-nigh fixed pattern of political allegiance they established continue to predominate in Yankee-settled areas in the state. In general, a political map of the most intensive Republicanism in Illinois follows along the same lines as a map of the areas settled by the Yankee stream. At the same time, the Yankee-settled areas have differed from other Republican areas in the state by virtue of their penchant for progressive Republicanism. More than a century ago, the Yankee counties led the way for the Free Soil party. Half a century ago, they rallied for Theodore

Roosevelt and the Progressive party (in fact, the areas of greatest Yankee settlement can be traced politically through the band of counties voting Progressive). Since 1912, there have been no such third parties to provide similar opportunities for measuring the progressiveness of the Yankee subculture. At the local level, however, the generally higher incidence of progressives who make themselves felt in local affairs and their particular concentration in those cities whose Yankee origins are most visible continues to be an affirmation of the larger generalization.

Despite its many successes, the Yankee stream in Illinois could only proceed so far before it encountered the other native stream with their particular subcultures. In the process of adjusting to the reality of the latters' existence, the Yankees' dreams of creating a new "city upon a hill" had to be substantially modified. This confrontation between the streams and its political consequences will be discussed in detail in Chapter Six.

In Wisconsin and Minnesota, on the other hand, the Yankee stream first flowed in virtually unimpeded by any others. Few Middle States emigrants and even fewer Southerners were deflected from their due westward course to try the Upper Midwest. The Yankees, in fact, initiated large-scale settlement in both states. Consequently they were able to mold the social and political systems of both substantially in the image of their own culture, achieving greater success in their efforts to create the New England of the West. The political cultures of both states were shaped by this Yankee drive for the good commonwealth; hence they came to demand a level of performance from politicians and public officials that has never been demanded in Illinois, with its different standards, products of a sharply different political culture (see Chapter Eight). Communal responsibility and public morality were essential ingredients shaping political behavior in both states from the first. In both, variations from the set standards of political morality (which, of course, occurred and do occur, as in any human society) were either local phenomena in specific civil communities or represented individual cases of backsliding. Not that the Yankees were unconcerned with commercial gain, but they separated politics and the marketplace.[9]

Characteristically, the first Yankees in the Duluth-Superior area were missionaries promoting Congregationalist-Presbyterian Christianity among the Chippewa Indians. Later, Yankees came as entrepreneurs, usually from St. Paul, to develop local business enterprises and to exploit the natural resources of the North Woods. However, the area was too far off the beaten track of the early Yankee migrations to be colonized by Yankees in the manner of cities farther to the south. Both cities were developed by rather polyglot groups of settlers twenty or more years later than the more southerly areas of Minnesota and Wisconsin. Still the small permanent Yankee communities that formed within each stood on the highest rungs of the political and social ladder and generally set the tone in local politics and society. In the process, they absorbed the representatives of other streams of the same status who settled locally.

Colorado, like Illinois, is situated at a geohistorical junction point where all three native streams (as well as others) came together. From the first, then, emigrants from all three streams were attracted to the future state. Most of the Southerners and many of those from the Middle States came to Colorado in search of gold or silver. Only the Yankee stream included substantial numbers of colonists who intended to settle in the territory from the beginning, either as farmers or to seek their fortunes by supplying the prospectors. As a result, when the mining booms played out and the fortune hunters left Colorado for greener pastures, the Yankees remained to mold the basic political institutions and culture of the new state before being joined by sizable numbers of settlers from other cultures. Ultimately the latter did come in numbers. Perhaps this explains Colorado's position somewhere between that of Illinois and Minnesota in its patterns of political behavior. Having a liberal leavening of settlers less concerned with creating the "New Jerusalem" on the plains, its pursuit of righteousness has been less pronounced than in Minnesota. Still, the Yankee influence set certain political standards that have had to be met from the beginning of the state's history as an American commonwealth.

Pueblo, by virtue of its geographic position, was situated on the very southern fringe of the Yankee migration. Relatively few Yankees settled in that civil community but those who did, as usual, became dominant in the business community and in civic affairs. The leading entrepreneurs were Yankees, as were the founders of the city's schools. The later influx of other elements only served to cut the Yankees and their descendants off from the main current of the Yankee streams while heightening their position in the economic and cultural life of Pueblo.

Though the major impact of the three native streams came in the early days of settlement of the greater West, the streams themselves persist. Since World War I, the Southern stream, transformed into one segment of the overall rural-to-urban migratory movement, has sent fingers northward again, establishing significant colonies of Southerners, particularly unskilled Southern mountain folk, in all the cities of the prairie in Illinois, even those such as Rockford, where none existed before. These groups have yet to become politically articulate in their new homes but their presence and nearly "alien" ways do present the civil communities with substantial minority group problems. To a lesser extent, the emigration from the farms of the Middle West to the cities of the prairie has also represented a continuation of the nineteenth-century streams. The original cultural patterns of those streams were best preserved in the rural areas where families, friendship cliques, and religious ties were most stable, having encountered less pressure to change. Thus many of the descendants of the original Yankee, Middle States, and Southern settlers, moving into the cities two, three, or more generations later, have brought with them infusions of a more faithfully preserved form of the original native cultures.

The Seven European Streams

Almost from the beginning of settlement in the greater West, but with increasing intensity as the nineteenth century progressed, the three native streams were supplemented by others which originated in Europe. There some ten thousand years of overlapping migrations, each with its own particular encounter with the local environment; political innovation and turmoil; and religious upheaval and reformation had left a mosaic of cultures contained within some ethnic and nationality groups and cutting across others.

While the European situation was far more complex than that which shaped the three American subcultural groups, it is possible to identify seven major streams that flowed directly across the Atlantic from that continent even though their precise Old World origins remain obscure. In most cases, these streams manifested themselves in currents composed of specific, ethnic, nationality, or religious groups.

The most prominent of these streams was what may be called the English stream, consisting primarily of those English, Welsh, and Cornish peoples within the fold of the Anglo-Catholic religious tradition and excepting those dissenters whose unorthodoxy stems from the Puritan tradition. The Scots (perhaps excepting the most isolated highlanders, who retained an ethnic and cultural affinity with Ireland), the Danes, the Norwegians, the Swedes of the coastal areas, the Dutch and some of the related peoples down the Rhine Valley as far south as Switzerland (such as Walloons and Huguenots) and along the Baltic Coast, and the dissenting English (who were concentrated in eastern and northern England where Danish and Norse influences had once been strong) constituted a North Sea stream united by certain ethnic ties, economic and political institutions that originated in the days when their lands were occupied by the Celts, and a common Calvinistic-Reformed religious tradition. The Jews constituted the only stream to come through Europe whose origins as a self-conscious cultural entity predated the rise of European civilization. Combining distinctive ethnic and religious characteristics within an undivided social framework, they were spread over most of Europe and came to the United States from all parts of that continent, yet, despite certain surface differences, they formed an essential unity. The Irish, with their ethnic and cultural uniqueness and puritan Catholicism, formed still another separate stream. The bulk of the German peoples, the central European peoples under German cultural influence such as the Bohemians and the Hungarians, as well as most of the French and Belgians, comprised the Continental stream. These peoples shared a common heritage from the Holy Roman Empire and its Bourbon and Hapsburg heirs with their politically absolutist tradition and conservative religious orientation, whether Catholic or Lutheran. The Eastern European stream, consisting of Russians, Poles, and other Slavic peoples, many of Orthodox persuasion, was a sixth. Finally, there was the Mediterranean stream consisting of Italians, Portuguese, Greeks, and the Balkan peoples.[10]

The French settlers who preceded the first American occupation of Illinois were of the Continental stream. They were the first Europeans to settle in any of the cities of the prairie but remained few in number and low in influence. Representatives of the English and North Sea streams from the British Isles were the first to arrive in significant numbers, beginning in the 1820's. The Continental, Jewish, and Irish streams and the European currents of the North Sea stream began to arrive in the 1830's. The flow of immigrants from these streams was heavy by midcentury, reached its greatest intensity during the Civil War era, and remained great until the 1890's. After the Civil War, but particularly after 1880, immigration from the Mediterranean and Eastern European streams commenced in earnest, dominating the immigration lanes into the cities of the prairie until the end of mass immigration in the early 1920's.

All seven European streams also started from the Atlantic coast, where the immigrants landed, and flowed westward, generally following the routes of the three native streams: first along the rivers and wagon roads that moved people from the Southern and Middle States across the Appalachians and then via the canals and railroads built by the Yankees. Many of the representatives of the streams stopped to settle at various points on the way west, where they added new layers to the social geology of already existing communities and states. Others pressed on to the frontier where they helped shape newly founded communities and states from the first. The settlers who came via four of the first five streams settled about equally in both rural and urban areas, spreading over the landscape in much the same manner as the people who came out of the native streams. Emigrants from England could be found in every community. Welsh and Scots were distributed widely if not evenly. Of the North Sea stream, only the Dutch confined themselves to a few selected locales, primarily in areas opened by the Yankees, such as western Michigan and northeastern Iowa. The Germans and the Irish spread themselves around the greater West almost as widely as Englishmen, and Hungarians tended to settle wherever there were large concentrations of the former. The relatively few French and Belgians, like the Dutch, settled in particular pockets. The Scandinavians flocked to the Upper Midwest and other Yankee-opened areas while the Jews scattered in small numbers throughout the sphere's cities and towns. Only the Jews were overwhelmingly townspeople from the first, settling widely if sparsely in virtually every hamlet in the sphere that offered commercial opportunities. Those who came out of the last two streams (as well as many of those of the first five who came at the same time) settled primarily in the centers of the urban-industrial frontier, which was in full swing during the years of their immigration, concentrating in the sphere's large and medium-size cities.

The cultural patterns transmitted by the ethnic groups comprising these streams can be roughly divided into those outward manifestations of a particular "old country" way of life (language, foods, family customs, and the like) which have tended to disappear in the assimilation process and those underlying values and patterns of behavior which, even in Europe, were in many respects supranational in character. Among the latter are many that are similar to the Yankee, Middle, and Southern values and behavior patterns considered native to the United States. These often latent but larger effects of the cultures carried by the streams of which the ethnic groups are a part have been worked into the overall culture of the country and the cities of the prairie in different guises, through which they continue to affect the body politic.

Each of the seven European streams brought in elements that both altered and reinforced the cultures and institutions established by representatives of the native streams where the latter had settled first. Where the immigrants who settled in a particular community reinforced the original cultural patterns, the level of political conflict between newcomers and old settlers was relatively low-key. Such was the case of the Scandinavians who reinforced the original Yankee settlers in Rockford. After the initial problems of status adjustment and the necessity to redivide political power (a task which was made less difficult since it did not involve serious value conflicts), both elements found that their common political and moral values bound them together far more than their different social customs divided them. In such cases, the original political culture and its institutional representations would be maintained more or less intact with community conflicts developing along other lines of cleavage, usually less intense.

However, where the new elements introduced values and behavior patterns that contradicted those of the established residents, intensive political conflict ensued, conflict not simply based on the adjustment of status or the redivision of political power among groups sharing essentially the same way of life, but a cleavage between different ways of life and conceptions of politics. A conflict of this nature needs much time to be resolved. Indeed there is reason to believe that, in at least some of the cities of the prairie, this fundamental conflict has never been resolved. It has only been transmuted into an apparently different conflict, which is interlaced with class and reference group cleavages. Peoria is a prime example of this and the foremost case in point. There, within the city itself, the "bluff" versus "valley" conflict seems to be a continuation of an old conflict between the heirs of an earlier alignment of both native and European streams, by other means.

Similarities and differences in religious heritage reveal much about the similarities and differences linking and separating the various European streams with their native counterparts. The English and North Sea streams were predominantly Protestant. The products of the latter who came from the Calvinist or Puritan tradition with their Congregational or Presbyterian patterns of ecclesiastical government set upon a social structure that had kept them freemen or yeomen during the feudal age reinforced the Yankee stream. So did the Jewish stream. Their very similar religious outlook stemmed from related theological "first principles," a similar commitment to the necessity of living in a community, a correspondingly high level of entrepreneurial talent and penchant for commercial activity, a common sense of mission and a strong sense of Biblical morality all produced by their common history of republicanism within a nationalistic (or proto-nationalistic) framework.

Those who came from the more hierarchical and liturgical Anglo-Catholic traditions of the English stream or its more democratic offshoot, Methodism, tended to reinforce those elements in the Middle stream which supported similar religious institutions. Because they, too, came from a social system that had been little affected by feudalism, both reflected much the same combination of entrepreneurial drive and "middle class values" as their Calvinistic brothers but with considerably less communal concern. In both cases, the native streams can be traced back to the same sources which produced their European counterparts in the Old World.

The products of the Continental stream, by and large Catholic or hierarchical Protestant, reflected the long history of classical feudalism and its classical breakdown in the countries of the old Holy Roman Empire and its peripheries. While many of them stemmed from peasant ancestry, they had been exposed to the postfeudal world in Europe and had at least begun to internalize the drive toward individual liberty, achievement, and success characteristic of modernism. By and large, they reinforced the individualistic tendencies of the already pluralistic Middle stream, which from its beginning absorbed most of the immigrants from the same European regions.

The Irish, Mediterranean, and Eastern European streams—the first overwhelmingly Catholic and the last two predominantly so with significant Orthodox minorities—were composed primarily of people of very traditional, rural, even peasant, backgrounds who not only changed location by crossing the ocean but entered into the mainstream of modern life for the first time. As subject peoples, their traditional societies had fostered in them a primary allegiance to family and kin-group with ties beyond kinship to community and polity clearly secondary. With the breakdown of that society, its orientation was diverted into a political concern for satisfying immediate individual and familial interests rather than in the development of the "good community" in any abstract sense. To this extent, the three streams had much in common with the native Southern stream—single dominant religion, strong kinship ties, essentially private goals—but without the native stream's advantage of an indigenous established elite to support their neotraditional ways. Moreover, the bulk of the people from these "Catholic" streams defined the good life in other than the puritan terms common to all the native streams. They had no "Protestant ethic" that made material success the measure of a man and that tended to enforce puritanical restrictions against most hedonistic indulgence. In this respect, the Irish came closest to the Protestant (particularly the Southern) streams and the Mediterraneans remained farthest removed from them. Consequently, while the Southerners were able to remain within the ken of their traditional culture even when they settled new territories so long as they remained in the majority, the three non-native streams, cut off from the sources of their traditional culture, blended in with the pluralistic (and hence more receptive) Middle stream from the first, adopting its individualistic orientation for their own. The Irish, with their long involvement with the English behind them, were particularly adept at the transition, especially in its political aspects. In this, they unwittingly set the pace for later cultural changes among native Southerners who moved away from their home bases.[11]

The English stream followed the path of the Middle stream from the first, coming in through the Ohio Valley and moving up the Mississippi and Illinois rivers. The vanguard of this stream came in preterritorial days, contributing commercial talent to the Madison and St. Clair Counties communities via St. Louis. From there they proceeded northward and were important figures in the founding of Rock Island and Davenport. As the number of English settlers increased, some settled in every one of the cities of the prairie, usually as members of the business community and secondarily as artisans and craftsmen, bringing with them their Episcopal churches and usually joining the higher status groups in the community with whom they shared a broad range of values and behavior patterns. Their spread was so wide and their assimilation into the native American streams so easy and thorough that their visibility was low from the first and their separate impact difficult to uncover.[12]

The major nationality groups from the North Sea stream had varying experiences in the cities of the prairie. For many of the same reasons as the English, the Scots migrated as individuals and spread themselves widely throughout the greater West. A colony of Scots settled near Rockford in the middle of the last century and only moved to the city when their colony failed. As Calvinists, they blended in very nicely with the like-minded Yankees and Scandinavians and did not acquire a separate political identity though they maintained a minimal church-centered identity a century later. Scots settled as individuals in all the other cities of the prairie, but only in Springfield was there any trace of a Scottish entity, which soon disappeared as a distinctive element, leaving a church behind them.[13]

The first Jews to have an impact as a group on the cities of the prairie had their European roots in the territories of the English, North Sea, and German streams. They came with the Germans and English in the mid-1840's and after, settling primarily in Springfield, Peoria, Davenport, Rock Island, Belleville, and Champaign as men of commerce, where many of them became important leaders in the local business community. After the turn of the century, Jews from Eastern Europe also settled in Rockford, Joliet, East St. Louis, and Decatur. Duluth developed the largest Jewish community of the cities of the prairie in the same period, as a result of its great boom, with Superior perhaps second or third. Pueblo's Jewish community dates from the later period but has always been small.

The Jewish communities of Duluth, Peoria, and the Quad Cities became the most important of their group, but in every community in which they settled, the Jews have assumed an importance beyond their numbers, as downtown business leaders, as professional men, and in the development of local "cultural" and philanthropic activities. Culturally they identified with the Yankee communitarian elements. Politically they made few demands and assimilated with relative ease into the dominant parties of their respective communities.[14]

Of the nationality groups from the Continental stream that settled in the cities of the prairie, the French, Germans, and Belgians were probably most significant. French influence was significant in St. Clair County in the eighteenth century and in Davenport in the nineteenth. The Davenport case is unique in that French settlers contributed to the American settlement of the Quad Cities. Antoine LeClaire, one of the city's founders, attracted a number of French Catholics, who organized the first church in the community, which was served by French priests until the Irish took over in the late 1850's. As an identifiable group, however, the French element has disappeared. The French who remain in St. Clair County are concentrated in their village of Cahokia and have had little impact as a group beyond their local parish, where they maintain a very distinctive subculture.[15]

The first mass migration from the Continental stream was of the Germans, who began to enter the greater West in substantial numbers after 1830. The Germans themselves were divided into different cultural groupings (or currents within their stream) separated primarily along Catholic (southern) and Protestant (northern) lines but also, among the Protestants, between northwestern (coastal and Rhine Valley) presbyterian and eastern (interior) hierarchical church groups. While substantial numbers of German immigrants did settle in the rural areas, the Germans as a group included the first true urbanites to reach the greater West. Accordingly, many of them settled in the embryonic cities of the prairie from the very first, not only as businessmen and small industrialists serving an agricultural economy but as people with urban skills who hoped to build an urban way of life. Even the Germans who settled in what is now Belleville, members of the so-called Latin Peasant movement whose urban-inspired romantic agrarianism led numerous German intellectuals "back to the soil," quickly turned their energy toward transforming that city into a predominantly German town, overwhelming the early deposits of the Southern stream and eroding even the Yankee outcroppings that had come (and become strong) in the interim. The Latin Peasants (who were neither Latins nor peasants) were followed by other Germans, many from the Catholic south and others from the Lutheran interior, who added other dimensions of German culture to the civil community. Belleville's early and leading industry was the brewing of beer, and until Prohibition beer gardens were the centers of the community's social life. To this day, the largest single element in Belleville's population is of German descent, its architecture has a Germanic character, and its peculiar local slang is derived from the German language.

The Belleville Germans, many of whom had participated in the revolutionary movements of the first half of the nineteenth century in the old country, seized the opportunity to participate in democratic politics. By the mid-1850's they had taken control of political life in their civil community. The Germans and the original Southern settlers were not very similar in background. At the same time, their political clashes were kept to a minimum during the early years since each element was settled in what were then the two separate and independent municipalities of East and West Belleville, which were not amalgamated until an indigenous (and American) generation came to maturity in the 1880's. Since each element tended to pursue its own concerns during the period of adjustment, there was little to bring them into conflict.

The Germans who settled in Alton, Peoria, and Davenport (where they concentrated most heavily) brought with them an urban orientation from the first. Those three cities soon became the leading urban centers between Chicago and the Trans-Mississippi West and are today centers of the three largest of the medium-size metropolitan areas examined in this study.

Of the three, Davenport's German heritage remains quite visible even today. The German settlers—most coming from northwestern Germany and the Rhine Valley—became the majority almost from the beginning. They actually began to arrive so close to the point of the civil community's initial settlement (the first came in 1836) that they were able to contribute substantially to the development of its basic social patterns. By 1890, close to 50 per cent of the inhabitants of Scott County were of German birth or descent. While the Germans, particularly the Protestants among them, contributed much to the community in the commercial and associational fields, setting a cosmopolitan and urbane tone which Davenport has maintained, at first they did not provide much leadership in the fields of religious organization and politics. Coming from a society where popular political participation was virtually unknown, political activity did not appeal to them until they became more Americanized. Later, their business leaders became politically involved as cosmopolitans, accepting positions on the more prestigious local government bodies such as the school and park boards. Many of the German immigrants, particularly the more communally minded, were freethinkers who rejected organized religion and sought social outlets outside the churches. They founded turnvereinen, cultural clubs, and singing societies, many of which continue to exist and to play an active role in community life. By and large they fitted in well with the other settlers of the Davenport area from the beginning, so that little political conflict based on ethnic divisions developed in that civil community, though the smaller number of German Catholics were relegated to a somewhat lower position in the social order.

Peoria also took on many characteristics of a German town, particularly as the German elements began to develop local brewing and distilling industries which made the city nationally famous. Peoria's national image as a German town was overdrawn, however. The balance between Southerners, Yankees, people from the Middle stream, and later ethnic arrivals limited the degree of German influence. The bulk of the German Protestants soon fitted into the middle-class elements in the community as they had in Davenport. They and the Yankees came to dominate the civil community's commercial life. Similarly, the German Catholics began integrating at a lower level on the social ladder.

Germans settled in some numbers in Springfield, Decatur, and Champaign-Urbana, where they followed the same pattern of middle-class activities and generally gained a degree of acceptance without prolonged conflict. Central Illinois, the heartland of Middle stream settlement in the State, also proved to be the area of the most intensive German settlement, in both the urban and rural areas, with both Catholic and Lutheran

Germans entering the area in number. Germans also settled in Joliet and Rockford, where they founded their own churches, entered politics, and became small but recognizable elements in both communities. Others, though far fewer in number, made their way to Superior, Duluth, and Pueblo, where they followed much the same pattern. By 1890, the flood tide of the German current had crested, though Germans continue to make up a large percentage of the contemporary overseas immigrants that settle in the cities of the prairie.[16]

At the turn of the century, a substantial number of Belgians settled in East Moline, making the Quad Cities area one of the two major centers of Belgian settlement in the United States. They were the last major group of the Continental stream to settle in the greater West, and their path was much like that of the Southern and Eastern European groups which arrived at the same time. Many of the Belgians in East Moline went into politics, where they remain influential. In general, their visible identity as an ethnic group is only beginning to lessen in the 1960's.[17]

Small but significant numbers of Hungarians and Bohemians followed the Germans to the cities of the prairie. They were even more likely to concentrate in the incipient urban centers where they were closely integrated with the German communities and paralleled their development.[18]

The Irish began to arrive at approximately the same time as the Germans, though in considerably fewer numbers. For the most part, they came in via the routes used by the Yankee stream, imported by the Yankees to supply the muscle power for the great public works projects that were to open the prairie; hence their first significant appearance in Illinois was in the northeastern part of the state. They arrived in the Joliet area as workers on the Illinois and Michigan Canal, the first great project in the greater West. Those who stayed after the canal was completed founded communities and churches and became active in politics from the start. Some of the others moved down the Illinois River to Peoria, where they settled and repeated the pattern. After 1850, the railroads brought the Irish to Rockford, Champaign, Decatur, Springfield, and the Quad Cities area, where they formed small but politically active minorities. Duluth attracted an Irish element which drifted up from the unsuccessful Irish colonization schemes that were tried after the Civil War in southern and central Minnesota. The Irish in the Madison-St. Clair Counties area came in somewhat later to work in the factories there while those who settled in Pueblo came as individuals to seek their fortunes in the gold regions.

Like the Germans, the Irish tended to settle in cities, in their case not because of any particular urban bias but because they initially lacked the skills or resources to do much other than contribute raw muscle power to the public works projects of their day. Few of them were prepared to undertake the already specialized task of farming the prairies for commercial gain (though Irish farming communities were developed in Champaign County, among other places) and, except for canal and railroad projects, their muscles were of use only in urban areas. This, of course, meant their consignment to the lowest and least influential levels of society in the cities of the prairie, as in the nation as a whole, for many years. As unskilled laborers, often barely literate, devoutly Catholic, and given to indulging in the pleasures of the poor, they represented the antithesis of the Protestant ideal of the good life. In this, they were unlike any previous element that settled in the northern cities of the prairie up to that time and suffered discrimination accordingly. Since the well-established people in those communities were Republicans, they entered the Democratic fold and became leaders of the local Democratic party organizations. Thus the proverbial Irish inclination for entering politics as a means for social advancement displayed itself even in the cities of the prairie, where their number remained relatively small. However, except in Joliet, where enough of them settled to ultimately come to dominate local politics, and, to a considerably lesser extent, in Rockford, where they gained power in a ward or two, they did not become influential as a group in the cities of the prairie, though they have produced their share of influential individuals as they have moved upward on the socioeconomic scale. Though the Irish have since risen and are now distributed among all socioeconomic levels, they have retained a unique sense of religious and even ethnic solidarity even where their communities are small.[19]

Scandinavians began arriving in the greater West after 1830 but did not arrive in sufficient numbers to affect the cities of the prairie until after 1850. They, too, came via the northern route and were among the first settlers to take advantage of the Yankee-built railroads. They generally settled in the same territory as the Yankees as well, concentrating wherever the railroad tracks ended at the time of their arrival or wherever the railroad companies promoted their colonization.

Because, of all the Illinois cities reached by the railroad in 1852, Rockford was the closest approximation of "home" to the first large group from Sweden to reach the greater West, it became the leading Scandinavian city in Illinois. With topography, vegetation, and a climate like the Upper Midwest, Rockford's very setting appealed to the Scandinavians. Moreover, the city's manufacturing orientation offered an outlet for the talents of Swedish craftsmen and mechanics just as its water power potential had first attracted the Yankees. Since 1852, Scandinavians have continued to come to Rockford to give that civil community its distinctive character as the largest and most visible element in its population.

The Quad Cities attracted quite a large number of Swedes as the railroad reached the Mississippi at Rock Island in 1854, for similar reasons.

That area offered a good test of the basic affinity between the Scandinavians and the Yankees. Rather than settle in more cosmopolitan and "wide open" Rock Island, the Swedish immigrants, who found work in the newly established agricultural implement factories of John Deere (a Yankee), established themselves in the adjacent village of Moline, a more staid Yankee community much like Rockford.

The Scandinavians, like the Yankees, moved northwest rather than southwest, so relatively few settled in the central or southern Illinois cities or in Pueblo. Being a northern people, they sought familiar northern lands to remind them of home. In doing so, they fell in with another northern people, the Yankees. Though relations between the two groups did not begin with great cordiality, the similarities between them generally brought about a reasonably rapid rapprochement. Protestant Scandinavians were much like the Yankees in their values, outlook, and behavior patterns. Their settlement in Rockford and Moline strongly reinforced the Yankee political patterns and added some new facets to the local communitarian spirit, in the way of an active cooperative movement and, later, a socialist political movement which functioned at the local level. In both communities the Scandinavian element remains highly visible, and the Swedes, Danes, and Norwegians maintained active ethnic identities in the 1960's.

Small groups of Scandinavians did settle in Joliet and Peoria, situated as they were on the border between northern and central Illinois. They have remained visible and politically identifiable at least to a limited degree, adding to the polyglot character of both civil communities that is so typical of Middle stream-dominated areas. The Illinois Central Railroad brought others into Champaign and Decatur and even Springfield, where their impact as a group was slight. Pueblo attracted a few on the same basis.

Duluth and Superior were in a different category entirely. They were properly placed geographically and were developed at the right time to attract large elements from all the Scandinavian countries plus Finland. To those cities, the Scandinavians became what the Germans were to Belleville and Davenport. In both, they overwhelmed the earlier settlers to establish their way of life as the visibly dominant mode in the community.

Unlike most of the other immigrant groups, the Scandinavian settlers tended to seek out the unsettled frontierlands from the first. They did not like to settle in large numbers in areas whose cultural patterns were already set, so they either settled new areas on their own or went into sparsely settled areas inhabited by people with a generally similar cultural background. This was not necessarily done by design, though, like the Yankees whom they resembled, the Scandinavians were colonizers who frequently settled in groups after first sending parties ahead to scout the land. Furthermore, they settled on the land as well as in the cities, thus integrating themselves into the overall environment and contributing to the maintenance of the ties between city and country that are characteristic of most of the cities of the prairie.

The extent to which the Scandinavians in the Upper Mississippi Valley fitted into the established patterns is revealed by their massive conversion to Republicanism so soon after their arrival in this country. By 1860 they, like the Yankees among whom they settled, were strong Republican partisans, an allegiance which they have generally retained—in Illinois almost totally and to a lesser extent in the other states. Their contribution to the Illinois Republican organization is the John Ericsson Republican League, which continues to function with varying degrees of influence in the northern half of the state. Contrast this with the Germans, who split in their party allegiance, at least partly along religious lines, depending on the level of their local acceptance, or with the Irish, whose social position literally drove them into the Democratic party.[20]

Elements from the Mediterranean and Eastern European streams arrived in the greater West even before the Civil War, but as groups with recognizable effects on the body politic, their appearance can be dated from the last two decades of the nineteenth century. About 1890, a substantial group of Italians came into the greater West, settling primarily in Rockford, Davenport, Joliet, Peoria, and East Moline in the north and in the industrial areas of Madison and St. Clair Counties in the south. Smaller groups of Italians settled in the other cities of the prairie. The Italians, like the other Mediterranean and Slavic groups, were drawn to the urban frontier and settled in the cities almost exclusively, where they became workers in the factories or in service industries serving an urban population. While they did not necessarily come from urban areas in Europe, they had been accustomed to living in relatively close quarters even in their "rural" villages. Their adjustment to the city was eased by this background, and they, like the Germans, brought a basically urban (though, in their case, not particularly urbane) quality into the cities of the prairie. Not unexpectedly, wherever they were numerous enough to constitute a recognizable group, they were relegated to the bottom rung on the social ladder, a position vacated by the Irish in their favor. This led them into a minority Democratic party, where they found a reasonably warm reception and into political activity as a means for economic betterment and social advancement.[21]

The Greeks also came at the turn of the century but, like the Jews, in relatively small numbers to engage in commerce rather than join the working class on the urban frontier. While they are rarely identifiable as a significant political element in any of the civil communities of this study, some have settled in virtually every one. East Moline and Davenport are the only civil communities with sizable Greek populations. Like the Jews, they have tended to avoid political activity as a group except in East

Moline, where they are reckoned as one of the important groups in the local political coalition of "ethnics."[22]

The complex of Slavic immigrant groups is often confusing to local "outsiders," who remain perpetually uncertain of who comes from where east of the Elbe River. Like the Italians, the Slavic groups all came late and settled on the urban frontier as its "hewers of wood and drawers of water." Joliet attracted Slovenians, Slovaks, Poles, Russians, Serbs, and Croatians, who came at the same time to work in the local steel industry. Rockford attracted small groups of Poles, Lithuanians, Ukrainians, and Russians. Similar groups scattered themselves throughout the Quad Cities area, in lesser numbers since the Belgians, Italians, and Greeks generally preempted the opportunities available to such groups there. Peoria attracted even fewer people of Slavic origin, most of whom settled across the river in the East Peoria area. Indeed, as one moves southward, fewer Slavic elements are found in the cities of the prairie. Springfield, Decatur, and Champaign attracted Italians and Greeks and, in some cases, Negroes, to fill the tasks that the Slavic groups handled in the northern cities, insofar as those tasks existed in basically nonindustrialized cities. The largest influx of Slavs south of Highway 6 was in the American Bottoms opposite St. Louis. East St. Louis attracted large numbers from Eastern Europe and the Balkans. Many more settled in the Madison County bottomland cities created for the industrial expansion of the post-1870's. In Illinois, the Slavic groups remained politically inarticulate for a long time, only recently showing any signs of political activity and concern.

As a general rule, Slavic and Balkan groups settled wherever there was a steel industry. This is partly because the steel companies engaged in active recruitment of men from both currents for their factories and partly because this type of heavy industrial employment offered the Slavs the best opportunities they could hope for on their arrival in the New World. Certainly the large Slavic and Balkan communities of Pueblo and Duluth, both off the beaten track of the American industrial belt, offer testimony to this effect. Duluth has substantial numbers of what are called locally "South Europeans," primarily Slovenians and Croatians, whose principal place of employment is the United States Steel plant in that city. Pueblo has a large population of Slovenians who were brought in to work at the Colorado Fuel and Iron Company mills. In both cities, these steelworkers became politically active with some rapidity, drawn as they were into the "party of the underdog" in each case. In both, their representatives have risen to positions of considerable importance. This was very likely a consequence of their settlement in cities so close to their original frontier stage that local patterns of political power and influence had not yet crystallized, leaving room for even the newest ethnic groups to penetrate.[23]

Most of the elements descended from the European streams which arrived earliest are today only slightly more identifiable to the naked eye than those of the three native streams. In some of the civil communities, generally those which have continued to attract immigrants from the same countries (such as the Swedes in Rockford and the Germans in Davenport and Belleville), their component groups have retained some sense of ethnic identity. In such communities they maintain a number of voluntary organizations as well as the usual churches through which they can still be identified. By and large, the Jews and the Scandinavians are the most ethnically conscious, the Germans next, and the Irish, while individually conscious of their Irish background, maintain the fewest specifically ethnic institutions. This is largely because, in most of the cities of the prairie, they dominate the Catholic Church, which preserves their identity in relation to non-Catholics while enabling them to set the standards for other Catholics the way the descendants of the Yankees do for Protestants, and are thus less constrained to work at maintaining a separate identity.

The most overt, visible ethnic manifestations in the cities of the prairie are found among those who are products of the later set of European streams. Generally speaking, there are substantial communities of first and second generation Americans drawn from those streams which can still be identified without much difficulty. This is true though the process of assimilation is much more rapid in the medium-size civil communities than in the larger ones or even the smaller ones (where such communities stand out more prominently). In 1960 it was still possible to find ethnic neighborhoods in cities like Joliet, Rockford, Peoria, Duluth, and Pueblo, though in most cases they are disappearing as the new generation moves out onto the suburban frontier.

The flow of the European streams radically diminished in intensity with the close of mass migration after World War I. The trickle that persists, continues to follow the same patterns as the earlier flows, like attracting like to each civil community. Since World War II, there has been somewhat of an increase in immigration. Just under four million immigrants from Europe have entered the United States since 1945, a percentage of whom came to the cities of the prairie to settle among relatives and friends, where their presence often reactivated latent ethnic impulses among their brethren who had preceded them generations earlier.[24]

The Two Canadian Streams

Usually overlooked in the history of immigration to the United States are the hundreds of thousands of Canadians who have migrated southward since the early nineteenth century. While certainly not foreign in the way the European streams were, Canada was something more than another North American filter for Old World cultures. Rather, it left its imprint on two streams which emanated from within its borders.

The French-Canadian stream, whose representatives migrated primarily to New England, contributed extremely little to the shaping of the cities of the greater West. Culturally, it was markedly similar to the Southern stream among the native ones and the Irish stream from Europe. As a stream, it touched the sphere only in the early days of the fur trade leaving some demographic residues on the southwestern peripheries of Duluth at Fond-du-Lac and scattered families wherever there had been permanent forts to serve the traders and trappers. In neither case has a French-Canadian "presence" been maintained.

The Anglo-Canadian stream was overwhelmingly dominated by descendants of English, Scottish, and Northern European stock. That, combined with the influence exerted by the Canadian experience, gave it a strong affinity for the culture of the native Yankee stream and close ties with the North Sea and English streams as well. As a consequence, while Canadians settled widely throughout the greater West, they mainly followed in the paths of the Yankees and rarely acquired a distinctive communal or cultural identity of their own. Hence their influence as a stream is extraordinarily difficult to isolate.

Anglo-Canadians settled most heavily in the northern reaches of the greater West, the areas closest to their native land. Among the cities of the prairie, Duluth and Superior led in attracting them. Substantial groups of Anglo-Canadians settled in both cities to quietly reinforce the relatively few Yankees and provide a leaven of New World leadership for the "ethnics" in the city. Other significant Anglo-Canadian concentrations developed in the Quad Cities, Rockford, and Peoria, in that order of magnitude, where they also reinforced the Yankee and similar streams.[25]

The Three "Excluded" Streams

The United States, and the cities of the prairie, have been touched with varying intensity by three non-European streams whose different or apparently different racial characteristics have led them to be excluded at one time or another from the mainstream of American life and degraded as irrevocably unassimilable into the larger American society. These streams, Afro-American, Hispanic, and Oriental, have in each case generated major social problems because of their non-European character and the exclusion they have been forced to endure—the problems of "the American dilemma"—which have not yet been solved. Despite great differences among these three streams, they share certain common characteristics ranging from an inward-orientation produced by their original relegation to lower caste status by white Americans and the differences in political values and behavior patterns between them and the other streams that stem from their common subject-orientation in politics extending back to their pre-American existence. The separate Negro churches produced by segregation, the linguistically segregated Catholic churches of the Hispanic stream, and the altogether unique Buddhism of the Orientals simultaneously reflected and heightened their caste-like separation.

The first, most widespread, and most important of these is the Afro-American stream, which is, in reality, as authentically native as any of the three native streams discussed earlier. Though African slaves were brought into every colony, the Afro-American stream as ultimately constituted flowed westward from the South, where the black population was concentrated, after as many generations of acculturation on American shores as the other native streams. The first blacks to enter Illinois and its civil communities were brought in as slaves. Indeed, the state's "compromise of 1824" barely managed to prevent the legalization of slavery in Illinois and then only at the price of a "black code" which effectively prevented free Negroes from settling in the state. Actually it was not until 1845 when new, Yankee-influenced state judges ruled slavery unconstitutional in any form that Negro slavery disappeared in Illinois, and it took the Republican triumph in the Civil War to achieve repeal of the black code. So, while there were black men in Illinois prior to 1862, the flow of the Afro-American stream really began with the migration of freed slaves northward from the Confederacy in that year.

Table 4–1 traces the growth of the black population in the cities of the prairie from 1820 to 1960. With the exception of the Peoria metropolitan area, every one of them recorded a spurt in black population between

TABLE 4-1

Cities of the Prairie: Afro-American Population, 1840-1960

	1840	1850	1860	1870	1880	1890	1900	1910	1920	1930	1940	1950	1960
Madison County	343	449	562	2,214	2,701	2,442	2,817	3,146	6,750	3,981	7,128	9,532	11,933
Alton	(10 slaves)	170	187	380	595	681	896	1,160	1,707	2,714	2,943	3,842	4,944
Granite City	—	—	—	—	—	—	154	18	7	5	3	12	55
St. Clair County	460	581	525	1,297	2,577	2,430	3,987	8,110	10,136	15,550	21,567	34,566	
Belleville	(59 slaves)	—	85	157	236	241	230	216	180	178	154	196	195
East St. Louis	—	—	—	100	513	772	1,799	5,882	7,437	11,536	16,798	27,555	36,338
Peoria County	9	86	126	155	512	966	1,535	1,737	2,334	3,216	3,091	6,276	10,157
Peoria	—	84	109	130	482	864	1,402	1,569	2,130	3,037	2,826	5,646	9,584
Tazewell County	20	36	43	64	87	60	24	25	57	42	16	38	14
Pekin	—	—	—	—	26	14	4	8	31	1	0	0	3
Sangamon County	175	253	311	1,166	1,822	2,339	3,106	3,633	3,256	3,635	3,609	4,479	5,923
Springfield	(6 slaves)	171	203	808	1,328	1,798	2,227	2,961	2,769	3,324	3,357	4,285	5,632
Macon County	3	3	83	235	352	605	656	906	1,283	1,976	2,144	3,482	6,004
Decatur	—	—	78	163	224	510	620	776	1,178	1,947	2,098	3,438	5,949

TABLE 4-1 (continued)

	1840	1850	1860	1870	1880	1890	1900	1910	1920	1930	1940	1950	1960
Rock Island County	8	2	24	137	534	379	601	822	1,553	1,488	1,517	2,426	4,290
Moline	–	–	1	25	132	261	488	281	338	302	318	42	338
Rock Island	–	–	21	60	180	126	282	397	754	680	705	156	2,754
Scott County	8	14	39	246	266	274	496	572	745	865	884	1,150	1,886
Davenport	–	10	25	210	231	261	488	569	681	787	801	1,120	1,778
Will County	10	33	57	242	703	503	1,244	1,134	1,374	3,131	3,410	5,886	11,915
Joliet	–	12	36	35	98	327	650	497	701	1,309	1,305	1,950	4,638
Winnebago County	4	12	34	121	140	170	238	257	581	1,305	1,419	3,882	8,574
Rockford	(1 slave)	–	33	83	99	143	212	197	490	1,110	1,190	2,499	5,323
Champaign County	–	2	48	233	462	411	551	950	1,620	2,040	2,135	4,533	6,770[a]
Champaign	–	–	31	123	273	250	404	759	1,234	1,598	1,802	3,118	4,520
Urbana	–	–	10	40	–	66	71	117	335	394	304	699	1,253
Douglas County	–	–	4	7	8	68	190	184	117	62	43	53	31
Superior	–	–	4	7	8	68	186	182	107	51	27	44	21
St. Louis County	–	–	–	22	13	228	370	439	531	453	349	383	624
Duluth	–	–	–	22	13	220	357	410	495	416	314	334	565
Pueblo County	–	–	–	27	147	904	1,404	1,689	1,455	1,333	1,420	1,714	2,247
Pueblo	–	–	–	14	–	877	1,213	1,498	1,395	1,305	1,381	1,441	2,026

[a]Total less than figures for Champaign and Urbana combined.

1860 and 1870. This spurt continued in all except Winnebago County through 1880, after which there was an absolute decline in black population in many of the civil communities, with growth continuing in Springfield and Decatur. The turn of the century brought another spurt in black migration northward, which ended in the 1920's. About the time of the Korean War, the flow began to accelerate again. In the more northerly cities, black people did not become a significant group on the local scene until the migration of the post-World-War-II period, which, however, was so extensive that it even reached as far north as Duluth. Generally speaking, however, the Afro-American stream has hardly touched them. The stream also slowed up as it reached the arid lands of the West, though, as in the case of the far north, in recent years it has picked up momentum in its westward flow, as the increase of the black population in Pueblo indicates. During the 1960's, the Afro-American stream has continued to flow in strength into the cities of the prairie, bringing them basically unskilled and undereducated elements for whom jobs must be found or relief provided and who are just beginning to gain a sense of political consciousness.

Table 4–1 also reveals the intensity of urbanization among the Negroes of the cities of the prairie. Despite their almost exclusively rural backgrounds in the South, they were forced by outside pressures to congregate in the cities as they moved northward. This is even true in the face of a tendency in those civil communities to force the Negroes into marginal unincorporated suburban slum areas outside the central city's corporate limits.

Within the civil communities with substantial Negro populations that extend back to the turn of the century or earlier, the Negro stream is not all of a piece. The oldtimers, usually the descendants of domestic servants or railroad workers who settled in their respective communities unobtrusively and quietly adjusted themselves into the local residential and educational patterns (always remembering their "place"), are frequently less than sympathetic toward the newcomers who come in large numbers from very different cultural environments and socioeconomic backgrounds, who by their very existence call attention, often unfavorable, to "the Negro problem." Before the eruption of the civil rights revolution, many of these oldtimers refused to have anything to do with their newly arrived brethren. In Champaign, for example, a number of them joined the Catholic Church in an effort to further separate themselves from those of their race whom they considered to be less desirable.

Politically, the Negroes were quiescent subjects within the civil community until the civil rights revolution. The oldtimers sought to enhance their protective coloration by supporting the majority party locally. In the predominantly Republican civil communities, this meant that they remained Republican while the newcomers, if they voted at all, were strongly Democratic in the national Negro pattern. The articulate newcomers, in turn, looked upon the oldtimers as "Uncle Toms," willing to kowtow to the dominant white community in return for the meager reward of anonymity. Since the early 1960's visible black political activity has increased measurably, but, while the old subject status is dying, no fixed patterns of local involvement have yet developed.[26]

The Hispanic (or Latin, as its members prefer to be called) stream is particularly unique in that it flows northward from the Caribbean area or from Mexico. Though its members are ostensibly of European descent, few do not share at least some Indian (or Negro) ancestry and all are products of some four centuries of Latin American culture, which has become dominant in their lives. The first wave of the Hispanic stream entered what is now the southwestern United States when it was Spanish territory in colonial days. Originally confined to an arc sweeping from Texas through Arizona and New Mexico and up the coast of California, it spread into Colorado beginning in the middle of the nineteenth century and eastward to the Mississippi about the time of World War I. By the end of World War II, it had established itself as far as the eastern limits of the greater West, occupying a place in the Anglo social order not unlike that of the Negroes in the northeast. Like the Negroes, the Latins share few of the dominant values and behavior patterns of Anglo society and find it difficult to advance up the social ladder even when presented with opportunities to do so.

Though a Mexican colony settled on the site of present-day Pueblo in the 1840's (before the arrival of the "Anglos"), the colonists were compelled to evacuate the area by the Indians, and Pueblo's present substantial Hispanic minority (the largest ethnic minority group in that civil community) is of almost contemporary origin. Latin Americans began to arrive in numbers about 1915 as agricultural workers to serve as field hands on the large farms located on St. Charles Mesa near the city and, after 1940, as urban dwellers to work in the city's heavy industrial establishments. They have formed a large, strongly Spanish-speaking minority in Pueblo, predominantly confined to the lowest socioeconomic levels, living in urban and suburban slum communities, dominated by bosses who control their political lives by dominating their relations with the larger civil community. In this way, the Mexicans are rendered politically inarticulate, though some among them, particularly veterans of military service in World War II who came to know the "outside world," have taken steps to change this system in the past half-generation. In this they have had help from the Catholic Church in the area.

Flowing eastward, a substantial Hispanic community has developed in the Quad Cities area with "branches" in Davenport and East Moline but centered primarily in Silvis, where their church is located. Many of these Latins came as migrant agricultural workers and found "permanent" industrial jobs. Most, however, were imported to work in the railroad yards and have had to adjust to the ups and downs of postwar railroading. Other communities have developed in Joliet and in the Madison-St. Clair Counties area, where they have entered local industry at the lowest level. Smaller groups have settled in Duluth, Decatur, Springfield, and Rockford. In the first four areas mentioned, they are an easily identifiable and still-unassimilated ethnic minority with problems somewhat like those of the blacks. As in Pueblo, they remain substantially alone and isolated from the larger community and have little political role or influence. There, too, their war veterans have sparked movements to change the situation. Unlike their southwestern brethren, however, they are considered by the Anglos to add "local color" to their respective civil communities; hence their ceremonies are featured in the local press and they are looked upon more sympathetically by the general population. In the last four, they are too few in number to be treated as other than local exotica. Like the Afro-American stream, the Hispanic one is continuing to flow as an identifiable stream of migration.[27]

The cities of the prairie have been little affected by the Oriental stream. Except for individual families, few Orientals have settled within their civil communities. Perhaps the greatest concentration of people of Oriental descent whose communal ties are still visible is in Duluth, where they settled in the days when that city was an important point on the overland route to the Far East. Like the Jews and Greeks, they tied to local commerce but at a very low level and have remained far more quiescent politically.[28]

By and large, the assimilation of these non-European streams into the mainstream of American society represents the major cultural problem facing the United States today. Since it is first and foremost a local problem, it becomes one of particular importance in the cities of the prairie, several of which are facing the problem for the first time in their histories. In the discussion of community politics in the following sections of this study, it will be easy to give the impression of smoothness and integration of the various elements within each civil community. With respect to these "minority groups," there has been little smoothness and often less integration, a matter of some concern in the maintenance of the political systems of the cities of the prairie.

The Streams and Their Contemporary Status

In substance, the social structure of the cities of the prairie has been determined by the settlement and fusion of the fifteen streams and their various currents into civil communities. The political systems of those civil communities reflect the social product of the fusion of some or all of those streams and the stresses and strains generated by their enforced proximity. Though all fifteen streams continue to flow into the cities, their diminished intensity means that the forms of their cultural deposits are generally established in each and are now subject to erosion by other migrations or to distortion, transmutation, and redirection through the simple passage of time.

Migration as a social phenomenon continues to be of the utmost importance in the cities of the prairie as in American life generally. As the number of foreign-born migrants in those cities has dropped to what is in all probability its lowest point in over a century (Table 4–2), internal migration has once again come to the fore as a means of disturbing local social and political patterns. Internal migration today has two aspects. On one hand there is the continuing cross-country flow of people seeking better opportunities of one sort or another. The predominant cross-country flow is still westward, though the northward flow from the greater South has become a close second and is apparently the most important in all the cities of the prairie except Pueblo. Table 4–2 indicates that, in 1960, the only cities having acquired less than 10 per cent of their total populations from outside their counties since 1955 were Alton and East St. Louis, both of which were experiencing the difficulties of older "central cities" whose new settlers are settling outside the city limits. Eliminating Champaign and Urbana, whose status as university centers brings in a large transient population, the remainder of the cities of the prairie have added from 10.4 to 17.5 per cent of their 1960 populations by the addition of migrants from other counties. This is true even of Superior, which has lost more population through out-migration than it has been able to gain through in-migration and births, and of Duluth, whose growth has been so slight as to constitute a relative loss. Six of the civil communities (Belleville, Davenport, Decatur, Peoria, Rockford, and Rock Island) actually gained 15 per cent or better from intercounty migration between 1955 and 1960.

At the same time, intra-metropolitan migration has become an even more important phenomenon. In not one of the cities of the prairie did as many as 56 per cent of the population reside in the same house in

TABLE 4-2

Nativity and Migration in the Cities of the Prairie, 1960

Civil Community[1]	Nativity: Per Cent Foreign Born	Nativity: Per Cent Native of Foreign/Mixed Parentage	Nativity: Total Foreign Stock	Migration: Residents in Same House[2]	Migration: Migrants from Different County[3]
Alton[a]	1.8	6.7	8.5	54.5	9.7
Belleville[a]	2.3	11.0	13.3	51.1	15.0
Champaign[a]	2.9	8.7	11.6	30.8	36.9
Davenport[a]	2.9	13.5	16.4	47.0	17.5
Decatur[b]	1.4	6.0	7.4	46.1	15.4
Duluth[a]	8.9	27.9	36.8	53.3	12.3
E. St. Louis[a]	2.1	6.1	8.2	51.6	7.8
Joliet[b]	5.3	21.0	26.3	54.9	13.8
Moline[a]	5.9	18.3	24.2	53.2	12.9
Peoria[b]	2.4	9.7	12.1	48.7	15.3
Pueblo[b]	3.9	13.5	17.4	49.9	13.5
Rockford[b]	6.1	17.2	23.3	46.4	15.4
Rock Island[a]	3.7	14.1	17.8	48.8	15.6
Springfield[b]	3.2	11.2	14.4	51.3	13.5
Superior[a]	7.2	27.5	34.7	55.9	10.4
Urbana[a]	4.5	8.2	12.7	31.6	37.5

[a] city
[b] urbanized area
[1] Approximate definition only since figures are available by city or urbanized area only.
[2] Residents in same house since 1955.
[3] Migrants who arrived from different county since 1955.

1960 as they had in 1955. Even excluding Champaign and Urbana, in six of the fourteen remaining civil communities, less than 50 per cent were residents of the same house. This great intra-metropolitan migration, a manifestation of the metropolitan frontier, does much to prevent the hardening of social and political patterns even within the civil community.

The intimate connections between the ebb and flow of the migratory streams and the state of the frontier can hardly escape unnoticed. As long as the rural-land frontier offered the greatest opportunities, the streams flowed in a generally westward direction into new territory, urban and rural. With the rise of the urban-industrial frontier and its spread westward and southward, the streams began to flow from rural to urban areas within each section as well. This shift in direction did not end the generally westward trend of migration in the United States, which continues to this day, but it did redirect the forward progress of all the streams into urban centers. More recently, the emergence of the metropolitan-technological frontier has again redirected the main flow of the now-modified streams, this time within the metropolitan areas from the urban centers into suburban and exurban locations, where their influence continues.

In Rockford, for example, the movement of the Yankee stream can be traced from the third ward (downtown on the west bank of the Rock River) into the fourth ward (somewhat north of downtown on the west bank) in the early years of the twentieth century and from there northward into the outer reaches of the fourth ward. In the 1950's the descendants of the Yankees crossed to the east bank of the river to settle in the outer reaches of the first ward, or even outside the city proper, in its upper-middle and upper-class suburban developments, where they were joined by those descendants of the other streams who had also prospered. Since they are, by and large, mainstays of the industrial, commercial, and professional elites in that very middle-class civil community, their move outside the city limits meant a loss of middle-class political power. Recognizing this, they began an annexation movement that added much of the suburban fringe to the city. Then, to restore their influence, they obtained a redistricting of ward boundaries in favor of the new settlers in those areas, the construction of a new high school within the first ward, and several other very tangible manifestations of a geographic shift in the locus of influentials within the civil community. At the same time, the influx of new people into those same annexed areas since World War II has forced older elites to reach an accommodation with them as well, thus forcing their relatively insular approach to the civil community's problems to open somewhat.

The erosive effects of time are clearly visible in the cities of the prairie. Because of their medium-size populations, the streams that came together within them have tended to blend more rapidly and more thoroughly than their larger sisters, since it is difficult to develop the "cities within cities" necessary for their clear-cut, visible preservation. In this respect, America's proverbial "melting pot" has melted with greater intensity in the medium-size metropolitan areas than anywhere else, including the small rural communities, where the lack of in-migration after the initial settlement period has helped the semi-isolated original ethnic cultures in their attempts to maintain themselves.

The various streams and currents in the contemporary cities of the prairie manifest themselves in several ways. (See Table 4–3.) Ethnic

TABLE 4-3

Characteristics of Comparable Streams in the Cities of the Prairie

Streams			Modal Characteristics
Native Stream	European Stream	Excluded Stream	
Yankee	North Sea Anglo-Canadian Jewish		Calvinistic Protestant (Congregational or Presbyterian), Communitarian, Entrepreneurial, Middle Class, Republican, fiercely loyal as a group to one party or fiercely independent.[a]
Middle	English Continental Irish		Catholic or Hierarchical Liturgical Protestant. Individualist and Pluralist, Multiclass, Entrepreneurial. Mixed party loyalties.
Southern	Mediterranean Eastern European French Canadian	Hispanic Afro-American	Single dominant religion or "color." Individualist but kinship oriented. Originally working class, Overt ethnic identity, Democratic.

[a]The Jewish stream deviates from these modal characteristics in several respects.

identification is still significant, particularly among the latest arrivals, but is diminishing in importance. In certain cases and under certain circumstances, secular ethnic associations continue to exist in the cities of the prairie, reinforcing the old divisions. The Germans have developed social clubs which continue to exist in the areas where the German minority is large, as in Belleville, Davenport, and Peoria. In the former city, German is offered in the elementary schools. The Scandinavians have been particularly successful in maintaining a number of institutions ranging from the John Ericsson Republican Club—strong in Rockford—to various singing societies and including a historical society which has social as well as scholarly functions. In Rockford, Swedish is offered in the high schools. The Jews maintain various quasi-religious associations such as B'nai B'rith, community welfare federations, and supplementary schools to teach their children of the Jewish heritage, as do the Greeks to a lesser extent. Among the third-wave ethnic groups, many clubs and associations, both political and social, are still active, but there is some question as to whether they will perpetuate themselves after the first and second generations pass from the scene. For the blacks, race is still a markedly important manifestation with *de facto* segregation widespread. In a few communities, the differences among streams or currents have crystallized along class lines while in a few others apparently unrelated associational ties have become vehicles for maintaining cultural distinctiveness.

The streams are best manifested today through the religious institutions and associations which their representatives organized upon settlement. Religious association has become the great universal and visible survival of the original cultures of each stream, and the primary institutional means for perpetuating those cultures by transmitting them from generation to generation and assimilating into them individuals from other streams. The Protestant religious associations themselves have crystallized into several interdenominational bands, each of which reflects a contemporary version of the original socioreligious patterns of the streams. These bands are not clear-cut, but they can be identified with reasonable accuracy. Among the Protestants, one, embracing most Congregationalists, northern Presbyterians, Unitarians, Reformed, and American Baptists, comprises a Calvinist-produced, socially oriented, doctrinally liberal grouping that reflects the cultural synthesis of the Yankee, North Sea, and Anglo-Canadian streams. Another, embracing most Episcopalians, the border state Presbyterian offshoots, northern Methodists, and Lutherans, represents the synthesis of the Middle, English, and elements of the Continental streams. Moving toward synthesis with those streams are the Mediterranean and Eastern European Catholics and the Eastern Orthodox.[29] A third, embracing the Southern Baptists, most southern Methodists and Presbyterians, "gospel" churches, and the Negro branches of all four, reflects the still clearly distinct Southern stream. Within its apparently monolithic structure, the Catholic Church is divided into two or three bands—the "puritan" churches, dominated by the Irish and English, the more indulgent churches founded by Southern Europeans, and a group in the middle composed of the moderately indulgent Central and Eastern European Catholics. The Jewish synagogue associations represent a final band. A partial listing of denominations by category is provided in Table 4–3.

The overall location of each of the cities of the prairie within the three broad bands of the indigenous currents, the flow patterns of all the currents which affected them, and the contemporary manifestations of the currents are shown in Table 4–4.

TABLE 4-4

The Streams and Currents and Their Contemporary Manifestations

Civil Community and Location in the Three-Stream Pattern	Initial Stream(s) of Settlement			Second Wave Stream(s)		
	Current(s)	Date of Initiation[a]	Present Manifestations	Current(s)	Date of Initiation[a]	Present Manifestations
Alton (S)	S[b], y[c], m	1815	Churches	G, e	1830	Churches
Belleville (S)	S, y, a	1815	Churches	G, e, j	1830	Churches, associations
Champaign (M)	M, Y, g, e, i, j, a	1855	Churches, associations	it, gr	1890	Churches, associations
Davenport (M)	M, Y, s	1835	Churches	G, sc, j, i	1845	Churches
Decatur (M)	S, M	1825	Churches	Y, M, S		Churches
Duluth (Y)	y, m, s, g, e, i	1855	Churches, upper middle class	EE, j	1890	Churches, associations, working class
E. Moline-Silvis (M)	B, EE, Gr, It	1905	Churches, associations, political clubs	—	—	—
E. St. Louis (S)	S, m	1810	Churches	g	1830	Churches
Joliet (M)	Y, M, I, G, s, sc	1835	Churches	It, EE, hu, gr, j, a	1890	Churches, associations
Moline (Y)	Y	1840	—	Sc	1855	Churches, associations
Peoria (M)	Y, S, m	1825	Churches	G, i, j	1850	Churches, associations
Pueblo (M)	S, Y, m, g	1860	Churches, country club	EE, It, j, p, a	1890	Churches, associations
Rockford (Y)	Y	1835	Church, upper class	Sc, g, i	1850	Churches, associations, political clubs
Rock Island (M)	S, M, Y	1830	Churches	Sc	1850	Churches
Springfield (M)	S, m	1820	Churches	M, y, g, c, j	1830	Churches
Superior (Y)	—	—	—	—	—	—
Urbana (M)	M, s	1820	Churches, political division	y	1860	Churches

TABLE 4-4 (continued)

Civil Community and Location in the Three-Stream Pattern	Subsequent Streams			Streams Presently Active	
	Current(s)	Date of Initiation[a]	Present Manifestations	Current(s)	Date of Initiation[a]
Alton (S)	EE, It, j	1890	Churches, associations	S	1940
Belleville (S)	—	—	—	S, g	1945
				St. Louis outmigrants	1950
Champaign (M)	A	1920	Churches, associations	A	1950
				University faculty and students	1945
Davenport (M)	it, gr, a	1900	Churches, associations	Hs	1920
				a, s	1950
Decatur (M)	a	1890	Churches	S	contin.
				A	1920
Duluth (Y)	none	—	—	a	1955
E. Moline-Silvis (M)	H	1917	Churches, associations	b	contin.
E. St. Louis (S)	—	—	—	A, s	contin.
Joliet (M)	a, s	1915	Churches, associations	A, s	1950
				Chicago outmigrants	1955
Moline (Y)	B	1910	Churches	a	1950
Peoria (M)	It, p, a	1890	Churches, associations	A, s	1950
Pueblo (M)	h	1915	Churches, associations	H	1940
				S, m, a	1950
Rockford (Y)	It, e, a, s, j	1890	Churches, associations, political clubs	Sc	contin.
				A, s	1950
Rock Island (M)	—	—	—	A	1950
Springfield (M)	a, g	1865	Churches, associations	S	1950
	H	1890			
Superior (Y)	—	—	—	A	1955
Urbana (M)	a	1920	Churches	University faculty and students	1945
				a	

[a]Approximations
[b]Capital letters indicate major impact.
[c]Lower-case letters indicate lesser impact.

Key:
S — Southern
M — Middle
Y — Yankee
A — Afro-American
AC — Anglo-Canadian
B — Belgian
E — English
EE — East European
G — German
Gr — Greek
H — Hispanic
Hu — Hungarian
I — Irish
It — Italian
J — Jewish
NS — North Sea
P — Polish
Sc — Scandinavian

The Cultural Geology of the Cities of the Prairie: A Historical Model

The real meaning of the geology of American migration lies in the social and political dynamics produced by the meshing and clashing of the various streams in particular localities and at various historical periods. The character of political life in the United States is rooted, to a substantial extent, in this human geology, and so any understanding of community politics can come only from a proper overview of the relevant historical geology of each community.

From the data available about the cultural streams and their currents, it is possible to construct a model of the historical geology of cultural integration and conflict which is generally applicable to the cities at the eastern edge of the greater West and, with slight modifications, to those farther west as well. It can be summarily stated as follows:

In the first generation of the civil community's history (approximately between 1815 and 1847), the first streams—usually native ones—arrive and deposit the initial settlers in the locality. These settlers create the basic local institutions, including the political institutions—county government, schools, a local post office, township or village government, and some uniquely local special districts (usually concerned with adjudicating land claims). These institutions are created in a manner and form appropriate to the geohistorical location of the new civil community but along lines reminiscent of the settlers' political and social experiences in their previous regions of residence. If more than one stream arrives at the same time, concurrent sets of political institutions (often in the form of separate cities) are frequently established. These are normally merged before the end of the first generation. At first, class and reference group distinctions are held to a minimum, as the great majority of the settlers begin to strive for "success" from a more or less equal base. Only at either extreme (the rich land speculator or banker who comes west with wealth to "get in on a good thing" and the "shiftless" squatter who does not have the drive necessary to improve his economic and social position) are class differences apparent. Reference group differences exist only to reflect the existence of different streams or currents in the civil community. Consequently, random individuals who settle in the community are able to assimilate in the cultural stream most congenial to them with little difficulty.

In the second generation (1848–1876) new streams arrive, settling within the already functioning civil community. Cleavages develop be-

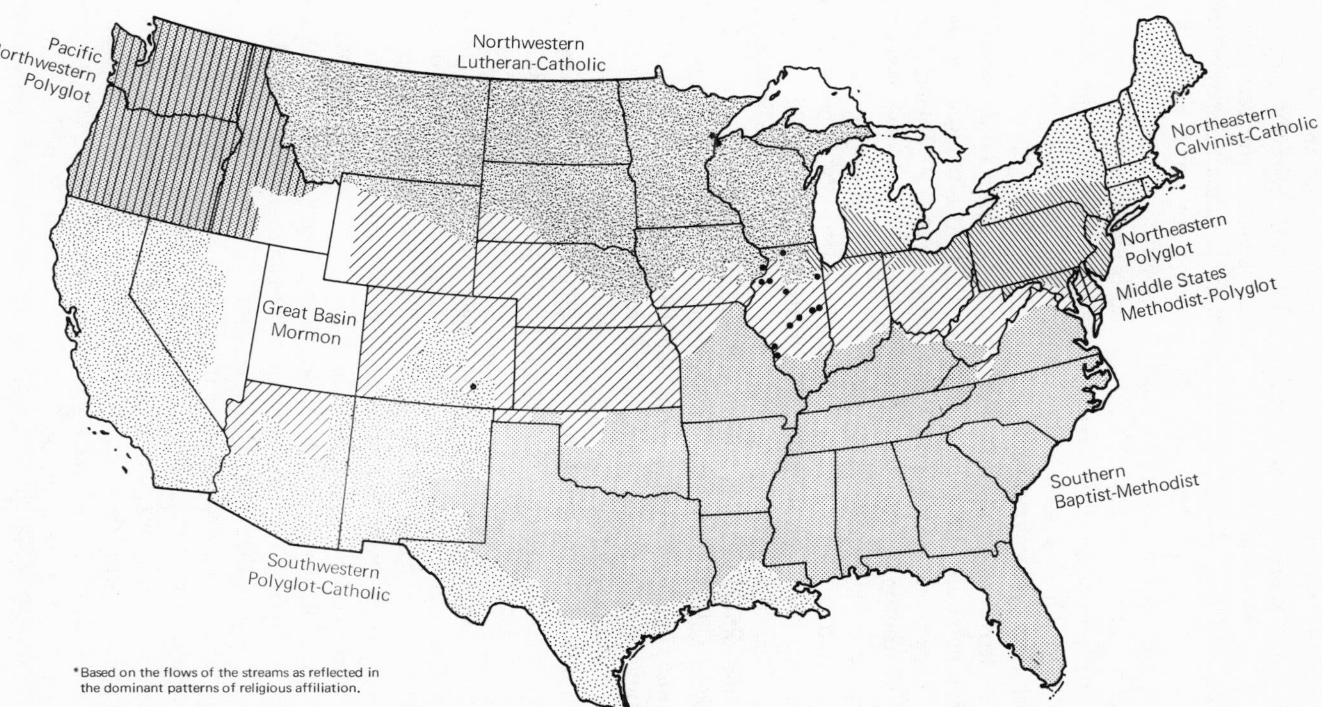

*Based on the flows of the streams as reflected in the dominant patterns of religious affiliation.

Map 10 The Cities of the Prairie and American Subcultural Areas*

tween the old settlers from the first stream(s) and the newcomers. If both streams share generally similar value and behavior patterns, the cleavage is minor and the political conflict between them relatively short. The focus of the conflict is on the adjustment of status and power arrangements to include the new elements but does not touch upon the basic "way of life" of the civil community. If, however, the new stream brings in different, or even antithetical values and behavior patterns, serious conflict is likely to erupt, based on a struggle which reflects the problem of adjusting to different ways of life, and which generally leads to intense and long-term political cleavage.

If the arrival of new streams occurs early enough in the community's second generation, the conflict may be somewhat reduced by the continued expansion of the civil community's political organization. The transition from village to city status, the expansion of local governmental services, and the expansion of the size of the governing bodies in the civil community, all tend to provide means for resolving political conflict by enlarging the political "pie" to be distributed. During this second generation, class and reference group distinctions, which are interlaced with the ethnic differences that divide the streams as well as socioeconomic differences within them, begin to emerge, making cross-stream assimilation more difficult. Almost from the beginning, these distinctions are institutionalized in the churches and church-related associations. Since the original settlers continue to directly dominate the political institutions through officeholding throughout the second generation, there is little evidence of class or reference group specialization in the political realm as yet.

The third generation (1877–1916) witnesses the arrival of the last of the new European streams and the first large-scale settlement of the "excluded" streams. These new migrations lead to political cleavages in almost every community, whose intensity varies in relation to the intensity of the cleavage between streams in the previous generation. Where the earlier streams were generally similar and conflict between them was minimal, the arrival of later, dissimilar streams tends to provoke severe conflict between the established old and the "invading" new. Where cleavage already existed between the older streams, the addition of the new cultural elements can be handled with greater ease, since many of the essential compromises have already been made. Often, the new streams harmonize well with their second-generation predecessors. In such cases, the descendants of the first generation streams are so overwhelmed numerically that they abandon open participation in politics and retreat to self-contained social preserves while maintaining as much political influence as possible through their economic dominance. In the case of the arrival of the "excluded" streams, their people can make so few demands on the civil community that they can hardly generate conflict, though they become victims of the most extreme forms of cleavage, virtual isolation by the "whites." Since the third generation represents a period of relative quiescence in regard to changes in local political institutions, there is little room for inclusion of new elements in the nearly static local political system. However, during this period members of the streams that came in the second generation generally begin to assume political positions within the civil community outside of their ethnic associations.

By the third generation, class differences have become entrenched. Social mobility is possible only in civil communities with expanding economies and then is keyed in some way to the degree of expansion. Reference groups have also matured as determinants of the local social system. Both class and reference groups are reflected to an increasing degree in the churches as the transformation from ethnic identification to religious connection becomes more pronounced. Since the religious institutions which replace the original ethnic ties represent the value patterns of the streams as a whole rather than the behavior patterns of the individual ethnic groups, assimilation from one ethnoreligious tradition to another begins to be possible, at least for favored individuals. The religious institutions are beginning to sort themselves into broad interdenominational bands, each of which reflects the values and behavior patterns of more than one stream or class. By the third generation, the cultural divisions brought into the community through the streams are being reflected in partisan political alignments, with the newer, low-status groups becoming predominantly Democratic in reaction to the solid Republicans of the older established groups.

By and large, the fourth generation (1917–1947) represents the most static one, an interregnum between the first growth of the community and its entrance upon a second long-term growth period. With little economic or political change locally, there is scarce opportunity for altering already fixed social patterns. The native and European migrations have declined, and the only active migration, if any, is from the excluded groups, who remain as excluded as ever. The tendencies of the third generation harden, though the visible ethnicism of the streams of the first and second generations continues to decline.

The fifth generation (1948 to the present) brings with it significant changes. New economic opportunities develop as a consequence of the opening of the metropolitan frontier. With them come new settlement patterns and an expansion of government activities, all of which contribute to political change and the expansion of political opportunities. Members of the later European streams enter the political arena openly and become public officeholders, partly because the older elements in the community are forced to grant them a "say." Even the excluded streams begin to be aroused and take tentative steps toward activating their latent power, such as it may be. Class lines become more fluid, returning to an approximation of the earliest periods in the community's history with a small, clearly outlined upper class that remains difficult to penetrate, a somewhat larger and equally sharply delineated lower class that remains difficult to escape, and a very broad and fluid middle class whose fuzzier class gradations can be traversed in one lifetime.

The continued decline in the visible influence of the ethnic groups heightens the role of the religious institutions in perpetuating the modified values and behavior patterns of the various streams, and individual assimilation from one stream to another becomes more common. There is a general fusion of values and behavior patterns into a community-wide subculture, which is manifested politically not only through an expansion of the recruitment of officeholders to include previously excluded elements but through a breakdown of older partisan loyalties and an increased willingness on the part of individuals to readjust their political ties on the basis of new influences. This is accompanied by a realignment of the component elements in the old system of cleavages. The cleavages generally continue, though perhaps with less intensity, but they are expressed through new issues and reflect the realignment of streams previously more influenced by forces from the outside along class and reference group divisions more characteristic of the local community. Though outside pressures remain strong and even increase, the local community in many ways becomes more autonomous as it develops local patterns of its own and an indigenous subculture which its articulate elements seek to preserve and enrich.

In the newer communities of the greater West which were founded a generation later, national pressures have tended to reduce this secular trend and compress it into four generations; the period of stasis is eliminated, with the fourth generation taking on the characteristics of the fifth. This lack of an interregnum period explains the tendency to greater social fluidity in those civil communities as well as the tendency to greater conflict between the still aggressive upper-class wealthy and the rapidly rising representatives of the lower-status streams.

The next chapter will explore some of the implications of the foregoing model in greater detail. What is most significant about the pattern within it is its potential for combining cultural continuity with social flexibility and increasing political openness. Many of the reasons for the uniqueness and viability of American society lie embedded within it.

NOTES

1. The concept of cultural streams and its relevance to the general problems of "political culture" and "national character" is discussed at greater length in Appendix B. The reader interested in the more technical aspects of this study is advised to read that appendix before examining the following chapters. Appendix B also contains a bibliographic note that sets forth the general sources for the analysis in this and the following chapter.

2. The importance of this method of transmission of values is often overlooked in political research. Its significance is spelled out in greater detail in Gerhard Lenski's recent study of contemporary religious communalism in Detroit, *The Religious Factor* (Garden City, N.Y.: Doubleday, 1961). Lenski traces many of the political manifestations of this interlocking intergenerational pattern of family-religious community-friendly clique relationship. The multidimensional ramifications of religious ties are explored in Morton King, "Measuring the Religious Variable: Nine Proposed Dimensions" in *Journal for the Scientific Study of Religion,* VI, No. 2 (Fall 1967), 173–190. King's bibliography (pp. 186–190) is a useful summary of other sources exploring this phenomenon. An extremely interesting study of the connections between religious conversion and pre-existing social relationships that help concretize the connections between religion and culture discussed here is Luther P. Gerlach and Virginia H. Hine, "Five Factors Crucial to the Growth and Spread of a Modern Religious Movement" in *Journal for the Scientific Study of Religion,* VII, No. 1 (Spring 1968), 23–40. I have suggested some ways in which religious communalism has influenced Rockford in "Churches as Molders in American Politics" in the *American Behavioral Scientist* (May 1961). The relationship of religious communalism to the patterns of migration is amply established in Edwin Scott Gaustad, *Historical Atlas of Religion in America* (New York: Harper, 1962) in which the state-by-state and county-by-county patterns of religious identification are traced, indicating a very high correlation between the streams as described here and the religious identifications of the residents in different parts of the country. For the role of individual religious denominations, see P. G. Mode, ed., *Source Book and Bibliographical Guide for American Church History* (Menasha, Wisc.: George Banta Publishing Co., 1921).

3. The foregoing generalizations, even though they are presented here in oversimplified fashion, can be shown to hold true despite a popular mythology that presents western settlement as a highly individualistic, atomistic, and even anomic, phenomenon. In point of fact, the process of migration, with its characteristic uprooting of people from the physical sources of their heritage of values and behavior patterns and its demands for readaptation to new and often very different environments and circumstances, tended to reinforce the role of religious communalism because a family's religious attachments were among the most eminently portable yet fundamentally stable items in its heritage. See, for example, Carl S. Meyer, *Moving Frontiers, Readings in the History of the Lutheran Church—Missouri Synod* (St. Louis: Concordia, 1964).

4. Based on U.S. Census Bureau statistics, the interstate migration rate has hardly changed at all in the past century. The figures today are approximately the same as in the post-Civil-War period, having been restored to that level by the post-World-War-II migrations after a slight dip from the early part of the twentieth century through the Great Depression. See U.S. Census Bureau, *Historical Statistics of the*

United States: Colonial Times to 1957, prepared with the cooperation of the Social Science Research Council (Washington, D.C., 1960). Unfortunately, the census data on the precise movements of people are very limited and quite inadequate for the purposes of this analysis; hence other means of calculating the flows of the streams have had to be used.

5. Sources useful in identifying the component elements of these three subcultures include:

(a) *General:* Frederick Jackson Turner's previously cited works; H. Richard Niebuhr, *The Social Sources of Denominationalism* (New York, 1929); Thomas G. Sanders, *Protestant Concepts of Church and State* (New York, 1964); William R. Taylor, *Cavalier and Yankee* (New York, 1961); H. H. Rammero and D. H. Aadler, *The American Teenager* (Indianapolis, 1957); Max Lerner, *America as a Civilization* (New York, 1957); Lloyd Warner, *American Life: Dream and Reality* (Chicago, 1953); Daniel J. Boorstin, *The Americans: The Colonial Experience* (New York, 1958); Daniel J. Boorstin, *The Americans: The National Experience* (New York, 1965); Edwin S. Gaustad, *Historical Atlas of Religion in America* (New York, 1962); W. W. Sweet, ed., *Religion on the American Frontier, 1783–1850*, 3 vols. (New York, 1931–1939); Frank R. Kramer, *Voices in the Valley* (Madison: The University of Wisconsin Press, 1964); George R. Stewart, *Names on the Land* (New York: Random House, 1945); Hornell N. Hart, "Selective Migration as a Factor in Child Welfare in the U.S. with Special Reference to Iowa," *University of Iowa Studies in Child Welfare*, Vol. I, No. 7 (Iowa: University of Iowa, 1921).

(b) *Southern:* W. J. Cash, *The Mind of the South* (New York: Alfred A. Knopf, 1960); Lloyd Warner et al., "Southern City" series; L. C. Gray, *History of Agriculture in the Southern United States to 1860* in Carnegie Institute, *Contributions to American Economic History*, 2 vols. (Washington, 1933); T. J. Wertenbaker, *The Old South: The Founding of American Civilization* (New York, 1942); James W. Silver, *Mississippi: The Closed Society* (New York, 1963).

(c) *Middle States:* Eric F. Goldman, "Middle States Regionalism and American Historiography: A Suggestion," in Eric F. Goldman, ed., *Historiography and Urbanization* (Baltimore: The Johns Hopkins Press, 1941); A. B. Hollingshead, *Elmtown's Youth* (New York, 1949); John R. Seeley et al., *Community Chest* (Toronto: University of Toronto Press, 1957); W. Lloyd Warner et al., *Democracy in Jonesville* (New York: Harper, 1949); T. J. Wertenbaker, *The Founding of American Civilization: The Middle Colonies* (New York: 1938).

(d) *Yankee:* A primary if popularized account of this stream and its impact can be found in Stewart H. Holbrook's *The Yankee Exodus* (New York: Macmillan, 1950). See also Merle Curti, *The Making of an American Community* (Stanford: Stanford University Press, 1959); Arnold M. Rose, "The Mormon Church and Utah Politics: An Abstract of a Statistical Study," *American Sociological Review*, VII (1942); Louis Kimbell Matthews, *Expansion of New England* (New York: Russell & Russell, 1936); Lloyd Warner et al., "Yankee City" series; T. J. Wertenbaker, *The Puritan Oligarchy: The Founding of American Civilization* (New York: Grosset & Dunlap, 1947).

Many very obvious but often neglected indices of the patterns of flow of the three native streams are available. The pattern of religious predominance, already mentioned, is one. Another important one is the pattern of the nation's railroad network, whose different lines follow their respective regional flows quite faithfully. In the case of the Middle stream, for example, the Union Pacific Railroad does not continue to the Pacific coast directly but curves northward into Oregon. In doing so it follows the pattern of the stream which produced it quite exactly. This is not surprising since the railroads were promoted on a regional basis to begin with. The ramifications of this are many and varied. Chicago was no doubt helped immeasurably in its rivalry with St. Louis by the fact that it is located at the confluence of the Middle and Yankee streams, both of which produced energetic entrepreneurs who seized the advantages offered by the new technology of the railroads, while St. Louis is located at the confluence of the Southern and Middle streams and may have lacked just that little "extra" needed to give it the same entrepreneurial vigor.

6. Though the French did have settlements in St. Clair County and on the present sites of Peoria, Duluth, and Superior before the Americans came and the Spanish had settled the Pueblo area briefly, with the exception of the small settlement of Cahokia, near East St. Louis, none of these pre-American settlements was in existence when the Americans arrived. While the political culture in the Cahokia area retains elements from the day of French rule (at least the tradition of political corruption has continued unbroken since the days of the French), the political system in operation there is unquestionably an American product. Hence it can reasonably be said that American beginnings are the beginnings for all the cities of the prairie.

For a discussion of the impact of the Southern and other streams in Illinois generally, see Ray A. Billington, "The Frontier in Illinois History" in *Journal of the Illinois State Historical Society*, Spring 1950. For the historical background in this chapter, I have relied heavily on Theodore C. Pease, *The Story of Illinois* (Chicago: University of Chicago Press, 1947), as well on the census materials and various local histories of the cities of the prairie listed in Appendix D. See also B. F. Wright et al., *Sources of Culture in the Middle West* (New York: Appleton-Century, 1934).

7. Turner, in *The United States: 1830–1850*, *op. cit.*, has prepared detailed maps of voting patterns in this zone for the period of his study, which show the historical roots of the political affiliations of the Middle stream counties of Illinois. Pease, *op. cit.*, also discusses this.

8. For a study of early Yankee influences in Illinois, see Carrie P. Kofoid, "Puritan Influences in Illinois Before 1860," in Illinois State Historical Society, *Transactions, 1905* (Springfield, 1906), pp. 261–339, and Matthews, *op. cit.*

9. This should not be interpreted as an overly sanguine appraisal of the Yankees and their subculture. The traditional stereotype of Yankees as "sharp" and highly legalistic in their approach to social obligations has more than a kernel of truth to it. What is of concern here, in discussing the aggregate behavior patterns of the Yankees, is the general predisposition of most Yankees to embrace a set of traditional (to them) ideals relating to communal responsibility and public morality and their general effort to live up to those ideals.

10. The background of these streams is amply discussed in Marcus Lee Hansen, *The Atlantic Migration* (Cambridge, Mass.: Harvard University Press, 1940); and Oscar Handlin, *The Uprooted* (Boston: Little, Brown, 1951). Hansen is also aware of the limits of ethnic group identification. He identifies four streams of migration: the Celtic (consisting of the Irish, Scots, and Welsh—the "genuine" Celts—and those Belgians, Dutch, Norwegians, and Germans from the upper Rhine Valley who came from areas on the European continent longest occupied by Celts, whose institutions continued to bear the mark of Celtic patterns), which predominated between 1830 and 1860; the Teutonic (consisting of the English, Germans from Prussia and Saxony, Austrians, Bohemians, Swedes, Danes, and Norwegians from the Scandinavian interior whose institutions bore the marks of a common Germanic or Teutonic origin), which predominated between 1860 and 1890; the Slavic (consisting of Finns, Latvians, Lithuanians, Poles, Karelians, and Ukrainians, and the Mediterranean (consisting of a whole complex of peoples from the Italian Peninsula, Greece, the

Balkans, and the Near East), both of which predominated between 1890 and 1914 (or 1920). Hansen's scheme is quite compelling. Its great virtue is that it avoids ethnic stereotyping by emphasizing geohistorical factors which internally divide the various ethnic groups themselves. In this respect, it comes close to the concept used in this study. However, Hansen's scheme ignores the effects of religious affiliation and later European historical developments such as those which divided the Celtic streams along Protestant and Catholic lines and the Teutonic stream into English and Continental components. These divisions, though couched most visibly in religious categories, actually reflect profound sociological differences which must be taken into consideration if they are to be meaningful for political analysis. Both Max Weber's *The Protestant Ethnic and the Spirit of Capitalism*, trans. Talcott Parsons (London: Allen and Unwin, 1939) and R. H. Tawney's *Religion and the Rise of Capitalism* (New York: Harcourt, Brace, 1937) with all their weaknesses are important as sources providing insights into those differences, despite their concentration on the European scene. When the socioreligious dimension which they explore is added to Hansen's geocultural dimension, it becomes possible to formulate the structure of the European-originated streams. For a compendious bibliography on the ethnic groups and their migrations, see *A Report on World Population Migrations as Related to the United States of America* (Washington: The George Washington University, 1956). Useful studies of the interrelationships of the various ethnic groups in Europe include C. T. Smith, *An Historical Geography of Western Europe Before 1800* (New York: Praeger, 1967), and Robert Lopez, *Birth of Europe* (Philadelphia: J. B. Lippincott, 1967).

11. There may be some relationship here between the style of religious orientation of the native Southern and Catholic elements and their similarities (which need not be overdrawn) in other respects. In the greater-South, the Southern Baptist Church is virtually a "national," if unestablished, church, embracing a majority of the population in a broad band from the Atlantic to eastern New Mexico, much as the Catholic Church is the national church in the Catholic countries. Needless to say, there are obvious and important differences between the two churches, particularly in their internal structure, but the relative uncompetitive universality of both within their particular cultural areas and their essential conservatism, strengthened by their ties to their respective political and economic "establishments," bring their adherents closer together than either group would be willing to acknowledge.

12. S. E. Johnson, *A History of Emigration from the United Kingdom to North America, 1763–1912* (London, 1913), and Thomas Brindley, *Migration and Economic Growth: A Study of Great Britain and the Atlantic Economy* (Cambridge, Eng., 1954) are the two best sources on the English migrations from the Revolutionary period to the end of the nineteenth century.

13. Material on the North Sea stream is available only in works on the several ethnic groups wholly or partially within it. See, in particular, John H. Finley, *The Coming of the Scot* (New York: Charles Scribner's Sons, 1940); Charles A. Hanna, *The Scotch Irish: Or the Scot in North Britain, North Ireland and North America*, 2 vols. (New York: G. P. Putnam, 1902); Ruth Putnam, "The Dutch Element in the United States," American Historical Association *Annual Report* (1909); H. T. Calenbrander, "The Dutch Element in American History," American Historical Association *Annual Report* (1919); John Paul von Grueningin, ed., *The Swiss in the United States* (Madison, Wisc., 1940); Douglas Campbell, *The Puritans in Holland, England and America*, 2 vols. (New York: Harper and Bros., 1892); Bertus H. Wabeke, *Dutch Emigration to North America* (New York: The Netherlands Information Bureau, 1944); George F. Huizinga, *What the Dutch Have Done in the West of the United States* (Philadelphia: private printing, 1909); Henry S. Lucas, "The Political Activities of the Dutch Immigrants from 1847 to the Civil War," *Iowa*

Journal of History and Politics, XXVI. The French Huguenots also fit into this stream. See Lucian J. Fosdick, *The French Blood in America* (New York: Fleming H. Revell, 1906). For additional references, see George Shepperson, "Writings in Scottish-American History: A Brief Survey," *William and Mary Quarterly* (April 1954); and Jacob Van Der Zee, *The Hollanders in Iowa* (Iowa City: The State Historical Society of Iowa, 1912).

14. Of the mass of material that has been produced by students of American Jewish history, little of a general nature deals with the concerns of this study. Perhaps the best sources are Abraham J. Feldman, *The American Jew: A Study of Backgrounds* (New York: Bloch Publishing, 1937); Max J. Kohner, "Some Jewish Factors in the Settlement of the West," *American Jewish Historical Society Publication*, XVII 1909); Anita Libman Lebeson, *Pilgrim People* (New York: Harper, 1950); Harry S. Linfield, *Statistics of Jews and Jewish Organization: Historical Review of Ten Censuses, 1850–1932* (New York: The American Jewish Committee, 1939); Daniel J. Elazar, "Sectionalism and the American Jewish Community," unpublished paper presented at the Annual Meeting of the American Jewish Historical Society, Philadelphia, 1962. See also the local and regional histories of Jewish settlement (many of which are cited in Elazar, *loc. cit.*), particularly W. Gunther Paul, *The Jews in Minnesota* (New York, 1959); Ida Libert Uchill, *Pioneers, Peddlers and Tsadikim* (Denver: Sage Books, 1957); Simon Glazer, *The Jews of Iowa* (Des Moines: Koch Brothers, 1904); Hyman L. Meiteo, *History of the Jews of Chicago* (Chicago, 1924). For additional sources, see Salo W. Baron, "American Jewish History: Problems and Methods," *American Jewish Historical Quarterly,* XXXIX (March 1942); and Moses Rischin, *An Inventory of American Jewish History* (Cambridge, Mass.: Harvard University Press, 1954).

15. For information on the French, see Fosdick, *op. cit.*, and J. G. Rosengarten, *French Colonists and Exiles in the United States* (Philadelphia: J. B. Lippincott, 1907).

16. The role of the German element in the Mississippi Valley is highlighted in Albert B. Faust, *The German Element in the United States* (Boston and New York: Houghton Mifflin, 1909), 2 vols. While a sample of the literature of ethnic apologetica, Faust's work does present a comprehensive study of German settlers in this country. See also Rachel DuBois and Emma Schweppe, eds., *The Germans in American Life* (New York: T. Nelson and Sons, 1936); F. F. Schrader, *The Germans in the Making of America* (Boston: The Stratford Co., 1924); Hildegard B. Johnson, "The Location of German Immigrants in the Middle West," *Annals of the Association of American Geographers* (March 1951). Other local studies of particular relevance include Hildegard B. Johnson, "German Forty-Eighters in Davenport," *Iowa Journal of History and Politics* (January 1946) and "Factors Influencing the Distribution of the German Pioneer Population in Minnesota," *Agricultural History*, XIX (January 1945). Additional material is cited in Dieter Cuny, ed., "Bibliography Americana Germanica, 1950," *American German Review*, XVI, No. 4 (April) and Emil Meynen, *Bibliography on German Settlements in Colonial North America* (Leipzig, 1937).

17. Lee W. Metzner, "The Belgians in the North Country," *Wisconsin Magazine of History* (March 1943), and Hjalman R. Helano, *Wisconsin's Belgian Community: An Account of the Early Events in the Belgian Settlement in Northeastern Wisconsin with Particular Reference to the Belgians in Door County,* in *Peninsula Historical Review*, VII (1933).

18. Emil Lengyel, *Americans from Hungary* (Philadelphia: J. B. Lippincott, 1948), and D. A. Saunders, "The Magyars in America," *Hungarian Quarterly* (Autumn 1941).

19. The Irish are a reasonably well-studied group, though again, the studies are

only indirectly helpful for the purposes of this volume. See, in particular, John O'Hanlon, *Irish-American History of the United States* (Dublin, 1903); Edward F. Roberts, *Ireland in America* (New York: G. P. Putnam's Sons, 1931); R. C. O'Connor, "The Irish Element in America," *American Irish Historical Society Journal*, IX (1910); Ina Ten Eyck Firkin, "Irish in the United States," *Bulletin of Bibliography* (Boston, 1917); Homer L. Calkin, "The United States Government and the Irish: A Bibliographical Study of Research Materials in the United States National Archives," *Irish National Studies* (March 1954). Sources directly pertaining to the cities of the prairie region include Charles M. Scanlon, "History of the Irish in Wisconsin," *American Irish Historical Society Journal*, XIII (1914); H. E. Eagan, "Irish Immigration to Minnesota," *Mid-American*, XII (October 1929, January 1930); George F. O'Dwynen, "Irish Colonization in Illinois," *Illinois Catholic Historical Review*, III (July 1920); Joseph J. Thompson, "The Irish in Early Illinois," *Illinois Catholic Historical Review*, II (October 1919).

20. The most useful material from the Scandinavian-American historical studies include Jacob Hodenfield, "Some Recent Publications Relating to Norwegian-American History," *Norwegian-American Society Studies and Records*, V–XI (1930–1938); Oscar F. Anders, *Guide to the Material on Swedish History in the Augustana College Library* (Rock Island, Ill.: Augustana Historical Society, 1934); K. C. Babcock, "The Scandinavian Element in the United States," *Studies in the Social Sciences*, III, No. 3 (1914); Albert Kamp et al., eds., *The Danish Way; Danish Pioneers and Work in Every Zone*, 2 vols. (Odense: Skandinavisk Bogforlag, 1950); O. M. Norlie, *History of the Norwegian People in America* (Minneapolis: Augsburg Publishing House, 1925); Lesla Marjorie Bergman (Nelson), *Americans from Norway* (Philadelphia, 1950); Helge Nelson, *Sweden and the Swedish Settlements in North America*, 2 vols. (New York: A. Bonnier, 1943); Adolph Burnett Benson and Nabath Wedin, *Americans from Sweden, 1638–1900* (Philadelphia: J. B. Lippincott, 1949); John Wargelin, *The Americanization of Finns* (Michigan, 1924); G. T. Flom, "The Scandinavian Factor in the American Population," *Iowa Journal of History and Politics*, III; Carlton C. Qualey, *Norwegian Settlement in the United States*, Ph.D. thesis (Northfield, Minn., 1938). Among the studies relating to the cities of the prairie are Thomas P. Christensen, "Danish Settlement in Minnesota," *Minnesota History Bulletin*, VII; Carlton C. Qualey, "Pioneer Norwegian Settlement in Minnesota," *Minnesota History*, XII (1931); G. T. Flom, *Chapters on Scandinavian Immigrations to Iowa* (Iowa City, 1906), and "The Danish Contingent in the Population of Early Iowa," *Iowa Journal of History and Politics*, IV (1907).

21. Philip M. Rose, *The Italians in America* (New York: George H. Doran, 1922); James Geddes, Jr., *Italian Contributions to America* (Boston, 1929).

22. Xenidis, *The Greeks in America* (New York: George H. Doran, 1922). Jerome D. Davis, *The Russian Immigrant* (New York: Macmillan, 1922).

23. See, for example, Alice M. Kenton, "Polish People in the United States: A Selected Bibliography," *Monthly Labor Review*, XXII (March 1926), 730–736; A. S. Walanin (comp.), "Some Recent Publications Relating to Polish American History," *Polish American Studies*, V (January), 37–41; (December) 112–114; Joseph S. Roucek and Patricia W. Pinkham, *American Slavs: A Bibliography* (New York, 1944); Mieczyslaw Haiman, "Problems of Polish-American History Writing," *Bulletin of the Polish Institute of Arts and Sciences in America* (January 1943); Thomas Capek, *The Czechs in America* (New York, 1920); Paul Fox, *The Poles in America* (New York, 1922); Joseph S. Roucek, "The Yugoslav Immigrants in America," *American Journal of Sociology*, XL (1935), and *American Lithuanians* (New York, 1940). For additional sources, see UNESCO *International Bibliography on Migration, 1953–1954* (Paris, 1955).

24. Little has been written on the continuing influence of these foreign-originated

streams. Handlin deals with recent immigration briefly in *Race and Nationality in American Life* (Boston: Little, Brown, 1957). The newspapers of the cities of the prairie record new admissions to American citizenship locally almost every week. They also record numerous instances of the new immigrants' contributing to the revival of latent ethnic attachments, particularly in Duluth, Superior, Rockford, Moline, Davenport, Joliet, and Belleville.

25. Leon E. Truesdale, *The Canadian Born in the United States: An Analysis of the Statistics of the Canadian Element in the Population of the United States, 1850–1930* (New Haven, 1943); Marcus L. Hansen, *The Mingling of the Canadian and American Peoples* (New Haven, 1940).

26. *The Report of the National Advisory Commission on Civil Disorders* (New York: Dutton, 1968) provides a good overview of the place of the Afro-Americans in American society. Its citations are also useful. On the blacks in politics, see Patrick Daniel Moynihan and Nathan Glazer, *Beyond the Melting Pot* (Cambridge, Mass.: MIT Press, 1963); St. Clair Drake, *Black Metropolis* (New York: Harper and Row, 1962). The vignettes of blacks in Studs Terkel, *Division Street; America* (New York: Avon, 1968) offer some useful insights into contemporary Afro-American life in Illinois. See also Elliott M. Rudwick, *Race Riot at East St. Louis, July 2, 1917* (New York: Meridian, 1967).

27. John H. Burma, *Spanish-Speaking Groups in the United States* (Durham, North Carolina, 1954); Lyle Saunders, "The Social History of Spanish-Speaking People in Southwestern United States since 1846," First Congress of Historians from Mexico and the United States, *Memoria* (1950); Carey McWilliams, *North From Mexico: The Spanish-Speaking People of the United States* (Philadelphia: J. B. Lippincott, 1949); see also Kingsley Davis and Clarence Senior, "Immigration from the Western Hemisphere," *American Academy of Political and Social Science, Annals,* No. 262 (March 1949); Clarence O. Senior and Josefina del Roman (comp.), *A Selected Bibliography on Puerto Rico and the Puerto Ricans* (New York, 1951).

28. There are a number of individuals of Oriental stock in Champaign-Urbana, where they are associated with the University of Illinois. They, however, are to be included with the University community as a whole just as the other University people. See Mary R. Coolidge, *Chinese Immigration* (New York, 1909); Rose Hiem Lee, "Social Institutions of a Rocky Mountain Chinatown," *Social Forces,* XXVII (October), 1–11; George R. Renner, "Chinese Influence in the Development of the Western United States," *American Academy of Political Science, Annals,* CLII (November 1930); Bradford Smith, *Americans from Japan* (Philadelphia, 1948).

Chapter 5 / Political Cleavages and Political Control

The Legacy of Frontier, Stream, and Section

THE COMBINED INFLUENCE of their sectional positions, the cultural streams which have created their particular geologies of settlement, and the impact of the successive frontiers upon them underlie and shape the patterns of political cleavage and control in the cities of the prairie. Analysis of these patterns can lead to a better understanding of the different ways in which political power is organized in American civil communities.[1]

Three basic forms of political control can be identified as existing or having existed in the various cities of the prairie either now or at some point in their historical development. In some fundamental way, they or their respective variations very likely encompass the range of community political systems encountered in the United States. They are described here in their simplest forms, as models or paradigms of what are necessarily complex arrangements somehow unique in every civil community. The models presented here are confined to delineating the forms of political control found specifically in the cities of this study [which means they reflect a synthesis of factors produced in civil communities: (1) located (with one exception) on the fringes of the country's three great sectional spheres, (2) socially organized through patterns crystallized by one of the three subcultural groups created by the amalgam of migrational streams into each, and (3) responding to one of the three frontier stages all have entered or passed through.] Were the same models to be applied to civil communities located elsewhere in space or time, some modifications no doubt would have to be made.

The *autocratic form,* based on hierarchical rule and pyramidal organization of power (either formally or *de facto*), reflects the existence of a person or an organization legally functioning as a person (such as a corporation), who (or which) virtually monopolizes the political power exercisable locally and, by being decisively involved in every significant local political decision, exercises well-nigh complete political control over the civil community. Three types of autocratic political control can be found to exist:

Perhaps best known is the simplified form of classic "boss rule," where a single man—usually a professional politician—holds full power to decide what is done in the community, does it, and distributes rewards. This type of autocracy (analogous to classic dictatorship) has always been rare in the United States and is becoming more so. In its pure and complete form it is feasible only in very small communities populated by particularly depressed and excluded groups, drawn primarily from the subject streams. As this combination becomes less common, the type of political control it produces also becomes less common. Among the cities of the prairie, this kind of boss rule is found only in certain of the little towns in the American Bottoms of Madison and St. Clair Counties and in unincorportaed "barrios" outside Pueblo. Brooklyn and Venice in the former area are the best surviving examples. Both have overwhelmingly Negro populations of a particularly depressed character and are governed by men who have made it their business to maintain autocratic control over the local populations. The towns are accordingly organized in plantation-like fashion reflecting the Southern influence, with the "boss" actually living in a more or less stately—and pillared—mansion in the midst of the shacks of his "constituency."

A second type of autocratic control is found in industrial domination of a particular civil community. The classic example of this is the "company town." Among the cities of the prairie, a number of cities in the American Bottoms were founded as company towns and were kept under control of their "parent" industry for many years. While some of these company towns were also subject to a form of "boss rule," in such cases the political leader was simply acting as a stand-in for the company, serving as its "political foreman," usually on a "fee" basis. This direct form of industrial autocracy was particularly associated with the currents of the greater South. Where it appeared farther north, it was almost invariably in communities populated by new immigrant groups which initially were so excluded from the American political system and so ignorant of the American political style that they would submit to such a system out of ignorance as well as out of economic necessity. This system, too, has tended to disappear as the local inhabitants have grown to feel their political oats. Moreover, the companies themselves began to discover the high cost of maintaining such extensive local control. They have since found less expensive ways to exercise control over those aspects of local politics which concern them while withdrawing from other political matters.

Occasionally a third form of autocratic political control has been found. In some civil communities, generally those lacking either a substantial industrial base or a significant immigrant population, a local business leader has maneuvered himself into a position of autocratic leadership. The classic example of this in the cities of the prairie was the rule of H. I. Green in Champaign-Urbana. Green, a lawyer by training and a man with many local and extra-local business interests, was able to exercise a very high level of political control in both cities and the county generally by combining his local interests, his connections with the railroad corporations, and his statewide political ties, for an entire generation from the mid-1920's to 1953. He was able to achieve this political power by working at it and only gained it because he wanted to work at it. While this is also true in the case of politician-autocrats, it is even more important for businessmen-autocrats, who operate within a political system that makes autocratic control much more difficult to achieve. Indeed, businessman-autocracy is never as absolute as either of the other types. Because other potential power centers are not fully eliminated, it comes closest to being a hierarchized form of oligarchy with the central businessman-broker as the premier power-holder.

In the last analysis, autocracy in its various forms was essentially a nineteenth-century phenomenon in the United States, closely associated with the urban-industrial frontier (or, in a few cases, the rural-land frontier). The opening of the metropolitan technological frontier has been the greatest single force in eliminating it. Whereas in other sections of the country, local autocrats were frequently members of older elite groups or, if not, were confined by the older elites to the same social status as their "subjects," in the greater West the autocrats were self-made men who rose to higher social status as they achieved economic and political success. Finally, autocracy thrived where the southern Negro, southern and eastern European, and Hispanic streams, with their strong tendencies toward a subject-like political culture, predominated.

Oligarchy is a form of political control in which a substantially closed group of men or a substantially closed grouping of interests represented by their leaders share the political power exercisable locally among themselves, virtually monopolizing that power by being decisively involved in every significant local political decision. Three types of oligarchical arrangements can be found.

The most simple is an oligarchy composed of a single element in the civil community, usually businessmen or politicians. The effects of such single-element oligarchies are frequently much the same as those of autocracies, except within the controlling element itself. Such oligarchies develop when no single individual possesses sufficient power to control the local political situation on his own but where a small group of individuals in the same general lines of endeavor, usually with interlocking relationships, can so monopolize exercisable local political power as to exclude all others. Such an oligarchy frequently exists when a political "machine" is able to control a community but is itself controlled by the ward (or similar unit) leaders acting in concert. Among the cities of the prairie its more common form is that of a business oligarchy, in which the local (usually "downtown") business, real estate, and banking leaders control the civil community by monopolizing local political and economic power.

Urbana is a case in point. Almost since its development as an urban community, it has been dominated by such a business oligarchy, centered around the leading local bank and a bipartisan collection of downtown merchants and lawyers. Co-opted by "Boss" Green (who came out of this group to begin with) during the days of his ascendancy, they returned to power within Urbana after his demise, though their present tenure will probably be limited, since the growth of the city is leading to the emergence of rival elements that appear to be gaining in influence and in ability to challenge the oligarchy. This is very significant. The business oligarchy in American history is almost invariably associated with a "main street crowd" in small towns or small cities. With almost equal invariability such oligarchies dissolve or are reconstituted as more complex oligarchies when the cities outgrow them (literally). This is what appears to be happening in Urbana.

Single-element oligarchies frequently are transformed into multiple-element oligarchies, usually combining industrial, business, and political elements. In such cases, political control still rests with a self-selected group which stands in more or less autocratic relationship with the remainder of the civil community. However, the group itself is not monolithic but an internal coalition of different elements, each of which has its own sources of power and which can only exercise maximum control in conjunction with the other group or groups. In a city like East St. Louis, the multiple-element oligarchy which dominates the community is composed of the leading industrial organizations (or their representatives) and the dominant local political organization. Chicago, as characterized by Banfield, is governed by a three-fold oligarchy of industrialists, "State Street" business interests, and the Democratic political organization.[2] A two-element oligarchy generally maintains a high degree of autocratic political control, often in conjunction with a "two-city" system. A three-element oligarchy, on the other hand, has already become sufficiently divided to allow a great deal of flexibility in political decision-making and demands considerably more interchange with elements outside the oligarchy proper.

Somewhat resembling the multiple-element oligarchies but even more broadly based and considerably more responsive to the articulate publics in the civil community are representative oligarchies, the third type. A representative oligarchy is one which exercises decisive control over the local political system and virtually monopolizes the political power exercisable locally through a closed system regularly composed of representatives from all—or nearly all—the different elements within the civil community. This type of oligarchy is frequently mistaken for a system of polyarchic leadership. Indeed, much of the recent debate over "power elites" versus "pluralism" in our local communities centers on the assessment of the "real" character of representative oligarchies (or organized pluralisms, the next type once removed). A representative oligarchy is not polyarchic because it is not readily open to new interests seeking a share in its power. The general character of its membership is likely to remain constant for relatively long periods of time, and the actors within its circle may indeed be reluctant to share their power with any individuals or groups defined as outsiders. Gaining representation in a representative oligarchy is more difficult than gaining representation in any polyarchic system, though access to members of the oligarchy is relatively easy.[3] By insuring at least indirect representation of the interests of the excluded elements until it is ready to co-opt their leaders, a representative oligarchy has great staying power.

Davenport offers perhaps the best example of a representative oligarchy among the cities of the prairie. There an oligarchy of this type has been functioning almost continually since the creation of the city. Decisions in Davenport are made through informal consultations and negotiations among representatives of the business community, the various local political groupings, the two major parties, the city government, the local public bureaucracies, lay representatives of the three major religious communities, organized labor, the ethnic reference groups, the welfare agencies, the manufacturers, and the "outside" governments. Belleville is governed through a similar oligarchy, which reflects the business community, the two major parties, the city bureaucracy, lay representatives of the three religious communities, and the local labor movement.[4]

The measure of influence in such oligarchies—as in the polyarchic systems described below—is two-fold. Influentials can be identified by their tacit veto powers (their ability to defeat projects they oppose by not approving them) and by their necessary inclusion in the development of the concurrent majorities required to initiate positive action in the civil community. These positive and negative powers represent the two sides of political influence in any local political system. It is their spread within any particular civil community which is the key to understanding what kind of power system exists within it.

Polyarchy represents the third form of local political control. Just what is to be considered "polyarchic" government is a matter of some dispute among social scientists; however, it should be possible to conceive of a polyarchic system as one in which no single individual, group, or element nor any exclusive combination of individuals, groups, or elements is able to monopolize the political power exercisable locally or to be decisively involved in every significant local political decision. Two essential elements may be said to characterize polyarchy: "openness" and "fluidity." In a polyarchic system, power is not only diffused among many groups, but different issues or situations are likely to increase the political relevance of different groups, giving them greater or lesser roles in the making of particular decisions or the formulation of particular policies. At the same time, the groups themselves are more likely to change internally within a reasonably brief span of time.

This does not mean that a polyarchic system necessarily has no continuing structure, as is sometimes assumed by those who tend to lump all social situations in which there are leaders and led, articulates and inarticulates, into the category of "oligarchy." Of the three identifiable types of polyarchy, at least one is highly structured though no less polyarchic.

Organized polyarchy is the type of political control most commonly encountered in the cities of the prairie. In an organized polyarchic system, there exists a more or less known variety of identifiable elements, groups, and individuals concerned with local affairs and possessing influence that can effectively help order the course of the local affairs which interest them. While their role and impact will vary from situation to situation, there are regular ways by which they are mobilized and known channels through which their influence is exercised. In a word, their participation is expected and their behavior generally follows recognized patterns.

Political control in Peoria, Joliet, Rock Island, Moline, Rockford, Superior, Duluth, and Pueblo represents organized polyarchy in its various nuances. Their chief common characteristic is a continuing division of power among a number of groups in such a manner that no ongoing set of influentials can be said to "control" decisions made locally but in which influential elements, groups, and individuals (and the issues which particularly interest them) can be identified without great difficulty. Moreover, coordination among them is both possible without excessive difficulty and frequent.

Other polyarchic systems diffuse power without possessing this potential for "easy" coordination, nor do their components coordinate their activities with much frequency. Such systems may be characterized as fragmented polyarchies in which power is dispersed past the point of easy determination of who has the power potential to do which things or to prevent which things from being done. When power is exercised in these systems, it is exercised by specific elements, groups, or individuals with relative ease so long as it is directed toward specific and limited ends, and new groups may become power exercisers with equal ease if they find open areas to fill. Champaign has a fragmented polyarchic system. Unlike Urbana, it had no strong local oligarchy that was able to survive the Green period and resume control after he had left the scene. Green's departure left an open field—a power vacuum—which has been only partially filled by this system of fragmented polyarchy. Civil communities with systems of political power so fragmented are reasonably rare, partly because such fragmentation tends to be a transitory phenomenon, a manifestation of a transition period during which the disintegrating power system is no longer able to organize influence while the emerging one is not yet strong enough to do so. A fragmented polyarchy is likely to last only in a civil community that is subject to few outside political pressures and which produces no serious claimants for political power from within, a rare combination at any time.

A sufficiently fragmented polyarchy may become chaotic polyarchy, the third type. Insofar as the cities of the prairie are concerned, this type is theoretically possible, but its occurrence has not actually been documented in this study. In essence its existence would signify a community in the last stages of dissolution, in which power was so fragmented that nobody could exercise it in an organized fashion. It would be a situation roughly comparable to Hobbes's "state of nature" or Marx's final communist society in which the community as an organized entity would barely exist, if at all.

Polyarchic and oligarchic political systems not only predominate in the cities of the prairie but, according to the written evidence of most community studies, also predominate in the country as a whole.[5] Polyarchy is, indeed, accepted as the most suitable way to organize power in the American civil community, meeting as it does the spirit of American institutions and reflecting as it does the exigencies of the American situation. Polyarchy, then, has been the widespread response of the civil community to the tides of changing frontiers, shifting populations, and changing sectional interests. Oligarchy, particularly in its more representative forms, has also proved to be a durable means of organizing political power locally, especially in the smallest and largest civil communities, where it offers chances for stability without denying access.

Both polyarchic and oligarchic systems have done well in relation to all three frontiers. The former, of course, are particularly suited to frontier situations, where fluidity is the order of the day, and the introduction of a civic order that can structure that fluidity without stopping it becomes a prime necessity. By the same token, it is no doubt true that the continuing existence of the frontier is a powerful bulwark of polyarchic political systems. Oligarchies have generally emerged only after the first period of each frontier has spent itself, allowing power relationships the chance to crystallize. As the record in the cities of the prairie indicates, there is no necessary movement from polyarchy to oligarchy. Whether such a movement takes place depends upon the sectional and especially the cultural factors infusing the particular situation of each civil community. In this regard, the character of each successive frontier that shapes the political system of each civil community has a great deal of importance in determining the kind of power distribution favored locally, with the first frontier having a special influence. The rural-land frontier probably favored both polyarchic and oligarchic forms, leaning toward the former; the urban-industrial frontier leaned heavily toward the encouragement of oligarchy in some form; if anything, the metropolitan technological frontier encourages polyarchy.

The pressures and possibilities of environment are so intertwined with the movement of the frontier in this country that the two are virtually inseparable. Their end product, sectionalism, has its influence on the forms of local organization of political influence as well. Broadly stated, single-element oligarchies have found fertile ground in the greater South. The greater Northeast has been most hospitable to the other two forms of oligarchy. Polyarchy in its several forms is particularly at home in the greater West. The sectional breakdown can be carried further. Even where the amalgam of cultural streams is not significantly different on its face, there were and are differences between the character of oligarchies (or polyarchies) in the civil communities of New England (where multiple-element to representative oligarchies predominate), those of the Middle Atlantic states (where single to multiple-element oligarchies predominate), and those of the Near West (where single-element or representative oligarchies predominate). Similarly, the character of Southern oligarchies, strengthened from the first by the sphere's old caste system, varies greatly from the rigid patterns of the Upper South (where old elites predominate) through the personalized patterns of the Lower South (where professional politicians predominate) to the business-entrepreneurial patterns of the Western South (where the business community almost invariably dominates). Patterns of polyarchic systems in the greater West range from the organized but open polyarchy characteristic of the Northwest, through the open polyarchy of the dominant caste coupled with the exclusion of non-"Anglos" characteristic of the Southwest, to the fragmented or close-to-fragmented polyarchy of the Far West, where the local publics are constantly shifting in several ways.

Finally, the impact of the several cultural streams on the organization of political influence within the civil community is crucial. The level of local homogeneity, the degree of potential relationship between the various streams, the order and spacing of their arrival—these are but a few of the factors that affect the organization of political influence locally. The next section treats these questions more fully in the discussion of political cleavage, one aspect of the issue of influence.

Figure 5–1 catalogs the nine variations in the organization of political control and graphically portrays them in their simplest form.[6]

Contemporary Political Cleavages

Perhaps the most important legacy of the pattern of settlement imposed by the flow of the streams on the organization of political influence in the cities of the prairie is the continuing pattern of political cleavage in each. While many factors contribute to the kind of political system emerging in each civil community, much depends upon the limits and possibilities of political linkage among the various groups that comprise its population. The limits and the possibilities are strongly affected by local ethnoreligious divisions which stimulate different kinds of power relationships community-wide.

Some form of basic political cleavage exists in every one of the cities of the prairie, varying in intensity from the kind of cleavage that affects every issue brought to public attention (high cleavages—Duluth, East St. Louis, Moline, Peoria, Rockford, Rock Island) through the kind that is reflected primarily in partisan political differences (medium cleavages —Alton, Decatur, Joliet, Springfield, Urbana) to the kind that manifests itself only on special issues that directly relate to the cleaved elements (low cleavages—Belleville, Champaign, Davenport, East Moline, Silvis, Pueblo, Superior).

The relative size of the cleaved elements apparently has little effect on the intensity of the cleavage. In some cases, the cleavage divides the city into nearly equal parts (Duluth, East Moline-Silvis, East St. Louis, Joliet, Peoria, Rockford, Springfield, Superior). In others, one element is about twice as strong as the other (Alton, Belleville, Champaign, Decatur, Rock Island). In some, the cleavage exists between the great bulk of the community on one side and a small minority element on the other (Davenport, Moline, Pueblo, Urbana).

The existence of the cleavage in each community may be expressed geographically ("valley" versus "bluff," east side versus west side, city versus suburb), in terms of reference groups ("cosmopolitans" versus "locals"), or as a division based on economic interest ("business" versus "labor"). While national party affiliation is sometimes a key to the cleavages in specific communities, it is not necessarily its most consistent manifestation, being apparent in only nine of the seventeen civil communities under study. Table 5–1 summarizes the contemporary patterns of political cleavage in the cities of the prairie in light of their historical origins.[7]

"Political cleavage" assumes the ability to articulate interests politically. In ten of the seventeen civil communities, one or more elements (usually Negroes or Latins) were so excluded from community politics until the mid-1960's that they could not be adequately placed within the cleavage pattern. This latent group has since bestirred itself and may either come to be a "third force" or may lead to the replacement of the older cleavage with one between it and the remainder of the community.[8]

Socioeconomic Interests and Local Politics

Analysis of Figure 5–1 reveals that culture is of first importance in determining the existence of cleavages; history determines the social ranking of their components, while geography determines their character and intensity. The organization of political influence reflects that synthesis of all three factors.

The alignments on either side of the cleavage reflect the cultural differences separating the socioreligious or ethnoreligious groups that have settled in each civil community. The status or position of these alignments is substantially determined by the time of arrival of the component groups in each, with earlier arrivals having attained higher status, except in the case of those groups unable to articulate their interests politically. Since location along particular migrational paths or the attractions of site strongly influenced which streams settled where, geographic factors contributed much to determining which cultures were to be found in each civil community—which, in turn, did much to determine what kind of interstream relationships there would be. Moreover, geographic factors, by directly or indirectly influencing economic development, contributed to shaping the intensity of the cleavage. The following pages treat these latter influences in greater detail by tracing the manner in which stream and section interact to shape the socioeconomic constitutions of the cities of the prairie, which have determined, in effect, what individuals and groups have been in a position to obtain political power or influence.[9]

By and large, the Yankee influence has been most important in the development of the commercial, civic, and cultural patterns of the cities of the prairie. From the first, the Yankee element provided a major share of the business talent and technological skills needed for the conquest of

TABLE 5-1

Fundamental Contemporary Political Cleavages and Their Historic Origins

Civil Community (and intensity of the cleavage)[a]	Contemporary Cleavage and National Party Orientation[b]	Historic Origins Streams	Waves[c]	Latent Streams
Alton (M)	Bluff (R)[d]	Yankee, Middle, English, North Sea, Continental	1, 2, 3	Afro-American, Recent Southern
	Valley (D)	Southern, Southern and Eastern European	4, 5	
Belleville (L)	East Belleville (D)	Old Southern, Continental	1, 2, 3	None
	West Belleville (D)	New Southern, Southern European	6	
Champaign (L)	The City (R)	Yankee, Middle, English, North Sea, Continental	3, 4	None
	Northeast Champaign (R)	Afro-American	5, 6	
Davenport-Bettendorf (L)	No commonly accepted local names	Yankee, Middle, English, North Sea Continental	2 3	Hispanic, Afro-American
Decatur (M)	No commonly accepted local names	Middle, Continental	2, 3	Afro-American, Recent Southern
		Southern	5, 6	
Duluth (H)	East Side (R)	Yankee, English, North Sea, Anglo-Canadian	3	None
	West Side (DFL)	Southern European	4	
E. Moline-Silvis (L)	Bluff (D)	Continental, Southern European	4	Afro-American
	Valley (D)	Eastern European, Hispanic	4, 5	
E. St. Louis (H)	North End (D)	Southern, Southern and Eastern European	1, 2, 3, 4	None
	South End (D)	Afro-American	5, 6	
Joliet (M)	West Side (R)	Yankee, Middle, English, North Sea, Irish	2, 3	Afro-American, Recent Southern
	East Side (D)	Southern, Southern and Eastern European	4	
Moline (H)	The City (R)	Yankee and North Sea	2, 3	None
	West End (D)	Continental	4	

TABLE 5-1 (continued)

Civil Community (and intensity of the cleavage)[a]	Contemporary Cleavage and National Party Orientation[b]	Historic Origins Streams	Waves[c]	Latent Streams
Peoria (H)	Bluff (R)	Yankee, Middle, English, North Sea, Continental	2, 3	Afro-American
	Valley (D)	Southern, Southern and Eastern European	4	
Pueblo (L)	The City (D)	Yankee, Middle, Southern, North Sea	3	Hispanic, Afro-American
	The Far South Side (D)	Eastern European	4	
Rockford (H)	North Side (R)	Yankee, North Sea, Irish	2, 3	Afro-American, Recent Southern
	South Side (D)	Mediterranean, Eastern European	4	
Rock Island (H)	Bluff (R)	Yankee, Middle, English, North Sea, Continental	2, 3	Afro-American
	Valley (D)	Southern, Southern and Eastern European	4	
Springfield (M)	West Side (R)	Yankee, Middle, English, Continental	2, 3	Afro-American
	East Side (D)	Southern, Southern and Eastern European	4	
Superior (L)	East Side (D)			None
	West Side (D)			
Urbana (M)	The City (R)	Middle, Continental	2, 3	None
	Northeast Urbana (D)	Southern	2, 3	

[a]H, High; M, Medium; L, Low

[b]Identified by the descriptive terms in common local usage where possible.

[c]Waves — 1. 1790-1820
2. 1820-1850
3. 1850-1880
4. 1880-1915
5. 1915-1945
6. 1945-1969

[d]Intensity of cleavage indicated by number of lines: ——, low; ═══, medium; ≡≡≡, high.

FIGURE 5-1
Forms of Local Political Control

A. Autocracy	B. Oligarchy	C. Polyarchy
1. Politician-Dominated	1. Single Element Oligarchy	1. Organized Polyarchy
2. Industry-Dominated	2. Multiple Element Oligarchy	2. Fragmented Polyarchy
3. Business-Dominated	3. Representative Oligarchy	3. Chaotic Polyarchy
Exemplary Design:	Exemplary Design:	Exemplary Design:

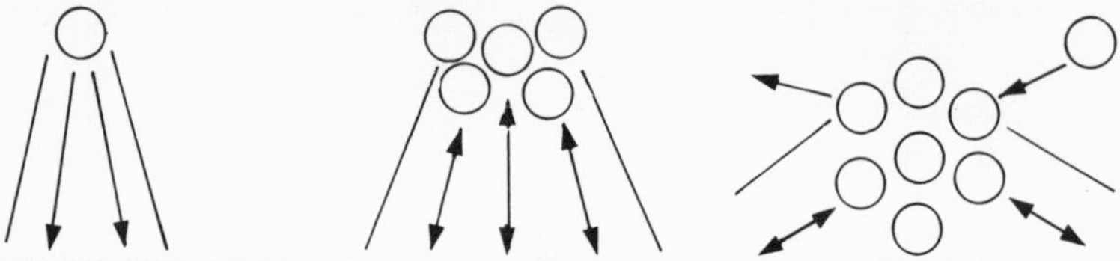

the greater West and the development of its potential. This meant that the civil communities which attracted Yankees in some number were in a better position to capitalize on favorable geographic conditions or to overcome the lack of same and hence had the best chance to develop as commercial and industrial centers. The major industries developed in the cities of the prairie (as distinct from those brought in by absentee owners) were, by and large, developed by Yankee entrepreneurs or by corporations which included significant numbers of influential Yankees. This is particularly so in the case of those communities which developed home-owned industries, such as Rockford and the Quad Cities and, to a lesser extent, Joliet, Peoria, Decatur, and Duluth (whose heavy industries were developed by the descendants of Yankees in Cleveland, where their home-owned industries are located). Since the level of home-owned industry appears to be directly related to the intensity of political activity and involvement on the part of local industrial interests, this is a political matter of no little importance. The general rule of thumb is still valid in regard to the cities of the prairie—the more Yankees among the original settlers, the greater the concentration of home ownership of industry today. Rockford and Moline, the two most Yankee communities among the cities of the prairie, and Peoria, with its substantially Yankee commercial class, remain the most important centers of home-owned industry.

By the same token, the more Southerners among the original settlers, the greater the concentration of absentee-owned industry today. The Madison-St. Clair Counties area is the prime example of this. In the American Bottoms, the original Southern settlers, who were largely unskilled, were reinforced by similarly unskilled Negroes and eastern and southern Europeans, most of whom were imported by the absentee-owned corporations to provide unskilled labor. All four streams served as sources of workers for outside industries rather than creating a pool of talent for the founding of local industries. When similarly unskilled workers came into Yankee-dominated communities, they were absorbed into locally developed industries. Where the local population was mixed, both forms of industrialization are found.

The extension of the corporate system into the cities of the prairie is primarily a contribution of the Middle stream and the English migration. It seems that the technologically talented Yankees were motivated first by a desire to be autonomous industrialists in the old entrepreneurial tradition rather than cogs in the corporate system. They turned to the corporation as a device only when it became a necessary alternative (as in the case of the great railroad companies), not as a preferred mode of operation. The products of the Middle States and the British had an interest in the development of big trading companies, the forerunners of the modern corporation, for exploitation of the riches of the greater West even before the Revolutionary War. Subsequently it was they who introduced the corporation economy into the cities of the prairie, first through those fur-trading companies whose posts were located in central Illinois, then through railroad and manufacturing companies, and farther west through the great mining and cattle companies.[10]

In point of fact, the economic system introduced by the representatives of the Middle stream triumphed throughout the greater West and in the nation as a whole, partly because the corporate system was very well suited to the task of taming such a large area and partly because the Middle States capitalists and their British colleagues worked at it. For the Middle States' more talented sons were the first to devote their energies almost exclusively to the achievement of economic success, with little regard for the civic (and hence the political) aspects of life except insofar as politics might affect their pursuit of economic goals. This characteristic mode of behavior functioned to hasten the political absorption of the Middle States element by other streams which produced a leadership interested in civic matters, either as professional politicians or as civic leaders. This locally apolitical condition was heightened by the general absence of many potential leaders from the westward movement of the Middle stream. This type of commercially oriented leadership was attracted eastward, to New York, Philadelphia, and Baltimore, as much as it was impelled westward. Moreover, unlike the leadership elements among the Southerners and the Yankees, many of the most aggressive Middle Easterners were not colonizers who wished to tame the land by settling it but commercial types who preferred to conquer through trading with others who colonized or through supplying the colonizers with capital. Thus the corporate system created to serve the cities of the prairie was developed outside the prairie and imposed on it by people who generally remained well away from the section. With this tradition, it is not surprising that the Middle Atlantic states should have become the hub of the American economic system and that "Wall Street" should have become the symbol of colonialist-style exploitation for the Populists. The latter, products of the colonizing streams, could not help but come into conflict with those commercial interests which did not share the colonizers' dreams and often worked to inhibit them.

Accordingly, absentee ownership of industry in the cities of the prairie, which is continuing to spread, appears to have developed first in those civil communities influenced most strongly by the Middle stream, such as Decatur, Rock Island, Davenport, Superior (whose polyglot population was weighted in favor of the Middle stream and its European counterparts), Pueblo (which was industrialized by absentee New Yorkers and Pennsylvanians anxious to exploit Colorado's mineral wealth), and even Joliet (where the Yankee influence grew less as northeastern Illinois grew more industrialized). The presence of other products of the Middle stream, plus a leavening of Yankees and representatives of the North Sea stream served to ameliorate the effects of absenteeism in some of those cities, where the local community had the energy, talent, and will to create a locally owned industrial base of varying magnitude to parallel the absentee-owned heavy industry and to produce a civic leadership that could talk to the absentee owners in their own language.

From the first, absentee owners have been much less concerned with local political matters than those who were both owners and citizens in the same civil community. Thus, even in the nineteenth century the absentee-owned companies made less effort to control local politics systematically and confined their efforts to securing favorable treatment where their interests were directly affected. The locally based industrialists, on the other hand, frequently attempted to control the entire local political system, as they did for many years in Rockford and Moline. If the latter were often authoritarian in their attitudes, they were generally community-minded in their approach, while the former did what they pleased with a minimum of regard for its effects on the community. Both of these approaches survived in nearly "pure" form in the cities of the prairie until the end of World War II. Since then there has been a great revolution, which has substantially altered the relations between the civil community and its local industries, limiting the political power of the overly paternalistic ones and expanding the civic involvement of the others. In some respects, this revolution brought a synthesis of Yankee and Middle stream patterns in all but the southernmost cities of the prairie; yet even in the synthesis the separate patterns of the two streams perpetuate themselves.

The vices of absentee ownership were best able to flourish in those cities of the prairie most influenced by the Southern stream. The manner in which they have flourished reflects the intimate interrelationship between economics and politics. The progenitors of the corporate system in the United States found a natural ally in the plantation system of the greater South, which provided them with a ready-made vehicle for the introduction of industrialization in Southern-influenced localities. Among other things, the plantation system supplied a method that made it possible to concentrate political and economic control in the same hands, hands that were generally unrestrained by what most Americans consider to be the "democratic" conception of the general welfare or the public good.[11]

Thus the absentee-owned corporations, often controlled by products of the other streams, particularly the Middle stream, were the ones primarily responsible for the industrialization of Madison and St. Clair Counties after the Civil War. They created company towns, little fiefs where they supplied the workers with housing on company terms and groceries in company stores and which were independently incorporated to preserve corporation control of such items as tax rates, annexation, public expenditures, and local police powers. Where they could not create their own cities, they gained control of the political apparatus of "going" cities and the two counties through their lawyers and the professional politicians the lawyers could "buy" or influence, with much the same result.

The people who originally settled in those communities lacked the requisite skills or experience to contribute an independent economic force or an independent body of civic and political leaders, and those who came in (or were brought in by the corporations) after them—the Italians and Slavs and Negroes, as well as the Southerners—were deficient in the same ways. Only in those civil communities where a large number of the residents were products of other streams, as in Belleville, with its heavy Germanic influence or in Collinsville and Edwardsville, with their Yankee and Middle States infusions, was this pattern successfully resisted. The contemporary differences in political behavior and economic structure between the communities in the bottoms and those on the bluffs are products of these culturally rooted sociological differences among the populations in each community, which were introduced by the different streams that settled in each segment of the metropolitan area.

The post-World-War-II revolution in Madison and St. Clair Counties necessarily has been of a different order than in the more northerly and westerly cities of the prairie, since it was perforce directed against an economic and political system quite different from that of their sister communities. Controlled economically from the outside, the area has had to rely upon outside intervention to generate changes in the status quo, to a far greater degree than the other civil communities.

The Germans who came to the greater West contributed to the local economy in much the same way as did the native products of the Middle stream except that they did so locally. At first their major contribution as Germans was the introduction of uniquely German family industries such as the brewing of beer (introduced by the South German current of the Continental stream) and skilled craftsmanship into the American setting. From these family enterprises, they developed corporations of their own, which frequently expanded into monopolies, such as that of the famous Peoria "whiskey trust" of the late nineteenth century. Running the gamut from artisans and small merchants to powerful newspaper editors and industrial leaders, the German element tended to supplement the earlier efforts of Yankees and Middle States emigrants. The same may be said of the Scottish, Scandinavian, and Jewish settlers. The former, from the Calvinist tradition, behaved economically like Yankees. The Scandinavians brought craft skills like the Germans and entrepreneurial interests like the Scottish. The Jews specialized in commerce, often replacing the Yankees who moved into industrial pursuits, to become the merchant princes of Peoria, Champaign-Urbana, Springfield, Superior, Decatur, and, to a lesser extent, Belleville, Davenport, Rockford, Rock Island, Duluth, Pueblo, Joliet, Alton, and East St. Louis. All four groups were attracted to civic life in one way or another, the Scandinavians primarily through practical politics, the Germans through practical politics and civic leadership and the political action that such leadership required.

The Irish came as manual laborers to supply the growing needs of the industrial activities developed by representatives of the other currents. Their background in Ireland discouraged most of them from moving southward into the corporate plantation region. Consequently, they stayed in the northern regions to complement the northern industrial economy and, never wary of self-assertion, quickly turned to politics in order to better compete with the older, established Protestant elements for benefits from the new urban-industrial frontier. Their brand of favor and kinship politics introduced something of the style more common to the Southern-influenced regions, but their general commitment to the twin goals of economic advancement and social acceptance and their knowledge of Anglo-Saxon ways and the English language prevented corporate exploitation of their situation in the same way that the less highly motivated, individualistic Southerners or the non-English speaking southern and eastern Europeans were exploited farther south.

The southern and eastern Europeans who reached the cities of the greater West were also unskilled workers for the most part, who took their places in the economic system at the lowest level. Without exception, the relative magnitude of the two streams within the cities of the prairie has reflected the extent of heavy industrialization in each civil community. They came close to becoming an authentic proletariat at one time but, in the process of assimilating into American society, lost most of the characteristics that contribute to the development of a working-class outlook and acquired in their place the middle-class outlook of the society around them. Only in Duluth has anything approaching a class cleavage developed. The predominantly peasant immigrants responded politically to the type of favor and kinship politics introduced by the Irish, which operated to ameliorate their position as economic underdogs by providing access to the governments of the civil community in return for political support at the polls and acceptance of the right of their politicians to take their "cut" for managing the government.

These two streams did introduce one new "industry" into the cities of the prairie—organized crime. Crime, as such, has been present in the greater West since the beginnings of settlement. Individual outlaws and small gangs operated in the older entrepreneurial tradition, and there was more than a little unorganized violence rooted in the explosion of human passions; but, while occasional efforts were made to organize the supply of illicit services in certain communities after the Civil War, it was not until the 1920's that crime was organized along modern business lines, to supply goods and services that were formally outlawed around that time. Liquor, gambling, and prostitution all had been legally and easily available in most of the cities of the prairie until World War I. The outlawing of these activities came at a time when the cleavage between the old settlers and the then most recent immigrants was strongest and the opportunity for the latter most limited. Consequently, it was easy for some of them to gravitate into society's marginal fields of activity to achieve economic success, particularly if their culture did not impose serious restrictions on any of the three activities they were called upon to supply.

The liquor question has been a benchmark of cultural cleavage in the cities of the prairie from the first. It was one of the original issues to confront most of them and, in one form or another, has remained a perennial one.[12] The temperance movement was introduced into the greater West by the more religiously active Yankees, as well as by products of the religious revivalism of the other native streams, as part of a reform "package" that periodically included such items as abolition of slavery, achievement of women's suffrage, and elimination of legalized prostitution. Resisted at first by "unrepentant" natives as well as by the Germans and Irish and later by the southern and eastern Europeans, reform later became identified with the growing conflict between Protestants and Catholics. At first, the temperance fight centered on the question of licensing establishments to sell liquor. Except for Rockford, the cities of the prairie did not take active steps toward total prohibition of the sale of alcoholic beverages until the first decade of the twentieth century, because the prohibition advocates were strongly outnumbered by free-drinkers and moderates. In highly Calvinistic Rockford full prohibition was a real issue from the first, but even there a restrictive licensing policy was adopted in its stead.

Prostitution, which was "wide open" and generally legalized even in medium-size and small cities in the days of the land frontier (again excepting Rockford, where it was always limited), clearly verged on the edge of the permissible because of its means of recruitment of prostitutes ("white slavery") and the ways in which the entrepreneurs and "madames" of the industry flouted other laws, such as those regulating the sale of liquor. Its elimination as a legally tolerated activity, like prohibition, came during World War I when local and national forces aligned against it found an opportune time to act.

As the reformers gained victory in the other two "crusades," they turned their attention to prohibition and prostitution. Just prior to and during the national emergency of World War I, they succeeded in securing prohibition, first by legislation in many states and local communities and then nationally by constitutional amendment. They also secured state and local legislation outlawing prostitution and federal legislation prohibiting the transportation of women across state lines for immoral purposes. The war itself brought active federal intervention in local communities to close down the red light districts "for the protection of the health of the servicemen." The great military raids of 1917 ended open prostitution in the cities of the prairie as in the rest of the country.

Gambling existed in conjunction with both the taverns and the brothels as well as independently. At first the province of professional gamblers, individual entrepreneurs in their own right, it was later reorganized into two wings. The first was structured along business lines with "outlets" primarily in the taverns of the working class. The other remained more "amateur," though it was institutionalized as a prime function of the fraternal orders to provide this service for the middle class. Both activities provided a lucrative source of revenue for local officials willing to officially overlook their existence and, at first, remained under the control of individual entrepreneurs or small operators. The simultaneous closing of both taverns and brothels drove gambling further underground.

Eliminating easy access to liquor, women, and betting did nothing to lessen the demand. The vacuum thus created was filled by those elements best able to do so—the newest immigrant groups. The reasons for this were many. These people were still excluded from equal economic opportunity in legal enterprises. They had fewer scruples about engaging in such activities since they were not necessarily considered bad in the context of their native cultures. They possessed the rudiments of an organization to handle the operations in their extended family ties and in the brotherhood societies they had imported from the old country. Their women (along with those of the lower classes from the South, who were in much the same position in the cities) had traditionally supplied the bulk of the prostitutes and were more frequently driven to that occupation by the limits placed upon them at home and in the community at large. While the extent of these twin industries varied from community to community, in virtually every case such industries as did exist were controlled by southern and eastern Europeans (often using properties owned by members of the upper and upper-middle-class Protestant ruling elite, who took their share of the profits in that way).[13] In Madison and St. Clair Counties, however, products of the native Southern stream such as the Shelton Gang took a direct hand in operating this industry, more or less dominating it to the exclusion of other ethnic elements. Regardless of who controlled this new industry, its survival depended upon the establishment of working relationships with the local authorities. Where the general ethos was more permissive, the local political system could accommodate such relationships with relative ease, and the industry flourished.[14] Otherwise, it was limited to survival in secret or semi-secret fashion with the relationships maintained *sub rosa.*

With the repeal of prohibition, the liquor issue again became a matter of conflicting ideas of proper regulation. Such questions as control over liquor sales, the number and location of taverns, local option, drinking hours, Sunday closing, and the transfer of liquor licenses are perennial matters of concern in the cities of the prairie. At the same time, the patterns of illicit control established in the 1920's were perpetuated in the still-illegal fields of gambling and prostitution. In several of the civil communities, the latter two activities flourished openly between the wars until another federal crackdown during World War II, then were revived until a statewide crackdown took place during Adlai Stevenson's administration. In most cases, they remained tied to the liquor industry in many communities, with underworld elements controlling licenses and distributorships for more or less legal profit and using retail outlets as centers for purveying both prostitution and gambling.

Excluding the Madison-St. Clair Counties area, where the supplying of illicit activities has been a major local industry in and of itself, it is possible to construct a "tolerance" continuum for the cities of the prairie with Rockford, which has strictly limited all such activities within its boundaries, at one end, and Springfield, which encourages a certain amount of prostitution, gambling, and after-hours drinking as "good for business," at the other. Table 5–2 summarizes the situation in the seventeen civil communities as of 1960. From an examination of the table, it is not only possible to learn of the relative extent of vice and organized crime in the cities of the prairie but to gain insight into the differences in local values in the various civil communities. These differences are highly correlated with the differences in the cities' demographic composition.

Until very recently, the attitude that black vice is a thing apart has

TABLE 5-2

Illicit Activities in the Cities of the Prairie

Civil Community	Historical Antecedents	Contemporary Manifestations	Local Attitude	Local Government Involvement
Champaign	Open prostitution until 1939. Relatively strict liquor licensing, some prohibition sentiment, gambling in private clubs.	Occasional B-girls; Some Negro prostitution; license limit maintained; gambling generally closed down except for annual affairs.	Opposed to white prostitution, casual toward Negro vice in all its forms. Moderate views on drinking liquor.	Payoffs until 1939. Opposed to Negro "houses." Licenses rarely transferred on "first come, first serve" but on "favor" basis. Gambling kept down by enforcement.
Urbana	Generally closed community, strong prohibitionist sentiment. Citizens patronized Champaign's services.	License limit maintained. Prostitution and gambling very limited.	Strong "anti-vice" sentiments.	Licenses granted on "favor" basis. Police enforcement strong.
Decatur	Semi-open prostitution until 1957. Moderate to free liquor licensing policy. Semi-open gambling till 1957.	Occasional B-girls and houses; some Negro prostitution. Large license limit, many taverns. Any gambling continues quietly, perhaps in clubs.	Opposed to prostitution, casual toward Negro vice in all its forms. Casual attitude toward liquor. Mixed response to gambling.	Tie-ins with local government and prostitution until closed down. Now strongly opposed. Extensive government enforcement of liquor laws. Strong city enforcement against gambling.
Joliet	"Wide open" prostitution and gambling until early 1950's, apparently under control of organized crime since 1920's. Many taverns, particularly on east side.	Some prostitution and more gambling remain available, apparently under a local "syndicate" tied in with organized crime in Chicago; easy attitude toward liquor licensing.	Accepts prostitution, gambling, easy drinking on the east side, and the reputed "syndicate" as "facts of life."	Reputedly considerable tie-ins with various local governments, particularly Will County and City of Joliet law enforcement agencies. Local authorities keep operations within limits.
Alton	Prostitution and gambling existed with little active opposition until 1950's. They served Missouri as much as Illinois. Taverns also active in serving Missourians.	Madison County as a whole supposedly "closed down" since late 1950's. What does exist exists quietly. Taverns continue to flourish without serious interference.	Generally apathetic toward all three issues and no feeling that their present status represents a "problem."	Manager government opposed prostitution and gambling and favored closer regulation of taverns. Rumors that all is not closed or regulated are widely circulated.
Belleville	Old brewery town; beer gardens once popular. Heavy gambling in private clubs and taverns. Occasional flurries of prostitution.	Many taverns, catering mainly to beer-drinkers. Gambling confined to some clubs after crackdown in recent years. In-city prostitution virtually nonexistent.	Casual attitude toward moderate drinking (beer) and continued interest in small-time gambling. Desire to keep prostitution out of town.	Strong opposition to prostitution and any threats by E. St. Louis crime syndicate to move into Belleville. Open gambling not allowed. Easier attitude toward gambling in clubs.

TABLE 5-2 (continued)

Civil Community	Historical Antecedents	Contemporary Manifestations	Local Attitude	Local Government Involvement
E. St. Louis	Traditionally a center of vice industry since early days. Since 1920's or earlier vice and crime highly organized into two-county syndicate independent of outside control.	Community serves as vice and illicit activities center for St. Louis metropolitan area under organized "syndicate" which ties together prostitution, gambling, liquor, racing, and entertainment.	Existence of vice and organized crime accepted by most as a matter of course, even of perverse local pride.	Organized crime and local government very closely linked, not only in "pay-off" alliance but in overlapping personnel.
Peoria	Traditionally characterized as a "wide-open river town" with good cause. Open prostitution and gambling closed down in early 1950's. Easy liquor policy.	The striptease-B-girl-prostitution chain continues to exist but operates less flagrantly and openly. Same true of gambling. Vice system apparently locally controlled with national tie-ins.	Some sentiment that a little bit of "action" is very good for business. General easy-going attitude toward these activities.	Collusion between local officials and vice elements once very pronounced. Now some protection is apparently provided, but "action" is kept within definite bounds.
Davenport	A lively town by Iowa standards, but tame compared to the cities across the river. Once "wide open" and still has tolerant attitude toward drinking; gambling always private.	No open prostitution and little, if any, covert. Beer sold legally, but liquor sold by the drink semi-legally or illegally only. Gambling in private clubs only.	Tolerant attitude toward drinking, unlike rest of state, but general opposition to prostitution and open gambling.	Bars are unofficially allowed to sell liquor by the drink in opposition to Iowa law. Prostitution kept down. Private gambling left alone by common consent.
Rock Island	Historically a "wide open river town" with prostitution, gambling, and liquor aplenty but handled in a "district" with considerable "western" flair.	Since the "district" was closed down during the Stevenson administration, prostitution has been confined to two locations, gambling to one or two or to the suburbs, and taverns better regulated.	"Western" best describes it—very tolerant so long as "things don't get out of hand."	Used to be very close. Now it is rumored that police keep things quite limited and get paid for doing so. Negroes given considerably freer rein.
Moline	Traditionally closed down tight. No organized prostitution within city limits. Gambling restricted to upper-class clubs. Liquor either prohibited or tightly regulated.	Much the same as in the past. Licensed taverns permitted in limited number. One known gambling club frequented by upper crust. No organized prostitution.	Highly puritan and actively in favor of strict enforcement. People who want "vice" go to surrounding areas.	Local authorities generally respond to public demands for strict enforcement, if only because demands are so actively made.

TABLE 5-2 (continued)

Civil Community	Historical Antecedents	Contemporary Manifestations	Local Attitude	Local Government Involvement
E. Moline-Silvis	Drinking, small-time gambling, and semi-professional prostitution traditionally allowed. Taverns mostly neighborhood clubs with political roles.	Much the same as in the past. Taverns are basically neighborhood clubs with political influence, though latter is declining.	Traditionally free attitude toward drinking, mild gambling, and semiprofessional prostitution.	Local authorities tolerant of all this. They are products of the general community mores and often of tavern-centered politics. They receive appropriate "campaign contributions."
Rockford	Strong puritan tradition. Liquor always an issue: prohibition vs. strict licensing. Little gambling, all private. Even less prostitution.	No organized prostitution in city or immediate environs. Perhaps some gambling in private clubs. Liquor licenses strictly supervised and limited.	Remains strongly puritan. Lunchtime drinking is greatest public deviation from local tradition.	Local authorities enforce laws strictly, even among Negroes. This attitude crosses all other lines of political cleavage locally.
Springfield	Generally "open" town. Prostitution, gambling, and free sale of liquor rarely interfered with or bothered by citizenry who accept the "obligations" of Illinois' capital city.	After a severe crackdown on prostitution and gambling and some regulation of liquor sales under the Reform (1955) there has been a moderate revival of all this.	Strong feeling that a certain amount of illicit activity is "good for business" in a state capital and convention center.	Local authorities have, with one exception, tolerated and allowed illicit activities, encouraged to do so by local business interests. They have also gained pecuniary benefit from these activities.
Duluth	Different historical patterns in each of Duluth's "two cities," the east end quite puritan and the west end more open in regard to all three activities, though more restrictive than Illinois.	In regard to prostitution and gambling, very little and nothing organized in any part of the city. The west end still allows more taverns than the near-dry east end.	The two cities' attitudes are merging into one generally puritan attitude except in the case of drinking.	In boom days local authorities were tolerant of activities in west end. Now they enforce laws strictly in response to community pressures as well as in reflection of community mores.
Superior	"Wide open" lumber and port town in which prostitution, gambling, and drinking were major local businesses.	City much quieter since boom has departed. All three "services" still provided quietly but kept in local hands.	Generally quite tolerant. Opposed to outside control of local vice. "Good for business" outlook.	Local authorities "keep things under control" and keep outsiders from encroaching. Otherwise no effort to close places down or to profit exceptionally from them.
Pueblo	Open red-light district in boom days since closed down. Liquor and gambling widespread in connection with it. Reasonably quiet since World War I.	No organized prostitution but continuing existence of B-girls. Private gambling only. Liquor controlled in city, freer in fringe.areas.	Generally pro-strict enforcement but with sense that some things are bound to exist because of "human nature."	Local authorities enforce laws rather strictly but without puritan bias. Hispanic element given more "freedom" from regulation. Minor amount of "payoffs."

FIGURE 5-2

Political Control in Selected Cities of the Prairie, 1820-1962

Civil Community	1820 – 1960
Champaign	Moderate and paternalistic business oligarchy — Business-dominated autocracy — Fragmented polyarchy
Urbana	Moderate and paternalistic business oligarchy — Business-dominated autocracy — Renewal of old oligarchy
Joliet	Strong, paternalistic industrial-political oligarchy — Industrial-political oligarchy / Politician-dominated autocracy — Organized polyarchy
Belleville	Representative oligarchy — Representative oligarchy
East St. Louis	Industrial-business political oligarchy — Industrial-business political oligarchy / Politician-dominated autocracy
Peoria	Fragmented polyarchy — Representative oligarchy — Industrial-business political oligarchy / Political oligarchy/autocracy — Organized polyarchy
Davenport	Representative oligarchy — Representative oligarchy
Rock Island	Fragmented polyarchy — Representative oligarchy — Industrial-business political oligarchy / Politician-dominated autocracy — Industrial-business political-oligarchy — Organized polyarchy
Moline	Organized polyarchy — Industrial-business oligarchy — Organized polyarchy
East Moline	Industrial-political oligarchy — Representative oligarch,
Rockford	Organized polyarchy — Representative oligarchy — Representative oligarchy / Political oligarchy — Organized polyarchy — Organized polyarchy
Springfield	Business-political oligarchy — Business-political oligarchy
Duluth	Fragmented polyarchy — Industrial-business political oligarchy — Industrial-business political oligarchy / Industrial-political oligarchy — Organized polyarchy
Pueblo	Organized polyarchy — Industrial-business oligarchy — Industrial-business oligarchy / Political oligarchy — Organized polyarchy

been well-nigh universal among all the civil communities. Viewed as members of a separate and excluded community, the blacks have been left to their own devices as long as they keep quiet and to themselves. As one police chief put it, "The niggers can cut and fuck each other as much as they want, as long as they keep it quiet." While this attitude has been useful to purveyors of vice and violence, it has prevented law-abiding black citizens from obtaining adequate protection for their persons and property.

The "Two Cities" and the Varieties of Political Control

The introduction of population elements from outside the Anglo-American political tradition into the northern and middle cities of the prairie threatened for a time to radically alter the pattern of politics within those civil communities. The often illiterate, generally unskilled, and politically inexperienced immigrants were not only easily captured by political machines which traded minimal services for votes and power, but even where full-blown machines did not emerge, the political cleavage that developed between the newcomers and the older settlers fostered the development of ruling circles in each civil community, drawn from among those who were products of the native streams or of the earlier waves of immigration.

Seeing the gap between the old and new elements, these ruling circles, who themselves had come from, and supported, democratic traditions, were tempted to limit democracy to their own group and to deal quite autocratically with those from outside their own cultures. Through their economic power, these better established elements could maintain themselves as a self-contained community, internally republican, while, by reaching an accommodation with the professional political "bosses" in their efforts to control the "masses," they could maintain their own positions more or less intact. The "two cities" produced by this system existed side by side, with the new immigrants controlled politically through the machine system and its professional political managers and economically through the factory system and its businessmen owners or managers.

The extent to which the "two-cities" system flourished varied from community to community, depending on the origins and relative strengths of their various elements. Still, four exemplary patterns can be identified. In the American Bottoms, it became solidly entrenched in its most intensive form very early, with the two "cities" actually separated by municipal boundaries in some cases. In Rockford, on the other hand, it hardly was attempted when the Scandinavians arrived but did succeed briefly when applied to the southern and eastern Europeans. In recent years it has been successfully challenged by the politically sophisticated element among the latter. In Champaign, its development was limited because of the lack of migrants from outside the American political tradition. In Duluth it led to the creation of two competing sections, each possessing reasonably equal political power drawn from different sources of strength, rather than two "cities" in the usual layered arrangement.

In the cities of the prairie, at least, the classic formulation of "boss rule" and "machine politics" as near-total dominance of a city or civil community by a hierarchical political organization led by a professional political "boss" is accordingly deficient when taken at face value. Except in rare cases, as when H. I. Green was the "businessman boss" of Champaign County and its cities, the control exercised by the political machine was confined to the newer elements in the community, who were as yet politically inarticulate and depended upon the favors of the machine system for sheer survival.[15] The other elements in the community, namely those that were socially established and politically articulate in their own right, may have turned the reins of most of the local governments over to the professional politicians and allowed them their surcharge fees for "running things" but, in matters affecting them directly, were generally quick to have their way. The locus of power within these established and articulate elements was determined in a "republican" manner, through reasonably open and equal competition among interest groups and their representatives.

The "two-cities" system could not last, given the American democratic ethos. Its elimination has been the central feature of America's great postwar revolution, whose political aspect began with the elimination of the old machine and continues today through the introduction of the blacks into the political process as equals. More concretely, the political aspects of the revolution began through the convergence of two factors. On one hand, the general predisposition of many Americans to strive for the creation and maintenance of a "good community" was transformed into active reform effort as a result of visibly flagrant abuses of power by the business-politician coalition. On the other hand, as the previously inarticulate immigrants became Americanized, they demanded a fair share in the decision-making process. The pressures put by the inhabitants of the "lower city" upon the inhabitants of the "upper city" in the name of the latter's own values and reinforced by the former's improved economic position led, sooner or later, to the breakdown of the division and the re-establishment of the original republican order, or a modern facsimile of it. The manner and extent to which these two factors developed and converged have varied from community to community, as have their effects on the status quo ante. However, it can be said that the half-generation since the end of World War II will be remembered as the time when the "two cities" of the late nineteenth and early twentieth centuries merged into one civil community, altering the pattern of community politics in the process.

Figure 5–2 presents an approximation of the historical trends in local political control in selected cities of the prairie since their founding, illustrating the rise and decline of the "two-cities" system, as well as the progression of forms of political control in each. Since accessible historical data for several of the civil communities is lacking, the comparison is limited to those whose political histories could be traced with accuracy.[16]

As the figure indicates, there is an overall trend to organized polyarchy as the dominant mode of local political control. This trend is by no means universal, nor is there any indication that it is the product of some unilinear evolutionary pattern. On the contrary, the effects of such sociocultural phenomena, as discussed in this and previous chapters, appear to substantially influence the evolution of the locus of political control in the different civil communities. What is apparent is the progressive elimination of the "lower city" and its incorporation with the "upper city" into a sociopolitically unified civil community, albeit with a political cleavage of greater or lesser intensity. This, in turn, by broadening the base of the politically articulate elements in the community, is contributing to the elimination of the autocratic and single-element oligarchic forms of political control, bringing most of the cities of the prairie into the range of categories extending from multiple-element oligarchy to organized polyarchy.

The significance of this phenomenon cannot be overstated, for in it lies the key which explains the near-total absence of class warfare in the American community despite certain "objective" conditions that could have encouraged it. While a certain amount of struggle has been necessary to achieve this political integration of the civil community, generally it has been achieved with relatively little effort, and the struggle for its achievement has left few scars. It is very likely that this is because the democratic values brought into the civil communities of the greater West—values such as individual responsibility within the community, which came from New England and later from the Scandinavian immigrants, and polyarchy as an integral part of republicanism, which came from the Middle States and was reinforced by the earlier demands of the Germans and the Irish for equal acceptance—made the citizens of the "upper city" more predisposed to recognize the validity of the political claims of the citizens of the "lower city," while the frontier-generated socioeconomic system of the greater West that allowed considerable room for social and economic mobility gave these values a viable social and material base.

The extent of this overall movement toward a single "city" is nowhere more evident than in the case of the excluded streams—Afro-American, Hispanic and Oriental—whose representatives have had the most difficulty in becoming citizens of even the "lower city". From the first, black men were brought or encouraged to come to the cities of the prairie to fill in where white men were not available, to do society's dirty work, as it were. In the nineteenth century, this meant domestic service or the like. After the industrial expansion of World War I, which coincided with the beginning of the upward movement of the immigrants of the post-1890 period into middle-class occupations, black labor became necessary to fill the lowest echelons of the factory system. This need became even more pronounced during and after World War II, by which time the immigrants of the post-1890 period and their descendants were no longer prepared to furnish the bulk of the unskilled labor in communities with going manufacturing operations. Negroes (and Southern whites from the depressed rural areas of that section) were imported—literally in many cases—from the South to fill this vacuum in increasing numbers, adding a new dimension to the social problems of the more industrialized cities of the prairie while filling an economic need that was to begin to disappear less than a decade after it was felt in its greatest intensity.

The Korean War marked the high point in heavy industry's need for traditional forms of unskilled labor. The cessation of hostilities in 1953 virtually coincided with the introduction of concerted efforts to automate even the traditional industries. In Rockford, particularly, where the dominant machine-tool industry was already well along the road to automation, and in the Quad Cities, Joliet, Decatur, Duluth, Pueblo, and Madison-St. Clair Counties as well, this meant that the workers imported in the early 1950's with the least seniority were the first to be laid off, creating an unemployment problem that was also a racial and ethnic problem. For a decade it seemed that the Afro-Americans and their Southern white brethren would remain politically inarticulate as they had in the past. Then in local manifestations of the nationwide trend, the black community began to arouse itself and to enter community politics in a manner reminiscent of the advance of the white immigrant groups except that, in a time when the two cities were merging into one, it was no longer ready to accept lower-city status. By 1962, Champaign had a Negro councilman, Negroes were members of elective school boards in several of the other civil communities, and in almost every community Negroes had been recognized through appointive positions.

Much the same course is being followed by the Hispanic migrants into the cities of the prairie. Originally migrant workers who were fast becoming an agricultural proletariat, they were attracted to cities with few Negroes, where they filled many of the same roles as did the Negroes elsewhere. There they, too, have felt the twin burdens of lack of training and racial-ethnic prejudice. Like the Negroes, the Hispanic element has been politically inarticulate until very recently. Since World War II and particularly since the late 1950's, they have begun to assert themselves in modest ways. The entrance into the political arena of these two groups, which is just beginning, marks the latest step in the sociopolitical revolution that has been taking place at the local level, a step which could only come after the first steps toward the elimination of the "two cities" of the "white" citizens had been taken.

Socioreligious Subcommunalism: The Contemporary Extension of the Streams

In the aftermath of the amalgamation of the "two cities," an undercurrent of cultural difference remains significant in the cities of the prairie, rooted in religious patterns that stem from the various streams. Why are religious patterns so important and how do they make themselves felt? The liquor question, birth control, school prayers and Christmas observances, Sunday closing laws—such issues exist and can become highly charged with public controversy from time to time. As questions of fundamental concern to the various religious denominations, they may engender direct involvement of organized religious groups and their spokesmen. Except in such cases involving matters of "conscience," there is relatively little direct consideration of specific denominational or even religious principles in political situations in most civil communities today.

The real political importance of the religious factor is not simply the manifest influence of organized religion on questions of personal and public morality, but the sometimes latent and sometimes not-so-latent influence of socioreligious groups in the civil community, groups which are descended from the original migratory streams that settled in each of the cities of the prairie. The transformation of the overtly ethnic identities of the streams into socioreligious affiliations has already been discussed. It is through these socioreligious subcommunities that the old ties of family and the friendship cliques that represent the primary group affiliations of most people are maintained. Since religious institutions, like political ones, are essentially conservative, they contribute to the maintenance of inherited patterns brought in by their streams of origin in the first place. If fewer people in the cities of the prairie are conscious of the ethnic origins of their ancestors today, their church affiliations frequently give those origins away.

A person's religious affiliation, then, is not just an indication of where a man may spend an hour Sunday morning. It often signifies a personal association with a way of life that goes beyond the specifically "religious" into fields that overtly have little or nothing to do with organized religion. Families tend to be religiously homogeneous, and, within broad limits, marriages tend to take place endogamously, within the same socioreligious subcommunities. Friendship cliques also tend to be religiously alike in large measure, unless transcended by other immediate pressures or interests. Much of a person's socialization, then, takes place within socioreligious subcommunities that exist within each civil community, both in his early years and even later in life.[17]

The increased recognition of the contemporary reshaping of American polyarchy around religious differences and the progressive consolidation of religious groups whose differences were based on doctrinal or ethnic separations that are no longer meaningful into larger, socially more meaningful bodies is symptomatic of this.[18] Indeed, the very conversion of people to different religions or religious denominations is today less symptomatic of intellectual or spiritual change than of a person's social assimilation into a new extra-church-centered way of life. What is happening, in effect, is that the older ethnic groups have been merging into churches which reflect the larger cultural streams of which they are a part. These churches then become the outward manifestations of different socioreligious communities whose links extend far beyond the church itself but which recruit new "members" through the church organization. The religious factor, then, becomes an extension of the influence of the streams, adjusted to new situations, by other means.

The specific effects of this new pluralism or socioreligious communalism in the civil community can be very extensive. Students of politics are already quite familiar with the influence of religious affiliation on voting behavior.[19] However, the effects of the religious factor, understood in the broader sociological sense, go beyond the act of voting itself. Several major areas of influence stand out in some or all of the cities of the prairie.

Religious affiliation affects the structure of power in most, if not all, of the cities of the prairie. Its significance is often so great that open reference to it, like reference to "religion" per se, is too volatile a subject to be tolerated, except where it becomes unavoidable. Thus there has developed a "gentlemen's agreement" among civic and political leaders, influentials, and actives to avoid open references to religion and religious cleavages while quietly taking them into consideration in a wide variety of ways. Very frequently, access to high-level political influence depends to a significant degree on one's church affiliation, with one or more churches either dominating certain fields of community leadership or sharing domination among themselves. Certainly membership in some churches rather than others makes a difference in the hearing one will get in certain civic matters. A member of the high-prestige Second

Congregational Church in Rockford will certainly have better access to the community business and industrial leadership than a "mere" Swedish Baptist, all other things being equal. The situation in Belleville is exceptionally clear-cut. There the civil community is divided into two "wings," Protestant and Catholic, both of which contribute "representatives" to each of the three important elements that make up the local oligarchy: "business," "labor," and "city hall." These "representatives" emerge, willy-nilly, from an internal influence structure within their respective socioreligious subcommunities of which they are parts. So, for example, the First Presbyterian Church is clearly the center for the leading influentials in the Protestant subcommunity, to the point where its members verbally acknowledge the extent of their influence, at least within the confines of the church itself. At the same time, the Catholics have their own influence structure tied to the offices of the Belleville Diocese (which has been in existence since 1887). The small Jewish group in town, though not sufficiently numerous to be considered a full-fledged "wing," also contributes a number of community leaders, who are, in part, recognized as Jewish "representatives."

The Belleville situation represents, in many respects, the extreme case of implicit public recognition of socioreligious subcommunities. However, its Protestant-Catholic-Jewish subcommunal substructure does represent the basic socioreligious division in community affairs that is found in most of the cities of the prairie. It is rarely a negative division but, rather, a positive and implicit recognition of a socioreligious subcommunalization that exists and which, as it replaces the ethnic differences that "counted" a generation or two ago, has become the major means of personal identification with these differing patterns of behavior and value systems that are acceptable within the community.[20]

In communities where the Catholic elements represent a later "intrusion" into a previously predominantly Protestant society, the division sometimes does take on some aspects of a negative cleavage. Again, Rockford is a case in point. Until the late nineteenth century, Yankee and Scandinavian Protestants, mostly from the free-church tradition at that, were virtually undisturbed in their civil community. With the arrival of numbers of Italians and later the Slavic groups—all Catholics—this situation was altered, and visible differences in attitude and behavior were associated with differences in religious attachment. Some Rockfordians responded by encouraging the development of a local branch of the American Protective Association, a nationwide anti-Catholic movement. In 1892, the A.P.A. actually elected a mayor, but he was defeated two years later in a large-scale repudiation of overt anti-Catholicism as being against the "Rockford way of life." The conflict that almost erupted in violence was then channeled into a quiet but more permanent political cleavage, which, while now much lessened in intensity, still exists. In recent years there have been signs that the old cleavage will be replaced by a form of cooperative subcommunalism as the differences in values and behavior patterns between northern stream Protestants and southern stream Catholics lessen.

In many respects, the cleavage between streams in Moline has taken on similar socioreligious overtones with northern Protestant Yankees and Swedes pitted against a small but visible minority of middle-Catholic Belgians. Across the river in Davenport, on the other hand, the situation has developed along lines similar to those in Belleville, with each of the three socioreligious subcommunities contributing "representatives" to a common representative oligarchy. A similar, if less obvious, situation prevails in Springfield and, very likely, in Champaign and Urbana as well. The extent to which it is true in the other civil communities is not as immediately apparent, but positive subcommunalism appears to exist in Joliet, Peoria, Decatur, Alton, Superior, and Pueblo while negative cleavages are found in East St. Louis (where the racial question is central) and Duluth (which resembles Rockford and Moline).

Those civil communities whose settlers came from a variety of different streams and currents, each of which has preserved its identity in some way, frequently carry the socioreligious extension of their subcultures beyond the basic three-fold division. In the first place, wherever a Negro community exists there is a fourth, Negro Protestant, subcommunity which is markedly separate from the white Protestant subcommunity and which plays an entirely different political role. In addition, both the Protestant and Catholic subcommunities may be divided (and are further dividing themselves *socially* despite the recurrent talk of *religious* ecumenicalism) into subcommunal groupings along the lines of the streams discussed in Chapter Four.

In Joliet and Rockford, for example, the Catholics are still divided among the "puritan" Catholic churches dominated by the Irish and the "free" Catholic churches dominated by the southern and eastern Europeans. The former contribute more people to positions of political leadership, but, because the parish system of the Catholic Church and the precinct (or ward) system in local politics tend to intermesh in the older "ethnic" neighborhoods, the latter are also given some place in the politics of both civil communities. The overall domination of the Catholic Church hierarchy by the Irish and the higher level of internal unity within the Church, as compared to Protestantism, make it difficult for the observer to distinguish these intra-church divisions and even more difficult to assess the possibilities for their future development.

The situation is somewhat more clear-cut among the Protestants. There appears to be an emerging three-fold division among them with a degree of political "specialization by subcommunity" within Protestantism. In most of the cities of the prairie, community civic leadership remains largely in the hands of the heirs of the Calvinistic-Reformed-Presbyterian tradition. The position of the hierarchical church groups differs considerably from community to community depending on the historical positions occupied by the streams they reflect. Representatives of the Episcopal Church tend to be the social and big business leaders while Lutherans may have less of a role in community life except insofar as they are specifically "represented." Members of both can be found among the local civic leadership, particularly where they are heirs to the right political subculture. While the fundamentalists are losing importance in the day-to-day decision-making process in the civil community, they have begun to demonstrate considerable power in issues which are taken to the public, by virtue of their numbers and their willingness to state their case vocally and publicly. Active fundamentalists can generally be found leading the fight against such "socialistic" and "atheistic" schemes as fluoridation, urban renewal, and dog-leash laws. They are minimally represented in the quieter processes of local government primarily because they have had little interest in politics, per se.

The socioeconomic aspects of the three-fold division in Protestantism are apparent. However, the standard socioeconomic explanations of this phenomenon are inadequate to analyze the complexities of each grouping's political involvement, particularly since the socioreligious communities themselves embrace a variety of socioeconomic groups and cut across class lines. It is their descent from the original streams of migration into the cities of the prairie that better explains their respective positions in the political systems of the contemporary civil community.

Socioreligious subcommunalism has a direct impact on two very important programmatic areas in every one of the cities of the prairie: education and welfare. In the field of education, every civil community has, in effect, a dual school system consisting of the public schools, which reflect the dominant values of the local Protestant "establishment," though perhaps to a declining degree, and the parochial schools, which are predominantly Catholic but which may include Lutheran and Seventh Day Adventist schools as well. The parochial schools have developed where subcommunities that stand substantially outside the original Protestant "establishment" have been strong enough financially and have felt strongly enough about the education of their children to seek to develop their own educational systems. Parochial school enrollment in the cities of the prairie ranges from better than fifty per cent in Joliet, a largely (estimated 70 per cent) Catholic civil community whose Irish and European Catholics are concerned with providing their children with a "Catholic education," to 15 per cent in Pueblo where, despite a Catholic majority among the religiously affiliated, the predominant Latins have little concern for providing such an education. The extent to which the existence of extensive parochial school systems affects public support for public education is hard to assess. In some communities there is a tendency for Catholics to oppose efforts to support the public schools beyond the minimum level.

In most civil communities, certain peripheral public-supported services are extended to students in the parochial schools. This is particularly true in the case of school health services. The Springfield situation is typical. There the public school district maintains a health program for all its enrollees while the city health department maintains a similar program for the students in the parochial schools. In some cities, library service to the parochial schools is extended by the city or county library while the public school district often maintains its own library program. School recreation programs may be similarly divided among public school districts and the city recreation department or the local park districts. This, of course, represents a political compromise based on the balance of power among the socioreligious subcommunities. The school district, which is usually dominated by Protestants, is rarely receptive to the extension of services to parochial schools. The city government, on the other hand, almost invariably has a high percentage of Catholics occupying key positions. They see the political value of extending certain public services to nonpublic schools and, where possible, do so. The extent to which they can do so is limited by the extent to which the Protestants will tolerate public support for services to essentially Catholic institutions.

While at least some degree of ticket balancing among representatives of the socioreligious subcommunities is well-nigh universal in the cities of the prairie, it is nowhere more evident than in the case of the school board elections. While Catholics may be given representation on the school board—even equal representation in communities like Belleville, which are equally divided between Catholics and Protestants—it is tacitly agreed that the Protestants have the "right" to dominate the public school systems, either through a clear majority on the school board or through Catholic acquiesence to policies that touch upon the essential interests of the Protestants.

There are indications that this arrangement is changing, less because of peculiarly local dissatisfactions than as a consequence of some nationwide trends which are reflected locally. In the first place, the decline of religiosity, in the traditional sense of concern for ceremonial observance, has weakened the interest of the Protestants in retaining a "Protestant" school system. This attrition of the peculiarly Protestant characteristics of the public school system is being pushed along by a nationwide effort to sharpen the lines of separation between church and state. While most of this nationwide effort has been concentrated at the national judicial level, there are periodic echoes of it in the cities of the prairie.

Champaign provided the point of origin for the well-known McCollum case, which ended in a United States Supreme Court ruling that outlawed released time programs of religious education using public school facilities. This was an exceptional situation. More frequently, local groups will agitate for the elimination or limitation of Christian observances or rituals in the schools with varying degrees of success. Referring again to Champaign, there has been action taken in recent years to play down Christmas observances in the district high school in response to the nationwide agitation against such observances, which has been echoed, albeit with a minimum amount of publicity, by some local groups.

By and large, however, these nationwide movements for more strict separation between church and state in public school activities are not translated into local public concerns, much less public issues, unless local groups agitate for them. More important, the growing number of Catholics making use of the public school system, either out of choice or because of lack of parochial school facilities, is reinforcing the already established non-Protestant (Jewish, secularist, and just unattached) clientele of the public schools. Together these groups are joining to eliminate some of the more overt "Protestantism" of the local public school systems.[21]

There is every evidence that in civil communities like Peoria, where more than one school district serves the local public school population as a result of the civil community's suburbanization, the continued interest shown in maintaining the separate existence of many school districts is a reflection of socioreligious concerns. The suburban school districts in the Peoria area are small enough to be reasonably homogeneous in population. This homogeneity has religious along with economic bases, even though suburban Peoria, like most suburban developments in the medium-size civil communities, is not, in the main, religiously segregated. Simply put, it is possible for a single socioreligious subcommunity to keep control of a small school district where it is difficult to do so in a larger district and, by doing so, utilize the public schools as institutions to help transmit their distinctive values and behavior patterns, such as they are.

Whereas socioreligious subcommunalism is recognized in the realm of education through dual, publicly financed and privately financed systems, in the realm of local health and welfare services it is recognized through a public-private mix of cooperatively financed systems. Perhaps the most clear-cut example of public recognition of the role of the socioreligious subcommunalism in the provisions of local health and welfare services is provided by the hospital system. Belleville is a good example. The Catholics established St. Elizabeth's Hospital as their contribution to the community. The Protestant leadership reacted by building Memorial Hospital as theirs. Both are equally recognized by the federal, state and local governments and get similar forms of public financial aid. Since Belleville has no governmentally operated hospital, these two must provide all the local hospital services for the civil community.

In Chapter Nine the public-private aspects of the public health program in Peoria will be discussed in some detail as an exercise in federalism. There the city and county public health districts work cooperatively with the Catholic and Methodist hospitals to provide hospital facilities locally. This arrangement has been recognized by the state and federal governments, which provide public funds through the Hill-Burton and other programs to hospitals controlled by different religious denominations as well as to government-operated hospitals, on an equal basis.

Nor are hospitals the only manifestations of the role of socioreligious communalism in the provision of local health and welfare services. Nursing homes, counseling centers, youth and family service agencies are frequently sponsored by different socioreligious communities with varying degrees of public support. These agencies are not simply designed to segregate people by "religion" but to contribute to the overall framework of public service institutions available to the residents of the civil community by implicitly recognizing the religious nature of these enterprises.

There is every indication that this socioreligious subcommunalism will increase in importance in the cities of the prairie, particularly as ethnic identifications continue to decrease. This "new pluralism" cannot help but be reflected in their local political systems, frequently through tacitly constructed "systems" of socioreligious "representation" and increasingly through the development of government-subcommunal collaboration in the provision of public services. As they are crystallizing, the socioreligious subcommunities are not so much new phenomena in the civil community as they are new manifestations of the legacy of the streams.

Streams, Sections, and the Practice of Politics

As settlers came into the cities of the prairie, the national influences to which they were subject prevented the development of an introverted, parochial politics isolated from national political trends. On the contrary, from the earliest days of settlement, local politics reflected national, as well as state, influences because its participants were products of streams spread nationwide. At the same time, the direct and specific influences of sectionalism enabled the local settlers in each civil community to develop specifically local variations of those national political patterns in the context of their communities as well as in their capacities as citizens of their respective states. These local variations have been sharpened and deepened over the years, as the accretions of local history grow, without ceasing to be part of the national system of politics.

Needless to say, the Southern stream was the first to place its imprint upon politics in the state of Illinois. Until the mid-1840's, politics in Illinois was conducted almost exclusively within the framework of Southern political mores and with a Southern orientation. In territorial days, "gentlemen" from the South created a system of interlocking family alliances which competed politically as two factions for access to the pecuniary benefits of an expanding society. Though this closed factional system was replaced by a more open system of two-party competition in the days of the Jacksonian revolution, the idea that politics was a business which men entered on a career basis for profit-making purposes became ingrained in the Illinois political culture. (See Chapter Seven). This conception of politics for personal profit was later reinforced by the arrival of large numbers of southern and eastern Europeans and, later, Negro and Hispanic immigrants, most of whom found this system to be of advantage to them, at least during the period of their struggle for adjustment to the new society.[22]

Observation of contemporary political behavior in the state reveals how deeply entrenched this kind of politics has become. Professional commitment to a political career is the norm among contemporary politicians in Illinois, and "amateurs" are clearly discouraged from becoming involved in the state's political system.[23] With rare exceptions, the only place in which nonprofessionals can become active in politics in Illinois is at the community level, in city politics and, even more prominently, in school and park district politics, which tend to be the preserves of amateurs in the cities of the prairie. Except in rare circumstances, the nonprofessionals active in community politics cannot hope to advance to higher political office. This is somewhat less true in the very northern part of the state, where the still predominant political culture fostered by the Yankees and the northwestern Europeans (see below) makes the professional grip slightly less complete.

While the system of family alliances as the basis for political activity was disrupted on a statewide basis by the rise of political parties after 1828, in Madison and St. Clair Counties it has survived in the nominal confines of the party system. County politics, particularly in St. Clair County, can be understood only when the extent of familial participation over the generations is understood. Certain families there go into politics generation after generation just as other families in other places go into the ministry or military service. Some families specialize in school politics; others in countywide politics with bases of operation in the cities and villages of the American Bottoms; and still others have carved out familial fiefs in municipalities, townships, and special districts in a manner highly reminiscent of a feudalistic society. To take just one example among many possible ones, one American Bottoms school district in St. Clair County has had three generations of the same family occupying the position of district treasurer. Each generation's representative has, in turn, been indicted or forced to resign for embezzling school funds, but in each case the family has regrouped to secure the office again. Though this case is almost a caricature, it is not as unusual as it appears to be. It is indicative of the permanency of the family alliance system in Southern-dominated sections of Illinois, even where subsequent streams have brought apparently radical changes to other facets of the civil community's life.

The "political family," though particularly strong in the Southern-influenced regions of Illinois, is not confined to those regions alone. These intergenerational family "dynasties" can be found in other cities and counties in Illinois as well, in some cases tied to families whose ancestors originally came from the South and in others to families produced by those European-originated streams in which family and kinship ties traditionally bulk large. The latter, particularly those of southern and eastern European origin, brought a tradition of family loyalties to this country not too different from that found in the South. Quite naturally, this tradition is carried over into the realm of politics and, where ethnic politics still exists in the cities of the prairie, plays some role. In most of the civil communities, however, the place of familial connections is relatively unimportant in the larger scheme of the political system. Only in the Madison-St. Clair area does it play an extensive role in the process of government.

Though the Southern stream also influenced the political development of parts of Iowa and Colorado, in these states its representatives arrived simultaneously with those of other streams. Consequently, they did not have the free hand to implant their "way of politics" onto the newly forming state political systems that they had in Illinois. Their contributions were substantially modified by the products of the other streams, particularly the Yankees, who contributed much to both states. What emerged in both were modified versions of the Yankee approach to politics, involving the incorporation of Southern (and Middle state) style of politics-as-a-system-of-favors-and-loyalties into a system of politics-as-a-responsible-public-enterprise. This meant, among other things, considerably less professionalization among political actives and much greater opportunity for amateur politicians to participate. In both states, political loyalties became more important among political actives than political principles, but politics did not become simply another profit-making business in either.

Since it has remained possible and even normal for nonprofessionals to capture any political office in those states, there has been considerably less separation between state-level and local-level politics in Colorado and Iowa and considerably greater mobility from one level to the other. This is not to say that city office in either state is a particularly good starting point for a political career at the state or national level, but it is one of several starting points for the suitably talented and is not considered to be a barrier to advancement as it often is in Illinois.

Still, the continuing division between the streams had led to a somewhat greater division between statewide politics and the politics of specific civil communities, which may be dominated by the products and traditions of one of the minority currents. This is true of both Davenport and Pueblo, the former because of its polyglot middle European background, which is well-nigh unique among cities of its size in Iowa, and the latter because of its southern European and Hispanic background, which is similarly unique in Colorado, though it is apparently not true in respect to their sister cities.[24]

The arrival of the Yankee stream on the Illinois scene brought a major political clash between its representatives and the managers of the Southern-style politics of the state, which ultimately changed the face of Illinois politics in many ways. This was fundamentally a clash of cultures whose political manifestations remain evident in the continuing pattern of state and national partisan political alignments and in the continuing character of state-local relationships.

During the twenty-year period preceding the Civil War, the Yankee emigrants to Illinois were involved in political warfare on several fronts. In national and state politics they were active advocates of the abolition of slavery or at least its elimination in the western territories. Since the struggle over slavery was essentially a political struggle, these Yankees were intensely involved in extra-community politics. However, the two major parties then existing in Illinois and the nation were essentially unsympathetic to these ideological goals, since their leadership was not interested in issue-oriented politics. Consequently, the more militant Yankees could find little succor within their ranks. This led many of them to leave the major parties and form Illinois contingents of such third-party movements as the Free Soil party. These rebels finally founded the Republican party in 1854 to carry their banner, which by then had come to include issues that promised to be of more direct benefit to them than the abolition of slavery. Within two to four years after the formation of the GOP, Yankee-Scandinavian northern Illinois had become Republican territory and the Republican party had made great inroads into traditionally Whig areas in central Illinois. Even the earlier moderates who had refrained from participation in third-party movements were so incensed over the Kansas-Nebraska Act and the Dred Scott decision that they left the disintegrating Whig party and the still-dominant Democrats en masse, to become Republicans and to bequeath their Republicanism to their children and their children's children. Northern and central Illinois, rural, urban, or metropolitan, has, with a few exceptions, remained the stronghold of Republicanism in the state ever since.

Table 5–3 reveals just how lasting this conversion was and how slowly

TABLE 5-3

Illinois Cities of the Prairie: Partisan Political Preferences, 1900-1964

Year	Illinois Statewide		Champaign Co. (Champaign-Urbana)		Macon Co. (Decatur)		Madison Co. (Alton, etc.)		Peoria Co. (Peoria)		Rock Island Co. (R.I., Moline, E. Moline)		Sangamon Co. (Spring-field)		St. Clair Co. (E. St. Louis, Belleville)		Will Co. (Joliet)		Winnebago Co. (Rockford)	
	Gov.	Pres.	Gov.	Pres.	Gov.	Pres.	Gov.	Pres.	Gov.	Pres.	Gov.	Pres.	Gov.	Pres.	Gov.	Pres.	Gov.	Pres.	Gov.	Pres.
1900	R	R	R	R	R	R	R	R	R	R	R	R	R	(R)	(D)	(D)	R	R	R	R
1904	R	R	R	R	R	R	R	R	R	R	R	R	R	R	R	R	R	R	R	R
1908	(R)	R	(D)	R	(R)	R	(R)	R	(D)	R	(R)	R	D	R	(D)	(D)	R	R	R	R
1912	(D)	(D)	(D)	(P)	(D)	(D)	(D)	(D)	(D)	(P)	(P)	(P)	(D)	(D)	(D)	(D)	(D)	(P)	(P)	P
1916	R	R	R	R	R	R	R	(R)	R	(D)	R	R	R	R	(D)	(D)	R	R	R	R
1920	R	R	R	R	R	R	R	R	R	R	R	R	R	R	R	R	R	R	R	R
1924	R	R	R	R	R	R	R	(R)	R	R	R	R	D	R	R	(R)	R	R	R	R
1928	R	R	R	R	R	R	R	R	R	R	D	R	R	R	D	D	R	R	R	R
1932	D	D	D	D	D	D	D	D	D	D	D	D	R	D	D	D	R	(D)	R	R
1936	D	D	D	D	D	D	D	D	D	D	D	D	D	D	D	D	D	D	(D)	D
1940	R	D	R	R	D	D	D	D	R	D	D	D	R	R	D	D	R	R	R	R
1944	R	D	R	R	D	D	D	D	R	R	D	D	R	R	D	D	R	R	R	R
1948	D	D	R	R	D	D	D	D	D	R	D	D	D	R	D	D	D	R	D	R
1952	R	R	R	R	D	R	D	D	R	R	R	R	R	R	D	D	R	R	R	R
1956	R	R	R	R	D	R	D	D	R	R	D	R	D	R	D	D	R	R	R	R
1960	D	D	R	R	D	R	D	D	D	R	D	D	D	R	D	D	D	R	D	R
1964	D	D	R	D	D	D	D	D	D	D	D	D	D	D	D	D	D	D	D	D
#GOP	11	9	13	13	7	10	7	7	10	11	7	9	9	13	3	3	12	13	12	14

( ) Indicates victory with less than 50 per cent of total vote.
Source: Samuel K. Gove, *Illinois Votes: 1900-1958*; and Richard M. Scammon, *America Votes*, Vol. 3.
R—Republican; D—Democratic; P—Progressive.

its aftereffects have been eroded by later events, even in the metropolitan centers of the Republican heartland. The table traces the electoral choices of the nine counties which contain the Illinois civil communities included in this study, in presidential and gubernatorial elections since 1900, indicating the victorious party in each election, by county, and in comparison with the statewide victor. Only presidential and gubernatorial elections are used, partly in order to simplify comparisons with counties in other states and partly to secure the maximum amount of deviation from party regularity by including the least consistent voters (who may vote only for these highly visible offices) and by injecting the maximum amount of extra-local pressures. The vote is recorded on a county-wide basis, partly because complete data are available back to 1900 only on that basis and partly because, short of attempting to calculate the limits of each civil community for each election and assembling voting data accordingly, the countywide vote is at least as accurate a reflection of political choices in the civil community as is the city vote alone, and probably more so. The former embraces considerably more area but not appreciably greater population, while the latter excludes everyone outside the city limits, which, particularly after 1920, leaves room for a substantial margin of error. Only in the cases of Rock Island, Madison, and St. Clair Counties are there several major civil communities with different patterns of voting behavior located within the same county. They will be dealt with separately.

With the exceptions of Macon, Madison, St. Clair, and Rock Island Counties, the Illinois cities of the prairie have remained predominantly Republican since their "conversion" in the nineteenth century, despite their greatly accelerated urbanization and metropolitanization. The extent to which this allegiance to the GOP has been maintained in national elections is even more graphically revealed in Samuel Gove's *Illinois Votes*.[25]

The influence of the streams is apparent. Those counties with the greatest number of Yankee and North Sea settlers have remained the most solidly Republican. The first to convert, for ideological reasons, they have generally remained in the Republican fold, excepting only 1912, when the same values which led their original settlers to become anti-slavery advocates led the then active generation into the ranks of the Progressive party. In some cases, they also broke ranks briefly during the depths of the Great Depression. Winnebago County (Rockford), the most solidly Yankee and northern European, remained the most solidly Republican until the New Deal. Then the pressures of economic necessity and the rise of the products of the newer streams combined to lower the county to second place. Still, except for 1936, the county has been carried by the Democrats only three times, by gubernatorial candidates that reflected the progressive image, Stevenson and Kerner (twice).

Will County, another center of Yankee settlement in the nineteenth century, has witnessed a progressive decline in the magnitude of its Republican majorities since 1920, when the newer immigrants apparently began to vote. This decline was temporarily accelerated in the 1920's as a consequence of the twin conflicts of Protestants versus Catholics and "dries" versus "wets" which were a feature of the decade. Overwhelmingly Catholic Joliet grew progressively less comfortable within Republican ranks and returned substantially smaller Republican majorities after 1920. However, the influence of its original culture bearers was such that Republicanism became a status symbol even for those descended from other streams. As they have joined the suburban middle class, they have entered (or reentered) the Republican fold, returning the civil community to the GOP column, where it has remained. Recently, the Democrats have been carrying Joliet Township proper, which is being abandoned to working-class elements as the other people move to Joliet's suburbs.

In a most revealing way, Champaign County (Champaign and Urbana have virtually identical patterns of voting behavior in state and national elections) has become the foremost Republican stronghold among the Illinois cities of the prairie. Like its northern sisters, it quickly converted to Republicanism when the party was founded but, with less of a population of northern stream origins, its Republicanism was less decisive until World War I. By that time, the immigration from the South had declined to a trickle, and the county's natives were lining up on the majority side of the fence. Since the county had received no major influx of potential Democrats from the later streams, its Republicanism could only intensify. As the other solidly Republican cities of the prairie found their majorities reduced by the arrival of the products of the later streams, Champaign-Urbana moved ahead by default.

What is significant about the Champaign-Urbana case is that it strongly implies that the changes in the voting patterns in the other counties are less a reflection of changes in individual voting habits (though such changes unquestionably do occur in times of crisis, as witness the very rise of Republicanism in the area) than an indication of the introduction of new groups into the active electorate, groups which do not share the norms of the dominant elements in the community and who vote accordingly where other norms are brought into play—in the more issue-oriented state and national elections. Where such groups are absent, even great political and economic events apparently have little effect on the voters' habits. A look at Table 5–4 reveals that in all cases except one, where the civil community is divided by high or medium cleavage on the basis of the "geologic" arrangement of the streams, the cleavage is expressed in the pattern of national party affiliations. (The one exception, East St. Louis, reflects a racial division which appears to be a sufficiently visible substitute for party ties.)

TABLE 5-4

Other States' Cities of the Prairie: Partisan Political Preferences, 1900-1964

Year	Scott Co., Ia. (Davenport) Gov.	Pres.	Douglas Co., Wisc. (Superior) Gov.	Pres.	Duluth, Minn.[a] Gov.	Pres.	Pueblo Co., Colo. (Pueblo) Gov.	Pres.
1900	R(1901)	R	R	R	D	R	(D)	(R)
1902	R(1903)	—	R	—	R	—	n.d.	—
1904	—	R	R	R	R	R	D	R
1906	(R)	—	R	—	D	—	(D)	—
1908	D	R	R	R	D	R	D	D
1910	D	—	R	—	(D)	—	D	—
1912	(D)	(D)	R	P	(D)	(D)	D	(D)
1914	(R)	—	R	—	D	—	R	—
1916	R	R	R	(R)	R	D	D	D
1918	(R)	—	R	—	R	—	R	—
1920	R	R	R	R	R	R	R	R
1922	R	—	R	—	R	—	D	—
1924	R	R	R	P	R	R	D	R
1926	R	—	R	—	R	—	D	—
1928	R	R	R	R	R	R	D	R
1930	R	—	R	—	FL	—	D	—
1932	D	D	R	D	FL	(D)	D	D
1934	D	—	(P)	—	FL	—	D	—
1936	D	D	P	D	FL	D	D	D
1938	D	—	(P)	—	R	—	R	—
1940	D	D	(P)	D	(FL)	D	R	D
1942	R	—	P	—	R	—	R	—
1944	R	D	(D)	D	DFL	DFL	D	D
1946	R	—	D	—	R	—	D	—
1948	D	(R)	(D)	D	DFL	DFL	D	D
1950	R	—	D	—	R	—	D	—
1952	D	R	R	D	DFL	DFL	D	(D)
1954	D	—	D	—	DFL	—	D	—
1956	D	R	D	D	DFL	DFL	D	R
1958	D	—	D	—	DFL	—	D	—
1960	D	R	D	D	DFL	DFL	D	D
1962	—	—	—	—	DFL	—	R	—
1964	D	D	D	D	—	DFL	—	D

[a]St. Louis County is clearly too vast to be at all representative of the Duluth civil community, hence figures are for the city of Duluth alone.

R — Republican
D — Democratic
P — Progressive
FL — Farmer-Labor
DFL — Democratic-Farmer-Labor
n.d. — data unavailable

This conclusion must be qualified to the extent that economic and political issues that are personally felt will alter established habits of voting. Belleville converted from Republicanism to the Democracy in 1928 in response to the prohibition issue. A community of heavy Germanic descent, accustomed to free consumption of beer and angry at being deprived of it by the GOP-led "government," its voters rallied to the cause of Al Smith and the "wet" Democrats and have remained predominantly Democratic ever since. That same year, the largely Southern-originated fundamentalist Protestant voters of East St. Louis, who were normally safely Democratic, reacted against Al Smith's Catholicism and "wet" position by voting for Hoover. In their case, however, this shift turned out to be an aberration that was quickly reversed with the coming of the Depression and the blow it struck against their immediate economic interests.

Despite this curious but understandable reversal in sources of Democratic voting strength that year, St. Clair County has had a record of consistent Democratic allegiance for generations. Just as the northern counties' Republicanism is a reflection of the geology of their settlement patterns, so is St. Clair County's Democratic allegiance a reflection of the serial impacts of the Southern, southern European, and Afro-American streams. Its sister, Madison County, which received a greater number of settlers from the other streams, was marginally Republican for a time. However, after the turn of the century, the great bulk of the migration into Madison County had its sources in streams generally Democratic. These new voters, as they became active members of the electorate, had already shaken the county's national Republicanism by 1912. The Great Depression did the rest, and the county has been solidly Democratic ever since 1932.

The civil communities in the middle—the ones settled originally from the Middle States and subsequently by many other streams—have also been the counties most likely to swing from party to party in response to national and state trends. In those counties, the balance of habitually committed voters from both parties has been so delicate that the independents have been able to swing the vote from one party to the other regularly. The reasons for the results in any given election in those civil communities are more closely related to immediate political issues than the reasons in the other civil communities. They will be further explored in Chapter Seven.

Though the Great Depression did deflect every one of the Republican counties from its normal pattern of electoral behavior at least once, its long-range effects upon voting behavior have been less than spectacular. By 1940, half of the metropolitan areas were voting Republican again, though by very slight margins. Indeed, since 1936 the Republican trend has been generally upward in all nine counties. By 1952, all except the

Madison-St. Clair area had returned to the Republican fold, and even in 1960, only Rock Island County joined the latter area in the Democratic camp. While the evidence is not clear-cut, the lowered Republican majorities of the post-New-Deal period can as easily be explained by the entrance of the last of the newer immigrant groups into the active electorate as by any shift in habitual voting behavior on the part of a substantial number of individuals, except in Rock Island County, where intensive party activity conducted by the strong Democratic organization may have produced sufficient changes in turnout among latent Democrats in the Rock Island and East Moline civil communities to really alter the previous voting patterns of the county, and in Will County, where the effects of the religiocultural cleavage of the twenties may have "permanently" weakened the Republican party.

While the role of the various states in determining who is placed on the ballot (both in the formal sense of legal determination and in the sense of the determinating force of political reality) and how frequently, prevents really clear-cut comparisons of the influence of the cultural streams on partisan political affiliations across state lines, some sense of their nationwide impact is provided when the same presidential and gubernatorial elections are compared in the other four cities of the prairie as well (Table 5–4).

Most of Iowa, like northern and central Illinois, was converted to Republicanism by the impact of the issues of the Civil War period. The Yankees and North Sea Europeans, and later those of the Middle and Continental streams, followed the same political path as their compatriots east of the Mississippi. Davenport, however, was not exactly like the rest of Iowa. Its more polyglot population included elements whose immediate local interests were not swayed by the same concern over the slavery issue but which reflected the cleavage between Protestants and Catholics in the state (usually, but inaccurately, referred to as the cleavage between "natives" and "foreigners"). So, while Scott County followed the general Iowa pattern of Republicanism in presidential elections, its voters periodically deviated from that pattern in gubernatorial contests.

The character of the cleavages in both Pueblo and Duluth were such that the observer would expect to find continuing bases of Democratic strength in both civil communities, regardless of the normal partisan preferences of their respective states. The southern Europeans who compose a large segment of the populations in both have traditionally supported the Democratic party. This expectation is borne out by the record. Even though Minnesota as a whole was predominantly Republican, with a continuing third-party movement in the period from the Civil War until the Depression, and Colorado as a whole has been a two-party state since it achieved statehood, there are great similarities between the voting records of Duluth and Pueblo.

If anything, "permanent" changes in the habitual voting patterns of the residents of all these civil communities have been made in response to religiocultural issues rather than to economic concerns. Students of voting behavior have pointed out that the real shift toward the Democratic party nationwide began in 1928, in response to the twin religiocultural issues of the 1920's and was only later reinforced by the economic crisis of the 1930's.[26] By the same token, historians have pointed out that the nationwide realignment of voters in the 1890's in connection with the Populist movement was more of a cultural conflict between city and farm than the product of a particular economic crisis, though the latter may have served as a periodic catalyst for action.[27]

The anti-Catholicism and the Prohibition question of the 1920's are only two examples of these politically significant religiocultural concerns. During World War I, the German elements in Davenport defected permanently from the Democratic party in reaction to "Mr. Wilson's War" against their "fatherland." The rise of the Republican party itself gained its greatest impetus from the "moral" (really religiocultural) issue of slavery rather than from any important economic concerns that could be felt directly by the public. (It is well and good to argue about the conflict between Northern industrialism and the free labor system versus Southern agrarianism and the slave labor system as economic determinants of the larger conflict, but these were not the felt concerns of the common people in the North who voted Republican. They were agitated, but about affronts to the religiocultural values and attitudes they held.)

In the 1960 elections, the older patterns of the streams, though considerably reduced in intensity, remained very much in evidence, despite a general turn away from the Republican ticket that year. Those patterns, diluted by the addition of new elements into the active voting population and modified by the influences of basic religiocultural concerns, remain to be reckoned with a century or more after their crystallization.[28]

NOTES

1. The argument over the nature of political control at the local level has waxed hot in recent years. Proponents of the "power structure" approach argue with the "pluralists." See Floyd Hunter, *Community Power Structure* (Chapel Hill: University

of North Carolina Press, 1953); Robert Dahl, *Who Governs?* (New Haven, Conn.: Yale University Press, 1961); Nelson Polsby, *Community Power and Political Theory* (New Haven, Conn.: Yale University Press, 1963); Thomas J. Anton, "Power, Pluralism and Local Politics," in *Administrative Sciences Quarterly* (March 1963); and Arnold Rose, *The Power Structure* (New York: Oxford University Press, 1967). Both groups tend to generalize for the country as a whole from single cases. As the number of studies of discrete communities increases, it has become apparent that there is no single kind of local political system in the United States while, at the same time, the range of differences among the country's local communities is quite narrow. This makes the development of both models and typologies feasible and relatively simple, provided that the individual cases are understood in the context of the three factors considered in this chapter.

2. See, in particular, Edward Banfield, *Political Influence* (Glencoe, Ill.: The Free Press, 1961).

3. For a discussion of access and representation as different phenomena in local politics, see Robert H. Salisbury, "Access and Representation in Local Politics," paper delivered at the 1961 meeting of the Midwest Political Science Association.

4. See Daniel J. Elazar, *The Politics of Belleville* (Philadelphia: Center for the Study of Federalism, 1969), for a detailed study of the Belleville situation.

5. Charles Press, *Main Street Politics* (East Lansing: Michigan State University, 1962), summarizes most of the useful community studies published between 1950 and 1962.

6. The nine-fold typology has an advantage in clarifying the locus of local political control in a given civil community which cannot be gained through identification of individual "decision-makers." Since the number of decision-makers as individuals is in every case limited to a small fraction of the total population, it is difficult to determine whether the particular decision-makers active at a particular point in time are functioning in a polyarchic, oligarchical, or autocratic system. Only through an understanding of the distinctions between these types and the addition of historical perspective is it possible to make reasonable judgments about the role of current actors in the local political process.

7. The data on political cleavages is based on the range of interviews conducted by the author in the civil communities in question as correlated with voting statistics for elections and referenda in the postwar period, and in some cases even earlier.

8. The problem of the politically inarticulate is just beginning to be studied in depth in the literature of political science. It is apparent to even the most casual student of political behavior that great numbers of otherwise eligible citizens do not participate in politics—at any level and particularly at the local level—even to the limited extent of voting. Students of local politics, regardless of their conclusions as to the nature of local political life, have agreed that the number of participants active in "decision-making" is relatively small while the number of "apathetic" citizens is incomparably greater. While this study was unable to devote proper attention to this phenomenon and its significance in the politics of the cities of the prairie, it does attempt to distinguish between those in the civil community who are politically articulate, those who may or may not be articulate themselves but are clearly represented by a politically articulate leadership, and those who are politically inarticulate and are not even represented by a politically articulate leadership.

9. Morris Janowitz, ed., *Community Political System* (Glencoe, Ill.: The Free Press, 1961) offers examples of the relationships between economics and politics, including industrial and business ownership. See also C. Wright Mills, *People, Power and Politics* (New York: Ballantine Books, 1963).

10. For a record of the influences of these streams on the development of corporate enterprise, see Douglass North, *Economic Growth of the United States: 1790–*

1860 (Englewood Cliffs, N.J.: Prentice-Hall, 1961); G. H. Evans, Jr., *Business Incorporations in the United States* (New York: National Bureau of Economic Research, 1948); and Louis M. Hacker, *Triumph of American Capitalism* (New York: Simon and Schuster, 1940).

11. W. J. Cash describes this relationship in *The Mind of the South* (New York: Alfred A. Knopf, 1960).

12. See Joseph Gusfield, *Symbolic Crusade* (Urbana: University of Illinois Press, 1963).

13. The record of prostitution in Illinois at that time is well documented in the 1913–1915 hearings of the O'Hara Committee of the Illinois Senate, published as "Report of the Senate Vice Committee," Lt. Governor Barrett O'Hara, 1916.

14. The study of organized crime and local politics has generally been left to sensationalist journalists and has been avoided by "respectable" political scientists, at least partly because "hard" data about such matters are hard to come by. Some material on the subject as it touches upon the cities of the prairie is available in Paul M. Angle's *Bloody Williamson* (New York: Alfred A. Knopf, 1962) which, though it concentrates on the coalfields of southern Illinois, discusses the history of the Shelton Gang in Madison and St. Clair Counties and in the Peoria area. The very rare report of the Congressional committee that investigated the causes of the East St. Louis race riot of 1917 includes the most extensive study of the tie-ins between local politics, business, and organized crime in that area. See Elliott Rudwick, *Race Riot at East St. Louis, July 1917* (New York: Meridian Books, 1967). Some more recent material can be found in the hearings of the Kefauver crime investigation committee. The O'Hara committee of the Illinois General Assembly investigated the prostitution industry in the State in 1913–1915. Its final report includes valuable material on conditions in the medium-size cities as well as Chicago.

15. While restricting my conclusions to the cases at hand, I believe that what has been true of the cities of the prairie has a more universal application. My studies of other larger cities have indicated that much the same "two-cities" system prevailed in each of them. Robert K. Merton's seminal article on machine politics in "Manifest and Latent Functions," which is included in *Social Theory and Social Structure* (Glencoe, Ill.: The Free Press, 1957), analyzes the functioning of traditional political machines.

16. While the assessments of political control are based primarily on the patterns of city politics, they take into consideration the politics of the other local governments as well, bound together as they all are in the civil community. The problem of obtaining historical data for urban communities of this size is a very difficult one. Few histories are available, and they are so written as to make the deduction of political data of this sort a matter of careful reading between the lines. Lacking full-scale historical research projects on this problem in each civil community, the summary outlines presented here must be considered as approximations, accurate in their general outline but perhaps subject to revision in their detail.

17. Several recent publications have begun to document this thesis. Among them are Gerhard Lenski, *The Religious Factor* (Garden City, N.Y.: Doubleday, 1961), a study of larger social differences among communicants of different religioethnic groups in Detroit, and Will Herberg, *Protestant-Catholic-Jew* (Garden City, N.Y.: Anchor Books, 1960), a more theoretical discussion of this theme. I have treated certain aspects of the relationship of religion and politics in my article, "Churches as Molders in American Politics," *American Behavioral Scientist* (May 1962). Other available materials of interest along this line include the series of books on different Protestant denominations as "ways of life" which have appeared in the past several years. Also Leo Rosten, ed., *A Guide to Religions of America* (New York: Simon and Schuster, 1955); Edwin Scott Gaustad, *A Religious History of America* (New

York: Harper and Row, 1966); Franklin Hamlin Littell, *The Free Church* (Boston: Starr King Press, 1957); Paul M. Harrison, *Authority and Power in the Free Church Tradition* (Princeton, N.J.: Princeton University Press, 1959); Wesley and Beverly Allinsmith, "Religious Affiliation and Politics—Economic Attitude: A Study of Eight Major United States Religious Groups," *Public Opinion Quarterly*, XII (Fall 1948). See also *The American Church History Series*, published in the 1890's.

18. This aspect of the trend toward church mergers has been largely neglected in the full flush of the ecumenical spirit, which sees the mergers as the beginnings of a single universal Christian church. In fact, the pattern of the mergers is in itself strong evidence for the hypothesis presented here.

19. Since the early 1940's, virtually every voting study published in the United States has considered the religious factor in this context. A summary of the best of these can be found in Seymour M. Lipset, Paul F. Lazarsfeld, Allen H. Barton, and Juan Linz, "The Psychology of Voting: An Analysis of Political Behavior" in *Handbook of Social Psychology*. Some of the better studies dealing with this question include Berelson, Lazarsfeld, and William N. McPhee, *Voting: A Study of Opinion Formation in a Presidential Campaign* (Chicago: University of Chicago Press, 1954) and Angus Campbell, Gerald Curin, and Warren E. Miller, *The Voter Decides* (Evanston, Ill.: Row, Peterson, 1954).

20. See Daniel J. Elazar, *The Politics of Belleville* (Philadelphia: Center for the Study of Federalism, 1969), for a detailed description of this phenomenon.

21. In 1967, for example, a very noisy challenge to Christmas observances in the Duluth public school system was initiated by a self-professed atheist recently moved into the community. He was at least partially successful. More respectable—and even more successful—was the Minnesota Attorney General's ruling that public high school baccalaureate services were no doubt unconstitutional that same year.

22. This study is not the place to trace the direct line of evolution of the professionalized politics of Illinois from the days of the Northwest Territory. However, the evidence is clear. The men and their parties from earliest times in the state have passed the system down to their heirs, making only such adjustments as have been necessary to meet external demands. The family factions gave way to the parties, the Whigs gave way to the Republicans, Chicago was given its seat at the table, there have been "blue-ribbon" tickets for national offices, but the system continues intact. For a short history of Illinois politics, see Theodore C. Pease, *The Story of Illinois* (Chicago: University of Chicago Press, 1947).

23. James Q. Wilson, *The Amateur Democrat* (Chicago: University of Chicago Press, 1962), discusses the plight of the amateur in Illinois politics in the 1950's in considerable detail.

24. There is some slight evidence that medium-size urban civil communities may be neither here nor there in their relationships to their respective states. That is to say, they may have considerably less access and influence than either the great cities, which have internal political power by virtue of their size alone, or the little cities, which are better connected to the overall state system because they are too small to be independent of it. The sample used in this study, including those cities examined less intensively, is too constricted to allow the writer to say more than this. In Illinois, the medium-size cities run the gamut from highly involved to nearly isolated. The four civil communities outside Illinois all appear to be more alienated from their state governments than their sister cities but, in each case, there are special local conditions which account for this.

25. Samuel Gove, *Illinois Votes* (Urbana: University of Illinois Institute of Government and Public Affairs, 1958).

26. See V. O. Key, Jr., *Politics, Parties and Pressure Groups* (New York: Thomas Y. Crowell, 1958).

27. Richard Hofstadter discusses this in his book, *The Age of Reform* (New York: Alfred A. Knopf, 1955). See also Richard C. Wade, "The City in History—Some American Perspectives" in Werner Z. Hirsch, ed., *Urban Life and Form* (New York: Holt, Rinehart, and Winston, 1963).

28. Though the foregoing analysis appears to concentrate on latent cultural and social phenomena rather than directly political considerations to explain differences in voting behavior in the several Illinois cities of the prairie, it should not be assumed that this is the case. It is clearly impossible to neatly separate "political" from "social" or "cultural" phenomena. However, it is also unwise to ignore the directly political influences on voting. The very fluctuation of voting behavior from election to election is indicative of the existence of political considerations in the determination of voters' choices. These political considerations affect the decisions even of those voters who ostensibly remain unmoved from their habitual patterns of voting. It is not the purpose of this study to investigate these political considerations, which are essentially individual. The concern here is with the elucidation of communal or social phenomena, hence the emphasis on the latter factors. However, the existence of political considerations need not go unnoticed. Much the same may be said in regard to other factors commonly discussed as contributing to the determination of voting behavior. While it is recognized that these other factors have affected voting patterns in the cities of the prairie, as elsewhere, the phenomenon of their continued allegiances seems to be best explained in terms of the streams, particularly since other variables do not appear to explain it. See Alice Ebel, "A Study of Illinois Elections, 1940–1954" (on file at the University of Illinois' Institute of Government and Public Affairs) for an analysis of county-by-county voting patterns in Illinois in a recent period in which other factors are taken into consideration and found wanting.

Chapter 6 / Political Culture and Politics in State and Community

General culture has its direct impact on politics from the outside, as it were. Political culture, that differentiated aspect of the overall culture which is itself a truly political phenomenon, has its direct impact from the inside. The role of cultural factors in shaping the political environment of the cities of the prairie has been a primary theme of this volume. The special role of political culture, alluded to in the previous chapters, is of crucial importance in shaping the cities' politics because of its directly political character.

"Political culture" has been defined as the "particular pattern of orientation to political action" in which each political system is embedded.[1] A political culture is related to the general culture of a particular society but is by no means identical with it. As Gabriel Almond says, "because political orientation involves cognition, intellection, and adaptation to external situations, as well as the standards and values of the general culture, it is a differentiated part of the culture and has a certain autonomy." Like all culture, it is so rooted in the cumulative historical experiences of particular groups that it has become second nature to those within its embrace.

Political culture, then, is the summation of persistent patterns of underlying political attitudes and values—and characteristic responses to political concerns—that is manifest in a particular political order, whose existence is generally unperceived by those who are part of that order and whose origins date back to the very beginnings of the particular people who share it. Political culture is an intrinsically political phenomenon which makes certain autonomous demands on particular political systems as well as affecting all other political demands within those systems. Political systems, in turn, are in some measure the products of the political cultures they serve and must remain in harmony with their political culture if they are to maintain themselves.

Political culture can best be understood in terms of the framework it sets for individual and group political behavior—in the political thoughts, attitudes, assumptions, and values of individuals and groups and in the range of permissible or acceptable action that flows from them. Political culture, as such, determines behavior in relatively few situations or in response to relatively few particular issues. Its influence lies in its power to set reasonably fixed limits to political behavior and provide subliminal direction for political action in particular political systems; limits and direction all the more effective because of their antiquity and subtlety whereby those limited are unaware of the limitations placed upon them.

The various aspects of political culture are made manifest through several cultural requisites or themes.[2] Political language, whether special political terms associated with particular cultures ("public servant," "good government") or the nuances of meaning inhering to common political terminology in a particular culture ("democracy," "freedom," "politics"), is of first importance in conveying and transmitting culturally determined value concepts within a framework implicitly understood by all who share in a particular political culture.[3] Every political culture can be identified by its particular forms of aesthetic expression or delight ranging from the aesthetically satisfying aspects of accepted political mythologies to the shared or recognized political symbols to accepted political styles. Standardized orientations to political life (recruitment, socialization, and appropriate behavior of political actors) and death (including the nature of and factors that bring about political death) are key aspects of political culture. Every political culture involves means for perpetuating the political system, its solidarity, and its norms, including common modes of political socialization, shared channels of political communication, and certain distinctive characteristics that animate its political institutions. Political culture plays a major role in determining the nature of people's demands for an ordered political life, the way which they organize to meet those demands, and the accepted "price of politics" in each political system. By the same token, the political culture plays a major role in defining the political needs of people in each political system—who is a person for political purposes in a particular political system; who gets what in the way of protection of life, rights, and property—and influences the way in which the system organizes to meet these needs.

A specific political culture may or may not coincide with a particular political system or civil society, since patterns of orientation to politics frequently overlap beyond the boundaries of specific political systems. Continental Europe may well have a single continent-wide political culture that crosses the national boundaries that otherwise divide it. The various national entities and, in some cases, the subnational and extranational ones as well, possess individuated subcultures of their own which give them meaningful distinctiveness without fracturing the overall universe of thought and action represented by the political culture shared across the entire continent.

The United States possesses a political culture of its own spread nationwide.[4] Each of the states of the American union possesses its own distinctive manifestation of that political culture. The manifestations—or, more properly, subcultures—operative in the American states and their component civil communities are products of the phenomena discussed in the first part of this volume—the interaction of geohistorical location, demographic streams, and patterns of the general culture, plus the influences of the national political process.

The Three Political Subcultures

Political cultural factors stand out as particularly influential in shaping the operations of the national, state, and local political systems in three ways: (1) by molding the political community's (the citizens, the politicians, and the public officials) perceptions of the nature and purposes of politics and expectations from government and the political process; (2) by influencing the recruitment of specific kinds of people to become active in government and politics—as holders of elective offices, members of the bureaucracy, and active political workers; and (3) by subtly directing the actual way in which the art of government is practiced by citizens, politicians, and public officials in the light of their perceptions. Furthermore, the cultural components of individual and group behavior make themselves felt in the kind of civic behavior dictated by conscience and internalized ethical standards, in the forms of law-abidingness adhered to by citizens and officials and in the character of the positive actions of government.

The American political culture is rooted in two contrasting conceptions of the American political order, both of which can be traced back to the earliest settlement of the country. In the first, the political order is conceived as a marketplace in which the primary public relationships are products of bargaining among individuals and groups acting out of self-interest. In the second, the political order is conceived to be a commonwealth—a state in which the whole people have an undivided interest —in which the citizens cooperate in an effort to create and maintain the best government in order to implement certain shared moral principles.

The commonwealth is animated by a mystique—a vision of the proper political order yet to be attained but that is in the process of being built upon existing foundations—and maintains its strength only by maintaining the vitality of that mystique. The marketplace, on the other hand, is animated by a desire to keep the peace through a balance of interests without any necessary commitments other than the preservation of the marketplace itself. Access to the political marketplace is open to all interests that in any way acknowledge its legitimacy and are willing to abide by its rules (at least most of the time). No independent criteria are used to judge the legitimacy of those interests as a condition of participation, so any individual or group that can make its presence felt acquires the functional equivalent of citizenship. In the commonwealth, on the other hand, citizenship, or the right to legitimately participate in the government process, is a matter of very serious concern, and *a priori* moral criteria can legitimately be applied to determine which individuals or groups have that right.

These two conceptions have exercised an influence on government and politics throughout American history, sometimes in conflict and sometimes by complementing one another. They are so intertwined as to be practically inseparable in any particular case or situation, with marketplace notions contributing to shaping the vision of commonwealth and commonwealth ideals being given a preferred position in the marketplace.

Overall, the national political culture is a synthesis of three major political subcultures that jointly inhabit the country, existing side by side in their grossest manifestations and frequently overlapping one another in their most immediate ones. All three are of nationwide proportions, having spread in the course of time from coast to coast. At the same time each subculture is strongly tied to specific sections of the country, reflecting the more or less orderly movement westward of the migrational streams discussed in Chapter Four. Considering the central characteristics that govern each and their respective centers of emphasis, the three political cultures may be called individualistic (I), moralistic (M), and traditionalistic (T).[5] Each of the three reflects its own particular synthesis of marketplace and commonwealth.

The Individualistic Political Culture

The individualistic political culture emphasizes the conception of the democratic order as a marketplace. It is rooted in the notion that government is instituted for strictly utilitarian reasons, to handle those functions demanded by the people it is created to serve. A government need not have any direct concern with questions of the "good society" except insofar as it may be used to advance some common conception of the good society formulated outside the political arena just as it serves other functions. Since the individualistic political culture emphasizes the centrality of private concerns, it places a premium on limiting community intervention—whether governmental or nongovernmental—into private activities to the minimum necessary to keep the marketplace in proper working order. In general, government action is to be restricted to those areas, primarily in the economic realm, which encourage private initiative and widespread access to the marketplace. Economic development activities—in the broadest sense—find great favor in such circumstances.[6]

The character of political participation in systems dominated by the individualistic political culture reflects this outlook. The individualistic political culture holds politics to be just another means by which individuals may improve themselves socially and economically. In this sense politics is a "business" like any other that competes for talent and offers rewards to those who take it up as a career. Those individuals who choose political careers may rise by providing the governmental services demanded of them and, in return, may expect to be adequately compensated for their efforts. Interpretations of officeholders' obligations under this arrangement vary among political systems and even among individuals within a single political system. Where the norms are high, such people are expected to provide high quality government services for the general public in the best possible manner in return for the status and economic rewards considered their due. Some who choose political careers clearly commit themselves to such norms; others believe that an officeholder's primary responsibility is to serve himself and those who have supported him directly, favoring them even at the expense of others. In some political systems, this view is also accepted by the public.

Political life within an individualistic political culture is based on a system of mutual obligations rooted in personal relationships. While in a simple society those relationships can be direct ones, societies with "I" political cultures in the United States are usually too complex to maintain face-to-face ties. So the system of mutual obligations is harnessed through political parties which serve as "business corporations" dedicated to providing the organization necessary to maintain it. Party regularity is indispensable in the individualistic political culture because it is the means for coordinating individual enterprise in the political arena and is the one way of preventing individualism in politics from running wild. In such a system, an individual can succeed politically, not by dealing with issues in some exceptional way or by accepting some concept of good government and then striving to implement it, but by maintaining his place in the system of mutual obligations. He can do this by operating according to the norms of his particular party, to the exclusion of other political considerations. Such a political culture encourages the maintenance of a party system that is competitive, but not overly so, in the pursuit of office. Its politicians are interested in office as a means of controlling the distribution of the favors or rewards of government rather than as a means of exercising governmental power for programmatic ends, hence competition may prove less rewarding than accommodation in certain situations.

Since the individualistic political culture eschews ideological concerns in its "businesslike" conception of politics, both politicians and citizens look upon political activity as a specialized business, essentially the province of professionals, of minimum and passing (if periodical) concern to laymen, and no place for amateurs to play an active role. Furthermore, there is a strong tendency among the public to believe that politics is a dirty—if necessary—business, better left to those who are willing to soil themselves by engaging in it. In practice, then, where the individualistic political culture is dominant, there is likely to be an easy attitude toward the limits of the professionals' perquisites. Since a fair amount of corruption is expected in the normal course of things, there is relatively little popular excitement when any is found unless it is of an extraordinary character. It is as if the public is willing to pay a surcharge for services rendered, rebelling only when the surcharge becomes too heavy.

Public officials in the individualistic political culture, committed to "giving the public what it wants," are not normally willing to initiate new programs or open up new areas of government activity on their own initiative. They will do so when they perceive an overwhelming public demand for them to act, but only then. In a sense, their willingness to expand the functions of government is based on an extension of the quid pro quo "favor" system which serves as the central core of their political relationships, with new services the reward they give the public for placing them in office. The value and legitimacy of change in the individualistic political culture are directly related to its commercial concern.

The individualistic political culture is ambivalent about the place of bureaucracy in the political order. In one sense, the bureaucratic method of operating flies in the face of the favor system that is central to the individualistic political process. At the same time, the virtues of organizational efficiency appear substantial to those seeking to master the market. In the end, bureaucratic organization is introduced within the framework of the favor system; large segments of the bureaucracy may be insulated from it through the merit system, but the entire organization is pulled into the political environment at crucial points through political appointment at the upper echelons and, very frequently, the bending of the merit system to meet political demands.

The individualistic political culture is a product of the Middle States stream with its overriding commitment to commercialism and concomitant acceptance of ethnic, social, and religious pluralism. It has been reinforced by the English, Continental, Eastern European, Mediterranean, and Irish streams whose products either brought that political culture with them or adapted to it as their traditional cultures broke down. Most recently, substantial segments of the Southern and Afro-American streams are adapting to it for similar reasons, as they are transplanted from their original areas of settlement. The individualistic political culture is strong or dominant in those areas where the products of the streams manifesting its characteristics are strong or dominant.

The Moralistic Political Culture

To the extent that American society is built on the principles of "commerce" in the broadest sense of the term and the marketplace provides the model for public relationships in this country, all Americans share some of the attitudes that are of first importance in the individualistic political culture. At the same time, substantial segments of the American people operate politically within the framework of two political cultures whose theoretical structures and operational consequences depart significantly from the individualistic pattern at crucial points.

The moralistic political culture emphasizes the commonwealth idea as the basis for democratic government. Politics, to the moralistic political culture, is considered one of the great activities of man in his search for the good society—a struggle for power, it is true, but also an effort to exercise power for the pursuit of justice in public affairs or the betterment of the commonwealth. Consequently, in the moralistic political culture, both the general public and the politicians conceive of politics as a public service centered on some notion of the public good and properly devoted to the advancement of the public interest. Good government, then, is measured by the degree to which it promotes the public good and in terms of the honesty, selflessness, and commitment to the public welfare of those who govern.

In the moralistic political culture, individualism is tempered by a general commitment to utilizing communal—preferably nongovernmental, but governmental if necessary—power to intervene into the sphere of "private" activities when it is considered necessary to do so for the public good or the well-being of the community, utilizing governmental resources for social regulation as well as for the promotion of economic well-being. Accordingly, issues have an important place in the moralistic style of politics, functioning to set the tone of political concern. Government is considered a positive instrument with a responsibility to promote the general welfare, though definitions of what its positive role should be may vary considerably from era to era.[7]

Since the moralistic political culture rests on the fundamental conception that politics exists primarily as a means for coming to grips with the issues and public concerns of civil society, it also embraces the notion that politics is ideally a matter of concern for every citizen, not just those who are professionally committed to political careers. It becomes each citizen's duty to participate in the political affairs of his commonwealth.

Consequently, there is a general insistence that government service is public service, which places moral obligations upon those who participate in government that are more demanding than the moral obligations of the marketplace. There is an equally general rejection of the notion that the field of politics is a legitimate realm for private economic enrichment. Indeed, even normal advancement in income and perquisites is frequently suspect as profiting from the public weal.

Since the concept of serving the general welfare or the public interest is at the core of the political relationship, politicians are expected to adhere to it even at the expense of individual loyalties and political friendships. Consequently, party regularity is not of prime importance. The political party is considered a useful political device but is not valued for its own sake. Regular party ties can be abandoned with relative impunity for third parties, special local parties, or nonpartisan systems if such changes are believed helpful in gaining larger political goals. Men can even shift from party to party without sanctions if the change is justified by political belief. In the moralistic political culture, rejection of firm party ties is not to be viewed as a rejection of politics as such. On the contrary, because politics is considered potentially good and healthy within the context of that culture, it is possible to have highly political nonpartisan systems. Certainly nonpartisanship is not instituted to eliminate politics but to improve it by widening access to public office for those unwilling or unable to gain office through the regular party structure.[8]

In practice, where the moralistic political culture is dominant today, there is considerably more "amateur" participation in politics. There is also much less of what Americans consider corruption in government and less tolerance of those actions which are considered corrupt, so politics does not have the taint it so often bears in the "I" environment.

By virtue of its fundamental outlook, the moralistic political culture creates a greater commitment to active government intervention into the economic and social life of the community. At the same time, the strong commitment to communitarianism characteristic of that political culture tends to channel the interest in government intervention into highly localistic paths so that a willingness to encourage local government intervention to set public standards does not necessarily reflect a concomitant willingness to allow outside governments equal opportunity to intervene. Not infrequently, public officials will themselves seek to initiate new government activities in an effort to come to grips with problems as yet unperceived by a majority of the citizenry. The moralistic political culture is not committed to either change or the status quo per se, but will accept either depending upon the morally defined ends to be gained.

The moralistic political culture's major difficulty in adjusting bureaucracy to the political order is tied to the potential conflict between communitarian principles and the necessity for large-scale organization to increase bureaucratic efficiency, a problem that could affect the attitudes of "M" culture states toward federal activity of certain kinds. Otherwise, the notion of a politically neutral administrative system creates no problem within the moralistic value system and even offers many advantages. Where merit systems are instituted, they are rigidly maintained.

The moralistic political culture is a product of Puritan New England in its efforts to create the holy commonwealth and its more secularized Yankee stream. It has been strongly reinforced by the North Sea and Jewish streams, who shared the same political culture when they came to the United States. It is strong or dominant in those areas where Yankees, Scotch, Dutch, Scandinavians, Swiss, and Jews are strong or dominant.

The Traditionalistic Political Culture

The traditionalistic political culture is rooted in an ambivalent attitude toward the marketplace coupled with a paternalistic and elitist conception of the commonwealth. It reflects an older, precommercial attitude that accepts a substantially hierarchical society as part of the ordered nature of things, authorizing and expecting those at the top of the social structure to take a special and dominant role in government. Like its moralistic counterpart, the traditionalistic political culture accepts government as an actor with a positive role in the community but in a very limited sphere, mainly that of securing the continued maintenance of the existing social order. To do so, it functions to confine real political power to a relatively small and self-perpetuating group drawn from an established elite who often inherit their "right" to govern through family ties or social position. Accordingly, social and family ties are paramount in a traditionalistic political culture, even more than personal ties are important in the individualistic where, after all is said and done, a person's first responsibility is to himself. At the same time, those who do not have a definite role to play in politics are not expected to be even minimally active as citizens. In many cases, they are not even expected to vote. In return, they are guaranteed that, outside of the limited sphere of politics, family rights (usually labeled "individual rights") are paramount, not to be lightly ignored even in matters such as education and hygiene. Like the individualistic political culture, those active in politics are expected to benefit personally from their activity though not necessarily through direct pecuniary gain.

Political parties are of minimal importance in traditionalistic political cultures, since they encourage a degree of openness and competition that goes against the fundamental grain of an elite-oriented political order. Their major utility is to recruit people to fill the formal offices of government not desired by the established powerholders. Political competition in a traditionalistic political culture is usually conducted through factional alignments, an extension of the personalistic politics characteristic of the system; hence political systems within the culture tend to have loose one-party systems if they have political parties at all.

Practically speaking, a traditionalistic political culture is found only in a society that retains some of the organic characteristics of the pre-industrial social order. "Good government" in that political culture involves the maintenance and encouragement of traditional patterns and, if necessary, their adjustment to changing conditions with the least possible upset. Where the traditionalistic political culture is dominant in the United States today, political leaders play conservative and custodial rather than initiatory roles unless pressed strongly from the outside.

Whereas the individualistic and moralistic political cultures may or may not encourage the development of bureaucratic systems of organization on the grounds of "rationality" and "efficiency" in government, depending on their particular situations, traditionalistic political cultures tend to be instinctively antibureaucratic because bureaucracy by its very nature interferes with the fine web of informal interpersonal relationships that lie at the root of the political system and that have been developed by following traditional patterns over the years. Where bureaucracy is introduced, it is generally confined to ministerial functions under the aegis of the established power holders.

The traditionalistic political culture is a product of the plantation agrarianism of the Southern stream. It was supplemented by the Afro-American stream, whose products were originally absorbed into the Southern way of life as slaves. Secondary reinforcement has come from the Hispanic stream. The traditionalistic political culture is strong only where it has become the dominant political culture, in those areas settled almost exclusively by the streams which manifest its characteristics. Where those streams have moved into environments in which other political cultures have been dominant, there has been a tendency for the traditionalistic political culture to break down. In fact, as the possibilities for maintaining more than semblances of traditionalistic life have continued to decline in the United States, traditionalistic political culture has also diminished, undergoing subtle but serious changes, generally in the direction of the individualistic political culture except where strong secondary tendencies toward the moralistic political culture are present.

The Political Cultures of the Cities of the Prairie

The character and degree of complexity in the geology of specific local settlements in the United States determines whether a particular state or civil community comes closer to resembling one of the three political cultural models or combines elements of more than one within its boundaries. Three of the five states of the cities of the prairie—Illinois, Iowa, and Colorado—are so situated geohistorically that representatives of all three political subcultures have contributed to their settlement and development in significant numbers. Settlements and bands of settlements dominated by all three can be found in those states in varying conditions of cultural development and change. Accordingly, their present statewide political cultures are amalgams created out of varying degrees of conflict generated by the initial meeting of the representatives of the three and the struggle between them for the dominant position of influence within the emerging state political systems. The general outcome of that original struggle has long since been determined. It created a relationship between political culture and political system in each of the states that continues to set the limits for political behavior within them. At the same time, within the framework of the statewide political subculture, the conflict between the products of the original political cultures, substantially modified and disguised though it may be, continues to be waged. Indeed, the very conflict itself has become institutionalized as one of the "moving parts" of the state political system.

Whatever the resolution at the state level, local pockets of the other political cultures frequently entrench themselves. This is certainly true in the case of the cities of the prairie in those states. As indicated in Chapter Five, with the exception of the smaller urban centers among them, the individual civil communities are too large and complex not to also have attracted a certain diversity of populations and cultures. Accounting for both population diversity and cultural change, the political cultures of the cities of the prairie of those three states are categorized in Table 6–1.

In Minnesota, and to a somewhat lesser extent in Wisconsin, a high degree of homogeneity in political culture has existed from the beginning. This means that the major political conflicts and cleavages have not been "culture conflicts" in their essence but have been intracultural. Consequently, the extent of the adjustment of the political system to the underlying political culture it serves has been well fixed from the beginning, at which time the relationship between political culture and political system was substantially settled more thoroughly than in the other three states. At the same time, some cultural diversity has always been present, manifesting itself particularly at the local level. The two cities of the prairie reflect both the overall statewise uniformity and local diversity.

Political Culture and the Purposes of Government

The development of these state political cultures and their impact on the cities of the prairie is discussed in the following chapters. Before turning to that discussion, however, some better delineation of the manifestations and consequences of political cultural differences is in order. The answer to the question of what are—or should be—the purposes, scope, and limits of government in the civil community is dictated in part by the external geohistorical environment. Beyond that, it is determined by the political culture. The two issues of education and planning are exemplary cases of current concern in all of the cities of the prairie that reveal the underlying political cultural differences among them.

It has been observed that, in most urban civil communities in America, there has been a shift in the orientation of government from its originally limited concern with providing some minimal level of public (read "police") services for its residents to a larger concern with participating in the management of community growth and change. This major shift in orientation at the local level is part of the change in the national climate that has taken place primarily in the twentieth century, which has seen an increased emphasis on the positive role of government in American society. While this new emphasis has affected every one of the cities of the prairie, the individualized legacy of political culture in each has contributed substantially to the manner and degree to which its residents have embraced this shift in orientation and the way in which their local governments have responded to it. The very conception of what constitutes positive government action, the perception of the legitimate scope and limits of such action, and the view of the direction such action should take reflect the underlying political culture in each civil community.

The question of the "proper" role of government in the civil community (and generally) is an old one in the cities of the prairie. Historical records show that there was a considerable division of opinion among those who settled them as to what should be the province of government and what should be left to private initiative virtually from the beginning of their respective histories. While there is no single explanation for it, this division of opinion seems to be directly related to the flow of the several streams into the cities, particularly the flow and influence of the native streams, since their products generally dominated local political decision-making bodies at least until late in the nineteenth century and set the tone for community decisions until the post-World-War-II generation.

Southern influence in the cities of the prairie has generally operated to limit the role of government. Southerners, reflecting their traditionalistic political culture, have historically displayed some willingness to use the

TABLE 6-1

City	Settlement Stages			Contemporary Synthesis
Alton	Tmi	I	IT	It
Belleville	Tm	It	It	It
Champaign	Im	I	tm	Im
Davenport	IM	Im	it	IM
Decatur	TI	Im	It	I
Duluth	im	MI	MT	Mt
E. Moline-Silvis	I			I
E. St. Louis	Ti	TI	Ti	IT
Joliet	Im	I	TI	Im
Moline	M	M	I	Mi
Peoria	TMi	It	It	I
Pueblo	TMi	Im	Tim	IMt
Rockford	M	Mi	Imt	Mi
Rock Island	Itm	IM	ti	Im
Springfield	Ti	Itm	It	I
Superior	Im	MI	Mi	MI
Urbana	It	Im	Itm	Im

powers and resources of government to encourage state economic development either by engaging directly in economic activities or by subsidizing favored private enterprises in a variety of ways. At the same time they have been extremely hesitant about supporting or encouraging government activity in the realm of regulation of private activities or the provision of social services. Since the high point of governmental activity of the first kind came in 1837, and the thrust of governmental expansion has since been in the latter two fields, the Southern outlook has tended to delay governmental responses to new situations in Illinois, Iowa, and Colorado to the extent that it is felt in state politics and to significantly retard it in those communities in which it has been strong. In the twentieth century, the heirs of the traditionalistic political culture seem to have modified their stance somewhat, perhaps because continued economic depression in their communities has forced them to seek both social and economic assistance from any quarter.

The Yankees, reflecting their moralistic political culture, have tended to look favorably upon government's role in promoting certain social ends, if only to insure a common public morality and a measure of equal economic opportunity. In the social realm, the Yankees have been inclined toward the promotion of public education and the regulation of the sale of liquor for similar reasons, relating to the advancement of individual and public morality. In general, government activities in the economic realm have been judged by the Yankees (and their "soul brothers" from other streams) from a moralistic perspective. That is to say, whether supporters of laissez faire or outright government ownership, "freedom of contract" or public regulation, their positions are justified on essentially moral rather than economic grounds—what they held would be best for the commonwealth.

Yankees have been found on all sides of these issues; what they have shared in common is their basic public concern. As a result, the impact of the Yankee stream in the cities of the prairie has been mixed, ranging from the advocacy of socialism to the most tenacious commitment to voluntarism and resistance to any expansion of the scope of governmental activity. This is particularly true in the twentieth century when, as the demands for change rose to new heights, the familiar patterns of the past were becoming virtually sanctified in those Yankee-descended communities where life seemed to go on as before. Ultimately, the higher visibility of the forces of change converted all but the most diehard to a perception of the need for governmental action as the most feasible means of manifesting the community's concern for its members.

The Middle States stream has built its basic conception of the proper role of government upon the individualistic political culture which it represents; hence it is a conception that begins and ends with the question of who benefits. Always pursuing "progress," roughly conceived as the expansion of commerce with the betterment of technology as its handmaiden, the pacesetters of the Middle stream have welcomed government activities aiding them in their pursuit. At the same time, those who have not benefited from that pursuit have not hesitated to look to government to aid them in redressing the political, economic, and social balance. In the nineteenth century, this situation led to a fluctuation of attitudes toward government action based on individual perceptions of what would be of benefit. In the twentieth century, it has meant a continuing shift of the majority in favor of positive government *action*—for some, especially on the national plane, where the relationship between government policy and the economy is most visible, and for others particularly on the local plane where they stood to benefit most. In any case, social (or moral) *regulation* by government has not been viewed with favor by those representatives of the individualistic political culture, since they have consistently held that such matters are the province of individual decision (unless and until they begin to openly affect the marketplace).

The nonnative streams added some subtle dimensions to the political cultures of the cities of the prairie. Most were accustomed to a greater government role in the life of the country than any native Americans were prepared to accept, though their attitudes toward positive government were not necessarily favorable. Here national as well as cultural differences were important. Scandinavians, Germans, and Dutch were generally well disposed toward direct government action to set the course of society, even when they wished to check the extent of government intervention. The Jews looked to government in America as an agency for the improvement of society from the first. The Irish were ready to use governmental opportunities for advancement against any established interests. The Continental and Eastern Europeans simply put up with government as a matter of course, while the Mediterraneans were generally antigovernment, distrusting its authority or the security it claimed to provide. Because of their centuries-long experience under slavery, the Afro-Americans looked to the governments of America with a mixture of fear of officially supported discrimination and expectation of paternalistic benefits. As these various groups became influential in the public life of the cities of the prairie, their attitudes contributed to shaping the local view of the proper role of government.

The history of public education in the cities of the prairie is an early example of the divergent approaches to the role of government influenced by differences in political culture.[9] The idea of free public education was originally brought into Illinois from the outside, a product of national influences in large measure stimulated by the federal common-school land-grant program. In the first decade of statehood, a few "enlightened" state leaders, mostly of Middle State origin, proposed that the state supplement the federal grants. The best they could get was legislation granting the localities the right to levy taxes for the support of common schools, passed in 1825. Not even the "local option" principle was sufficient to overcome Southern hostility to the idea of public education. The act remained a dead letter and was repealed a few years later. The predominantly Southern Illinoisians held that those who wanted schools for their children should pay for them themselves.

Though the General Assembly did allow local organization of the Congressional townships established by the federal land survey to manage the federal common-school grants, it was not until 1845 (at the height of the Yankee in-migration) that it again allowed localities to exercise local option to levy special school taxes. Not until 1855, after the Yankees had captured a significant position in state affairs, was state legislation passed providing for even minimal state support for public elementary education.

Not only was state action necessary to secure the establishment of a truly free public school system, even in a locally oriented state such as Illinois but, from the first, state action determined the mode of organization of that system. Proponents of public education wished to have the educational function handled through a system of local school governments independent of the other local authorities. The network of school districts established in 1855 was based on that principle. Though since modified many times, it remains the basis for school government in Illinois.

From 1818 to 1856, federal grants provided the only public revenues for education in Illinois other than minor allocations from general purpose local taxes. Still, some civil communities established schools, financed by tuition payments plus such public funds as were available.

The first schools in Southerner-settled Belleville were private subscription schools supported by the relatively few families that wished to educate their children. Moreover, the first of these was organized in 1815 by a Yankee missionary, one of several sent west by the Congregational churches of Massachusetts and Connecticut to help "civilize the frontier." Public education did not even become an issue until the arrival of the Germans after 1830. By the mid-1840's the German element, with its particular intellectual interests, was sufficiently strong to carry the issue. The first city school board, the School Association of Belleville, a semiprivate group, was elected in 1847, and the first semipublic school in town opened in 1848. It was supported by tuition and grants from the school fund based on the federal land grant. Not until 1855, when the state school law was enacted, was a public school district established. The first fully free public school was organized in 1856. Belleville has since developed a reputation for maintaining a strong interest in education, based in part on the fact that its record is exceptional for its region. It was one of the first civil communities in its part of the state to promote high school (1916) and, later, junior college (1946) education at public expense, and the otherwise fiscally conservative local residents continue to support their schools with greater willingness than other governmental functions.

The other Southern-influenced communities also appear to have been dependent upon non-Southerners to initiate public education efforts. Alton, a community strongly influenced by a Yankee minority in its early years, established a semipublic school in the 1820's and the second free public school in the state (after Yankee-influenced Chicago) in 1837. As the Yankee influence declined in the face of the continued influx of Southerners and others, so did public concern with the schools. Though few settled there, Yankees appear to have been instrumental in the establishment of the state's third or fourth free public school in Springfield in 1840. The leading Middle States settlers (who formed the local majority) in that civil community perceived the advantages of basic education in promoting local progress and continued to support the public schools.

As the northern civil communities were established, free public education spread. Schools were among the first public or quasi-public institutions created in each of them, invariably under the auspices of the Yankees. Where the Yankees represented the bulk of the community, the founding of public schools preceded the establishment of any other governmental institutions. Rockford was notable in this regard, as was Moline. In both, the soon-to-come Scandinavian majority carried on the Yankee pattern.

The civil communities in the other four states did not face the problem of securing public educational facilities locally before gaining support from the state. In all four, general laws establishing free public school systems were enacted in territorial days, usually to take advantage of the available federal grants but also reflecting the values of the Yankee stream which was so strong in their initial settlement. Except in the case of Davenport, these laws preceded the organization of general purpose local governments in the cities of the prairie in those states. Provision of public education, then, was considered a cardinal function of government in those civil communities from the beginning.

Lest it be assumed that culturally influenced differences in educational standards are a thing of the past among the cities of the prairie, the 1960 census figures show that the impact of the streams in the realm of education is still of some importance. Table 6–2 shows the rank order of the cities of the prairie in terms of median school years completed and per cent of population that has completed high school or more. Excluding Urbana and Champaign, where the presence of the University of Illinois faculty and student body raises local educational achievement levels all out of proportion, and Rockford, whose high percentage of foreign-born means a higher number of people who had less opportunity to attend school, the Yankee-influenced Upper Midwestern civil communities stand out as having the highest level of educational achievement, while the Southern-influenced civil communities on the fringes of the greater South stand out as significantly poorer in educational achievement.

In the mid-nineteenth century, public education was the "radical" program whose acceptance and support can be used with considerable reliability as an indicator of community attitudes toward local government services. In the mid-twentieth century, the complex of activities that come under the heading "community planning" may well be considered equally suitable indicators of local conceptions of the "proper" role of local government. By the end of 1961, every one of the cities of the prairie had initiated local planning in some form. Once again, the variation in the nature and extent of community planning was substantially explained by differences in local political culture.

Eleven of the civil communities have professional planning staffs, annual planning budgets that run into five figures, and general plans either completed or in preparation. Duluth, with the oldest planning department and one of the largest professional staffs, probably has the most important planning program of any of the cities of the prairie. Not only does its planning program extend back to the 1920's, but the plans made over the years by its planners have generally been implemented under their guidance. Its planners have successfully promoted a 9,000-acre city forest reserve, a new campus for the Duluth branch of the University of Minnesota, a public port terminal, a network of public school sites, a high bridge connecting Duluth and Superior, and other projects and programs of this caliber. They have, in effect, supervised much of their civil community's public development. In Duluth, where the Scandinavians have been the dominant element almost from the first, planning is accepted as a legitimate government activity that fills an important communal need. In this respect, the Scandinavian influence so prevalent in Minnesota is almost undiluted in Duluth.

TABLE 6-2

Cities of the Prairie: Relative Educational Achievement, 1960

City	Median School Years Completed	Per cent Completed High School or More
Urbana	12.8	66.7
Champaign	12.4	60.3
Duluth	11.5	46.5
Moline	11.4	46.4
Rock Island	11.4	45.7
Davenport	11.4	45.4
Superior	11.3	45.3
Springfield	11.1	44.3
Decatur	11.1	43.7
Rockford	11.0	43.1
Joliet	10.9	42.1
Pueblo	10.6	40.8
Peoria	10.5	40.0
Alton	10.2	38.7
Belleville	9.8	34.6
E. St. Louis	8.7	23.2

Planning is less dynamic but almost as well accepted in Davenport. The civil community's more conservative Germans, though considerably less planning-oriented than the Scandinavians, are highly predisposed to orderly development. Organized local planning was begun relatively early in Davenport, and the city had a comprehensive plan by 1945. Though the city's planning department has not accomplished any spectacular feats, it has pioneered most of the local development programs in the last half-generation.

Rockford also entered the planning field early in the 1940's with a joint city-county planning operation designed to reflect the extra-municipal scope of the civil community. Despite this early interest in planning and a continued public commitment to the planning idea characteristic of a civil community with Rockford's background, little "successful" planning has been done compared to Duluth. In part, this is a result of local political conflicts. Just as the civil community's planning activities were about to enter the implementation stage, a major change in municipal regimes in 1957 cut the base of support out from under the planning staff. Since the professional planners were identified with the previous regime, they were rendered ineffective. Though some of their plans were implemented, their agency was given no substantive role in their implementation. After several years of fruitless conflict, the entire planning staff left Rockford. Despite these problems, the local planning commission has been concerned with planning as such and not just with zoning regulation, as are most of its sisters. In this it reflects something of the ambivalence toward planning present in a civil community dominated by a native stream whose leading representatives, even though theoretically committed to planning, are reluctant to accept the technocratic aspects of professionally prepared plans with their limitations on local decision-making based on moralistic considerations. In an effort to develop effective planning mechanisms without the technocratic aspects, the planning commission has attempted to assume the role of broker between influentials and interests. This effort, initiated by the politically "savvy" commissioners, was resisted by the professional planning staff and contributed considerably to the decline of their influence with the community. Since their departure, the planning commission may well have returned to the broker role conceived to be the proper one by the community leadership.

Moline has had problems between commission and staff not unlike those of Rockford, for many of the same reasons. There, too, the idea of planning as a legitimate function is apparently well entrenched despite the quality and impact of the planning program at any given time. At the same time, the conflict between its technocratic and communitarian aspects remains unresolved, a matter of conflict within the planning "establishment" itself.

Planning in the remaining civil communities rests upon the narrow edge of conflicting attitudes which are characteristic of the articulated public reaction to planning generally. On one hand, there is a national trend (financed, in part, with federal funds) toward the establishment of local planning agencies as symbolic hallmarks of the "progressive" community. This must help to explain the near-universality of organized planning institutions in civil communities of over 25,000 population. This trend has a substantive side as well in that every one of these civil communities does have apparent and visible need for planning in some form, if only for zoning and subdivision control. Every one of these communities also has at least a few influentials who are committed to planning as an idea and as a useful tool in community development and who are sincerely interested in developing local planning facilities.

On the other hand, there are substantial numbers of community influentials in all those communities who oppose planning as an infringement on private rights and a threat to established patterns from which they benefit. (The two reasons are intertwined in their overall position and cannot easily be separated.) They, in turn, can usually muster considerable popular support when planning questions are brought before the general public. In between the advocates of planning, on one hand, and its opponents, on the other, there stand the bulk of the community's influentials who are willing to support planning operations for their symbolic value and for any services they may be able to render on behalf of economic development or to promote governmental "efficiency" but who do not wish to see their particular interests touched adversely for the sake of "long-range planning" or the "planned community."

These three elements are represented in some proportion in every civil community. Clearly, the way in which the proportions are distributed provides the basis for determining the place of planning in the community. In the civil communities along the nation's middle, where the individualistic political culture predominates, the quality of the planning program depends upon the extent to which the representatives of that culture are won over to support particular planning activities and—most important—particular planners. Though timing is of the essence in determining the chances of acceptance for particular planning activities, the personalities of the planners are even more important for their effect on the status of planning in those communities. Decatur, Pueblo, Rock Island, and Springfield have had some notable (though limited) successes in the planning realm in the past decade because of the talent of the professional planners that have served them and the ability of those planners to work with the local influentials. Champaign has utilized its planning apparatus somewhat less, perhaps less as a consequence of the planners and more as a consequence of other factors on the local political scene. Peoria has achieved little rapport between planners and influentials, and the planning program has been limited accordingly (and, for that matter, fragmented as well). In all six civil communities, the demands placed on planning are limited to the preparation of the way for further economic development or to the suggestion of means to economize in government projects.

The same factors supporting and opposing planning are present in civil communities dominated by the heirs of the South and the traditionalistic political culture, but the balance is definitely against planning as a necessary or legitimate local government activity. The differences between Alton and Joliet serve as a case in point. Civil communities of roughly the same size but located in different sections of Illinois and with visibly different demographic compositions, both have planning programs that began with the preparation of general plans in the fashion of the 1950's without having professional planners in residence. In both cities, the local planning commissions have been involved in "planning" projects and do not confine their activities to zoning matters only. In both, the hiring of a professional planner has been a matter of public discussion and, by 1960, a budget line for such a position existed in Joliet. In both cases, opposition from politically articulate elements prevented the hiring of any professional. One consequence of this has been to transform the planning commissions in both cities into strategic centers for the negotiation of group differences over specific projects, moving them away from the traditional function of planning commissions as providers of citizen endorsements of the planning fiats of the professionals.

In Alton, however, the general attitude is less than favorably disposed to the idea of planning, except as a means to insure the implementation of the short-range desires of the business and industrial leadership. Public attitudes toward planning were exemplified in the early 1960's by Alton's rejection of even a minimal housing code required by the federal government to comply with the standards set down by Congress to obtain urban renewal grants. The city council had only hesitatingly approved the proposed code, after the Urban Renewal Administration had lowered their requirements to the absolute minimum just to get Alton's urban renewal program under way, only to have the city's voters reject it at the polls. The fight against the code was led by the John Birch Society, whose major argument was that it restricted the individual's right to use his own property as he saw fit and that government restrictions on private use are not different from outright confiscation.

Planning is somewhat better accepted in Joliet, not as a technical activity but as a reasonable way in which to maximize return on local effort while satisfying a more broadly based group of interests and influentials. This may explain why no action was taken to hire the planner provided for in the city budget while, at the same time, the planning commission was actively involved in examining, reviewing, and modifying proposals for all the city-supported long-range improvement projects under consideration. In 1962, the planning commission was actively involved in shaping two urban renewal projects, a project for a new city hall or city-county building and a proposal for the construction of high-rise housing for the elderly on the fringes of the central business district.

Pueblo's planning efforts also reflect the marketplace orientation of the individualistic political culture but with an unusual twist. The director of the city-county planning agency, a professional planner, was himself responsible for directing the planning commission into a broker role at the strategic center of development decision-making. From the first, the Pueblo planning district was set up to embrace the entire civil community—the city proper and its unincorporated fringes—while excluding the greater part of Pueblo County, whose size and relative emptiness really remove it from the city's immediate ambit. The planning director, in an instinctive appreciation of the local political culture, turned his agency away from the development of a master plan whose utopian overtones are inevitably more appealing in a moralistic environment and put his staff to work on collecting and organizing data that would be useful to local developers of all kinds. Simultaneously, he worked to turn the planning commission itself into a broadly representative body (including members who had openly opposed its creation) with a membership that was personally influential in the civil community so that it would become a negotiating instrument rather than simply a body that ratified professional productions. He was successful in his efforts because the influentials in the community quickly perceived the utility of that kind of planning operation both as a source of good data (a substantive benefit) and as a place for important negotiations (a procedural benefit).

Belleville, the last of the cities of the prairie to enter the planning field, established a planning and zoning commission in 1961 after nearly fifteen years of false starts and aborted efforts that reflected a widespread opposition to formal planning and zoning in that civil community. There again, the conflict between planning as a symbolic "good" and a technocratic interference with individual rights lay at the roots of the delay. Even so, some steps had been taken in the direction of a planning program out of sheer necessity. By 1961, the city had pieces of a "master plan" prepared by a local engineer on a voluntary basis and a weak subdivision control ordinance. It had no zoning ordinance at all. Though the Chamber of Commerce officially encouraged the enactment of a zoning ordinance, not even the business community for whom the Chamber ostensibly spoke was eager to see one developed.

Planning in East St. Louis is a problem so different in character that it is difficult to discuss it meaningfully in this context. All such efforts initiated locally must fit into a political system in which planning is considered to be of very little value and even a detriment to its "proper" functioning. Most of the planning done in that civil community has been done through the intervention of an "outside" agency, Southern Illinois University (see Chapter Seven). The University has outflanked, as it were, the local planning institutions, which have always been so much windowdressing for a political organization dedicated to other goals.

Size seems to be an additional factor affecting the scope of planning in the three smallest of the cities of the prairie, though it has no bearing on the cultural dispositions of the civil communities concerned. In East Moline, Urbana, and Superior, local planning commissions exist primarily to handle zoning questions and to make recommendations on same to the city council. Though East Moline has a general plan (acquired in 1959 in response to a general trend in the Quad Cities area to have outside consultants prepare such plans), it is not really used. Since none of the three has professional planning staffs, their advance planning work is virtually nonexistent. Still, there exist differences in attitude toward planning among the politically articulate elements in the three communities.

Superior officially and publicly supports the planning principle in the style of Duluth. Only its poor economic position and declining population have prevented that city from developing a more extensive planning operation. As it is, the planning commission operates as a conservation agency with powers far in excess of those exercised in most communities, limiting "urban sprawl" within the city by controlling the issuance of building permits to specific areas so that the city will not be burdened with excessive costs for providing services. This device is also used to preserve the natural beauty of the area, a matter of some local concern.

East Moline publicly supports planning because it is considered the right thing to do in the Quad Cities metropolitan area. Though its political culture is far more individualistic than those of its sister cities, as their junior its city fathers feel compelled to follow their lead. "Planning" in that metropolitan area, however, is conceived of as a more moderate enterprise than in Superior—an advisory activity, as it were, even in those cities possessing planning staffs—so it has not become an onerous burden for East Moline. The city, which does not have any professionally trained people in its municipal government, can do little more than give lip service to the idea of advance planning.

In Urbana, perhaps the most homogeneously individualistic civil community of all, the planning idea was not even given lip service by the planning commission or its leading backers during the 1950's. The city's small size enabled it to remain concerned exclusively with individual zoning cases without the necessity for considering larger planning issues. This predisposition was brought out into the open late in 1962 when a leading member of the commission resigned after publicly charging that the commission was refusing to concern itself with planning. His resignation caused no significant stir in the community. Though Urbana was then acquiring parts of a general plan, it was as a result of efforts made by one of the minority aldermen on the city council rather than a serious city effort. He arranged for graduate students of planning at the University of Illinois to prepare a land-use map and secured council approval because he was able to get their services free.

While it would be inaccurate to infer the existence of a single-minded "community" attitude toward the purposes and functions of local government, or even the existence of single-minded "community" attitudes toward public support of education or planning, from the sectional location of the cities of the prairie and the distribution of the migrational streams among them, certain "general predispositions" can be seen in each community. When kept in proper perspective, those predispositions can be related to sectional and demographic patterns of political culture in the greater West.

After accounting for size differences and the idiosyncrasies present in each local situation, it is possible to discern a strong predisposition to accept a broadened view of the local government's planning function in those cities of the prairie dominated by the moralistic political culture and located in the trans-Mississippi states. In them the combination of a sectional tradition of greater government activity to cope with the conquest of the several frontiers and the settlement of communal pacesetters from the Northern streams is the crucial determinant leading to the acceptance of orthodox planning efforts as the starting point. The broadest view of the role of planning, and the planning program that has been most successful in providing community leadership, is found in Duluth where the combination of Northern streams has been most pronounced. There the utopian aspects of orthodox planning are attractive in and of themselves while the high importance of government as the major innovator in the civil community has given the planners considerable authority to act on their plans. In Davenport and Pueblo, where the Northern and Middle Streams are mixed, planning as a form of negotiated development has attracted broad support. In both civil communities, less utopian planning programs have been relatively strong and quite successful in contributing to community development. Superior, closer to Duluth and the trans-Mississippi West than to the rest of Wisconsin, shares Duluth's acceptance of comprehensive planning and, indeed, implements a comprehensive plan more fully than any of its sisters.

Within the state of Illinois, where the trans-Mississippi sectional configuration is absent, the cities most influenced by the Northern streams—Rockford and Moline—have shown a general predisposition toward public planning but have had minimally successful programs, apparently because of their influentials' conflicting attitudes toward orthodox planning. In the absence of a clear tradition of visibly heavy government involvement in their previous development, accompanied by a substantial dose of Yankee individualism, their willingness to accept utopian-style model-building was reduced without any proper substitute developed to take its place. Those civil communities influenced by the Middle streams and dominated by the individualistic political culture have programs whose importance has varied in relation to the planners employed and whose directions have, in any case, been limited. The key to successful planning operations in those communities has been the ability of the planners or planning commissions to get away from planning orthodoxies, adapt to a market-oriented culture by demonstrating the utility of applying planning techniques to commercial development, and then become the strategic centers of negotiation in development decision-making. Springfield and Decatur offer some notable examples of planners able to do just that while Joliet's planning commission has tried much the same route.

The civil communities most influenced by the Southern streams have been most reluctant to embark upon government-sponsored planning programs, since neither the promise of utopian improvement nor the support of commercial development appeals to their traditionalistic political cultural orientation *per se*. Hence, they have created planning institutions only as a consequence of outside intervention or in response to the overwhelming pressures of necessity accompanying urbanization. The unique situations in Alton, Belleville, and East St. Louis illustrate this.

The full meaning of the foregoing differences in local political cultures can be better understood when the cities of the prairie are viewed in the context of the political cultures of their respective states.

NOTES

1. This definition and its elaboration are taken from Gabriel A. Almond, "Comparative Political Systems," *The Journal of Politics*, XVIII (1956), 391–409. Almond is the first political scientist to systematically attempt to define and explore the relationship of political culture to the political system. His work and the work of his colleagues have been the starting point for the theoretical aspects of my exploration of the concept, but its application has been limited because of their cross-cultural concerns as against the intracultural concerns of this study. Let it be clearly understood that this discussion of political culture and the treatment of the concept that follows is not meant to imply some kind of crude "cultural determinism." "Political culture" as a concept is difficult enough to isolate in the context of a materialistically oriented phenomenology of "science," and is that much more difficult to identify and delimit empirically. Despite this difficulty—or perhaps as a consequence of it—it remains all too easy to attribute too much to "political culture" and to overdraw the effects of political culture on political behavior. Such error invariably leads to an implication of a facile and false determinism that becomes virtually apolitical in its very nature.

2. These six themes are adapted from the works of Clyde Kluckhohn. See, particularly *Mirror for Man* (New York: McGraw-Hill, 1949). See also Charles S. Sydnor, *American Revolutionaries in the Making* (New York: Collier Books, 1962).

3. The relationship between language and culture is universally recognized as one of the utmost profundity. Kluckhohn, *op. cit.*, treats the relationship well. For a most sensitive exposition see Edward Hall, *The Silent Language* (Garden City, N.Y.: Doubleday, 1959), and *The Hidden Dimension* (Garden City, N.Y.: Doubleday, 1966). The "value-concept" as a means of expressing important ideas in other than systematically philosophical or definitional ways is effectively advanced by Max Kadushin in *Organic Thinking* (New York: The Jewish Theological Seminary of America, 1938), and *The Rabbinic Mind* (New York: The Jewish Theological Seminary, 1952). The value-concept idea is an eminently useful one in the study of language and culture, particularly in the American political setting where reliance upon implicitly understood terms is extensive.

4. Gabriel A. Almond and Sidney Verba deal with the American national political culture comparatively in *The Civic Culture* (Princeton, N.J.: Princeton University Press, 1963).

5. The names given the three political subcultures are descriptive rather than evaluative. The three subcultures are delineated here as models or ideal types and, like all models, oversimplify the complexities of reality.

6. This description and the ones following it must be considered very carefully and only after first abandoning many of the preconceptions associated with such idea-words as *individualistic*, *moralistic*, *marketplace*, etc. In this case, for example, nineteenth-century individualistic conceptions of minimum intervention were oriented toward laissez faire with the role of government conceived to be that of a policeman with powers to act in certain limited fields. In the twentieth century, the notion of what constitutes minimum intervention has been drastically expanded to include such things as government regulation of utilities, unemployment compensation, and massive subventions to maintain a stable and growing economy—all this within the framework of the same political culture. The demands of manufacturers for high tariffs in 1860 and the demands of labor unions for workmen's compensation in 1960 may well be based on the same theoretical justification that they are aids to the maintenance of a working marketplace. Culture is not static. It must be viewed dynamically and defined so as to include cultural change in its very nature.

7. As in the case of the "I" political culture, the change from nineteenth to twentieth century conceptions of what government's positive role should be has been great—for example, support for prohibition has given way to support for wages and hours regulation. At the same time, care must be taken to distinguish between a predisposition toward communal activism and desire for federal government activity. For example, many "M" types oppose federal aid for urban renewal without in any way opposing community responsibility for urban redevelopment. The distinction they make (implicitly at least) is between what they consider legitimate community responsibility and what they believe to be central government encroachment, or between "communalism," which they value, and "collectivism," which they abhor. Thus, on some public issues we find certain "M" types taking highly conservative positions despite their positive attitudes toward public activity generally. "M" types may also prefer government (inevitably local) intervention in the social realm as a protector of morals—as censorship or screening of books and movies—to similar government intervention in the economy.

8. In this context, it should be noted that regular party systems are sometimes abandoned in local communities dominated by the "I" political culture to institute nonpartisan electoral systems in an effort to make local governments more "businesslike" and to take local administration "out of politics." Such antipolitical efforts are generally products of business-dominated reform movements and reflect the view that politics is necessarily "dirty" and illegitimate. In this context, see Edward C. Banfield, ed., *Urban Government* (New York: The Free Press of Glencoe, 1961), Sections III and IV.

9. See Theodore Calvin Pease, *The Story of Illinois* (Chicago: University of Chicago Press, 1949) for a brief history of public education in the state.

Chapter 7 / Competing Political Cultures in Illinois

Two Political Cultures and Their Sources

IT HAS ALREADY become clear that Illinois, whose cities are of central concern in this study, is one of the most heterogeneous states in the Union. In its social structure and its patterns of political response it is very likely the nation's most representative state.[1] In the heart of the Middle West (as traditionally defined), it stands at the geohistorical center of the United States. While its physiographic personality is relatively undistinguished, it combines within its boundaries most of the social, economic, historic, and geographic diversities found in this country. The careful observer will notice sharp regional contrasts within the state, which have had their influence on its settlement patterns. Illinois is simultaneously the western anchor of the industrial and megalopolitan greater Northeast and the gateway and chief trading center for the greater West. In its southern reaches it also includes a substantial extension of the physiographic and demographic elements which combine to form the distinctive character of the greater South.

Overall the state contains within its boundaries the western edge of the Eastern woodlands, the northern limits of the Southern hill country, a southern projection of the Northern lake and forest country, and the easternmost projection of the Western prairies.[2] It is both a major agricultural and major industrial state and has an extensive extractive industry as well. As described in Chapters Four and Five, the patterns of settlement and economic development that were implanted in Illinois closely follow the state's physiographic divisions.

In view of this fundamental heterogeneity of environment and general culture in Illinois, it is not surprising that there should be a certain heterogeneity in its political culture as well. Actually, two regional political cultures of unequal population, political strength, and geographic spread—the individualistic and the moralistic—have had to coexist within the boundaries of the state. The unequal competition between their respective representatives has been a continuing factor in the shaping of the Illinois political system and in the ordering of the political institutions which have molded its citizenry from the early days of statehood.

The individualistic political culture is dominant in Illinois. Its beginnings lay in the breakdown of the kinship-oriented traditionalistic subculture brought into the state by its early Southern settlers under the impact of the frontier and the force of the individualistic political culture brought in from the Middle States (whose products soon represented the major portion of the state's in-migrants). This "T" culture was reinforced by later migrants from similarly oriented nonnative cultures; southern and eastern European, Afro-American and Hispanic. True to its mixed roots, the values and attitudes which characterize the individualistic political culture in Illinois contain elements of a traditionalistic cast, particularly in the southern third of the state. Thus "private activities" immune from governmental intervention are very broadly defined and the rights of traditional local elites strongly protected. Government action is frequently structured with an eye to providing private economic benefit (in the form of either favors to individuals or supports for businesses) even when it is ostensibly for larger purposes.

Conservative in a quite individualistic way, most Illinois public officials are reluctant to exercise the powers of government, doing so only in response to immediate and unavoidable pressures and generally avoiding advance planning or even middle or long-range policy-making. The mechanisms of government are extensively used to provide economic rewards for the state's professional politicians, who are bound together by various networks of individual loyalties and friendships, ranging from common ethnic backgrounds to association with the American Legion, and cemented by a quid pro quo "favor" system. Ideology or even a concern with issues is notably lacking. Democratic professionals are vaguely committed to the mainstream views of their party, while the Republicans tend to be to the right of center. In both cases, the relative conservatism of men at home in a particular system makes itself manifest. Party politics are competitive but not overly so, with interparty "arrangements"—actual or tacit—not infrequently determining the allocation of offices from the township to the governorship. Since office is sought as a means to control the distribution of the "favors" of goverment rather than as a means of exercising governmental power for programmatic ends, it is often more appealing to the professionals to divide up the cake rather than engage in bloody fighting on an all-or-nothing basis. "Politics" is conceived to be a specialized activity for professionals but, at the same time, it has a kind of cynical fascination for the citizens of Illinois, most of whom believe it to be a "dirty" and corrupting business. Local administration is either tied to politics in the most direct sense or has been bureaucratized in the hope of insulating it from politics in any sense.

As the dominant political culture, individualistic values and attitudes and their functional expressions are operative throughout Illinois state government, in most, if not all, of the state's counties, and at the civil community level in much of the state as well. It is weakest in the state's northwestern counties, roughly those dominated by the descendants of Yankees and Scandinavians easily identifiable as those where the Progressive party was strong in 1912. It is in this latter area that the minority political culture survives as a force.

The values and attitudes which characterize the minority political culture are significantly manifested only at the civil community level, even in those areas. They include a strong public service orientation, which places heavy moral obligations upon those who participate in government to maintain community goals, particularly in opposition to the individualistic political culture that surrounds them. Local action, both governmental and nongovernmental, to improve the civil community, is relatively intense and regularly encouraged by community "liberals" and "conservatives" alike. Political conflict, accordingly, tends to revolve around questions of (or be couched in terms of) the public good or community improvement. Governmental powers are frequently used for at least middle-range planning and policy-making, not just for ad hoc responses to immediately pressing problems. While the two-party system is very much in evidence because of state demands, local nonpartisanship, special local parties, or—in extreme cases—third-party movements are characteristic of the local political scene. Politics in these moralistic enclaves is viewed as a practical vehicle for coming to grips with the issues and public concerns of civil society. Accordingly, every effort is made to convince every citizen to become as actively involved as possible in the political life of the community. Local administration tends to be highly professionalized with a great deal of emphasis on employing qualified higher civil servants in key positions but without trying to insulate or emancipate them from the political process.

In the early 1960's a team of investigators from the Office of Community Development of the University of Illinois, seeking to identify the University's potential role in meeting problems of the contemporary urban scene, found a marked resemblance between the politics of Springfield and Peoria, on one hand, and Rockford on the other, and the two political cultures identified above. Their utilitarian-oriented observations offer independent confirmation of the thesis advanced here. They characterized the first type, which they see as dominant in Springfield and Peoria, as follows:

The bedrock political culture of these cities, which tends to manifest itself whenever claims are made for mobilization of the *public* interest, shows the following outcroppings [summarized] as "Type I politics."

a. The world is to be understood primarily in economic terms, and the mechanism of social adjustment to be guarded above all else in the economic marketplace. Therefore, private action, *ceteris paribus*, is always to be preferred over public action.
b. The purpose of politics is to allocate rewards to individuals. Politics serves as a substitute for the economic marketplace in cases where the market is not allocating rewards to "deserving" individuals, or where people wish to utilize political power as one of their counters in the economic market itself . . .
c. Because b. (above) is the expected mode of behavior, politics is denigrated as dirty business, and it is expected that people who enter politics voluntarily will be as venal as they dare . . .

However, they also see a second type of politics, which exists in Rockford (and which may be emerging in the other two cities) having the following characteristics:

a. The world is still to be understood in economic terms, and the major mechanism of adjustment is the market. But it is admitted that in spheres of action which are essential to public peace and safety *and* in which a monopoly of coercion is necessary in order to accomplish the job, the marketplace is an inappropriate mechanism . . .
b. The purpose of politics is to provide a mechanism that is capable of formulating and enforcing general rules for the efficient performance of public functions. Efficiency, economy, and impartiality are the major goals.

To the extent that a variant of Type II politics emerging is in Springfield and Peoria, it takes on characteristics of a response to the dominant political culture, thus:

By the nature of things, [public] spheres of action are quite circumscribed; they are limited to traditional municipal functions of public safety, public health, and public works.

and

Because of the general view of politics . . . , the best elected official is assumed to be a successful businessman. He is safe because he needs neither the prestige nor the pecuniary rewards of public office, and he is most able to organize for efficient performance.[3]

Rival Political Cultures in Early Illinois

An examination of the constitutional history of Illinois in the perspective of political cultural change in the state illuminates the conflict between its cultures, exposing the reasons behind the separation of the state and some local governments alluded to above and elucidating the manner in which the political systems of each of the cities of the prairie has evolved.

The first constitution of the new State of Illinois was adopted in 1818 by a voting population made up almost exclusively of immigrants from the American South or from the southern reaches of the Middle States. The constitution was actually modeled on the constitutions of Virginia and Kentucky (and, to a lesser extent, on those of Ohio and Indiana, which were also modeled on the first two). From first to last, in its progressive sections as well as in its traditional ones, it reflected the then-current Southern approaches to government as well as the realities of the Illinois situation.

There was apparently no thought on the part of the state's political leaders that there would be any separation between state and local politics. On the contrary, the linkage between all levels of politics, like the ties between state and local governments, was taken for granted. Counties—the primary local governments—were considered to be instruments of the state government for the administration of justice, first and foremost. The historical record shows this to have been a reasonable assumption. Probably more than at any other period in the state's history, the same men were politically active at both levels. No provision was included for township organization, a form of government alien to the South, even though civil townships as administrative subdivisions of the county were a feature of the territorial period when local government organization was prescribed by Congress along New England lines. Where villages were established, their founders tended to be either political leaders who were also land speculators interested in selling town lots or politicians instructed to lay out county seats. Perhaps most important, virtually all the political actives in the state either came out of the same political culture or had embraced its values upon arrival in Illinois.

Politics in Illinois came early to be centered on personal influence, patronage, distribution of federal and later state benefits, and the availability of economic gain for those who were professionally committed to politics as their "business."[4] Even the change from a Whig-leaning to a predominantly Democratic state in the late 1820's and early 1830's did not affect the practice of politics in Illinois. It is true that, while the ruling elite that became the backbone of the Whig party consisted of "gentlemen" politicians who were only "semi-professionals" and the Democrats were led by out-and-out professional politicians from the first, both types shared the same approach to politics, impregnating the state's political system with their shared political culture by the Jacksonian era.

The influx of settlers from other parts of the United States and the world, coupled with the changing pattern of politics and economic organization on the national scene and the changing society of Illinois itself, created the felt need for constitutional revision in the 1840's. The agitation for constitutional revision involved more than a few specific demands. It also signified the interjection of a different political culture onto the Illinois scene.

The new arrivals, particularly the Yankees among them, soon dominated most of the emerging cities and the economic life of Illinois through their energetic efforts to do so. The Yankees' concern for the development of a commercial society within the context of the Puritan attitudes they brought with them (in modified form), led them to think of community action for the common good as an important social—even moral—duty. This outlook led to immediate demands for increased government activity of a positive character, ranging from aid in the construction of railroads to the provision of free public schools. In their efforts to implant towns (not just settlements) on the prairie, they reflected their conception of politics as an extension of man's struggle to create the good society as well as a source of personal opportunity.

The Yankees soon discovered, undoubtedly to their intense dissatisfaction, that their hopes for a new society on the prairie ran right up against a pattern of state government and a traditionalistic-cum-individualistic political culture already well rooted in the civil society of Illinois. Thus they were brought into almost immediate conflict with the dominant political interests in the state, whom they looked upon as desperately in need of "civilization." The Yankees were confronted with the problem of working themselves into the political system and, at the same time, modifying it insofar as possible to meet their goals for the good commonwealth. In demanding their share of political power, the newcomers also demanded more than a redivision of the existing political pie. They wished, in effect, to remake the pie itself. While they were ultimately successful in establishing themselves as political participants through their possession of undeniable geographic bases of power from which to negotiate, as something less than a majority in the state they had only limited success in altering the existing political institutions. From time to time, and after varying degrees of effort, they were able to achieve certain concrete "reforms," such as gaining the right of individual counties to adopt the township system of government by local option; the creation of a statewide system of public education; the repeal of the "black code" that had prevented Negroes from entering Illinois and had reduced those already in the state to virtual slavery; the inauguration by local option of such "supplemental" government activities as the support of public libraries and parks; and the other similar additions to the range of government services that they favored. These innovations, however, made only the barest of changes in the state's political culture and climate. As it turned out, even in those areas where the Yankees were able to settle first, the subsequent arrival of European streams whose products were culturally in harmony with the Southerners and Middle Americans—the Germans, the Irish, the Southern and Eastern Europeans—led to a lessening of their influence as a cultural force.[5] Only where the heirs of the Puritans were reinforced by Scandinavians was their strength maintained.

In the end, Yankee influence statewide raised popular sights as to the possibilities of politics, even when it did little to alter the popular conceptions of political reality. This may well be the source of an apparent political cynicism which is prevalent among the state's citizenry, particularly in its northern parts. As the Yankees discovered that it was considerably easier to change a power relationship than it was to alter the fundamental culture within which the power relationships were acted out, something akin to a social "trauma" occurred. The Yankee "men in the street" saw the gap between their ideals and political reality widening, and they reacted by developing a cynicism which has sunk deeply into the core of Illinois political life, profoundly affecting the public's political attitudes and expectations and perhaps the quality and extent of the average citizen's participation in politics as well.[6]

In effect, the representatives of both political cultures were forced to settle for a compromise which ultimately led to the separation of Illinois' political system into two separate though interacting segments. The individualistic political culture retained and even increased its dominance over the state as a whole, with a few traditionalistic survivals and moralistic increments built in. Indeed, not a few of the Yankees found this system to their liking once it became apparent that they would have to live with it. At the same time, the various civil communities were tacitly given the option of remaining largely outside the state political culture and maintaining a culture—traditionalistic or moralistic—of their own choosing. Confronted with this reality, the one political resource left to the Yankee leadership in their efforts to build the greater New England was to take advantage of the option offered them and develop reasonably autonomous civil communities within the areas of the state which they dominated. They were aided in their efforts by the traditional localism of the New England culture, which had encouraged local religious and political autonomy back home. The separation could not be complete, since the state was still the central government and source of local authority, but it could be sufficiently sharp to allow a great deal of local leeway even in matters of statewide concern. Of course, the civil communities which exercised their option gave up the possibility of forging good connections with the state political system as a whole—none has even contributed a major-party gubernatorial candidate, for example—and has frequently suffered for it.

Rockford and Moline, both founded after the Yankee migration had begun, are the chief examples of this isolationist effort among the cities of the prairie. Characteristically, very few people who have been active in local politics in these civil communities have ever advanced in statewide politics. Rock Island, Decatur, Joliet, Peoria, and Champaign were also influenced by the minority political culture, though to a considerably lesser extent. They are also less isolated from state politics and occasionally contribute someone who has risen through local politics to a position of statewide importance. Springfield, no doubt because of its position as state capital, is the only city of this group in the northern two-thirds of Illinois which has contributed a significant number of men with local political connections and interests to the state political scene. The situation is far different in the southern Illinois cities of the prairie. There even Belleville, which strives for the isolation of its political system from that of St. Clair County for reasons internal to that area, has contributed its leaders to the state.

The Constitution of 1848 formally ratified the new balance of political power in Illinois. Unlike the 1818 document, it made specific provision for local government, set forth definite limitations upon the state in regard to state-local relations, and provided for tie-ins between the state and local political systems in a manner that could be used to encourage local political autonomy. For example, rather than simply providing for the election of the state legislators by "the several counties or districts to be established by law," the new constitution provided that "districts shall be composed of contiguous territory bounded by county lines . . . *Provided* [Italics in the original] that cities and towns containing the requisite population may be erected into separate districts" (Art. III, Sec. 9). Thus cities were constitutionally recognized in Illinois for the first time. Even though there were still relatively few incorporated places and even fewer chartered cities in the state in 1848, the number had increased seven-fold since the arrival of the Yankee migration, and there was every expectation that the number of cities would soon increase even further. This was partly a simple assessment of socioeconomic trends. More important, it seems to reflect an effort on the part of some of the framers to provide a political locale in which the minority political culture would be able to sink roots.

The judicial article (V) of the new constitution, in its very first section, incorporated a provision authorizing the General Assembly to establish "inferior local courts, of civil and criminal jurisdiction" in the cities, in addition to the regular state-county court system. This new grant of opportunity to as-yet-unformed cities in the realm of the administration of justice clearly added to the potential for local autonomy. It was all the more significant when it is understood that the Illinois judiciary was already highly intermeshed with state politics by 1848 and was one more means for systematic reflection of the dominant political culture. Indeed, so extensive was the tie-in that the representatives of the dominant political culture were not willing to abdicate any significant portion of it, on the entirely reasonable (if unexplicit) grounds that nowhere is the conflict of political cultures more apparent than in the administration of justice. They were not willing to subject themselves or their allies to any justice other than their own. The General Assembly never authorized the creation of city courts other than the police magistrate's court with its very limited jurisdiction, except much later in the city of Chicago, after its political leadership had been absorbed into the state's dominant political culture.[7] Otherwise, the state-county system of the first constitution was simply expanded to provide for the election of state's attorneys in each county as well as the range of county judges, justices of the peace, court clerks, and sheriffs, all of whom function in dual capacities as county and state officers and are, accordingly, attached to the state political system.

The Constitution of 1848 included an article (VII) entirely devoted to counties and their government. The provisions of the article were designed to effectuate a compromise between the old settlers and the demands of the new ones. In it the General Assembly's authority to alter county boundaries or move county seats without the consent of the residents of the county involved was severely limited. This represented a victory for the proponents of the status quo, who did not wish to see the new settlers secede from the established counties to create their own, as had been happening in all parts of the state in the late 1830's and early 1840's. It also included a major concession to the Yankees and their efforts to secure a political base for their political culture, since it granted the individual counties the right to reorganize under the township system of government by local option, after a referendum and subject to legislation on the subject by the General Assembly.

The Revenue Article (IX) of the new constitution explicitly provided for the levying and collection of taxes for local purposes by "the corporate authorities of counties, townships, school districts, cities, towns and villages," subject to the provisions of the General Assembly. This relatively broad grant of taxing powers was a further step in the direction of making a certain degree of local autonomy possible. As in the case of the earlier steps, it was part of an overall effort to make formal provisions for handling cultural differences that were aggravating the state.

This "live and let live" approach was subsequently implemented by the General Assembly through the practice of inaugurating new programs by opening up local options which could later be followed by statewide action if the programs came to be accepted widely throughout the state. At first, public education was left to local option in this manner. Only later was it made a mandatory governmental function statewide. The option for township organization remains within each county, where it was first placed in the Constitution of 1848. Later in the nineteenth century, the provision of public library service, the establishment of parks and recreation programs, and even the development of local roads became matters of local option. Today the list of optional programs ranges from annexation of adjacent territories by municipalities to the enactment and enforcement of city or county zoning ordinances. Cities have local option in such important fields as the form of government they may choose; the institution of local planning and zoning; prohibition of the sale of alcoholic beverages; the levying of an additional sales tax to be collected by the state for local use, a utility tax for local purposes, a motor vehicle wheel tax, or all three; and the establishment of local human relations commissions to deal with minority group problems, to name only a few fields. School districts may operate under three or more different organizational forms. Park districts can be organized under three different options, each of which is governed by separate state legislation.

The entire Constitution of 1848 is permeated with this effort to compromise the interests of people who came out of two political cultures. The end result was a frame of government that satisfied few people and was found seriously wanting within less than a decade after its ratification. Efforts to alter it, however, foundered on the strains generated within the state during the Civil War period. As the ideological elements in the moralistic and traditionalistic political cultures intensified as a result of the struggle over slavery, polarizing the individualistic political culture that held the nation together and engendering efforts to divide the nation into two separate civil societies, the State of Illinois was caught in the middle. It was not until the question of disunion was settled that the state could see to the remodeling of its fundamental charter, and then the remodeling was undertaken in such a way as to meet the same problems of potential disunion that had confronted the nation as a whole.

In the intervening period, many cultural and demographic changes had taken place within Illinois which influenced the state's constitutional development directly or indirectly. After 1850 the most important elements to settle afresh in the state originated in Europe. The manner in which they either reinforced or came into conflict with the native streams that had preceded them (see Chapter Four) added another dimension to the conflict of political cultures in Illinois.

The Yankees' efforts at local isolation or autonomy were reinforced by the Scandinavians, who shared many of the same values and came to seek much the same right to be left alone. No doubt this contributed to the emergence of Rockford and Moline as the most self-contained of the medium-size civil communities in the state. The Middle State and Continental European commercially oriented migrants, while not overly interested in advancement in the political realm, were concerned with economic expansion and hence found isolation of limited value and often impolitic. They were supported in this by the Irish, who quickly became interested in politics as a means for economic advancement. Whether by accident, design, or inevitable coincidence, they settled in civil communities already dominated by the individualistic political culture, which they reinforced. Thus the most important aspects of political life in the commercially expanding river towns such as Joliet, Peoria, and Rock Island were absorbed into the state political system despite the efforts of a determined minority in all of them to foster a politics rooted in the moralistic political culture. Springfield, as state capital, could hardly escape involvement and continued to attract people who sought it. The central Illinois cities not particularly well located for commerce, such as Decatur, Champaign, and Urbana, attracted fewer immigrants from Europe but deepened their own commitment to the individualistic political culture through the continued influx of settlers from the Middle States.

In 1854, the creation of the Republican party introduced onto the Illinois political scene, a politics committed to achieving power to attain programmatic goals first and foremost. The founders of the party were predominantly Yankees who opposed the extension of slavery to the territories as an immediate issue and who, in the long run, opposed slavery and the Southern influence in American government in general. Most of them reached the Republican party after first experimenting with several antislavery third parties on the state and national scene. By and large, they were from the same element that had worked hard to secure the concessions to the Yankee political culture that were written into the 1848 Constitution. The Republican party *as they created it* represented a different political tradition as well as a new political force, unambiguously conceived to be dedicated to the values and aspirations of those groups sharing the moralistic political culture. Thus the cleavage between the early Republican party and the Democratic party was of a different order and went much deeper than the older cleavage between Democrats and Whigs, to bring the increasing moralistic fervor of the 1850's into the party system and accelerate the polarization of both state and nation.

Prior to the emergence of the Republican party, competition between Illinois Democrats and Whigs had been conducted within the same frame of reference—the same political culture—and was generally confined to who should control offices and gain the pecuniary benefits of government. Outside of the periodic espousal of specific programs in particular elections, there was virtually no long-range party commitment to any conflicting ideas, even in general terms. In fact, when critical issues such as the future of slavery in the state came to the forefront as matters of political concern, the parties studiously refrained from either active or passive participation in their resolution.

Between 1854 and 1860, the Whig party, which had been composed of an uneasy alliance between conservatives of both traditionalistic and moralistic political culture, became a casualty of cultural-cum-ideological polarization and gave up the ghost; while some of its political actives, particularly those in the southern third of the state, entered the Democratic party, whose practical political ethos was more congenial to them, the bulk of the ex-Whig politicians opted for the Republican party, which gave every indication of being the party of the future for office-seekers and the party of greater popular appeal to the ex-Whig voters. Indeed, the new party encouraged them to enter its ranks, knowing that it needed their support to win statewide and national elections. Their affiliation with the GOP gave it the strength to become the new majority party in the state, but they also introduced a strong element of the individualistic political culture into its organization. Between 1856 and 1872, representatives of the two trends battled quietly for party control. In the latter year, the schism in both the national and state party organizations drove many of the founders out of the GOP. Those that remained reached a *modus vivendi* which enabled them to remain political bedfellows but, in doing so, increased the sharpness of the cleavage between the two political cultures. Once again, individualistic ways triumphed at the state level while moralistic one were confined to localities where the representatives of that political culture were strong. Those among the latter who were not satisfied with this arrangement seceded from the GOP. A few returned to Democratic ranks. Others made an effort to create a third-party movement in the state. As a consequence of their efforts, the period of the 1870's and 1880's was the only one in which third-party activity took on any continued significance in Illinois.

When the efforts to repeat the success of the previous generation failed, the dissidents returned to the ranks of the regular parties, choosing the one they felt to be more likely to respond to their particular political demands. By doing so, they managed to establish "permanent" wings in both parties that do give the moralistic political culture some voice. These wings continue to exist, varying in strength from era to era but always in competition with the representatives of the dominant political culture. It is only in so-called reform periods, when they are needed to lead the party to victory with a "reform" candidate or ticket, that they become temporarily important in the party councils and sometimes exert some temporary influence on state government. They have never been able to substantially alter the state political system, however, because they run up against the dominant political culture shared by the majority.

The Emergence of a State Political Culture and the Rise of Civic Reform

The rise of the Republican party and the change in the origins of the migrants to Illinois coincided with major changes in the state's overall economic order. The land-frontier period in Illinois came to an end just before the Civil War. The war itself had a major effect in stimulating the industrialization of the state which had begun in the late 1840's and 1850's (see Chapters Two and Four). By the time of the adoption of the Constitution of 1870, economic power in the state had effectively passed into the hands of the new industrial entrepreneurs, particularly those involved in the building of the modern corporate economy. The political impact of this newly concentrated economic power was heightened after 1870 by the economic decline of the southern third of the state and its lapse into the hands of absentee owners, who managed the major portion of its economy according to their own dictates and without regard for local needs. The system of absentee ownership in southern Illinois took on a particularly venal character as the years went by, reducing that section of the state to virtual colonial status. The rise of Chicago as both the locus of one third of the state's population and the center of its economic life added still another dimension to the growing concentration of economic power.

The Constitution of 1870, which remains in force today, was built around three major adjustments. On one hand, the southern Illinois political leadership endeavored to write into the document a number of features to safeguard their declining influence. At the same time, the representatives of the new economic elites sought to gain constitutional concessions for their group. Finally, the spokesmen for the state's minority political culture made another effort to write their conception of the good commonwealth into the state's fundamental law, either to extend its application statewide or to further protect their local bases of power. Hovering over the constitutional convention, to the concern of all three groups, was the problem of recreating the unity of the state which had been damaged during the war, when Illinois was rent by the same conflict of cultures that nearly sundered the Union.

As the constitutional convention developed, it became apparent that the first two groups had much in common. They found themselves able to collaborate in the creation of the system of minority representation in the General Assembly whereby three legislators were to be elected from each district through a system of cumulative voting that would enable minority party voters to cast up to three votes for one man, and in the incorporation of other features into the constitution which enabled them to protect the lion's share of their fundamental interests. The end result of their collaboration was the development of a system whereby careful manipulation of the state's organs of government and maintenance of long tenures in the legislature served to reinforce the political positions of the southerners while, at the same time, serving to support and favor the interests of the favored economic elites from Chicago, Peoria, and the other newly industrializing cities. As time wore on, the alliance between the legislators representing the state's backwash areas and the economic interests acting (sometimes quite illegally) to preserve their favored position served to strengthen the previously dominant political culture in Illinois as well as to limit state-level action to meet statewide problems.

Once again the representatives of the communitarian tradition, reduced in number, had to be content with securing the constitutional right to maintain their local political systems reasonably independently of the state political system. This time their task was actually made more difficult. In the first place, they were more clearly in the minority than in 1848, if only as a consequence of the combination of the other two groups, one of which had not existed earlier. In the second place, many of the provisions written into the earlier constitution to secure local autonomy and which had been found to interfere with the operation of the dominant interests in the state had already been circumvented by the development of informal techniques for doing so. Ultimately, the clash between their desires and those of the other interests led to the abandonment of several provisions which had been favorable to their cause. The new system of legislative apportionment was a case in point. Minority representation meant that the same fifty-one relatively large districts would be used for the apportionment of both senators and representatives, eliminating the smaller assembly districts that had made it possible for cities other than Chicago to elect their own representatives to the General Assembly.

Where their demands coincided with those of the southern Illinois "protectionists" and the new economic interests who wished to restrict the possibilities for legislative interference in their affairs, the advocates of local autonomy did gain some concessions. Thus the new constitution included more limiting detail than its predecessors, particularly detailed limitations on the legislature. In Article IV, Section 22, the legislature was prohibited from passing local or special legislation in a number of specific cases, among them several that had direct bearing on the functioning of local government. The most important of these prohibitions was the elimination of the incorporation of cities by special charter and the corollary creation of a general law governing municipal corporations in the state.

The all-embracing scope of this provision has been reduced by various commonly accepted legislative devices that reintroduce special legislation via the "back door." Nevertheless, its importance in furnishing a new basis for the development of local government in Illinois should not be underestimated. The Cities and Villages Act, passed in 1872 as a consequence of this provision and amended many times since, has become the fundamental charter of all but a handful of Illinois cities, particularly since even the Constitution of 1870 is relatively silent about municipal government, leaving the power to create, limit, and direct same to the General Assembly within very broad limits.

Other provisions were included in the new constitution which guaranteed at least a minimum of local autonomy for those who sought it. A selected list is contained in Table 7–1. The constitutional aspects of the conflict between political cultures did not end with the adoption of the Constitution of 1870. Soon the representatives of the minority political culture found themselves confronted with increased legislative intervention into local affairs and—to their way of thinking, much worse—an increasing encroachment of the dominant political culture into their communities. The sources of their anxiety were two-fold. On one hand, the post-1870 influx of Southern and Eastern Europeans introduced elements that were strongly attracted to the same attitudes and values that underlay the state's dominant political culture. As they were assimilated into the individualistic political culture, they created what amounted to a "fifth column" even within the civil communities previously dominated by the moralistic political culture without serious challenge.

In addition, the period after 1870 witnessed the rise of organized labor as a factor to be reckoned with in state and local affairs. At first a discontented but repressed element which had only a mimimum of power derived from its nuisance value, by the late nineteenth century organized labor began to threaten the balance of power in the state and in the growing metropolitan communities. The reaction on the part of the economic elites was not long in coming. Many of them who had previously supported the communitarian goals and moralistic procedures of the minority political culture found that they could gain greater protection from the rising labor and new immigrant groups by allying themselves with the professional politicians who would support their economic interests in return for the right to "boss" the "lower city."

This turnabout on the part of elements previously committed to the moralistic political culture was hastened by two other factors as well.

In the first place, simple passage of time led to an erosion of the values of the secondary political culture particularly among those who were born into an environment dominated by a market culture. The more mixed the community was to begin with, the sooner the dominant political culture made inroads among the descendants of its minority counterpart. Furthermore, the rise of demands for a regulated capitalism encouraged many of the businessmen who had been raised in the milieu of the moralistic political culture to look more sympathetically upon a style of politics that encouraged a "live and let live" or laissez-faire posture in government. Most of the state's business and manufacturing interests, who had always been well known for their desire to be left alone, found that they could become highly tolerant of the dominant political culture in Illinois, which promised them this in return for payment of a "tax" of petty corruption for the privilege. Indeed, they came to prefer to pay this "tax" (often while publicly denouncing the system which demanded it) rather than run the risk of having an energetic issue-oriented government which might interfere with their patterns of doing business.

The bargain was struck in most of the growing cities in the state as well as on a statewide basis. The "two cities" emerged, with the leadership of both functioning as partners in an effort to secure their respective economic interests. The idealists, the populists, and the progressives—products of the moralistic culture who remained faithful to it—found themselves outgunned and undermined even in the bailiwicks which they had claimed for their own. At first they turned once more to third-party movements in an effort to recoup their losses within the political arena. When this tactic failed again, they turned to administrative and constitutional reform, inaugurating an era of periodic waves of "municipal reform" that persisted in the state and the nation (for much of what happened in Illinois was a reflection of what was occurring in other parts of the country as well) for two generations or more into the early 1960's.

Reform waves developed periodically in this context because the overall situation generally tolerated in the new political climate occasionally became inadequate for the conduct of business (it failed to provide needed services, the "tax" became too heavy, it gave the local community or the state a bad image) and intolerable for the middle-class elements that dominated the business community, who retained certain moralistic values (it became too corrupt or too "inefficient"). When this occurred, the business community would sometimes unite with the populist-progressive reformers who were otherwise too weak to initiate "reform" by themselves. Together the two elements could introduce changes of varying degrees of superficiality or intensity. The most recent wave of reform generated by that business-populist alliance took place between the close of World War II and the early 1960's, and provides the focus for this study.

TABLE 7-1
Selected Constitutional Provisions Shaping Local Government in Illinois

Article	Section	Provision
IV	22	The general assembly shall not pass local or special laws . . . for— Laying out, opening, altering, and working roads or highways; Vacating roads, town plats, streets, alleys, and public grounds; Locating or changing county seats; Regulating county and township affairs; Regulating the jurisdiction and duties of justices of the peace, police magistrates, and constables; Incorporating cities, towns, or villages, or changing or amending the charter of any town or village; Providing for the election of members of the board of supervisors in townships, incorporated towns, or cities; Providing for the management of common schools; The opening or conducting of any election, or designating the place of voting;
	23	The general assembly shall have no power to release or extinguish, in whole or in part, the indebtedness, liability, or obligation of any corporation or individual to any municipal corporation in the state.
VI	13	Counties with populations exceeding 100,000 or with populations exceeding 50,000 where circuit court business shall occupy nine months per year may be designated separate circuits by the general assembly.
	17	Judges of all inferior courts must be residents of the jurisdiction in which elected.
	18	Each county shall have a county court with elected judge and clerk as a court of record with original jurisdiction in probate matters, matters of taxation and assessment, and any other matters as provided by general law.
	19	Right of appeal from county courts as may be provided by law.
	20	Probate courts may be established in counties of over 50,000 population by the general assembly.
	21	Justices of the peace, police magistrates, and constables shall be elected in and for such districts as are, or may be, provided by law, and the jurisdiction of such justices of the peace and police magistrates shall be uniform.
	22	State attorneys to be elected in and for each county.
IX	3	Property of counties and other municipal corporations may be exempted from taxation by general law only. County tax levies shall never exceed 75 cents per $100 valuation unless authorized by referendum.
	9	The general assembly may vest the corporate authorities of cities, towns, and villages with power to make local improvements by special assessment, or by special taxation of contiguous property, or otherwise. For all other corporate purposes, all municipal corporations may be vested with authority to assess and collect taxes; but such taxes shall be uniform in respect to persons and property, within the jurisdiction of the body imposing same.
	10	The general assembly shall not impose taxes upon municipal corporations, or the inhabitants or property thereof, for corporate purposes, but shall require that all the taxable property within the limits of municipal corporations shall be taxes for the payment of debts contracted under authority of

TABLE 7-1 (continued)

Article	Section	Provision
		law, such taxes to be uniform in respect to persons and property, within the jurisdiction of the body imposing same. Private property shall be liable to be taken or sold for the payment of the corporate debts of a municipal corporation.
	11	Public defaulter, ineligibility for municipal office. Pay of municipal officer not to be increased or diminished during his term.
	12	No county, city, township, school district, or other municipal corporation, shall be allowed to become indebted in any manner or for any purpose, to an amount, including existing indebtedness, in the aggregate exceeding 5 per cent on the value of the taxable property therein, to be ascertained by the last assessment for state and county taxes, previous to the incurring of such indebtedness. Any county, city, school district, or other municipal corporation incurring any indebtedness as aforesaid, shall before, or at the time of doing so, provide for the collection of a direct annual tax sufficient to pay the interest on such debt as it falls due, and also to pay and discharge the principal thereof within twenty years from the time of contracting the same.
X	1	No counties to be formed of less than 400 square miles nor any existing counties reduced to less than 400 square miles.
	2	Division or reduction of counties by local referendum only.
	3	There shall be no territory stricken from any county, unless a majority of the voters living in such territory shall petition for such a division; and no territory shall be added to any county without the consent of the majority of the voters of the county to which it is proposed to be added. Stricken portions to remain liable for their share of the debts of their former county.
X	5	The general assembly shall provide, by general law, for township organization, under which any county may organize whenever a majority of the legal voters of such county, voting at any general election, shall so determine, and whenever any county shall adopt township organization, so much of this constitution as provides for the management of the fiscal concerns of the said county by the board of county commissioners, may be dispensed with, and the affairs of said county may be transacted in such manner as the general assembly may provide. And in any county that shall have adopted a township organization, the question of continuing the same may be submitted to a vote of the electors of such county, at a general election, in the manner that now is or may be provided by law; and if a majority of all the votes cast upon that question shall be against township organization, then such organization shall cease in said county; and all laws in force in relation to counties not having township organization, shall immediately take effect and be in force in such county. No two townships shall have the same name, and the day of holding the annual township meeting shall be uniform throughout the state.
XI	4	No law shall be passed by the general assembly granting the right to construct and operate a street railroad within any city, town, or incorporated village, without requiring the consent of the local authorities having the control of the street or highway proposed to be occupied by such street railroad.

The general rule that the urge for community reform, when it arises, develops on a nationwide basis but is expressed locally in different ways was fully as valid in the early years of the twentieth century as it is today. By 1900, the center of the reform movement in Illinois had moved from the farms to the cities, reflecting the urbanizing trends of the time. Municipal reform became the order of the day. The reformers believed that by "kicking the rascals out" of their city governments they would be able to rebuild their cities according to the dictates of their political culture and, from there, move on to capture control of the state. Success in the battle for municipal reform was, to no small degree, contingent upon success in the legislature where constitutional change—either through amendment of the constitution itself or through alterations in the Cities and Village Act—had to be obtained to open the gates of change. At the turn of the century, the state's urban civil communities could incorporate either as villages with the village president-trustee system of government or as cities under the mayor-aldermanic system. In effect, they had no significant options for structural change. As the commission form of government (developed in Texas) and the city manager plan (developed in New York, Virginia, and Ohio) began to attract national attention, the Illinois reformers attempted to secure legislation permitting cities and villages to opt for them as alternate forms. In 1911 a coalition of reformers drawn from Chicago and the medium-size cities in the state was able to secure the passage of an act granting cities the option of choosing the commission form of government by local referendum.

Among the Illinois cities of the prairie, adoption of the new form of government was contingent on several factors. Perhaps most immediately important was the presence of an active group of reformers seeking its adoption who could make their voices heard. However, reformers alone were not enough. Those civil communities which were least affected by the conflict of political cultures within their limits made little or no effort to change the form of their city government. This was the case regardless of whether their local political systems fitted into the state's dominant political culture or stood outside it.

Alton, East Moline, Urbana, and Belleville, four civil communities which operated within the statewide political culture and had relatively few reformers to challenge their established systems, also saw no particular need to alter their institutions. "Reform," to them, was more a matter of replacing the "ins" with "outs" not too different from them but who had not yet had access to the rewards of local government and were willing to provide new services to the public for the opportunity. By the same token, Rockford and Moline, both reasonably secure within their own boundaries against the extensive penetration of the dominant political culture, retained the traditional form of city government despite the presence of and disproportionate number of reformers. Without any change in the structure of city government, Rockford underwent what can only be described as a major reconstitution in that period, which climaxed in 1921 with the election of a socialist mayor and city administration and transformed that civil community into a socialist stronghold until the early 1950's. Rockford's socialists were drawn from the ranks of both Scandinavians and Yankees and were of the conservative "sewer socialist" variety. They were successful in overthrowing a tight, if benevolent, industrialist-dominated Yankee oligarchy which had controlled local politics up to that time. Through their domination of the local party system, the socialists were able to control the city and township governments for thirty of the next thirty-six years. Moline, like Rockford, saw the rise of a socialist element which, however, was less successful in winning city elections than in influencing the dominant oligarchy to incorporate some of its proposed reforms.

Because these reform movements represented struggles for power within a common political culture rather than clashes between representatives of rival political cultures, even relatively radical reformers like those in Rockford felt little or no need to alter the basic political institutions of their civic community on the assumption that only radical institutional change could "throw the rascals out." They merely wished to capture control of those institutions for their own ends and were satisfied that the same institutions could be used to further those ends.

The reformers in the cities of the prairie most affected by the conflict of political cultures were the ones who felt the necessity for changing the local constitutions—and institutions—most keenly, hoping to utilize governmental structural change as a means of regaining control of their civil communities. Consequently, it was in those civil communities that the most strenuous efforts were made to adopt the new form of government as soon as it became legally possible to do so. Indeed, their reformers were the most active lobbyists for legislative authorization of the option at the state level, since they were the most interested. For them, as for reformers throughout the United States, the commission plan seemed to offer much. It introduced "full-time city government," which would presumably eliminate the political hacks and raise the level of the city's elected officials to that of at least semiprofessional administrators. At the same time it was nonpartisan, so professional politicians would presumably be excluded. "Politics," meaning the professionalized political system which was a feature of the individualistic political culture, would presumably be eliminated, once and for all. Finally, it presumably was to be "efficient and businesslike," without the old system of ward and local logrolling and checks and balances to impede the flow of city business. This last appealed not only to the reformers but to the "cosmopolitan" (as distinct from "local") business and professional elements who otherwise accepted the dominant political culture while desiring a form of efficiency that recognized their area-wide interests rather than those of the neighborhoods and whose support was needed to secure the adoption of the new plan.[8]

Champaign, Decatur, Joliet, Rock Island, and Springfield adopted the commission form of government within a decade after its introduction into Illinois. Though all five were dominated by the individualistic political culture, all were caught, to a greater or lesser extent, in the conflict between political cultures. In all five communities the drive for structural reform was initiated as a consequence of the reformers' grave dissatisfactions with the political status quo within the individualistic political culture, but reform itself was a product of the coalition of two diverse groups, products of different political cultures. In Rock Island, it literally took a gun battle to drive out the old regime—temporarily, at that. The transition in Champaign, Decatur, and Joliet was less difficult and reflected the continued influence of the progressives (generally representatives of the moralistic political culture) in those communities. The small minority of progressives in Springfield capitalized on a particularly blatant public scandal in the city government, involving the embezzlement of relatively large sums of public money through the issuance of duplicate warrants by the city officials of the "old regime," to rally the cosmopolitan business-and-professional community (which was really part of the dominant political culture) to support reform at the polls.

It would be erroneous to assume that the division between reformers and anti-reformers was based on political culture alone, or that the products of the individualistic political culture were—or have been—anti-"reform," per se, while the moralistic political culture is "reformist" per se. In every one of the five cities, it was the added support of many products of the state's dominant political culture which made the difference. While representatives of the moralistic political culture were more likely to be in the vanguard of reform, political cultural differences were crucial not so much in determining who would support reform issues when they became issues, but in shaping conceptions of when (under what conditions) reform was needed and what it should accomplish.

By and large, the moralistic reformers, reflecting the communitarian political values of their political culture, were interested in developing a continuing reform movement which would lead to increased public responsibility in matters political (if not to increased governmental activity, which was only one aspect of increased public responsibility to their way of thinking). That is to say, they were interested in reforming politics—making politics more democratic, as they saw it—not in eliminating politics from government. This led them to espouse such causes as the direct primary, nonpartisanship, proportional representation, and commission government, all of which they saw as opening up politics to greater participation rather than eliminating political activity.

The people amenable to reform within the individualistic political culture did not think of reform as a continuing activity but as a "one-shot" effort to introduce efficiency, economy, and "businesslike" procedures into government. Since their view of politics was cynical, to say the least, they saw little hope in reform through politics. To them, reform could only be secured by eliminating politics from government as fully as possible. Since this view tied in very nicely with the business ethic of "efficiency and economy" which meant so much to them in the economic realm, it led naturally to the development of a "government as against politics" dichotomy in their thought. Such a view was not designed to promote public responsibility but, on the contrary, to create the "perfect" mechanism that would obviate the necessity for continued public responsibility, beyond voting at election time or perhaps occasionally petitioning the city government for special services. Their interest in reform was limited to a concern with changing the form of the government but did not imply any dedication to maintaining the quality of the personnel that were to implement the new form and certainly did not indicate a willingness on their part to become regularly active in politics.[9]

In one of the cities of the prairie which adopted the commission plan, "reform" was exclusively the product of the individualistic political culture. There was no conflict of political cultures in East St. Louis; however, municipal government was so overwhelmingly corrupt in that civil community, even by the lowest standards of the individualistic political culture, that "reform" appeared to be vitally necessary in the minds of the cosmopolitan business-and-professional community who were no longer ready to pay their political "specialists" such a heavy tax. The professional politicians in control, apparently realizing that the commission form of government could be even more easily controlled by them for their purposes than the mayor-aldermanic form, allowed the adoption of the new plan, then proceeded immediately to take control of it. Since the element sponsoring reform followed the pattern common among reformers in their political culture and abandoned their general interest in city government after adoption of the new system, the politicians had only to wait and step in.

Peoria was the only major city among the Illinois cities of the prairie that, according to the theory presented here, "should" have adopted commission government and did not, defeating the proposed plan in a 1911 referendum. The reformers in Peoria were numerous enough and strong enough to secure an immediate referendum on the adoption of the commission plan. However, they were not able to secure the support of the cosmopolitan business-and-professional element which they needed to win. The leadership of that element, the "big businessmen," were just not interested in reform.

A closer look at the Peoria situation reveals why this was so. Peoria's history, demography, and economic development, examined in earlier chapters, indicate the manner in which that civil community came to be a miniaturized version of the larger, more complex metropolitan centers in the Mississippi Valley. The emergence of a "big business" leadership that remained located in Peoria gave that civil community a dimension absent in others of similar size. This leadership element was originally drawn, in large measure, from the ranks of the Yankees who had come from the moralistic political culture. However, as their business enterprises expanded, they found it much more in their interest to make their peace with the dominant political culture, partly because their economic interests were better served by doing so and partly because their horizons of personal interest were raised beyond their local community or even their state, so that state and local politics came to interest them only insofar as their economic interests were directly affected. A vicious circle developed as their lack of personal concern led to a lack of interest in the conflict between the individualistic and moralistic political cultures, leading them, in turn, to accept the former as dominant. The victorious politicians rewarded them by providing easy means for securing the protection of their economic interests, which, in turn, discouraged any interest on their part to alter the political system in the name of values put forth by the representatives of the minority political culture.

In any case, within four years at the most, the old-line politicians regained control of the municipal governments of those cities which did change. Considering the difficulties involved in changing political culture and the fact that the reformers had to rely upon alliances with products of the dominant political culture, it is not surprising that governmental structural change failed to "restore good government" in them. This failure is even less surprising when it is recognized that the structural change itself was effected by narrow margins in almost every case and only after public exposure of scandal, vice, and corruption in most of the cities. In only one city—Springfield—did the change to the commission system make a difference. There the commitment of A. G. Spaulding, the moving spirit behind the change, to a public-service career as one of the commissioners made the difference. His exceptional personality and long tenure in office gave the forces of change a permanent and effective share of power in the civil community. The Springfield case is an excellent illustration of the truth of Pope's couplet—"For forms of government let Fools contest/What e'er is best administer'd is best"—though, in all honesty, it was the structural change that enabled a good man to gain a significant position in the city government.

On the eve of World War I, however, this failure had yet to become apparent. Fresh from a few municipal victories, the reformers proceeded to assault the bastions of the statewide system as part of the concerted effort at reform that characterized the Progressive Era. They succeeded in obtaining state administrative reorganization in 1917 through a statewide alliance with the cosmopolitan business-and-professional elements similar to the alliances at the local level. Thus encouraged, they felt the time was ripe to attempt serious state constitutional reform. Included among the proposed reforms was one to establish constitutional home rule for the cities in the hope that this would enable them to maintain local autonomy from the dominant political culture and the system which manifested its values.

The reformers secured passage of a resolution calling for a constitutional convention from the 1917 General Assembly. The voters approved it in 1918, and in 1920 the convention, consisting of a very diverse group of delegates representing every conceivable division in the state, met. After two years of deliberation, they emerged with a document that made no significant alterations in the state-local relationship other than to provide limited home rule for Chicago (much of which was already embodied in a constitutional amendment that had been ratified in 1904) and which was so evidently an unsatisfactory compromise from a convention that could barely agree on any document that it was decisively defeated at the polls. This setback virtually ended the momentum for local reform in Illinois until after World War II.

Political Culture and the Contemporary Reform Movements

The intervening years between the municipal reform movements of the Progressive Era and the end of World War II brought great changes nationally, culminating in the great expansion of governmental activity brought about by the Great Depression and the New Deal. During the 1930's public attention was focused on Washington as the states and localities proved fiscally and otherwise unable to handle their problems without generous federal aid. During those years, reformers interested in changing their communities worked actively for federal financial and technical assistance rather than for local constitutional change. Though the greater part of the assistance obtained involved state action as well as federal, and state supervision of funds and projects decisively influenced the manner in which the civil communities could use the federal help available, in the *minds* of the reformers, the role of the states had diminished radically.

Perhaps more important, the magnitude of the crisis made the by then essentially marginal or residual conflict between political cultures of clearly secondary importance. So much needed to be done that the agreement on goals to be pursued reached virtual consensus, though they may have been reached from different points of view. Much indeed was accomplished in those years in the way of rebuilding local communities physically through this convergence of interests, which united those who valued public improvement and increased communal activity as legitimate in and of themselves with those who accepted the expanded role of government as a temporary economic device to meet an emergency situation, in a common coalition.

The Depression was followed by World War II, which turned public concern away from domestic issues entirely. It was only after the end of the war that interest in domestic problems, including renewed interest in state and local activities, was revived. The Illinois scene, still following national trends, has been radically altered in the interim. The "two cities" of the previous generation were in the process of becoming one as the last wave of European-originated immigrant groups and organized labor rose to positions of political equality within the civil community as well as outside of it. Political power at the local level was either being redistributed as the war ended or was ripe for redistribution.

Furthermore, in Illinois as a whole and particularly in those communities which had earlier been on the front lines of the conflict between political cultures, the subtle changes of time as expressed through the rise of a new generation lessened the potential for conflict by virtually eliminating the moralistic culture as a factor in state politics. Only vestigial remnants remained, expressed through the positive political activities of individual reformers and the negative political attitudes (produced by experience with the dominant political culture) among much of the cosmopolitan business-and-professional element. Only in the northern and northwestern parts of the state, particularly in Rockford and Moline, where the moralistic political culture had continued to be locally dominant in an area geographically contiguous with the Upper Midwest (where that political culture has always been and continues to be dominant) did it remain a potent force.

Urbanization was no longer the central dynamic force in the life of the state, the nation, or the civil community. Just as it had replaced ruralism two generations earlier, so it was being replaced by metropolitanization in turn. The impetus for reform was shifting to the suburban areas (either within or outside the boundaries of the central cities), along with the population. Despite the virtual disappearance of an overt conflict between political cultures even in those cities which had gone through an earlier reform as a consequence of that conflict, reform was again rearing its head, this time within the framework of the dominant political culture, though stimulated by the vestiges of the other.[10] As in the earlier period, the interest in local reform was part of a nationwide trend, but in Illinois it took on some unique characteristics of its own.

Much as in the preceding generation, municipal reform in postwar Illinois was tied in with reform efforts at the state level. The election of Adlai Stevenson to the governorship in 1948 signaled the beginning of a renewed effort to change the character of government in the state. Stevenson's nomination and election was, in itself, the product of the regular political organization's sensing of the temper of the voters. After a series of particularly nasty scandals in the Republican-controlled statehouse and in Democratic-dominated Chicago, the voters clearly indicated their desire for some measure of political change. The Democratic organization responded by giving them "blue ribbon" tickets, starting in 1947 with Martin Kennelly for mayor of Chicago and continuing in 1948 with Paul H. Douglas for United States Senator and Stevenson for governor. The maneuver worked, and all three were elected, with the support of the remaining pockets of the moralistic culture (solidly Republican Rockford was carried by Stevenson, the only Democrat to do that in years) as well as with the votes of those from the dominant culture who wanted a change.

Stevenson, however, was not about to become a figurehead representative for the regular political leadership. With considerable dedication but with much less political "savvy," he went about trying to change the state's political system to bring it into conformity with the values of the moralistic political culture, of which he was a product. Of course he could not succeed in this effort. Within months after taking office, he had antagonized the leaders of his party, who could not comprehend his "unprofessional" (in their sense of politics) approach to his office and responsibilities. While his programmatic achievements on the state level were severely restricted by a hostile opposition from both parties, he was able to make significant impressions on a wide range of political situations, not the least of which was local government reform.

Stevenson's greatest contributions to the stimulation of local reform movements came from quite disparate aspects of his brief involvement in state politics. From the very first, the Stevenson gubernatorial campaign had taken on aspects of a "crusade," much as his presidential campaigns were to do a few years later. Many of the original Stevensonians who had looked for a leader to take them out of the wilderness of "politics" lost heart after Stevenson's failure to create a utopia in Illinois and his subsequent failure at the national level. Most of them returned to their previous position, reaffirming that politics was a dirty business and unfit for decent men. They, as "decent men," got out. These people were, of course, reflecting one aspect of the individualistic political culture. Others, the remnants of the moralistic political culture, saw in Stevenson the chance they had been waiting for to move into positions of power in the various echelons of the Illinois governmental system. They embraced his cause with a vigor that was no less impressive because of their fundamental naiveté about Illinois politics. Even after it became apparent that few opportunities would present themselves for most of these dedicated Stevensonians to become active on the state level, they remained ready to become active in promoting his presidential candidacy or, among those who found politics, as such, to be interesting and who wished to continue the fight they had started, to begin activity in their own communities. Among the latter were many of those who became active in the civic reform movements of the cities of the prairie in the 1950's.[11]

After Stevenson took office, his state police began raiding centers of gambling and prostitution in every part of Illinois, drawing public attention to the "wide-open" conditions that prevailed and, by inference, exposing the tie-ins between local government officials and those illicit activities. It was this very simple and easily understood action that triggered widespread public concern with local reform, not so much because of any objections to either gambling or prostitution as such but because the extent of the illicit activities caused them to receive nationwide publicity and reflected poorly on their communities. Rock Island, Peoria, Joliet, Decatur, Springfield, and even the Madison-St. Clair Counties area all felt the Governor's hand in this respect. A decade and more later, with the exception of the last-mentioned area, none had recovered from the Stevenson raids or from the follow-up local action stimulated by them.

The revelations of corruption that emerged from this assault on the status quo, combined with the nationwide renewal of emphasis on local government action and the increasingly visible problems of the metropolitan frontier, fanned public interest in local reform. Available to advance that interest were the more vocal supporters of Stevenson in both parties. Furthermore, many of the cosmopolitan business-and-professional "independent Republicans" who had voted for Stevenson without becoming Stevensonians, were aroused. Whatever the reasons for their concern, they were now ready to support and even lead local reform efforts. Since it was from this group that the top economic leadership in the cities of the prairie was drawn, their cooperation made reform possible in a way in which it had not been before.

Since the commission governments had "failed" to change those aspects of municipal government which aroused dissatisfaction in the minds of reformers and cosmopolitans, the major visible thrust of this new reform movement in all but a few of the cities of the prairie was to once again alter the structure of government, this time to introduce the city manager plan. As in the previous generation, it was argued that what was needed to achieve "good government" was a new governmental structure, one which would eliminate "politics" and introduce businesslike "efficiency."

The "fallacies" of the commission plan were pointed out in detail—the lack of central direction, "empire building" by the different commissioners, the absence of executive leadership, the lack of professionalization and administrative expertise, the lapses of commission government into "politics"—all leading to the conclusion that commission government was just not "businesslike."

Despite some apparent surface similarities, the new reform movement in Illinois was not like the older one. Though they were encouraged and stimulated by the surviving heirs of the populist-progressive tradition, the businessmen and professionals out of the individualistic political culture were the ones who now set the pace, whereas in the earlier era of reform they had but followed behind. The interest of these new reformers was not the reform of politics but its elimination, the development of apolitical, "businesslike" governments, managed by professional apolitical administrators and responsible to the public through a system of nonpartisan (read "nonpolitical") elections.

The rash of adoptions of the council-manager system of government represented an effort to implement this theory of reform within the context of the individualistic political culture. With culture conflict no longer an immediate factor, support or opposition to the change followed the lines of the cosmopolitan-local division. The cosmopolitans, oriented primarily to the civil community as a whole and especially concerned with its image in the state and nation, generally advocated the change as a means of "keeping up" while the locals, with their primary orientation to an immediate environment based on a neighborhood, a social class, or an occupational interest and no particular interest in the opinions of the larger world, opposed it for fear of upsetting established patterns which they had mastered and from which they felt they benefited. Despite the differences in the reformers' goals, however, the variation of the cities' response to reform efforts remained much the same as it had a generation earlier.

The first step in this new wave of governmental structural change was to gain enactment of state legislation allowing larger cities to adopt the council-manager plan as their form of government by referendum. Theoretically, a city manager could have been appointed by ordinance in those cities, but such an arrangement would not have released the constitutional city officers from their primary responsibilities or introduced the hoped-for apolitical nonpartisanship into city government. Thus the full plan was required if reform were to do more than provide for the appointment of an administrative manager within a still "political" system. Appropriately, legislation to this effect was introduced in the General Assembly by one of the representatives from Peoria, whose leading businessmen, by this time, had become strongly interested in "reform." It was backed by Governor Stevenson, who considered this a necessary step in his overall program. The necessary legislation was enacted in 1951, following the traditional pattern of state permissiveness in matters of local concern.

In direct contradiction to its earlier reluctance to change its governmental structure, Peoria became the first of the Illinois cities of the prairie to adopt the council-manager system two years later. Still the little metropolis, its reasons were quite in line with those that led it to reject governmental structural change in 1911 and subsequently. Simply put, the traditional system of Peoria politics had become almost a caricature of the most cynical observations about the nature of politics as conducted in the individualistic political culture. The highly professionalized politicians who controlled Peoria's city hall were not only utilizing politics for pecuniary reward but had become greedily corrupt. Government was characterized by inefficient management of the standard municipal services and complete reluctance to undertake new activities or even to upgrade old ones. Nothing visible was being done to meet the problems of the postwar period or to respond to the renewed interest in local action that had become the badge of the progressive community in the nation at large. Gambling and prostitution were "wide open" in the civil community and a lucrative source of wealth for the politicians in power. Peoria's reputation for "sin" and corruption had become common knowledge in the state and around the nation. Peorians in the armed forces came home embarrassed by their experiences in the service, where their hometown had been the butt of a variety of obscenities. Leading businessmen and industrialists found that the city's reputation was "bad for business." In short, the "taxes" of corruption and inefficiency had become too heavy to bear without sufficient return for their money.

Accordingly, sparked by the Peoria Association of Commerce, which spoke for such major interests as the Caterpillar Company, the downtown banks, and the leading retailers, Peorians picked up the hitherto neglected demands for reform preached by the handful of local populist-progressives and adopted the council-manager system in 1953, with all its "efficiency and economy" and "nonpartisan" trimmings. Once that was accomplished, and a few more details of community reform taken care of in the other governments of the civil community, the top economic leaders of the community were satisfied to leave the realm of political activity, relying on the "nonpartisan" mechanisms just established to maintain the goals of reform as they saw them. The populist-progressive originators of the reform idea, not particularly influential in the cosmopolitan community which had provided the bulk of their support, were left to remain concerned about continuing political reform alone and with little public support.

Rock Island, Joliet, Decatur, Champaign, and Alton all adopted council-manager government between 1953 and 1957. In all five cities, the synthesis of political cultures produced as a result of the conflicts of earlier generations led to the same kind of interest in reform as that in Peoria—an interest in businesslike, efficient, economic, apolitical government, as they defined it, stimulated in the first place by the populist-progressive heirs of the moralistic political culture and adapted by the more conventional cosmopolitan business-professional element for their own purposes.

Joliet, the most traditionally political of the five cities (from both sides of its cultural inheritance) was virtually sold a bill of goods by the same Caterpillar leadership that had been instrumental in securing adoption of the council-manager plan in Peoria, but, after adopting the plan by referendum, the cosmopolitans almost immediately withdrew from the fray. The older politicians were returned to office by the locals and reduced the plan to a dead letter. The mayor reasserted control, and the city manager was reduced to the level of an administrative assistant to him. After the one professional city manager who had been hired left in disgust, the mayor and council appointed a local engineer to replace him, a man who knew how to function as a chief administrator within a political context and who did not try to be a city manager "by the book."

Rock Island adopted council-manager government in an effort to eliminate "politics" from city affairs and to close down the remaining prostitution within its limits. Champaign and Decatur chose the same form of government for the same antipolitical reasons though neither had suffered any great public scandals to encourage the change. In both of the latter cases it was a matter of doing the "progressive" thing, as dictated by national fad and the political norms rooted in the community. In all three cities it was the cosmopolitan business-and-professional group which turned out to vote for the system while the locals stayed home. As the majority in Rock Island, the cosmopolitans won handily. In Champaign and Decatur they won because the opposition voters were apathetic about the issue and did not turn out in the numbers they possessed.[12]

In all three, as in Peoria, Joliet, and Alton, the opposition consisted of the professional politicians and those who stood to benefit from maintenance of the status quo. Organized labor was in the forefront of the opposition in every one of these communities. Its rank and file members, virtually all locals, mostly from racial and ethnic groups not yet fully assimilated into the community or with cultures so different that the cleavage between them and the cosmopolitans took on a cultural dimension, relied upon the ease of access they felt they had under forms of government already familiar. This was particularly true in Peoria, Rock Island, and Alton, which had mayor-aldermanic government with partisan ward elections offering neighborhood representation. It was less true in commission-governed Champaign and Decatur, and the opposition of organized labor in those communities was much less intense. The leadership of organized labor, though less confined by their constituents' localistic outlook, rightly perceived that the city manager profession was predominantly business-oriented and would not be easily accessible to them. Moreover, they were fearful of the police power the city manager would possess, which potentially could be used against them for strike-breaking. Hence they opposed the system as inimical to their basic political interests. Both the leadership and the rank and file hesitated to support a system which called for a city council elected on a citywide basis, invariably to the detriment of the locals.

Alton adopted the manager plan almost by a fluke, in a wave of reform brought on in the wake of the exposures of corruption in local government throughout its metropolitan area. Dissatisfaction with the system soon developed among cosmopolitans and locals, business and labor, alike. Once the new system was installed, neither group liked the efforts of the city manager to operate by the "objective, nonpolitical" standards of his code. Alton was really not interested in nonpolitical government; its political culture mitigated against such an approach. After tolerating the system for five years, the voters chose to abandon it and returned to the clearly political mayor-aldermanic system in 1962.

One other city, East Moline, adopted the council-manager plan. That smaller community did so also through a fluke, during the height of the interest in city manager government in the Quad Cities area. After a succession of poorly qualified professional city managers—all the city could afford on its limited budget—the council tacitly abandoned the plan by just not hiring a new manager. The local residents, all from backgrounds that did not value the ostensible benefits of nonpartisan city manager government in any case, appeared to be quite satisfied with that arrangement.

The remaining cities of the prairie in Illinois did not embark upon programs of governmental structural change. Their reform movements pursued other courses of action to achieve their ends. Referenda for the adoption of the council-manager system were conducted in both Rockford and Moline, at the instigation of local groups who placed them on the ballot by petition. In both cases, these were groups who represented the values of the individualist political culture. In both cities the proposals were soundly defeated by publics which saw no need to change their governmental structures, particularly in a manner calculated to make them less politically responsive and responsible. In Rockford, even the League of Women Voters opposed the adoption of council-manager government.

As in the previous generation, reform in Rockford was initiated by the formation of a new local party, this time consisting of a coalition of middle class populist-progressives and local businessmen, backed by the descendants of the old Yankee oligarchy, which pledged itself to end the by-this-time conservative and pinchpenny administration of the last of the nominally socialist mayors. Stimulated by pressing problems of suburbanization and aroused by an increasing 1930's-style militancy in the local labor movement, this party won control of the city administration in 1957 and proceeded to institute a straightforward, if not elaborate, program of municipal improvement (most of which they had borrowed from their immediate predecessor, a progressive who had been supported by the old party and defeated because of that).

Rockford liberals and progressives had been among the first to support the Stevensonian movement in Illinois through the Democratic Federation of Illinois. Their local group, named the Democratic Victory Club, did not give in when the statewide collapse of that organization came. Having turned their attention to the local scene even before the DFI had decided to disband, its members began a five-year battle against the regular Democratic organization for control of the county Democratic party. Putting together a coalition of political amateurs—teachers, professional men, and unionists—much like that which forms the basis of the Democratic-Farmer-Labor party in Minnesota (where their political culture is dominant), they forged an organization of their own which finally succeeded in capturing control of the local party organization early in 1963.

During this struggle many of the same DVC actives had become involved in Rockford city politics as well, contributing to local reform efforts through participation in both local parties. However, as the originally reform-oriented All Rockford Party lost its reformist momentum and settled down to become a holding operation for the local business community, most of the DVC people within its ranks began to seek other outlets for stimulating local reform. After the intraparty victory, the DVC decided to move into city politics to provide this outlet. In April 1963, they introduced national party labels in the city elections with some success for the first time in Rockford's history, indicating that they were beginning to identify the local Democratic party with the civil community's political values in a manner which no national party had been able to achieve since the Civil War period.

The course of reform in Moline was similar but less intense. The influence of the John Deere Company was finally reduced to reasonable proportions in the years following World War II, as a result of efforts by a local populist-progressive movement, coupled with a change in company policy to adjust to the postwar conceptions of the "proper" role of industry in community affairs. Attainment of that objective within the existing political structure dampened any drive to change that structure.

The citizens of Belleville, East St. Louis, and Urbana, all within the dominant political culture, also felt no apparent need to alter their municipal governmental structure. A reform movement affected great changes in Belleville, and other movements became active in both East St. Louis and Urbana relatively late. In all three cases, they were geared clearly and explicitly to the local situation and have been satisfied to function within the existing political framework and culture.

Springfield, like Peoria, has apparently reversed its overt pattern of political behavior in the past generation, this time by rejecting proposals to adopt council-manager government. In truth, this rejection merely confirms Springfield's position within the state's dominant political culture. A highly political city, its articulate citizenry, reform-oriented or not, is not in the least interested in taking its city government "out of politics." Since commission government, though nonpartisan, was not at all apolitical in orientation, it had been an acceptable change. However, city manager government represented a step not in keeping with the Springfield tradition. Hence the reform movement in that civil community which wrought great changes in the 1950's was undertaken within the framework of the existing governmental structure.

The universality of reform efforts in the cities of the prairie during nationally recognized periods of reform is another indication of how governmental concerns in the United States—even those centered on local government—become nationwide concerns. At the same time the precise actions in those civil communities reveal how mistaken it would be to think of the local responses to those concerns as equally universal in content, even where there are similarities in format. Similarities in format are often misleading. There are, after all, relatively few options for governmental organization within any political culture, or even within every political culture, at any one time.

At any given period in American history, a few options for change stand out. They are utilized or rejected by communities caught in the throes of change for a variety of reasons, resting on their relations to the current frontier, their sectional position, and, above all, the particular political culture in which they are embedded. The diversity of political cultures in Illinois has insured a diversity of responses in that state's cities of the prairie, within the limits of the possible.

NOTES

1. There are a number of good studies of society and politics of Illinois available. The reader interested in a good brief review of Illinois as a political system might choose to explore the following selections: Federal Writers' Project, *Illinois: A Descriptive and Historical Guide* (Chicago: A. C. McClurg, 1947), rev. ed.; Theodore Calvin Pease, *The Story of Illinois* (Chicago: University of Chicago Press, 1949) rev. ed.; Austin Ranney, *Illinois Politics* (New York: New York University Press, 1960); Gilbert Y. Steiner and Samuel K. Gove, *Legislative Politics in Illinois* (Urbana: University of Illinois Press, 1960); and Neil F. Garvey, *The Government and Administration of Illinois* (New York: Thomas Y. Crowell, 1950). The publications of the Institute of Government and Public Affairs, University of Illinois,

particularly the Institute bulletin, *Illinois Government*, and the annual publications of the papers and proceedings of the Illinois Assembly, are valuable sources of information on the Illinois political system which cover a wide range of questions dealing with Illinois politics. For a description of the overall pattern of local politics in Illinois, insofar as one exists, see Lois Pelekoudas, ed., *Illinois Local Government* (Urbana: University of Illinois, 1961), and Samuel K. Gove, "Local Politics: The Illinois Experience," paper presented at the annual meeting of the American Political Science Association, September 1962.

2. The physiographic position of Illinois can be delineated from the *Goode's World Atlas*, 11th ed. (Chicago: Rand McNally, 1960), particularly A. W. Kuchler's map of "Natural Vegetation" pp. 54–55. It is also discussed in historical perspective in Walter Prescott Webb's classic, *The Great Plains* (Boston: Ginn and Co., 1931), and by Baker Brownell in *The Other Illinois* (New York: Ruell Sloan and Pearce, 1958).

3. James G. Coke, "Some General Characteristics of Middle-Sized City Political Systems in Illinois, A Working Paper on Urban Political Capabilities" (Office of Community Development, University of Illinois, March 1963).

4. Pease, *op. cit.*, provides a thorough if unsystematic analysis of the origins of the Illinois political system in the "favor-centered" politics of the territorial period, in chaps. 5, 6, and 7 of his book.

5. The Yankees did not give in without a fight. They even went so far as to attempt to secede from Illinois and join Wisconsin, whose political culture was more congenial. A convention met with that aim in mind in Rockford in 1842, with representatives from the fourteen northernmost counties in the state, all predominantly Yankee. Though the movement failed, the sentiment for secession remained, and most of the civil communities in those counties engaged in "internal secession" after that was made possible by the Constitution in 1848.

6. The existence of comparable situations in other states with conflicting political cultures adds some credence to the thesis suggested here. Massachusetts is a prime example. There the clash of political cultures widely known as the struggle between the Yankees and the Irish had many of the same qualities of the clash in Illinois, only in reverse and with greater intensity. One consequence of the past century of the conflict of political cultures in that Commonwealth apparently has been the development of a high proportion of alienated voters—people who are so cynical about "politics" that they avoid even minimal participation or serious consideration of the alternatives offered to them on the grounds that it is all meaningless. The alienated voters of Massachusetts generally and of Boston in particular have been studied by Murray B. Levin in *The Compleat Politician: Political Strategy in Massachusetts* (Indianapolis: Bobbs-Merrill, 1962), and *The Alienated Voter: Politics in Boston* (New York: Holt, Rinehart and Winston, 1960).

7. There was even an effort to formally regionalize the court system in Illinois in such a manner as to provide representation on the bench for products of both political cultures. The justices of the State Supreme Court were to be elected from three grand divisions in the state. Because of the circuit system of court sessions then in use, the rest of the court system would automatically be structured to fit into this scheme. Though provision was made for the General Assembly to alter the grand and lesser divisions established in the Constitution itself, the framers did include a specific apportionment of the counties into three grand divisions, clearly in the hope of maintaining them. As drawn, the three grand divisions clearly separated the Yankee-settled areas of the state, giving them their own division and—hopefully—their *entrée* into the court system. In point of fact, this never came to pass, for the same reasons that the cities were not given their own judicial systems, only more so.

8. The cosmopolitan-local dimension is one of the crucial factors in shaping community conflict. For further discussion of "cosmopolitan" versus "local" attitudes, see Robert K. Merton, *Social Theory and Social Structure*, 2nd ed. (Glencoe, Ill.: The Free Press, 1968). Alvin Gouldner, *Studies in Leadership: Leadership and Democratic Action* (New York: Russell and Russell, 1965), and Daniel J. Elazar and Douglas St. Angelo, " 'Cosmopolitans' and 'Locals' in Contemporary Community Politics," in *Proceedings of the Minnesota Academy of Science,* XXXI, (1964). The last piece discusses recent reform movements in the cities of the prairie.

9. Coke, *op. cit.*, describes the conception of reform current among the cosmopolitan-business-and-professional elements as manifested in the most recent wave of reform in his three cities, in some detail, and in the same vein as the above discussion.

10. It is quite possible that, in the large metropolitan regions of Chicago and St. Louis, where suburbanization is being channeled into independent suburban cities and villages, the conflict of political cultures is being revived. Some of the smaller and newer suburbs have been settled by products of the moralistic political culture who migrated from the central cities. In their former homes they were politically submerged and remained politically inarticulate, but in the suburban settling they have found themselves in the majority and are taking steps to enthrone their type of politics as the dominant type in their civil communities. This is not only reviving old conflicts but is heightening old desires for local autonomy. Such situations are clearly in the minority in Illinois suburbia. Even among the suburban reform movements more of them appear to reflect the reformist interests of the individualistic political culture—the interest in creating a political and "businesslike" local government. This study, of course, cannot deal with these phenomena other than to suggest their existence.

11. Perhaps the best example of the problem facing the Stevensonians was furnished by the history of the abortive Democratic Federation of Illinois. Originally organized by people who entered politics to support Stevenson, it attempted to do for Illinois what the California Democratic clubs had done for that state, namely introduce amateurs into positions of influence within the party machinery in an organized fashion. DFI-affiliated clubs came into existence in civil communities across the state and then joined together in a statewide coalition. Illinois was not California, however; its political culture mitigated against the success of even organized amateurs. After a brief and unsuccessful career in which they discovered how unwanted amateurs were among the professional politicians and how well the professionals could operate to exclude amateur "interference," the members of the DFI were forced to dissolve their organization and either retire from politics or make their way as individuals into the party ranks as best they could. James Q. Wilson discusses the history of the DFI in *The Amateur Democrat* (Chicago: University of Chicago Press, 1962).

12. Formal nonpartisanship does not necessarily mean that otherwise active politicians from the state political system do not intervene in local nonpartisan elections in some civil communities. What it does mean is that they must do so as individuals (or as precinct committeemen able to secure votes for individual candidates) rather than as official representatives of their parties. It is a rare politician who will not rise to the bait of an election, either for reasons of economic self-interest or simply from love of the "game," but that is a very different story than party participation as a party. While this effort has not succeeded in removing state influence on the civil community, it has succeeded quite well in lessening the civil community's influence within the state.

Chapter 8 / Variations in State Political Cultures and Their Political Meaning

THE INFLUENCE of political culture is not confined to the relationship between the states and their local governments nor to the course of municipal reform. It can be traced in virtually every aspect of local political life. Understanding political cultural differences is particularly useful because of what they reveal about the differences in meaning of apparently similar actions that occur in states and civil communities across the nation. In this connection, the contrast between the political cultures of the Illinois cities of the prairie and those of the other states is illuminating.

With all their common bonds of sphere and section, frontier experiences, and migrational flows, each of the five states of concern in this study possesses a clearly distinctive political "profile" of its own. Many of the distinctive features which set the states apart have been alluded to or can be deduced from the information presented in previous chapters. Even the gross differences in area, total population, population density, extent of urbanization, extent of metropolitanization, per capita income, median family income, and total per capita direct state and local expenditure are revealing (Table 8–1).[1] While area and population differences contribute to the differences among the states, size itself is not the source of their distinctiveness. Nor is geographic proximity particularly significant.

Though Illinois shares common boundaries with Iowa and Wisconsin, the three states are no more alike than Illinois and Minnesota and less alike than Illinois and Colorado, which are separated by nearly one thousand miles.[2]

Statistically measurable socioeconomic and demographic differences are not the only ones to strike the eye in an "across-the-board" comparison of the five states. Even more striking are some of the differences in partisan political allegiance visible from even a casual reading of their voting records in light of their respective geohistorical settings. Students of American history from the national perspective alone are likely to assume that all five states share a common political pattern usually labeled "midwestern," one of continued Republican dominance since the Civil War with periodic Democratic successes in times of crisis punctuated by occasional third-party movements of varying strength and duration. The voting pattern for each of the five states since attainment of

TABLE 8-1
Five-State Comparison of Gross Statistical Indicators[a]

State	Area	Rank	Population	Rank	Pop. per Sq. Mile	Rank	% Pop. in Urban Places	Rank	% Pop. in SMSA's	Rank	Per Capita Income	Rank	Median Family Income	Rank	Total Per Capita Direct State-Local Expenditures	Rank
Colo.	104,247	(1)	1,743,516	(5)	16.9	(5)	73.7	(2)	68.0	(2)	$2,253	(2)	$4,812	(3)	344.14	(1)
Illinois	56,400	(3)	10,005,955	(1)	180.3	(1)	80.7	(1)	76.9	(1)	2,592	(1)	5,589	(1)	286.68	(5)
Iowa	56,290	(4)	2,742,753	(4)	49.2	(3)	53.0	(5)	33.2	(5)	1,987	(5)	4,240	(5)	293.84	(3)
Minn.	84,068	(2)	3,391,348	(3)	42.7	(4)	62.2	(4)	51.3	(3)	2,013	(4)	4,674	(4)	328.98	(2)
Wisc.	56,154	(5)	3,930,312	(2)	72.2	(2)	63.8	(3)	46.3	(4)	2,147	(3)	5,173	(2)	290.16	(4)

[a]1960 data.

statehood belies such casual assumptions. If one takes the statewide vote for president to indicate national party preference in a reasonably meaningful and comparable way over time and the statewide vote for governor to indicate a similar state party preference, (Table 8–2), a variety of interstate differences is immediately visible. These differences, more pronounced in gubernatorial elections than in presidential contests, have at least remained constant and may even be increasing. Careful examination of the table in light of what is known of each state's history and political culture explains much about those differences.

First of all, the impact of the geohistorical framework from which each state has evolved on the overall pattern of partisan political preference is apparent. Illinois, the historical center of the United States, has never seriously deviated from reflecting the national image of partisan preference in either the national or its major statewide elections, maintaining a competitive two-party system throughout its history with both major parties

TABLE 8-2

State Partisan Political Preferences, 1818-1962
(Based on Presidential and Gubernatorial Elections)

Year	Illinois (1809-1818)		Iowa (1838-1846)		Wisconsin (1836-1848)		Minnesota (1849-1858)		Colorado (1861-1876)	
	Gov.	Pres.	Gov.	Pres.	Gov.	Pres.	Gov.	Pres.	Gov.	Pres.
1818	N	-								
1820	-	D								
1822	*N*[a]	-								
1824	-	D								
1826	*W*	-								
1828	-	D								
1830	W	-								
1832	-	D								
1834	W	-								
1836	-	D								
1838	D	-								
1840	-	D								
1842	D	-								
1844	-	D								
1846	D	-	D							
1848	D	D		D	D	W				
1850	-	-	D	-	D(1849)	-				
1852	D	D	-	D	W(1851)	D				
1854	-	-	W	-	D(1853)	-				
1856	*R*	D	-	*R*	D(1855)	R				
1858	-	-	R(1857)	-	R(1857)	-	D(1857)	-		
1860	R	R	R(1859)	R	R(1859)	R	R(1859)	R		
1862	-	-	R(1861)	-	R(1861)	-	R(1861)	-		
1864	R	R	R(1863)	R	R(1863)	R	R(1863)	R		
1866	-	-	R(1865)	-	R(1865)	-	R(1865)	-		

TABLE 8-2 (continued)

Year	Illinois (1809-1818) Gov.	Illinois Pres.	Iowa (1838-1846) Gov.	Iowa Pres.	Wisconsin (1836-1848) Gov.	Wisconsin Pres.	Minnesota (1849-1858) Gov.	Minnesota Pres.	Colorado (1861-1876) Gov.	Colorado Pres.
1868	R	R	R(1867)	R	R(1867)	R	R(1867)	R		
1870	-	-	R(1869)	-	R(1869)	-	R(1869)	-		
1872	R	R	R(1871)	R	R(1871)	R	R(1871)	R		
1874	-	-	R(1873)	-	D(1873)	-	R(1873)	-		
1876	R	R	R(1875)	R	R(1875)	R	R(1875)	R	R	R
1878	-	-	*R*(1877)	-	*R*(1877)	-	R(1877)	-	R	-
1880	R	R	R(1879)	R	R(1879)	R	R(1879)	R	R	R
1882	-	-	R(1881)	-	*R*(1881)	-	R(1881)	-	D	-
1884	*R*	R	R(1883)	R	R	R	R(1883)	R	R	R
1886	-	-	R(1885)	R	*R*	-	*R*	-	D	-
1888	*R*	R	R(1887)	R	*R*	*R*	R	R	R	R
1890	-	-	*D*(1889)	-	D	-	*R*	-	R	-
1892	*D*	D	*D*(1891)	*R*	*D*	*D*	*R*	*R*	*P*	P
1894	-	-	*R*(1893)	-	R	-	*R*	-	R	-
1896	R	R	R(1895)	R	R	R	*R*	R	D	D
1898	-	-	R(1897)	-	R	-	DP	-	D	-
1900	R	R	R(1899)	R	R	R	*R*	R	D	D
1902	-	-	R(1901)	-	R	-	R	-	R	-
1904	R	R	R(1903)	R	R	R	*D*	R	D	R
1906	-	-	R	-	R	-	D	-	R	-
1908	*R*	R	R	R	R	R	D	R	D	D
1910	-	-	*R*	-	R	-	R	-	D	-
1912	*D*	*D*	*R*	*D*	*R*	D	*R*	*P*	*D*	*D*
1914	-	-	*R*	-	*R*	-	*D*	-	*R*	-
1916	R	R	R	R	R	R	R	*R*	D	D
1918	-	-	R	-	*R*	-	*R*	-	R	-
1920	R	R	R	R	R	R	R	R	R	R
1922	-	-	R	-	R	-	*R*	-	D	-
1924	R	R	R	R	R	P	*R*	R	R	R
1926	-	-	R	-	R	-	R	-	D	-

TABLE 8-2 (continued)

Year	Illinois (1809-1818) Gov.	Illinois Pres.	Iowa (1838-1846) Gov.	Iowa Pres.	Wisconsin (1836-1848) Gov.	Wisconsin Pres.	Minnesota (1849-1858) Gov.	Minnesota Pres.	Colorado (1861-1876) Gov.	Colorado Pres.
1928	R	R	R	R	R	R	R	R	D	R
1930	-	-	R	-	R	-	FL	-	D	-
1932	D	D	D	D	D	D	FL	D	D	D
1934	-	-	D	-	*P*	-	*FL*	-	D	-
1936	D	D	D	D	*P*	D	FL	D	D	D
1938	-	-	R	-	R	-	R	-	R	-
1940	R	D	R	R	*R*	D	R	D	R	R
1942	-	-	R	-	*P*	-	R	-	R	-
1944	R	D	R	R	R	R	R	D	R	R
1946	-	-	R	-	R	-	R	-	D	-
1948	D	D	R	D	R	D	R	DFL	D	D
1950	-	-	R	-	R	-	R	-	R	-
1952	R	R	R	R	R	R	R	R	R	R
1954	-	-	R	-	R	-	DFL	-	D	-
1956	R	R	D	R	R	R	DFL	R	D	R
1958	-	-	D	-	D	-	DFL	-	D	-
1960	D	D	R	R	D	R	R	DFL	D	R
1962	-	-	D	-	D	-	DFL	-	R	-

[a]Italics denotes election by less than a majority of the total vote cast.

Sources: *Illinois Blue Book*, *Iowa Official Register*, *Colorado Year Book*, *Minnesota Legislative Manual*, and *Wisconsin Blue Book*. No data is shown prior to statehood.

Key: N – No party designation
W – Whig
D – Democratic
R – Republican
DP – Democratic-Populist
P – Progressive
FL – Farmer-Labor
DFL – Democratic Farmer-Labor

having strong regional bases. Illinois has deviated from the national pattern in presidential elections only twice since 1852 and, with two exceptions, has chosen governors and presidents from the same party at every election in which partisan designations existed. Even the few periods in which major party candidates won only by plurality (invariably an indication of a strong third-party movement) reflect the national situation.

Illinois, with its long tradition of strong and deeply entrenched party organizations, has maintained a particularly close relationship between state and local politics. Minor party efforts have been as weak in county-wide as in state and national elections. Consequently, those civil communities with sentiments which, in Minnesota and Wisconsin, would very likely have been channeled into third-party movements have generally been forced to create special local parties or institute nonpartisan electoral systems for municipal and township elections to insulate local politics from the pressures of state political patterns as well as to provide an outlet for their maverick inclinations.

At the same time, the continued existence of an active and competitive statewide two-party system in Illinois has permitted those civil communities most closely connected to the state political system to vote in opposition to the state's overall partisan tendencies without suffering serious political disability, provided they abide by the "rules of the game," that is, remain within the confines of the regular two-party system and the political values it reflects; accept the agreed-upon limits of policy differences; and do not try to create third-party movements or even attempt to sharpen the differences between the regular parties. St. Clair County offers the best example of this tacit understanding. Since 1900 its voters have deviated from the statewide pattern in presidential and gubernatorial elections fourteen times and, in addition, have voted predominantly Democratic throughout that period. In both respects, the county differs radically from any of the other counties of the cities of the prairie in Illinois, even including Madison County, its neighbor to the north. Yet at no time has it been alienated from the state political system. On the contrary, its political leadership is as much a part of that system as the leadership of any other county, because they have constantly abided by the commonly accepted rules of the state's political game, which include certain standards of political "professionalization," demands for loyalty among persons, and a "businesslike" approach to political activity but which do not demand partisan conformity.

Political Culture and Political Isolationism in Minnesota[3]

Minnesota stands in great contrast to Illinois in almost every respect. Illinois stands at the geohistorical center of the United States and reflects a kind of mainstream Americanism because it contains almost all the variations on the theme of American civilization to be encountered at any given time or place. Minnesota is located in a relatively sequestered part of the country where people from an extraordinary variety of ethnic backgrounds but sharing a common political culture settled. They have since gone about maintaining their own way of doing things as much as is possible in our intensely cosmopolitan society, to create one of the most unique states in the Union. The Duluth civil community is an integral part of Minnesota civil society in these respects. In fact, its isolation from the main currents of American economic development and political life is considerably more extreme than that of the state as a whole. Such isolation at the local level is made possible, in part, by the state's functioning as a buffer between its civil communities and the rest of the nation. Duluth benefits extensively from Minnesota's protective services in this regard. This fundamental fact governing state-local relations stands in great contrast to the situation in Illinois, where civil communities that wish to be different must create their own immediately local buffer zones against the state, if not against state and nation.

Despite its continental centrality in a purely geographic sense, geohistorically Minnesota is a relatively isolated part of the American Trans-Mississippi West. Off the main routes of the westward movement, the advance of the land frontier in fits and starts made it the farthest outpost of American penetration into the Northwest for many years and one of the last of the continuous states to have an open land frontier. As in Illinois, three major regional physiographic patterns meet in the state, each of which has demanded its own forms of social organization and technology. First encountered by the Americans were the lowland prairies, to which could be applied essentially the same forms as had been used on the Illinois prairies. North of the prairies were found the so-called Big Woods, in part an extension of the forest-and-rock desert known as the Canadian or Laurentian Shield. Settlement on the shield required adaptations not dissimilar from those required to settle the mountain deserts of the far West. The western third of Minnesota, though initially thought to be simply a continuation of the humid prairie, was discovered by its settlers to be a transition zone between the humid grasslands and the high, dry plains, which required modification of lowland prairie patterns to accommodate human needs in a climatically harsh, semi-arid environment.

All told, approximately two-thirds of Minnesota represents a difficult physical environment even by the standards of the greater West. This fact led, in turn, to the establishment of a marginal civilization, one which was prone to seek more radical solutions to its recurrent problems.

The initial American settlement of Minnesota came relatively late in the history of the land frontier, and its settlement period lasted long, well into the twentieth century, to overlap the next frontier stage with hardly any break in momentum. The history of its settlement parallels the history of American settlement on the West Coast, one of many indications of how isolated from the main stream of American development Minnesota was during its formative years and, in some respects, continues to be.

Minnesota emerged as a civil society in the decade immediately prior to the Civil War, the decade with the most ideologically intense cleavage in the history of American politics. Between 1849, when Minnesota Territory was created, and 1858, when the state entered the Union, the fixation of the country as a whole on the problems that led to the Civil War was reflected even in Minnesota. The cleavage within the emerging civil society between the Republicans—mostly antislavery Yankees—and the Democrats—mostly Middle State and Southern moderates who accepted Stephen Douglas' position of "popular sovereignty"—which had ethnic overtones as well, became so intense that the representatives of the two parties would not even sit together in a single constitutional convention. The state constitution was drafted separately, in two conventions, and the two documents harmonized by a conference committee after a bitter struggle. Since neither group of partisans would sign the final document with the other group, to this day Minnesota has two official "original constitutions."

Since the state took shape in the period in which politics nationally and locally was dominated so intensively by issues, the most important of which were highly moral in character, the objective political environment encouraged the development of a strongly issue-oriented politics (at least in comparison to the nation as a whole) from the first. This commitment to issues was subsequently reinforced in the post-Civil War generation by social and economic factors relating to the creation of a marginal society on the Minnesota frontier. The commitment to issues was further reinforced by a majority of Minnesota's first settlers, who stemmed from the moralistic political culture. Mostly New Englanders or descendants of New Englanders from upstate New York, northern Illinois, or southeastern Wisconsin, they combined moral concern with the desire to become economically successful that led them to the frontier. These products of the Yankee stream settled in the southeastern part of the state, on the humid prairie, applying the technology developed by their compatriots for the Illinois prairies a decade earlier. Unlike the

Yankee settlers of Illinois, however, they were virtually the first to occupy their future commonwealth, so they did not have to compromise their communitarian individualism with any "rugged" individualistic elements already entrenched in power. Nor did their environment encourage the latter type of individualism, since even on the prairies cooperation was required for survival. Actually, in light of the migrations that were to follow, the first Yankee settlers came in time to be considered the symbols of extreme individualism in Minnesota.

Minnesota's second wave of settlement came during and after the Civil War and was dominated by immigrants who came directly from Europe—from the Scandinavian countries, Germany, and Ireland. Most of them were farmers, but substantial numbers of Germans and Irish settled in the burgeoning urban communities along the state's navigable waterways. From the very first, the role played by these immigrants has had important consequences for Minnesota's political culture, for the most part serving to reinforce the original contributions of the Yankees in much the same manner as in northern Illinois. Most of the Europeans who came to Minnesota shared a version of the communitarian ethic similar to that found among the descendants of the American Puritans. This has been true even of the Catholics, predominantly Germans and Irish, who represented something of a self-selected population. Many of the latter were attracted by the great Catholic Americanist, Bishop John Ireland, for just those qualities, to establish farming colonies in Minnesota's hinterland. Perhaps even more important, the overwhelming majority of those European emigrants came directly to Minnesota, where they settled on virgin land. Thus, unlike their compatriots who settled in the cities or in rural areas already occupied by others and who had to adjust their ways to established patterns, they could retain many of the basic attitudes of the cultures which they had brought with them from the Old World, if not their overt manifestations. This, too, contributed to Minnesota's uniqueness in the national picture, to the state's ultimate desire for a degree of semi-isolation, and to the particular political culture which is dominant within its boundaries. As the nineteenth century drew to a close, they were joined by Southern and Eastern European farmers, brought in by the railroads, along whose rights-of-way they created replicas of Old World farm villages, each with its own distinctive culture.

Sometime after 1880 a third wave of settlement began in the state. Like the first two, its representatives also sought the still-plentiful vacant areas on the land frontier. Though this wave included many farmers (predominantly Scandinavians), the element which gave it a distinctive character was composed of miners, mostly Southern and Eastern European in origin, who settled the three iron ranges on the Laurentian Shield to extract ore. The settlement of the iron ranges was already a response to the demands of the national corporate economy produced by the urban-industrial frontier. The settlers themselves were employees of large companies from the first. The lumberjacks who entered the state in great numbers at the same time were brought by the large lumber companies then engaged in cutting the forests of the "Big Woods." Even the farmers who pioneered this stage of the land frontier in the state, though still in the entrepreneurial pattern, were frequently settled on the prairie by the great land-grant railroad companies of the Northwest eager to populate their rights-of-way. The miners and those lumberjacks who stayed to settle in the state brought a kind of proletarian radicalism to add to an already radical (by American standards) tradition of politics in Minnesota. Most of them settled in the northeastern part of the state, and Duluth's demographic base has been strongly influenced by them.

After the turn of the century, a fourth wave of settlement occupied Minnesota's far north. Because of the length of Minnesota's land frontier period, this fourth wave was dominated by a group which had actually been born and bred within the state, the descendants of the Yankees of the southeastern counties. Their efforts to establish themselves permanently in the north country ran right into the post-World-War-I agricultural depression, which transformed them into seekers for social solutions for their problems along lines most appropriate to the twentieth century but in a spirit of communalism and political responsibility akin to that found among their fathers.

The fifth and, to date, last wave of settlement to enter Minnesota, while not particularly radical, has served to reinforce the state's distinctive American subculture. Moving from the rural sections of Minnesota's great Upper Midwestern empire (the Dakotas, Montana, and parts of Wisconsin, Nebraska, Iowa, and the Upper Peninsula of Michigan contribute most of this fifth wave) to the state's metropolitan centers, particularly the Minneapolis-St. Paul metropolitan region which embraces most of the section's frontier zones on the metropolitan-technological frontier, they have sought new social and economic opportunities similar to those sought by rural and small-town Americans across the country. In the process, they have helped to create one of the most demographically self-contained sections in the United States with the States of Minnesota at its heart. Drawn from the same cultural streams, these new migrants naturally reflect the same cultural background as the section's—and the state's—original settlers. Hence they reinforce the patterns of political culture already rooted in the state's political system. Minnesota's unique subculture is further protected by a gross out-migration of population from the state, which tends to leave the "hard core" Minnesotans in control of every facet of the state's life.

Out of these five waves of settlement have emerged Minnesota's dominant socioeconomic groups. Agriculture, the predominant industry in the state for many years, has provided two very divergent elements: the more conservative farmers of the relatively prosperous southeastern and central counties and the populist types from the more marginal farm areas in the rest of the state. Both groups have been very strong on the state political scene, even though their relative population strength has drastically declined in recent years and Minnesota has become statistically "urban," because of the large role agriculture continues to play in supporting subsidiary businesses and industries. Only since the opening of the metropolitan frontier has urban Minnesota begun to develop a substantial economic base divorced from "agribusiness." Because of the forest-and-rock desert in which it is located, Duluth's northeastern hinterland did not develop from an agriculturally based economy, a fact which heightened its differentiation from the rest of the state.

By and large, the dominant elements in the state's business community are descended from the early Yankee entrepreneurs. Since World War I, they have been joined by entrepreneurs from the other streams, many of them Jews, who have developed enterprises of various sizes in a spirit similar to that of the Yankees. The largest enterprises in the state have institutionalized this spirit even where they have passed out of the hands of their founding families. Consequently, the entrepreneurial tradition particular to the communitarian culture remains reasonably strong in Minnesota. With some few but well-known exceptions, business and industrial concerns in the state have remained moderate in size and are locally controlled regardless of size, even when they have become international in concern. In the twentieth century some of the locally owned companies—General Mills, Pillsbury, Cargill, Minnesota Mining and Manufacturing, to name only a few—have expanded into nationwide corporate giants, but the continued location of their headquarters in Minnesota means that the local pattern of "home-owned" industry has not been substantially altered. One consequence of this is that Minnesota businessmen and industrialists have remained active in civic life in a manner reminiscent of the older, prebureaucratic business system that is only now beginning to come back into vogue on the national plane.

The rapid rise of a locally created electronics industry in the past ten years is testimony to the survival of the entrepreneurial tradition as a major factor in the state's economy. The Twin Cities area is the third major center of electronics work in the United States, despite its handicaps of location and its lack of federal defense contracts. Even Duluth is beginning to attract smaller electronics concerns. The bulk of the area's electronics industry was developed locally by individual Minnesotans who wished to establish themselves in their native state despite its economic and climatic disadvantages, rather than by large corporations or outsiders seeking a more favorable business climate. It is primarily a product of local resources, from financial support by Twin Cities banks to the supply of skilled manpower in the tradition of Scandinavian craftsmanship and German precision. Duluth is the one significant exception to this pattern. Since the 1870's it has been an industrial colony of the lower Great Lakes cities, particularly Cleveland, and a business colony of the Twin Cities. One result of this is that its politics in part reflects the struggle between a labor force that remains tied to its locality and corporate stewards serving absentee owners while holding great political power locally.

In view of the state's past history, it is not surprising to find an important labor movement in Minnesota, composed to a very large extent of highly skilled workers. Organized labor is strong in politics, local as well as national, and is exceptionally successful in its ability to gain community support for its demands. This is in no small measure because unions in Minnesota have been able to organize middle-class elements, such as the retail clerks and state and local government employees, in a basically middle-class population. This, in turn, has created a labor movement with some markedly different goals from those of the labor movements in other areas (including most of Illinois), one concerned with civic responsibility as well as "bread and butter" issues. The organization of government employees has also increased the level of labor activity in the political realm by creating a dual stake in politics for a large segment of the local labor movement. In this respect, Duluth is like Minnesota, only more so, with what is very likely the strongest and most active labor movement in the state, combining within its ranks three unions noted for civic activity: the State, County and Municipal Employees, the Retail Clerks, and the United Steel Workers, all of which are actively involved in local politics and civic affairs.

An industrial base which rests primarily on skilled labor drawn from much the same population base as the business and professional people has prevented the development of the divergencies in outlook between the business-professional subcommunity and the labor subcommunity in Minnesota consistently found in other cities of the prairie where the two subcommunities have, to a great extent, been drawn from culturally different streams as well as from different ethnic groups. In the latter, the earlier arriving native streams had supplied the bulk of the business and professional elements while the latecoming European elements were more or less automatically assigned to the working class upon arrival and were forced to "work up" as individuals. Perhaps paradoxically, however, the similarity in cultural background between the two elements seems to have stimulated class conflict to an extent not experienced in the other civil communities. The situation in Duluth offers a paradigm of this phenomenon.[4]

While the complex origins of class cleavage in politics are not easily unraveled, two factors stand out as important in a civil community like Duluth. In the first place, because the Old World-originated streams flowed into Duluth directly from Europe at the outset of its settlement, some of the class consciousness more common to European politics went into the very formation of the civil community's political system. Furthermore, class differences could not be masked by ethnic or cultural ones. Rather, the similarity in cultural backgrounds between those who became the business and professional classes and those who entered the working class made the latter more conscious of class as a factor.

Since obviously inferior status and economic conditions could not be explained away by pseudo-historical rationalizations about the "rights" of earlier groups or pseudo-racial theories about a "superior northern and western European stock," resentment between the two elements grew as the labor subcommunity demanded a better place in the local sun. In time, this led to a sharp cleavage between the two subcommunities which, in the European manner, has come to be expressed through politics. This cleavage was aggravated by the absentee ownership problem, which sharpened the social cleavage between the local managers and those people to whom Duluth was all the home there was. It is now beginning to diminish since labor has won much of what it has demanded, including a dominant position politically, while business-labor cooperation on common projects (often forced by the city government) has brought both elements to a new level of communication with and understanding of each other. However, though greater harmony is coming to replace near-implacable hostility, the two subcommunities still remain apart from one another, separated socially as well as geographically.

Another aspect of Minnesota's uniqueness is the existence of a strong cadre of academics and members of the intellectual professions who participate in civic and political affairs with a considerable degree of vigor and success. The very existence of such an element bespeaks the reality of Minnesota's special culture. It is a sign that the state's political order is sufficiently attuned to the kind of issues which generate intellectual (and moral) excitement and stimulates the participation of such elements and that its political culture is so constituted as to make their participation natural.

Academics and members of the intellectual professions are particularly important in the state's party system. In the 1950's the Democratic Farmer Labor party (DFL), in particular, was the focal point of these elements. That party rose to power after 1946 led by a collection of ex-college teachers such as Senators Hubert Humphrey and Eugene McCarthy and Minneapolis Mayor Arthur Naftalin, who retained their "amateur" standing as politicians while retaining their ties to the academic community, in one way or another. Even Duluth, whose predominantly working class democracy has produced fewer indigenous political figures of this type, has benefited from the leadership the relatively few members of the intellectual professions have provided. In essence, the DFL there and in the state as a whole is a coalition of political "amateurs" such as these, who are interested in the party as a vehicle for implementing progressive or liberal policies, and the labor movement, which furnishes the bulk of the party workers who have an economic as well as an ideological interest in politics.

Nor is the Republican party lagging far behind in the attraction and use of intelligence. By the early 1960's, cadres of young academics and intellectually attuned lawyers were rising from the grass roots to articulate new programs for a party in need of new blood. Reluctantly or not, the GOP leadership discovered how important this element was and began to accommodate them within the party framework. Thus, in 1963, the Republican Speaker of the State House of Representatives was a graduate of Phillips Exeter Academy, Harvard College, and the Harvard Law School.

All these elements, operating together within the state's political system, have generated a spirit of public concern with community problems that has led to popular recognition of Minnesota as one of the nation's most progressive states. The state's voting record indicates one way in which this progressivism has manifested itself.

Minnesota deviates most from the national voting pattern, not so much in the final results of its elections (which, in the case of the presidential elections at least, were virtually forced into the two-party mold) but because, for so much of its history, it maintained an entirely atypical party system. Minnesota became a state after the Republican ascendancy had already begun. The Democratic party, which had controlled the territorial government through presidential patronage, was almost immediately relegated to a residual role. Though Minnesota voters were even more committed to Republicanism in national elections than those of Wisconsin or Iowa, they have been the least faithful to the party's state candidates. Since Minnesota's second party was virtually nonexistent, these progressives rarely turned to the two-party system as an outlet, preferring to create their own third-party organizations from the first. Indeed, as the number of elections decided by plurality indicates, for most of the years between 1886 and 1944, Minnesota actually had a multiparty system for interstate politics, operating under a Republican umbrella, in which the progressive parties won elections only when they could unite among themselves or form a pre-election coalition with a Democratic party that often polled a smaller vote than the largest "third" party. By 1932, this arrangement had so sapped traditional loyalties to the Republican party that Minnesota voters began swinging Democratic nationally as well. However, only after the amalgamation of the Democratic and Farmer-Labor parties in 1944 made the successful progressive coalition permanent was the old allegiance to the GOP in state politics, which had been honored in the breach for two generations, replaced by a new one.

Minnesota is second only to Wisconsin in the number of times (six) it has elected governors and presidents from different parties, a sure sign of an effort to separate state and national electoral politics. Even the state's formal arrangements have been pointed toward that end, with two-year terms for state officers allowing for significant "off-year" state elections. The 1958 constitutional amendment increasing the governor's term of office to four years made this effort explicit by providing for his election in non-presidential years.

For many years political debate in Minnesota has been chiefly concerned with questions of how large a role government should have in society, not whether government should play a part in the first place. The state's pioneering role in railroad and utility regulation, conservation of natural resources, public ownership of public utilities, development of a progressive system of taxation, and creation of the cooperative movement is well known. Whether through governmental or public nongovernmental agencies, Minnesotans have a nationally acknowledged record for communitarian activities. Minnesota's widespread communal concern has not necessarily implied a simple bias toward governmental activity. On the metropolitan frontier, however, communal responsibility has almost invariably come to mean a relatively high level of government participation on both the state and local planes and Minnesota's state and local governments are moving actively in that direction.

Minnesota progressives turned to nonpartisanship as well as to third partyism and, by World War I, had just about eliminated formal partisan competition for all except the highest political offices in Minnesota. Today only 22 of approximately 32,500 state and local elective offices are filled on a partisan basis in that state.[5] The state's constraints against partisan elections were applied to the localities as well, placing them in the same nonpartisan mold. Local nonpartisanship in Minnesota, however, did not signify an effort to escape participation in the state political system, as it did in Illinois, but represented an effort on the part of the progressives to capture their state whole. Party organization was accordingly identified as antiprogressive and, indeed, antidemocratic for many years. It was only in the 1920's that strong party organizations developed among the progressives, and they were connected to the Farmer-Labor party, an outgrowth of progressive Republicanism. Though that party was later to run into trouble, in part because of its strong organization, it showed the progressives that political organization and progressivism were not incompatible. This, in turn, led to a renewed interest in strong political organization to promote progressive aims.

Unlike the situation in Illinois, politics in Minnesota consistently has been an activity open to and dominated by amateurs. This may be due to the persistence of issues as a central element in determining alignments in Minnesota politics, which in turn has meant the recruitment of new elements into the parties as issues change and their domination by issue-conscious people rather than by people interested in politics as a form of business. In such an environment, the number of people who earn their livelihood from politics is correspondingly reduced, particularly since the use of politics for economic advancement flies in the face of the accepted local morality. This, in turn, has a feedback effect. Since there are so few pecuniary benefits to be gained, professional politicians are few and far between (and the ones that do exist are very different in style), thus opening the ranks of political leadership to even more amateurs. This is not to say that at times in the state's history, party organizations have not followed their natural inclinations to become ingrown and exclusive groups of cronies interested in making a profit, but, whenever they have moved in that direction to a point where their activities become perceptible to those outside the "inner circle," either other party actives or the state's voters have removed them from power and created conditions which have forced such movements to their own destruction.[6]

Minnesota's recent political history is a case in point. The Farmer-Labor party was organized by a typically Minnesotan group of political amateurs in the 1920's. After the party gained power in the 1930's, they developed into just such an inner group, becoming well-nigh professional in their interests after a decade of office-holding. Typically, the newly developed professionals began to look upon politics as their "business" and began to indulge in the kind of monetarily self-rewarding activities quite common in Illinois and other states dominated by the individualistic political culture. Their actions were discovered, and a public scandal ensued, egged on, of course, by the opposition Republicans. The voters swept the Farmer-Labor party out of office with such force that the party was utterly crushed. Six years later, out of the depths of their hopelessness, the survivors were forced into an amalgamation with the Democratic party in order to revive the possibility of any Farmer-Laborites attaining high public office again.

The miniscule Minnesota Democratic party with which they amalgamated long had been centered in (and almost confined to) St. Paul, where it was run by a group of professional politicians of the type that manned urban political organizations throughout the country. It was so thoroughly out of character with the rest of the state that it had managed to win more than 12 per cent of the statewide vote for governor only three times between 1918 and 1946. When FDR was elected President, he preferred working with the Farmer-Laborites and did not even give the Minnesota Democrats exclusive rights to federal patronage. Finally, they too were forced into this amalgamation, with FDR's active encouragement. In the process of amalgamation the positions of both groups of professionals were destroyed, and a new group of DFL leaders, more in keeping with Minnesota's style, arose out of it. They have been careful to maintain their "amateur" standing, if only because the party rank-and-file has challenged them whenever they have shown signs of becoming too "professional." In the 1956 presidential primary campaign, the leaders of the DFL tried to deliver the state for Adlai Stevenson by virtually dictating to the rank-and-file DFL'ers that they vote for him in the name of party unity. The spontaneous reaction of the voters was to give Estes Kefauver the victory as a message pointed toward Hubert Humphrey. Humphrey got the message and, at the next DFL state convention, virtually apologized for overstepping himself. In 1960, there developed some feeling in DFL party ranks that their then national committeeman (an Irishman from Duluth) was gaining material benefits for his law firm above and beyond what he should have been, as a consequence of his official position in the party. He was accused of becoming "professional," was retired from his post, and has never regained his influence in party affairs.

The Republicans have been equally subject to the effects of this aspect of Minnesota's political culture. The Republican party has traditionally been less organization-prone than the Democratic party throughout the country, perhaps because of the early influence of its founders. In Illinois, this has meant that the party has been able to organize on a statewide basis only under some strong political leader holding either the governorship or a seat in the United States Senate and otherwise has consisted of a number of relatively independent factions and local organizations. In Minnesota, even Republican governors and senators have had a difficult time knitting the party together.

After replacing the Farmer-Labor party in the state capitol in 1938 with the election of Harold Stassen to the governorship, the Republicans gave Minnesota a succession of organizationally independent governors. None of them was able to build their personal power through the party apparatus, though some, particularly Stassen, tried hard to do so. These governors won elections not through the strength of the party organization, but through their personal ability to attract voters. Their personal followings, no matter how loyal, could not be "delivered" to other candidates in other elections. When the DFL did put together an organization of devoted amateurs, they acquired the extra momentum which took the statehouse and the state away from the Republicans. Since 1956, the Minnesota Republican party has been trying with increasing success to build a winning organization within the confines of the Minnesota tradition along the lines laid down by the DFL. Young Republican suburbanites in the Twin Cities area and young professional men with GOP ties out of state have begun to repeat the pattern of the immediate postwar years as the aging DFL leadership develops organizational hardening of the arteries.

The Minnesota political culture also allows and even encourages local communities to extend their control over matters involving public morality. Municipally owned liquor stores and tight liquor regulation, limitations on Sunday sales, and similar forms of local law enforcement are features of the Minnesota scene, which has accepted this form of public activity as legitimate for a century. Horse racing, like gambling in any other form, is prohibited in the state. While gambling and other illicit activities are certainly carried on underground in Minnesota, as elsewhere, their managers are considerably less influential politically than their counterparts in Illinois and are even subject to continued harassment by law enforcement agencies in most localities.

Duluth may well be the most straitlaced seaport in the world. Despite its role as a center of Great Lakes and foreign shipping, the city strictly regulates the sale of alcoholic beverages, maintains Sunday as a publicly enforced "day of rest" in many ways, and keeps gambling and prostitution to a bare minimum. Visiting sailors know that for such entertainment they must cross the state line into Superior, Wisconsin. Moreover, there is no apparent pressure on the part of state or local commercial interests with a stake in the port's development to relax those standards.

Here, too, Minnesota acts as a buffer protecting Duluth's way of life. The state's service in this regard points up a very significant aspect of state-local relations in Minnesota: the state's role in maintaining an environment in which local variations of the Minnesota political culture and style can operate. It is particularly apparent in the case of Duluth, whose local political patterns deviate even more from the American norm than those of the state as a whole.

The Yankee tradition in Minnesota has placed a high premium on local self-government. At the same time, other indigenous traditions developed in response to sectional demands have encouraged statewide action in ways which, in Illinois, would be considered an unseemly exercise of state control over local options. The result has been the development of strong positive state involvement in most Minnesota governmental activities, from education to municipal reorganization to law enforcement, but with the preservation of a high degree of latitude at the local level within the framework of state standard-setting or assistance. The state government, in essence, guarantees the right of its civil communities to develop acceptable local variants of the state political system in line with variations in local need while simultaneously insuring that no important civil community will develop a political system not in harmony with the state's political culture.

The state's requirements for nonpartisan local elections and its permissiveness in the realm of local control over issues of public morality furnish two divergent examples of this. Another is provided in the peculiarly limited form of "home rule" authorized under the state constitution. While cities, townships, and, since 1958, even counties are granted the right to draft their own charters and theoretically to assume all permitted municipal powers, the state legislature has either limited the effects of the constitutional provisions or, in the case of counties, simply refused to pass the necessary implementing legislation. Thus the legislators elected from each of the three major cities in the state must still caucus together publicly and regularly to present the united front required to gain legislative assent to meet local demands, including such basically local issues as the redistricting of the Hennepin County (Minneapolis and suburbs) Board of Commissioners. A whole series of formal and quasi-formal legislative procedures has been developed to deal with local matters, ranging from a scheme for classifying cities that approaches legitimation of special legislation to procedures for expediting passage of legislation presented by unanimous county delegations.

Another central feature of Minnesota's political culture is its implicit acceptance of the legitimacy of politics. This is reinforced by the values and attitudes of the moralistic political culture in at least two ways. First of all, the communitarian orientation of the political culture means that social action is considered legitimate. It is not difficult to move from acceptance of the principle of social action to the realization that social action in a democratic society must, by its very nature, be political action. Second, the belief that "politics" is not necessarily dishonest makes it possible for the kind of people who in other political cultures tend to seek apolitical solutions to political problems and would certainly avoid personal involvement in partisan political activity to utilize the political system to meet their problems and even to devote a share of their time to party and other political affairs. The belief in the efficacy of politics remains strong among a substantial segment of the population in Minnesota, to an extent unmatched in states dominated by the individualistic political culture.

This conjunction of values and attitudes makes it possible for the citizens of Minnesota to conceive of the possibility of social reform through political change. As in any political system, social change occurs only as a consequence of accumulated dissatisfaction. It certainly is not an end in itself, nor is it initiated for "light and transient reasons." Minnesota has embraced social reform movements more frequently than most states, but there again, unlike Illinois, the dissatisfactions that have led to the expression of the demand for social change as a demand for political change are rarely those that arise from popular disgust with the political system as structured, but those that arise from a belief that the system is being perverted internally or threatened by external forces seeking to alter its essential ends. In such cases, there tend to be temporary uprisings, designed to gain satisfaction on specific issues, rather than attempts to change the structure of the system. It is no accident that Minnesota is still operating under its original state constitution despite the problems attendant upon its adoption and occasional drives to rewrite it. Nor should it be surprising to discover that there has been relatively little change in the structure of local governments in Minnesota in the past decade, despite the almost nationwide tendency to translate the current urban revolution into movements for government structural change.

The achievements of local reform movements in Minnesota provide a particularly clear reflection of the basically political character of reform in the state. Unlike the situation in most of the Illinois civil communities, local reform has not been apolitical. Even when nonpartisanship was the keynote for reform, it rarely took on an antipolitical character. It was simply a device for overcoming the traditional Republican commitment of the bulk of the local electorate, which frequently enabled anti-reform candidates to win elections by identifying with that party. The nonpartisan elections were no less political, nor were they intended to be so. In fact, as soon as a competitive two-party system dominated by amateurs was developed in the larger cities, the DFL developed an informal system of party endorsements covering offices from the state legislature to local school boards. As this endorsement system took hold, it was adopted by the Republicans as well. Since the change did not alter the state's basic political character, it met with little public interest. By the late 1950's, Minnesota's formal system of nonpartisan elections had been effectively subverted on a statewide basis by both parties, without interfering with the unity of the state's political system or changing its fundamental orientation.

Duluth, like the rest of the state's civil communities, has had nonpartisan local elections for better than half a century. Until the post-World-War-II period, the elective governments in the civil community were generally controlled by Republican businessmen who gained power through use of the nonpartisan system while the voters were otherwise supporting Farmer-Labor party candidates on the state level and, after 1928, Democratic presidential nominees. Only after the merger of the Democratic and Farmer-Labor parties was a strong local DFL organization developed that successfully challenged the business coalition through the endorsement system—still under the guise of nonpartisanship, of course.

The final demonstration of the difference between political nonpartisanship in Minnesota and the apolitical nonpartisanship of other states lies in that state's general resistance to council-manager government. Of the 106 incorporated cities in Minnesota in 1960, only fourteen had adopted council-manager government. Commission government, a highly political form of nonpartisanship, was slightly more popular in Minnesota. In its day, it was adopted by both Duluth and St. Paul, among other cities. Minneapolis, on the other hand, has retained its mayor-aldermanic system since its incorporation. While St. Paul has kept the commission system, in 1956 Duluth changed its form of government again, one of the few cities in the state to do so in recent years, to an even more visibly political form.

When the abandonment of Duluth's commission government was first suggested by the local League of Women Voters and the business and professional leadership, the council-manager system was proposed as the alternative. It was soon made clear that organized labor and the local DFL would strenuously oppose any effort to institute city-manager government. The local business community, whence the suggestion came, was really interested in improving the city's administrative structure in the hope that this would lead to greater economy in government and in its gaining better representation on the city council, which, under the "nonpartisan" commission system, had been dominated by the Labor-DFL coalition for a decade. Its people had seized upon the manager plan because it was the one called to their attention as the current reform panacea by the national organizations with which they were associated. However, lacking any real commitment to the apolitical aspects of the plan, they were willing to accept a substitute establishing a modified "strong mayor-council" system which gave them a mayor with strong executive powers, to be assisted by a professional administrative aide who would handle the day-to-day administration of city affairs; plus a fourteen-member council, part of which was to be elected from districts to insure representation for all segments of the city, and part at large. This plan was modeled in part after the state's device for combining administrative efficiency with political control, which has provided the governor with a commissioner of administration since 1939.

The new charter was passed in a public referendum in 1956 with the generally active support of the business and professional community and the DFL amateurs and the generally tacit support of the labor leadership. It has brought little change in the city's day-to-day operations since there was little that could be altered by charter reform, and it has been difficult to find the proper type of administrative assistant to provide the continuing administrative direction necessary to effectuate operational changes. However, it has apparently satisfied the business community by offering them a chance to elect some city councilmen while remaining politically dominated by the DFL, through which it maintains the proper connections with the state's political system, culture, and traditions.

The Melding of Political Cultures in Colorado[7]

Colorado's primary urban political problems are not those of Illinois—achievement of urban reform to eliminate political corruption, the "two cities," or governmental lethargy. Nor are they problems of economic revival and social improvement as in Minnesota. First and foremost, its cities are faced with the need to cope with the unprecedented physical expansion and economic growth that has made the post-World-War-II boom in the mountain West.

Not only are the sources of Colorado's urban concerns different from those of the other two states, but the political culture and social structure upon which its civil communities must draw is also substantially unique, though its basic components are the same as those found in the others. Colorado's political culture represents a melding of the political subcultures encountered in Illinois and Minnesota, only in reverse order, with the individualistic political culture secondary in Colorado and the moralistic culture dominant. Its politics partake of the commonwealth concerns of Minnesota leavened by the marketplace concerns prominent in Illinois. In short, if it were possible to construct a continuum of state political characteristics with Illinois at one end and Minnesota on the other, Colorado would very likely fall close to the middle.

Allowing for the differences in its geohistorical location, Colorado possesses some of the centrality of Illinois and some of the isolation of Minnesota. Geographically it is the central state of the Trans-Mississippi West. In the nineteenth century, however, its topography—particularly the Rocky Mountain barrier rising seven to nine thousand feet from the plains across the entire state—caused most of the westward migration to go around it, either to the north or south. Only with the coming of the air age in the twentieth century has Colorado been able to capitalize on the central position geography gave it. Those migrants who did come to the state in the days of the land frontier chose to do so much in the way that Minnesota's settlers did. An energetic lot, they overcame the state's geographic disadvantages to build Denver into the empire city of the Rocky Mountains and, since the coming of the airplane, the central metropolis of the interior West. At the same time its major concentration of population remains separated from the two main bodies of American population by a thousand miles in either direction. Like Illinois, its original settlers were a mixture of Southerners (who came to dig gold), Northerners (who came to settle and became the dominant element—socially, economically, and politically), and people from the Middle States (who did both), plus a later (though much smaller) immigration of people from every part of Europe. It also has a substantial "non-Anglo" minority of Mexican-Americans and much smaller minorities of Negroes and Orientals. Like Minnesota, however, it was not greatly touched by the huge ethnic immigration that has colored the character of metropolitan life in the northeastern third of the United States. Colorado is unique among the states of this study in that its population is still being visibly augmented by an in-migration that could potentially alter its political culture. The state's population nearly doubled between 1940 and 1960, increasing by approximately 35 per cent between 1950 and 1960 alone.

Geographically, Colorado is pulled in three directions: northeastward into the northern plains country and the Missouri River basin, southward into the desert southwest, and northwestward into the grazing-and-mining country of the Intermountain West. These geographic cleavages are reflected in the fundamental regional cleavages which are publicly recognized as highly significant in the state's politics. The northeast, which includes Denver and most of the state's major population centers, dominates life in the state, to the intense displeasure of the southeast-south central area (which includes Pueblo and Spanish Colorado) and the western slope. While water is the major public issue which divides the regions, political representation, industrial development, tourism, and the allocation of state expenditures are also perennial issues of regional concern. Overall, however, Colorado is Western and highly conscious of it. Its people are also highly conscious of their state identity, perhaps even more visibly so than are Minnesotans.

The first "European" settlers in Colorado were the Spanish-speaking Mexicans who came up from New Mexico in the 1840's to settle in the area located roughly south of the Arkansas River. Unlike the pre-American settlers in Illinois and Minnesota, who were few and easily overwhelmed when the Americans came in, a significant number of the Mexicans have remained rooted in Colorado's southern reaches to become a prominent ethnic group that has taken on certain aspects of a racial minority. They have been periodically reinforced by their countrymen from Mexico and the American Southwest who have come to work in the fields of Colorado over the years. The "Mexican question" is a perennial issue in Colorado, much like the "Negro question" east of the Mississippi River.

The first wave of settlement from the United States to permanently occupy land in Colorado came as a result of the abortive Pike's Peak Gold Rush of 1859. Thus both Southerners and Northerners came west in response to the lure of gold, and some stayed to battle for control of the new territory. While most of those who came to Colorado at that time were primarily interested in personal gain, hoping to strike it rich in the gold fields, the intensity and pervasiveness of the sectional conflict over states' rights, secession, and the slavery question were such that it even penetrated into the lives of the isolated gold-seekers of the Pike's Peak region, as Colorado was then called. The first decade of political conflict in the Territory of Colorado (created in 1861) revolved around Civil War issues in many subtle and not-so-subtle ways. In this period the basis for the state's highly competitive two-party system was established by competing pro-Southern and pro-Northern elements. Also established in the same period was the basic division between those interested in politics for personal economic gain and those desirous of fostering a politics more clearly oriented toward questions of the public weal, which was to become a standard feature on the Colorado scene, even though the latter group soon became the dominant one in the state.

The first real boom of permanent settlers began toward the end of the Civil War when both the agricultural and mining frontiers were opened in earnest. Northeastern Colorado, which became the center of the state's agricultural production, was settled by Yankees and Middle Western descendants of Yankees, most of whom were involved in the establishment of a social order on the parkland between the mountains and the semi-arid plains that was to be a continuation of the way of life they had developed in the prairie settlements to the east, based on a similar technology (with one very significant addition—an irrigation system which required a high degree of community cooperation) and with similar political values. Some of the Yankees even attempted to establish utopian colonies on the plains where the values they represented could be fully implemented. A smaller number of Yankees went to the new cities and mining camps to become entrepreneurs, supplying the miner's basic needs —at a price—but at the same time imposing a measure of law and order upon the boom towns so that they would be fit places to raise a family in the manner to which the Yankees were accustomed. They and the Jewish entrepreneurs who joined them became the moving spirits behind the development of communities in or near the mining areas.

The mining frontier attracted a polyglot in-migration from all over the world, most of whom moved on as the boom passed. However, enough of these fortune-seekers stayed to become the nuclei of three different elements that were to contribute to the emerging Colorado civil society: a small entrepreneurial element, mostly Yankee in origin; a managerial class, often from the British Isles or the Middle States, that supervised the property of absentee owners located "back East" or overseas in Great Britain; and a proletarian element of both New and Old World origins whose frustration and disappointment at becoming workers for others rather than successful fortune-hunters in their own right led them to become radical anti-capitalists with syndicalist leanings.

A fifth element that arrived in the state during the second migration period between the Civil War and the turn of the century consisted of Southerners, particularly Texans, who came northward with the cattle industry. These were highly individualistic men, either cattle barons who resisted the "encroachments" of organized society on the grazing lands they had appropriated for themselves or cowboys who drifted from job to job as the spirit moved them, always guarding their independence. With rare exceptions, neither the cattle barons nor the cowboys were concerned with questions of the public welfare, nor were they interested in developing institutions of government to serve any purpose other than those of immediate economic benefit to them.

In the clash of interests that developed at the state level between these divergent migratory trends and their internally divergent components, the Yankees and their allies who devoted themselves to commonwealth-building while others were seeking quick ways to get rich succeeded in entrenching their value system as the ideal in Colorado politics. Nevertheless, the representatives of the individualistic political culture (and those from traditionalistic backgrounds who assimilated with them) succeeded in modifying that ideal sufficiently in practice to permit satisfaction of their basic economic interests in the context of the state political system. Consequently, if politics in Colorado has never become a business, as in Illinois, it certainly has revolved openly around economic interests more than around issues considered within a moral framework. Thus public officials with high standards of personal integrity and the best conceptions of public service for many years did not hesitate to use troops against strikers at the behest of the (usually absentee) mine owners if they felt that their economic interests were threatened by unionization. What was of vital importance, however, was that the same men could ultimately be persuaded that such actions were not only unprofitable but unjust. Perhaps the state's ability over the years to maintain a tension between the ideals of "good government" and the striving for economic advantage through politics has remained possible because the state has continued to expand economically and there has been no need to resolve that tension permanently one way or another.

Toward the end of the nineteenth century, a small third wave of settlement came to Colorado, consisting primarily of Europeans who came to form agricultural colonies on the high plains and in the mountain valleys or to work in the smelters that processed the ores being brought out of the mountains. As their colonies failed and the mining industry settled down into a formalized corporate mold, the surviving settlers moved to the cities to give many of them something of a polyglot texture. Many of these Europeans came from middle-class backgrounds, which lessened their overtly "ethnic" characteristics in the eyes of the native

Americans who came to know them personally and eased their assimilation into Colorado society. Even so, their adjustment to the American milieu required time.

Only in Pueblo were Southern and Eastern European migrants brought in specifically to work in heavy industry. They came in such numbers and for so clearly a proletarian purpose that they were typed as "foreigners" by the native population from the start. This discrimination did not lessen their own interest in developing a middle-class environment, even if it had to be a segregated one at first. They did not become the urban proletariat they were marked out to be, but a highly stable population that from the first cultivated the private-home-with-immaculate-lawn tradition so highly valued by their "American" neighbors. Consequently, it was not too long before they assimilated the basic values of the state's political culture and began to develop political strength to go with their evolving status.

Almost from the beginning of its history, Colorado's economy has developed within the framework of large-scale national and international capitalism. Emerging as a civil society after the country's simple free enterprise system was well on its way to being transformed into the more complex economy of the large corporation, the state has had to live with absentee ownership, managerial control, and bureaucratic organization of its farms, mines, and mills. Despite intense efforts early in the state's history to create an agricultural society based on the family farm in the manner of the more humid lands back east, agriculture on the arid plains quickly proved to be successful only on a large-scale basis and, in the twentieth century, primarily as a corporate endeavor. Hence, Colorado did not develop a widespread rural population base in the manner of Illinois and Minnesota. Moreover, few of the industries which located in Colorado were dependent on agriculture. Based on mining, they generally demanded an urban social structure for extractive, supply, and service purposes, so Colorado has been a basically urban state since its founding. Certainly after the 1880's, the greater share of the migrants coming into the state located themselves in the cities. Even the agricultural workers, the Mexicans brought in to work in the fields during World War I, settled in semi-urban areas on the cities' peripheries, from which they could move out to the farms where they worked. At the same time, mining was a boom and bust activity whose fixed costs soon came to demand large-scale corporate organization, able first to shoulder the burden of exploration and investment and then to unload specific operations when they were no longer profitable. Corporate decisions controlled the life and death of mining towns and the economic lives of those who lived in them.

Both agriculture and mining, then, contributed to the development of a restless migratory population which wandered about within the state working on its farms and in its mines when work was available, a population which soon developed strong industrial union and even radical leanings. The social and political effects of this colonial or neocolonial condition have contributed their share to the molding of Colorado's distinctive political culture.

The Mexican agricultural workers represented a fourth wave of migration into Colorado, the last before the great postwar boom. Kept segregated and relegated to subcitizen status, it would be another generation before they (or their children) would begin to enter Colorado's political life. Their neighborhoods in Denver and their barrios located around Pueblo and the state's smaller cities became Colorado's equivalent of the black ghettos of the east.

By the 1920's a number of powerful political groups had emerged in Colorado which, while functioning according to the canons of public responsibility of the moralistic political culture, were primarily concerned with advancing their own economic interests. A coalition of absentee-owned industries and local businesses that served them dominated the commercial industrial sector. The big agricultural corporations and the cattlemen's associations vied with the Farmers' Union as the spokesmen for agriculture. Labor was represented by increasingly conservative middle-class craft unions after the more militant miners' organizations were crushed or destroyed themselves by resorting to near-guerrilla warfare against the established order. The older citizens comprised a unique and very influential group on the political scene, perhaps the state's most active lobby. By and large, these groups and their smaller cohorts, all the direct and immediate heirs of Colorado's land frontier experience, had developed a *modus vivendi* that gave each a seat in the state's political game and discouraged any activities that might rock the boat. They were served by cadres of politicians drawn in the main from the liberal professions who never became professionals in politics in the accepted sense but, rather, maintained their status as amateurs through their outside sources of livelihood.

All of these interest groups have maintained themselves in the post-World-War-II era, but the structure which they had erected has undergone substantial modification as a result of the impact of the fifth migration. The effects of that migration began to be translated into political terms in the mid-1950's, interjecting a substantial measure of conflict and flux into what had become a somnolent political system.

The fifth, and by far the greatest, single wave of settlement in the state's history has come into Colorado since the close of World War II, primarily between 1945 and 1960. Some idea of the magnitude of this migration may be gained by noting that the population of metropolitan Denver increased by 51 per cent between 1950 and 1960 while Pueblo's boosters lamented their civil community's failure to compete in attracting in-migrants by citing its "mere" 43 per cent growth in the same period. The postwar migration was induced by and directed toward the metropolitan frontier. In general, the migration reinforced the populations who came in previous waves, consisting primarily of a mixture of Southerners coming particularly from Texas, Oklahoma, and Missouri; the descendants of earlier Yankee and Scandinavian migrations to the Upper Midwest, particularly Minnesota and Iowa; and people from the Middle States, particularly Illinois. Their distribution, however, was somewhat different than in earlier waves. In particular, their tendency to concentrate in three metropolitan areas and, secondarily, in a handful of smaller cities, brought large numbers of Southerners into the orbit of the other streams for the first time. There is another difference between this last and the earlier migrations. The talents of the most recent migration are those of the organization society, and their values reflect the new impulse to choose a place to live the "good life" of leisure—in this case centered on outdoor living—rather than a place whose primary attraction is economic.

The problems generated by such a heavy in-migration, added to the already growing problems of suburbanization, provoked the postwar urban revolutions in Denver, Pueblo, Colorado Springs, and other burgeoning urban centers in the state, revolutions which have had repercussions on the local level since the early 1950's and, after 1960, began to influence the government of the state as a whole. First in local and now in state politics, the suburbanites, some natives and most newcomers, are becoming increasingly significant. They have shaken up the statewide structure of interests and have injected new talent into the state's political bloodstream. While the new migration is clearly stretching the fabric of Colorado's political culture in some ways, it has not really set out to break down the old traditions and replace them with something new and different. On the contrary, most of the new Coloradoans have been anxious to adapt to the Colorado way of life and, the longer they live in the state, the more like their predecessors they become. In fact, defense of "the Colorado way of life" is a political issue that has served to unite new and old Coloradoans alike.

The "Texan" problem is one example of this common struggle to maintain the established patterns of Colorado's identity. As part of the business and commercial expansion that accompanied the population boom in the immediate postwar period, large numbers of Texans began to invest in the state. Their investments ranged from the oil industry to the development of the Denver central business district to the purchase of extensive tracts of agricultural and grazing lands in the San Luis Valley. The Texans' interest in Colorado was heightened by their own desires to escape the Texas summer by vacationing in the state or to enjoy skiing in the Colorado mountains in the winter. Thus their influence was felt not only in the world of finance but on the streets of every major city in Colorado. In the early 1950's, the influence of these Texans, all proverbially millionaires, was growing visibly stronger year after year and, in the manner of Texans, was being proclaimed openly in the press, on the buildings they were erecting, and through the visible presence of Texan drivers on Colorado's highways and fliers in its airways.

Soon a reaction set in. Native Coloradoans and those originally from other parts of the country began to resent the "Texanization" of their state. Recollections of conflicts, dating back over a century to the days when the Texas Republic claimed the heart of what is today urban Colorado, were revived. Stories of the Texans' efforts to invade Colorado during the Civil War and the heroic efforts of Colorado troops in the Battle of La Glorieta Pass (1862) were printed in the newspapers, as if to remind the public that the struggle between Texans and Coloradoans was an ancient one. Interpreting the latest wave of Texan investment as an effort to conquer Colorado by other means, the local citizenry proceeded to challenge the newcomers and investors from the Lone Star State. Letters to the press about Texans' behavior became common, and public discussion of the matter grew. This even carried over into the business world. Texan investments were bought out by Colorado-based syndicates. The Murchison brothers' plan to name their newly erected Denver skyscraper "Murchison Towers" was scrapped and the building itself sold to local interests. Even in Pueblo, whose leadership appeared to be seeking people and investment funds from every quarter, the local business community became aware of the Texas "menace," not only within Colorado itself but in the increasing importance of Amarillo as a rival commercial center that was cutting into "normal" Pueblo markets.

One element among the new migrants has caused an unanticipated measure of cultural conflict in the state. The Southern migrants, coming from a different political culture and settling in the midst of the older population, have generated some strains on accepted patterns of political behavior. The Denver police scandal was one serious consequence of this unanticipated mixture. When a burglary ring was discovered within the Denver Police Department, the first reaction in that city and the state as a whole was one of disbelief: "Such things just don't happen in Colorado." Then it turned out that most of the police involved were postwar migrants, and mostly from the western South at that. This, combined with the Texas question, led to a renewed concern on the part of those Coloradoans who are products of the state's dominant political culture (including the new Coloradoans from areas of similar political culture "back East") with the problem of preserving their state's communitarian and "good government" values.

At the same time, the alienation of the products of the traditionalistic-cum-individualistic political culture of the western South from the essentially moralistic political culture has led many of them toward the radical right or at least an ultraconservatism based on the conspiratorial theories of the radical right. Their challenge to state politics is the first real expression of traditionalistic norms in the state in nearly a century.

While the outcome of the present struggle may still be in doubt, there is considerable evidence that Colorado's dominant political culture is maintaining itself. Certainly, the traditionalistic thrust has been confined to the right wing while continued prosperity has prevented the development of serious economic demands on the political system that could cause a culture crisis. On the contrary, the majority's interest in "the good life" as they defined it probably strengthens their commitment to honesty and openness in politics and to the larger political culture which has spawned those values.

Colorado's two parties, though not as issue-oriented as those in Minnesota, are composed of much the same kind of people. Both are coalitions of issue-oriented middle-class cosmopolitans and "bread and butter" labor (Democratic) or business (Republican) groups, leavened with a sprinkling of professional politicians. While the adoption of extreme positions is no more common in the Colorado parties than in those of other states, the existence of a substantial radical element for much of Colorado's history has given each party its share of radicals during different periods of the state's history. Both the Republican and Democratic parties had a leavening of radicals in the years immediately following the Civil War, but after the rise of populism the more militant progressives generally aligned themselves with the Democrats, becoming quite influential in that party in the 1890's. Ultimately they helped convert the party into a bastion of twentieth century political liberalism. Yankee communitarianism has kept the voice of moderate progressivism alive and influential in the Republican party also. More recently, the ultraconservative right has aligned itself with the GOP in the hope of capturing that party. Though a small minority in the state party, their influence grew in the early 1960's but received a major setback after Goldwater's defeat. Still, the parties are not divided along ideological lines, not in a state whose two United States Senators, one a Democrat and the other a Republican, a few years back could maintain a joint office for Colorado affairs on Capitol Hill.

Colorado most nearly approximates the classic model of two reasonably equal competing parties marked by recognizable differences in their orientation to political issues. Coming into existence after the bloom of Republicanism had faded and something like two-party competition had been restored at the national level, its settlers not only came from many different streams, but arrived with ties to both parties. Except for the period between 1926 and 1938, no party has held the governorship for more than eight consecutive years, and even that length of tenure has only been achieved or exceeded three times. Presidential elections reflect this competitive situation equally well. As in Minnesota and Wisconsin, geography functioned to heighten Colorado's insurgency movements, which were particularly intense and widespread in that state. However because the two-party system was viable, one of the parties was usually able to channel most protest movements into its own ranks.

Since party competition for state office in Colorado has always been intense and neither party has ever been able to claim a clear and continuing statewide majority, the mavericks, who are spread statewide in their influence, have been cultivated by both parties as holders of the balance of power. They, in turn, have been able to channel their energies into one or the other of the two regular parties (usually the Democratic party) in efforts—frequently successful—to gain control of the regular party organizations. At the very least, they have been able to wring concessions from both parties. This has generally obviated the necessity for them to develop third-party movements, even at the local level.

Uncritical party regularity is relatively rare among Colorado voters, and is even suspect. Senatorial nonpartisan arrangements of the kind described above have worked well as a result. In fact, it is quite likely that the willingness of voters to support candidates from either party has kept the two vying for the political middle and avoiding the extremes demanded by their more radical elements. The independence of the electorate and the mutually modifying effects of the mixture of issues and economic concerns—all aspects of Colorado's political culture—contribute to the importance of candidates' personalities in the state's electoral struggles. Personal appeal is considerably more important in Colorado than in Minnesota and far more than in Illinois (where it is rarely important at all). The most appealing candidates in Colorado state and local politics are those that have a kind of rugged sophistication—men of the world with cowboy boots.

This situation has had a contradictory effect on Pueblo. Puebloans, the most "regular" voters in Colorado, have been constrained to act within a system in which party regularity is not only rare among the voters, but is even suspect. Pueblo's statewide image as being "boss-ruled" has led it to be ignored and even disliked by the rest of the state for being outside the pale of political independence. At the same time, its very regularity makes it important to the Democratic party because its electorate represents one of the few concentrations of consistently Democratic voters in the state, and the votes of its citizens are needed to win elections. Pueblo's constant struggle to gain consideration from the rest of Colorado, and the greater frequency of conflict between its Democratic leadership and their party colleagues at the state level are both products of the difficulty the civil community has in fitting its unique pattern into the Colorado electoral and party system, despite its intense involvement in other aspects of the state's political system.

The Colorado public has much the same set of expectations regarding politicians' behavior as the Minnesotans, though they are applied less rigorously. The honest economic self-improvement of political figures is accepted, though Coloradoans are clearly unwilling to tolerate the kinds of pecuniary gain available to politicians as a matter of course in Illinois. Actually, Colorado has so few professional politicians in the Illinois sense that the category cannot really be said to exist. Pueblo County, which is considered to be "machine-ridden" in the rest of the state because it has a Democratic party organization that is bound together by interpersonal loyalties and a sense of party regularity, is barely organized by Illinois standards and its political leadership would be considered incorruptible in the latter state. Pueblo's style of party organization, though a response to local cultural variations, is sufficiently in tune with the state's political culture so that the civil community's permanent residents can easily find their places within it if they so choose. At the same time, the absentee-owned industries and businesses have enough political access and are assured of sufficient political regularity to feel that their immediate interests are protected without their having to be more directly involved.

The problem of political cultural differences enters most pronouncedly into the pattern of state involvement in local activities. Just as the representatives of the individualistic political culture who control state politics in Illinois make demands upon every local community in some way, so do their counterparts representing the moralistic political culture in Colorado. In fact, the intervention of the latter is in many ways more intense. Almost by definition it is to be expected that representatives of the moralistic political culture would be more concerned with deviations from their standards and more willing to intervene to prevent such deviations where the power to intervene is available to them. Rejecting the "live and let live" approach to political life of the individualistic political culture, they must insist upon certain standards of political behavior simply to maintain the fabric of their culture intact. This is clearly evident in Colorado. Its state level political leadership is almost invariably drawn from the moralistic political culture or at least conforms to its norms but, unlike Minnesota, that leadership cannot count upon every civil community to function according to the standards of that political culture. Thus the temptation to constantly intervene in local affairs, to maintain the "accepted" state standards, is always present.

The relationship between Pueblo and the state government illustrates this very clearly. As indicated earlier, Pueblo is a suspect civil community in the eyes of the rest of the state, particularly in the eyes of northeastern Colorado, where the bulk of the political power lies. Its heavy industrial base, until recently a unique phenomenon in the state; its high percentage of Southern, Southern and Eastern European, Afro-American, and Hispanic-originated inhabitants, who make it the state's only Eastern-style "melting pot"; its penchant for political organization and party regularity and the fact that elements held to be "less desirable" by the state's opinion molders are not only represented but actually hold considerable political power locally; all tend to make it different and suspect.

It is indeed true that the Pueblo political system represents something of a mixture of political cultures. The demands of an industrial community with many foreign-born citizens have led to the development of a service-oriented political organization manned by politicians who have a stake in staying in power that differs significantly from the kind of loose aggregations of volunteers that pass for organization in the rest of Colorado. Nevertheless, the organization itself has embraced the Yankee-originated values of Colorado politics. Its leaders are not professional politicians but hold nonpolitical jobs to support themselves. They seek power and prestige (status benefits which are of particular interest to many of Pueblo's lower-middle-class political actives) but rarely direct pecuniary gain from their political associations. It is true that there is an element of indirect economic benefit that comes from political participation (as there is in almost every political system); Pueblo's "crime" is that its citizens openly accept this as a legitimate reward rather than denouncing it. Similarly, the quest for "access," something which obviously exists among political actives in every political culture, is openly accepted in Pueblo while it tends to be politely veiled in northeastern Colorado.

All these differences do not add up to a different political culture. Puebloans have merely developed a modified version of the state's dominant political culture which just as truly is Coloradoan. The other Coloradoans are not so easily convinced of this, however, and a state administration can invariably make political capital by intervening in Pueblo affairs on the grounds that it is necessary to make that civil community conform to the state's political mores. The forms this intervention may take are various—some revolve around the state's important role in the local economy through its institutions (see Chapter Nine)—and politically articulate Puebloans are quick to perceive and react to them, feeling, as they do, that the rest of the state looks down upon their community.

As a result, Puebloans seek political influence at the state level not only for the material benefits it brings but for the prestige and status it can provide to a very prestige-conscious and status-hungry community. The years in which Pueblo was known throughout Colorado as "Pewtown" have left their mark on the community's psyche. Its people would like nothing better than to be accepted as Coloradoans of equally good standing with their brethren in the rest of the state. Statewide acceptance on that scale requires both a change in Pueblo's public image and a change in the civil community's real role in state affairs as well. Even in the Democratic party, which relies upon Pueblo's regularity while publicly expressing disgust at its "machine voting habits," Puebloans have had no more than a minimum of influence. Since the days of Senators Adams and Costigan in the 1920's, Pueblo has not contributed a single important statewide political leader who has been able to transcend his identification with Pueblo and win the respect of the state. Pueblo's role has been forced to be obstructionist only, utilizing its bloc of votes in the primary elections against candidates its leadership has opposed. The Republicans, though clearly the minority party in Pueblo since 1932, have had to bear much the same stigma.

Finally, entrance into full participation in the Colorado political system is attractive in and of itself, since the system represents a political culture whose values are attractive to most politically articulate Puebloans. Unlike the situation in Illinois, where even the political leadership in most of the cities of the prairie desires to preserve a certain degree of independence from the state political system because the image of that system is not particularly attractive (even though connections with it may be useful), Puebloans view the Colorado political system as basically a good one, worth being a part of for the values it represents.

The ramifications of the differences in Pueblo's political culture are felt in the civil community's local politics as well. Reflecting the moralistic aspects of their political culture, Puebloans have not eschewed political solutions to political problems. At the same time, the presence of strong elements from the individualistic political culture has led them to make certain efforts to guard against the problems of marketplace politics.

During the first generation of civic reform, Pueblo's commitment to progressivism, coupled with an apparent dissatisfaction with the high degree of political control exercised by the then dominant Colorado Fuel and Iron Company, the leading local industry, led to the adoption of the commission plan for the city government. Since Pueblo County, like all Colorado counties, is governed by county commissioners who are clearly political figures, commission government certainly had few antipolitical overtones in the minds of those Puebloans who were interested in the change. It is apparent that their concern was to "restore politics to the people" and, at the same time, eliminate the corrupting relationship between the absentee-owned industries that dominated the community economically and the local politicians who stood willing to serve them in return for their share of the potential economic rewards. The latter arrangement was, of course, familiar in Illinois. There it was reinforced by the individualistic political culture and proved hard to root out. In Colorado—

even in Pueblo—the dominant moralistic political culture provided a basis through which to mobilize the citizenry (including many politicians) to root it out.

In the 1940's, representatives of the local business community became interested in the council-manager plan apparently out of sympathy for its "businesslike" orientation toward "efficiency and economy" in government. Their idea was to create a strong city manager supported by a small city council to be elected at large (they were, after all, cosmopolitans). Timing their action well, they proposed the adoption of the new charter at the height of local dissatisfaction with the incumbent city commissioners, who had developed reputations as heavy drinkers and dispensers of favors beyond the civil community's tolerated limits. Still, the local population was reluctant to adopt a form of government which, to them, seemed clearly apolitical (and that is, after all, what the opponents of the plan are really saying when they accuse it of being undemocratic). The local labor unions, who were (and are) one of the mainstays of the local Democratic party, recognized the virtue of acquiring a professional administrator to handle the tasks of municipal administration but did not want a government that would not be clearly responsible politically. They proposed an alternate plan, calling for amendments to the existing city charter to create a city council of fourteen members, elected by districts, who would appoint a city manager but would effectively retain executive as well as legislative power in their hands as under the commission plan.

Labor's scheme was adopted by referendum in 1950 but soon proved to be most unsatisfactory because it made no provisions for an executive leader with power to act, and the enlarged council could not develop sufficient internal unity to create a surrogate. A new compromise charter was drawn up by a committee representing all factions in the civil community that formally authorized the appointment of a city manager and provided for a seven-man city council, four of whom were to be elected from districts. This plan met the business cosmopolitans' demands and labor's objections. It was adopted by the voters in 1954. Since then, the remaining antipolitical aspects of the plan have been further neutralized in practice. After a succession of city managers brought in from the outside, who tried to govern in approved city-manager fashion, the city council has settled down to choosing local men for that position, men who know the distribution of power and interests in the local community and the limits of their mandate.

Colorado law provides that council-manager cities shall not elect a mayor independently. The council elects one of its number to serve as mayor, ostensibly for ceremonial purposes. In Pueblo, there is some evidence that the position of mayor is taking on more importance as an executive position, to provide some direction for a city unwilling to grant that prerogative to its city manager. Having no need to secure or maintain an "independent" city manager whose function it is to "kick the rascals out," Puebloans are not interested in depoliticizing their city government, much as they may be interested in professionalizing its bureaucracy. Their solution is characteristic of representatives of the moralistic political culture.

Iowa and "The State of Scott"[8]

Iowa presents a public image of internal homogeneity and overall stability unexcelled among the other states of the Union. Even its pattern of metropolitanization appears to have developed evenly statewide. The state is not dominated by any large city. Six of its seven metropolitan areas are approximately the same size and serve approximately the same functions in their respective regions. (Des Moines is slightly larger.) Politically and culturally the Davenport metropolitan area is the one maverick among them, so much so that it is popularly known in other parts of Iowa, after its county, as "the State of Scott."

The differences between Davenport and Iowa as a whole reveal a good deal about the political culture of the state. Iowa, like Illinois and Colorado, has had to blend the moralistic, traditionalistic, and individualistic political cultures into a workable state political system, but in proportions unique to its own situation and as a product of its own geohistorical location. Like Colorado, the moralistic political culture emerged as the dominant one but, like the Illinois situation, only in reverse. Counties and groups of counties dominated by the other two political cultures remain as local pockets within the overall state pattern. The cities of eastern Iowa are "pulled" by Illinois, both as a consequence of geographic factors (the Mississippi River, in particular) and because their population components are descended from the same streams that settled the western and west central areas of the latter state. Iowa's southern tier of counties has been strongly influenced by the political culture of the South, brought into them from Missouri. Both of these disruptive factors are offset by the influence of the Yankee and Northern European streams in the rest of the state and the "pull" exercised by Minnesota over its northern two-thirds.

Unlike the other three states, however, Iowa suffers from a relative out-migration of population, so its cultural patterns have not been disturbed by any radical changes in the state's demographic base in recent years. Since population patterns, including the pattern of population change, are so uniform in Iowa, even urbanization and metropolitanization appear to have had little disruptive effect on the state's political culture.[9] One result of this even development has been to smooth over the original differences among the state's people; hence there is no sharp cleavage between political cultures, even in the case of the eastern cities such as Davenport. The cultural differences that lie at the root of the uniqueness of the "State of Scott" are primarily differences in general rather than political culture. The Iowa case clearly reveals the separation between the two.

Iowa has been the most solidly Republican of the five states, as well as the most regular of them all; though it seems to be sharing in the transition to a competitive two-party system that has been general in the Upper Midwest since the end of World War II. Beginning its political history as a two-party state with Democratic leanings, the influx of Yankees and Scandinavians opened it to conversion to Republican dominance when that party made its appearance on the scene. At the same time, pockets of Democratic strength reflecting the political ties of other immigrants remained which, in times of crisis or general discontent, could attract sufficient support from other elements in the state to gain occasional statewide victories. While the farmers' revolts of the late nineteenth and early twentieth centuries periodically generated third-party movements that drew away enough Republican strength to place the issue in doubt in certain gubernatorial elections, the state's basic conservatism prevented the development of significant, ongoing third-party movements such as those which appeared in Wisconsin and Minnesota.

The demographic composition of the Davenport civil community could well have been conducive to the development of a third-party movement. In fact, in the generation before World War I, several of the national or regional third parties entered unsuccessful candidates in the Davenport city elections. However, Iowa's general resistance to third-party movements made the local efforts seem futile, and no third party was able to remain politically alive for more than two elections. Scott County was forced to assert its difference from the rest of Iowa before 1918 by periodically voting Democratic in statewide elections counter to the general Republican tide. After American intervention against Germany in World War I alienated the German-descended Democratic voters of Davenport (many of whom had voted Socialist when the one or two serious opportunities to do so presented themselves) from their previous party ties, the absence of any alternative led the county into the Republican fold, at least nominally, until Prohibition and the Depression shook many of them loose once again. Since 1952, Scott County has again asserted its individuality by giving its votes to the Democratic candidate for governor while supporting the Republican candidate for the presidency.

Davenport's goal in seeking a measure of local autonomy is not to preserve an ostensibly higher (or to maintain a lower) standard of political morality. Its residents' conception of politics does not appear to be appreciably different from that of most Iowans. Its aim is to be able to maintain a less puritanical way of life.

Iowa's general culture is the embodiment of the erstwhile rural outlook often described as Midwestern American puritan. Among the characteristics of this culture is a heavy emphasis on the maintenance of public morality regarding such matters as liquor and sex. As a result, Iowa's citizens tend to support a high level of state and local regulatory action in those realms. Issues of public morality invariably become politically important because of the state's general cultural predispositions and the conflicts that may be generated by them.

Perhaps the most burning point of political contention between Davenport and Scott County on one side and the state of Iowa on the other is the liquor issue. The state, long a Prohibitionist stronghold, until 1963 prohibited the public sale of "hard" liquor by the glass at any time and the public sale of spirits in any form on Sunday. Davenport, with its European and particularly Germanic background, is emphatically not prohibitionist and does not like to be restricted in this way. Since no such restrictions obtain in the Illinois cities just across the river, Davenport is additionally constrained to oppose the state law in order to meet its competition. Since Scott County has never had the political strength to have the laws changed, it has devised various ways to circumvent them. In the days before sale of liquor by the drink was legalized, one of the most useful was the "private club." Taverns (which could sell beer legally) and restaurants become "private clubs," able to sell liquor to their "membership," broadly defined, of course. In less fashionable surroundings even this rigamarole is dispensed with, and hard drinks are sold directly over the counter.

The local police have made it a point not to enforce the state law unless the taverns violate the unwritten mores of the civil community. Though the residents of Davenport want to enjoy the right to lift a glass in public, they do not appreciate the free and easy ways of Rock Island, at least not for Davenport. There are unwritten but well understood limits to illegal sales of liquor, which are enforced. When Davenporters wish for a more exciting evening, they go across the river, where they can find whatever they are looking for. Their political leaders are convinced that they like it just that way.

Periodically Scott County's semipublic flaunting of state law publicly raises the eyebrows of the Iowa legislators. It is this aspect of the state-local relationship (coupled with the city high school's athletic prowess) that has led to the appellation "State of Scott" being bestowed on the metropolitan area. Occasionally a state administration seeking either reform or political credit will intervene to enforce the law, to the disgust and anguish of the local residents. The city is then closed down temporarily, but such waves of reform do pass and things return to their previous state.

The political leadership of Davenport can make common cause with political leaders from Iowa's other Mississippi River towns which share the same "liberal" heritage on issues involving government regulation of private morality and with the political leadership of the state's other medium-size civil communities on issues involving urban interests. Thus Davenport is not really isolated from its state in matters of politics. While in neither case does the combination command a majority position in the state, both represent considerable minorities with many crossties which reduce intrastate divisions to manageable proportions.

The Iowans' attitudes toward government provision of public services is more ambiguous. While committed through its basically moralistic political culture to the use of public authority to achieve communitarian goals, Iowa's rural biases and relatively recent urbanization have functioned until recently to keep the expression of that communitarianism local and, frequently, nongovernmental. Until the mid-1960's, positive state government action in the realm of public services was kept to a minimum with the state granting the option of action to its local communities in a number of specific fields. Thus Iowa has a record that places it close to the bottom among the states in state financial support of public education while, at the same time, it has one of the very best records of literacy and maintains an acknowledged high level of educational achievement. Public education is very important in the Iowa scheme of things; it is considered a means for democratic salvation as it is wherever the moralistic political culture is dominant. The first public schools in Iowa were founded—with public support—when it was still part of Michigan Territory, and public high schools came early to the state. Modeled after the New England system from the first, education has continued to enjoy strong public support but primarily through local financing.

Another way in which Iowa's political culture is tempered by its rural outlook that is only now diminishing is a certain statewide hesitancy to embrace federal aid programs directed to the cities, perhaps because they symbolize and concretize the facts of urbanization in the state. Though Iowa does not share the kind of antifederal bias common in the South and has easily accepted federal aid programs tailored for an agricultural society in the past, even the people in its cities were not particularly interested in the urban programs until the "Great Society" came along.

Coupled with this rather conservative rural orientation is a genteel system of "courthouse circle" politics, particularly in the southern third of the state and in the most rural areas, that has encouraged a certain amount of professionalization in Iowa political life, to a greater extent than in Minnesota but to a much lesser extent than in Illinois. This system also makes allowance for a certain amount of personal economic gain through political means, provided the professionals' economic gain conforms to the local standards of public (not business) morality in each community and is kept local. By and large, the kind of "professionalism" involved in those communities combines political specialization with widespread interpersonal ties locally, of the kind described by Vidich and Bensman.[10] The system has encouraged party regularity since the parties serve as means to hold together perennial office-seekers as well as vehicles for the expression of different positions on public concerns.

Nevertheless, positions on public concerns are of some importance in Iowa partisan politics, and the system does leave considerable room for amateurs to participate fully in the party organizations. Many "amateurs" or semiprofessionals are active in all parts of the state, but they are particularly strong in the rising urban and metropolitan centers. Indeed there is good reason to believe that, as Iowa becomes increasingly urbanized, the role of the amateurs is becoming more important. This would be quite in line with the general tenor of the moralistic political culture and very likely represents a contemporary manifestation of what took place earlier in Minnesota and Colorado. As in Colorado, in particular, as time goes on the professional politicians find themselves increasingly limited to county politics or to lower echelon positions in the state service. This is much the case in Davenport, where there was apparently greater room for professionals in the past than at present.

The ability of professionals and amateurs to work together in Iowa is some indication that the state apparently has not suffered the political trauma that occurred in Illinois. Even where politics is in the hands of courthouse gangs, the essential political tradition in the state is that of the Yankee and northern European streams modified by those of the Middle States and western Europe. Politicians in the state, of whatever stripe, know what is expected of them in the way of public responsibility, even when they fail to live up to expectations.

Iowa's moralistic conservatism is reflected in Davenport's internal politics, particularly in that civil community's conservative approach to governmental structural change. The city of Davenport has been governed by a weak mayor-aldermanic system since its incorporation. The development of extralegal centers of political power and community leadership has enabled this system to continue to function over the years and adjust to changing times. It is an eminently political system in a civil community that accepts the role of politics in dealing with political questions and the possibilities of using political mechanisms to arrive at solutions that reflect the public interest as they define it.

During the periods of nationwide interest in civic reform, suggestions have been made within Davenport to change the structure of city government by adopting one of the more "modern" systems currently in the public eye. Partly out of a conservatism reinforced by the civil community's oligarchic system of control, partly from satisfaction with the existing system, and partly out of the conviction that any reforms that need to be made can be made within the civil community's traditional constitution, all such suggestions have been rejected to date, usually by the civic leadership, before they can gain enough momentum to be put on the ballot.

Political Culture and Ethnic Cleavage in Wisconsin[11]

The currents that shaped Wisconsin were primarily northern, whether American or European. One of the most ethnically mixed of all the states, as in Minnesota, its immigrants from overseas settled much of the state directly upon arrival on these shores and prior to any other settlers. Moreover, they came as highly visible ethnic groups, most with great cultural self-assurance.

Wisconsin's first European settlers, the French, settled along the state's major waterways. They were notably uninterested in assimilating to an "Anglo-Saxon" culture. The Yankees, the first Americans to arrive, concentrated first in the state's southern reaches but, as Wisconsin's land frontier was slowly pushed back, they spread all over the state. German Protestants and Catholics settled in Wisconsin's eastern half, where they actively endeavored to preserve their language and culture, often through their religious institutions (Wisconsin is a stronghold of both Catholic and Lutheran schools, most of which emphasized the German language until World War I). Irish, Polish, Slavic, and Italian people followed the Germans into the same parts of the state and were encouraged by their environment to retain their ethnic consciousness. The Scandinavians, predominantly Norwegians and Danes, settled in northwestern and central Wisconsin to create the state's most visibly distinct political region while the Swiss created a small society of their own in the hills and valleys of the unglaciated southwest. Southerners in some numbers settled the state's far southwestern tip, drawn originally by the lead mines. As the different ethnic groups scattered to all parts of the state, they carried their Old World ideas with them, even when they gave up Old World customs, to create a checkerboard of cultures within the American consensus.

The sense of communal responsibility that was part of the mainstream culture of Wisconsin's dominant migratory currents has become rooted in the political culture of the state and in most of its civil communities. The moralistic political culture is dominant in Wisconsin but, with the exception of a few small pockets, even those groups which fall within the range of the individualistic political culture share a strong commitment to (or at least an acceptance of) activist government because of their particular Old World backgrounds. In such a political environment, Superior does not have to isolate itself from the state's political system. As in Minnesota, the state itself serves as a protective barrier that helps to prevent the intrusion of "alien" influences into the civil community.

This does not mean that Wisconsin is free of serious intrastate cleavages or that state-local conflicts do not exist. While most of those that do exist are based on disagreements over specific programs, or administrative and fiscal issues, there is also an element of culture conflict involved, based, as it were, on differing conceptions of what "communal responsibility" should mean.

The regional cleavages that developed from the state's pattern of geoethnic settlement have carried over into politics. The center of agrarian progressivism has been in the basically Scandinavian and Protestant northwest, which extends in ethnic terms down through the Madison area. Socialism has been locked in combat with conservatism in the predominantly German southeast. The strongly Catholic northeast has been the bastion of isolationism and ultraconservatism, the home ground of the late Senator Joseph McCarthy, the German-American Bund, and the John Birch Society. Political individualism flourishes in the far southwest. These regional political cleavages are ethnic and ideological and hence deeper in Wisconsin than in any of the other four states (excepting perhaps the social-psychological Chicago-downstate cleavage in Illinois).

The party division in Wisconsin was an even sharper reflection of a basic cultural cleavage between the original Yankee settlers who came to the state as Whigs and later became Republicans and the Germans who arrived on their heels and generally attached themselves to the Democrats. The former were substantially reinforced by the Scandinavians and the latter by the Slavs. For a number of years, political protest movements, which came frequently in Wisconsin, were either channeled through the dominant Republican party or into the Democratic party, mobilizing the latter's latent strength and giving it some temporary victories. However, the Yankee and Scandinavian farmers in Wisconsin encountered problems of geography, soil, and climate unlike those encountered in fertile Iowa. Political palliatives did not help them as easily, so they became increasingly radical. Their views were echoed with increasing frequency by the socialists located in the state's urban areas and primarily of German descent. Perhaps, because of the conflict between national party regularity and the penchant for progressive action on the state level, Wisconsonians have shown greater willingness to split their tickets along state and national party lines than any of the five states, having done so in eight elections. When the more radical elements in the state no longer felt that the two-party system could satisfy their demands, they bolted both parties and created a more or less continuing third-party movement. Before the twentieth century, these third parties could not mobilize enough support statewide to do much more than cut into the margins of Republican victories or to allow the minority Democratic party to gain office. By the 1920's and 1930's, however, the original tradition of Republicanism was sufficiently weakened to allow charismatic leaders to develop a temporarily successful third party known as the Progressive party at the state level. The period of Progressive party success came to an end with the death of Wisconsin isolationism after World War II. It was followed by a massive realignment of party strength as the younger Progressives moved into the Democratic party that ultimately led to the emergence of a Democratic majority in state politics.

State government in Wisconsin has acted more frequently and with greater effect than in any of the other states, excepting perhaps Minnesota. Wisconsin has a long and distinguished record as an innovative state, a pioneer in the development of government regulation of public utilities and government-sponsored public services. Despite the Yankee localism of its birth, it is a state that has gone further toward centralizing regulatory and social services than all but a handful in the nation. Consequently, the pattern of state-local relations is rather highly centralized. By legislative authorization state agencies are charged with stimulating and encouraging local action often according to some form of statewide plan, in a wide variety of fields. In many cases, local administration is allowed until such time as it appears that an overriding statewide interest requires more direct state intervention.

Partisan political organization in Wisconsin stands somewhere between Colorado's and Minnesota's in character and orientation. As in Minnesota, agricultural and labor organizations represent a large segment of the population and furnish an even larger share of the nonprofessional political actives, particularly for the Democratic party. Wisconsin's large number of small nonmetropolitan cities are a breeding ground of nonprofessional political participants for the Republican party. Statewide the parties are much less "profit-making businesses" and more agglomerations of interests and ideas. When they occasionally lapse from the latter standard, there always lurk reformers in the wings ready to step in and return them to what Wisconsonians consider "the straight and narrow."

In sum, the bundle of values colloquially known as "good government" represents the essence of the political culture of Wisconsin, a state with a national reputation for "good government" and progressivism for better than two generations. Professional politicians must share party leadership with amateurs whose interests revolve around matters of principle, and state action in a variety of fields is the norm. While certain of these values are challenged from time to time by geo-ethnic dissident elements, they remain of statewide concern, a reflection of the influence of the northern currents, particularly those of western and northern Europe.

Superior's position in this framework is somewhat similar to Duluth's position within the Minnesota civil society; however, the Wisconsin city is even farther removed from the centers of its state's economic and political life and is far less important among the state's cities. Isolated from the Wisconsin heartland by miles of virtual wilderness, its relations with the state government are clearly affected by its detachment from the mainstream of Wisconsin life. Its residents chronically complain of neglect at the hands of the state government. Regardless of the justice of this claim, it seems clear that Wisconsin's economic and commercial interests lie in the development of its Lake Michigan coast and southern interior communities as permanent concentrations of population and industry while reserving the northern half of the state for tourism and outdoor recreation. This, of course, leaves Superior in just the position it finds itself—a declining commercial center with little to support its declining population and few prospects for improvement. The areas of closest cooperation between the Superior civil community and the state are those involving the promotion of tourism and outdoor recreation. At the same time, Superior does remain the undisputed urban center of Wisconsin's northland. This means that the regional offices of state agencies and regional state institutions such as the state college are located there, providing economic benefits and encouraging political ties that might otherwise be absent.

Douglas County has been turning in close to two-to-one majorities for Democratic candidates at least since the late 1940's, to become perhaps the most solidly Democratic county in the state. At the same time, the Superior Democrats and their counterparts in the rest of northwestern Wisconsin do not share the outlook of the socialist-and-organized labor Democrats of Milwaukee and the urbanized southeastern sections of the state but remain the heirs of the populist-progressive tradition, which is essentially middle class and agrarian. The differences between the two groups have led to intraparty cleavages within Democratic ranks as in the case of the 1960 presidential primary when northwestern Wisconsin supported Hubert Humphrey and the southeast supported John F. Kennedy. They continue to be reflected in the personalities of the party's leadership.

Since Superior residents share the same political culture that is dominant in the rest of the state, there are no barriers to state-local collaboration from that angle. Indeed, when Superior was still a major city in the state, during the Progressive years, it contributed its share of statewide leaders, through the Progressive party. Its mayor at the time of this study was one such old Progressive who was once a leader in the state party organization and a close friend of Senator Phillip LaFollette. A registered Republican since the demise of the Progressive party, his ability to win election as mayor in Wisconsin's strongest Democratic bastion is testimony to the continuing Progressive sympathies of Superior's population.

Superior's recent internal politics is suggestive of the role its particular branch of the state's political culture may play in maintaining a certain degree of tension with other components of the state system. In 1958, as one aspect of its response to the urban revolution of the 1950's, Superior voted to abandon council-manager government and return to the mayor-aldermanic system. The overt reason for the abandonment was that the mayor-aldermanic system would be less expensive by obviating the necessity to pay a full-time professional city manager (something of a reverse "efficiency and economy" argument for municipal reform).

It is likely that city-manager government, which is very popular in lower Wisconsin because it offers "orderliness" even at the expense of popular political control, had been originally adopted in Superior in response to a statewide trend. When dissatisfaction with the system's apolitical tendencies, particularly among the labor groups, was coupled with the desire to economize fostered in the business community, the system was defeated with relative ease. Having no fear of "rascals" infiltrating a more political form of city government, the residents of Superior had no objection to restoring the mayor-aldermanic system. In this respect Superior may have a more positive commitment to the old Progressive idea of popular government than many civil communities in other parts of Wisconsin.

NOTES

1. The eight variables included here are but a few "tracers." For a fuller analysis of statistically measurable interstate differences, see Thomas R. Dye and Brett W. Hawkins, eds., *Politics in the Metropolis* (Columbus: Merrill, 1967).

2. Analyses of the Dye data by Ira Sharkansky in *The Utility of Elazar's Designations of Political Culture: A Research Note*, unpublished paper, University of Georgia (January 1968), reveal both the regional ties and the state by state differences for the fifty states. Their respective analyses, though involving different methodologies and somewhat different questions, support the theses advanced in Part One of this book while also demonstrating that, in the last analysis, each state is significantly unique.

3. Minnesota has been exceptionally well studied by political historians and political scientists. The reader interested in further exploration of that state may well begin with the following works: Federal Writers' Project, *Minnesota: A State Guide* (New York: Viking Press, 1938); William W. Folwell, *A History of Minnesota* (St. Paul: Minnesota Historical Society, 1921–1930), 4 vols.; William Anderson and Edward W. Weidner, "Intergovernmental Relations in the United States as observed in the State of Minnesota." (A series of ten monographs published by the University of Minnesota Press); G. Theodore Mitau, *Politics in Minnesota* (Minneapolis: University of Minnesota Press, 1960); and John Borchert, *Minnesota's Changing Geography* (Minneapolis: University of Minnesota Press, 1960). The publications of the Minnesota Historical Society, including its quarterly journal, *Minnesota History*, are excellent sources of first-rate political studies.

4. For a fuller discussion of this, see Daniel J. Elazar, "Constitutional Change in a Long-Depressed Civil Economy: A Case Study of the Duluth Civil Community," *Proceedings of the Minnesota Academy of Science*, XXXIII (1965).

5. Theodore Mitau, *Politics in Minnesota* (Minneapolis: University of Minnesota Press, 1960), p. 42.

6. Lincoln Steffens describes such a situation in Minneapolis at the turn of the century in *The Shame of the Cities* (New York: McClure, Phillips, 1904). The differences between "boss rule" there and in the other cities he studied which he describes—often unwittingly—are most revealing of the differences in political culture between Minnesota and other states.

7. The literature on the politics of Colorado is considerably more limited than in the case of Illinois and Minnesota. Among the items that are available and of some value are: Federal Writers' Project *Illinois* (Chicago: A. C. McClurg, 1939) and *Minnesota* (New York: Viking Press, 1938); Leroy R. and Ann W. Hafen, *Colorado* (Denver, Colo.: Old West Publishing Co., 1952); Carl Ubbelohde, *A Colorado History* (Boulder: Pruett Press, 1965); and Roy E. Brown, "Colorful Colorado: The State of Varied Industries," in Thomas C. Donnelly, ed., *Rocky Mountain Politics* (Albuquerque: University of New Mexico Press, 1940). *Colorado, The Yearbook of the State of Colorado*, published biennially by the State Planning Commission is more than a statistical compendium, containing, as it does, useful features on government and politics in the State. John Gunther's chapter on Colorado in *Inside USA* is quite useful for the immediate postwar period.

8. Since the civil communities of this study located in Iowa and Wisconsin are treated primarily because of their relationship to civil communities in Illinois and Minnesota, the treatment of their statewide environment is purposely held to a minimum. Further information on Iowa politics and political history can be found in Federal Writers' Project, *Iowa: A Guide to the Hawkeye State* (New York: Viking, 1938); The State Historical Society of Iowa, "Iowa Centennial History," Series; and Russell M. Ross, *The Government and Administration of Iowa* (New York: Thomas Y. Crowell, 1957).

9. Harlan Hahn, *Urban-Rural Transition: The Iowa Case* (unpublished doctoral dissertation, Harvard University, 1964), relates urbanization to the political and social variables of concern in this study, including cultural and migrational data, to offer useful background material for identifying the patterns of politics and settlement in Iowa.

10. Arthur J. Vidich and Joseph Bensman, *Small Town in Mass Society* (Princeton, N.J.: Princeton University Press, 1958).

11. Wisconsin has had an active university and historical society for better than three generations, and much material relevant to the study of its political life is available. The best comprehensive sources for a brief exploration are: Federal

Writers' Project, *Wisconsin: A Guide to the Badger State* (New York: Duell, Sloan and Pearce, 1941) and Leon D. Epstein, *Politics in Wisconsin* (Madison: University of Wisconsin Press, 1958). See also Fred L. Holmes, *Old World Wisconsin* (Eau Claire, Wis.: E. M. Hale and Co., 1944) for a picture of the state's ethnic composition, virtually county by county.

PART III

CITIES, STATES, AND NATION

Chapter 9 / The Cities of the Prairie and the American Partnership

Civil Community and Civil Society

THE CITIES of the prairie, as civil communities, possess reasonably complex and actively functioning political systems of their own. Some of those complexities and their sources were explored in Parts One and Two. Nevertheless, it would be a distortion to view them or their political systems as autonomous. The casual civics student knows that local governments are creatures of the state and that the states are linked in union under a federal government whose influence is widespread and whose hand is felt in the local community in many ways. It is equally misleading to view local political systems as limited to a particular sphere by the state and federal governments but otherwise autonomous within that sphere. Since the founding of the Republic, operations in the American federal system have been predominantly cooperative, involving the sharing of functions by all planes of government in partnership, a mode which has avoided either separation of functions by level or system or centralization of power in the national government. This system of collaboration has been the norm, ideological pronouncements to the contrary notwithstanding. The dynamic character of American society has so mitigated against anything other than collaboration between governments and levels that periodic attempts to force disengagement have all ended in failure.[1] Thus the civil communities are part of larger and more complex political systems which impinge upon them "every day in every way" (and which they impinge upon in turn) to the point where neat separation of activities is existentially impossible and theoretically inaccurate.

Nor is it possible to accept this integration of activities, acknowledge its existence, and then proceed to ignore it in studying particular local political systems. While it is possible to explore local polities as real entities within the larger systems, the exploration must be conducted in a manner that accounts for the influence of the larger systems upon them. Under the American system of government, each state, as well as the nation, possesses its own political system as part of its general social order. The states and the nation may be characterized as "civil societies"; relatively complex social entities which encompass a wide variety of social and economic interests, organized politically, charged with considerable responsibility for satisfying the needs of their citizens, and capable of authoritatively mobilizing the resources necessary to do so sufficiently well for their own continued maintenance. Their "wholeness" (or, in the case of semi-sovereign states in a federal system, their potential wholeness) in this regard distinguishes them from the civil communities, which, as local systems, are quite limited in their complexity and in their ability to maintain themselves autonomously.[2] Though the civil community cannot be autonomous, it remains the essential building block in the constitution of civil societies. One of the central questions in the relationship between civil communities and the civil societies of which they are a part is the extent to which the former can formulate and execute policy or influence the formulation and execution of policies which determine their future.[3]

Every civil community, then, is located within a civil society which is capable of supplying those things which it cannot supply alone. Civil communities in the United States are located in two civil societies simultaneously, each of which places certain demands on the community and also satisfies certain of its needs. This arrangement linking semi-separate systems exists and thrives despite the great intermeshing of the actual functions of government. The fact that this system of systems functions cooperatively does not lessen the structural discreteness or independent policy-making functions of its constituent entities. While the active participants in the governmental process can often barely see the separation between communities, societies, and functions, the observer looking at the process as a whole can see the distinct effects of that separation in every case.

The existence of two governmental complexes which impinge on the civil community often makes life confusing, and not only at the local level. For the civil community, however, it is both a limiting factor and an opportunity. The civil community can frequently gain greater influence over matters which affect it by playing one government against the other or by using one to gain influence over the other.

Such opportunities are enhanced by the American predilection for the values linked with local government. One basic premise of American politics is that the promotion of freedom is possible only by limiting the power of government, primarily vis-à-vis the individual. As a corollary, it is widely believed that where government is necessary, it is best controlled by being kept local or at least subject to a great deal of local control. Thus a rarely challenged hierarchy of "goods" has developed, beginning with a preference for individual nongovernmental action, followed by a preference for local governmental action, then by a willingness to accept state and federal action if the localities retain a substantial amount of influence over their activities. Public debate on the role of government is generally directed to questions of how to translate these principles into action.

The history of governmental activity in this country belies the common assumption that this hierarchy of values has always been used as an actual model for determining when or how the various planes of government should act. Federal and state initiative has generally been required to stimulate most local governments to take action to meet specific problems.[4] But even when the values of the American political consensus are transcended by pragmatic considerations, they remain a powerful source of leverage for civil communities to use. Perhaps because of a widespread reluctance to betray those values or perhaps simply out of a desire to hold to them as much as possible in the face of the upsetting demands of reality, federal and state programs have been developed in a manner calculated to give as much discretion and influence to the local authorities as possible. This desire for decentralization of state and federal programs is strongly reinforced by a generally noncentralized political system which gains many advantages from the maintenance of maximum local control. Consequently, the civil community that has energetic and aggressive leadership is put in a good position to capitalize on the system.[5]

The Universality of Public Concerns

Historically, the need for collaboration between federal, state, and local governments has been generated by the emergence of frontier-created problems which stem from a universality of experience that to some meaningful extent transcends the country's very real sectional and subcultural differences. The common concerns ancillary to the advancing frontier in the nineteenth century included the planning and execution of a program of migration, settlement, and development of the frontier regions; the promotion of public education to create a literate citizenry capable of maintaining the system of self-government inaugurated by the founders of the nation; the development of an adequate system of internal communication to bind the far frontiers of the nation to its centers and to simultaneously encourage greater access to those frontiers; the development of an economic system and technology that could be used to conquer the land frontier and exploit its riches; and the solution of the problems of slavery and secession which were aggravated by the impact of the newly settled frontier on the older sections. In each of these areas, specific problems arose which made demands on the political systems of nation, state, and civil community.[6]

In the middle of the twentieth century, the metropolitan-technological frontier has promoted a similar set of demands on the country's several political systems: the planning and execution of a settlement, housing, and development program for the metropolitan area; the enrichment of public education to develop a citizenry with the social and technical skills required to cope with the problems of a highly complex society; the development of an even more elaborate system of internal communication to meet the pressures of population growth, urbanization and metropolitanization, and defense; the expansion of our economic system to embrace the new technologies, to meet the problems of international discord and competition, and to continue the conquest and exploitation of physical frontiers now beginning to extend beyond the earth itself; and the refinement of our social system to provide greater equality for the descendants of the slaves and other deprived elements while maintaining the noncentralized system of government of our traditional constitution.

In some way, these common concerns have confronted all political systems at roughly the same time. In some form, every American civil community has had to confront the problems of land settlement, urbanization, and metropolitanization as they have presented themselves in the American context. Moreover, from the outset, the simple fact of location at a specific period in time and in a specific segment of American space has determined much of the specific agenda of every civil community. Thus the cities of the East Coast have had to deal with these three problems before their sisters to the south and west and, hence, under somewhat different conditions.

Consequently, it is not surprising to find that the cities of the prairie have been faced with the well-nigh universal public concerns that have emerged to confront American cities in the half-generation since the opening of the metropolitan frontier, conditioned by the particular geohistorical factors of their region and shaped by certain elements of scale. One of the factors which characterizes the medium-size civil communities is the profusion of public concerns found within their limits. In fact, they appear to share the same profusion of concerns as their larger sisters. The smaller civil communities in the same metropolitan areas share somewhat fewer concerns, indicating that at some point size has an effect upon the range of community concerns.[7] Apparently a community must be large enough to support a sufficient variety of "specialists" who are sufficiently concerned with specific issues to raise them publicly. Once a community reaches that level of complexity, however, size increments do not cause new issues to be raised so much as they add to the expression of the same ones.

The chief issues to be found confronting the cities of the prairie can be categorized as follows. In their specifics, almost all are new—reflections of new forms of settlement such as metropolitanism and its urban ghetto byproducts, new technological developments such as the automobile and cybernetics, new social problems arising from the impact of the foregoing phenomena, or economic concerns that arise because of changing settlement patterns and technological demands. Yet almost all of these public concerns can be traced back to the universal experiences which have been the sources of public concern in the United States from the days of the first frontier.

1. Issues relating to the long-range economic and physical development of the civil community to enable it to share in the advances of the metropolitan frontier, concretely manifested in such questions as:

a. The institutionalization of efforts to promote economic development through governmental agencies or public nongovernmental agencies with government cooperation.
b. The promotion of better highway, particularly freeway, connections with the outside world.
c. The construction and improvement of airports and aviation service.
d. The improvement or renovation of business districts, particularly the central business district.
e. The improvement of traffic control and local streets to enable them to handle the expanded flow of traffic, and the development of necessary parking facilities.
f. The maintenance of public transportation within the community.
g. Urban renewal, neighborhood redevelopment and conservation.
h. The maintenance and improvement of zoning regulations.
i. The adoption or improvement of the various building codes.
j. The promulgation and enforcement of regulations for the proper construction of new subdivisions.
k. The development of professionalized planning agencies.
l. The extension of city services to newly settled suburban areas.

2. Issues relating to the long-range social and cultural improvement of the civil community and economic advancement of its residents created by frontier-generated demands, concretely manifested in such questions as:

a. The expansion and upgrading of local educational systems.
b. The development or expansion of higher education facilities.
c. The upgrading of community welfare services.
d. The provision of health, recreation, and housing services for the aging.
e. The provision of supervised recreation and guidance activities for youth.
f. The initiation of concern for problems of mental health.
g. The advancement of the scope of public health activities (including the fluoridation issue).
h. The expansion of local park systems and their facilities.
i. The development or expansion of public cultural (theatrical, orchestral, artistic) and recreation programs.
j. Perhaps most important of all in the end, the emergence of concern with the problems of intergroup relations, particularly the provision of more equal housing, employment, and social opportunities for nonwhites.

3. Issues relating to changes in the structure of local government to accommodate frontier-generated changes in the scope and functions of the local political system, concretely manifested in such questions as:

a. Changing the forms of city government (as from mayor-aldermanic to council-manager government).
b. The realignment of existing political boundaries (as through annexation) to take into account recent population shifts.
c. The creation of special purpose districts (airport districts, recreation commissions, port authorities, sanitary districts, and the like) to provide new services.
d. The creation of special agencies within existing governments (planning commissions, housing authorities, traffic departments, civil defense agencies and the like) to handle new governmental tasks.
e. The formation of areawide governments or councils of governments, either general or for specific purposes, to serve metropolitan populations.
f. Increasing the level of professionalization in local administrative agencies.

4. Issues generated by the advancing urbanization and mechanization of society generally and the metropolitan civil communities in particular, concretely manifested in such questions as:

a. Improvement of the quality, standards, and facilities of fire and police protection.
b. Development of improved or additional sources of water supply.
c. Regulation of sewage disposal in local waterways.
d. Control of air pollution in its most gross manifestations.
e. Regulation of Sunday sales by local merchants.
f. Passage of ordinances requiring the leashing of dogs in public places.
g. Maintenance and general esthetic enhancement of the local environment.

5. Recurrences of the perennial issues that confront American communities in much the same form regardless of time and place, particularly such questions as:

a. Provision of adequate revenues for governmental expenditures.
b. Control of governmental corruption.
c. Maintenance of the symbolic activities that provide the basis for community identification such as parades, festivals, and celebrations.
d. Liquor and narcotics control.
e. Control of vice, particularly gambling and prostitution.

While all of the foregoing matters figured among the public concerns of the cities of the prairie in the fifteen or eighteen years before 1962, not all were of equal prominence in the public eye and certainly not all were of equal importance. The very length of the list raises the question as to what constitutes a public concern. Some might argue that a number of items included on it are not legitimately "public concerns" since they were not translated into issues which attracted substantial public attention or which involved major segments of those assumed to be "influentials." Quite clearly, the simple cataloguing of concerns is no indication of the attention given each within the context of any specific political system, and it need hardly be said that the importance of any concern depends on who is concerned, when, and how. Contemporary students of local politics have generally singled out those concerns that provoke overt conflict or wide popular interest as the important ones "by definition." This definition of what is important is particularly widespread among those social scientists seeking to measure the relative power or influence of different individuals or groups. This has the deleterious effect of limiting attention to those concerns which can provoke public attention because of their "visibility," ignoring the very real possibility that a concern which can capture public attention or even the attention of a majority of the articulate elements in the civil community may well be of only transient interest or importance while a less visible concern may be crucial in its long-range effects on the community's sociopolitical system.

Thus, in Champaign in 1962, the question of whether to require dog owners to leash their pets when taking them outside their own yards received more public attention than any other issue to confront that civil community in those years, save that of imposing a local utility tax. The city council engaged in a "great debate" over the issue, which was avidly followed by citizens who appeared before the council in person and by the press. The "letters to the editor" columns of the local newspapers were flooded with correspondence on the subject, including a sharp exchange on the Biblical view of dogs (whether they were not really unclean animals proscribed by the Bible and thus deserving of regulation by the City of Champaign) and another between lovers of dogs ("How can I leash my pooch who has always roamed free and still retain his affection?") and lovers of children ("My child was nearly mauled last week by a wandering canine.").

While this issue was being considered with such popular fervor, the city planning commission was engaged in a controversy with the mayor, city council, and certain local developers over the propriety of reducing the space requirements per unit specified in the local zoning ordinance for high-rise apartment buildings to be erected near the central business district, ostensibly to make it possible for the developers to construct apartment buildings to house the community's aging. This controversy involved some of the more influential citizens in town (by any standard of measurement of influence currently in use) since it concerned the setting of standards that would very likely determine the pattern of residential development near downtown Champaign for the immediate future. Though it was covered by the local press, it received little or no public attention outside of immediately involved circles.

Even less public attention was accorded to a third event that occurred at the same time, the initiation of action by a small group of citizens interested in improving the job opportunities of local Negroes who had otherwise displayed little interest in local politics and could not be said to have possessed any significant amount of political influence except that accruing to them by virtue of the cause they represented. Even the "influentials" paid it scant attention, except for a brief period when some downtown stores were picketed.

All three of these events reflect local public concerns. The first, reflecting one aspect of Champaign's effort to come to grips with its recent growth into medium size, involved a large number of citizens for a relatively brief time whose public concern was hardly more than a multiplication of their private concerns over the leashing of dogs. The second event involved men whose public and private concerns are so closely intertwined that they are regularly and perennially involved in public issues of this sort. The third event represented but one stage in the efforts of a group of citizens who, by all current measures, were far from the seats of influence. Their public concern had only rarely entered the realm of public controversy in the cities of the prairie and has attracted the attention of the "influentials" only when forced upon them through the most extreme public pressures. Whatever success they have, they owe as much to the march of events outside the civil community as to their own efforts locally; yet they, too, by virtue of their translation of a general trend into local terms, are reflecting a public concern just as much as the briefly enraged citizenry or the continually active influentials.

Judging the "significance" of public concerns such as these requires something more than the usual measurements of "community power." Five years later, the leash-law controversy had disappeared into the limbo of historical curiosa, while the zoning decision has had some important medium-range consequences, though the issue itself has been reconsidered in one form or another again and again. On the other hand, the successful integration of the employees in a handful of downtown stores was the first step in a major drive to redefine the place of the Negro minority in the civil community, one which could only lead to major changes in its social structure. If history is any guide, the latter act will be viewed someday as a decisive milestone in the mid-twentieth century reconstitution of Champaign as a community. Furthermore, while all three concerns can be found nationwide—many communities just grown into cities have been confronted with the leash-law question, and this type of zoning problem appears ubiquitously and perennially—only the last was truly historical in a national as well as local sense.

The list of public concerns is accordingly a long one, based as it is on something more than the premise often implicit in community studies that community issues are limited to those which concern the business-bureaucratic-political elite and are accordingly most visible in the formal governmental activities of the civil community. It must include all those concerns which have constituencies and find expression through those public agencies or institutions, formally governmental or quasi-governmental, whose actions contribute to the total government of the civil community and have significant consequences in the continual shaping of its sociopolitical system. Identifying public concerns in this way requires a historical perspective and a sense of the larger whole so that proper distinctions can be drawn, particularly since what is of public concern in the civil community is a product of social influences so widespread that it must be of public concern in the civil societies as well. And what is of public concern in this country is also ultimately of governmental concern—on all planes.

The meaning of this approach to an understanding of public concerns must be reemphasized. That the local labor unions are more likely to be concerned with public welfare distributions handled by the county welfare department and may not be concerned with zoning decisions made by agencies of the city government does not mean that their concerns are not of equal public significance in the civil community. In fact, both are liable to have great long-range impact on the local sociopolitical system, though the paths of their impact may be substantially different. If the more specific question of the location of off-street parking lots on one or another nearly adjacent site in the central business district is compared with the concern over distribution of surplus commodities to the community's unemployed, it is likely that the latter is of greater significance in the long run than the former, even though the business-bureaucratic-political influentials who compete over parking lot locations because they stand to gain economically or politically from the decision show little or no interest in commodity distributions (which provide them with no visible gain) and dismiss those who are so concerned as peripheral to the central "power structure" of the community and, hence, to the community's central concerns.

The delineation of local public concerns is further enhanced by determining what local public action the concerns have stimulated. "Public action" in this context refers to positive observable action taken by some group or groups in the civil community in conjunction with governmental and public nongovernmental institutions (both local and extra-local) to deal with perceived local problems. Public action need not be "positive" action, in the sense of successful achievement of the aims of those taking the action. It may be the consideration of an urban renewal proposal and its rejection in a public referendum over a bond issue, as in Pueblo in 1961. It need not involve the mobilization of large segments of the community but, as in the case of the efforts to increase job opportunities for Negroes that were made not only in Champaign but in Springfield, Decatur, Peoria, and Joliet as well, it may mean intensive activity on the part of relatively small and otherwise "peripheral" groups. Public action need not be primarily government action. It may be the mobilization and operation of large numbers of volunteers, Boy Scouts, and the county medical association with the cooperation of county, state, and federal agencies to implement a mass polio immunization program, as in Champaign County in 1962. By the same token, sheer discussion of a problem, even by a local elite or by leaders in local government, without positive steps taken publicly in some form or public rejection of proposed courses of action cannot be considered to be "public action."

The wide range of public concerns in every civil community eliminates the likelihood of finding civil communities with neat bundles of political activity. It also renders the focus of attention on one local government, no matter how broad-gauged, something less than useful. Instead, it makes the concept of civil community as the bundle of public activities and services even more meaningful. Moreover, the broad range of public concerns means the heightened involvement of other planes of government in the activities of the civil community, since many of the groups responsible for the local expression of public concern in matters generally adjudged to be peripheral by the local influentials draw their inspiration and such influence as they possess from these extra-community sources.

What may be surprising to those who observe community political systems through the spectacles of today's "powerholders" is the frequency with which the actions of today's peripheral groups are the historically important ones. The situation of the Negroes is today's classic example of this fact. Two generations ago, public nongovernmental community welfare agencies were looked upon by the "influentials" of the day as peripheral manifestations of "do-goodism" by essentially powerless individuals. Yet it was the combined effort of community welfare agencies across the country preparing the way, even before the opportune moment provided by the Depression of the 1930's, that secured the enactment of federal and state public welfare programs after 1932. And it was this extra-community action which, when brought back to the local level whence it had originated that overturned the balance of political power in almost every civil community in the United States, forcing a whole series of local political realignments and role redefinitions, including the virtual elimination of the old-fashioned political boss. In the long run, the political revolution triggered by this coalition led to the assault on the division of American civil communities into "two cities" with all of its momentous consequences. It is now quite evident that these once "peripheral" actions and their consequences have been responsible for many aspects of the local revolutions of the past half-generation.[8]

The Historic Roots of the Partnership

From the beginning, American civil communities were limited corporations designed to handle certain local aspects of what were already universally felt concerns throughout their colonies and, very shortly, throughout the embryonic federation of states. They were not self-contained civil societies as were the city-states of the European continent that were later amalgamated into larger nation-states. Their social and economic interests were simply manifestations and variations of the larger interests of an expanding society faced with a seemingly limitless frontier to conquer. They had no opportunity to become parochial in the premodern sense since any parochialism on their part was a virtual guarantee of decline in an expanding society.

Actually, even the first urban civil communities of the United States are the direct or indirect products of a world-wide commerce and a modern technology. Their fate from the very beginning depended on markets in England, on African slave expeditions, and on agricultural production from the West Indies as well as the contributions of the American West, while their populations were always dominated by the spirit of transience and the real possibility of migration to "better" climes, rather than being bound by the commitment to place and tradition found in premodern cities. Contrary to the common mythology, since the last third of the eighteenth century at least, this country has had a national society based on a modern culture. This does not mean that all parts of the United States have always participated in this modern culture to the same degree or that a national society cannot live with subcultural and regional differences. What it does mean is that American society as a whole was founded on the economic, social, technological, and political principles of the post-medieval era, along lines which in Europe were only implanted upon a premodern base after a long struggle against the forces and patterns of medievalism and feudalism. Modernism, as such, was planted in virgin territory on North American shores at every point, to produce both the common ideas which became the foundation stones of the American persuasion and the social order in which those ideas were rooted.[9]

As American settlement moved westward, an increasing preoccupation with problems of internal development came to obscure public recognition of this international involvement, but the cities of the Trans-Appalachian West were no less products of modernism and universalism than their eastern counterparts. The cities of the prairie are cases in point. The American settlements in Madison and St. Clair Counties which, in 1816, were no more than villages on the far frontier were profoundly affected by the depression that hit Europe after the fall of Napoleon and cut off the markets for war-induced American grain surpluses. The growth of every one of the Illinois cities of the prairie was severely retarded for a decade or more as a result of the great national depression that followed the panic of 1837 and stopped the construction of the roads, canals, and railroads needed to promote commerce in the new west. Duluth was born, virtually died, and was reborn because of market manipulations in New York and London in the 1870's. And every one of the cities of the prairie was involved in interstate and even international commerce before it was fifteen years old.

Confronted with these universal interests, it is quite natural that all political systems should actively respond to them regardless of any finely spun webs of theory. Though the complexity and "velocity" of government (the amount of government activity relative to the total activity of society) have increased in our own day, there has never been a time when it was possible to put neat labels on separate "federal," "state," or "local" programs. Federal and state grants of land, money, and services have long stimulated local activity in fields where local governments have hesitated to act on their own resources alone. Direct federal and state activities in the civil community, ranging from river and harbor improvements to youth work with potential juvenile delinquents have supplemented local government efforts and have become expected parts of the "package" of government aids available to civil communities. Federal and state "government locally"—the post office, the state employment office—have become integral parts of the bundle of government activities included in the political system of every civil community.

Higher levels of government were substantially involved in the creation of the cities of the prairie. Belleville, Decatur, Springfield, and Urbana were established by the Illinois General Assembly to serve as seats of government for newly created counties and were first settled in order to serve that purpose. Davenport, Joliet, Peoria, Pueblo, Rockford, Rock Island, and Superior, though settled earlier, took form as cities only after—and coincident with—legislative designation as county seats. Of the latter, Davenport, Peoria, and Rock Island first originated to serve federal military posts established earlier as outposts of the advancing American frontier; Fort Peoria in 1813 and Fort Armstrong in 1816. Duluth and Superior were at least partly created to serve as termini for the Northern Pacific Railroad built with federal and federal-state land grants, while Champaign was established as a division point for the Illinois Central Railroad, a federal-state-private enterprise. Superior's original settlement was directly stimulated by the construction of the Soo Canal around the Sault Ste. Marie rapids three hundred miles to the east in 1855, a federal-state project which opened Lake Superior to larger vessels and made mining and lumbering along its shores profitable. Similarly, Joliet was a product of the construction of the Illinois and Michigan Canal, a major federal-state project of a decade earlier. Only Alton, East Moline, East St. Louis, Moline, and Pueblo were founded by anything like "private enterprise" in the classic sense, which only means that the federal and state contributions to their establishment were less visible. And, as indicated in Chapter Two, regardless of the scope of outside governmental participation, all of the cities developed at least partly in response to national considerations, with the speed and extent of their development dependent on their evolving positions in the national scheme of things. The fundamental concerns of civil communities whose development depended upon national trends and needs could hardly be other than those universal throughout the nation.

The development of governmental institutions in each civil community followed a similar pattern, involving the early establishment of local agencies of the state and federal governments as well as the creation of specifically local governments. Indeed, the original symbol of civil community in the greater West was almost invariably a federal agency—the post office, whose establishment not only preceded municipal incorporation in most cities, but legitimized their names as cities. Recognition of a post-office name by Washington was—and still is—a necessity for every city and, in most cases, the post-office name was the one under which later incorporation took place. Where Washington did not make the final decision on name, the state legislature invariably did.

The early post offices played a major political role as well, frequently serving as the civil community's first institutionalized connection with state and national politics. Its nationally determined political function as the first source of local patronage made it the center of partisan politics for its district while the postmaster was frequently the key political figure in his locality. Tied closely to the post office as a source of employment patronage were the mail contracts; prime sources of financial patronage that could enrich local political influentials by enabling them to enter the transportation business on a grand scale.[10]

The burgeoning of federal and state government locally is, indeed, one of the most significant manifestations of the partnership system. The situation in Rockford provides an exemplary case, repeated with minor variations in each of the cities of the prairie. The first federal or state agency to locate in the Rockford civil community was the United States Post Office, established in 1837, only two years after the town's settlement and two years before it was incorporated as a village. The local post office was established the same year that the government of Winnebago County was organized, and the two share the honor of being the first civil governments to specifically serve Rockford. The post office remained the only permanent government agency not responsible to the local voters until the Civil War as state business was handled by the county government and other federal business was handled in Chicago. During the Civil War, federal and state recruiting officers and federal internal revenue agents made their appearance in the community. The Illinois National Guard and the United States Weather Bureau were the next two agencies attached to "outside" governments to be established in the Rockford area and were the last to come before the turn of the century.

The great expansion of both federal and state government locally came after 1913 and particularly after 1933. By 1960, thirty-three of the 107 separate government offices (city, township, special district, county, state, and federal combined) serving the civil community were local offices of federal and state agencies (Table 9–1). The federal government alone had virtually the same number of offices as Winnebago County, the local government with the largest number of departments, and had more than the city of Rockford. Eight of the ten cabinet departments were represented. The state of Illinois, with fewer governments locally since many state functions are performed by county departments, still ranked fourth on the list. The existence of these federal and state agencies as permanent fixtures in the local community is a fact, despite the public position taken by a majority of the Rockford "influentials" in opposition to any federal—or even state—"interference" in local affairs.

In addition to federal and state government locally, federal-state grant and service programs, ranging from school land grants which made possible the establishment of the first public schools in the cities of the prairie through a variety of different grants for internal improvements that provided the impetus for connecting them to each other and to the rest of the country, became increasingly common even before the inauguration of the great twentieth-century cooperative programs. These programs, which were developed in response to the universal problems

TABLE 9-1

Federal, State and Local Government Offices in the Rockford Civil Community, 1960

I. Federal Agencies with Local Offices (24)

A. Civilian (13)

1. *Department of Agriculture*, Soil Conservation Service, Winnebago County A.S.C.[a]
2. *Department of Commerce*, Civil Aeronautics Administration, Federal Mediation and Conciliation Service, Weather Bureau
3. *Department of Defense*, Selective Service Boards,[a] Veterans Administration
4. *Federal Housing Administration*
5. *Department of Health, Education and Welfare*, Social Security Administration
6. *Department of Justice*, Federal Bureau of Investigation
7. *Department of Labor*, Bureau of Apprenticeship
8. *Post Office Department*
9. *Treasury Department*, Internal Revenue Service

B. Military (11)

1. *Department of the Air Force*, Air Reserve Center, Chicago Air Procurement District (Production Representative), Industrial Property Office, Air Force Recruiting Office
2. *Department of the Army*, Army Recruiting Station, Army Reserve Area Command
3. *Department of the Navy*, Inspector of Naval Material, Organized Naval Reserve, Navy Recruiting Substation, Marine Corps Recruiting Station, Marine Corps Reserve Company

II. State Agencies with Local Offices (9)

1. *Military and Naval Department* Illinois National Guard
2. *Illinois Public Aid Commission*
3. *Department of Public Welfare* Division of Vocational Rehabilitation
4. *Secretary of State* Drivers License Department
5. *Department of Public Works and Buildings* Division of Highways Maintenance Garage
6. *Department of Mines and Minerals*, Oil Inspection Laboratory
7. *Youth Commission*
8. *Veterans Commission*

III. Local Government Offices (66)

A. City

1. Rockford (20)
2. Loves Park (8)

B. Winnebago County (27)

C. Rockford Township (5)

D. Special Districts (9)

E. School Districts (3)

---

[a]Formally a state office as well but listed as a federal one in the telephone directory.

of the nineteenth century, led directly into the cash-grant and service programs of more recent years.

In the case of Rockford, money from the state internal improvement fund, which had been created through the sale of federal land grants for that explicit purpose, was instrumental in the construction of the state road from Chicago to Galena that first connected the new village with the outside world. Today, that road has been transformed into the city's major transcontinental connection, U.S. 20, which still benefits from federal funds and, in Rockford, is still State Street, the city's main east-west thoroughfare. Additional funds appropriated by the Illinois General Assembly from the state internal improvement fund were used to build the original network of county roads in Winnebago County that fixed Rockford as the county's trading center. The first public transportation to serve Rockford, the stagecoach line connecting it with Chicago, was able to operate because of the federal mail subsidy. Rockford's school system originated in a series of schools created in 1837 and thereafter, which were supported in part by the payment of tuition and in part by appropriations from the county school fund, which was composed of revenues from the federal school land grant of one section (640 acres) per township and was later increased by the proceeds of the swamp land grant. With all that, Rockford was exceptional because it was somewhat off the beaten track of westward migration and so received comparatively *little* in the way of federal and state aid prior to the twentieth century.

Finally, the civil communities have also been the sites of various federal and state institutions which have contributed to shaping their development over the years. The widespread distribution of these institutions reflects an effort to give as many communities as possible the economic benefits accruing from them and is clearly accepted political policy at all levels. While each specific institution is, perforce, unique to each civil community, their existence as a class is so common that their contribution must be considered in the study of local political systems.

Table 9–2 indicates the widespread distribution of federal and state institutions in the cities of the prairie. Only three civil communities—Belleville, East St. Louis, and Rockford—failed to acquire either one or the other in their early years, though all three were situated close to such institutions located in adjacent civil communities. At least since World War I, none of the civil communities has been without some such institution located within its limits.

Intergovernmental Sharing and Local Fragmentation

The political structure of the civil community seems sufficiently complicated by the "vertical" fragmentation of governmental activities brought on by federal and state involvement locally. The situation is even further complicated, however, by the high level of "horizontal" division of local government within the civil community as well. The number of local governments involved in meeting the demands generated by the public concerns is as great or greater than the number of federal and state agencies involved. The effects of this further division of functions at the local level are twofold. In some cases, it is simply a question of specific programs falling under the jurisdiction of specific governments. In others, the responsibility for a single program is shared by several governments.

"Fragmentation" of government at the local level is widely discussed and frequently denounced. However, rather than simply dismissing it as an unfortunate aspect of American local government badly in need of reform, the very universality and persistence of the phenomenon should raise the question as to whether it may not fill certain very real local needs in the context of American politics.[11]

Actually, the division of authority locally appears to be another corollary of the basic American proposition of limited government. It is derived, in part, from the great divergency of interests that must compete for the limited attention and resources of governments, resources which are particularly limited at the local level. Those interested in specific programs are consciously or implicitly aware that this is the case and seek to secure some independent governmental body devoted entirely to the concern they are promoting. An independent government has three basic advantages. With its organization generally comes the continuing right to a tax levy, which gives it a more or less permanent share of the limited fiscal resources available locally, insuring continued public support of its program. Furthermore, its very existence as a government vests its program and supporters with a legitimacy that enables the latter to better compete with the other public concerns for attention and support and to go to other levels of government for both. Considering the nature of the federal system, this latter is no mean advantage. Finally, the boundaries of each functional government can be set to coincide with the area it is designed to serve, thus allocating the tax burden among users and overcoming the difficulties attendant upon efforts to change the boundaries of established governments—particularly general-purpose ones.

TABLE 9-2
Major Federal and State Institutions in the Cities of the Prairie

Civil Community	Immediate Cause of Founding	Early Federal Institutions	Early State Institutions	Contemporary Federal Institutions (as of 1960)	Contemporary State Institutions (as of 1960)
Champaign	Illinois Central RR[a] Division Point		University of Illinois[a]	Chanute Air Force Base	University of Illinois[a]
Urbana	Designated County Seat by State		University of Illinois[a]	Chanute Air Force Base	University of Illinois[a]
Decatur	Designated County Seat by State			U.S. Signal Corps Depot[b]	
Joliet	Center of construction for Illinois and Michigan Canal[a]		Illinois and Michigan Canal,[a] State Penitentiary	Joliet Ordnance Depot, Illinois Waterway Locks	State Penitentiary
Alton	Riverboat landing		State Penitentiary (1829-1861)	Alton Lock and Dam	Alton State Hospital[a] Southern Illinois University[a]
Belleville	Designated county seat by Territory			Scott Air Force Base	
E. St. Louis	Ferry crossing and terminus of National RRs.				Southern Illinois University[a] Cahokin Mounds State Park
Peoria	Federal military post (Ft. Peoria)	Fort Peoria			Peoria State Hospital
Davenport	Federal military post (Ft. Armstrong)	Rock Island Arsenal		Rock Island Arsenal	

TABLE 9-2 (continued)

Civil Community	Immediate Cause of Founding	Early Federal Institutions	Early State Institutions	Contemporary Federal Institutions (as of 1960)	Contemporary State Institutions (as of 1960)
E. Moline-Silvis	Location of factories for National Corps.	Rock Island Arsenal		Rock Island Arsenal	E. Moline State Hospital[a]
Moline	Industrial site	Rock Island Arsenal		Rock Island Arsenal	
Rock Island	Federal military post (Ft. Armstrong)	Rock Island Arsenal		Rock Island Arsenal District Office: U.S. Eng. Corps.	Black Hawk State Park[a]
Rockford	Industrial site and stage coach crossing	Camp Grant (1917-1918, 1940-1946)			
Springfield	Designated County Seat by State	U.S. Land Office	State Capital State Fair	Federal regional offices	State Capital State Fair
Duluth	Designated terminus for Northern Pacific RR[a]	U.S. Land Office Federal Harbor Control		Federal Harbor Control USAF Air Defense Force	University of Minnesota (Duluth)[a]
Superior	Lake Port and Designated County Seat by State	Federal Harbor Control		Federal Harbor Control	State College[a]
Pueblo	Gold Rush	U.S. Land Office		Pueblo Ordnance Depot	Colorado State Hospital Colorado State Fair Colorado State Museum

[a] Received or receives extensive federal aid.
[b] Terminated in 1961.

These reasons might not be sufficient in and of themselves to stimulate such heavy reliance on so many independent governments locally, but they are reinforced by another and even more pragmatic one. Few political or civic leaders have broad-gauged interests at the local level. With the exception of some of the top leadership, even the small minority of civic actives generally limit their active concern to one or two programs. Examination of the roster of office-holders and candidates for office in the several local governments in the cities of the prairie reveals little overlap in personnel.[12] Those interested in the school board are rarely among those who will run for city council, while city councilmen rarely seek positions on the airport or park boards. Like their counterparts among the professional administrators, their concerns are often not governmental per se, but programmatic. They are interested in schools or parks or airports—or zoning—and they do what they can to separate the agency that will manage the programs they are interested in from other agencies of government, frequently under the guise of separating a particular function from "politics," which is considered "dirty" or "inefficient" and hence potentially damaging to the program in question.

In some cases—public housing authorities and public health districts are the foremost examples—the federal government has been instrumental in the creation of independent local governments. In other cases—particularly school and park districts—state policy lies at the root of their independent existence. Still others, such as fire protection and airport districts, are created to satisfy purely local inclinations. Many of these local governments are established in order to take advantage of federal and state grants-in-aid. Contrary to most assumptions, however, they do not represent the imposition of an outside will upon a reluctant civil community, since the groups advocating the programs locally are no less eager to obtain an independent voice than are their counterparts in Washington or the state capital who are eager to develop special channels to handle the aid they disperse.

The pattern of diffused local government is as old as the country itself. When and where municipal governments were added, they were almost invariably superimposed upon existing counties or townships so as not to supersede or eliminate them. Special-purpose governments standing independently of the more traditional forms of local government were also superimposed virtually from the beginning, particularly in the settlement of the greater West. As the number of tasks requiring local governmental action expanded rapidly in the latter part of the nineteenth and twentieth centuries, many, if not most of them, were allocated to special-purpose governments created by the states or by local referenda pursuant to state law—from school districts to fire protection districts to quasi-independent agencies of the municipalities. The end result of all this was the accretion of separate local governments upon most localities in the several states and the growing formal division of governmental authority in the local community.

While the perceptive observer can see how these disparate governments and their related institutions coalesce into a civil community, the very difficulty of viewing the local world in these terms is enhanced by the tradition of noncentralized local government. Of course, this noncentralization also enhances the need for considering the local community as a *civil* community—a polity that is clearly something more than a legally defined city in its political structure but less than a *communitas* in the relationships of its inhabitants to each other.

One practical effect of this multiplication of local governments is to enhance the strength of the vertical sharing system. The specialized functional local governments are encouraged to cooperate with their state and federal counterparts with whom they share common programmatic interests while their separation—often physical as well as legal and functional—from the other local governments makes interlocal cooperation even more difficult. Thus the civil community is virtually forced to make an effort to develop institutionalized (though not necessarily formal) means to coordinate the diverse activities of its various local governments if there is to be any overall community control of its own government. While this may be difficult for the civil community to accomplish, insofar as it is able to do so, it is enhanced as a civil community.

The foregoing generalizations do no more than trace the outlines of intergovernmental collaboration in the American federal system. A closer examination of cases throws more light on the character of the partnership. Take the field of public health. Every organized county in the United States is served by a public health official whose official title is "sanitarian." Sometimes he is employed by the county itself, sometimes by the major city in the county, sometimes by a regional health department. His office, created as a product of a formal cooperative effort to improve public health facilities throughout the nation, provides an excellent, if extreme, example of the intermeshing of federal, state, and local functions from the perspective of the public servant. Look at the sanitarian in a county of 25,000 population in a state in the lower Mississippi Valley. He is appointed by the state under merit standards established by the federal government in collaboration with the sanitarians' professional association. Most of his salary as sanitarian comes from state and federal funds but is supplemented by the largest city in the county, which pays him for his services as city plumbing inspector. His office and its equipment are supplied by the county, assisted by the city, and part of his expenses are paid from county funds.

His day-to-day operations are equally intermingled. He carries out his task of enforcing the pure food and drug laws under federal standards, though he enforces state law when inspecting commodities that have not been in interstate commerce. To make the system more complex, he inspects milk coming into the county from another state as a local official operating under authority granted him by his state. He acts as a federal officer when he impounds impure drugs imported from a neighboring state; a federal-state officer when he distributes typhoid immunization serum; a state officer when he enforces standards of industrial hygiene; a state-county officer when he inspects the purity of his city's water supply; and completes the circle as a city officer when he compels the city butchers to adopt more hygienic methods of handling their garbage. To cover any situations not otherwise provided for in his various mandates, he is a deputy sheriff and an ex-officio member of the city police force.

It is apparent that our sanitarian friend is responsible for all public health and sanitation business in his own county. He considers all such business his business and does not stop, in the course of his work, to con sider what hat he is wearing at any particular time unless forced to.

In the counties of the cities of the prairie, health departments are generally autonomous governments under the law, relatively large and complex organizations, with specialists available to handle these divergent tasks. The spread of their concerns is even greater; the pattern of their response remains as involved. The greater resources and larger staffs of their departments enhance the possibilities of local decision-making by providing local sources of expertise that make state and federal "interference" less necessary. At the same time, the larger local programs increase their involvement in the overall system through larger federal and state grants, the sponsorship of "pilot projects," and the like.

Similar pictures of intergovernmental involvement can be drawn for many other programs. Here, too, the caricatures point out the realities of intergovernmental entanglements even though they obscure the generally harmonious relations that accompany the vast majority of them.

Street maintenance and traffic control are generally considered to be entirely local matters. In Illinois, as in many other states, local streets which bear state or U.S. highway designations are subject to control by the state highway department even in matters such as curbing and traffic control and must meet specifications approved by the Federal Bureau of Public Roads since they are partly financed by federal grants. When it snows in Champaign, Springfield Avenue (Illinois 10 and U.S. 45) is cleared by locally based state highway department equipment, while it remains snow-covered in Urbana because the state route turns northward at the latter's city limits. A few years ago, when Rockford wished to place a stop sign at a particularly bad intersection caused by temporary rerouting of traffic because of other road construction, its mayor, traffic engineer, and city council had to negotiate with the state highway department at the district and state levels because one of the streets was also the route of U.S. 20.

Nor is this simply a matter of arranging harmonious relations between levels of government. Often the problem is complicated by divergent local interests. Federal control over navigable waters is well established by a specific grant of power in the Constitution itself. Joliet is bisected by the Illinois Waterway, which is under the jurisdiction of the United States Corps of Engineers. The bridges which span the waterway in the center of the city have been constructed through state or local action (depending on whether they serve state-maintained highways or not) but are managed locally by the Corps of Engineers. Their frequent raising for barge traffic has continually played havoc with city traffic patterns. Under strong public pressure to "do something about it," the city authorities used their political influence in Springfield and Washington and were finally able to negotiate an agreement with the Engineers to hold up the barges during morning and evening rush hours. The agreement immediately aroused the opposition of the very influential local manufacturers' association, which is more concerned with promoting commerce on the waterway than in meeting the city's traffic problems.

The complexities of collaboration are often spectacular. When Rock Island desired to build its own bridge across the Mississippi River two decades ago, it had to obtain state legislative authorization to create a toll bridge commission; secure passage of a local referendum authorizing the issuance of bonds and establishing the commission as a quasi-independent city governmental body; obtain permission from Congress to bridge the river; secure approval of its plans by the Corps of Engineers; get authorization from the Iowa state legislature because of the project's interstate character; and, finally, obtain the approval of the City of Davenport in order to purchase the land for the bridge's western approaches. The end result was a bridge whose western terminus is located in Iowa but which is owned by a municipal subdivision of the state of Illinois, built according to federal specifications, maintained in part with state and federal funds because it is a U.S. highway, regulated by the state as a state route, and controlled and exploited by a local political clique which is beholden to the Rock Island County Democratic party organization.

The Special Character of State-Local Relations

THOUGH EVERY civil community is part and parcel of the overall system of American federalism, there remains a qualitative as well as quantitative difference in the character of state-local, as distinct from federal-local, relationships. This is partly a matter of formal or legal lines of authority;

it is also a reflection of the basic pattern of the diffusion of power in American politics.

Despite the great increase in *de facto* local autonomy in the past two generations, the accepted constitutional position that all local governments are creatures of their respective states still remains the underlying principle from which any analysis of the state-local relationship must begin. It is possible to list five broad, though by no means mutually exclusive, fields in which every state enjoys a special and even immediately overriding relationship with its local subdivisions.

In the first place, the state is constitutionally the source of authority for all its creature local governments. The state constitution defines the terms and sets forth the framework for their creation and establishment. It is supplemented by state legislative enactments pursuant to the constitution, often organized into a code or codes, which also bear a constitutional relationship to the civil community. In Illinois, all cities are subject to the Illinois Municipal Code (as the state's Cities and Villages Act is designated) which, along with the few sections relating to municipal government in the Illinois Constitution, represents the fundamental constitutional instrument for all municipalities in the state other than the few which have retained their special charters from before the adoption of the present constitution in 1870.[13]

Before the opening of the urban-industrial frontier, general rule-making for local government was minimal and special legislation the rule. The urban-industrial frontier made the governmental problems confronting cities so general that special legislation became both inadequate and unjust. In 1872, the state legislature enacted the first municipal code. Since then, the legislature has relied upon general legislation to establish the allowed variations in the structuring of local government. Changes in the laws governing the incorporation of new municipalities in metropolitan areas, providing for easier annexation of unincorporated territory into existing cities, or encouraging local government consolidation, all must be made at the state level. The variations themselves are now debated as questions of statewide interest rather than as matters of local concern only and changes are usually hard to come by, in Illinois and in the other four states.

The transfer of the question of local government structure from the specific to the general realm has also resulted in the development of new legal limitations on local governments. The "home rule" question in Illinois is a case in point. Cities which obtained special charters prior to 1872 frequently possess greater powers of local autonomy than cities incorporated under the general laws of the state. Rockford, for example, secured a municipal charter in 1852, which granted the city government the power to establish and maintain free public schools. This power, which, except in the case of Chicago, is otherwise vested in specially created school districts under the terms of the state school act of 1855 and subsequently, has been retained by the City of Rockford, making it unique among the cities of the prairie in this respect.

As the cities generally began to agitate for greater autonomy at the very end of the nineteenth century, their reformer representatives suggested the adoption of general provisions granting municipal home rule to all cities that wished to take advantage of it. Such a general grant of power has been rejected by the state's lawmakers time and again. The extent to which the absence of formal home-rule provisions in Illinois law has actually affected the government of the state's civil communities is hard to determine. On one hand, Illinois cities can choose between all the options currently in use in the United States in the organization of city government. At the same time, the absence of provisions certainly does legally limit their operations, particularly in connection with matters likely to be challenged in the courts.

Iowa, like Illinois, does not have any formal municipal home-rule provisions in its constitution, and its cities are governed under the appropriate sections of the Iowa Code. However, four of the cities, including Davenport, have retained their special charters, granted them by the General Assembly before the adoption of the Constitution of 1857, which eliminated that power. As in Illinois, this gives them some additional local autonomy.[14]

The other three states provide for local home rule in their constitutions. The Minnesota constitution grants counties, cities, and villages the right to draft their own home-rule charters by popular action. The major cities in the state, including Duluth, have all taken advantage of this provision which, in theory, gives them greater flexibility in the formal structuring of their governments than is possible in Illinois.[15] Wisconsin's home-rule provisions are similar to those of Minnesota in extent and in their subsequent construction.[16] Colorado's constitution also has a home-rule provision, perhaps the broadest of any of the states. It explicitly grants all cities adopting home-rule charters all powers not otherwise reserved to the state government or involving substantial state interests, almost federalizing the formal state-local relationship.[17]

Second, the immediate determination of the legal rights and powers of local government is vested in the state government as written into state law and as interpreted by the state courts. In Colorado, for example, state court rulings that the legislature has the final power to determine what is of substantial state concern have reduced the effective scope of home rule in that state to local determination of the formal structure of local government and the salaries of local officials—in reality, hardly any more power than that available to Illinois cities.

Regardless of the degree of federal functional involvement in the affairs of the states and localities, it is a fundamental principle in American law that (a) there is no federal common law and (b) federal law is primarily interstitial—that is, it only fills in the gaps left by the existence of a separate corpus of law in each of the fifty states.[18] This means that federal legal intervention into state and local legal problems is restricted at the outset. Furthermore, the federal courts have constantly reaffirmed their hesitation to intervene in the majority of the legal issues raised in connection with local government, on the grounds that they are primarily local matters to be settled in the state courts under the inherent police powers of the state. Historically, then, each state has developed its own reasonably unique body of law, *which is even enforced by the federal courts functioning within its boundaries*. One authority on local government has summarized the practical consequences of this arrangement succinctly:[19]

> The subordinate legal status of cities makes it necessary that the question of whether or not a particular city has the power to perform a particular function in a particular way be decided by the courts. Because the city is merely a creature of the state while the state itself is a sovereign body, the courts have established a rule of a narrow construction of municipal powers and a broad construction of state powers.

If this is true of cities, which legally are municipal corporations, the most autonomous form of local government, it is doubly true of other local governments. The cities of the prairie are very much within this framework.

The most widely cited rule limiting the autonomy of municipal corporations is Dillon's Rule, framed half a century ago by a leading Iowa jurist:[20]

> It is a general and undisputed proposition of law that a *municipal corporation possesses and can exercise the following powers, and no others:* First, those granted in *express words;* second, those *necessarily or fairly implied* in or *incident* to the powers expressly granted; third, those essential to the accomplishment of the declared objects and purposes of the corporation—not simply convenient, but indispensable. Any fair, reasonable, substantial doubt concerning the existence of power is resolved by the courts against the corporation, and the power is denied.

This rule has become part and parcel of each state's constitutional tradition, though with some differences in its interpretation from state to state and from era to era.

It has been said, with justice, that every political question in the United States ultimately becomes a judicial question, through legal challenges of political decisions upon which the courts are ultimately required to rule. It is certainly true that all the cities of the prairie have been involved in litigation in one form or another in the past half-generation in the process of implementing many of the programs they have undertaken. This litigation has ranged over such questions as the legality of the annexation of certain territories, the legitimacy of enacting changes in city governmental structure, the validity of zoning regulations, the propriety of devoting public funds to planning, or off-street parking, or urban renewal, the justice of special assessments, the legality of certain forms or methods of taxation, and many others. In every case, the role of the state courts has been to make plain the power of the state to intervene in local actions, even when the decisions have been made in favor of the local authorities.

This continuous process of litigation has, in turn, bred a perhaps inordinate amount of caution in local officials, who tend to think twice about doing anything out of the ordinary for fear of arousing some individual taxpayer or, more seriously, some corporation or taxpayers group, who will bring suit against them in the state courts. The precise effects such experiences have on limiting the discretionary courage of local officials is hard to gauge, particularly since few of the same local officials seem to be inclined toward new courses of action in any case. Whether it is a primary reason for their conservatism or a rationalization, the possibility of state judicial intervention is a felt concern among the local authorities in the cities of the prairie, one used to justify a "go slow" attitude in their own minds, if nothing else.

The State as Master and Regulator of Its Subdivisions

State policies affect the governmental structure of the civil community in yet another way. Each state has the exclusive right and obligation to regulate the manner in which its elections are to be conducted (within the very general limits of the framework imposed by the United States Constitution as interpreted), the right and obligation to set the time and place for every election (within the limits imposed for presidential and national congressional elections); and the right and obligation to recognize and regulate political parties, candidates, form of ballot, and the other instruments of the electoral process. Because of the directly political consequences of this power, the influence of the states upon their civil communities is appreciably heightened simply by the manner in which each state regulates its electoral calendar and procedures. In fact, each state's political system dictates the framework of choices for most elective offices within each civil community by determining who shall be on the ballot in general elections and under which party designations. National and state electoral politics are directly shaped by the state-imposed framework. County offices are similarly affected because of their ties to state party politics. As we have seen, in some cases, party ties reach down to embrace municipal offices, bringing them into the system as well.

Third, the states maintain a special, continuing, and omnipresent relationship with their civil communities in the realm of public regulation—of transportation, of public utilities, of matters involving public health and morals. The highways, the railroads, and even the local public transportation systems are state-regulated. In the states under study here, this means that such immediately local decisions as where to place a stoplight and how long its "stop and go" intervals are to be are frequently decided by, or in concert with, state authorities. Railroad crossing guards and the length of time trains may block crossings are matters for state regulation, often to the intense dissatisfaction of the locality involved. The initiation or abandonment of local bus service is ultimately decided in Springfield, or Denver, or St. Paul, or Des Moines, or Madison. Water and telephone rates, the price and availability of gas for heating and cooking, are all regulated by the state.

The only way in which localities have been able to exercise any reasonable control over the public utilities which serve them in so many crucial ways is through public ownership. Springfield, under the leadership of City Commissioner Willis Spaulding, who was aware of the many possibilities inherent in municipal ownership, embarked on a program of municipal ownership of electric power production facilities at the time of World War I. Though the city shares the Springfield area market with a private utility regulated by the state, its average electric rates are only two-thirds of those of its sister cities because the municipally owned system has established an effective price "yardstick" against which the private company must compete, thus effectively superseding the state's rather weak rate regulation program.

Springfield is the exception among the Illinois cities of the prairie, none of which has embarked on more than minimal municipal ownership programs (Table 9–3). Municipal ownership of sewage treatment plants (made possible primarily since World War II by virtue of federal and state financial and technical assistance, encouragement, and where necessary, direct pressure), and, in some cases, water supply systems actually leads to even closer state regulation over local government because both of these utilities are very closely regulated by all five states. Supply of water to the public was among the first functions to be regulated by the states when utility regulation by administrative agency was still in its infancy in this country. Today, continuous sampling and testing of public water supplies is an accepted state function that involves a most direct supervisory relationship by state authorities over local officials. Municipal sewage treatment is a more recent innovation, stimulated by state and federal governments acting in concert and enforced through federal and state regulatory measures that are harmonized for the most intensive effect locally. Thus Belleville, a civil community not noted for its rapid embracing of new governmental functions, was forced to construct a sewage treatment plant through the combined pressures of the Illinois Sanitary Water Board, which forbade the further dumping of raw sewage into the waterways in the Belleville area, and the Federal Housing Administration, which refused to guarantee mortgages of new houses constructed without adequate sanitary sewer connections.

State powers to regulate public morals are legally extensive but are used less frequently than others. The extent of their use is directly related to the culture of each state (see below). In Illinois, where various stand-

TABLE 9-3

Municipal Ownership of Public Utilities, 1962

City (by size category)	Utilities Owned
Duluth	Gas distribution facilities, sewage treatment plant, water supply system
Peoria	[a]
Rockford	Water supply system
Davenport	Sewage treatment plant
Decatur	Water supply system
East St. Louis	[a]
Joliet	Sewage treatment plant, water supply system
Pueblo[b]	Sewage treatment plant, water supply system
Rock Island	Sewage treatment plant, water supply system
Springfield	Electric generation and distribution, water supply system
Alton	Sewage treatment plant
Belleville	Sewage treatment plant
Champaign	[a]
Moline	Sewage treatment plant, water supply system
Superior	Sewage treatment plant
Urbana	[a]
Bettendorf	Sewage treatment plant
East Moline	Sewage treatment plant, water supply system

[a]Sewage treatment plant owned and operated by independent sanitary district.
[b]Pueblo subsidizes the private bus company in return for control over its level of service.
Sources: *Municipal Year Book*, 1962; and author's field notes.

ards of public morality prevail, for various reasons, this power has been used sparingly, when used at all. Occasional increases in its use have generally been due to the election of reform-oriented governors who have been willing to act in the face of considerable political opposition. In Minnesota, on the other hand, where a more or less common standard of public morality prevails statewide, a certain level of state regulatory action in this realm is expected and even encouraged, despite a strong tradition of localism in such matters.

Where the states do not regulate local action directly, they are involved in local government matters through the enactment of permissive legislation (and appropriate administrative regulations) allowing local governments to act. The constitutional necessities for this have already been outlined. Since this field is so broad, encompassing as it does all areas of local activity not otherwise accounted for, its ramifications need not be singled out for discussion here. They are apparent throughout the entire study.

The State as Direct Actor and Supporter

Direct state action in the local community ("government locally") represents a fourth field of state involvement locally. In some cases the state finds it expedient to directly operate its own programs within the civil community. The local functions of the Illinois Youth Commission are a case in point. The Commission was established to manage the custodial facilities provided for juvenile offenders and also to undertake an action program in the state's urban areas to attempt to reduce juvenile crime and delinquency. In fulfillment of the latter function, the IYC has maintained resident youth workers in the state's medium-size and large metropolitan areas since the mid-1950's. These youth workers not only operate as field workers among potential juvenile delinquents but also serve as catalytic agents to encourage local efforts—government and nongovernmental—to meet the problems that may lead to the development of juvenile delinquents. In Rockford the IYC leader has been active in encouraging the development of a politically articulate Negro leadership that will be able to participate actively in the affairs of the civil community and, by doing so, gain a better place for the black subcommunity. He has also been active in promoting local urban renewal and community conservation efforts to upgrade Negro housing conditions, both inside Rockford proper and in the unincorporated suburban fringe areas of the civil community. The IYC workers in Springfield and in the cities of Rock Island County have been involved in similar endeavors.

In some cases, direct state action is not a product of generalized statewide programming but a consequence of uniquely local situations. In the Madison-St. Clair Counties area, the bulk of the public park and recreation facilities are provided by the State Department of Conservation. Better than a generation ago, the state acquired some 1,275 acres of land of archeological, historic, and scenic interest, which were developed as Cahokia Mounds State Park, Grand Marais State Park, and Cahokia Court House State Memorial. During the 1930's these parks were developed as recreation areas with the help of federal public works appropriations.

Meanwhile, the intensive urbanization of the two counties led to an increased need for such park and recreation facilities and the *de facto* conversion of these scenic and historical preserves into urban parks serving few of the functions normally served by state parks. For a variety of reasons, the local residents of the area have shown little interest in creating new parks or in developing existing facilities, though some limited action has been taken in recent years in the four larger cities—Alton, Belleville, East St. Louis, and Granite City—continuing to rely upon the state's open space acreage to handle local needs.

State intervention of a different order has developed in the Madison-St. Clair Counties area through the offices of Southern Illinois University. Indeed, the intervention of that institution has become the most important single factor in raising the level of government and public services in the two counties, perhaps the greatest factor since their original settlement 265 years ago. Shortly after the end of World War II, Southern Illinois State Normal College was reorganized as Southern Illinois University. Its new administration took upon itself the task of upgrading the economically depressed southern third of the state, whose problems had been growing since the Civil War but which had reached crisis proportions in the 1930's and 1940's. The Madison-St. Clair Counties area, though little conscious of its relationship to rural Southern Illinois, was among the most blighted sections of that region.

As part of its efforts to meet this self-imposed obligation, SIU inaugurated a community development program to reach into its region's urban areas including the Illinois section of the St. Louis metropolitan area. The University established a "Southwestern Illinois" branch divided between East St. Louis and Alton to provide college opportunities for potential students in that area who could not afford to leave home for the main campus in Carbondale. The establishment of these two divisions was made contingent upon both cities' acceptance of the University's right to intervene to stimulate local social and economic change, including efforts to improve the position of the clearly "excluded" Negro communities in both cities. The major effort to achieve that end was soon directed to the greater East St. Louis area, unquestionably the most deficient of the two in terms of the commonly accepted standards and amenities associated with urban living in the United States. The very arrangement for leasing a dilapidated school building in East St. Louis for use as a temporary campus by SIU was utilized to encourage the construction of new school facilities by the local authorities to replace the leased ones and to increase the opportunities for Negro youth to continue their education.

Several years after the establishment of the East St. Louis division, in 1957, SIU added another intervenor, in the form of its Department of Community Development. The field workers of that department sent into the area, backed up by the University administration, organized Community Progress, Incorporated, a citizen-directed, community-wide organization formed to give shape and impetus to civic redevelopment. The political leadership of East St. Louis, though not disposed to support the existence of such an organization whose avowed intentions were to alter the status quo, was unable to resist the combination of financial blandishments and political pressure exerted by the University. They accepted CPI (as it soon was designated) with reservations and became at least publicly cooperative since its establishment, having no other recourse.

With a staff provided by SIU, CPI began to organize neighborhood committees and to promote immediately local activities to clean up and "beautify" the city. From this, CPI moved to stimulate the adoption of a city urban renewal program and to secure the passage of a referendum for an urban renewal bond issue; to encourage the development of a large park improvement program by the East St. Louis Park District; to foster the inauguration of a multimillion dollar school construction and improvement program by East St. Louis School District 189; and to inaugurate the preparation of a master plan for the civil community as a whole. The unusual record of successes compiled by CPI through this complex of activities, in a very difficult political environment at that, led to national recognition in the form of the Look Magazine-National Municipal League All-American City Award in 1960.

Along with the promotion of the foregoing major programs, the SIU people working through CPI and other groups stimulated the initiation of a wide range of public nongovernmental activities, utilizing existing public service and community welfare organizations or stimulating the creation of new ones, such as neighborhood associations or a Humane Society, where necessary. They conducted a survey of local attitudes toward the civil community and assessments of the community's deficiencies and problems, whose highly negative results they used to establish public study committees to investigate the major (and obvious) problems identified by the public.

From this beginning, the local Community Development staff was emboldened to tackle the local political situation more directly. They arranged for an "efficiency and economy" type study of the East St. Louis city government—a revolutionary step in that community—which was issued publicly in 1961. Even more significant, they stimulated the creation of CAPS 189, a citizens group dedicated to reforming the school system by removing it from local partisan politics. CAPS 189 has been running candidates for the school board since 1961, with increasing success.

While the Department of Community Development has concentrated its efforts on East St. Louis, its local staff has been available for advice and consultation to all the communities in the area. From time to time they have been brought in on a wide range of problems in most of the communities. Where they have not been able to be of service, other agencies of SIU located in the Madison-St. Clair Counties area or in Carbondale have been ready to step in.

All told, SIU contributed better than half of the budget of CPI, through its payment of Department of Community Development personnel serving the civic development organization. Through its other local divisions, it pumped even more money into local community development programs. Most important, it supplied the people and the stimulation necessary to develop local concern and response. Whatever changes have been made in the East St. Louis civil community in the past half-generation are due, in great measure, to this form of specialized state intervention.

Operating in a very different context, the State of Minnesota has had a similar impact on the Duluth civil community in the past half-generation. Of the five major projects which have contributed most to the reshaping of Duluth in that period, three have involved direct state intervention. The expansion of the Duluth branch of the University of Minnesota into a full college program with an entirely new campus and a research and teaching program geared to the needs of northern Minnesota was undertaken by the University directly. Though some of the local influentials—particularly the union leadership, the foremost influentials in the DFL, and the higher civil servants in the city hall—were active in encouraging the University in this regard, still others, primarily from the upper echelons of the business community, were quite pessimistic about the value of the project. If local initiative alone had been the determining factor, it is unlikely that the facility would have been developed.

The weight of state intervention was even more vital in the development of the public Port of Duluth. Though the construction of the St. Lawrence Seaway made expansion of the port facilities at Duluth a significant matter for local concern, the same local business influentials who had been cool to the development of the University were downright hostile to the development of the port, fearing it as a source of competition. They, in turn, were opposed by the same labor and government influentials. Had the matter been determined locally, the opposition would have successfully vetoed any efforts to appropriate sufficient funds to create new public port facilities. However, the State of Minnesota was interested in the potentialities of the Seaway too. The governor and legislature were encouraged to take action by the concerted efforts (perhaps unusual) of the DFL leadership and the Twin Cities business community. The state appropriated five of the ten million dollars needed for the project and established the Port of Duluth Authority, virtually forcing the leadership of the Duluth civil community to take action. Even the opponents had to acquiesce in the face of this statewide effort, and the city and county contributed the other five million dollars, leading to the construction of the first facilities in time for the opening of the Seaway.

The third project involved the construction of interstate highway connections to link Duluth with the Twin Cities, its western hinterland, and its immediate markets in Wisconsin and the Upper Peninsula of Michigan. This has also been a matter for direct state intervention, within the context of the national defense highway construction program. The first and most immediately beneficial link in the interstate network focusing on Duluth was a high bridge to connect Duluth and Superior. All three of the existing bridges were better than half a century old and were deteriorated, and all were subject to interruption by ship traffic. Again, many of the conservative business elements opposed the construction of a high bridge, fearing its economic consequences rather than accepting it as opening new economic opportunities. Only the state policy decision, as well as the state's unequivocal role as the constructor of the project, led to its incorporation in the interstate system and completion in 1962.

Some kinds of state involvement in Pueblo affairs, though presenting certain problems, are eagerly sought by Puebloans for its economic benefits. During the period of this study, the state government controlled the second largest payroll in the Pueblo civil community through two major state institutions—the Pueblo State Hospital for the Mentally Ill and the Colorado State Fair—along with several other smaller state agencies. The major institutions are so important that a problem in either of them almost invariably becomes a community problem. Pueblo civic and political leaders are acutely aware that any cutback in state support for either institution is immediately felt locally because of their very size. This point was brought home during the administration of Governor Steve McNichols when there were major hassles between the governor and the Pueblo leadership over plans for both institutions and the governor took the time-honored public position that the political "bosses" in Pueblo were seeking ends subversive of the state's sense of public morality.

Pueblo's dependence upon the state in this respect has already grown since 1962. Both the State Hospital and the State Fair were expanded (much to the delight of the local community leadership, of course). In addition, Puebloans secured the establishment of a four-year state college, which opened its doors in 1963, adding another potential source of economic benefit and state-local contention. While Pueblo's case is somewhat out of the ordinary, the relatively small population of Colorado means that virtually every significant civil community in the state has some state institution that makes a real contribution to the local economy and provides the state government with a bridgehead for intervening in local affairs.

Rather than seeking to eliminate state intervention locally, the civic and political leaders of Pueblo are seeking to tie their community more closely to the state political system, to gain a greater voice at the state capital. There are several reasons for this. In the first place, long experience as an uninfluential entity on the state scene, constantly subject to state pressures but unable to influence the course of those pressures, has persuaded the local leadership that influence at the state level is an absolute necessity if Pueblo hopes to achieve its stated goals.

This belief has been reinforced by a growing series of successes in Denver, all of which have come as a consequence of concerted local efforts to influence the state government by presenting a reasonable and united front as a civil community, using the appropriate symbol system to reach the powers that be in the state. First the Pueblo Chamber of Commerce was able to develop a scheme that unified local requests for state highway aid into a single package which, when presented to the state highway commission at its annual hearing, was almost certain to be accepted because of the unanimous local support behind it. From this came the Pueblo expressway, a crosstown connection as well as a link to Denver. Other successes followed. Most recently, a concerted local effort overcame intense opposition on the part of Denverites and others from northeastern Colorado in the state legislature to secure the establishment of Southern Colorado State College. This major achievement has convinced the Pueblo leadership of the soundness of their course of action.

Every one of the cities of the prairie can point to some form of specially directed state intervention that has contributed to its local political picture in the years since World War II. Such intervention has ranged from the central and continuing activities of the state university in Champaign-Urbana and the state government in Springfield to the state police crackdown on prostitution and gambling in Rock Island County, the Joliet area, and the Peoria civil community over the heads of the county and city law enforcement officers during the Stevenson administration. Intervention in the first case not only provides the Champaign-Urbana civil community with the heart of its economic base but also has provided such diverse "extras" as additional police and firefighting support; a "free" airport facility of first rank for a civil community of that size; and a new auditorium which is making it possible for the civil community to become a convention and entertainment center in its part of the region. In the latter three cases, the brief intervention of the state law enforcement authorities led to such revelations of local government corruption that it stimulated reform movements which successfully altered the structure of city government in all three civil communities.

Where the state does not intervene directly, it frequently affects the course of local government and politics through the provision of financial aid for programs and projects of statewide concern. The state-local fiscal relationship has been well studied from the viewpoint of public administration. Elaboration of its general character and effects is not necessary here. For all intents and purposes, the bulk of the federal aid that reaches the cities of the prairie is provided as state aid. In most cases the local officials who handle the funds cannot distinguish between the two sources.

Table 9–4 summarizes the general state payment programs to local governments in the five states in 1957 and 1962, indicating the various ways in which states contribute to local government programs and the extent to which federal funds are included in state payments. Table 9–5 summarizes the total local government revenue in each of the designated (or adjusted) metropolitan areas of the cities of the prairie in 1957 and 1962, indicating the state and federal contributions to that total. While these figures have since been increased, they can serve as reasonable indicators of the extent of state (and federal) financial assistance to local government and the variety of purposes toward which such assistance is directed. The changes that have taken place since then have tended to increase both the extent of this outside aid and the variety of uses to which it is put, in most cases further tying the civil communities to their states.

At the same time, the broadening in the range of services offered by local governments, which, in large part, has been fostered by federal and state financial support, has also led to an increase in the powers of local government, despite the rise of local involvement in intergovernmental relations. Indeed, it is the growing ability of local governments to utilize the facilities and resources of the federal government to gain local ends that is contributing to their increased position of influence within their respective states. The lines of this evolution still remain unclear and its course undetermined. The signs point simultaneously in different directions.

Among the cities of the prairie, enlarged local ability to undertake projects of ever-increasing magnitude is related to the greater importance of the cities and special districts as the active agents on the local scene. They are the governments generally responsible for initiating new programs locally and maintaining them. At the same time, the locus of organized political power remains in the counties and townships in most of the civil communities, with the latter also dominating the civil community's political connections with its state. Table 9–6 summarizes the various ways in which this is so. The dominance of county political organizations is particularly marked in Illinois. While it is not possible to generalize about the situation in the other four states, it is striking that in all four non-Illinois civil communities (and in Rockford, which so resembles them) the municipal and county (or township) governments share more equally in serving these functions.

The Origins of the American State-Local Relationship

The uniqueness of the American city, in contrast to the model or paradigm of "the city" familiar in the cities of the classical world and Europe, has much to do with the characteristically American relationship between the states and their creature civil communities. Cities originated in the classical world and in most of the ancient Near East as civil societies—or city-states, as they are more commonly called in the history books. Indeed the term *polis*, the closest Greek equivalent of the English term "civil society" describes just that type of small, sovereign city-state. In its original form the city or polis was politically autonomous, combining both local and central governmental authority.[21] The city, then, preceded the development of larger political units in much of the Western world, retaining both civic identity and political autonomy even when larger polities began to emerge.

Colonization in the ancient world consisted, in the main, of the foundation of new cities; hence even the first empires did little to alter the solidarity of the polis. In the days of the Hellenistic and Roman empires, the basic subimperial unit in most of the known world was the polis, which possessed its own constitution duly recognized by the imperial authorities.[22] In fact, the polis system was fostered by the imperial authorities even where it was previously nonexistent to replace previously existing kingdoms which had been conquered and then had to be divided. By creating new cities and granting them new constitutions offering some local autonomy (particularly in the religio-cultural sphere) but dependent upon imperial favor, it became possible to substantially reduce potential nationalistic movements.[23]

The cities of northern and central Europe evolved later in much the same manner. The citizens of each of the early cities, which first appeared in feudal times when centralized government was nonexistent, won the right of self-government for themselves, their city, and perhaps a small hinterland as well. Later, when nation-states developed, these cities were, perforce, absorbed within them but remained conscious of the fact that they had antedated their central governments, often by centuries.[24]

Unlike the situation in the classical world or medieval Europe, cities as governmental units developed relatively late in the Anglo-American world, after both central and centrally organized rural local governments had become well established. This chronological factor has set the development of the American city on a radically different course. When cities were founded in the United States, they were creatures of their central

TABLE 9-4

State Payment Programs to Local Government, 1957-1962

Field	Illinois	Minnesota	Colorado	Iowa	Wisconsin
	State				
Education	Common School Fund Transportation Education of Handicapped Special Tuitions County Supervisory Services Junior Colleges Normal Schools School Lunch and Milk* Vocational Education*	Per Capita Aid Permanent School Fund* Special State Aid Basic Aid Equalization Aid Transportation Education of Handicapped Other Special Aids Gross Earnings Tax Replacement Reimbursement for Tax Losses* Vocational Education* School Lunch and Milk* Indian Education* Junior Colleges	Attendance Distribution Equalization Program Emergency Aid Junior Colleges School Transportation Education of Handicapped Vocational Education School Lunch and Milk	General Aid Equalization Aid Transportation Education of Handicapped Other Special Aids Agricultural Land Tax Reimbursement Public Land Tax Reimbursement Permanent School Fund* Homestead Exemption Reimbursement Military Service Tax Credit Reimbursement Vocational Education* School Lunch and Milk*	Elementary and High School Aid Transportation Education of Handicapped and Exceptional Children County Normal and Agricultural Schools and Supervising Teachers Permanent School Fund* Utilities Property Tax Vocational Education* School Lunch and Milk* Indian Education* Forest Cropland Income
Highways	Motor Fuel Sales Tax Federal Highway Aid*	Motor Fuel Sales Tax Road and Bridge Allotment*	Highway User Revenue Distribution* Maintenance of State Highways Motor Vehicle Property Tax	Road Use Tax Fund City Maintenance of State Highways	County Truck Highways* Street Improvement* Supplemental Highway Aids Connecting Streets and Bridges* Reimbursements to Counties* Flood Damage

TABLE 9-4 (continued)

	State				
Field	Illinois	Minnesota	Colorado	Iowa	Wisconsin
Public Welfare	Categorical Assistance* Public Welfare Administration* General Relief Care for Children	Categorical Assistance* (Including Public Welfare Administration) General Relief Equalization of Welfare Costs Children under Guardianship	Categorical Assistance* Public Welfare Administration* Child Welfare Services	Categorical Assistance* Administration Expenses*	Categorical Assistance* Aid to Indians* Public Welfare Administration*
Health and Hospitals	Local Health Services* Tuberculosis Hospitalization Hospital Construction* Hospital and Medical Services*	Tuberculosis Sanatorium Public Health Nursing Hospital Construction* Medical and Hospital Services*	Tuberculosis Aid Health Service* Hospital Construction*	Mental Aid Hospital Construction*	Tuberculosis Sanatorium Care of Insane Medical and Hospital Services* County Nurses Local Health Services* Hospital Construction*
General Local Government Support	a	Alcoholic Beverage Sales Tax Cigarette Sales Tax Bank Excise Tax Death and Gift Taxes Gross Earnings Tax Replacement Taconite R.R. Tax Mineral Rents and Royalties	Motor Vehicle Penalty Assessments	Homestead Exemption Reimbursement Alcoholic Beverage Monopoly Sales	Income Taxes Utilities Property Taxes "Highways Privilege Tax" Alcoholic Beverage Sales Tax Telephone Tax Rural Electric Association Tax RR. Terminal Tax Forest Cropland Income
Miscellaneous and Combined Purposes	County Veterinarians Airport Construction*	Insurance Premiums Tax Soil Conservation Airport Construction* Civil Defense* Federal Forest Reserve Revenue*	Insurance Premiums Tax Property Tax Civil Defense and Disaster Relief* Federal Forest Reserve Revenue* Federal Mineral Leasing Revenue*	Aid of Soil Conservation Districts	County Forests Federal Forest Reserve Fund* Insurance Premiums Tax Insurance Claims Civil Defense* Income Taxes

*Includes federal funds.
[a]Since 1957 Illinois has enacted a sales tax rebate for cities.
Basic Source: *State Payments to Local Governments* (1957 Census of Governments, Vol. IV, No. 2).

governments, legally endowed with powers of local government only, through central government charter as municipal corporations. They were not sovereign units or even the fundamental building blocks of their states, nor did they originally assume broad governmental powers and then relinquish some of them to central authority as in the Old World. This is true even of cities founded in colonial times and is particularly so in the case of the cities created in the post-Revolutionary West.[25] It is true that the first local governments to be instituted on these shores—the counties and towns of the Eastern seaboard—took on some of the characteristics of small republics (particularly in New England) but they, too, were formally and primarily instruments of their colonial governments.

TABLE 9-5

Cities of the Prairie: Sources of Local Government Revenues, 1957 and 1962

Metropolitan Area	Total Revenue		State Funds (thousands of dollars)		Federal Funds	
	1957	1962	1957	1962	1957	1962
Champaign-Urbana	a	24,524	a	4,301	a	1,201
Decatur	16,436	24,486	2,910	5,309	b	48
Joliet	18,297	33,764	2,485	6,020	170	385
Madison-St. Clair	57,802	92,972	12,968	21,306	992	1,746
Peoria[2]	22,004	34,616	3,185	5,027	386	567
Rockford	27,779	41,879	4,336	8,380	34	65
Rock Island-Moline-Silvis	22,546	35,357	3,825	6,318	37	432
Springfield	21,476	33,652	3,402	5,774	c	77
Duluth[3]	58,387	83,710	11,736	20,833	469	432
Superior	9,497	11,693	4,767	6,488	132	145
Pueblo	20,406	28,666	6,903	9,588	321	718
Davenport	14,009	25,312	2,800	2,534	36	233

[a]Not included in census figures.
[b]Peoria County only.
[c]Includes all of St. Louis County.
Sources: *Local Government Finances in Standard Metropolitan Area* (1957 Census of Governments, Vol. III, No. 6) and *Local Government in Metropolitan Areas* (1962 Census of Governments, Vol. V, No. 12).

In the United States, the central government charged with the creation and supervision of local governments has always been and continues to be the state. Incorporation—the formal granting of legal existence and authority to a local community—could (and can) only come from a state or a state-surrogate (a colony or a territory). Not only is this a legal requirement but it is an accurate reflection of the basic fact that most American cities originated not as complete communities in the classic sense but as local service centers to serve local needs, first in an agricultural and commercially oriented society and later in more urbanized variations of that society.

If there is any precedent for this mode of urbanization it is to be found in the "cities" of Israel described in the Bible. The Israelite city

TABLE 9-6

Loci of Local Action and Political Power in the Cities of the Prairie

Civil Community	Locus of Local Action	Locus of Political Control	Locus of State Political Connections
Champaign	City, school, and special districts	Township and county political organizations	County political organization and University of Illinois
Urbana	City, school, and special districts	City, township, and county political organizations	County political organization and University of Illinois
Decatur	City, school, and special districts	Township and county political organizations	County political organization
Joliet	City, school, and special districts	City, township, and county political organizations	County political organization
Alton	City, school, and special districts	Township and county political organizations	County political organization
Belleville	City, school, and special districts	City and township political organizations	City political organization
E. St. Louis	City, school, and special districts	Township and county political organizations	County political organization
Peoria	City, school, and special districts	City, township, and county political organizations	County political organization
Davenport	City and county, school and special districts	City and county political organizations	County political organization
E. Moline	City, school, and special districts	Township political organizations	County political organization
Moline	City, school, and special districts	City and township political organizations	County political organization
Rock Island	City, school, and special districts	City, township, and county political organizations	County political organization
Rockford	City, township, and special districts	City and township political organizations	County political organization
Springfield	City, school, and special districts	City, township, and county political organizations	County political organization and influential individuals
Duluth	City and county	City and county political organizations	Congressional district political organization
Superior	City and county	City and county political organizations	County political organization
Pueblo	City, county, school, and special districts	City and county political organizations	County political organization

is the classical predecessor of the American city. Israelite cities were not founded as separate autonomous civil societies but as civil communities, creatures of their respective tribes which provided their immediate supra-local governmental structure under the umbrella of the national constitution.[26] Local governments in the countries informed by this second pattern have traditionally been instituted by supra-local authority to serve local purposes primarily, while central government (or "sovereign") authority remains vested in higher echelons of the civil society. Accordingly, they have never had a claim to local autonomy like that of their European counterparts. Indeed, except for the largest among them, which have come to more closely approximate the European model, American cities have been hard put to develop identities of the kind that will encourage their residents to conceive of themselves as "citizens" of "the city," with a concomitant civic pride. Cities have been looked upon by their residents primarily as useful vehicles for providing specific public services rather than as the centers of society in any normative sense. This explains part of the difficulty civil reformers have in persuading the residents of cities to undertake radical and comprehensive programs of civic development (usually designed to make the cities more "citified"). Lacking a sense of "the city," people are not likely to respond to calls to action predicated on the existence of such sentiment. Their pragmatic view of the city as a utilitarian device for the satisfaction of specific needs may make them receptive to proposals for specific programs (if they are designed to meet felt needs) but no more than that.

This outlook has been reinforced by America's traditional agrarian outlook described in Chapter One. It has been additionally strengthened by the nearly "nomadic" tendencies that are found so deeply embedded in the patterns of American life. Such tendencies function to lead masses of Americans, particularly the most articulate citizens, to move out of their native cities to seek "opportunity" without constraint and often to migrate from city to city in the course of a lifetime. Among such people loyalty to one's city of residence at any particular time is heavily diluted by a sense of transience and impermanence on one hand, and by emotional and familial attachments to an original "home town" on the other. Finally, the average American's essentially private and economic-oriented interest in his city, which is almost invariably the limit of his civic concern, is both the product of this historical pattern of development and a means of reinforcing that pattern in our own day.[27]

The "home-rule" struggle, which has dominated the attention of reformers and city officials alike for better than two generations, and the manner in which "home rule" has failed even where written into state constitutions is but one reflection of this. The entire question of local government structure is another.

Since local governments have been instituted by higher authority in response to specific local governmental needs as they have been perceived, their establishment has come about piecemeal as new tasks have developed for local authorities to undertake. With no demand for the development of a central government for the city, there was little or no demand for the development of a centralized government there either. On the contrary, it was frequently advantageous for both the state and those local citizens interested in increasing local functions to secure the creation of separate local authorities.

Today, problems relative to the establishment of new local governments are confined almost entirely to municipal incorporations and the creation of special districts. The national pattern of counties was fixed in the days of the land frontier and has remained generally stable since then. No county in Illinois is less than one hundred years old, and even the counties of Minnesota and Colorado are, with one exception, at least fifty years old. The township pattern was also fixed in the same period, though the rise of the urban-industrial frontier led to the creation of city townships in Illinois (which serve Peoria, Champaign, Springfield, Belleville, and East St. Louis among the cities of the prairie); the separation of cities and villages from towns (the equivalent of townships) in Wisconsin; Iowa's abolition of township governments in all but in name; and the statewide limitation of township functions, as well as outright abandonment of township organization in the northern counties in Minnesota. At the same time, there has been a great growth in the number of municipalities and special-district governments with municipal powers, particularly since the opening of the metropolitan frontier. These new local governments are occasionally created by direct state action but are more commonly established through local referenda conducted under the terms of state law.

The Civil Community and Local Autonomy

Given the extent of intergovernmental collaboration that ties the political systems of nation, state, and locality together, where does this leave the civil community? In what way can it be considered to be a political system in its own right in light of its virtually total involvement in intergovernmental relations on one hand and its fragmented character on the other? To what extent does it possess the necessary power or influence to control the bundle of governmental services and activities that are maintained within its boundaries?

The very reaction of the localities to the cooperative system is an indication of the way in which they are able to carve places within it for themselves as civil communities. Though local leaders may denounce this intricate system of collaboration in general terms for political reasons, with a few exceptions they do not view it with hostility. Local communities seek federal aid in many ways and for many purposes. City officials in Springfield seek expert advice on building a jail; park commissioners in Rock Island seek financial aid in developing a park; local businessmen in Rockford seek funds for airport improvement and for transfer of an old military installation to their city; public and private parties in Pueblo seek lands for industrial development and grants of fire-fighting equipment under the civil defense program. It is apparently an impossible task even to list the federal aids and services available to the civil community—from model plumbing codes to construction of marinas to disaster relief—since no one seems to know exactly how many hundreds there are. And these federal activities are not viewed locally as a forcible intrusion of a distant central government but, almost invariably, as the successful consequences of local activity in steering federal programs to serve local ends in a manner good for community and nation both.

This local view, developed over time through concrete experiences rather than by abstract logic, is historically correct because it reflects the noncentralized nature of the American system. Because it is not a hierarchical system in which orders flow neatly from top to bottom nor even a circular one in which decisions flow from the center, it often appears to be mildly chaotic. The lack of centralized authority, however, does not mean that some order does not exist within its bounds. On the contrary, the creators of American federalism purposely sought to establish order without centralization. Their solution was an orderly but not ordered matrix linking numerous power centers on several planes. Such a matrix of dispersed power centers provides the essential design underlying the cooperative system. While every plane of government is involved in all governmental activities, each operates from its own position of power within the matrix and together they provide a series of focal points for the organization of the system.

Let us return to our exemplary and apparently over-divided sanitarian. With all the hats that he may wear from time to time he remains, first and foremost, a local official whose formal position and informal ties revolve around his location within and attachment to the civil community he serves. Indeed, it is the civil community he serves which determines the extent of his service. While his office is charged with certain basic responsibilities by the state, on behalf of both the state and federal governments (in a strict sense, he is never a federal officer except insofar as he is mandated by the state to enforce federal laws), the full range of his activities is determined locally.

Thus the three sanitarians in Pueblo County are officers of the City-County Health Department and are directly responsible to a department director who is officially the county health officer and clearly a local public servant, though his department obtains much federal and state aid. The Pueblo Health Department performs many services beyond the Colorado minimum requirements and is the pride of the Pueblo civil community. The expansion of departmental functions has been a matter of local initiative. The organization of the department as a joint one was decided upon by the city and county governments after pressure from the local Community Welfare Council (a federation of local nongovernmental public welfare bodies), which sought to develop coordinated countywide public health services, and in conformity with state law. The means and form of local financing are products of the same city-county negotiations and are based on a formula devised by the department engineer. The health director was appointed by the local Board of Health under provisions of state law. The Public Health Building, which was partly financed by federal aid under the Hill-Burton Act, was authorized by public referendum only after agitation by the Health Department staff and authorization by the city council and the county board. Aside from the usual range of functions, by 1961 the department had opted to provide medical care for county welfare patients, establish a mental health program, operate a diagnostic and evaluation center for the mentally retarded, and develop a medical education program, all by local decision and all with outside financial aid.

Virtually every program of the Pueblo department has been assisted by federal funds and, sometimes, by personnel from the United States Public Health Service. Federal money has given it much of its flexibility to develop new programs. As one staff member put it, "We would be in real hot water if some congressman wanted to see how federal funds are used." Once the funds are granted, it is the local agency which, within broad limits, determines their use locally. In this it is supported by its state counterpart. All federal funds are channeled through the State Health Department, which employs and distributes them in such a way that the local people do not know what is state money and what is federal. Furthermore, the state health people assume, in essence, that Congress does not know the local situation well enough to specify uses for the funds it grants, so they have little hesitation in taking federal money for one purpose and then diverting it for other purposes which seem more vital to them wherever possible. In this they have the active support of the district health departments (of which Pueblo's is one). As the Pueblo health director put it, "Almost all federal grants are for specific purposes. This is quite an imposition for us at the local level, to use the money as the grants intend." With the assistance of the state, they find ways to avoid this "imposition." When his department diverts funds from a mental retardation program to a health education project, the state department certifies the local reports without asking too many questions. Furthermore, in Colorado every local health department is allowed to develop its own personnel and merit system, which the state automatically certifies as complying with the Hatch Act requirements.[28]

In the Peoria civil community, the sanitarians are attached to separate city and county health departments. The division of functions in the county among the two departments is a matter of local choice, as is the measure of consolidation gained by the appointment of a joint director of health to head them both. In 1960, state and federal funds supplied 15 per cent of the county department's expenditures. In Illinois, as in Colorado, state control over all but a few special federal grants makes it virtually impossible for the local agency to distinguish between the two sources. Additional local leverage over federal grants is gained through the involvement of a wide variety of nongovernmental organizations which administer programs partially supported by the two government agencies. Cooperation with organizations such as the local Methodist and Catholic hospitals (the jointly sponsored poison control center exemplifies this collaboration), the Forest Park Foundation (the area's major philanthropic foundation), the Peoria-Tazewell County Heart Association, the Peoria County School Health Council, the Senior Citizens' Council, the local Cancer Society, and others enable the local health departments to engage in services which would otherwise be outside their purview and beyond their budgetary limitations. This locally established policy differs from Pueblo's, where the Community Welfare Council, a strong organization able to provide central community leadership for most of the similar agencies, provides direct support for health department-administered activities. The difference, itself a product of the different environments in the two civil communities, is illustrative of the possibilities for local discretion within the sharing system.

In the Joliet civil community, the Will County Health Department was actually founded through federal action. Because of the nearby Joliet Arsenal, the federal government took a hand in local health matters during World War II, intervening to create a defense zone health department in 1942 to control venereal disease. This department was subsequently made a local government by county-wide referendum. It is now supported by county taxes plus grants-in-aid and provides minimal health services for both the city of Joliet and the surrounding county. Additional city services are provided by the quasi-governmental Public Health Council, which serves the city and township of Joliet and gets some financial support from the county health department. Unlike either the Pueblo or Peoria health agencies, the Will County department's functions have remained substantially those required of it by federal and state law. Created by outside pressures, it has apparently failed to capture the imagination of any influential groups in the local community and remains little more than a local agency for the administration of programs deemed to be in the national and state interest. Even in this case, the department essentially governs itself, using local resources to emphasize one function or another as local needs seem to demand.

Three central factors aid the localities in their ability to exercise substantial control over the bundle of governmental services and activities provided locally, regardless of their formal point of origin. In the first place, the localities which do exercise control at any level of significance do so because they are organized as civil communities. It is the ability of the Pueblo City-County Health Department to draw upon the fiscal resources of the city and county to support its continuing activities and to serve as "bait" to attract outside funds; to utilize the political skills of the county's delegation in the state legislature and the region's congressman; to mobilize influentials in the community through the Community Welfare Council to support its plans; to convince voters of its value through services rendered and thus gain a constituency that will support it in its relations with the city council and county board; and to share its range of interests with the public nongovernmental agencies concerned with public health within the Pueblo civil community (such as the hospitals and the antidisease associations) that makes it possible for it to shape its programs to meet local needs no matter what the sources of their support. All these reflect the set of interacting institutions and relationships within a given locality that goes to make up a civil community.

It is in this sense that the civil community can be said to consist of the complex of local institutions organized to substantially control the bundle of public services and activities within its boundaries. The federal-state-local distinction loses much of its force at this point. The post office is as much a part of the civil community as the park district; the postmaster as much a member of the community as the park director, if not more so. Paradoxically, the postmaster is invariably appointed from among the local residents, often from among the political actives, while the park director is usually a professional, brought in for the job from outside the community, and is likely to move on should a more attractive opportunity in another community present itself. Neither is the "public-private" distinction of much importance here, since the political system of the civil community includes all institutions concerned with public life within it, regardless of their formal identification as "public" or "private." A chamber of commerce is as much a part of the civil community as a city council, an active family service agency as much as a sanitary district. There is, in effect, a continuum between the "public" and the "private" spheres.[29]

The ability of the civil community to exercise control over the bundle of governmental activities and services within its boundaries is enhanced by the complexity of the local bureaucracy it possesses to exercise that control. The lonesome sanitarian in the small Southern county is kept so busy performing functions of state and federal origin that he is hardly in any position to develop a community health policy and to implement it. Not so in Pueblo or in Peoria. The Peoria County Health Department, with its public health nursing staff of nine, its sanitarian staff of four, its two public health educators, dental director, business administrator, and its full-time director of health, an M.D., can not only provide a full range of services at the minimum level demanded by state law and national standards, but can develop additional programs to serve specific local needs or experiment with new programs in fields not yet covered by state and federal policy. It can do all this only with outside assistance, but it assimilates the assistance within the framework of a community health policy developed within the civil community. Thus professionalization and bureaucratization within the civil community can enhance its position vis-à-vis the professionals and bureaucrats of the other planes.

Finally, the ability of the civil community to control the bundle of governmental services and activities within its boundaries is enhanced by its position within the state civil society. In confronting the national pressures which are evident in everything that concerns it, the civil community is strengthened by its position as part of a civil society which is subnational in scope and accordingly has interests which not only need not be identical with those espoused on the national plane, but which can even go counter to them; which is concerned with its own subdivisions to a substantial degree; and which also is large enough and strong enough within the national civil society to take appropriate action to successfully defend its own concerns and those of its component civil communities, where necessary.

The value of membership in the state political system is apparent in many specific ways. Every state possesses considerable political power vis-à-vis Washington by virtue of its position in the constitutional and political system of the United States. Its two senators and the rest of its congressional delegation stand ready in Washington to run political interference for the legitimate (and, sometimes, not-so-legitimate) interests of the civil community in matters involving federal action. Every state has a well-developed bureaucracy which tends to be more professionalized the more it is involved in cooperative programs. This bureaucracy is in a position to shape federal programs along the lines it deems most appropriate for the state it serves. In doing so it is in a position either to help a local bureaucracy tailor the programs to fit its civil community or to provide the same assistance for civil communities too small to have local bureaucracies of their own. The state government not only provides a shield for localities in their relationship with the federal government but also provides technical and political support for aggressive local governments that wish to lead the way in negotiating specific new programs with their federal counterparts.

It is true that for these benefits, the state exacts its price. Most civil communities must compete for attention from their states before they can hope to obtain federal assistance. Securing state attention may depend on many factors, not all of which appear to the outside observer as immediately relevant to the issue at hand. The more energetic states, which run the best interference, also tend to exert the most control over local use of federal aids while the least energetic states actually jeopardize their civil communities' chances to get federal assistance, since the federal system is so constructed as to make state action almost mandatory before localities can get a proper hearing. This is particularly true in the case of medium-size and smaller civil communities, which do not possess sufficient political power to obtain direct access to Washington in and of themselves. The largest metropolitan centers, the so-called big-city blocs, do possess that power. They, in turn, often feel frustrated by their states' insistence on controlling their access as well. This frustration is heightened when state policies differ from those of the big cities. For, in the last analysis, the states do not exist just to "run interference" for their civil communities. They have policies and interests of their own, articulated or not, to which the civil communities must bend.

By and large, the medium-size civil communities and their smaller counterparts benefit considerably from association with their states. Their policies are in most cases reasonably similar to state policies, and their needs can best be satisfied with state assistance. Not only that but, as components of the state civil societies whose leadership, political and professional, can and usually does have face-to-face contact with their opposite numbers at the state level, they can also influence state policies, generally even more than they can hope to influence national ones.

In the last analysis, the extent to which any specific civil community can capitalize on the opportunities available to it within the national civil society depends on the character and constitution of its political system and the individual local governments which are embodied within it. Though the system gives every civil community and its local governments a multiplicity of "cracks" (both in the sense of blows against the state and federal political systems and fissures through which the locally generated blows can penetrate) to use to bend any given program in the direction desired locally, it is the responsibility of the individual civil community to make use of these cracks. If local initiative is not present, the opportunities will remain unrealized.

As one focal point within the national civil society, the civil community serves in five major capacities: as an acquirer of outside aids—governmental and nongovernmental—for local needs; as an adaptor of government actions and services to local values and conditions; as an experimenter with new functions and services (or readaptations of traditional ones); as an initiator of governmental programs of particular relevance locally that may or may not become widespread later; and as the means through which the local population may secure an effective voice in governmental decisions that affect them.

The combination of local organization as a civil community to coordinate the public activities of the locality, development of a professionalized local bureaucracy to handle the programs of government within the civil community, and utilization of the state as a means by which to gain access to Washington and control over federal programs makes it possible for the civil community to be a meaningful political system despite its lack of "autonomy" in the classic sense of separateness. It also makes it possible to talk about "local political systems" as real entities and in realistic terms.

NOTES

1. For a fuller exposition of this point, see Morton Grodzins, *The American System: A New View of Government in the United States* ed. Daniel J. Elazar (Chicago: Rand McNally, 1966), and Daniel J. Elazar, *The American Partnership* (Chicago: University of Chicago Press, 1962).

2. The concept "civil society" is derived from the political philosophers who, in recognition of the fact that society does not exist without government, used it to characterize the social organization of mankind in accordance with nature and for the realization of some form of justice on earth [see Leo Strauss, *Natural Right and History* (Chicago: University of Chicago Press, 1953), pp. 130–132]. The good civil society, as the first political philosophers conceived of it, was a small, closed society, identical with the city-state of the ancient Greeks. They could not conceive of the possibility of a truly just (even by limited human standards) civil society larger than that in which every "mature [member] could find his bearings through his own observation, without having to rely habitually on indirect information in matters of vital importance" (Strauss, *op. cit.*). The small civil society, capable of (though not necessarily successful in) perfecting man when constructed under the proper constitution, was termed the "city." What this writer calls the civil community is roughly comparable *in size* to the classic civil society. The latter became practically obsolete even while it was being delineated theoretically. The concept of "civil society" was reconstructed and expanded by the political philosophers of the seventeenth and eighteenth centuries, who adapted it to the modern nation-state. This enlarged conception of "civil society," in its federal modification, is the basis for the present usage. In legal terms, such a civil society would be termed "sovereign." However, the modern situation has made the classic conception of sovereignty obsolete, even in the case of so-called sovereign nations, hence the more cautious definition of a political system possessing relative autonomy advanced here. For an elaboration of the concept of the political system, see David Easton, *The Political System* (New York: Alfred A. Knopf, 1953), Chapter 5.

The nation and its states are civil societies because they are defined primarily in political terms. Their political boundaries determine their outer limits, and they are distinguishable from other societies in large measure because of the particular political ends they serve. In a real sense there is no form of society other than civil society since mankind, naturally social, does not exist in society ungoverned, and the existence of government implies a society organized politically, based upon certain principles of justice and possessing institutions with reasonable power to implement those principles or to make them effective agents of social control within its boundaries.

3. It should be pointed out that the largest cities in the United States may well have many of the characteristics of individuated civil societies. This, in part, accounts for the conflict between these great cities and their states over matters of public policy and public finance. I have dealt with this distinction in *American Federalism: A View from the States* (New York: Thomas Y. Crowell, 1966), Chap. 7.

4. Recent research has indicated that, regardless of the local origins of demands for governmental action, the initiation of such action has come from the higher levels of government—federal and state. See Elazar, *The American Partnership*. The series of monographs on intergovernmental relations in Minnesota, edited by William Anderson and Edward Weidner, documents the thesis of higher level sources for governmental action in depth for that state, one which has as good a record of public willingness to accept an expanded role for government as any in the Union.

5. For an analysis of the noncentralized political system and the elements that support it, see Elazar, *American Federalism: A View from the States* and Grodzins, *The American System*.

6. See James G. Coke, "The Lesser Metropolitan Areas of Illinois," and Samuel Gove, ed., *Illinois State Government* (Urbana, Ill.: Institute of Government and Public Affairs, 1958).

7. For a discussion of the effects of these universal concerns on American government prior to 1913, see Elazar, *The American Partnership*, Part III.

8. For a more detailed exposition of this phenomenon see Clark Chambers, *Seedtime of Reform* (Minneapolis: University of Minnesota Press, 1963), and Arthur Schlesinger, Jr.'s trilogy, *The Age of Roosevelt* (Boston: Houghton Mifflin, 1957).

9. It is to be hoped that this obvious oversimplification will be understood as a generalized description of the aggregate situation in the United States. The author is quite aware of the neofeudalistic elements in the early colonization of this country and of the effects they had, even in their ultimate failure, on the American socio-political system. The full fruition of modernism did not come until the Americans crossed the Appalachian Mountains and began the settlement of their own West. However, none of this negates the essential and vital truth that the institutions of American society, including those of the urban civil community, are products of the modern era that emerged in Europe in the middle of the seventeenth century after a century's gestation and which were implanted on these shores from the very beginning of English settlement. American institutions have, without exception, been developed in an effort to meet the problems of modernism.

10. For an analysis of the role of the post office in local politics in the cities of the prairie, see Ion E. Fehrenbocher, "The Post Office in Illinois Politics of the 1850's," *Journal of the Illinois State Historical Society*, XLVI, No. 1 (Spring 1953), 60–71.

11. The question of "fragmentation" is discussed more fully (and with specific reference to the cities of the prairie) in Daniel J. Elazar, " 'Fragmentation' and Local Organizational Response to Federal-City Programs," *Urban Affairs Quarterly*, Vol. II, No. 4 (June 1967), pp. 30–46.

12. For a summary of this phenomenon that goes beyond the limits of this study, see Urban Politics Research Group, *Memorandum No. 5* (July 1962).

13. *Illinois Constitution*, Article X, Sections 1 to 7, and Illinois Municipal Code. Smith Hurd, *Illinois Annotated Statutes*, Permanent Edition, Chapter 24, *Cities and Villages 1942* (Illinois, 1942). For a history of "home rule" in Illinois, see pp. 22, 25, 47, 65.

14. *Iowa Constitution,* Article II, Section 30; Article XI, Section 3 (Special Charters: Davenport, Muscatine, Wapello, Camanche).

15. *Minnesota Constitution,* Article XI, Sections 1 to 4.

16. *Wisconsin Constitution,* Article XI, Section 3.

17. *Colorado Constitution,* Article 20, Section 6. For an examination of home rule in Colorado, see Benjamin Schuster, "State-Relations with Home Rule and Non-Home Rule Communities: Colorado and Illinois," unpublished paper, Temple University, Department of Political Science (1968).

18. For a full and authoritative discussion of this fundamental principle, see Henry M. Hart and Herbert Wechsler, *Federal Courts and the Federal System* (Brooklyn: Foundation Press, 1953).

19. Charles R. Adrian, *Governing Urban America,* 2d ed. (New York: McGraw-Hill, 1961), p. 171.

20. John F. Dillon, *Commentaries on the Law of Municipal Corporations,* 5th ed. (Boston: Little, Brown, 1911), Vol. I, Sec. 237.

21. The most recent and perhaps most comprehensive historical review of the origin, development, and meaning of cities is Lewis Mumford's monumental *The City in History* (New York: Harcourt, Brace, & World, 1961). While this work is limited through its reflection of the pronounced views of its author, which are unhesitatingly expressed with all the vigor at his command, it remains a most valuable guide to the unfolding of urbanism as a form of social organization. A further description of the ancient city may be found in Numa de Fustel de Coulanges, *The Ancient City,* tr. Willard Small (Magnolia, Miss.: Peter Smith, 1952).

22. Herbert Muller provides us with a convenient description of this phenomenon in *Freedom in the Ancient World* (New York: Harper, 1961).

23. The purpose of the *polis* in the imperial systems of that epoch is discussed in Victor Tcherikover, *Hellenistic Civilization and the Jews* (Jerusalem: Magnes Press, The Hebrew University, 1959), particularly Part I, Chapter 2, and Part II, Chapter 2.

24. Erwin Austin Gutkind's multi-volume series, *International History of City Development* (New York: The Free Press of Glencoe, 1964–1967), is an excellent source of data about medieval cities. See also Henri Pirenne, *Medieval Cities* (Princeton, N.J.: Princeton University Press, 1925).

25. For a brief but comprehensive summary of the development of local government in the American colonies and the early United States, see Clyde F. Snider, *Local Government in Rural America* (New York: Appleton-Century-Crofts, 1957).

26. There is some historical and archeological evidence to show that the difference in the origins of the classical and Biblical cities should be of considerable interest to students of urbanization in the contemporary world, since the differences were subsequently reflected in different patterns of growth as well. While the classical city became increasingly "urban," urbane, and self-contained, the Biblical city remained predominantly a "non-city"; rural in outlook and orientation and—the exigencies of military security permitting—diffuse and almost "metropolitan" or "suburbanized" (to use two highly anachronistic terms of description) in structure. In the former, the distinction between urbane and rural ways of life grew sharp with the passage of time and tended to increase the political cleavage between "city" and "country." The sociological distinction between "urban" and "rural" tended to remain minimal in the latter and little political cleavage developed. Social change in the land of Israel during the Biblical period tended to be more or less uniform throughout the country. Furthermore, the Israelite cities were predominantly oasis cities for reasons of climate and topography. All told, they provided a prototype for city development that differed considerably from that of the classic polis, and which, without any direct connection, has found its home in the New World. Unfortunately, there are

few studies bearing directly on the nature of the Biblical-Israelite city. The Israelite city is described in Gaalyahu Cornfield, *Pictorial Encyclopedia* (New York: Macmillan, 1965), and the *Book of Joshua,* Chaps 12–13. Mumford, *op. cit.*, is also useful in this connection.

27. The author elaborates on this thesis in his chapter, "Are We a Nation of Cities?" in Robert Goldwin, ed., *A Nation of Cities* (Chicago: Rand McNally, 1968).

28. Since this study was completed, the Public Health Service and Congress have taken cognizance of state and local demands for greater flexibility and have replaced the categorical allotments with block grants that, *ipso facto,* legitimize many of the things which the Pueblo department—and others—were doing under the table.

29. For a discussion of the interaction of public and private groups at the local level, see Grodzins, *The American System*, Chapter 9.

Postscript / The Civil Community at Midfrontier

The Twin Tasks of American Politics

THE PATH which American society has chosen—or had thrust upon it—imposes a dual burden on American political institutions. On one hand, they share major responsibilities for opening new frontiers and, on the other, they carry the major burdens of solving the problems generated by those frontiers. The governments of the United States have always been called upon to encourage the scientific and technological development needed to break the ground for new frontiers, create a political framework without which nongovernmental and individual enterprise could not move out onto those frontiers, and provide the necessary public infrastructure for their conquest. The very process of conquering each frontier has in every case generated a host of problems, positive and negative, ranging from those immediately incidental to the development of the frontier's resources and the shift of population to the frontier zone to long range problems requiring the opening of yet newer frontiers for their resolution.

The governments of the United States, singly and collectively, have not only been expected to solve the frontier problems facing American society at any particular time (not simply *meet*, but *solve* them) but the political system and its subsystems are blamed when the problems are not, or cannot be, solved. State and local political institutions, constitutionally located on the cutting edge of the frontier, have had to bear more than their share of the blame in such cases. The major thrust of American politics, then, has been toward coming to grips with one frontier after another. The political history of the cities of the prairie stands as stark evidence of this fact.

Since many of the frontier-generated problems which cannot be solved by being met head-on have a way of diminishing with the passage of time and changing frontiers, the political systems that must deal with them are able to outlast them without having to undergo serious change if they can simply keep them under control. Perception of this (conscious or unconscious) can—and sometimes does—lead to a very conservative response on the part of the nation's political leaders to the challenges of frontier problems, even among those who avidly support governmental assumption of the responsibilities for opening new frontiers. Such a response is particularly characteristic of the traditionalistic political culture. However, a majority of the political leaders, like their constituents, share the outlook fostered by America's other two political cultures (as a consequence of other frontier experiences) that problems are meant to be solved by men. So they also expect the political institutions to rise to the occasion once the problems are recognized and defined.

Out of the frontier challenges and these institutional responses there has developed a dialectic of intergenerational change that has already persisted for at least two centuries through three frontier stages and three renegotiations of the social compact which gives the United States its shape as a nation. The ways in which the cities of the prairie have come to grips with the problems of the metropolitan frontier in the half-generation following World War II offer some insights into the overall dialectic and into the variations in local responses due to the differing challenges that emerge from each local synthesis of the forces of frontier, culture, and section.

The Frontier and the Continuing American Revolution

Inevitably, the movement of the frontier is initially more rapid than the political response to it can be. In the first place, it takes time for people to recognize that a new frontier stage with its attendant new problems has begun. The sheer political problem of translating that recognition into requisite political action increases the time lag while the cumulative impact of the frontier continues to add to the degree of political response needed.

The extent of the response needed in any particular generation depends upon the point in each frontier stage at which that generation is called upon to respond. Particularly in the early stages of a new frontier, the demands for revolutionary action in the political realm are great. In every case, including the most recent one, not only do the problems of dislocation and readjustment which attend every frontier advance have to be dealt with but new communities—territorial, ethnic, or racial—have had to be integrated into the body politic.

This has necessitated certain kinds of political reconstitutions that at times have had revolutionary force and impact. These revolutionary forces become particularly intense just after the first burst on the new frontier when sufficient change has taken place to unleash them while the momentum of the frontier itself is at least momentarily diminishing. This study was concluded at the beginning of that point in the history of the metropolitan frontier, and so it deals with the easier aspects of political reconstitution in the cities of the prairie, the ones that paved the way for the release of the harsher revolutionary forces of the 1960's. Recognition and understanding of those aspects are important in understanding the larger political impact of the frontier on American society.

Even aside from the political revolutions it may trigger, the burdens arising from the frontier often appear to be overwhelming, too heavy a price to pay for what is otherwise accepted as "progress." Nor should they be underestimated. Frontier-caused dislocations can and do breed maladjustment, alienation, and anomie. Crime, mental illness, juvenile delinquency, and the high divorce rate, to name only a few of the plagues afflicting contemporary America, in all probability have been exacerbated by frontier conditions. The historical and statistical record, fragmentary as it is, shows all these and other similar problems to have been present in abundance on all of America's frontiers. To take one example, Americans are inherently no more and no less violent than other men, but the American frontier has encouraged a certain kind of violence in every one of its stages. The violence of the 1960's is not a result of any "frontier heritage"—only the choice of weapons can be blamed on that—but a response to an immediate frontier situation. There is no minimizing any of this. Perhaps the cost now comes to more than value received. That is a judgment that Americans must make in every generation. But first it is necessary to understand the source of the costs.

At the same time, the regular recurrence of the highly visible pressures generated by the frontier has prepared Americans to undertake the periodic social and political reconstitutions necessary in any society if it is to remain an open and vital one. The way in which reform has been institutionalized in American political life is a matter of great fascination and significance. Since the Revolutionary War, every generation has gone through a period of *reform* activity of greater or lesser magnitude. The periodic *reconstitution* of American communities is less frequent. Only three such reconstitutions have taken place to date. But, because they have involved changes in the fundamental distribution of political power and even in the *de facto* or *de jure* definition of citizenship, they have had even wider ramifications for the reintegration of a civil society under continued stress. To date, they have been able to keep revolutionary drives within the bounds of the nation's larger constitution, offering an alternative path to change rather than either simple reform or drastic revolution.

If the frontier has generated many of the problems and most of the stress faced by Americans, individually and collectively, in every generation, the federal system has dictated how these problems would be considered and handled governmentally by decisively influencing the kinds of issues raised in American politics and the way in which issues are developed and resolved. Within the complexities of the country's intergovernmental partnership, the problems and stresses that lead to efforts at reconstitution develop on a nationwide basis, often in an immediate response to a depression or war that demands national effort under federal direction. However, it is the lot of the civil community to be the first to make the major adjustments inherent in the reconstitution and then to be the ultimate concretizer of such national reconstitution as does finally take place.

World War II was the catalyst for a new era of reconstitution in American history. The shaking loose of populations, the renewal of prosperity, and the opening of the metropolitan-technological frontier on a grand scale all combined to demand drastic changes in American civil communities and civil societies alike. In the half-generation immediately following World War II, the civil communities of the nation became the major battlegrounds in the fight to meet those demands, the focal points for myriad local revolutions and reconstitutions that were the first steps toward the struggle for national reconstitution that began in earnest in the 1960's.

Almost all of the first responses to the metropolitan frontier, involving the provision of new public services tailored to its demands, came in the civil communities. Sometimes they acted with direct federal and state assistance, but frequently they began to act without either except where particular civil communities could redirect existing aid programs. In fact, the problems toward which the services were directed were hardly perceived to be other than local ones by almost all concerned until close to the end of the 1950's.

Local efforts in the field of education alone (the nation's second largest public enterprise, after national defense, in terms of dollar expenditures and largest in terms of employment) would have put them in the forefront of the governmental response to the new frontier. With very minor exceptions, the full burden of the expansion of the public education system below the college level fell upon the civil communities, albeit with some state aid. Education has been but part of a larger local effort. The major burden of providing the public infrastructure for settling the new frontier

—organizing the new subdivisions and supplying them with all the services they demanded plus raising the level of services in the community as a whole to meet new qualitative demands—fell upon the civil communities.

In all cases, the response to these demands on the part of the nation's many civil communities was highly localized. With few exceptions, the particular demands placed upon them were met. This was certainly true of the cities of the prairie, among which demands and responses varied widely. Despite the myths to the contrary, local government cannot be said to have failed to exert itself in the provision of services. The expansion of federal and state assistance in the 1960's has come on top of these exertions to extend their impact, not because the exertions were not made.

Even more important than the provision of new services, the crucial steps necessary for the further democratization of American politics were taken in the civil communities. In the most direct sense, the demise of machine politics in its several variations with the concomitant introduction of new kinds of political activists into local political systems has broadened the distribution of political power in the country. At first the redistribution was primarily local but, as the new men have advanced their own political careers, it has been felt on the state and national planes as well. Of the seven members of Congress representing the cities of the prairie in 1968, at least five have emerged as political leaders on the metropolitan frontier, as have eight of their states' ten senators. They simply represent the top of the iceberg. Equally important are the many state and local officeholders, public officials, party workers, and civic leaders brought into public affairs from hitherto untapped sources as a result of the changes in community politics in the postwar years.

The key to the democratization of the civil community lay in the merging of the "two cities" created *de facto* during the century of the great Atlantic migration. The opening of civic life to people from all ethnic or racial groups, religions, and cultural streams as equals was undoubtedly a byproduct of the mixing of populations during World War II, but its first meaningful fulfillment came in the civil community as a response to the new world of the metropolitan frontier. What was started there has since spread upward and outward, encouraged by national conditions and the opportunities opened up by the metropolitan frontier and, in the case of the Afro-Americans, by federal action as well.

In fact, the black revolution is the culmination of this merging of the two cities, the last stage in the process. A good case can be made that racial integration, which is clearly the most revolutionary aspect of the reconstitution of contemporary American society, involving as it does the renegotiation of the nation's social compact to eliminate racism from its political and social life, was only made possible by first integrating the new white immigrant groups with the old ones. Once integration of populations under the precepts of the Declaration of Independence gained momentum, there was no stopping it along racial borders. Again, the beginnings were made in the cities (and states) where employment opportunities raised the black population *and* its aspirations, where the first modern antidiscrimination legislation was enacted, where the first positive programs to meet Negro problems were inaugurated and where Afro-Americans began to enter politics in the usual way. Minnesota's strong fair-employment and fair-housing legislation; the emergence of Negro school board members and elected officials in a number of the cities of the prairie; the role of the Illinois Youth Commission, particularly in Rockford, and Southern Illinois University in the East St. Louis area all typify strictly state and local responses to the problem of racial equality that not only came while the federal government was still paralyzed by the powerful southern Democrats but pioneered the national laws, programs, and progress of the next decade. Though the revolutionary front was briefly shifted to Washington (principally between 1963 and 1966), it has since returned with a vengeance to the local scene where the racial revolution will ultimately have to complete its tasks.

In short, the thrust of national reform and reconstitution of the 1960's and the public ferment that has accompanied them must be viewed as extensions of the local reform and reconstitution movements of the late 1940's and 1950's. It is the civil community which first assumed the once-in-a-century burden of reconstituting American civil society, a burden the country has not had to shoulder since the Civil War.

The "Westernization" of the United States

A major aspect of the metropolitan-technological frontier's impact has been the increasing "westernization" of the entire country. In a sense, this newest frontier has brought the greater West into its own, not simply in the shift of population westward and certainly not in the redistribution of national power—though there has been some of both since World War II—but in becoming the decisive social force in the nation, the crucial influence on the changes in human behavior and social organization which have characterized the new frontier. In the process, America's life style has been radically changed in some vital ways.

The greater West in its two major sections has always stood for what is archetypally American in the American mystique. The Middle West has represented the archetypal American at home, presiding over the fundamental continuity of American values, while the Far West has symbolized the archetypal American adventure, the individual's search for wealth, excitement, and new things at the end of the rainbow. In both manifestations, the greater West has been the quintessence of the American frontier and, as such, the sphere most easily adaptable to changing frontiers.

This may well be because of the geohistorical context within which the greater West was formed. While the United States as a whole has been able to capitalize on the greatest technological revolution since the emergence of civilization, it may be truly said that the greater West is the product of that revolution. The greater Northeast has been enriched by the new technology but only after paying the price which was demanded of it, namely the recasting of those parts of its original social order developed in the pre-industrial colonial period which were not entirely suited to an industrialized society. The greater South actually resisted the technological revolution for many years, raising its plantation-centered agrarianism to the level of an ideologically endorsed socioeconomic system. The Civil War reflected its resistance to the technological revolution to no little extent. Even after succumbing to necessity and embracing the new technology, the South has continued to make every effort to mold it in the image of that sphere's lost agrarian past. In the greater West, there was no past, for all intents and purposes, prior to the arrival of the new technology. Hence the very fabric of its society is rooted in the technological revolution which made its settlement possible.

The chain reaction generated in the greater West by that technological revolution has today spread throughout the country so that, just as the nineteenth century saw the easternizing of the West, the twentieth is witnessing the westernizing of the East. The physical structure of the contemporary American city is a case in point. Its basic architectural patterns are, to an increasing degree, developing along lines pioneered in the cities of the greater West. The traditional Eastern city, whose structural patterns were established in colonial times, was characterized by relatively high population density spread more or less uniformly throughout its relatively small area in buildings of medium height, with a minimum of open space preserved within its built-up areas. In cities like New York and Boston, the coming of the industrial revolution simply reinforced that pattern as single-family row houses gave way to medium-rise tenements jam-packed together around the central business district. Where greenery was valued, as in Philadelphia, low and medium-rise row housing that mixed residential and commercial uses continued to predominate at uniformly high densities throughout the city. The traditional Southern city resembled its Eastern sister in many respects except that it emphasized lower densities and less well-defined limits. Half buried in the forests which inevitably surrounded it, its buildings were even lower and far less uniform than those of the Northeast, and its center far less well defined. In the twentieth century, both of these patterns, in both spheres, have given way to one that more closely approximates the tower and village combination characteristic of the American city as it evolved west of the Great Lakes, first at the city's edges and slowly, through urban redevelopment, in its very core.

The skyscraper with its steel frame construction and its own internal transportation system (the elevator), which stands at the central core of the American urbanized area, was first developed in Minneapolis, Chicago, and Kansas City. It has provided a means to conquer and "settle" yet another kind of previously unconquered space. The two basic styles of the contemporary mass-produced free-standing single-family home common on the suburban frontier throughout the country were evolved in the greater West as urban adaptations of the quickly erected balloon-construction farmhouse of the prairies or the ranchhouse of the plains. They were brought east to provide housing in the agrarian style favored by Americans for larger urban populations, of a kind which had previously been available only to the well-to-do who could afford the solid, custom-built dwellings produced in the Eastern mode. The principle of sharply separated commercial districts and residential neighborhoods is another product of the greater West. So is the idea of low-rise commercial and industrial structures for outlying districts, designed to keep the overall density of urban settlement low and to maintain the feeling of spaciousness which Americans (particularly Westerners) have valued at least since coming out onto the prairies better than a century ago. Combined, these elements have furnished the basic ingredients for the design of the urban centers that dominates contemporary American society in all three spheres.

The contemporary American transportation system also reflects the influence of the greater West. The chief characteristic of movement in that sphere has always been the traversing of vast empty spaces between settled oases, out of touch with humanity except at a few specific points of human occupation. Air travel and the limited access highway have created highly analogous situations in the other two spheres. Where the spread of population had previously made travel through an easily accessible settled landscape the rule, men now move in new dimensions from earthbound oasis to oasis as cut off from their fellows in the interim as the Deadwood stage once was. What population growth and technology have tied together, men have found new ways to tear asunder. In Illinois, the travel facilities that puncture the isolation of the state's toll roads are formally called oases. Every major city around the country becomes something of an oasis within the new air-land transportation system.

As part of the creation of a new spatial dimension in the United States, the limited access highways, with the airways, have changed the space-time relationship in normal communications. Measurement of distance is increasingly a matter of hours and minutes rather than mileage, with the crucial factor the time it takes to move from point to point rather than the space to be traversed. One result of this has been the development of a willingness in the Eastern megalopolis to travel hundreds of miles for a day's activity, an attitude formerly found only among the people of the greater West. In doing so, the new highways and skyways have opened new vistas from which to gain perspective on the land and its settlement patterns, creating a new sense of spaciousness and vastness where confinement and often unpleasant intimacy of scale were once the only perspectives available.

The sense of spaciousness characteristic of the greater West has spread eastward and southward for another reason: the actual increase of open space virtually on the doorsteps of the great megalopolis and the other metropolitan areas in those spheres. The abandonment of the Appalachian countryside has created ever larger areas in northern New England, New York, Pennsylvania, Virginia, and West Virginia with land-frontier-like densities of less than six and, in places, even less than two people per square mile. The reappearance of this kind of open space within easy freeway access of the nation's most densely populated areas is beginning to restore or foster a concern with the outdoors common in the greater West but hitherto absent in the greater Northeast. Much of this area is being turned into nature reserves of one kind or another with the federal government beginning to make its presence felt in a manner reminiscent of (though far less than in) the West.

The restoration of woodlands even in relatively densely populated suburban areas has further enhanced the natural character of the environment, to the point where wildlife—deer, raccoons, rabbits, and the like—is even found within the major cities today. Despite the sensationalist reports about the destruction of open space in the megalopolis, more land along the East Coast is now wooded than at any time since the early nineteenth century as farms have given way to suburbs and trees are planted to increase suburban amenities.

Low-density settlement is responsible for this enhancement of the natural environment within urbanized areas while metropolitanism is responsible for the opening of land space in their hinterlands. This, too, reflects the westernization of the East. Urbanization in that sphere had originally consisted of the development of a few commercial centers which served as metropolitan magnets and many discrete and fundamentally self-sufficient cities and towns with their own industrial or agricultural basis that were neither magnets nor tributary to magnets. In contrast, the cities of the greater West were almost all founded for commercial purposes, to be magnets for their hinterlands. The metropolitan frontier has encouraged similar kinds of commercial magnetization in the greater Northeast, drawing many of the formerly discrete cities and towns into the orbit of some metropolis and, in general, drawing people from the countryside into metropolitan areas.

In this respect, the greater South has been even more affected by "westernization." There scattered rural settlements have coalesced around crossroads into metropolitan magnets where no cities or towns of any consequence had previously existed, emptying a countryside that had been the paradigm of diffused settlement in the United States. The metropolitan frontier has changed the map of the South far more than that of any other sphere or section and, there too, the changes have been along lines pioneered in the greater West.

The westernization of the United States has been nowhere more noticeable than in the realm of intergovernmental relations. The greater West grew up with the federal government. It was there that the system of federal-state-local-private collaboration that has become the American partnership was forged at a time when the South was becoming ideologically committed to an antifederal position and the Northeast was unconsciously reaping indirect federal benefits without actively participating in the sharing process.

The states and localities of the greater West learned how to live with a powerful federal government and benefit from its powers without losing their identity or diminishing local loyalties. Thus they have taken the twentieth century increase in federal activity more or less in stride. In the Northeast, the sudden visibility of the federal government in fields that previously had seemed to be exclusively matters of state and local concern has come as something of a shock, turning people's attention away from their states and localities to assess the federal role as more significant than it really is. In the South, a kind of schizophrenia has developed, coupling intensive efforts to obtain federal aid with continued assaults on "federal encroachments" on the rights of the states. In fact, as the twentieth-century expansion of intergovernmental activity increasingly involves the entire country in common programs, the old distinctions between the sections' relations to the federal government are rapidly diminishing even if sectional differences in the perception of those relations are lagging behind.

Cultural Foundations and Cultural Change

The westernization of the United States has been particularly visible in the social and cultural arena. The loosening of ties to family, community, and place; the casualness of life; the emphasis on leisure—particularly outdoor leisure—these and similar aspects of the frontier West which have reached their apotheosis in our time on the West Coast, have come to influence life throughout America. The character and meaning of these phenomena cannot be discussed here. Nevertheless, they and the other social and cultural changes generated by the contemporary metropolitan frontier must be considered in any full discussion of the American civil community in this generation because of their impact on its political life and political change in general.

No doubt, the freedom inherent in the aforementioned changes has contributed significantly to the breaking down of the "two cities" and the further democratization of American politics as well as American life generally. Consider only the question of pluralism in the United States. Within the acknowledgedly pluralistic American society there are substantial differences in the way that pluralism is manifested.

In the two easternmost sections of the greater Northeast and the large cities of the third, a "pluralism of communities" has evolved whereby people are somehow identified by their ethnoreligious group whatever their other status attributes or desires may be. This process of communal identification is so well rooted in the culture of those sections that it has become largely unconscious. Politicians think in terms of ethnic blocs automatically, and even ostensibly "emancipated" Easterners somehow understand the communal ties that bind.

In the three sections of the greater South, the fundamental pluralism is founded upon an original caste system dividing whites and blacks. Within their respective castes, people are tied together or divided by place or by their formal associations, particularly their church attachments, which represent the common denominators of identification without any particular reference to matters of piety. Ticket-balancing in the South is traditionally a matter of balancing Baptists, Methodists, Presbyterians and the life at the local level and people from different localities in state politics.

Two forms of pluralism have emerged in the greater West. In the Northwest (plus the small cities of the Near West), a "pluralism of associations" has emerged, giving people more freedom as individuals to choose their societal ties while organizing social and political life around a continuing system of voluntary associations covering a very wide range of interests. People in the Upper Mississippi and Missouri valleys can choose their points of social affiliation, whether a church or a camera club. Emphasis, of course, is on associations like the former with their kindred associations such as political parties (which have often become secular churches or binding fraternities in those states), fraternal orders, business and professional groups, and labor unions (whose other-than-economic functions are frequently very important without being as ethnically stratified as in the Northeast). Such associations represent the core of the social structure, but any legitimate association can gain a meaningful place in the structure of any particular community simply by seeking it. What is most important about this form of pluralism is its combination of lasting yet voluntary qualities. Once they choose their primary associations, people are expected to stay with them, leaving only for serious cause; hence the stronger associations are long-lived, uniting the generations as well as contemporaries. Still, the notion that individuals can choose is a very real one. All that is demanded of political office-seekers in such a system are some legitimate associational ties, but neither group balancing nor the wooing of ethnic blocs is considered a primary strategy for electioneering.

The freedom of choice implied in the Northwest's pluralism of associations has been carried a radical step further in the Far West to become a "pluralism of individuals." Particularly on the West Coast, people even have been freed from the necessity of establishing any long-term social ties. Within that subculture, there are no special expectations that people should be permanently committed to a particular church, profession, or even a particular family, much less to a place or an ancestral group of any sort. The ideology of individual freedom is taken literally and carried to its logical extreme in theory and often in practice. One consequence of this is an amorphousness in group participation that virtually rules out strong and continuing organizations of any kind. The turnover in participants is just too high. Only where there are dedicated professionals with values that are attractive to the nonprofessionals who drift in and out of their organizations do associational structures persist, to be filled and refilled by individuals with shifting interests. Nowhere is this more strongly felt than in politics, where organization is consistently at a minimum and office-seekers rely upon a combination of personality and ideology to attract voters without facing any serious public expectations that they be tied to any particular associations or other primary groups.

The fact is that, of the four forms of pluralism, the first two are increasingly becoming residual phenomena while the last two are becoming more widespread throughout the country. Though they have by no means disappeared in the last twenty years, ethnic and class divisions are reeling under the pressures generated by the metropolitan frontier. They are either diminishing or are being restructured (and weakened) as associational ties offer far more free choice to their members. Caste lines are undergoing even more radical assault. Moreover, the radical individualists are multiplying in every section (though outside of the Far West they are still being forced into loose associations or "communities of individualists" as a matter of hard necessity). The political consequences of these forms of American westernizing range from the decline of bloc voting and a massive increase in the number of political independents to demands for the repeal of laws establishing public standards of morality, particularly in personal and sexual matters.

When we come up against the social changes of the last twenty years, with the benefits they have brought and the problems they have created, we quickly come up against the limits of politics. The increasing bureaucratization of private as well as public interpersonal relations, the new emphasis on hedonism; the collapsing of distinctions, particularly those based on age and sex; the problems of widespread affluence; and the breakdown of old community ties—all major social problems that have come upon this generation—ultimately are not susceptible to political solutions. Proper political action can help harness bureaucratic tendencies, but such action is inevitably restricted by the American public's fascination with technological change, its demands for ever more material advantages, and its willingness to put up with the organizational complexity and intensive competition needed to sustain both. Legislation can limit public display of some of the more gross aspects of the pursuit of hedonism but cannot change men's minds regarding the ultimate values of life. Laws maintaining the established morality and traditional social distinctions have been among the first casualties of the change in public attitudes. The mastery of private affluence barely comes within the purview of politics as it is practiced in the United States. Political decisions can indeed make the forging of communities easier (or more difficult) but the kinds of decisions needed to do so can come only after enough people are committed to building communities to turn the political process in that direction.

Whether or not the social changes presently taking place are leading to fundamental cultural changes in the United States and its civil communities remains to be seen. The amount of behavioral variation possible within a particular cultural matrix before the matrix itself is altered is quite substantial. Whatever the other changes, there is little, if any, evidence of fundamental changes in the country's *political* culture. Even the three political subcultures appear to be moving along established paths to date. Changes in the culture patterns of particular states and civil communities are another matter. The tempo and thrust of the continuing internal migration, added to special sectional and local impacts of the metropolitan frontier, can and have brought about already visible changes in the general or political cultures of some, or both. Thus environment, in-migration, and particular frontier technologies have apparently strengthened the radically individualistic elements in California's general culture to the point where they have become dominant, without altering its essentially moralistic political culture. Other states and communities—in and including Arizona, Florida, and New Jersey, to mention a few—are undergoing similar changes with differing consequences. No such radical changes appear to have occurred among the cities of the prairie or in their states, even in Pueblo with its high rate of in-migration. This offers some testimony as to the strength of cultural bedrock once formed. Only the most intensive upheavals seem to shake it.

The American political system and its political culture may indeed emerge substantially intact after this wave of social change, demonstrating an ability to assimilate great social innovation and absorb the shocks of great social conflict now as in the past. Still, there is no question but that the great and growing sense of unease about the social changes that have been taking place is being translated into political terms, regardless of whether political solutions to the problems generated by the changes are possible or not. One consequence of this is that the extensive efforts and very real successes of the local political reconstitutions of the 1950's have been submerged in the public eye by the social revolutions of the 1960's which, though inspired by the events of the previous decade, pose problems of indeed another dimension.

The Future of the Partnership

Lack of recognition of the great strides made in the 1950's has been compounded by the nearly exclusive public emphasis on national affairs that has developed at least since the 1930's and intensified with the development of national television. If they do not take place in Washington, New York, or (sometimes) Los Angeles, revolutionary developments that are not accompanied by violence are virtually ignored by the mass media. Television, moreover, has become a kind of "seal of truth" in its own right. Consequently, even if people know what is happening in their own communities—a big "if"—they tend to discount it as being of no larger significance if they do not see it reported on television.

These unhappy facts have given rise to the myth of local failure, the most pervasive assessment of local government abroad in the land today. This myth has been fostered with a vengeance by those who dislike the fundamental character of the American city and reject the American public's preference for urbanization without citification. They view the country's overall response to the metropolitan frontier as appalling, opposing the decentralization of population as "urban sprawl"; the mass construction of single-family homes as the creation of "ticky-tack" suburban slums; the accommodation of the automobile through the improvement of roads as "the paving of the country with asphalt" and, in general, calling for cities that are planned to meet the aesthetic, cultural, and other life-style demands of a very small but very articulate minority. The myth is reinforced by those who wish government on all planes to enter fields of social planning and engineering that have not found widespread public favor. It is propagated with particular force by those who are ideologically committed to the notion that the federal government can do anything better than local government. Its widespread acceptance is due in large measure to unrealistic public expectations as to the abilities of any government to solve all the problems of the metropolitan frontier through political action, increased by the very real magnitude of the racial problem and the undeniably worsening crisis in the nation's very largest cities.

This is not to say that the expansion of federal urban assistance programs in recent years was a consequence of erroneous public opinion. Federal involvement need not be promoted or justified on the basis of reputed local failures, nor are local successes likely to reduce the federal role. One thing is clear about the American federal system: where nationwide problems are involved, the federal government will be asked in, regardless of whether the state and local governments are doing their jobs properly or not. In fact, the very achievements of the cities and states during the 1950's, which were reflected in new or expanded programs that raised their taxes and public debt (far faster than that of the federal government) to unprecedented levels, led them to demand new federal assistance in a wide variety of fields they had previously pioneered. Thus local successes invite federal involvement to deepen their results and spread their fruits to other civil communities as much as local failures invite federal efforts to remedy them. It is an old lesson of American history that local initiative breeds federal imitation while local stodginess demands federal stimuli. Certainly the continuing problems of the metropolitan frontier are likely to demand more government activity—and more federal aid—in the immediate future.

Though the case for local failure cannot be substantiated, this does not mean that the federal system does not have real problems. The problems of the partnership today lie in its increasing complexity coupled with a kind of inexorable pressure to expand the federal government's power in domestic affairs. Increasing complexity has generated a renewed consideration of the questions of what government should do and how governments should do it, even to the point of provoking clashes between the "what" and the "how." The very prosaic problem of the proliferation of project grants, perhaps the most notable feature in the expansion of federal aid programs in response to the metropolitan frontier, is symptomatic of this conflict. While it is not difficult to justify the "what" of most project grants, the "how" has become a serious problem indeed, causing duplication of effort as many federal agencies try to get into the act, needless delays in getting work under way because of bottlenecks in Washington, difficulties for civil communities less adept at grantsmanship to acquire aid, and far more federal control over the day-to-day use of grant funds than in previous grant programs, not to speak of the problems it inflicts on the state-local relationship. Project grants are just one aspect of the new complexity and the question "how" which it has generated. There is every indication that it will be one of the major questions to confront the partnership in the last half of the present generation.

Intimately connected with the question of "how" is the widespread idea that all nationwide problems require solutions imposed hierarchically by the federal government. A byproduct of the bureaucratic theories of social organization imported from Germany in the late nineteenth century that have come to dominate American business and governmental thinking, this idea has increasingly tended to direct efforts to solve such problems to Washington first. This tendency not only ignores the realities of the American federal system's mosaic-like character but is coming in for increasing criticism from liberals as well as conservatives as an inefficient way of utilizing governmental power in the United States. The challenge to hierarchical thinking is one of the major aspects of the new ferment in American society. It is even beginning to be felt in the business world. There is every reason to believe that it will be a matter of increasing concern in the political world as well. In this sense, the idea and practice of federalism may well turn out to be the key to transforming theories of nonhierarchical relationships into political realities.

If the basic fact of sharing is not likely to be changed, this does not mean that shifts in the modes and means of cooperation will not take place. Considering the growing questioning of present trends, there is some evidence that such shifts may be in the offing already, based on a new recognition of the role of localism and the diffusion of power even in a very cosmopolitan society. For, if the recent accomplishments of the civil community are not yet recognized, the necessity for and virtues of strong local communities having the capacity for self-government are beginning to be rediscovered.

The growth of alienation in America, of a sense of powerlessness in shaping the public decisions that determine so much of one's life, may very well reflect the consequences of the strong pressures leading to the breakdown of communities that have dominated the twentieth century in most, if not all, of its social and technological manifestations and which have become particularly intense since the opening of the metropolitan frontier. Moreover, the increase in social disorganization in the cities reflects, in no little measure, the absence of stable communities where neighbors know and are concerned with one another and thereby provide each other with a kind of protection (including protection from the consequences of one's own personal weaknesses) that no police force can possibly supply, while at the same time subtly maintaining community standards without the necessity of resorting to formal legal or bureaucratic processes. Politics alone cannot solve the social problems delineated above but, by using politics to help re-create proper civil communities which will be the most appropriate places for solving or resolving such problems, it can play a major role in creating the best possible climate for coming to grips with them.

The crucial role of the local community in preserving and adjusting the social order is not unique to the United States, even if particular manifestations of that role are. Local ties are the primary ties even for the mobile people of the mass society. It is clear that, in the United States, they are not and cannot be the ties of a *gemeinschaft*, the rooted, homogeneous, organic community of medieval Europe. Rather, they must be based on the realities of a contractual civil society—social and geographic mobility, pluralism, and voluntarism. Hence they are likely to remain limited ties with political, or civil, ends first and foremost. As past American experience itself has shown, such communities are feasible in a contractual civil society and in no way contradictory to it, provided that a true pluralism of communities is fostered by the nation as a whole so that people can make choices from among many options. A metropolitan society, which links many communities together for economic purposes while allowing them to remain separate for other purposes, offers unparalleled possibilities for such a pluralism of communities without creating the problems of choice inherent in such a system in the past. The multiplicity and diversity of civil communities that can emerge in such a setting may well offer working examples of differing notions of the scope of the political.

Nor are the psychic satisfactions communities offer their members the only reasons for seeking to restore a sense of civil community. All the arguments advanced about grass-roots parochialism, conformity, and supposed venality notwithstanding, Americans are beginning to realize that the only way most men will ever participate in political decision-making is as functioning members of meaningful local communities. A man who has no love for his community, however delineated, is not likely to love his country either. Few men love their country abstractly. Rather, they love that system which protects the immediate way of life to which they are attached. An entity as large and necessarily as abstract as the United States draws its strength from millions of people who see it in light of personally meaningful benchmarks—that is, as their own local world writ large.

Strong civil communities, then, are not only a proper means of enabling people to participate meaningfully in public life but are vitally necessary to the health of the whole body politic. Hence the future tasks of local self-government within the framework of the American partnership are great indeed. The problems of defining those tasks more carefully and reshaping American political institutions to undertake them, begun in the 1950's, will become matters of increasing importance in the coming decades.

The future of the civil community depends to no little extent upon the role of the states. The states are the only entities that can offer the advantages of larger than local scale where necessary yet remain manageable civil societies within the reach of ordinary men's influence. Already definers, coordinators and administrators of so many programs of urban and metropolitan significance; the states will have to develop "backstopping" skills that will both support and raise local aspirations. The states are already beginning to make substantial efforts to serve their civil communities in these capacities, and there is every reason to believe that they will be able to rise to the challenge if the overall process of redefinition is successful.

The New American Town

The new recognition of the virtue of and necessity for strong local self-government is a product of the latest stage in the metropolitan frontier, triggered by the efforts of the Afro-Americans to join the upper city and reflecting the ever more apparent failure of the nation's super cities to function as truly local governments. Though the cities in question (broadly defined) contain little more than 10 per cent of the nation's population, they are the real loci of the urban crisis. Formally defined as local governments, their sheer size makes them too massive and complex to be civil communities even to the extent of being able to coalesce their various components into a "package" sharing common public interests and values, much less in providing opportunities for meaningful political life for their residents. Consequently their residents find themselves locked within still another impersonal governmental framework without any significant opportunities for local political expression.

Black Americans have been the first to openly articulate this problem, but two decades earlier the migration of white big city residents to the suburbs was at least partially a vote for local government reduced to local scale. The virtual impossibility of consolidating metropolitan areas or even groups of suburbs within metropolitan areas reflects this commitment to the maintenance of proper scale, whether by those who have become truly active in community politics or by those who simply wish to be able to have some voice in matters affecting the maintenance of their physical environment, through zoning, the provision of law and order through the police and lower courts, and the education of their children in local schools. Now the Afro-Americans, and others remaining in the big cities by choice or otherwise, are demanding similar rights of community self-determination, calling for decentralization of powers and functions to "neighborhoods" that are really large enough to be medium-size or large cities in their own right.

The drive to create civil communities within the big cities is simply the latest indication that the medium-size urban polity may well be coming into its own as the local political system most characteristic of the metropolitan frontier. Substantial evidence of this can be read in the statistics of city growth and decline, which clearly reveal a trend from both directions toward the predominance of cities in the 25,000 to 250,000 range. There is some logic behind these statistics. Supported by the sharing of functions inevitable in the American system, civil communities more or less within that range are large enough to be functional, given the demands for services placed upon them today, yet small enough to be democratic in the sense of offering significant possibilities for meaningful political communication and participation.

The growing tendency of Americans to concentrate in local political jurisdictions that fall within the range of potentially authentic civil communities may reflect some dimly felt perceptions of proper scale for political communication or some unspoken appreciation of functional realities. At least since the days of the Greeks, philosophers who have considered the problem of political community have concluded that truly meaningful political communication can take place only when no citizen is more than one person removed from the political decisions of his immediate polity; that is to say, when every citizen at the very least is in a position to know someone well who knows the relevant political decision-makers well. Simple calculations based on this principle lead to the conclusion that 250,000 is (roughly) the upper size limit for any true civil community, with somewhere between 120,000 and 150,000 a more reasonable maximum for communication without strain.

In studying the cities of the prairie, it became apparent that local governmental institutions sufficiently sophisticated to meet the demands of the new frontier did not emerge until civil communities reached a population of forty thousand. Around the forty thousand mark, there is a radical shift upward in the availability of resources—human and economic—to provide the range of talents necessary to operate a sophisticated local government and the fiscal wherewithal to do so, without any serious diminution of political communication in comparison with their smaller sisters. Past forty thousand, professionalization of the local public services—governmental and nongovernmental—is almost assured while salaries can be set high enough to attract good men to fill the available positions. The bundle of local interests becomes sufficiently complex to prevent political dominance by any single group or collection of individuals. Somewhere around that point, the civil community's economic base has expanded sufficiently to be able to begin supporting the range of public services demanded from local governmental and nongovernmental institutions. Moreover, it has begun to be sufficiently diversified to provide economic support for the new diversity of local interests. Perhaps most important of all, a civil community reaching that size can produce from among its own people sufficient talent to manage its more sophisticated public and private institutions and, more than that, can provide sufficient opportunities to keep many of them at home (or attract others with equal talents to settle locally). At the same time, the sense of neighborliness based on wide acquaintance characteristic of small cities remains more or less undiminished. The tendencies toward greater sophistication and opportunity could be seen continuing to unfold without any basic changes in the larger cities of the prairie, up through the largest, which hovered around the 150,000 mark, without any visible changes in ease of access, neighborliness, or community-wide political communication. This common effort to temper increasing sophistication with a strong dose of small-town atmosphere is in itself a phenomenon especially characteristic of the civic aspirations of the metropolitan frontier.

There is even some reason to believe that efficiency as well as democracy is enhanced at the scale of the medium-size urban civil community. It is well documented that school systems of larger than medium size have a tendency to bog down in bureaucracy with a resultant gap between the administrators and the teachers in the classroom. Other agencies of government have similar histories. Cost analysis has revealed that cities of above 250,000 population suffer increasing diseconomies of scale. Meaningful civic participation reaches it apogee in such civil communities. The medium-size suburb makes a contribution to better metropolitan coordination as well. Inter-local collaboration in matters of area-wide concern has come easier in metropolitan areas that have many cities within the same medium-size range—the Los Angeles-Orange County area is a prime example—that can join forces without fearing for their very existence. In such situations, their combined strength has helped to balance the role played by an outsized central city whose very scale makes most suburbs afraid to cooperate with it.

As the etymology of the words themselves reveals, the key to community is to be found in the ongoing existence of a particular sphere of communication among relevant communicants—communication in its original sense of sharing as well as in the sense of transaction. Obviously, the key to civil community is the existence of a particular sphere of political communication. It is not at all amiss to see the problem of creating and maintaining civil communities as a problem of communication, especially in the sense of the sharing of a particular kind of political life. Since the existence of a civil community is more a matter of the interrelationships between its public and private, governmental and non-governmental, political and civic parts than simply a question of political boundaries, the primary measure of that existence is the ambit of a particular kind of local political communication while the primary measure of its effectiveness rests on the level and pattern of political communication between and among its parts. That is where the question of scale takes on added significance. Some political jurisdictions, even if they are called cities, are simply too large to foster the requisite kind of sharing among their components necessary for the existence of a civil community even though their leaders may be able to manipulate the organized media of communications so as to give the illusion of community. The proof of that pudding is invariably shown when the city has to confront internal and external pressures and cannot produce anything like a common front. By the same token, some political jurisdictions are simply too small to contain a complete local communications network. They become, in effect, neighborhoods within some larger civil community.

What constitutes the ambit of a local political communications network in the United States has changed over time as the density of population in the nation's settlements has increased. In the days of the land frontier, the Yankee town, the Middle Western township, and the rural Southern county were models of the kinds of civil communities which were ideally suited for sustaining a complete local political communications network on their respective geographic scales. Today, on the metropolitan frontier, the medium-size civil community, whether free-standing metropolis, suburb, county seat-and-hinterland, or inner city corporation, appears to be the best equivalent of those earlier forms of settlement, offering sufficient ambit for the development of a complete local communications network while maintaining a level of interpersonal communication sufficiently high to encourage sharing on a face-to-face basis. The medium-size urban civil community, then, could possibly become the contemporary version of the classic American town.

Toward the Next Frontier

By the mid-1960's, the first bloom of the metropolitan frontier had faded. The line of suburban settlement continues to advance, but the settlement of new suburbs has become routine. Increasingly, the problems of suburbia are becoming second generation problems, not unlike the second generation problems of communities created on earlier frontiers. The very political turmoil of the 1960's is indicative of the fact that the country as a whole has entered a period of consolidation in the aftermath of the rush to the frontier of the 1950's.

All this is not to say that the metropolitan frontier has come to an end. It certainly does not mean that there are no more frontiers in the offing. In the dynamic world of today, the sheer passage of time opens new frontiers for each generation. Off on the horizon somewhere is yet a fourth frontier stage, to be based perhaps on megalopolitan settlement patterns and on the explosion of information technology. Already the pattern of urban settlement in the Northeast and on the West Coast and increasingly in parts of the South and the Middle West has become linear rather than nodular, combining discrete towns, cities, and counties into long, relatively thin magnets that are attracting much of the human energy in the country. Marshall McLuhan may well be on the right track in his discussion of the transition, its technology, and the impact of that technology on social forms and processes.

Before any new frontier stage will be opened, however, there are great social needs that must be met and great political tasks that must be undertaken to help meet them. The first task that demands immediate attention is the renewal of the covenant that binds Americans together into a civil society. Other nations, whose origins are lost in the dimness of time, can afford great social traumas because they have attained the status of organic societies. Frenchmen know that they are and will continue to be Frenchmen come war, revolution, or *coup d'état*. Americans know all too well how the United States came to be. Ours is an artificial (meaning manmade) civil society in the best sense of the word—an artifact created by men sharing certain high common purposes. The health of our society, and perhaps its very existence, is contingent upon the maintenance of those high purposes in common and the continuation of efforts reaching toward their fulfillment. Lincoln knew this when, in the throes of a prior renegotiation of the compact, he called us the "almost-chosen people" and demanded our complete rededication to the principles upon which the nation was "conceived and dedicated." Our social and political compact is both our burden and our glory, the opportunity to make adjustments to new frontiers and new times as free men and the necessity for periodically doing so. Since we are presently in the midst of one of those periods and may continue to be well into the 1970's, we must give it our fullest attention.

A major aspect of the renewal of the national covenant must be a renewed sense of localism, a "community-defining federalism" that will lead to a "federalism of communities." Here the creation or restoration of civil communities of proper scale will be of the utmost importance because the fostering of proper political communication on the local plane is a necessary step toward the re-creation of meaningful political communication throughout the American federal system. Fortunately, difficult as this task may be, the possibilities for the development of a community-defining federalism have not been better at any time since the Civil War, both in will and in wherewithal.

Finally, or perhaps first and foremost, effort will have to be exerted toward the forging of a renewed public conscience, a renewed inward sense of what is decent and proper, moral and just, socially as well as politically, shared in common by Americans of all streams and strains. This task is complicated by its essentially extra-political character. It is additionally complicated by the fact that we are presently at a watershed in world history. After three hundred years, the modern epoch has come to a rather fiery end. The values and ways of life which it had fostered and sustained relatively unchallenged since the middle of the seventeenth century are undergoing serious assault and desperately require reintegration or replacement. In short, we are facing a particular kind of crisis of confidence, one bred out of a crisis of conscience that has spread throughout western civilization.

Community politics seems far removed from such weighty concerns. Yet, in an era of collapsing society-wide values, it may well be that men will once again have to gather in communities of their choice to work out common ways of life on a more restricted scale—as a prelude to the renewal of public conscience for our larger civilization. It may well be that the greatest contribution that politics can make to this extra-political quest is the restoration of the possibilities of community as a means of searching out the values and way of life that will serve us for the next epoch.

APPENDIX A

The Method of the Exploration

I

THE OVERALL STUDY OF THE CITIES OF THE PRAIRIE, the results of which are partially reported in this volume, was conducted over approximately four years (preparation for the field work was initiated in October 1959, intensive field work was begun in January 1960 and concluded in July 1962, and systematic observation of political developments in Champaign and Urbana was continued through June 1963), primarily by one trained political scientist (the author) assisted in his office by various graduate and undergraduate research assistants, never more than one at a time. Consequently, the study represents such limitations as are inherent in work done by one human being as well as the advantages of a high level of control over comparability of perception, field work techniques, and data analysis. Continued consultation and collaboration with colleagues, some of whom had studied or were studying some of the same metropolitan areas for other purposes has, hopefully, overcome some of the possible deficiencies of a one-man project. Nevertheless, it is clear to this writer that some limitations tied to this fact remain.

Because one man was studying ten metropolitan areas in less than three years (and with other responsibilities which prevented him from devoting full-time to this project), it was manifestly impossible to come to know any of the ten areas as intimately as have many of the participant observers among the sociologists and anthropologists who have devoted full-time to participant observation in single communities for a year or more, though the author's residence was in Champaign-Urbana for the entire period and longer, during which time he systematically observed local politics. As it was, an average of three months was spent on each metropolitan area, divided as follows: two to four weeks of preparation in the office prior to going into the field (reviewing background data and existing research on the community, selecting the particular issues and cases to be studied in light of the overall scheme, refining the questions to be asked, and acquiring the names of people to interview); very intensive field work in the metropolitan area itself of from eight days to seven weeks, depending on the number and size of the central cities in each metropolitan area and based on approximately two weeks per central city; approximately five weeks spent after returning from the field in reviewing and digesting the interview transcripts and the collected documentary material and ordering it so as to present a sociopolitical profile of each metropolitan area; and an additional two to four weeks of library research to fill in needed historical background and other necessary follow-up work. During this entire process, continued research and reading were done on the general background of the entire complex of civil communities considered in this study.

The author discovered, after two trial runs, that the period of approximately two weeks per central city would enable him to gather as much information as possible short of spending a year in residence as a participant observer in each civil community. The surface and immediate subsurface information which leads to a good general outline of community politics, plus in-depth information for one or more case studies, could be obtained through intensive interviewing and gathering of documentary materials in that period of time, while extensions short of a year yielded diminishing returns. A full year or thereabouts of virtually single-minded study in each community would be necessary to penetrate into the more subtle nuances of its politics. This field-work pattern was adhered to in six of the metropolitan areas and in one city of a seventh. The complexity of the Madison-St. Clair Counties area would have required three months of field work under the formula. Fortunately, by cooperating with two political scientists of the Institute of Public Administration and Metropolitan Affairs, Southern Illinois University, it was possible to share the field work with the author concentrating on Belleville. In Peoria, a parallel study being conducted by four colleagues (a political scientist, a geographer, and two sociologists) from the University of Illinois Office of Community development made possible a cooperative approach which reduced the amount of field time spent by the author to eight days over a two-week period plus spot interviews. Previous political and social research projects conducted under the auspices of the Institute of Government and Public Affairs in Decatur had so exhausted the community's informants that it was considered best to eliminate extensive field work and to rely on the earlier studies and the field notes of previous researchers as corroborated through personal conversations with them and with some of the leading actors on the Decatur scene. In Champaign-Urbana, though intensive field-work time approximated the formula of two weeks per central city, continuous observation of local politics for the three-year period provided the study with at least one long-term observation point. The field-work timetable for each metropolitan area can be approximated as follows:

Rockford: sixteen days over a three-week period in January 1960 plus a special one-day followup in November 1961.

Quad Cities: seven weeks over a two-and-a-half-month period in May–July 1960.

Duluth-Superior: eighteen days over a three-week period in August 1960.

Springfield: eight days over a three-week period in July 1961 plus subsequent spot interviews.

Pueblo: thirteen days over a two-and-a-half-week period in July–August 1961.

Champaign-Urbana: four weeks during the winter and early spring, 1961–1962, plus continuous observation and spot interviewing from January 1960 to June 1963.

Madison-St. Clair Counties: one day in March 1961, one day in February 1962, and two weeks in April 1962, plus exchange of data and joint field work with the Institute of Public Administration and Metropolitan Affairs, Southern Illinois University.

Peoria: eight days over a two-week period in May–June 1962 plus continuing cooperative research with the Office of Community Development, University of Illinois.

Joliet: twelve days over a two-week period in June–July 1962.

Decatur: spot interviewing plus utilization of data gathered in previous studies conducted under the auspices of the Institute of Government and Public Affairs.

The research program undertaken in this fashion was predicated on the feasibility of combining (1) selective interviewing of political and community actives in depth, (2) limited on-the-spot observation of events, (3) extensive review of the local press, (4) utilization of other relevant studies of the ten metropolitan areas or their component civil communities, (5) collection of basic socioeconomic data prepared for each metropolitan area by other agencies, (6) review of relevant historical materials available, (7) compilation of significant election data with judicious analysis based on reasonably rigorous hypotheses, and (8) systematic unobtrusive observation of all visible aspects of the civil community. From twenty to seventy people were interviewed in each civil community, with interviews ranging in length from half an hour to fifteen hours (over several days). Persons interviewed were selected from a list that included (1) all locally elected officials, (2) appointed heads of government and major government agencies in the area, (3) major political leaders, (4) major civic leaders, (5) officers and executives of civic associations, chambers of commerce, and the like, (6) representatives of the local press and mass media, (7) major business, professional, and industrial leaders, and (8) people suggested by others interviewed as particularly good sources of information. No list was covered exhaustively, both because of time limitations and because a number of the people simply were unavailable during the period of field work in each area. The writer believes, however, that the distribution was wide enough to be representative of the categories on the list and that the informants were generally astute enough to have provided him with information as detailed and accurate, and even more perceptive, than that available through survey research and other ostensibly "harder" data.

The author attended all public and private meetings of governmental bodies, political organizations, civic groups, chambers of commerce and business groups, and private gatherings of political actives held during his stay that were open to him. Even in the relatively short time available in each city, this was of substantial value for watching people who had been interviewed "in action" and for getting the "feel" of politics in the community. It was also valuable as a starting point for reinterviewing participants in the meetings, usually in an informal setting after the meeting had concluded, at which time the writer was able to ask more pointed questions that, by tying in with the more general questions asked in the formal interview, served as both an addition to and a corroboration of the latter. Since access into even the most intimate meetings of a political or civic nature was rarely denied, this was a highly productive aspect of the field work.

All the newspapers published in each metropolitan area were intensively reviewed for the field work period. This was coupled with a review of older material relevant to specific issues being examined in depth, such as council-manager referenda, and with interviews of editors, publishers, and reporters for elaboration on the published accounts. The newspapers were used as sources of information on matters directly political and for background on the metropolitan area as a whole. Of course, the mass media were studied as actors on the local scene as well as chroniclers of it, particularly since, in more than one case, the character of the chronicles was directly related to the interests of the newspapers as actors.

Such studies, academic, quasi-academic, and reform-oriented, as existed for each of the metropolitan areas, few as they were, were critically examined and, where possible, the studies were discussed (and the data on which they were based reviewed) with those who had commissioned them or carried them out. Relatively few academic studies were available for the ten areas, and even fewer were directly concerned with political phenomena. There were a number of doctoral dissertations, particularly on Champaign-Urbana (which has been frequently used as an exemplary case because of the location of the University of Illinois), Rockford, and the Quad Cities. A few of those dissertations focused on political matters. Several are cited in the Bibliography. In addition, the writer was fortunate in being able to benefit from colleagues carrying on other research projects within one or more of the ten areas contemporaneously. Charles S. Liebman had studied the transition to city manager government in Decatur just prior to the author's study and was a valuable source of ideas as well as data. During the first year of research, Richard Robbins was engaged in a study of the effectiveness of local human relations commissions and allied bodies in many of the same cities, which was particularly useful in uncovering information pertaining to the Negro communities in those cities. The following year, Rondal G. Downing studied judicial politics in Illinois and included within his study the Rockford and Madison-St. Clair Counties metropolitan areas. His data helped confirm the writer's analysis of the regional relationships of those metropolitan areas as well as filling in gaps in our knowledge of a major area of political activity in the State of Illinois and its subdivisions. Acknowledgment of the assistance of others has been made above.

Aside from these academic studies, the League of Women Voters chapters in most of the communities studied had prepared descriptions of the formal governmental systems of their communities of varying scope and quality, all of which proved useful. Similar material, often with interesting appendages on the less formal processes of government, had been prepared by chambers of commerce in some of the cities studied for use in their practical politics courses. Public administration and planning studies were also of use in providing background information. None of the civil communities studied was without at least one of these. Often there were several, prepared over a forty-year period and valuable as historical as well as contemporary documents. All told, a reasonable body of this kind of literature, of varying quality, could be unearthed for almost every metropolitan area to supplement other forms of data gathering.

Basic socioeconomic data in a variety of forms were collected from the census reports, planning agencies, industrial development groups, private industry, chambers of commerce, and other state and federal sources. Many governmental and private agencies assemble statistical data on a wide variety of matters. These data were used as indicators of a similarly wide variety of patterns and trends in the civil community. Furthermore, standard publications, such as city and telephone directories, carry within them many implicit indicators of the same sort. Historical "indicators" taken from the records and from secondary sources available for each metropolitan area were examined as thoroughly as possible. Scholarly histories were used wherever they were available. Semischolarly and filio-pietistic histories of cities and counties were of particular use in tracing patterns over time, despite their obvious deficiencies. Some communities are fortunate in having active local historical societies with collections of documents and with members who themselves have written articles and papers on local history. In addition, city records and reports and general books and articles dealing with the areas in question were reviewed.

Voting returns for selected national, state, and local elections and state and local referenda were assembled with decreasing thoroughness back to the earliest days of organized government in each metropolitan area. Significant gaps exist in the availability of voting data at the local level in the communities studied, limiting the extent of data analysis possible.

The author systematically observed the physical manifestations of life in each civil community along the lines subsequently set forth in *Unobtrusive Measures*.[1] Street and land-use patterns; characteristics and distribution of business, residential, industrial, and recreational areas; architectural styles; public advertising; the character and availability of newspapers, magazines, and books; the quality of merchandise available in various kinds of stores; and many other such measures available through unobtrusive observation reveal much about the character, concerns, and underlying values that influence politics in each civil community.

Underlying these eight facets of community research was the outline and guide for studying the civil community included as Appendix B.

II

Unlike many other recent studies in the fields of political behavior and community politics, this one did not rely upon survey research or the administration of a rigorously designed and pretested questionnaire for its basic data. While these methods have their value, their weaknesses for research in depth without predetermining outcomes are particularly apparent in the kind of study undertaken here. The research for this study was done in a manner which the writer believes is consistent with his approach to the study of political systems as political phenomena with roots in specific space and time. This is not to imply that this is, in any sense, the only valid approach to community research or that other methods are not more useful in appropriate situations.

This writer believes that which can be measured quantitatively in studies of political systems is not necessarily of greatest importance to the understanding of the system while that which is of greatest importance more often than not cannot be quantified. What is necessary, then, is a method of research which combines reasonable rigor with sufficient flexibility to allow imaginative analysis. Reasonable rigor is a necessary aspect of scientific research of any kind, in order to allow replication of research and to promote the comparability of the results of research. However, the meaning of "reasonable rigor" and the methods for its achievement vary from discipline to discipline and even from project to project within a discipline. In a study such as this one, the best results are obtained by developing sound questions that can be studied through field research, proceeding to undertake the necessary field research in a manner designed to elicit information in the greatest possible depth from the widest range of knowledgeable actors and observers available in each community; formulating propositions that best answer the questions raised at the outset of the study; and, finally, developing and refining hypotheses that best explain the propositions in light of the available data.

In essence, this type of research suggests that the crucial problem in community studies is not the isolation of "decision-makers" or the identification of individual members of "power structures," but delineating and describing community political systems, placing them in their larger social and political context, and, by determining their patterns of systematic evolution, abstracting the persistent political roles which must be filled in order for them to function as political systems. Only by first delineating the system being explored and its components is it possible to develop questions which can be dealt with empirically and which, at the same time, permit some level of generalization. The results of such an exploration will not be predictability of future political action but the development of reasonably sound hypotheses that can be applied to forecast the order of probabilities for future political behavior within the context of a particular political system.

In this context, it may be well to say a word or two about the writer's conception of the functions of social research. This, in turn, should help clarify the value commitments with which he undertakes his work.

The central task of the branch of social research of which community studies is a part is to explore man's changing social environment with maximum precision and to maximum depth in order to make known its character and content to mankind. This task is central because all other tasks of social research, such as scientific generalization about social phenomena or interpretation of their meaning for purposes of taking action, flow from this basic exploration function. The historical context in which this branch of social research has developed offers testimony as to the truth of this statement. Social research as we know it today, as a *social* activity of recognized importance and value (as distinct from its "purely humanistic" value as the pursuit of knowledge), is essentially the product of the modern, or scientific, epoch which opened up in the seventeenth century, an epoch in which change has become the dominant characteristic, in which human society, for all appearances, changes with such rapidity that one generation does not easily understand the life and works of its forebears, the direction of its heirs, or even its own identity, without the applied effort of students of society. The questions that demand the attention of social research are, of course, manifold, ranging from theoretical inquiry into the entire problem of conservation and change to more practical questions of how to manage change in specific contexts.

Regardless of more intraprofessional theoretical considerations, then, the first function of social research dealing with particular community configurations is to make known what is unknown and to make it well enough known so that men may understand their communities to the limits of their capacity. Social research of this type is a form of exploration, a frontier activity which has its origins in the great frontier of the Western World which has opened in the past five centuries, though it did not emerge as a discreet kind of exploration until the nineteenth century. It is a latecomer to that frontier precisely because it did not develop as a recognized social function until the social need for it became apparent, namely, when the social manifestations of the frontier became too complex to be explored in the traditional ways of the philosophers. It is this exploration function that gives social researchers their fundamental *social* justification.

Disclosures of this writer's conception of the central task of social research should also indicate the character of his values. Indeed, any discussion of the distribution of power in society *ipso facto* involves a consideration of values. The conflict between the power elitists and the pluralists (discussed below) is a case in point. Basically, both groups agree that a limited number of individuals are actively involved in most "decisions" in the local community. The elitists view this group as consciously limited to be representative of the community's more or less closed "power structure" rather than its population as a whole, establishing "undemocratic" local control by the power elite. The pluralists consider the activist group tc oe limited by objective necessity (only so many people can participate in any given decision for purely physical reasons) but withal drawn with sufficient breadth to be representative of the articulate elements in the community and sufficiently open to accept representatives from any element willing to become articulate, so that community decision-making may be considered "democratic." The power elitists, generally inspired by Marxian theory, tend to advocate radical changes in the community power structure to "democratize" it while the pluralists, generally inspired by Madisonian theory, tend to affirm the moral legitimacy of the existing system and look for local improvement within its confines.

The functioning of these different value premises here does not need elaboration. Nor is it out of place for political scientists, who live as citizens as well as scholars, to be concerned with the value implications of the distribution of power within a key segment of the American political system. Values unclarified, however, are values unconsidered—unconsidered as to their implications and unconsidered as to their effect. The best way to handle the value problem is to place empirical studies of politics within the framework of the historically fundamental political questions from the first. Such a course is an implicit recognition of the inseparability of value considerations in the study of things political, a conclusion reached by men like Aristotle (and the author of the *Book of Joshua*) at the beginning of political inquiry and reaffirmed by men like John Dewey in our own day. Rather than attempt the impossible elimination of value considerations, it becomes possible to view political phenomena as responses to different sets of values by viewing them in light of central concepts which impute value themselves. Such concepts must, of necessity, be related to those larger questions of political thought which are of permanent or continuing concern to men as men and as citizens.

If this writer's political values need to be made more explicit, for all practical purposes he is committed to the maintenance of progressive federal democracy which, in the form that we know it is largely the product of the world of the great frontier. Brought down to the level of this study, the analysis of the cities of the prairie in some measure reflects the writer's own commitments to the values of democracy, equality of opportunity, social justice, and individual self-realization, as they have developed in the context of the American value system and, more precisely, in the context of the immediate worldview which animates the greater West of the "cities of the prairie."

Acknowledgment that federal democracy and its values are products of a particular world does not diminish their worth. Twenty-five centuries ago Aristotle, the erstwhile founder of our discipline, analyzed and compared the constitutions of the various polities of his day, and came to two conclusions. One was that the political system of every polity was understandable in the social context in which it was erected and accordingly justifiable at least to that extent. The second was that this fact did not preclude judgments that some political systems were better than others and, in fact, that some were good and others bad in the context of the laws of nature which reflect transcendent right. Aristotle reconciled these apparently contradictory conclusions by formulating the theory that, while every political system is the product of a particular coincidence of factors that shape it, some political systems are products of better coincidences of factors than others. The good constitution, then, is seemingly a product of chance, of the apparently fortuitous coincidence of the right factors. Though this means that only certain constitutions can be good constitutions in the very nature of things, and that the others must be understood accordingly, it does not mean that judgment must be suspended. The coincidence of factors may be rare, even unlikely, in the world as we know it, but that does not detract from the fact that the polity it would produce provides the standard of judgment against which to measure the goodness of all polities.

III

One more point must be made in regard to method. Prior to, and concurrently with, the conduct of this study, the author was obliged to consider the larger questions raised in connection with community studies by social scientists and political practitioners in recent years. The central question raised in recent urban studies is one which has concerned Americans, citizens, and social scientists alike, in contexts beyond that of the local community, namely, who holds or exercises power (or influence) in American (urban) government and how do they exercise it.

While many students of American society have discussed this question since the days of *The Federalist*, the two most notable schools of thought on the subject in American social science today are those of the "power elitists" and the "pluralists." Among the former are the late C. Wright Mills, Floyd W. Hunter, and numerous sociologists. The latter are perhaps best represented by Robert A. Dahl, Herbert Kaufman, and numerous political scientists. The most representative works of each "school" are those of Hunter and Dahl, respectively. Briefly summarized, the power elite school views power in the urban community (as in the nation as a whole) as essentially the power to make policy. They believe such power to be centered in the hands of a relatively small socioeconomic elite which rests atop a power pyramid. As Hunter has stated:

> The top group of the power hierarchy has been isolated and defined as comprised of policy-makers. These men are drawn largely from the businessmen's class in Regional City. They form cliques or crowds, as the term is more often used in the community, which formulate policy. Committees for formulation of policy are commonplace, and on community-wide issues policy is channeled by a "fluid committee structure" down to institutional, associational groupings through a lower level bureaucracy which executes policy.
>
> Intra-community and extra-community policy matters are handled by essentially the same group of men in this city, but there is a differentiation of functional activity within this policy group. Some men operate on different levels of policy decisions, particularly in matters concerning governmental action. . . . [I]t was found that the [power] structure is held together by common interests, mutual obligations, money, habit, delegated responsibilities, and in some cases by coercion and force.[2]

Appearance of Hunter's study of "Regional City" (Atlanta) led to a series of attacks on the power structure theory by political scientists. One group of political scientists, led by Robert Dahl, has conducted extensive investigations of another city (New Haven) which have led them to conclude that power, which they view as a measurable and quantifiable entity, is not held hierarchically but is diffused among reasonably wide segments of the population. Dahl, refuting the "power elite" theory in his study of New Haven, *Who Governs? Democracy and Power in an American City*,[3] acknowledges the one-time existence of a controlling power elite, but he concludes further that:

> In the political system of the patrician oligarchy [before 1850], political resources were marked by a cumulative inequality: when one individual was much better off than another in one resource, such as wealth, he was usually better off in almost every other resource—social standing, legitimacy, control over religious and educational institutions, knowledge, office. In the political system of today, inequalities in political resources remain, but they tend to be *non-cumulative*. The political system of New Haven, then, is one of *dispersed inequalities* [italics in the original].

While most students of urban politics have lined up on one side of this question or the other, several have been led to reconsider the entire framework of the discussion. They have concluded, essentially, that both answers were the natural outcome of the questions each school has asked, that they were unavoidable in light of the *a priori* assumptions established in each case prior to beginning the research.[4] Among them is the implicit assumption that the decision-making process can be pinned down precisely through location of the "decision-makers" and measurement of the extent of their decision-making power, either generally as part of a continuing power structure (the power elitists) or in each specific situation (the pluralists). Concurrently, both groups limit their studies entirely to the local community under consideration, with little, or no more than perfunctory, obeisance to the idea that the local community may be part of a larger social and political system as well as possessing a system of its own. This limitation necessarily follows the first assumption since the "decision-making process" can be meaningfully studied as a whole only if it can be shown to be reasonably self-contained, in this case within the local community.

Herbert Simon, in the introduction to the second edition of his book *Administrative Behavior*,[5] has pointed out the inherent fallacy of the "decision-making" approach in a somewhat different but no less relevant context:

> Discussions of administrative centralization and decentralization often bog down on the question: "Who *really* makes the decisions?" Such a question is meaningless—a complex decision is like a great river, drawing from its many tributaries the innumerable component premises of which it is constituted. Many individuals and organization units contribute to every large decision. . . .

While Simon is speaking of decisions within bureaucracies, much the same can be said for decisions made within local political systems, or any other systems, for that matter. Furthermore, as this study should have demonstrated, local political systems, in the United States at least, cannot be adequately considered apart from the larger whole. The nature of the American partnership precludes the facile separation of the local community, particularly for purposes of identifying those who decide its destiny. The local community can be meaningfully studied as a political system, but only in the context of the larger system of which it is an active part.[6]

Another serious limitation found in both schools lies in their repeated attempts to generalize from the immediately particular without fully grasping the degree of "particularity" involved in their "sample." This is not so much a question of particularity of place alone (each has studied only one city and honestly makes the reader aware of this as a possible limitation) or of time alone (though Dahl and some of the elitists do provide an historical background, both studies and the others like them are seriously deficient in that they concentrate on perhaps a five-year period in the post-World-War-II era and generalize about local politics from this basis) but of a particularity that lacks any sense of the geohistorical universe. There is little spatial or temporal perspective in these studies. The dynamics of time and space are, at best, referred to in passing while the connections between the local political system and the larger world are virtually ignored.

The foregoing critique is not meant to imply that the work that has been done in the field of local political research in recent years is not of considerable value or that the two examples cited here are not significant contributions to our understanding of political phenomena. It is simply that the next step in the study of urban political systems is to raise our sights above the "merely local" and the "merely momentary" to view the urban political systems of America (and, by implication, more generally) without falling into needless logical traps and in the light of the larger universe of which they are a part.

NOTES

1. Eugene J. Webb, Donald T. Campbell, Richard D. Schwartz, and Lee Sechrest, *Unobtrusive Measures* (Chicago: Rand McNally, 1966).

2. *Community Power Structure* (Chapel Hill: University of North Carolina, 1953).

3. New Haven, Conn., and London: Yale University Press, 1961.

4. For a major critique of the power elite position, see Nelson W. Polsby, "The Sociology of Community Power: A Reassessment," *Social Forces* XXXVII (March 1959), 232–236. The pluralist position is, in turn, subjected to a similar critique by Thomas J. Anton in "Power, Pluralism, and Local Politics," *Administrative Science Quarterly*, Vol. VII, No. 4 (March 1963).

5. New York, Macmillan, 1960.

6. Perhaps the best critique of the study of local politics as a self-contained subject is to be found in Morton Grodzins, *The American System: A New View of Government in the United States,* edited by Daniel J. Elazar (Chicago: Rand McNally, 1966). It should be mentioned that Edward Banfield, though considered a leading pluralist, is less bound by these assumptions than most of his colleagues. In his book *Political Influence* (Glencoe, Ill.: The Free Press, 1961), he at least relates decision-making in Chicago to politics in Illinois in the most obvious cases. The two best theoretical statements about the study of local politics to have emerged in recent years are both by Norton Long, "Aristotle and the Study of Local Government," *Social Research,* XXIV, No. 3 (Autumn 1957), 287–310, and "The Local Community as an Ecology of Games," *American Journal of Sociology*, LXIV, No. 3 (November 1958), 251–261.

APPENDIX B

The Research Outline and Guide

AUTHOR'S NOTE: This guide was developed in 1959 and 1960 for the "Cities of the Prairie" study used as the basis for the research done in connection with it. It has undergone some modification and expansion in light of the results of that project and my other community studies but is reprinted here in its original form for accuracy's sake. The revised version is available from the Center for the Study of Federalism, Temple University.

I. *An Approach for the Analysis of Local Political Systems*

QUESTIONS OF LOCAL political behavior can be approached and analyzed through eight general categorizations, each of which covers a basic concept whose manifestations in the world of action concern the political scientist yet all of which overlap to provide different means of focusing on the same phenomena. They are: *Civil Community, Frontier, Federalism, Constitutionalism, Democracy, Republicanism, Metropolitanism, Regionalism.* These eight categorizations may be viewed in the following manner:

CIVIL COMMUNITY

Scope: Covers the system of population components within the locality; their overall culture and specific subcultures; the general institutions in which these are expressed; and the manner in which they are represented by the governments and quasi-governments which function in the locality.

Hypothesis: The political style, questions, issues, and processes of the locality are in large measure determined and guided by the culture of the civil community as developed and manifested over time. Consequently, analysis of the phenomena of local government must rest on an identification and understanding of the culture of the civil community, particularly through the identification and understanding of the political style, questions, issues, and processes recurring over time.

Means of Testing Hypothesis: Identification of the culture and subcultures of the civil community and their institutionalized expressions. Identification of the salient questions and issues in the history of the civil community, particularly those recurring over time. Comparison of the data that emerge with the data emerging from investigation of the other seven categorizations.

FRONTIER

Scope: Covers the impact of socioeconomic development and change on the civil community and its political institutions.

Hypothesis: American society in its commitment to the conquest of nature (in its broadest sense) by civilization and in its actions directed to that end, has been a frontier society since its origin. The civil communities which make up the larger American society are deeply involved in, challenged by, and forced to respond to the pressures and demands generated by the frontier (namely a high degree of socioeconomic change in the society as a whole and in at least a certain portion of its component parts in every generation with its consequent pressures for cultural and political adjustment). The degree to which a given civil community is involved in, challenged by, and forced to respond to the pressures and demands generated by the frontier strongly influences the political issues and problems that confront the civil community, and are recognized by it, and the means and processes involved in meeting those issues and problems.

Means of Testing Hypothesis: Identification of the position occupied by the specific civil community relative to the great frontier. Identification of the socioeconomic impacts of the great frontier on the civil community. Correlation of those impacts with the local political culture. Comparison of the results in communities with varying degrees of involvement in the great frontier.

FEDERALISM

Scope: Covers the relations of the civil community with the larger civil society, particularly the intergovernmental relations that are manifest in the United States in the federal-state-local partnership.

Hypothesis: Virtually all governmental activity in the United States is shared activity—shared by the three planes of government and their constituent institutions and agencies. Consequently, not only is there no single government for any civil community but the multiplicity of governments is not confined even to the local plane. This means that decisions affecting the civil community, including many of the most basic and vital ones, are made, fully or partially, outside its boundaries. The very concept of the civil community revolves around the local response to this problem of federalism. The civil community consists of the sum of the governments and quasi-governments that function in a given locality and that are tied together in a single bundle of governmental activities and services. Local government then comes to mean the manner in which this bundle of governmental activities and services is manipulated in the locality to serve the local political value system.

Means of Testing Hypothesis: Identification of the shared governmental activities and functions in the civil community, including the ways in which they are shared. Identification of the loci of decision-making for given questions confronting the civil community, within the collaborative system. Identification of the means whereby the governments and quasi-governments of the civil community are able (or the situations in which they are unable) to manipulate the bundle of governmental activities and services to serve the local political value system.

CONSTITUTIONALISM

Scope: Covers the overall constitutional structure of the civil community and the component elements of the civil community's constitution.

Hypothesis: Every civil community develops, over time, a constitution that embodies an outline of the civil community's formal political structure and the fundamental allocation of power, responsibility, and influence within it. Generally speaking, this constitution consists of a frame of government, modifying nonstatutory documents, and modifying customs and traditions for each constituent government (and quasi-government) in the civil community, encompassed by the customs and traditions of the civil community as a whole. Identification of this constitution is fundamental to, and a key to, the understanding of the process of government in any civil community. Furthermore, certain issues—particularly those relating to governmental structure and the scope of formal jurisdiction, the planning process, and the alteration of the internal equilibrium of the civil community—are constitutional issues and, as such, arouse a greater degree of community response and generate a greater degree of conflict in the civil community.

Means of Testing Hypothesis: Identification of the components of the civil community's constitution. Tracing the development and modification of the constitution over time. Studying cases of breakdowns in the constitutional pattern or attempts to change the constitution. Identification of the "constitutional issues": when and how they are raised; the reactions of various groups and interests in the civil community; and how they are resolved (or circumvented). More specifically, these may include attempts at changing forms of government, attempts at community planning, annexation of territory, redistricting and reapportionment, and similar issues that concern the alteration of the internal equilibrium of the civil community.

DEMOCRACY

Scope: Covers the participation of the people as a whole, in groups, or as individuals in the process of government in the civil community, through elections, associational and interest group activity, individual responses, and the like.

Hypothesis: The role of socioeconomic variables in determining the character, scope, and forms of popular participation in the decision-making process is generally accepted. The operation of specific socioeconomic variables within specific communities requires further investigation. In addition, in contemporary American society with its predominantly middle-class orientation, the division in frame of reference and activity between those who are extensively involved in the community (cosmopolitans) and those whose involvement is constricted (locals) has become more significant in the decision-making process, particularly in community conflict situations. The ramifications of the cosmopolitan-local division extend beyond electoral alignments and into the structure and functioning of governments, government agencies, and quasi-governments in the civil community. The "power structure" of the civil community is fundamentally pluralistic. Government (insofar as it involves decision-making) rests upon the mobilization of concurrent majorities developed from among the various group and individual interests represented in the civil community. This means that a wide variety of groups and individuals hold the power of the tacit veto over given issues, by preventing the formation of the requisite concurrent majority. The strength of their tacit veto power varies by group and by issue. Some groups and individuals have wide powers of tacit veto. The power of others is confined to limited areas. The determination of which groups and individuals have what degree of tacit veto power provides the basis for identifying the community's "power structure."

Means of Testing Hypothesis: Analysis of cases of community conflict in light of the socioeconomic and political data referred to previously (using voting returns, intensive interviewing of political actives and, where possible, survey research data). Analysis of voting behavior on specific issues (such as tax referenda, school support, and public improvements) by geographic area and over time. Identification of the sources of citizen pressures on various governments, governmental agencies, and quasi-governments with a view to determining which groups and individuals involve themselves with which governments. Identification of the groups possessing tacit veto powers, the ways and means by which they may exercise those powers, and the realms in which they may do so.

REPUBLICANISM

Scope: Covers the interaction between the functioning of the governmental and political institutions in the civil community and their structure.

Hypothesis: Within the formal local governments, there is a tendency to abdicate power. The pressures of the local political value system are on the side of the dispersal of power among a wide range of elements. These pressures are tied to the use of the various formal governments and government agencies by different elements in the community—political and economic interests, socioeconomic groupings, and frame of reference (cosmopolitan-local) groups. Within the intragovernmental framework, these pressures have often made any concentration of executive power impossible. Where this is so, local government has more often followed the pattern of a parliamentary system (whereby the executive agencies are controlled by a committee, or committees, of the legislative) rather than that of a presidential system (in which a strong executive controls his branch of the government subject to checks imposed by the legislature).

Method of Testing Hypothesis: Identification of the actual functions of the local governments in the civil community (particularly those of the city government) and comparison with their allowed functions. Investigation of the actions of local governments in handling the functions they do undertake. Investigation of the origins, compositions, and operations of special governments in the civil community (school district, park district, sanitary district, airport district, and the like). Examination of the relations between specific interests, groupings, and groups and their "governmental counterparts." Identification of the operational procedures within the local governments in reference to legislative-executive and legislative-agency relations: preclearance systems, legislative committee systems, and actual foci of power within the formal governmental structure. Determination of perceptions of the executive and legislative functions by local political executives and other officeholders.

METROPOLITANISM

Scope: Covers the functional relationships of the political subdivisions of the civil community to each other.

Hypothesis: The several local governments within the civil community were originally created or have evolved in such a way as to separate themselves and their functions from one another. One result of this is the existence of a greater degree of collaboration between agencies of the federal and state governments and specific local governments which share responsibility for the same programs than between the various local governments themselves. Nevertheless, the pressures and problems of metropolitanism are leading to a greater degree of inter-governmental collaboration within the civil community. The government most likely to benefit (in terms of increased scope and power) from the political changes introduced by metropolitanism is the county government. The most important political changes that will take place in response to metropolitanism are likely to be at the county level because of the ubiquity of county governments, the absence of political vacuums (such as exist on the fringes of cities) between counties, the relative equality of county governments due to their shared position in the state's local government pattern, and the traditional location of political power at the county level. The growing impact of metropolitanism is not likely to lead to formal metropolitan integration of governmental structures but to functional integration of governmental activities and services with the county playing an increasingly important role.

Means of Testing Hypothesis: Identification of the county government's functions and their change in recent years. Examination of the formal and informal interrelations of the various local governments. Identification of politicians and officeholders' responses to inter-local collaboration and the expansion of specific governments' activities and services.

REGIONALISM

Scope: Covers the political, cultural, and socioeconomic relationships of the the civil community to the larger geographic areas of which it is a part.

Hypothesis: The nature and functioning of the civil community, in terms of federalism, its relationship to the frontier, and forms of its construction, the nature of its democracy and republicanism, and the character of its metropolitanism are, to a significant extent, determined by the way in which these concepts are translated into actions in the regions of which the civil community is a part. Regional influences are important factors in shaping its culture, its politics, its forms and processes of government, its history, and its economic conditions.

Means of Testing Hypothesis: Identification of the particular regional patterns referred to above. Determination of the specific relations of the civil community to those patterns, individually and collectively.

II. *A Guide to the Mapping of a Civil Community's Political Characteristics*

A. *Purpose of This Guide:*

This outline guide is designed to provide an inventory of information needed to develop a political map of a civil community, a pattern by which to organize that information, a series of questions to be used in analyzing the information, and a check-list that can be used to classify the data originally gathered and periodic supplements.

A political map, in this sense, is an outline of the patterns of political behavior in the civil community as a whole and in its various subdivisions. It includes socioeconomic, voting, and influence patterns as related to political behavior and is intended to indicate the political character of the community.

The term "civil community" is used in reference to cities and their metropolitan areas. A civil community consists of the sum of the governments and quasi-governments that function in a given locality and that are tied together in a single bundle of governmental activities and services. This bundle of governmental activities and services is manipulated in the locality to serve the local political value system. There is no standard set of political jurisdictions that can be used to delineate the individual civil community. Each civil community must be delineated in its own terms. In any particular case, the civil community may consist of a city itself, an entire county, a school district, a regional planning district, or the like.

B. *Why Map?*

In order to embark on a course of political or governmental action appropriate to the civil community concerned (or any of its parts) and developed with every possible effort to promote its success, it is necessary to understand the community's political characteristics. This means that something must be known about:

1. The community's history, particularly its political history and traditions.
2. The local political framework, what may be called the community's "constitution," particularly which governments or governmental agencies are officially involved in which activities.

"Constitution," as used here, refers to the outline of the formal political structure and the fundamental allocation of power and influence within it. As applied to civil communities, the term is used more in the sense of a collection of basic documents, fundamental laws, and established customs that set basic political patterns than in the sense of a single organic law or charter (that may or may not exist in any particular civil community).

3. The structure of individual and group interests that are brought into play on political and governmental questions in the community.
4. The political process through which issues are selected and funneled and decisions made.

C. *Relevant Information That Should Emerge:*

The following general questions should be at least partially answered when the political map is developed. In each case, the general answers will no doubt have raised specific questions that may or may not be answerable with the information assembled. These questions serve, on the one hand, to check the accuracy of the information and, on the other, to point out its limitations. In addition, specific questions relating to each community in its uniqueness will also emerge, many of which will be answered in the same manner through the development of the political map. Every community includes certain basic patterns common to all communities, yet these patterns are always uniquely arranged within each. Identification of the common patterns can lead to the understanding of community processes; identification of those unique to a specific community can lead to an understanding of those processes as applied to it.

1. Questions stemming from the community's general history
   What have been the settlement and growth patterns in the community?
   What have been the social and industrial patterns that accompanied them?
   What religious and ethnic group patterns have been developed?
   What political patterns have capped these others over time?
   What kind of community is it as a whole?
2. Questions relating to the community's political framework
   Identify the community's constitution.
   What are the means, frequency, and types of constitutional change?
   What governments are involved in providing the bundle of services for the civil community? How do they cooperate to provide those services or initiate new ones?
   Given the political framework, what kinds of things can or cannot be done by government? Who can do them?
3. Questions relating to the structure of individual and group interests
   Where do the various groups in the community live? Why?
   Who makes up the various groups in the community?
   Which individuals and groups participate in community, particularly governmental, affairs: Generally? On specific issues (which issues)? Rarely or not at all?

Which individuals and groups can influence government in the community, directly and indirectly? Generally? On specific issues (which issues)? Rarely or not at all?

4. Questions relating to the operation of the political process
   Who participates in the outright political process?
   What is the nature of the party system in the community?
   What is the nature of the intra-governmental political process? (Who initiates policies? What are the informal relations between the branches and departments of government?)
   Which individuals and groups have tacit vetoes in the community?

D. *How To Go About Mapping:*

The key to political mapping is proper utilization of previously prepared sources rather than the intensive development of new ones. The best sources are:

1. Previous studies of the community
   Usually available in local governmental offices, civic associations, and public utilities offices, local libraries, local colleges, or the state university (farther afield, in institutes of governmental or related research at major universities). These include academic studies, studies of specific problems, "practical" studies, studies by private consultants, studies by planners and planning commissions, and studies by private interests directly or indirectly related to the local political and governmental situation.
2. Government and public documents
   These include reports of governments and governmental agencies, government publications dealing with the community, maps, budgets, audits, and so on. Also included here are reports and publications of civic groups, "watchdog" organizations, labor unions, and other public nongovernmental organizations.
3. Voting records
   These include maps of the community showing electoral districts; voting results for candidates and issues in recent elections and relevant past elections recorded by electoral districts and subdistricts; and records of voter registration and turnout.
4. Newspaper records
   These should include the local daily press, weeklies, special interest (labor, church) newspapers, and any regional newspapers that carry news of the locality. Within limitations, newspaper sources can be used to provide a continuous look at the community. They can provide case studies on issues, records of local politics, accounts, and background material on local problems, as well as nonpolitical background material.
5. Interviews
   These could consist of formal interviews with key government officials, civic leaders, and community members or records of pertinent informal information gathered through the normal course of business and other contacts.

III. *An Outline for Mapping the Civil Community's Political Characteristics**

A. *The Civil Community and Its Citizens:*

FOCUS: To assemble historical and contemporary data descriptive of the development of the general ethos and character of the civil community and its citizens.

1. Definition and boundaries of the civil community
2. General descriptions of the character and ethos of the civil community
   A more or less impressionistic summary of what the population data suggest, comments of local interviewees, data provided by other studies, conclusions from the researcher's own investigations, and suggestions from historical materials.
   a. Conservative-progressive-innovating
   b. Cosmopolitan-local
   c. Frontier-transitional-hinterland
3. Characteristics of the population of the civil community
   a. General population and mobility data
      Number of persons
      Rate of growth
      Growth of central city and peripheries
      Geographical direction of growth
      Population density
   b. Housing—home ownership
      Conditions of housing, types of housing
   c. Employment
      Industrial, commercial, services, professional, governmental unemployment
      Employment trends
   d. Family and household data
      Family income
   e. Nonwhites
      Number, rate of growth, location, income, home ownership, employment patterns, direction of community growth
   f. Ethnicity and national origin
      Variety of groups, number, patterns of settlement, history of settlement, employment pattern, assimilation-cohesiveness
   g. Religious affiliation
      Variety and number of groups, backgrounds of church mem-

* Originally prepared in collaboration with Kenneth E. Gray.

bers, membership statistics, location of churches, ethnic churches, social status of churches

h. Educational and cultural background

Educational level, schools, colleges, libraries, museums, and so on

Clubs, organizations, and societies (of a generally nonpolitical nature)

i. Popular identification with the general community or sub-communities, neighborhood, city, suburb, metropolitan area

j. Special demographic data

Available studies

Data of particular relevance in the specific community

4. Characteristics of the population by electoral divisions and census tracts. See III, A 1 and 2.
5. Characteristics of the civil community relative to its larger environment
   a. Regional position
   b. Transportation and communication facilities
6. General history of the civil community

B. *Political Organizations in the Civil Community:*

1. Background—the character of conflict
   a. Historical background
   b. A general overview
   c. The local political tradition(s)
2. The formal structure
   a. Charters and organic laws (identify the local written "constitution")
   b. Organized governments (names, types, number)
   c. Electoral systems
   d. Constitutional, statutory, traditional, and informal functions of governments
   e. Constitutional, statutory, traditional, and informal functions of departments and officers
   f. Institutionalized operational arrangements within the governments and their subdivisions
   g. The public service (merit system and patronage)
3. The character of the political parties

   Focus: To classify the kinds of parties, delineate their respective characters, and show the internal relationships of their active components.

   a. Special local parties
      i. Nonpartisan (no permanent factions or alliances)
      ii. Permanent antimachine alliances
      iii. Ad hoc, special reform alliances
      iv. Traditional local parties (unaffiliated nationally)
      v. Persistent local factions in one-party situations

b. Standard political system
  i. Democratic party
  ii. Republican party
c. Relationship between special and standard parties in city, county, area, state, and national affairs
d. Noninstitutional influences on the character of the parties
  i. Interest groups
    (a) Labor
    (b) Business
    (c) Minorities (racial, ethnic, and religious)
    (d) "Good government" groups
  ii. General influences
    (a) Intellectuals (innovators, manipulators, and carriers of ideas)
    (b) Conservatives and liberals
    (c) Personalities
    (d) The press

4. The Character of Intraparty Organization
  a. Ward organizations and leaders
    i. Old-style machines (based on patronage, racial, and ethnic appeals)
    ii. New-style organizations (based on organized mobilization of consent through precinct work and the press)
  b. Intraparty factions and alliances
    i. Origins
    ii. Cohesiveness
    iii. Leadership

C. *Electoral Behavior in the Civil Community:*

Selected voting data and background information for the civil community as a whole and as subdivided politically. Where significant, contrast city and noncity electoral behavior. In all cases, a "ward" in incorporated areas is equivalent to a "township" in unincorporated areas. Be sure to list dates of changes in electoral district boundaries during last twenty years. The usefulness of ward voting returns selected will depend upon whether maps of earlier districting arrangements are available.

1. Voting participation in elections.
   Where possible secure voting statistics in table form for most recent year and last twenty years, for (a) city, partisan local, state, and national elections (b) local and state referenda. Include registration by party if available.
   a. Population and voter registration by ward and precinct: most recent year
   b. Comparative registration and population by wards (over time)
   c. Registration and voting totals: city primary and general, county and state primary and general elections—twenty-year period

d. Number voting in city, state, and national elections—twenty-year period

2. Campaigns for local office
    a. Candidates (identification and brief description)
    b. The character of the campaign (issues, personalities, tactics)
    c. Voting returns for local officials (major cities, special local governments, townships where relevant)
        i. Voting by ward and precinct for mayor, council, and other elected officials, last election and selected others
        ii. Vote on candidates for city council, last election and selected others
        iii. Vote for other significant local officials (when relevant)
3. Referenda campaigns
    a. Issues in each campaign
    b. Development of proposed solutions
    c. Proponents and opponents
    d. The character of the campaign (issues, personalities, tactics)
    e. Voting returns
        i. Vote on state and local referenda and money issues by wards and precincts, for selected elections
        ii. Vote by ward and precinct on school taxing and bond issues, for selected elections
        iii. Total vote on local constitutional referenda over past half-century (list of elections and their results)
    f. Voting in county-wide, state, and national (partisan) elections
    Vote by wards and precincts for selected county, state, and federal officials in last election and selected others (offices should be selected to show partisan voting patterns)

D. *Intergovernmental Relations:*
FOCUS: Relationships between the central city(s) and other political levels, units, and actors.
1. City-state
    a. Special districts
    b. Suburbs
    c. County
    d. State government locally
    e. State (as a whole)
2. City-federal
    a. Federal government locally
    b. National agencies
3. Interstate (particularly for border cities)

E. *The Character, Goals, and Political Roles of Interest Groups:*
FOCUS: To identify the interest groups, their composition, history, activities, leadership, interests, goals, political participation, and relationships to other interest groups.

1. Labor
    a. Unions
    b. Labor as a class
2. Business
    a. Chamber of commerce
    b. Business "elites"
    c. Outside business interests
3. The Press and the Mass Media
    a. Newspapers
    b. Radio and television
4. Negroes
5. Ethnic groups
6. Religious groups and churches
7. Individuals and social class
8. Reformers and good government groups
9. Public administrators
10. Other groups

F. *Issues and Problems:*

FOCUS: To identify the major issues of the present and recent past to show how politics is carried on in the civil community.

Some basic questions are: How are community problems agitated to become political issues? What kinds of problems do or do not become issues? What groups or individuals are instrumental in the selection of issues—what part do the politicians play in the selection and resolution of issues? What kinds of issues can be settled locally? What kinds of settlements depend upon decisions made outside of the civil community? What groups and interests are served by the resolution or nonresolution of particular issues? How does the selection and treatment of issues relate to the organizational maintenance needs of groups?

Note: Try to locate illustrative case studies.

1. Governmental structural change (charter revision, home rule)
2. City finances
    a. General policy
    b. Financial structure
    c. Taxation and taxes
    d. Referenda on financial matters
    e. Budgeting and budgets
    f. Sharing of revenues
3. Conditions of employment in the public service
4. Community conservation and development
    a. City planning and zoning
    b. Urban renewal, redevelopment, and conservation
    c. Housing (as an issue)
    d. Freeways and highways
    e. Local streets and traffic

5. Economic development
    a. Industrial development
    b. Economic decline, unemployment
    c. Promotion and "boosterism"
6. Public transportation and public utilities
7. Regional planning and metropolitan reorganization
8. Annexation
9. Schools and colleges
10. Libraries and cultural institutions
11. Parks and recreation, open space
12. Law enforcement and crime
    a. Governmental corruption
    b. Vice and prostitution
    c. Gambling
13. Liquor
14. Air and water pollution problems
15. Water resources problems
16. Human-needs problems
    a. Aging
    b. Public welfare
    c. Juvenile delinquency
    d. Public health and hospitals
17. Human relations problems

G. *Aids to Further Research: (Additional references and sources)*

1. Informed persons (names, addresses, identifications)
2. Governmental offices
3. Nongovernmental organizations and offices
4. Academic sources
5. Bibliography of published and unpublished documents, articles, case studies, and the like
6. Library collections

H. *A Selection of Supporting Maps and Documents:*

1. Maps
    a. Maps showing political boundaries, census tracts, and electoral divisions (drawn to the same scale or with enough detail so that scale maps can be constructed).
       Note: Secure maps with electoral boundaries corresponding to past election returns.
    b. Historical development and annexation map(s)
    c. Map of social geography
    d. Redevelopment plans and renewal projects
    e. Public housing
    f. Business and commercial districts
    g. Park and school locations

2. Documents
   a. City charter
   b. Special reports of governments and government departments
   c. Annual reports of governments and government departments
   d. Yearbooks
   e. Special publications on city government and politics
   f. Descriptions of city government and politics
   g. Planning reports and research papers
   h. Reports and publications of chamber of commerce, local development groups
   i. Reports and publications of other interest groups
   j. Newspapers and clippings
   k. Civic, community, and business organizations

I. Suggestions for Specific Research

APPENDIX C

The Concept of Cultural Streams

I

THE CONCEPT OF cultural streams that forms the basis for the analysis in Part II of this volume is related to the general problem of "political culture" and some of the more specific aspects of "national character." It represents an effort to uncover, in the words of Inkeles and Levinson, "relatively enduring modal patterns of behavior in large social aggregates with cross-generational ties" usually, but not necessarily, located in specific territories that affect political values, perceptions, and actions in the various American political systems. Questions of modal behavior patterns and national character have concerned historians, anthropologists, and social psychologists for many years. They have received increasing attention (in various guises) from political scientists. The study of these phenomena properly seeks (1) to discover coherent, persistent, and unique patterns of culturally defined values and behavior expressed through institutional as well as individual actions which are found in particular communities and societies and (2) to uncover the various geohistorical influences which have shaped those patterns as well as (3) the ways in which they have been transmitted through time by the appropriate institutions and disseminated through space by human migration.

Social psychologists speak of the phenomenon of modal behavior as "the regularity with which certain values, themes, or patterned behavior sequences are expressed or manifested by the individuals participating in any culture." Ralph Linton, in his book *The Cultural Background of Personality* conceives of national character as modal personality structure, the one among a great variety of individual personality characteristics and patternings in any society that appears with sufficient frequency to be recognized as the norm. Inkeles and Levinson elaborate on this idea in "National Character: The Study of Modal Personality and Sociocultural Systems." All quotations in this Appendix are taken from that article unless otherwise identified. *Basic personality structure* as used here "refers to the sociocultural matrix rather than to that which is 'deepest' in the person." It "consists of those dispositions, conceptions, modes of relating to others, and the like, that make the individual maximally receptive to cultural ways and ideologies, and that enable him to achieve adequate gratification and security within the existing order." See Kardiner, *The Individual and His Society.* For the relationship between culture and personality with particular emphasis on the American political scene, see Erikson, *Childhood and Society.*

Using this concept of modal personality structure as representing the central ingredient in the determination of national character, and understanding its limitations, it is possible to speak of cultural streams in the manner used in this study. *Cultural stream* does not imply a unimodal distribution of personality variants in a given culture or subculture. It certainly is not meant to revive nineteenth-century stereotypical theories of national character or inherent racial characteristics. Rather, it focuses on the modal personality pattern that can be discerned within a multimodal social environment but one which is not necessarily coterminous with national boundaries or any civil society. The term is intentionally somewhat imprecise since the streams are themselves but trends which are blurred at their outer edges. The analogy to the movement of water which comes to mind is intended and apt. However, since these are human phenomena it should also be understood that the aggregate behavior they are meant to describe does not preclude the existence of many individual departures from each stream's "mode" within every stream.

Focus on the cultural stream as the basic configuration of certain cultural patterns adds a spatially dynamic element to the study of culture since it offers a means for following the movement of cultures via human migration—one of the constants of human history—and the mixing of cultures in the course of such movements. In this and in other ways, the concept can enhance our understanding of the complexities of cultural configurations in any nation, political system, or civilization. Some sense of the complexities is inherent in the very imagery of "stream," which has direction but whose flow and limits are not self-determined but are set by the ground it traverses except insofar as its very flow modifies that ground. Furthermore, streams have currents within them to further differentiate their composition and flow. Cultural streams share the same kind of internal differentiation. Even at this stage it is possible to recognize currents within the cultural streams discussed above and further research should sharpen our recognition of such divisions.

Anthropologists, more interested in the cultural than the individual manifestations of this phenomenon, have written of the dynamic character and movement of what are here termed cultural streams. See, in particular, Arensburg, "American Communities." Other useful sources from related social sciences include Edward T. Hall's two exceptional works, *The Silent Language* and *The Hidden Dimension*, Henry A. Murray, ed., *Myths and Mythmaking*, Kluckhohn, "Culture and Behavior," Lipset and Lowenthal, *Culture and Social Character,* and Mead, "The Study of National Character." Two classical studies deserving of attention are those of the Baron Montesquieu, *The Spirit of the Laws* and *Persian Letters.*

The concept of political culture and its relationship to general culture has been explored in recent years by Gabriel Almond and his colleagues whose most significant works are listed in the bibliography at the end of this appendix.

II

The terms "stream" and "current" are used here for purposes of generalizing about the overall patterns of migration and settlement in the United States. They are designed to convey a sense of the dynamic yet somewhat blurred nature of migrational patterns in this country and the directional character of the various migrations that have molded American settlement patterns. Streams are not ethnic groups. In fact, the concept of streams is deliberately used as a means to overcome the limitations of conventional "ethnic group" concepts. Discussions of "ethnic groups" usually focus on what are more appropriately termed nationality groups, usually delineated according to the national boundaries (or the nationalistic claims) of early twentieth-century Europe. This leads to two significant errors. On one hand, important intranational ethnic divisions disappear within larger general categories that cut across those divisions (for example, all residents of Germany as unified by Bismarck are lumped together as Germans without distinction, ignoring fundamental, if seemingly hidden, differences between northern Protestants and southern Catholics, Prussians and Rhinelanders, Bavarians and Saxons, and so on). On the other hand, deeper transethnic patterns of similarity of great significance rooted in common religious and cultural ties are equally ignored because they disappear within the framework of the various national divisions and loyalties which have captured the consciousness of the people involved (for example, no distinction is made between coastal and interior cultural patterns in Northern Europe). Furthermore, traditional ethnic analysis ignores the existence of quasi-ethnic groups within the older "American" (white Anglo-Saxon Protestant) population that is just as meaningfully divided by general and political cultural differences as are the more visible "immigrant" groups. The concept of cultural streams and currents is designed to get at just those problems by focusing on divisions that combine ethnic groups whose members stem from a particular geocultural background, taking into account patterns that often lie deeper or extend more broadly than the level of ethnic division, patterns which may reflect subcultures within specific ethnic groups or geocultural patterns which transcend them.

The description in Part II may give the impression of too even a "flow" of the streams as they course across the country. In point of fact, while the streams can be properly conceived of as flows, they have always been broken up by various obstacles or by intermixture with each other. Different streams deposit different groups of different sizes in different places. The local sums of their "deposits," the populations of specific places, are accordingly uneven and generally conglomerate. Thus the geology of human settlement in any particular community, which when taken alone appears to be unique, often obscures the essential geohistorical relationship between the particular community and the overall national pattern. Yet this relationship contributes much to the explanation of similarities of political behavior in apparently diverse communities and the differences in political behavior in apparently similar ones.

The extensive documentation available for the hypotheses put forward in Part II necessarily has been reduced to the citation of general sources only. While relatively little has been done to examine the influence of migrational streams on American political behavior, there is a great deal of evidence presently available to support the broad generalizations about the role of migrations in the diffusion of American cultural diversity. In point of fact, the study of migrations in this sense has been a central concern of the entire school of "frontier" historians from Frederick Jackson Turner to the present. Consequently, the several guides to the literature of the frontier cited in the footnotes to the text represent good starting points for background data.

Central to the entire study of migrational patterns and cultural streams are the decennial compilations of the United States Census Bureau, particularly the statistical atlases published between 1870 and 1920, that graphically delineate migrational patterns and many other kinds of social statistics that can be correlated with each other. Unfortunately the published census data on in-migration and internal migration are relatively limited and their classifications highly conventional, which lessens their usefulness for the kind of analysis called for here. In order to utilize the data on overseas migrations to even roughly approximate the cultural streams involved, this writer developed the categories shown in Table C–1.

Delineation of the native streams is possible primarily through use of data on religious affiliation. If migrational data are inadequate, the census data on religious affiliation are even worse. Only four full-scale censuses of religion (at decade intervals from 1906 through 1936) have ever been taken in this country. Prior to them, fragmented data were assembled and, subsequently, a sampling in 1957. These data were classified according to the categories shown in Table C–2.

Among the historio-geographic sources of particular value are the works of Turner, particularly *The Frontier in American History, The Rise of the New West*, and *The United States 1830–1850*. The Turner Papers at the Henry E. Huntington Library, San Marino, California, are invaluable, containing as they do considerable data on the role of the various ethnic groups in settling the country. Geographic studies include Charles O. Paullin, *Atlas of the Historical Geography of the United States*, Frederic L. Paxson, *History of the American Frontier 1763–1893*, Lawrence U. Rath's "The Growth of American Cities," a useful city by city analysis of nineteenth-century urban development, and Edwin Scott Gaustad, *Historical Atlas of Religion in America.* The latter source is particularly important since it sums up many other social factors of importance in the various migrational currents in order to illuminate the relationship of religious affiliation to general social trends.

W. Lloyd Warner's team study of Morris, Illinois, a community that appears to be sociologically a miniaturization of the Illinois cities of the prairie in many ways, is of great value as background material to the problems of culture, class, and current in the greater West. See, particularly, *Democracy in Jonesville.* On larger national questions of migration, ethnicity, and class and particularly useful in studying the rise and fall of the "two cities," see E. Digby Baltzell, *An American Business Aristocracy.*

TABLE C-1

Proximate Alignment of Census National Origins Divisions by Cultural Stream

Political Culture	Cultural Stream	National Origins Divisions
Moralistic	North Sea	Scotland, Northern Ireland, Norway, Sweden, Denmark, Iceland, Netherlands, Switzerland, Finland, also diffused among English.
	Jewish	Diffused among all national origins divisions, identifiable by native language classifications in some cases. Especially prominent in Russian, Polish, Austrian, German, and other Central and Eastern European countries and, since 1948, Israel.
	English Canadian	Canada (English-speaking)
Individualistic	English	England (generally), Wales, Australia[a]
	Irish	Ireland
	Continental	Belgium, Luxembourg, France, Germany, Czechoslovakia, Austria, Hungary
	French Canadian	Canada (French-speaking)
Traditionalistic	Eastern European	Poland, Russia (U.S.S.R.), Latvia, Estonia, Lithuania, Rumania, Bulgaria
	Mediterranean	Yugoslavia, Turkey, Greece, Albania, Italy, Spain, Portugal, Armenia, Palestine, Syria, Azores, Atlantic Islands
	Hispanic	Cuba, Mexico, Puerto Rico, Central and South American countries
	Oriental	China, Japan, India, Philippine Islands, Pacific Islands

[a] English of Puritan stock properly belong among the moralistic streams.

TABLE C-2

Classification of Major Religious Denominations by Political-Cultural Leaning

Moralistic	Individualistic	Traditionalistic
American Baptist Convention	Assemblies of God	African Methodist Episcopal Church
American Lutheran Church	Churches of Christ	African Methodist Episcopal Zion Church
Christian Reformed Church	Disciples of Christ	All Baptist bodies except American Baptist Convention
Church of Christ, Scientist	Eastern Orthodox Churches	Church of God
Church of Jesus Christ of the Latter Day Saints (Mormons)	Evangelical United Brethren	Church of God in Christ
Congregationalists (now United Church of Christ and dissident Congregational churches)	Free Methodist	Church of the Nazarene
Friends (Quakers)	Lutheran Church—Missouri Synod	Evangelical United Brethren Church
Jewish Congregations	Lutheran General Conference	Pentacostal Churches
Lutheran Church in America	Methodist Church	Presbyterian Church in the United States
Reformed Church in America	Methodist and Episcopal	
United Presbyterian Church in the USA	Protestant Episcopal	
	Roman Catholic	
	United Lutheran Church	
	Wisconsin Evangelical Lutheran Synod	

III

The role of religious movements (in the largest sense of belief systems) in shaping the streams and currents cannot be explored here. However, all signs point to such movements as the keys to cultural continuity and the transmission of cultural modes, the transcendence or division of ethnic and national groups, and fundamental change within a particular culture that leads to the emergence of new cultures or subcultures. Religious experience seems to be the only force sufficiently strong to cause the kind of deep personality change within a substantial population that leads to cultural change. Such religious experience may range from the Jews' experience at Mount Sinai to the American Indians' ghost dance, from the Protestant Reformation to the spread of Communism. It may be generated by a host of factors, some inexplicable in scientific terms. Once a religious experience takes hold in in a particular population group, however, it becomes a force promoting fundamental change in its own right, probably the most powerful single force to influence man.

Two corollary points: Specific religious movements, even as they change culture, are generally most successful among groups already culturally predisposed toward their fundamental demands. (Thus Calvinistic Protestantism found its strength among elements with a common cultural heritage along the shores of the North Sea. Their American descendants created Yankee Puritanism. Mormonism was founded by upstate New York Yankees and has had most success in proselytizing among the same elements that were originally attracted to Calvinism plus the Scandinavians who came from a similar cultural milieu.) The decline of the force of a particular pattern of religious belief and experience within the culture it has molded invariably leads to a cultural crisis of the first magnitude and the search for religious substitutes to overcome that crisis. (The Roman Empire underwent that experience after the first century of the Christian era, and there are strong indications that the Western World is experiencing it today.)

BIBLIOGRAPHY

Gabriel A. Almond, "Comparative Political Systems," *Journal of Politics,* XVIII (1956), 391–409.

Gabriel A. Almond and James Coleman, eds., *The Politics of Developing Areas* (Princeton: Princeton University Press, 1960).

Gabriel A. Almond and C. Bingham Powell, Jr., *Comparative Politics: A Developmental Approach* (Boston: Little, Brown, 1966).

Gabriel A. Almond and Sidney Verba, *The Civic Culture* (Princeton: Princeton University Press, 1963).

Conrad Arensburg, "American Communities," *American Anthropologist,* Vol. LVII (1955).

E. Digby Baltzell, *An American Business Aristocracy* (New York: Collier, 1962).

James Bryce, *Modern Democracies* (New York: Macmillan, 1921), Chapters XXIV, XXV.

Murray Edelman, *The Symbolic Uses of Politics* (Urbana: University of Illinois Press, 1964).

Erik Erikson, *Childhood and Society* (New York: Norton, 1950).

Edwin Scott Gaustad, *Historical Atlas of Religion in America* (New York and Evanston: Harper, 1962).

Edward T. Hall, *The Hidden Dimension* (Garden City, N.Y.: Doubleday, 1966).

———, *The Silent Language* (New York: Doubleday, 1959).

Alex Inkeles and Daniel J. Levinson, "National Character: The Study of Modal Personality and Sociocultural Systems," in Gardner Lindzey, ed., *Handbook of Social Psychology* (Cambridge, Mass.: Addison, 1954).

Abram Kardiner, *The Individual and His Society* (New York: Columbia University Press, 1939).

Clyde Kluckhohn, "Cultural Behavior" in Gardner Lindzey, ed., *Handbook of Social Psychology* (Cambridge, Mass.: Addison, 1954).

Harold D. Lasswell et al., *The Language of Politics* (Cambridge: Harvard University Press, 1965).

Ralph Linton, *The Cultural Background of Personality* (New York: Appleton-Century, 1945).

Seymour Martin Lipset and Leo Lowenthal, *Culture and Social Character* (New York: Free Press, 1961).

Margaret Mead, "The Study of National Character" in Daniel Lerner and Harold Lasswell, eds., *The Policy Sciences* (Stanford: Stanford University Press, 1961).

Henry A. Murray, ed., *Myths and Mythmaking* (New York: Braziller, 1960).

Charles O. Paullin, *Atlas of the Historical Geography of the United States* (Washington: Carnegie Institute, and New York: American Geographical Society, 1932).

Lawrence U. Rath, "The Growth of American Cities," *Geographical Review,* V, No. 5 (May 1918).

Frederic L. Paxson, *History of the American Frontier* (Boston and New York: Houghton, 1924).

Frederick Jackson Turner, *The Frontier in American History* (New York: Holt, 1920).
———, *The Rise of the New West* (Gloucester, Mass.: Peter Smith, 1959).
———, *The United States 1830–1850* (New York: Holt, 1935).
W. Lloyd Warner, *Democracy in Jonesville* (New York: Harper, 1949).

APPENDIX D

A List of Source Materials

AUTHOR'S NOTE: The material cited here includes only those items not otherwise acknowledged in the Preface or appendices or cited in the text. It represents only a selection of the data gathered for this study. Only the most important interviews, documents, and secondary sources are included. In some cases, important interviews are not cited to preserve confidences. City and regional plans, maps, telephone and city directories, city codes and ordinances, local government budgets and financial reports, minutes of meetings of local government bodies and their relevant committees, reports of local governments and government agencies, office files, local newspapers and newspaper files were routinely examined in every civil community and are not cited individually in Section III unless of special importance beyond their obvious purposes. The data gathered for the study are available at the Institute of Government and Public Affairs, University of Illinois and the Center for the Study of Federalism, Temple University.

I

General Works on the Central Themes of This Volume

Adrian, Charles R. *Governing Urban America.* 2nd ed. New York: McGraw-Hill, 1961.

Anderson, William. *Intergovernmental Relations in Review.* Minneapolis: University of Minnesota Press, 1960.

Banfield, Edward C. (ed.). *Urban Government.* New York: The Free Press of Glencoe, 1961.

———, and James Q. Wilson. *City Politics.* Cambridge, Mass.: Harvard University Press and MIT Press, 1963.

Bell, Daniel. "Crime as an American Way of Life," *Antioch Review,* XIII, No. 2 (1953), 131–154.

Bendix, Reinhard, and Seymour Martin Lipset (eds.). *Class, Status and Power.* Glencoe: The Free Press, 1953.

Bollens, John C. (ed.). *Exploring the Metropolitan Community.* Berkeley: University of California Press, 1961.

———, *Special District Government in the United States.* Berkeley: University of California Press, 1957.

———, and Henry Schmandt. *The Metropolis: Its People, Politics, and Economic Life.* New York: Harper, 1965.

Converse, James B. *The Bible and Land.* Morristown, Tenn.: Rev. James B. Converse Publisher, 1899.

Davis, Allison; Burleigh B. Gardner; and Mary R. Gardner. *Deep South: A Social Anthropological Study of Caste and Class.* Chicago: University of Chicago Press, 1965.

Dobriner, William M. "The Natural History of a Reluctant Suburb," *Yale Review* (Spring 1960).

Donovan, Frank. *Wheels for a Nation.* New York: Thomas Y. Crowell Co., 1965. (A study that delineates the frontier aspects of the automotive revolution.)

Elkins, Stanley M. *Slavery: A Problem in American Institutional and Intellectual Life.* Chicago: University of Chicago Press, 1959.

Federal Reserve Bank of Chicago Monthly Bulletin, 1959–1967.

Federal Reserve Bank of Kansas City Monthly Bulletin, 1959–1967.

Federal Reserve Bank of Minneapolis Monthly Bulletin, 1959–1967.

Fite, Gilbert C. "The Agrarian Tradition and Its Meaning for Today," *Minnesota History,* XL, No. 6 (Summer 1967), 293–299.

Frazier, E. Franklin. *The Negro Family in the United States.* Chicago: University of Chicago Press, 1966.

Frederick, William L. *State Technical Assistance to Local Governments: A Review of Selected State Services.* Chicago: Council of State Governments, 1962.

Friedmann, John, and William Alonso (eds.). *Regional Planning and Development.* Cambridge, Mass.: MIT Press, 1964.

Fuchs, Lawrence H., "American Jews and the Presidential Vote," *American Political Science Review,* XLIX (June 1955), 385–401.

Furlong, William Barry. "Small Town Smack in the Big Time," *New York Times Magazine,* October 14, 1962.

Goodnow, Frank J. *City Government in the United States.* New York: Appleton-Century-Crofts, 1904.

Gosnell, Harold F. *Negro Politicians: The Rise of Negro Politics in Chicago.* Chicago: University of Chicago Press, 1935.

Gove, Samuel K. *The Lakewood Plan.* Urbana: Commission Papers of the Institute of Government and Public Affairs, University of Illinois, May 1961.

Hughes, Jonathan. *The Vital Few.* Boston: Houghton Mifflin, 1966. (A study of the contributions of outstanding gifted and influential individuals to American economic and social development which adds a useful dimension to the frontier hypothesis presented here while adding evidence to support the "three frontiers" theory.)

Johansen, Dorothy O. "A Working Hypothesis for the Study of Migrations," *Pacific Historical Review,* Vol. XXXVI (February 1967).

Johnson, Charles S. *Shadow of the Plantation.* Chicago: University of Chicago Press, 1934.

Keil, Charles. *Urban Blues.* Chicago: University of Chicago Press, 1966.

Lubell, Samuel. *Revolt of the Moderates.* New York: Harper, 1956.

Maass, Arthur (ed.). *Area and Power: A Theory of Local Government.* Glencoe: The Free Press, 1959.

Mandelbaum, Seymour J. "Spatial and Temporal Perspectives in the U.S. City." University of Pennsylvania, mimeo.

Martin, Roscoe C. *Metropolis in Transition: Local Government Adaptation to Change.* Washington: Housing and Home Finance Agency, 1963.

———, et al. *Decisions in Syracuse.* Bloomington: Indiana University Press, 1962.

Munger, Frank (ed.). *American State Politics.* New York: Thomas Y. Crowell, 1966.

Patterson, Samuel C. *The Political Cultures of the American States.* Iowa City: University of Iowa, 1966.

Press, Charles, and Oliver P. Williams. *Democracy in the Fifty States.* Chicago: Rand McNally, 1966.

Rossi, Peter H. *The Middle-Sized American City at Mid-Century.* A paper presented at the twenty-seventh Annual Conference of the Graduate Library School of the University of Chicago, August 8, 1962.

Rostow, W. W. *The Stages of Economic Growth.* Cambridge, Mass.: MIT Press, 1963.

Schmid, A. Allan. "Economic Theories of Space for Land Settlement Policy Analysis." A paper prepared for a Land Settlement Policy Seminar sponsored by the Southern Land Economics Research Committee, Washington, April 22–23, 1968.

Sealey, J. R.; R. A. Sim; E. W. Loosley. *Crestwood Heights: A Study of the Culture of Suburban Life.* New York: Basic Books, 1956. (For an examination of space, time, and culture in a small North American city, much of whose culture resembles that of the cities of the prairie and medium-size civil communities generally.)

Spear, Allan H. *Black Chicago: The Making of a Negro Ghetto, 1890–1920.* Chicago: University of Chicago Press, 1967.

Steffens, Lincoln. *The Autobiography of Lincoln Steffens.* New York: Harcourt, Brace, and World, 1931.

U.S. Census Reports, 1810–1960.

Warren, Roland L. *The Community in America.* Chicago: Rand McNally & Co., 1963.

Whitlock, Brand. *Forty Years of It.* New York: D. Appleton & Co., 1914.

Wilbern, York. *The Withering Away of the City.* University: University of Alabama Press, 1964.

Wilson, James Q. *Negro Politics: The Search for Leadership.* New York: The Free Press of Glencoe, 1960.

II

The States of the Cities of the Prairie

Colorado

Colorado State Planning Commission. *Yearbook of the State of Colorado.* Denver, 1956–1966.

Colorado Writers' Project. *Colorado.* New York: Hastings House, 1941.

Donnelly, Thomas C. (ed.). *Rocky Mountain Politics.* Albuquerque: University of New Mexico Press, 1940.

Hafen, Leroy H., and Ann W. Hafen, *History of Colorado.* Denver: Fred Rosenthal, 1943.

Jonas, Frank H. (ed.). *Western Politics.* Salt Lake City: University of Utah Press, 1961.

Martin, Curtis. *Colorado Politics.* Denver: Big Mountain Press, 1960.

Stone, Wilbur Fisk (ed.). *A History of Colorado.* Chicago: S. J. Clarke, 1918.

Illinois

Collections of the Illinois State Historical Library, 1909, Vol. IV. Executive Series, Vol. I. *The Governor's Letter—Books, 1818–1839.*

Constitution of the State of Illinois and the United States. Secretary of State of Illinois, Springfield, n.d.

Emancipation Centennial Issue. *Journal of the Illinois State Historical Society.* Springfield, Autumn 1963.

Government in Illinois. Secretary of the State of Illinois, Springfield.

Illinois: A Descriptive and Historical Guide. Originally compiled and written by the Federal Writers' Project for the State of Illinois. Revised 1946. Chicago: A. C. McClurg, 1939.

Illinois Blue Book, 1881–1967.

Illinois Government. University of Illinois, Institute of Government and Public Affairs.

Journal of the State Historical Society of Illinois. 1921–1968.

Memo to Bureau of Community Planning Staff from W. Lamont. Re: *Summary Analysis of Four Midwestern Metropolitan Planning Programs,* January 16, 1959.

Report distributed to the Members of the Council on Community Development, January 24, 1961, by Dr. Merle R. Sumption, Chairman of the Metropolitan Area School District Organization Committee, "A Study of Metropolitan Area School District Organization in Illinois, December 28, 1960.

Ackerman, William K. *Early Illinois Railroads.* Chicago: Fergus Printing, 1884. Read before the Chicago Historical Society, February 20, 1883.

———, *Illinois Central Rail Road.* Chicago: Fergus Printing, 1890.

Allen, John W. *Legends and Lore of Southern Illinois.* Carbondale: Southern Illinois University Press, 1963.

Althoff, Phillip, and Samuel C. Patterson. "Political Activism in a Rural County," *Midwest Journal of Political Science*, X (February 1966), 39–51.

Banfield, Edward C. *Political Influence.* New York: The Free Press of Glencoe, 1961.

Barnard, Elizabeth. "Settlement Along the Illinois River," unpublished manuscript prepared for Frederick Jackson Turner, n.d., 26 pp.

Bateman, Newton, and Paul Selby (eds.). *Historical Encyclopedia of Illinois.* Vol. I. Chicago: Munsell Publishing Co., 1916.

Blair, George. *Cumulative Voting.* Urbana: University of Illinois Press, 1960.

Busch, Noel F. *Adlai E. Stevenson of Illinois.* New York: Farrar, Strauss and Young, 1952.

Calkins, Carnish Elmo. *They Broke the Prairie.* New York: Scribner's, 1937. (A study of Galesburg, Illinois, that is illustrative of western Illinois development.)

Calley, Charles C. *Pilot Study of Southern Illinois.* Carbondale: Southern Illinois University Press, 1956.

Chicago Home Rule Commission. *Modernizing a City Government.* Chicago: University of Chicago Press, 1954.

Derge, David R. "Metropolitan and Outstate Alignments in Illinois and Missouri Legislative Delegations," *American Political Science Review* LII (1958), 1051–1065.

Faith, Emil F., and Richard G. Browne. *Government and History of the State of Illinois.* Chicago: Mentzer, Bush, 1956.

Federal Reserve Bank of Chicago. *Annual Report.* 1959–1964.

Fisher, Glenn W. *Financing Illinois Government.* Urbana: University of Illinois Press, 1960.

Frost, Richard T. "On Derge's Metropolitan and Outside Legislative Delegations," *American Political Science Review*, LIII (1959), 792–795.

Gamberg, Herbert V. *A Working Paper on Urban Political Capabilities.* Urbana: University of Illinois, Office of Community Development, March 1963.

Garvey, Neil F. *The Government and Administration of Illinois.* New York: Thomas Y. Crowell, 1958.

Gosnell, Harold F. *Machine Politics: Chicago Model.* Chicago: University of Chicago Press, 1937.

Gove, Samuel K. (ed.). *Illinois State Government: A Look Ahead.* Urbana: University of Illinois Press, 1958.

——— (ed.). *State and Local Government in Illinois: A Bibliography.* Urbana: University of Illinois Press, 1953.

——— and Alvin I. Sokolow (eds.). *1958 Supplement to State and Local Government in Illinois: A Bibliography*. Urbana: University of Illinois Press, 1958.

——— and Gilbert Y. Steiner. *The Illinois Legislative Process. University of Illinois Bulletin*, Vol. LI, No. 75 (1959).

Howards, Irving. *Selected Aspects of State Supervision Over Local Government in Illinois: A View of State-Local Relations.* Carbondale: Southern Illinois University, 1964.

James, F. Cyril. *The Growth of Chicago Banks.* Vols. I, II. New York: Harper, 1938.

James, Herman G. *The Preamble and Boundary Clauses of the Illinois Constitution.* A paper read before the Chicago Historical Society, January 18, 1910.

Johnson, Claudius O. *Carter Henry Harrison I.* Chicago: University of Chicago Press, 1931.

Littlewood, Thomas B. *Bipartisan Coalition in Illinois.* Eagleton Institute Cases in Practical Politics, No. 22 (1960).

MacRae, Duncan, Jr., and James A. Meldrum. "Critical Elections in Illinois: 1888–1958," *American Political Science Review*, LIV (1960), 669–683.

Masters, Nicholas A.; Robert H. Salisbury; and Thomas H. Eliot. *State Politics and the Public Schools.* New York: Alfred A. Knopf, 1964.

Mendota Centennial Committee. *Magnificent Whistle Stop.* Mendota, Ill.: MCC Inc., 1953. (A study of Mendota, Illinois, that is illustrative of north central Illinois development.)

Municipal Human Relations Councils. The Institute of Government and Public Affairs. *Illinois Government*, No. 6 (February 1960).

Nodger, Carl F. *Illinois Negro Historymakers.* Chicago: Emancipation Centennial Commission, 1964.

Pelekoudas, Lois M. *The Illinois Constitution.* Urbana: University of Illinois Press, 1962.

——— (ed.). *Illinois Local Government.* Urbana: University of Illinois Press, 1961.

——— (ed.). *Illinois Political Parties.* Urbana: University of Illinois Press, 1960.

Plate, Nick. *Along the Line in Illinois.* Cleveland: The Industrial Development Department, Nickel Plate Road, 1945.

Putnam, James William. *The Illinois and Michigan Canal.* Chicago: University of Chicago Press, 1918.

Ranney, Austin. *Illinois Politics.* New York: New York University Press, 1960.

Rosen, Harry and David. *But Not Next Door.* New York: Avon, 1962.

Snider, Clyde F., and Irving Howards. *County Government in Illinois.* Carbondale: Southern Illinois University, 1960.

Steiner, Gilbert Y., and Samuel K. Gove. *Legislative Politics in Illinois.* Urbana: University of Illinois Press, 1960.

Vogel, Virgil J. *Indian Place Names.* Springfield: Illinois State Historical Society, Pamphlet Series No. 4, 1963.

Walton, Clyde C. (ed.). *John Francis Snyder: Selected Writings.* Springfield: Illinois State Historical Society, 1962.

Wendt, Lloyd, and Herman Kogan. *Lords of the Levee.* New York: Bobbs-Merrill, 1943.

Whitlock, Brand. *The 13th District.* New York: Grosset and Dunlap, 1962.

Wilson, William E. *The Wabash.* New York: Farrar and Rinehart, 1940.

Woodely, Carroll Hill. *The Case of Frank L. Smith.* Chicago: University of Chicago Press, 1931.

Iowa

Annual Statement, Cities and Towns, 1959–1961.

Federal Writers' Project. *Iowa: A Guide to the Hawkeye State.*

Gold, David, and John R. Schmidhauser. "Urbanization and Party Competition: The Case of Iowa," *Midwest Journal of Political Science* (1960).

Iowa Legislative Manual, 1891–1967.

Porter, K. H. "The Deserted Primary in Iowa," *American Political Science Review* (1945).

Ross, R. M. *The Government and Administration of Iowa*. New York: Thomas Y. Crowell, 1957.

Salisbury, Robert H., and Gordon Black. "Class and Party in Partisan and Non-Partisan Elections: The Case of Des Moines," *American Political Science Review*, LVII (1963), 584–592.

Schmidhauser, John R. *Iowa's Campaign for a Constitutional Convention in 1960*, Cases in Practical Politics No. 30 (1963).

Minnesota

Anderson, William, and Edward Weidner (eds). *Intergovernmental Relations in Minnesota*. 10 vols. Minneapolis: University of Minnesota Press, 1950–1960.

Blegen, Theodore G. *Minnesota: A History*. Minneapolis: University of Minnesota Press, 1964.

Christianson, Theodore. *History of Minnesota*. New York: American Historical Society, 1935.

Federal Writers' Project. *Minnesota: A State Guide*. New York: Viking Press, 1938.

Flinn, Thomas. *Governor Freeman and the Minnesota Budget*, Inter-University Case Program, No. 60 (1961).

Folwell, William Watts. *A History of Minnesota*. 4 vols. St. Paul: Minnesota Historical Society, 1921.

Minnesota Economic Regions: Their Delineation, Description, and Development Potential, Dr. John S. Hoyt, Jr., Consultant, December 2, 1966, for the Review and Comments of the State Planning Advisory Committee.

Minnesota Historical Society. Collections, vols I-XVII.

Minnesota History, 1919–1968.

Minnesota Legislative Manual. 1881–1967.

Mitau, G. Theodore. "The Governor and the Strike," in Richard T. Frost (ed.), *Cases in State and Local Government*. Englewood Cliffs, N.J.: Prentice-Hall, 1961.

———. *Politics in Minnesota*. Minneapolis: University of Minnesota Press, 1960.

Morlan, Robert L. *Political Prairie Fire: The Non-Partisan League*. Minneapolis: University of Minnesota Press, 1955.

Ylvisaker, Paul N. *The Battle of Blue Earth County*. Inter-University Case Program, No. 25 (rev. 1955).

Wisconsin

Anderson, Theodore A. *A Century of Banking in Wisconsin.* Madison: State Historical Society of Wisconsin, 1954.

Baggalay, Andrew R. "Religious Influence on Wisconsin Voting, 1928–1960," *American Political Science Review*, LVI (1962), 66–70.

Epstein, Leon D. "American Parties: A Wisconsin Case Study," *Political Studies*, IV (1956), 30–45.

———. *Politics in Wisconsin.* Madison: University of Wisconsin Press, 1958.

———. "Size of Place and the Division of the Two-Party Vote in Wisconsin," *Western Political Quarterly*, IX (1956), 138–150.

Federal Writers' Project. *Wisconsin: Guide to the Badger State.*

Greenhill, H. G. *Labor Money in Wisconsin Politics, 1964.* Princeton, N.J.: Citizens' Research Foundation, 1966.

Johnson, Walter K. "The Wisconsin Experience with State-Level Reviews of Municipal Incorporations, Consolidations, and Annexations," *Wisconsin Law Review*, 1965, No. 3 (Summer 1965), 462–475.

Leopold, Aldo B. (ed.). *Round River: From the Journals of Aldo Leopold.* New York: Oxford University Press, 1954.

Mills, Warner E., Jr., and Harry R. Davis. *Seven Cases in Decision-Making.* New York: Random House, 1962. (For the flavor of smaller city politics in Wisconsin.)

Quaife, Milo M. *The Attainment of Statehood. Publication of the State Historical Society of Wisconsin*, Vol. XXIX. 1928.

——— (ed.). *The Convention of 1846.* Vol. XXVII. Madison: State Historical Society of Wisconsin, 1919.

———. *The Struggle over Ratification: 1746–1846.* Vol. XXVIII. Madison: State Historical Society of Wisconsin, 1920.

Schlenbert, Leroy (comp.). *Subject Bibliography of Wisconsin History.* Madison: State Historical Society of Wisconsin, 1947.

Thwaites, Reuben Gold (ed.). *Collections of the State Historical Society of Wisconsin.* Vol. XVIII. Madison: State Historical Society of Wisconsin, 1908.

Wisconsin Legislative Manual. 1881–1967.

III

The Cities of the Prairie

Belleville

SELECTED DOCUMENTS AND MAPS

Report of the Southwestern Illinois Area Study Commission to Governor Otto Kerner and Members of the 73rd General Assembly. Submitted April, 1963.
Proposed Zoning Ordinance, City of Belleville, Illinois.

SELECTED INTERVIEWS

(NOTE: A number of important interviews from the Belleville area have not been cited to preserve confidences. They are available in the Files of the Institute of Government and Public Affairs.)
Joe Adam, *Belleville News-Gazette* reporter.
R. G. Dabson, Belleville Chief of Police.
Gene Graves, Southern Illinois University Community Development worker, E. St. Louis.
Peter Kern, Publisher, *Belleville News-Gazette.*
Devereaux H. Murphy, St. Clair County Highway Commissioner.
Charles E. Nichols, Mayor of Belleville.
P. C. Otwell, Attorney, Former Democratic City Chairman.
Clifford Peake, Belleville Chamber of Commerce Manager.
Al Pierce, Belleville Town Auditor.
Leroy Roberts, Office Manager for Belleville Township.
John Thompson, City Engineer.
Jack Wellinghoff, President, Belleville-St. Louis Coach Co.
Gene Widman, Attorney, Former Democratic City Chairman.

Champaign-Urbana

BOOKS AND ARTICLES

History of Champaign County.

Powers, Richard F. *Federal Aid to Impacted Areas: Some Local Observations.* Unpublished paper.

Steiner, Gilbert Y., and Phillip Monypenny. "Merger? The Illinois Consolidation Case," in Richard T. Frost, *Cases in State and Local Government.* Englewood Cliffs, N.J.: Prentice-Hall, 1963, pp. 267–290.

SELECTED DOCUMENTS AND MAPS

"Basis for Decision," Panel on Urban Renewal in Champaign-Urbana, WILL-TV.

Champaign-Urbana Courier, Champaign Centennial Issue, July 3, 1960.

———, Special Sections, June 16, 1963.

———, 25th Annual Report of the City of Champaign, June 23, 1963.

Files of the Institute of Government and Public Affairs, University of Illinois.

SELECTED INTERVIEWS

(NOTE: Perhaps because of their proximity to the university, the public officials of Champaign-Urbana were most reluctant to be cited by name; hence I have chosen to omit the names of all those who did not give me direct permission to be cited.)

Rubin Cohn, Professor of Law, University of Illinois and Democratic gubernatorial advisor.

Edward Dessin, Champaign political active.

Jerry Dobrovolny, Professor of Engineering, University of Illinois, and leader of Champaign County Republican party.

James V. Edsall, University of Illinois Physical Plant.

William Goodman, Professor of Planning, University of Illinois and city planning consultant.

Samuel K. Gove, Professor of Government and Public Affairs, University of Illinois.

Charles Hagen, Professor of Political Science, University of Illinois.

Robert D. Harvey, Professor of Finance and Chairman of the Champaign City Planning Commission.

Charles Kneier, Professor of Political Science, University of Illinois.

Arthur Lerner, Champaign Republican active.
Phillip Monypenny, Professor of Political Science, University of Illinois.
Robert W. Oldland, Champaign City Manager.
Connie Pelekoudas, leader of the liberal wing of the Champaign County Democratic party.
Lois Pelekoudas, Urbana Democratic active.
Charles Silverman, Champaign liquor dealer.
Gilbert Y. Steiner, Director, Institute of Government and Public Affairs, University of Illinois.
Dennis Sullivan, Assistant Professor of Political Science, University of Illinois.
Mike Wolin, Urbana Alderman.

Decatur

BOOKS AND ARTICLES

"Growth and Prosperity in Five Midwest Cities," *Annual Report.* Federal Reserve Bank of Chicago, 1955.
History of Decatur and Macon County.
Katz, Elihu, and Paul F. Lazarsfeld. *Personal Influence.* Glencoe, Ill.: The Free Press, 1955.
Liebman, Charles S. "First Manager, First Month." *Illinois Government.*

SELECTED DOCUMENTS AND MAPS

Files of the Institute of Government and Public Affairs, University of Illinois. Particularly the data collected by Charles S. Liebman for his study of Decatur.

SELECTED INTERVIEWS

Samuel K. Gove, Professor of Government and Public Affairs, University of Illinois.
Charles S. Liebman, Research Assistant, Institute of Government and Public Affairs, University of Illinois.
Alvin D. Sokolow, Research Assistant, Institute of Government and Public Affairs, University of Illinois.
Gilbert Y. Steiner, Director, Institute of Government and Public Affairs, University of Illinois.

Duluth

BOOKS AND ARTICLES

Let's Get Acquainted with Duluth and the Public Schools: A Handbook for New Teachers. Duluth, Minn.: Board of Education, 1953.
School Record, Vols. X–XII (1958–1960).
The Bridge: Between Departments, City of Duluth, October 10, 1959–November 10, 1960.
The Duluthian, 1958–1959 Annual Report Edition, Vol. XII, No. 1, October, 1959.
Havighurst, Walter. *Vein of Iron.* Cleveland: The World Publishing Company, 1958.
MacDonald, Dora Mary. *This Is Duluth.* Duluth, Minn.: 1950.
———. *Our Public Schools.* Duluth, Minn.: Board of Education, 1958.
Minnesota Arrowhead Country, compiled by Workers of the Writers' Program of the Work Projects Administration in the State of Minnesota. Chicago: Albert Whiteman and Co., 1941.
Nute, Grace Lee. *Lake Superior.* New York: Bobbs-Merrill, 1944.
Stub, Halger R. *Migration to Duluth, 1958–1959.* Social Sciences Research Trust Fund, University of Minnesota, No. 4, 1961.
Woodbridge, Dwight E., and John S. Pardee (eds.). *History of Duluth and St. Louis County, Past and Present.* Vols. I and II. Chicago: C. F. Cooper and Co., 1910.

SELECTED DOCUMENTS AND MAPS

Accommodation and Shopping Guide.
Amended By-Laws, Duluth Democratic Farmer Labor Coordinating Committee.
Annual Report, Duluth Health Department, 1958–1961.
Annual Report, Housing and Redevelopment Authority of Duluth, Minn., December 31, 1951.
Annual Report, Staff Research Assistant of the City of Duluth, Minn. 1959.
Apportionment of Tax Levy, 1950–1957.
Arrowhead News, Official Publication, Minnesota Arrowhead Association, Vol. I, No. 3, April 1959 to Vol. II, No. 3, April 1960.
Brief of the Contents of the Comprehensive Plan for the City of Duluth.
Budget Appropriations, City of Duluth, 1931–1960.
Bulletin of the Duluth Campaign Review Council.
Charter of the City of Duluth, June 11, 1956.
Description of Office of City Attorney of the City of Duluth.
Description of Office of Department of Public Finance and Records.
Directory of Manufacturers, Duluth, Minn., 1960.
Duluth Chamber of Commerce, Policy on Public Solicitations.
Duluth Employment Developments, 1947–1956, State of Minnesota Department of Security, St. Paul, Minn., 1957.

Duluth Employment Trends, Special Edition, January 1959.
Duluth Employment Trends, No. 158, July 15, 1959.
Duluth Overall Tax Outlook.
Duluth Public Schools, Duluth, Minn. *Annual Report.* July 31, 1959.
Facts on Duluth–Superior Harbor, Corps of Engineers, U.S. Army.
Fifth Annual Report, Staff Research Office of the City of Duluth, 1961.
Foreign Trade—General Cargo—Twin Ports, April 26, 1960–August 9, 1960.
Governmental Research Bureau, Duluth, Minn. *A Tale of Three Cities.* December 26, 1951.
———. *Should Taxing Powers Be Determined at Home?* January 20, 1953.
———. *The Kraeger Report.* September 8, 1953.
———. *Duluth Population Trends,* No. 6.
———. *New Taxes,* No. 9.
———. *1954 Tax Levy,* No. 11.
———. *The Relegation to the State House,* No. 12.
———. *Budget vs. Property Taxes,* No. 15.
———. *Open Letter,* concerning Board of Equalization proposal to equalize property tax values, No. 16.
———. *Social Welfare Trends,* No. 26.
———. *Duluth Population Trends,* Utility Report, No. 31.
———. *Tax Analysis,* No. 32.
———. *County Taxes and Services,* No. 33.
———. *St. Louis County Welfare Costs in July 1961,* No. 39.
———. *St. Louis County Welfare and the 1960 Census,* No. 40.
———. *Duluth Population Trends,* No. 41.
———. *Taxes Up, Services in Demand, Economy Encouraged,* No. 42.
———. *Apportionment of Tax Levy in the City of Duluth,* No. 44.
———. *Duluth Population Trends,* No. 45.
Hearing on the Needs and Advisability of Harbor Improvements at Duluth–Superior for Present and Prospective Deep–Draft Commerce.
Minimum 10-Year Duluth Trunk Highway Needs.
Minnesota State Employment Service, *Supplementary Statistical Data.*
An Opportunity. International Duluth Seaport Corporation, Duluth, Minn., and Winnipeg.
Port Authority Information, 1959.
Port of Duluth-Superior. *General Rules and Regulations, 1960.*
Profile of Duluth's Health and Medical Facilities. Prepared by AFL-CIO Community Services Activities, 400 Moore Memorial Building.
Proposed Reorganization Plan, City of Duluth, Minn., Presented to the City Council November 12, 1956, by Eugene R. Lambert, Mayor, H. G. Bower, Administrative Assistant.
Citizens' Committee on Parking, *Report.*
Report of the Duluth Civil Defense Agency, 1959.
Report on Harbor Improvement.
Report on Present Downtown Parking Space Needs.
Special Number, *Legislative Daily,* 84th Congress, First Session, Vol. IV, No. 116, June 28, 1955.
Testimony by Roy H. Anderson, Manager, Duluth Office of Minnesota Department of Employment Security, Before U.S. Senate, Special Committee on Unemployment Problems, November 19, 1959.
"Where to Turn," A Guide to the Uses of Social Services in Duluth, Duluth Welfare Council.
Your Police Department, Walter L. Wiske, Chief of Police.

SELECTED INTERVIEWS

Ray Allen, AFL-CIO Community Services Activities Director.
Chester Barnes, City Auditor.
Emmett Davidson, Professor of Political Science, University of Minnesota.
Dr. Fisher, Public Health Director.
Mark Flaherty, City Planner.
Gerald Heaney, attorney, labor lawyer, former Democratic National Committeeman for the State of Minnesota, and local political leader of the DFL.
Richard Hicks, Duluth Civil Service Director.
Richard Humes, Duluth Housing and Redevelopment Authority.
John Humner, Director, City Planning Department.
Dorothy Kennedy, staff research assistant-secretary.
Mr. Miller, Assistant Director and Researcher, Governmental Research Bureau.
Harry Nash, Duluth Recreation Director.
Bert H. Parson, Duluth City Clerk.
Harry Reed, Director, Governmental Research Bureau.
John Rutford, Executive Secretary, St. Louis County Republican party.
Robert Smith, Duluth Port Authority Director.
Alvin Stalen, Duluth Superintendent of Schools.
Harry Weinberg, Duluth City Attorney.
Louis G. Wendlant, Chief Clerk, Duluth Municipal Court.
Colonel Fred G. Wood, Duluth Civil Defense Director.

Joliet

BOOKS AND ARTICLES

Baker, Ruth E. *This Is Cook County*. Chicago: Cook County Council of the League of Women Voters.

Carper, Edith T. "Illinois Goes to Congress for Army Land," in Edwin A. Bock and Alan K. Campbell, *Case Studies in American Government*. Englewood Cliffs, N.J.: Prentice-Hall, 1962, pp. 223–263.

Hansen, Harry. *The Rivers of America: The Chicago*. New York: Farrar and Rinehart, 1942.

Lyon, Leverett S. (ed.). *Governmental Problems in the Chicago Metropolitan Area*. Chicago: University of Chicago Press, 1957.

Merriam, Charles E., Spencer D. Parrott, and Albert Lepawsky. *The Government of the Metropolitan Region of Chicago*. Chicago: University of Chicago Press, 1933.

SELECTED DOCUMENTS AND MAPS

"Public Water Supply, Drainage, and Sewerage Services in Northeastern Illinois," Public Administration Service, 1956.

SELECTED INTERVIEWS

Sam Bason, Joliet Park District Superintendent.
Louis Battino, Assistant Superintendent, Joliet School District.
George Comerford, Joliet City Manager.
Verne E. Corckel, Will County Superintendent of Schools.
J. L. Crittenden, Managing Editor, Joliet *News-Herald*.
Vance Cummens, Public Relations Officer, Joliet Federal Savings and Loan Assn.
Ruth Dillon, Secretary, Will County Health Department.
Verness E. Dillon, Illinois State Employment Service.
Roy C. Doerfler, Will County Treasurer.
James P. Hennessy, Mayor of Joliet.
Gilbert A. Kanter, Sheriff, Will County.
Albert A. Kryzwonos, Regional Director, United Steelworkers of America.
George P. Lloyd, Chairman, Joliet Planning Commission.
Francis J. Longham, State representative.
John Lux, editor and publisher, *Joliet News-Herald*.
C. H. Peterson, Will County Republican Chairman.
Robert Pilcher, President, Joliet Park Board.
Bernard Prola, Joliet Public Works Director.
Harold Schilling, Joliet Police Chief.
George Shipley, Executive Vice President, National Bank of Joliet; President, Joliet Region Chamber of Commerce.
Eugene G. Silvers, Joliet Region Chamber of Commerce.

Peoria

BOOKS AND ARTICLES

John Bartlow Martin, "The Town that Reformed," *Saturday Evening Post,* October 1, 1955.

SELECTED DOCUMENTS AND MAPS

District No. 1 Map of the City of Peoria, 1958.
District No. 2 Map of the City of Peoria, 1958.
District No. 3 Map of the City of Peoria, 1958.
District No. 4 Map of the City of Peoria, 1958.
Map and Business Directory of Pekin, Illinois, 1961, Pekin Daily Times.
Official Zoning District Map of Peoria, Ill.
Zoning Map of Hallis Township, Peoria County, Ill.
Zoning Map of Kickapoo Township, Peoria County, Ill.
Zoning Map of Limestone Township, Peoria County, Ill.
Zoning Map of Medina Township, Peoria County, Ill.
Zoning Map of Richwoods Township, Peoria County, Ill.

SELECTED INTERVIEWS

Dr. Bills, Peoria School District Superintendent.
Ilion Crabel, Peoria City Clerk.
Joseph K. Gilchrist, Manager, Industrial Development Commission.
G. Louis Heller, Executive Director, Tri-County Planning Commission.
Charles W. Iben, Judge, Peoria.
Herbert Johnson, Peoria Association of Commerce.
William Kampf, Peoria County Recorder of Deeds.
L. P. Murphy, Peoria Area Director, U.S. Corps of Engineers.
Mrs. Maybelle Murphy, Peoria County Treasurer.
Mr. Radley, County Zoning Officer.
William Rutherford, attorney.
Art Walsh, Administrator, Forest Park Foundation.

Pueblo

BOOKS AND ARTICLES

Civic Design Study: Rocky Mountains and Great Plains Area. By the Civic Design Study, Colorado College, Colorado Springs.
Colorful Colorado and Rocky Mountain Outdoors, Vol. I, No. 4, Spring 1966.
"Steve the Big Issue," Special Report on Colorado Politics by Tom Gavin, *Denver Post* Staff Writer, Parts I and II, June 24, 1962; July 1, 1962.

James H. Risley. *How It Grew: A History of the Pueblo Public Schools.* Denver: University of Denver Press, 1953.

SELECTED DOCUMENTS AND MAPS

All American Cities Contest, Nomination of Pueblo-Colorado, by Russell W. Rink, City Manager, 1954.

Amendment to Charter of the City of Pueblo, Article 15.

An Evaluation of Pueblo's Economic Potential, Bureau of Business Research, University of Colorado, 1960.

Better Business Sales Policy, Pueblo Chamber of Commerce.

Brief of the City and Chamber of Commerce of Colorado in the Kansas-Oklahoma Local Service Case before the Civil Aeronautics Board, May 29, 1959.

Buyers' Guide 1960–1961, Pueblo, Colorado's Second Largest City, Pueblo Chamber of Commerce.

City of Pueblo, *Annual Reports,* 1953–1960.

City of Pueblo, Ordinance No. *2165*, An Ordinance Establishing Procedure for Zoning Amendments.

City of Pueblo, Ordinance No. *2367*, An Ordinance Amending Chapter 30 (Zoning) of "The Code of Ordinances, City of Pueblo," by Providing for Transition Zones.

City of Pueblo, Colo., Zoning District Map.

Colorado's Second Largest City, Annual Report of Pueblo Chamber of Commerce, 1960.

Commemorating the Opening of the Pueblo Freeway, July 1, 1959 (booklet), Public Relations Division of Colorado Department of Highways.

Eleventh Annual Report, Arkansas River Compact Administration (1959). Lamar, Colo., December 8, 1959.

First Annual Report of the Pueblo Regional Planning Commission, 1960.

The Fryingpan-Arkansas Project, Southeastern Colorado Water Conservation District.

Goals, Programs, and Projects, Pueblo Chamber of Commerce, 1960.

Biennial Report, 1960–1961, Pueblo City-County Health Department, Vol. I, No. 1.

"Hi Podner," Welcome to Pueblo Ordnance Depot, Pueblo Ordnance Depot.

Joint Petition of the City of Pueblo and the Pueblo Chamber of Commerce for Leave to Intervene and Petition of Intervention before Interstate Commerce Commission, Docket Nos. 21334, 21335, 21314, 21315.

Let's Talk About Pueblo, Pueblo Chamber of Commerce 1961–1968.

Opinion, Pueblo Chamber of Commerce. By Charles Thompson, June 5, 1961.

Petition for Annexation to the City of Pueblo.

Plats, Subdivisions, and Annexations, City of Pueblo, Reprint, Chap. 20, "Code of Ordinances, City of Pueblo."

Proposed Charter for the City of Pueblo—Submitted at a Special Election to be Held Tuesday, April 6, 1954.

Pueblo: A Great City to Live In, Annual Report of Pueblo Chamber of Commerce, 1961.

Pueblo Business and Economic Trends, Pueblo Chamber of Commerce, 1961–1968.

Pueblo City-County Health Department Budget Message, 1962.

Pueblo, Colo., *Taxation.* The third of a series of studies sponsored by the Pueblo, Colorado, Chamber of Commerce, 1946.

Pueblo Facts, "100 Years of Progress," Chamber of Commerce of Pueblo, Colorado.
Pueblo Region Map, prepared and published by the Pueblo Regional Planning Commission.
Pueblo Regional Fact Book. Report No. 2, March 1961, prepared and published by the Pueblo Regional Planning Commission.
Pueblo Regional Zoning Proposal, Report No. 3, October 1961. Prepared and published by the Pueblo Regional Planning Commission.
"Pueblo Reports to Its Citizens," *Pueblo Star-Journal and Chieftain,* 1960.
The Pueblo Schools at a Glance, School District No. 60.
Recommendation for a Four Year College, to Serve the Pueblo Region and Southern Colorado, Citizen's Legislative Advisory Committee, November 1, 1960.
Report Number One: Regional Planning for Pueblo, October 15, 1960, prepared and published by the Pueblo Regional Planning Commission.
Report Number Five: Pueblo Regional Growth Policy Paper, March 1962, prepared and published by the Pueblo Regional Planning Commission.
Report to The Colorado General Assembly, *Urban Renewal in Colorado,* Colorado Legislative Council, Research Publication No. 39, November 1960.
Request for Highway Construction to Colorado State Highway Commission from Pueblo County Commissioner, Pueblo City Government and Pueblo Chamber of Commerce, November 14–16, 1960.
Revised By-Laws of Pueblo Chamber of Commerce, November 1959.
Secretary-Treasurer's Report to the Board of Education and the School District No. 60. Pueblo, Colorado, for Calendar and Budget Year 1960. (For 1959–1960 also.)
Sheet News, United Steelworkers of America AFL-CIO, Vol. XVII, No. 7, July 1961.
Taxes—fact sheet.
The Union Avenue Project for the City of Pueblo. Urban Renewal Authority.
Welcome to Pueblo, First National Bank.

SELECTED INTERVIEWS

Dr. John Anderson, City-County Health Officer.
Allan Blomquist, Regional Planner.
John Bonforte, Contractor.
Sam Cocharo, City Traffic and Planning Engineer.
Terry Curran, City Hall reporter.
Frank Evans, attorney and state legislator.
Dr. John B. Farley, Democratic party leader.
George E. Fellows, Pueblo City Manager.
Louis E. Gelt, Denver attorney.
Roy F. Harper, Police Chief.
Tom Healy, real estate salesman.
John E. Hill, County Commissioner.
Gordon Hinds, Pueblo City attorney.
Frank S. Hoag, Jr., publisher, Pueblo newspapers.
Mrs. Patricia Jenkins, County Superintendent of Schools.
Don Jones, Assistant Director, Colorado Municipal League.
A. L. Koehenberger, County Clerk.

John Krutka, Sheriff, Pueblo County.
Levi Martinez, attorney, leader of Hispanic community.
Cecil Osborne, courthouse reporter.
Wayne Price, President, C.F. & I. Local, United Steel Workers.
Sam Rowe, Member, Regional Planning Commission.
Mary E. Shower, County Treasurer.
Owen Smith, Associate Superintendent of School District 60.
Marvin L. Starkweather, County Commissioner.
Franklin Stewart, attorney and Democratic candidate for Congress.
Charles "Tommy" Thompson, Chamber of Commerce Secretary.
Dale Tursi, State senator.
Joseph Venta, Republican County Chairman, attorney.

Quad Cities

BOOKS AND ARTICLES

Baldwin, Sara Mullin. *Who's Who in Rock Island, 1929*. Rock Island, Ill., 1929.
League of Women Voters of Moline, *Moline: It's Your City*.
League of Women Voters of Rock Island, *Rock Island County Government*.
Tillinghost, B. F. *Rock Island Arsenal in Peace and in War*.

SELECTED DOCUMENTS AND MAPS

Davenport, Iowa: In the Heart of the Rich Mississippi Valley, courtesy of Davenport Chamber of Commerce.
Facts on Davenport, Iowa, Davenport Chamber of Commerce.
Quad-City Commerce Quarterly, 1957–1968.

SELECTED INTERVIEWS

A. V. Bargmann, Davenport Building Inspector.
Grace Bryant, Iowa State Welfare Department.
Mrs. Lillian Carlton, Moline City Clerk.
Elmer Clayton, Scott County engineer.
Stanley Erikson, Rock Island City councilman and professor at Augustana College.
Robert Fernsterbusch, Director of Davenport Chamber of Commerce.

M. A. Fulton, editor, *Davenport Daily Times.*
Rick Gage, Rock Island County Courthouse reporter.
Dr. Earl Hansen, Rock Island Superintendent of Schools.
Robert Heitsch, Rock Island City Manager.
Henry Houk, Davenport Publicity Director.
Harold Johnson, Rock Island County Clerk.
Ken Jones, Rock Island Chamber of Commerce Executive Director.
Irvine Katz, Rock Island attorney.
William R. Klatt, Rock Island City Planner.
Henry Knacik, Assistant County Engineer and Zoning Officer, Scott County.
Martin D. Leir, Scott County attorney.
Theodore Lirengen, Davenport Alderman.
Herb Lowry, Democratic Chairman, Rock Island County.
Bob Lucken, Rock Island City Hall reporter.
William Luhmin, Moline Assistant Planner and Traffic Engineer.
Anthony Marinaceis, Davenport School Superintendent.
John J. Martin, Davenport politician.
Roy W. Osterman, President, Rock Island Bank and Trust Co.
E. H. Rassou, Rock Island insurance agent.
Stan Redick, Moline Traffic and Planning Director.
George F. Reeder, Moline Chamber of Commerce.
Fred Sandemann, Research Assistant, State University of Iowa, Institute of Public Affairs.
Claire M. Schroeder, Clerk of Moline City Court.
Don Shetter, Rock Island attorney.
Thomas Sinnet, Rock Island attorney.
Arnold Smith, Mayor, Moline.
Henry Smith, Research Assistant, State University of Iowa, Institute of Public Affairs.
Richard Stregh, Rock Island attorney.
Jack Sundine, editor, *Moline Dispatch.*
William J. Tacey, City Clerk of Rock Island.
Mr. Thompson, State Welfare Director, Scott County.
Richard Turnland, Rock Island City Official.
Leo Tyler, Rock Island County Map Department Director.
William F. Voss, Scott County auditor.
Pale Wahlstrom, Rock Island County Deputy Auditor.

Rockford

BOOKS AND ARTICLES

Bateman, Newton, and Paul Selby (eds.). *Historical Encyclopedia of Illinois and History of Winnebago County*, Vol. II. Chicago: Munsell Publishing Co., 1916.
Daniel J. Elazar. "Rockford, Illinois: A Preliminary Report on the Political Characteristics of Medium-Size Illinois Metropolitan Areas," unpublished manuscript.

SELECTED DOCUMENTS AND MAPS

Maps Outlining a General Renewal Plan called "Saybrooke Renewal Area," Rockford, Ill.

Neighbors, Rockford Chamber of Commerce, 1960–1967.

Statement of Special Assessment, Revenue and General Obligation Bonds, and Tax Anticipation Warrants Payable on December 31, 1959, City of Rockford, Ill.

Urban Renewal Report Nos. 1–18, A Case Study of Public Urban Renewal in the Rockford Metropolitan Area.

SELECTED INTERVIEWS

Richard Arms, Regional Planning Commission Director, Winnebago County.
Bill Collins, Corporation Counsel.
Mrs. Davison, Dean of Women, Rockford College.
Earl F. Elliott, Park District Superintendent.
Jay Fisher, reporter.
J. Herman Hallstrom, former Mayor.
Rick Johnson, reporter on *Rockford Register Republic.*
Tad Johnson, Commissioner, Department of Public Works.
Rick Johnston, Illinois State Youth Commission worker.
Robert Lindsey, City Clerk.
Robert McGan, Rockford political leader.
Holton Odegard, Associate Director of the City-County Planning Commission.
Stanley Parsons, Professor of History, Rockford College.
Ronald N. Pennock, County Forester.
Owen Pollard, Rockford political leader.
Ben E. Schleicher, Mayor.
John Schleicher, optometrist, Commissioner of Rockford Park District.
Daniel Smith, Chief Clerk, Rockford Board of Election Commissioners.
Frank Spence, Institute of Commerce Executive Director.
Sal Stern, bail bondsman.
Barney Thompson, editor emeritus.

Springfield

SELECTED INTERVIEWS

Ira Becker, County Auditor.
Willard Bunn, President of SCADA.
Hugh Campbell, Sheriff.
Lester E. Collins, Mayor.
Charles Hartman, Chief Clerk, City Election Board.
Inez Hoffman, Commissioner of Finance.
Nelson Howarth, former Mayor.
Charles Kirshner, City Planner.
William E. Montague, Executive Director of SCADA.
Conrad Noel, Attorney.
Frederic O'Hara, Commissioner of Health and Safety.
Albert Oswald, Administrative Assistant to Mayor Collins.
Pat Palmer, Secretary of Civil Service.
A. L. Sargent, Illinois Municipal League.
Willis Spaulding, former City Commissioner.
Gilbert Y. Steiner, Director, Institute of Government and Public Affairs, University of Illinois.
Bradley Taylor, Executive Director, Sangamon County Regional Planning Commission.
J. E. Thoman, County Clerk.
Walter Wagner, Executive Director, Association of Commerce and Industry.
Jack Weiner, attorney.

Index